THE DIARY OF
SAMUEL PEPYS

THE DIARY
OF
SAMUEL PEPYS

A new and complete
transcription edited by

ROBERT LATHAM
AND
WILLIAM MATTHEWS

CONTRIBUTING EDITORS
WILLIAM A. ARMSTRONG · MACDONALD EMSLIE
OLIVER MILLAR · T. F. REDDAWAY

VOLUME I · 1660

HarperCollins*Publishers*

University of California Press
Berkeley and Los Angeles

Published in the UK by
HarperCollins*Publishers*
77-85 Fulham Palace Road
Hammersmith, London W6 8JB
www.**fire**and**water**.com

UK paperback edition 1995
Reissued 2000

Published in the USA by
University of California Press
Berkeley and Los Angeles, California

First US paperback edition 2000

1 3 5 7 9 8 6 4 2

First published by Bell & Hyman Limited 1971

ISBN 0 00 499021 8 (UK)
ISBN 0 520 22579 1 (USA)

Printed and bound in Great Britain by
Clays Ltd, St Ives plc

PRINCIPAL EDITORS

ROBERT LATHAM, C.B.E., M.A., F.B.A.
Honorary Fellow and formerly Pepys Librarian,
Magdalene College, Cambridge

WILLIAM MATTHEWS, M.A., Ph.D., D.Lett.
Late Professor of English, University of California, Los Angeles
Fellow of Birkbeck College, University of London

CONTRIBUTING EDITORS

(*Theatre*)
WILLIAM A. ARMSTRONG, M.A., Ph.D.
Professor Emeritus of English Literature, Birkbeck College,
University of London

(*Music*)
MACDONALD EMSLIE, M.A., Ph.D.
Honorary Fellow, University of Edinburgh

(*Pictures and Works of Art*)
SIR OLIVER MILLAR, K.C.V.O., F.B.A.
Surveyor of the Queen's Pictures

(*London Topography*)
T. F. REDDAWAY, M.A., F.S.A.
Late Professor of the History of London, University College,
University of London

★ ★ ★

(*Text assistant*)
LOIS MATTHEWS, B.A.

CONTENTS

LIST OF MAPS

PUBLISHER'S NOTE

This edition comprises eleven volumes – nine volumes of text and footnotes (with an Introduction in volume I), a tenth volume of commentary (the Companion) and an eleventh volume of Index. The text volumes are designed so that each of the first eight contains one whole calendar year of the diary, from January to December. The ninth volume runs from January 1668 to May 1669.

The preparation of this edition has gone through several phases. In 1929 the late Mr Francis Turner (Fellow of Magdalene College, then Pepys Librarian, later Tutor and President) began work on a revision of the Wheatley edition published by this firm in 1893–9. He examined the text for errors, planned a number of additions to it and started to make some necessary changes in the footnotes. His labours were, from the beginning, interrupted by his college duties, and were brought to a halt by his service in the Second World War. It then became clear that his growing responsibilities at college made it unlikely that he would be able to complete the work. In 1950, therefore, Mr Robert Latham was asked to help, and at his request the project was remodelled so that it involved the construction of a systematic commentary on it. Some years later Professor William Matthews was asked to become, with Mr Latham, a Principal Editor of the edition, his main assignment being to prepare a new and complete text. The typewritten and printed forms of this text, prepared by him with the assistance of his wife and carefully checked against the manuscript, have been closely examined from an historian's point of view by Mr Latham, who has also checked the longhand and the punctuation. The Introduction is the joint work of the two Principal Editors, as indicated by their initials. The commentary in the footnotes and Companion is mainly the work of Mr Latham. Professor Matthews criticised all those parts of it lying within his field *of interest. Other scholars (Professor Armstrong, Dr Emslie, Sir Oliver Millar and the late Professor Reddaway) were invited to act as contributing editors to deal with certain specialised topics, and have provided footnotes which are marked by their initials. In the text volumes and also in The* Companion and Index, *invaluable help has been given by Professor A. Rupert Hall, Dr R. Luckett, Dr C. E. Newman and Dr D. J. Schove. Other acknowledgements are made in the Prefaces to the* Companion *and* Index.

The design and direction of the work as a whole, and the major part of the onerous task of seeing the volumes through the press, has been the responsibility of Mr Latham.

PREFACE

The diary[1] of Samuel Pepys runs from 1 January 1660 to 31 May 1669, covering over nine years of the diarist's life, between the ages of 26 and 36. He wrote it in shorthand (with occasional words in long-hand), and abandoned it because of an unfounded fear that he was going blind. He later kept other journals, but none to compare with this. The diary passed after 1669 into a limbo from which it did not emerge until its publication in abbreviated form in 1825. A succession of new editions, re-issues and selections published in the Victorian age, when the English reading public was expanding more rapidly than in any previous period, made the diary one of the best-known books, and Pepys one of the best-known figures, of English history. But, for all its interest and significance, the diary was never adequately printed and edited. Lord Braybrooke, editor of the first edition, brought out three more (all highly selective); the Rev. Mynors Bright, a Fellow of Magdalene, produced another incomplete edition in 1875-9; and H. B. Wheatley, a London antiquary, published the best and most complete of the nineteenth-century editions, in ten volumes, in 1893-9. But in none of these versions - not even in the Wheatley, which for long has stood as the standard edition[2] - was there a reliable, still less a full, text, and in none of them was there a commentary with any claim to completeness.

The text printed here includes all words and passages omitted from previous editions, whether by accident or design. It is based on a transcription of the original manuscript made by Professor Matthews in the course of several readings of the unique copy in the Pepys Library at Magdalene College, Cambridge. His text has been

1. Pepys more often referred to it as his 'Journal' and had all six volumes given that title by the binder. But he also spoke of it, particularly towards the end of his life, as his 'diary' (see below, p. xli, n. 1), and by that name it has become known to all his English-speaking readers. The present Editors have not attemped to fly in the face of that tradition.

2. For all its faults, this has been of the greatest help in the preparation of the present work.

scrutinised, at various stages of drafting, by Mr Latham. It is, in fact, only by some such co-operation between students of seventeenth-century shorthand, language and history that many of the difficulties peculiar to Pepys's manuscript can be tackled.[3]

The methods used in the transcription and editing of the manuscript and in the design of the commentary are explained below.[4] It should be emphasised that the text is in some ways a reconstruction rather than a reproduction. Like many private documents, the diary will in fact never be printed exactly as Pepys wrote it. His hand, it is true, was remarkably clear – very few words are doubtful – but he used a method (mixing shorthand with heavily-abbreviated longhand, and occasionally adding scrambled shorthand and full longhand) which presents many difficulties in transcription and publication. It allows of no certainty, at very many points, about the spelling, capitalisation or punctuation which the author had in mind. The most that can be done by an editor is to aim at printing Pepys's words in the order in which he used them and in their original paragraphs. It is impossible, without rendering the text hideous, to reproduce all Pepys's scribal usages, and to indicate (e.g. by square brackets) all the editorial extensions of longhand.

The primary aim of the Principal Editors has been to see that the diary is presented in a manner suitable to the historical and literary importance of its contents. At the same time they have had in mind the interests of the wide public of English-speaking people to whom the diarist himself, rather than the importance of what he wrote, is what matters. They cannot hope to have achieved all they set out to do, but at least they feel confident that not even academic editors and eleven-volume editions can spoil the appeal of Pepys.

3. Professor Matthews also transcribed (for the purposes of this edition) Pepys's 'Navy White Book' (PL 2581; q.v. below, 7 April 1664, n.) – a memorandum book of office business, mostly in shorthand, which complements the diary at many points.

4. See pp. liv +, cxliii +. They are also given in summary in the Reader's Guide.

ACKNOWLEDGEMENTS

The Principal Editors wish to acknowledge their gratitude to the many individuals and institutions whose co-operation has made this work possible. The Master and Fellows of Magdalene College, Cambridge, owners of the manuscript, granted permission for the edition to be undertaken and for the diary to be photographed. They afforded Mr Latham (while he was a teacher at Royal Holloway College, London) many months of hospitality. Mr Victor Montagu allowed his family papers (the Sandwich MSS, now at Mapperton, Dorset) to be examined; so, too, did the 6th Marquess of Bath, of Longleat, Wilts. Royal Holloway College and the University of California, Los Angeles, speeded the enterprise by the grant of periods of study leave. Both his university and the American Philosophical Society generously made financial grants to Professor Matthews.

A number of scholars have closely shared in the work of preparing the edition. Dr E. S. de Beer, the editor of Evelyn, scrutinised two entire drafts of the text, notes and Introduction, to their very great benefit. He has been a constant and invaluable counsellor. Mr H. M. Nixon, of the British Museum, criticised everything in the commentary which concerns books and bookbinding, and has also given invaluable advice in the composition of those parts of the Introduction which deal with the diary manuscript. Professor A. R. Hall and the late Professor D. H. McKie criticised the footnotes on science; Drs W. S. C. Copeman and C. E. Newman those on medicine; Dr H. G. Roseveare those on public finance; Mrs E. Ettlinger those on folk-lore; Dr J. E. Stevens those (for 1660-1) on music. Mrs H. Truesdell Heath read several parts of the Introduction and commentary. The Editors' obligations to all these friends of the edition are extensive and profound. Numerous other scholars – whose names are given in a List of Acknowledgements in volume XI – have kindly answered enquiries on particular points. No one but the Editors themselves, however, is responsible for the errors and inconsistencies which remain.

A large debt is owed to the custodians of the libraries and archives in which most of the work has been done. Dr R. W. Ladborough, Pepys Librarian at Magdalene, has given every possible help. Mr D. Pepys Whiteley, formerly Deputy Pepys Librarian, has answered many queries and has read not only parts of the Introduction in typescript but also a large number of proof-sheets. Mr G. P. B. Naish of the National Maritime Museum, Greenwich, Dr A. E. J. Hollaender of Guildhall Library, London, Dr Neville Williams of the Public Record Office and Dr J. P. C. Kent of the Department of Coins and Medals at the British Museum, have readily given expert help to the project over several years. Mr A. W. Aspital, formerly of the Department of Prints and Drawings at the British Museum, has been of great assistance (along with the contributing editors, the late Professor Reddaway and Mr Millar) in the choice of illustrations. The staffs of several libraries and record offices have unfailingly co-operated in the task of ransacking their collections: in particular, those of the Bodleian; the British Museum; the Public Record Office; the Corporation of London Records Office; the Institute of Historical Research, London; Somerset House; the Wellcome Historical Medical Library, and Royal Holloway College. The Society of Genealogists has courteously allowed access to its valuable collection of copies and abstracts of parish registers and London city company records. Thanks are due also to Miss M. Swarbrick, archivist of the city of Westminster; Miss D. Coates, formerly Librarian of Longleat; Dr C. H. Josten, of the Museum of the History of Science, Oxford; to the county archivists of London, Middlesex, Dorset, Huntingdonshire and Cambridgeshire; to the bursars of Magdalene College and Christ's College, Cambridge, and to the archivists of the University of Cambridge, of Lambeth Palace, and of the Museum Enschedé, Haarlem.

The work done by a number of secretaries and assistants has been indispensable. Mrs D. Hopkins typed the diary text with exemplary skill and accuracy. Mrs H. Murdoch and Mrs G. Jackman coped admirably with a succession of manuscript drafts and typescripts, as well as with a large correspondence. Miss D. Ensor and Mrs H. J. Hunt aided in the construction of a card-index of persons. Miss M. R. Pryor and Mrs R. Miller independently read the galleys of the first three volumes against the typescript.

The late Mrs Robert Latham read many of the proofs. Beyond that, she gave help which can never be measured.

Last, and not least, the Editors place on record their thanks to the publishers for the courtesy, co-operation and quite extraordinary patience which they have shown in the production of this edition.

INTRODUCTION

I The Diarist[1]

When he began to keep his diary in 1660, Pepys was a young man of close on 27, employed in a double capacity – as a household official in the service of his cousin Edward Mountagu (Cromwellian politician and naval commander), and as a clerk in the Exchequer. He had been educated at St Paul's School and at Cambridge, and in 1655 had married Elizabeth St Michel, an Anglo-French girl seven years his junior. He and his wife – they had no children – had settled in 1658 in a house in Axe Yard, off King St, Westminster, within a short walking distance both of Mountagu's official lodgings in Whitehall Palace and of the Exchequer building close by Westminster Hall. Almost a mile to the east, reached through crowded streets or more easily by river, lay the city of London, which was not only the commercial and financial capital of the country but also at that time a place where people lived as well as worked. It was to the city – to Seething Lane, not far from the Tower and the port – that Pepys moved house when in June 1660 he took office as Clerk of the Acts to the Navy Board, there to begin his career as a naval administrator. In later life, after the diary period, Pepys settled in other houses, but always (until his last illness, when he moved to Clapham) in London or Westminster.

His natural habitat consisted of these few square miles of urban territory. He was as much a Londoner as Samuel Johnson, and his diary is in one sense a history of his London neighbourhood. Never, even in his affluent retirement, did Pepys try to become a country gentleman. He enjoyed visits to East Anglia, the homeland of his forebears, and he took a townsman's pleasure in short retreats to the countryside, but, as we may gather both from his diary and from his letters, he always felt life in the country to be a form of exile.[2] London was the centre of Pepys's civilisation. It was at that time unchallenged in its eminence among English cities. The metropolitan area held about

1. This section summarises Pepys's career principally before and during the diary period. Additional biographical details (with fuller references than are given here), together with some account of his intellectual interests, will be found in the *Companion* articles ('Books', 'Health', 'Music', 'Science', 'Theatre', etc.).
2. Cf. 14 July 1667; *Priv. Corr.*, ii. 1. He rented a weekend villa at Parson's Green near Fulham, c. 1667–81: Bryant, ii. 183, 360.

half-a-million inhabitants – perhaps five-eighths of the total urban population of the country. (Bristol, its nearest rival in size, had only about 30,000.) Yet, from the point of view of the people living in it, London was not over-large. All that Londoners needed for a full life was there, yet contained in a space so small that it was easy to escape for an hour's airing to fields or river walks. It had taverns, clubs, shops and (after the Restoration) public playhouses. Its musical life – at a time when music held a high place in English culture – was the best in the country. It housed scholars, writers, artists and publishers. In its churches and conventicles was offered an inviting variety of sermon and service. Above all, it was the centre of English political life – the home of royalty, of parliament, of high finance and of the governing *élite*.

Politics fascinated Pepys. As an impressionable boy he had lived through civil war and revolution; he was now to witness the miracle of a bloodless restoration – even to play a small clerical part in it. In an age of violent partisanship – but also of widespread neutralism – Pepys came to have no very strong political convictions, unless a belief in governmental efficiency may be counted as one. By 1660, he was ready, although a servant of the Republic, to welcome a return to monarchy simply because it would give stability. Similarly, his ecclesiastical views (at any rate when he was a young man) did not spring from doctrinal principles or from the inner motions of a spiritual life. They were simply the working rules of a worldling who favoured ecclesiastical uniformity for the sake of civil peace. In religion, as in all things, he was curious; he enjoyed sermon-tasting in several churches on a single sabbath, and was willing to listen even to the Presbyterian preachers who preached long and hard. But he was clearly in 1660 an Anglican by habit and by sentiment, and had for some years been attending by preference the illegal prayer-book services which so often had little difficulty in prospering in Cromwell's capital.[3] The puritan fanatics he abhorred and distrusted.

Pepys had not been born to wealth or power, and he had not inherited any great legacy of culture from his parents,[4] but by the time

3. See esp. 4 March, 8 April 1660; Grey, ii. 426. He did not, however, attend communion: below, 30 March 1662.

4. They were not highly cultivated (his mother was quite uneducated), but his father's possessions included maps, books and virginals (*Family Letters*, pp. 13–15), and his younger brother Tom, a working tailor, knew French (15 March 1664).

the diary opens he was clearly beginning to be ambitious to take a place of his own among both the politicians and the virtuosi of London. He had grown up to think of himself, in the words of his favourite Baconian essay, as '*faber fortunae*', and there were means of entry to these circles, even to young men of small inheritance, provided they had the right abilities and connections.   Politicians, such as his cousin Mountagu, needed their 'men of business' to keep their accounts, manage their households and fend off importunate petitioners.   The other side of Pepys's ambition – that of becoming a virtuoso – may have been slower in forming because it was not so directly associated with the business of making a career.   But by 1660 he had already acquired (like so many of the lively-minded young men of his genera-tion) the elements of the best general culture of the day: a classical and mathematical education, together with a curiosity about the fine arts and the sciences, if not yet an informed interest in them.   Besides cultivating his music, he was beginning to make collections of books, prints and mathematical instruments.

The 'man of business' and the 'virtuoso' – both important and fash-ionable types in late seventeenth-century England – were perhaps the two roles in which Pepys in his serious moments saw himself most clearly in 1660.   Another favourite role (also fashionable) was, in the language of the time, that of the 'goodfellow' – the man of pleasure. London offered him all the diversions he craved for: music and women (to the beauty of both he stood in a 'strange slavery'[5]), friendships, the casual sociableness of the taverns, above all – what only a great town can give – the constant stimulus of new experience.   Pepys was always 'with child to see any strange thing'[6] – living and savouring every moment of his life with an intensity which never failed, despite occasional spasms of guilt.   There can have been few young men in London with an appetite for pleasure to compare with his in sharpness and range.

He had been born on 23 February 1633 in Salisbury Court, off Fleet St.   There, in a roomy house backing on to the churchyard of St Bride, his father John carried on his business as a tailor.   John Pepys had married Margaret Kite, sister of a Whitechapel butcher, seven years before, and Samuel was the fifth in a line of eleven children born to them.   His father had several relatives at this time who had settled in business in London, but by origin the Pepyses were country-folk who, from the thirteenth century onwards, had held land as

5. 6 September 1664.   6. 14 May 1660.

villeins in or near Cottenham in Cambridgeshire. In the fifteenth century they had produced several men of ability who had served the Benedictine house of Crowland as reeves and bailiffs, and in Elizabeth's reign the grandfather of John Pepys had by a shrewd second marriage equipped himself to buy the manor of Impington, near Cambridge. His daughter Paulina had been married in 1618 to a brother of the 1st Earl of Manchester, Sir Sidney Mountagu, who in 1627 had acquired the house and estate of Hinchingbrooke, near Huntingdon. The Pepyses had thereby established a connection with one of the most prominent of East Anglian families. Another branch of the family, established at South Creake, Norfolk, in the reign of Henry VIII, had prospered in trade, become landowners, and since at least 1563 had been allowed a coat of arms.

Numerous and widespread by the time of the diarist's birth, the Pepyses enjoyed a certain pride of achievement and kinship, and counted among their number a variety of types: yeomen and gentry, tradesmen and lawyers. The lawyers were particularly noteworthy. The administrative ability which had marked many of the Pepyses in medieval times seems to have shown itself in the seventeenth century in a flowering of legal talent. In the generation to which Pepys's father belonged, there were three cousins who all became lawyers of some distinction: Richard Pepys (d. 1659), Cromwellian Lord Chief Justice of Ireland; Roger Pepys, M.P. (d. 1688), Recorder of Cambridge (as was his father before him); and John Pepys, LL.D. (d. 1692), civil lawyer and for a time Fellow of Trinity Hall, Cambridge. A more distant relative of the same generation, John Pepys of Ashtead, Surrey (d. 1651), served Chief Justice Coke as his confidential and much-loved secretary.

Family tradition might easily have led Pepys himself to a career in the law. Perhaps only the accident of civil war and the influence of the Mountagus determined otherwise. Eldest of four surviving children by the time he was seven, he was sent off after the outbreak of war in 1642 to Huntingdonshire, where he lived in all probability with his uncle, Robert Pepys of Brampton, a man of some substance, who appears to have served in the household of his relatives, the Mountagus of nearby Hinchingbrooke. Samuel almost certainly attended the grammar school at Huntingdon, which counted among its ex-pupils not only Oliver Cromwell but also Edward Mountagu, the young squire of Hinchingbrooke. The latter – eight years Pepys's senior – inherited the estate in 1644 from his father, Sir Sidney. It was in his service that Pepys was to find his chance of making a career, following much the same path, *mutatis mutandis*, as many of his medieval forebears. They had served abbots; he, in the new fashion, was to serve the lay landlord who had succeeded to monastic property. (Hinchingbrooke was founded on the spoils of a nunnery.) Edward Mountagu, with his more prominent cousin of Kimbolton, Huntingdonshire, the 2nd Earl of Manchester, now acquired in the civil war a new importance as a leading member of the parliamentary army of the Eastern Association. He saw active service as one of Cromwell's 'young colonels' and sat in parliament as member for Huntingdonshire.

Pepys returned to London after the war had ended and entered St Paul's School, there to be given a grounding in classics and mathematics. He later recalled in his diary[7] that with a schoolboy's enthusiasm he had rejoiced in the execution of Charles I. Mountagu, on the other hand, broke with his army colleagues over this and other acts of extremism. He went out of politics between 1648 and 1653 and lived quietly at home as a country gentleman. Meanwhile, his young kinsman had passed from school to Cambridge with the help of a leaving exhibition. He was entered first at Trinity Hall (very much a lawyer's college), and then transferred to Magdalene, whose Master John Sadler was a neighbour in Salisbury Court.[8] His election to college scholarships in 1651 and 1653 suggests some academic success. He retained throughout life a taste for the Latin classics – particularly for Cicero and Ovid – and an interest in mathematics. He learned shorthand.[9] His intellectual interests, if yet a little superficial, were wide. Music, an early passion, was first among them. By 1660, when the diary opens, he played the lute, the viol and the flageolet, was interested in other instruments, sang well, and was about to make an attempt at composition.   As a boy he had been cast for a female part in a privately produced play,[10] and as an undergraduate he had tried his hand at writing a romance. In 1664 the manuscript still survived, unfinished, but impressively entitled: '*Love a Cheate*.[11]

He took his bachelor's degree in March 1654, and it is likely that it was not long before he entered the service of Edward Mountagu as his secretary and agent in London. Mountagu had returned to politics

7. 1 November 1660.
8. J. Hutchins, *Hist. Dorset* (1796–1815), i. 260.
9. See below, pp. xlix–l.   10. 30 May 1668.
11. 30 January 1664.

in the summer of 1653 when he sat in Barebone's Parliament; soon afterwards he was serving on the Council of State and on two of its committees. Like so many of his sort, an empiric rather than an enthusiast in politics, Mountagu now cast in his lot with the cause of firm government; the old association with Cromwell was restored, and with the establishment of the Protectorate in December 1653, he quickly became an active member of the new Council of State and of the Treasury Commission. He received a salary of £1000 p.a. for each of these posts and was given official lodgings in Whitehall Palace. He now needed a secretary and London agent, while Pepys, trained for no profession, needed a career. By late 1654 or early 1655 it is probable that Pepys had begun to work for him, although there is no documentary proof of the fact until a year or so later.[12] The supposition is strengthened by the fact that by December 1655 Pepys had married the fifteen-year-old daughter of a penniless Huguenot exile[13] – Elizabeth St Michel, a wife he could not have taken without having an assured income.

In Mountagu's household Pepys mastered his first lessons as an administrator. For many men of ability but limited means, the route to state preferment lay through private service. Attachment to the household of a great personage gave a blend of the right experience and the right acquaintance.[14] Pepys, living with his wife in a single room in his master's lodgings,[15] looked after Mountagu's Whitehall household and helped with his London business generally. Mountagu's duties mounted rapidly. He was soon appointed to the Admiralty Committee in addition to his other posts, and in January 1656 was made a General-at-Sea. In the four successive summers of 1656–9 he was abroad on naval service; in the winters he would spend weeks on end out of London with his large and growing family at Hinchingbrooke. With every absence Pepys's responsibilities were enlarged. He

12. There is among Mountagu's papers a memorandum of 15 December 1655 in Pepys's hand (Carte 74, ff. 18–19) and a letter of 11 March 1656 addressed by Mountagu to 'my Servant Samuell Pepys at my Lodginges in Whitehalle' (ib. 223, f. 170r).

13. This is the date of the civil ceremony. It seems likely that a religious ceremony had taken place in the previous October: see below, ii. 194 & n. 3.

14. Among Pepys's contemporaries, or near-contemporaries, Sir Stephen Fox, Paymaster-General of the Army, started off as a household servant of Lord Percy; James Carkesse, of the Ticket Office, later a junior colleague of Pepys, graduated from the household of the 1st Marquess of Dorchester.

15. 25 February 1667.

managed the servants, collected Mountagu's salaries and fees, and conducted the multitude of transactions with tradesmen and bankers which
the affairs of a scattered and busy family demanded. There was at
least one lapse of vigilance: in December 1657 Mountagu had to
replace one of the London maidservants, and it appeared that a contri-
butory cause of the trouble was that the young and pleasure-loving
major-domo was not always at home.[16]   But Pepys was on the whole
a faithful steward – prompt in the execution of orders, punctual and
systematic in his financial accounts, a servant whose diligence and
honesty were coming to be taken for granted.

He was introduced by Mountagu some time after 1656 to a post in
the public service, becoming clerk to George Downing, a Teller of the
Receipt in the Exchequer.   In return for a small salary, supplemented
by fees and gratuities, Pepys there performed duties (mostly of paying
out cash) which did not require long or fixed hours of attendance.
His posts suited him well, and he was on the whole a happy and
successful young man.   But he had his setbacks.   At some unknown
date in 1656–8 and for some unknown reason, he and his wife had
'differences' and separated, Elizabeth going to live for a short time at
Charing Cross.[17]   And in March 1658 he underwent a dangerous
operation for the removal of a bladder stone.   For years afterwards he
celebrated his recovery by an annual banquet.   In August 1658, or
thereabouts, a new phase of his life began, when he and his wife set
up their own household in Axe Yard, Westminster.[18]   He remained
attached to Mountagu's service, though by the time the diary opens
in January 1660 his duties had been for the most part reduced to a
supervision of the family accounts.

Shortly after the Pepyses moved into their new home Oliver
Cromwell died, in September 1658, and the state lost the only leader
capable of holding together the revolutionary government.   Mountagu
was identified with the late Protector's personal following.   He had
supported (in vain) every proposal to make the protectorate here-
ditary, as well as the more radical proposal of 1656–7 to make Oliver
King.   In early 1658 he had accepted a Cromwellian barony and membership of the short-lived Upper House.   After Oliver's death he
transferred his allegiance to the successor, Oliver's son Richard, but the

16. Carte 73, ff. 175r, 187r, 190r.
17. 13 August 1661; 15 August 1663.
18. The date is roughly established by his reference at 26 August 1661 to
having then had a maid of his own for exactly three years.

new Protector was too diffident a politician to survive for long in the jungle rivalries which now broke loose. With Richard's overthrow in April 1659, Mountagu became in effect alienated, like so many other moderate 'Presbyterian' politicians, from the revolutionary cause. He continued to serve the state, but with silent and significant reservations. Despatched with a fleet to the Baltic in March 1659 to mediate in the war between Sweden and Denmark, Mountagu found himself more and more at loggerheads with the government, in which outright republicans were now in the ascendant. Not only did he take part in secret negotiations with the exiled Charles II, but in August he brought home his fleet in circumstances which suggested that he was eager to make contact with the royalist risings of that month. Arriving too late, he found himself in disgrace, and retired to Hinchingbrooke for the winter. Pepys, who at the end of May had paid him a brief visit in the Baltic carrying letters from the government,[19] remained in charge of his affairs in London. His letters to Mountagu on public as well as private affairs were one of the means whereby his master kept in touch with events.[20]

In October 1659 the general officers of the army took over the government, dismissing the Rump which had been in session since Richard's fall in April. Thereupon it gradually became clear that, if anarchy

19. *Sandwich*, pp. 33, 35. Pepys was with the Baltic squadron for two days.
20. Carte 73, ff. 320r, 322r, etc.

KEY TO MAP opposite

169 Hamlin's Yard	184 Bowman's Court	200 Vine Court
170 Duffin's Alley	185 Poulterers' Yard	201 Green's Alley
171 Sea Alley	186 White's Alley	202 Little Sanctuary
172 Bell Court	187 Clinkers Court	204 Red Cross Alley
173 Rose and Crown Inn	188 Falcon Alley	205 Ogilby's Yard
174 Chequer Alley	190 Antelope Alley	244 King's Alms Houses
175 Pensioners' Alley	191 Blue Boar Yard	245 Little Almery
176 Brewer's Yard	192 George Yard	246 Gatehouse
177 Rhenish Wine Yard	193 Bell Alley	263 Fish Yard
178 Stephen's Lane	194 Fountain Court	264 Westminster Hall
179 Lady Court	195 Frogget's Alley	265 Exchequer
180 White Horse Inn	196 Spread Eagle Alley	266 House of Commons
181 Braceby's Alley	197 Star Alley	267 House of Lords
182 Whiting's Alley	198 Scott's Alley	
183 Pitman's Alley	199 Round Court	

The gateway across King St was Holbein's Gate

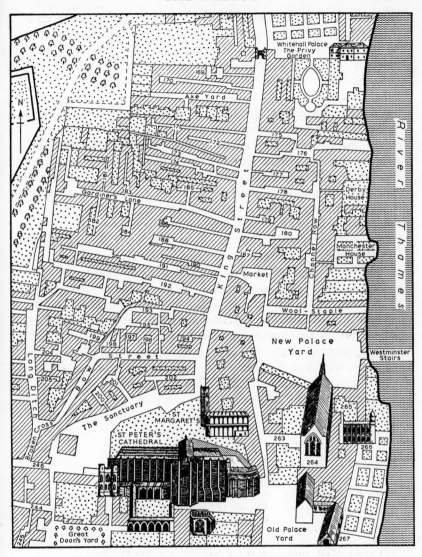

WESTMINSTER: AXE YARD AND KING STREET

Map prepared by the late Professor T. F. Reddaway from R. Morden and
P. Lea, *A prospect of London and Westminster* (1682)

were to be avoided, the choice before the country was between military dictatorship and a Stuart restoration.   Other methods – the reformed protectorate which Mountagu had once favoured, or the parliamentary republic which leaders of the Rump stood for – were proven failures.   The public, sick with fear of another civil war, and tired of sterile experiments, high taxation and irresponsible leadership, gradually set what hopes it had in the direction of a return of the old scheme of things, or something like it – a monarchy and a parliament. The army officers no longer commanded a revolutionary army worth the name.   They had no confidence that their men, with pay badly in arrears, would any longer obey orders.   Moreover, the most powerful section of the army, under General Monck in Scotland, had declared its opposition to the October *putsch* and had moved south towards the border, giving silent encouragement to the hope that it would support the cause of a restored parliament.   It was in or near to London, where Pepys was watching developments, that a succession of events occurred in December 1659 which had the effect of completely altering the political situation by the end of the year.   On 5 December the apprentices in the city mobbed the soldiers.   On the 13th the fleet in the Downs declared for a parliament, its example being followed soon afterwards by the Dublin garrison and most of the army in Ireland. On the 19th the Common Council of the city of London, already in touch with Monck, secured a promise of a free Parliament from Fleetwood, Commander-in-Chief of the army, to whom a parliament now represented the only hope of pay for his men.   On Christmas Eve the rank and file of some of the London regiments demonstrated in favour of a parliament, and on Boxing Day the Rump was allowed to reassemble.   Finally, on 1 January 1660 Monck moved his leading troops over the Tweed, and began to march south.

On that same New Year's Day Pepys began to keep his diary. Probably it was his first attempt – certainly he later spoke of it as though he had never kept one before.[21]   The impulse to do so now came principally from the alarms and excitements of these public events of December 1659.   The first five months of the diary, before the restoration of Charles II, are crowded with political news.   This political crisis may explain his choice of the moment at which to begin the diary, but no doubt there were other impulses which led him to

21. 9 March 1669.   It is perhaps remarkable that he does not appear to have kept a journal of his Baltic voyage in 1659.

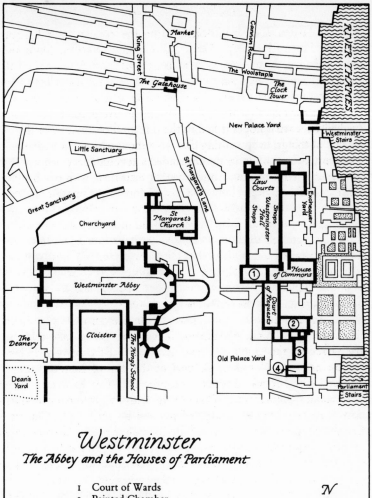

Westminster
The Abbey and the Houses of Parliament

1 Court of Wards
2 Painted Chamber
3 House of Lords
4 Prince's Chamber

Based on a map prepared by the late Professor T. F. Reddaway

keep it.[22]   After all is said, the origins of so deeply personal a document must themselves be personal.   One origin is certainly the vanity which is so clearly marked a feature of Pepys's character.   Another, equally certainly, is his love of life.   The diary is a by-product of his energetic pursuit of happiness.   The process of recording had the effect, as he soon found out, of heightening and extending his enjoyment. It enabled him to relish every experience more than once – not only at the moment of its happening but also in its recollection.   But possibly the most important part of the explanation may have been his concern for neatness, which showed itself throughout his life in many forms – in his carefully arranged library of books marshalled by size, or in his taste for formal gardens and English Renaissance architecture.   His handwriting was small, shapely, controlled.   The very inditing of the quick slim symbols of shorthand probably gave him a palpable satisfaction.   Similarly, it is likely that the diary itself, fully and regularly kept, tidy and neat, had the effect of making life itself seem neat and tidy – the quotidian chaos reduced to order, each day's events packaged and tied up in a rounded summary.   He was by nature a man of system,[23] and one to whom the keeping of records was necessary to the art of living.   The diary was one of a series of records, which by the 1660s included petty-cash books, account books, letter-books, memorandum books and also more idiosyncratic records such as his 'book of tales' and his list of private vows.[24]   All were means to a disciplined life, methods of canalising the stream of experience – the diary best of all, because it was the most comprehensive and the most intimate.   As a young man, he took vows on several matters of conduct, but never a vow to keep a diary; that came naturally.   In the whole diary there is

22. Cf. below, pp. cvi+, cxiv. His patron Mountagu was by 1660 already keeping notebooks and admiral's logs, but they were very different in character from Pepys's diary and cannot be assumed to have had any influence on it. There is a pocket-book of Mountagu's notes (1655–68) in the Bodleian (MS. Lyell empt. 29), and miscellaneous jottings, astronomical calculations, etc. (1652–9) in the first volume of his 'Journals' (ten vols, with App., in the Sandwich MSS at Mapperton, Dorset). His journals, strictly so-called, in that collection are admiral's logs (covering his voyages during 1659–65, printed by R. C. Anderson in 1929).   The rest (and much the greatest part) of the 'Journals' consists of miscellaneous travel-notes and drawings dating principally from the time of his embassy to Spain (1665–8). Sections of the ten volumes were written out by his clerks, but none by Pepys himself.

23. Clarendon later said of him: 'No man in England was of more method': below, 14 February 1667.

24. For these two last, see, e.g., 24 October 1663; 21 August 1664.

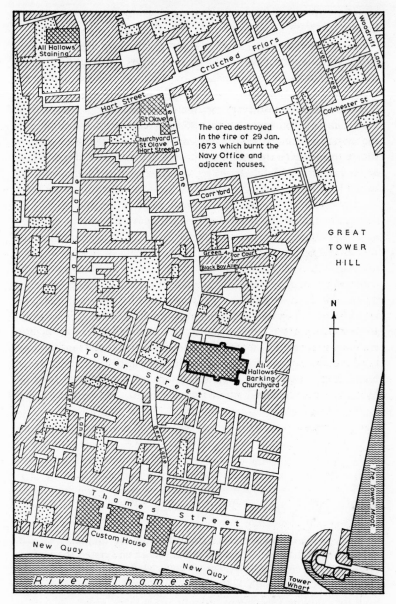

The area destroyed in the fire of 29 Jan. 1673 which burnt the Navy Office and adjacent houses.

THE CITY: THE NAVY OFFICE AND TOWER HILL

Map prepared by the late Professor T. F. Reddaway from J. Ogilby and W. Morgan, *A large and accurate map of the city of London* (1677)

no complaint that it was a drudgery to keep it, although there must have been occasions when to make time for it was not easy.

He had begun it at a time when his own affairs as well as those of the nation were about to take a sudden turn. By 25 April 1660, when the newly elected parliament demanded by public opinion had met, agreement had been reached secretly between Monck and the exiled court on the terms of a royalist restoration. Mountagu, back in office (as Councillor of State and General-at-Sea) as soon as Monck took over the government in February, joined the fleet in the Thames on 23 March, carrying Pepys with him as Admiral's secretary. John Creed, another of his East Anglian *protégés*, had held this post in 1659 and was to hold it again under other admirals, but Mountagu preferred Pepys on this occasion. Perhaps there were personal reasons, or Creed's strong Puritanism disqualified him; or Pepys's knowledge of shorthand and ciphers (already considerable) was in the circumstances of 1660 held to be an advantage. On 11 May the fleet sailed to Holland to bring Charles II back to his kingdom. Pepys worked hard at his letters and accounts, as well as at the notes for his diary; he delighted in the friendliness and excitement on board the *Naseby* (soon renamed the *Royal Charles*); he wandered ashore, agape and marvelling, through the strange Dutch streets. He was presented to the King and his brother the Duke of York at The Hague; he made himself useful and pleasant to naval officers and courtiers; above all he established his reputation with Mountagu himself. On the return of the fleet to England, Mountagu was showered with titles and offices – and property worth £4000 p.a. to sustain his new dignities. He became a Knight of the Garter, Earl of Sandwich, Vice-Admiral of the Kingdom, Master of the Great Wardrobe, and Clerk of the Privy Seal. He now promised Pepys that they would 'rise together',[25] and in June 1660 he acquired for his assistant a government post of some importance – that of Clerk of the Acts to the Navy Board – as well as making him one of his deputies at the Privy Seal. Pepys, alone among Mountagu's entourage to be so highly favoured, moved house from Axe Yard to the Clerk of the Navy's official lodgings in Seething Lane in the city. The lodgings were part of a range of buildings which housed (besides the office itself) several senior officials, some clerks and a housekeeper. There Pepys lived, with his growing family of servants and clerks, until the building was destroyed by fire in 1673.

With this appointment Pepys's apprentice days were over. He was

25. 2 June 1660.

now one of the Principal Officers of the Navy, with the rank of esquire, two clerks at his beck and call, a salary of £350 p.a. and prospects of making handsome 'profits' far greater than his official pay. The Navy Board, under the direction of the Lord High Admiral of the Kingdom (the Duke of York, 1660–73), dealt with the civil administration of the navy (stores, provisions, victuals, shipbuilding, ship-repair and dockyard management) in much the same way as it continued to do until its abolition in 1832. Reconstituted in 1660 after the Interregnum, when it had been replaced by committee rule, the Board now consisted, apart from Pepys, of six officers: the Treasurer of the Navy (Sir George Carteret, head of the office), the Comptroller (Slingsby in 1660, Sir John Mennes after 1661, busiest of the Board if he were to live up to his title), the Surveyor (Sir William Batten, in charge of ships and stores), two Commissioners with general duties (Sir William Penn and Lord Berkeley of Stratton) and a resident Commissioner at Chatham, the largest of the yards (Peter Pett, the shipbuilder). Except for Berkeley, a courtier and royalist soldier, all had seen considerable service at sea or in naval administration. Pepys was young: in naval affairs he was a tyro with only a few weeks of pen-pushing to his credit. But he had what was to prove of greater worth than either the rank or the experience of his colleagues – he had the mental powers, the physical vitality and the love of order which go to the making of a great administrator.

The diary contains the story of his developing skill and reputation between 1660 and 1669. Within a few days of beginning work, he had resigned his Exchequer clerkship and, characteristically, was making an inventory of the Navy Board's papers; within a few months, he had familiarised himself with much of its routine and had asserted his rights as Clerk against the claims of his colleagues. By his capacity for hard slogging – starting work at 4 a.m. in summertime when necessary – he was setting a pace which no rival on the Board could match. Not that he was ever in danger of becoming a drudge. He lost few opportunities of conviviality with friends, colleagues or business acquaintances. He devoted himself almost as systematically to music and the theatre as to work, and (acting hopefully on his maxim 'nulla puella negat')[26] he snatched all possible (and some impossible) chances that came his way of brief debauches with the complaisant shopgirls and servant-girls who in such numbers found him irresistible.

The year beginning in January 1662 with the issue of the Duke of

26. 4 September 1660.

York's Instructions to the Navy Board marked a special advance in Pepys's progress as an official. He redoubled his attendance at the office, gave up his part-time work as Sandwich's deputy at the Privy Seal, and took vows to protect himself against wine, women and plays. The diary for the spring and summer of 1662 speaks a new note: for months on end it chronicles the life of a virtuous and single-minded official, learning a new pleasure – that of following his business. He abstracted all the contracts made since the Restoration, rearranged the books of the office and began to take frequent lessons from experts in the technologies of his work – in shipbuilding, the measuring of timber, the stoving of hemp. From being a clerk registering the Board's decisions, Pepys had become a leader among his colleagues: able to sway the Board, against the arguments of their technical expert Batten the Surveyor, in the award of an important contract for masts;[27] more knowledgeable than the rest of his colleagues on most matters, and the only one among them with a synoptic view of office business. His growth in confidence and maturity is shown by his boldness in deliberately risking the loss of Sandwich's goodwill in November 1663. Sandwich had been openly conducting a love affair in Chelsea which threatened his family happiness and led to his neglecting attendance at court. Pepys screwed up his courage, and, after much hesitation and consultation with others of Sandwich's entourage, wrote him a 'great letter of reproof'.[28] The *protégé* had become the censor. His intervention earned him Sandwich's displeasure, but the love affair was broken off, and after a few months patron and *protégé* had resumed their old relations.

'Chance without merit' had brought him into the navy, he wrote on 1 November 1665; only diligence, he added, could keep him there. The test came in 1664–7 during the Second Dutch War, when the national effort turned on the navy, and when the scrutiny of parliament was fastened on the conduct of naval officials. Ships and men had to be provided. Material and provisions were needed in unprecedented quantities, quickly, in the right places, at the right prices (and very often on credit). At every turn the Board was hamstrung by lack of finance. Generous though parliament was, it was not generous enough. Seeing so much at stake and so much going wrong, Pepys drove hard on colleagues, clerks and contractors; he roused the dockyards by surprise inspections; he rooted out some of the worst effects of corruption. Troubles mounted and multiplied; disaster and disgrace often seemed

27. 10, 21 September 1663.   28. Below, iv. 387–8.

close at hand.   The war was indecisive.   The summer campaign of
1665 was fought to the accompaniment of the Plague; that of 1666 was
followed in September by the Great Fire of London.   1666 saw also
the loss of Pepys's patron: Sandwich was removed to Spain as ambassador to escape the disgrace which followed the discovery of his having
permitted irregularities in the disposal of prize goods (from which
Pepys also had allowed himself to benefit).   In June 1667, while peace
negotiations were under way, the Dutch had the triumphant impertinence to invade the Thames and Medway.

Through all these difficulties Pepys kept his head, though not without fears for the outcome.   He throve on hard work.   In 1664 he was
appointed a member of the Fishery Corporation.   In 1665 he undertook the Treasurership of the Tangier Committee, in addition to his
other duties – an arduous appointment, but lucrative, gained in competition with a well-placed and high-born rival, Henry Brouncker.   To
live in the company of crises stimulated Pepys.   Friendships and love
affairs multiplied; theatre visits became more frequent; diary entries
longer.[29]   In February 1665 he was elected a Fellow of the Royal
Society, where he took his place as one of the interested amateurs of
miscellaneous learning who formed a large proportion of the Society's
membership.   The Society included a number of Pepys's colleagues
and friends – Sandwich and his secretary John Creed, the Navy Commissioner Viscount Brouncker (an able mathematician who served as
first President of the Society), Peter Pett the shipwright, Thomas
Povey of the Tangier Committee, Sir William Petty, and John Evelyn.
Such men as these helped to establish the close connection between
science and the practical arts (including that of administration) which
was such an important feature of the Society's work.   But Pepys also
delighted, like other members, in attending the discourses and demonstrations on all manner of subjects – from comets and hydrostatics to
French methods of baking bread – though he did not always have
'philosophy enough to understand them'.[30]

But his work for the navy remained Pepys's first concern.   It was,
of course, impossible for the Navy Board, under the spur of war – and
of Pepys – to become, of a sudden, quite united and thoroughly
efficient.   It remained a prey to delays and corruption – its accounts
improperly kept and in arrear, its meetings irregular.   But it was on
the whole successful.   It handled greater sums of money than had ever
been granted for war purposes before, and made larger contracts; in

29. 1667 is the longest year in the diary.   30. 1 March 1665.

three years of war it despatched (according to Pepys's calculation) twelve times the amount of paperwork that had been dealt with in the one and a half years of Cromwell's Dutch War.[31] Some reforms were achieved. In 1665 Pepys improved the victualling arrangements by a scheme of control, with surveyors in each of the main ports and himself as Surveyor-General, and in January 1666 he reorganised the method of keeping pursers' accounts. A proper oversight of general expenditure, next to impossible as long as the comptrollership remained solely in Mennes's weak hands, was made more likely in January 1667 by the appointment of two assistants, and in 1669 by a new method of keeping and checking storekeepers' accounts, with special officers appointed to each yard. Soon after the end of the war, in 1668–9 (at Pepys's instigation), the Lord High Admiral made a thorough investigation of the work of all the Principal Officers, by which he established (at Pepys's prompting) that all (except Pepys) had fallen short in the performance of the duties placed on them by the Admiral's Instructions of 1662. Meantime the ubiquitous Clerk of the Acts had become the Board's leading spokesman against parliamentary criticism. His speeches to committees of the Commons, in answer to charges about the defence of the Medway (22 October 1667) and about pay-tickets (5 March 1668), were notable performances. The latter – three hours long – earned him, according to his own account, an orator's fame. (Perhaps he could, like so many of his kin, have become a successful legal advocate; he already had some hopes of joining others of the Board as a member of Parliament.) More typical of the profession he was beginning to adorn was the elaborate memorandum which he submitted in November 1669 to the Parliamentary Commission of Public Accounts: a document justifying the whole conduct of the Navy Office during the war.[32] Like his parliamentary speeches, it was long, detailed and crushing.

By the time the diary ended in the spring of 1669, Pepys's professional success was well established. He was the acknowledged 'right hand of the Navy';[33] master of an elegant household; owner of a coach and a pair of black horses; a man rich enough (mostly from his fees and gratuities) to retire and live 'with comfort, though not with abundance'[34] if parliamentary critics should oust him, as they had ousted Pett and almost ousted Penn. But although prosperous and successful,

31. PL 2242, p. 100.   32. Ib., pp. 509+.
33. The phrase was Albemarle's: 24 April 1665.
34. 20 April 1669.

Pepys was by no means free from care. He was just recovering from
the effects of his wife's discovery in October 1668 of his affair with her
companion, Deborah Willet. (He was often inclined to forget whose
companions these pretty young women were supposed to be.) He
was worried to distraction at times both about Deb and about his eyes,
which since 1664 had been causing him such discomfort that at times
they would 'ake, ready to drop out'.[35] The eye-strain imposed by the
hard work of the war years had not been eased by any of the remedies
recommended by advisers and friends – spectacles, paper tubes, bleed-
ings and pills. Strong light now hurt his eyes acutely; the writing of
the diary became so difficult that he convinced himself that he was
going blind, 'which [is] almost as much', he wrote, 'as to see myself go
into my grave'. Sadly he drew the entries to a close at the end of May
1669. In the following autumn he took a long holiday in Holland,
Flanders and France with his wife.   A bare fortnight or so after their return Elizabeth died (at the age of 29) from a fever caught on the journey.

Pepys's marriage had survived the strains created by his infidelities,
but principally because only one of them – the affair with Deb – had
been brought to light. Others had been suspected, but had lain successfully hidden. Pepys's attitude to his wife had often been selfish
and insensitive,[36] and although on occasion he was capable of understanding the loneliness and neglect she felt, he would usually assume
that it was enough to pity her, or to buy her a present, or to arrange
for her to take lessons in music and drawing. Yet of his genuine
affection for Elizabeth there can be no doubt. Perhaps one of the
reasons for his selfishness was that they had no children. At first, he
had felt the lack of them; by September 1664 he was reconciled to
childlessness, even glad of it.[37]

As for the other members of his family, his mother had died in
March 1667 at Brampton, Hunts., the property left to Pepys and his
father by the diarist's uncle, Robert Pepys, in 1661. On receiving
this inheritance, Pepys's father had handed over his tailoring business
to his second surviving son, Tom, who died a bachelor in March
1664. Old John Pepys lived until 1680, made comfortable by an

35. 8 June 1664.
36. It is perhaps significant that her birthdays are never mentioned in the
diary.
37. See below, p. 1; 6 November 1663, 26 July, 22 September 1664. By
28 June 1661 Pepys and his wife were sleeping in the room they had called the
nursery.

annuity paid him by Samuel to supplement Robert Pepys's legacy. Pepys's youngest brother John, eight years his junior, had been sent to Christ's College, Cambridge, after leaving St Paul's School, and was intended for the Church. He took orders but never held any living, drifting rather fecklessly into semi-dependence on his brother, who obtained for him the clerkship of Trinity House in 1670. In 1673 he became also joint-Clerk of the Acts of the Navy Board (with Thomas Hayter, Pepys's old clerk). He remained an ineffectual pluralist, in both posts, until he died, unmarried, in 1677. Samuel paid his debts. Paulina, their only surviving sister, was seven years younger than Pepys, to whom she seemed a forlorn hope for marriage, hard as he tried to find a suitable match. In February 1668, however, she was married off to a country neighbour, John Jackson of Ellington, Hunts. It was their second son John who ultimately became Pepys's heir.

Pepys's life at the conclusion of the diary in 1669 had reached only its mid-point, and, as for his career, the major part of it still lay ahead. With the retirement in 1668 of the Admiral's secretary, Sir William Coventry, Pepys had become beyond dispute the most skilled and powerful of all English naval officials. In June 1673 he left the Navy Board for the Admiralty, where he became Secretary of the commission[38] which took over most of the Lord High Admiral's duties when the Duke of York was extruded from office by the Test Act against Papists. Pepys now went to live in new official lodgings at Derby House, in Cannon Row, by the Thames, south of the Strand.[39] The problems of the Third Dutch War (1672–4) occupied his first four months of office. Afterwards he directed an epoch-making programme of recovery and reform, in the course of which not only were thirty new ships built, but also some of the basic elements of a professional naval service laid down. The practice of half-pay and super-annuation-pay was extended; the duties of lieutenants defined for the first time, and an establishment introduced for naval chaplains. By 1678 the navy was a sizeable, disciplined force, and the Lord High

38. This was a committee of the Privy Council. Pepys was its servant and spokesman in parliament (to which he was elected in 1673), but not a member of it.

39. He had suffered the loss of his old home in the fire of January 1673, which destroyed the Navy Office and several surrounding buildings. (Few of his possessions were burnt, if we may judge by the almost complete lack of evidence to the contrary: cf. *Further Corr.*, p. 280.) For some months immediately after the fire he seems to have lived with his friends the Houblons in Winchester Street in the city.

Admiral's office (previously small and almost informal) had been converted into a government department equipped with a systematic
body of records. For all this, Pepys himself – typical of a new school
of civil servants who were transforming several parts of the public
service at this time – was mainly reponsible. In the House of Commons (in which he sat for Castle Rising, Norfolk, in 1673–8, and
for Harwich in 1679 and 1685–7) he now spoke as the voice of the navy
itself; a shade too portentously, his opponents thought – 'rather like
[a Lord High] Admiral than a Secretary'.[40] But he could be forgiven
a little pride. Not only was he, more than any other person of his
time, the architect of a new fighting force, and of the administrative machine which ran it, but he was also among the first to see that
executive efficiency could never be achieved without an understanding
with the parliament which provided the money. It was on lines laid
down by Pepys that future developments in these matters were to run.

His career was at its peak when in 1678–9 it was checked by sudden
disaster. His old master the Duke of York was suspected, in the irresistible crisis of the Popish Plot, of being involved in a French-
inspired Catholic conspiracy to take over England by force. Samuel
Atkins, a clerk of Pepys's, was tried and acquitted on the charge of
being accessory to the murder of the Protestant victim, Sir Edmund
Berry Godfrey; Pepys's private musician, Cesare Morelli, was ru-
moured to be a Jesuit; Pepys himself was accused in the Commons of
being a secret Papist. He resigned office in May 1679 and spent six
weeks in prison under suspicion of having sold naval secrets to France.
In the end no charges were preferred against him, somewhat to his
chagrin, since he had gone to vast pains to prepare a comprehensive
defence and to unmask both his accusers and their agents as knaves
and dupes.

He remained out of office for the next five years, apart from a few
months in 1683–4 when he served as secretary to an expedition to
Tangier sent to supervise its abandonment. He then kept once again
a shorthand diary in his own hand, recounting the events of the official
visit to Tangier and of a private journey he afterwards made to South-
ern Spain.[41] The affinities which this Tangier diary had with the

40. Grey, v. 388 (11 May 1678).
41. Rawl. C 859B, Rawl. C 859C; the best edition is that by E. Chappell
(1935). Pepys also kept a shorthand diary of parliamentary proceedings in
1677 (Rawl. C 859A) which has never been printed. For these and the other
(less personal) journals he wrote after 1669, see below, ix. 565, n. 1.

great diary of 1660–9 arc, however, few and slight.   On his return he was suddenly rewarded with office again – with higher office than he had ever held before.   In June 1684 the King ended the inept rule of the Admiralty Commission appointed in 1679 and made Pepys his Secretary for Admiralty Affairs – a new post which Pepys continued to hold when the Duke of York succeeded to the throne as James II in 1685.   In modern terms, he now combined the duties of a permanent secretary of a department with those of a Secretary of State.   At Pepys's suggestion, James set up a Special Commission in 1686 to perform most of the work of the Navy Office.   With its help, Pepys set about a restoration of the good governance of the navy – again carrying out disciplinary reforms (e.g. the prohibition of carriage of plate in royal ships), some reorganisation (e.g. in the creation of an establishment for midshipmen), and some shipbuilding.   In the only book he ever published – *Memoires relating to the state of the royal navy* (1690)[42] – Pepys wrote a business-like account of this achievement.

With the fall of James II at the Glorious Revolution, Pepys, as one of his most intimate servants, fell too.   He resigned in February 1689, never to hold government office again.   In 1690 he was in custody for three months on the unfounded suspicion of being an active Jacobite. He now retired, with a touch of unwillingness,[43] to the consolations of private life, to enjoy what his friend the shipbuilder Sir Anthony Deane called 'the ould soldier's request, a little space between business and the grave'.[44]   Since 1679 he had lived in a fine new house in York Buildings, off the Strand, which he shared with Hewer, his old clerk, now a man of wealth.[45]   Here (and after 1688 in the neighbouring house) Pepys – himself grown rich in the service of

42. There is a modern edition (1906) by J. R. Tanner.

43. In 1689 and 1690 he tried (unsuccessfully) to enter Parliament.   He might have been tempted back into office had he had friends at court.   But he could hardly have become Secretary to the Admiralty again, for by then the office was occupied by a senior clerk who received only a quarter of Pepys's salary.

44. Deane to Pepys, 29 October 1689: *Letters*, p. 211.

45. Hewer had prospered in government service, becoming Treasurer of Tangier (1680–4) and a member of the Special Commission of the Navy (1686–8).   According to Evelyn, he 'got a very Considerable Estate in the Navy' (25 July 1692).   He served in Parliament for Yarmouth (I.O.W.) in 1685–7, was Master of the Clothworkers' Company in 1685–6 and later (after the Revolution) a Director and Deputy-Chairman of the old East India Company.   Pepys referred to him in his will as his 'most approved and most dear Friend'.

the state[46] – lived the life of a connoisseur, bibliophile and patron of the arts, especially of music. He gave occasional service to a few chosen causes. He took the lead, for example, on the board of Christ's Hospital in reorganising its constitution and in reforming the mathematical school which the Hospital, in conjunction with Trinity House, ran for the training of boys to become pilots. For this work he was given the freedom of the city in 1699. He had now perhaps achieved most of his ambitions. In his public career he had established himself, both at the Admiralty and in parliament, as 'the *Oracle* of the Navy'.[47] He had served as Master of Trinity House (1676-7, 1685-6), where he left his mark as an active reformer, and he had held the quieter and less onerous mastership of his city company, the Clothworkers' (1677-8).

In his library he had gathered a collection – of manuscripts, books, ballads, prints and drawings – which was coming to be known as one of the most interesting in London. Now, in his retirement, he made many purchases, and twice, in 1693 and in 1700, spent a great deal of time and loving care in overseeing the compilation of a catalogue. In 1698 he sent his nephew and heir, John Jackson, on a lengthy tour of Italy to complete his worldly education and to acquire books and prints for his uncle. Pepys was by this time well known to the learned world of the metropolis and of Oxford and Cambridge. Books had been dedicated to him in recognition of his services as a friend of learning. He had served on the Council of the Royal Society and for two terms (1684-6) as its President. He conducted a large correspondence with men of learning – John Evelyn, Isaac Newton, John Wallis, Arthur Charlett. 'The worse the world uses me' (he wrote, referring to his fall in 1689) 'the better, I think, I am bound to use myself.'[48] In these last years he enjoyed a quiet and well-regulated domesticity, his household being presided over by Mary Skinner, with whom he had had a long and affectionate association, never consecrated by marriage but accepted as respectable by all his friends, since shortly after his wife's death in 1669.[49] He refreshed himself, particularly after his health began to break down in 1700, by prolonged visits

46. In his will (1701) he claimed that the government still owed him (for his service to the navy and to Tangier) over £28,000.

47. Jeremy Collier, *A supplement . . . to the dictionary* (1705), n.p.

48. Pepys to Deane, 23 November 1689; *Letters*, p. 212.

49. In a codicil of 13 May 1703 to his will, Pepys refers to her 'Steddy friendship and Assistances' to him over a period of thirty-three years.

to Hewer's country house at Clapham.   It was there, on 26 May 1703, at the age of 70, that he died after a long and painful illness.

On the day of his death his friend John Evelyn wrote of him in his diary: 'This day dyed Mr. Sam: Pepys, a very worthy, Industrious & curious person, none in England exceeding him in the Knowledge of the Navy . . . [He] was universaly beloved, Hospitable, Generous, Learned in many things, skill'd in Musick, a very great Cherisher of Learned men, of whom he had the Conversation.'   In this miniature of Pepys in his last years it is not difficult to discern the Pepys of the 1660s, now grown more sober and responsible, a little stiffer and more dignified with age, but still the same vivacious character – the man of business, virtuoso and goodfellow – whose everyday life for nine-and-a-half years he had made a part of both history and literature in the entries of his diary.

R. L.

II The Diary

(a) The Manuscript

The diary, or 'journal' (to use the term that Pepys normally used at the time of its composition[1]) covers the period 1 January 1660 to 31 May 1669. It contains about 1,250,000 words in some 3100 pages (excluding blanks).[2] The daily entries vary greatly in length;[3] the years contain approximately the following number of words:

1660,	117,000	1665,	121,000
1661,	84,000	1666,	151,000
1662,	105,000	1667,	201,000
1663,	159,000	1668,	128,000
1664,	132,000	1669,	52,500

The manuscript is in six volumes, and about their binding Mr H. M. Nixon writes as follows:

'All are bound in lightly-mottled brown calf, with raised bands and two red lettering pieces on the spine. That in the second panel is lettered in the form: 'IOVRNAL/Vol./V.' and that in the third panel has the dates of the period covered in the volume, e.g. '1666./1667./1668.' or '1668./1669./∵'. The covers are gold-tooled in similar but not identical styles. They have a rectangular panel with small tools in the angles, mitred to a gilt two-line border and in the centre the bookstamps found on all the books in the Pepys Library; on the upper cover a mantled shield over crossed anchors is surmounted by Pepys's crest and bears the inscription: SAM. PEPYS CAR. ET IAC. ANGL. REGIB. A SECRETIS ADMIRALIÆ; on the lower cover an elaborate mantling surrounds his arms, crest and motto. The stamps were added by Pepys's nephew according to the instructions in the codicil of 13 May 1703 to his will (*Pepysiana*, p. 266).

They are not, however, uniform except for volumes V and VI. Volume I is an octavo, $7\frac{1}{4}$ inches tall; the other five are quartos of different width and thickness, and varying between $8\frac{5}{8}$ and 9 inches

---

1. But cf. below, pp. lxxi, 243.
2. The diarist did not number the pages.
3. There are only twelve words in 3 April 1662, but over 1800 in 2 September 1666.

in height. Volumes I, II, V and VI have five raised bands, but III and IV have only four. There are differences in the treatment of the edges of the leaves and the edges of the boards, in the ties, the headbands and the endleaves, which make it clear that only volumes V and VI were bound at the same time and that the others were all bound on different occasions.

The volumes were probably bought from John Cade of Cornhill, who is often referred to in the diary as Pepys's stationer. Cade was also probably responsible for binding the volumes. There is a significant similarity between the diary and PL 2193 ('Mr Holland his first discourse of the Navy'), which is pretty certainly one of the two volumes which Pepys directed Cade to bind in December 1662 (below, iii. 286). On its covers is used a distinctive tool which is also found in the angles of the covers of volume III of the diary, the entries in which begin on 1 July 1663. But whether Cade himself did the binding is doubtful. Although he was in business until 1678 at least, his name does not occur among the list of 82 bookbinders (or booksellers employing their own binders) who signed *A general note of the prices of binding all sorts of books ... presented to the Master* [etc.] *of the Worshipful Company of Stationers, August the 2d. 1669.* William Richardson, the only binder mentioned by name in the diary, may have worked for Cade: see below, 27 May 1667.'

The bookplates pasted on to the pages immediately before and after the diary entries in each volume are described and illustrated in *Pepysiana*.[4] Except in volume I, the portrait-plate faces the first page of writing, and except in volume IV the anchor-plate comes at the bottom of the last page of writing.

There are several indications that the manuscript was written in these same six volumes, not on separate sheets or smaller books that were later bound together. There are several blots on the edges of the pages, and particularly four in volume III, each affecting many pages. Moreover, Pepys normally in his diary entries refers to the diary as 'a book' ('this book of two years', etc.).[5] Although the volumes each contain paper of different quality and texture, some sheets being stout and opaque, others so thin that the writing on the versos shows through very plainly, it seems likely that each of the volumes was an ordinary stationer's notebook, bought at different times as needed.

4. pp.63-4 ('large portrait – plate' and 'Anchor plate').
5. See 30 June 1663 and 30 June 1665.

The pages have margin-lines in red ink, giving margins of approximately $\frac{5}{8}$ inch at the top and $\frac{7}{8}$ inch at the left of the page. Volume I, which is considerably smaller than the rest, has left-hand margins varying between $\frac{1}{2}$ and $\frac{1}{4}$ inch and top-margins of about $\frac{5}{8}$ and $\frac{3}{4}$ inch. It seems likely that Pepys himself inserted these marginal lines. Into the left-hand margins are inserted the numerals representing the days of the month; in the centre of the top margin is inserted the month. Pepys occasionally wrote the days and months incorrectly and later corrected the errors.[6] New months are begun on a new page, but there is no space between the daily entries. Occasionally there is a rubric or annotation in the margin.[7] The entries are written close to the margin, within $\frac{1}{8}$ inch on the left (at times the writing almost touches the margin line) and $\frac{3}{16}$ inch at the top. At the bottom of the page a space is ordinarily left which varies from $\frac{1}{2}$ to $\frac{3}{4}$ inch. The writing on left-hand pages goes deep into the binding, probably as a result of the rebacking and tightening of the volumes in modern times. The writing on right-hand pages comes close to the edge of the pages (very often it touches) so that at first sight it seems the pages must have been shaved. This possibility is ruled out, however, by the blots we have mentioned, by there being no *lacunae* at these places and by the fact that the ink of a symbol sometimes goes over to the edge of the page. From the standpoint of penmanship, what is quite remarkable in the manuscript is the evidence of the diarist's skill in taking his lines to the very edge of the page and in maintaining the clarity of his forms even in physically awkward positions. Some touches of editorial work appear in marginal notes and rubrics.

The physical characteristics of the writing vary from section to section. In some sections the writing is so clear-cut that it must have been done with a newly cut pen; in others it is blunter. The size of the symbols varies from section to section, sometimes slightly and sometimes (for reasons that will be suggested later) greatly, and such differences are often accompanied by slight variations in the angle and slope of the symbols. Similarly, the ink varies from heavy black in some sections to thin brown in adjoining ones. Such differences in writing style and ink often suggest that the entries were made in blocks of days, and sometimes they seem to contradict the diarist's own

6. These and other errors and corrections in the manuscript are recorded in the textual footnotes to this edition.

7. See 7 November 1660, 17 October 1661, 4 and 13 October 1663, etc.

statements about when entries were made.[8] They therefore raise problems in relation to the status of the diary as it exists in the final manuscript. These problems are discussed later in this Introduction.[9]

The penmanship is remarkable. There are enough variations to make it unlikely that Pepys used guide-lines or a ruled backing-sheet; but his lines are extraordinarily straight and horizontal – the only exception is that there are some pages in which the bottom lines rise slightly from left to right. Spacing between the lines is pretty uniform; the ordinary page contains between twenty-four and twenty-eight lines. The writing – the shorthand more than the longhand – is precise and clear. It was manifestly done far more carefully than was necessary simply for the writer's own reading. Very few blots mar the pages, although a few have been scratched out. There are many corrections and changes, perhaps 4000 all told, but they are made so neatly that only close examination reveals their existence; often they are perceptible only to a reader who knows the shorthand. When a daily entry is very long it sometimes runs over a page; but the great majority of pages begin with a new entry and end with the last words of the same or another entry. This neat disposition of the material on the pages is achieved at times by writing the last lines of a day's entry in small characters and by crowding the lines. The tiny writing and crowding, however, is sometimes used for a whole page, sometimes for several pages.[10] These passages may afford manuscript evidence that Pepys occasionally left blank pages for a series of entries and filled them up later, after he had entered a section that bears a later date – and that this was an occasional practice of his is certain from other evidence.[11] Insertions, also in small writing, are sometimes put between lines or in the spaces left at the ends of paragraphs and daily entries. They, too, must have been inserted later. Occasionally, but rarely, insertions of diary material as distinct from rubrics are made in left-hand margins. During the last months of the diary, when the diarist was suffering sorely with his eyes, the writing is sometimes less meticulous, the characters being larger and less well formed, the lines widely spaced and

8. See, e.g., 5 August 1662, 26 October 1662, 29 April 1665, 10 May 1667.
9. See below, pp. xcviii+.
10. See 16–28 September 1666, 1–7 October 1666, 10–27 February 1667.
11. See the discussion of the Great Fire entries and the two sets of rough notes which serve instead of regular entries, below, pp. c–ci.

sloping up to the right.[12] It is surprising though, that even in the period when Pepys was writing with the help of an optical tube, most of the shorthand in the diary is well formed and legible, though larger than usual.

The neatness of the diary manuscript is remarkable if the entries were jotted down directly into the diary-books. Some of Pepys's other manuscripts are rough, untidy drafts; it is only their perfected copies that display him as he wished to be seen in public. Some people who have glanced at the manuscript of the diary have believed that it must be a fair copy, made from a preliminary draft. The suggestion has generally been ignored by Pepysian scholars; but it is a notion not to be scouted, and later we shall need to consider it in some detail. Certainly, the care that Pepys took to ensure that the manuscript should seem clean and shapely, together with his pride in it and his pains to ensure its preservation in the library which he bequeathed for the use of future scholars, must mean that he intended it to have some of the qualities of a printed book, something akin to the Book of Psalms in shorthand that had recently been printed.[13] Moreover, given the fact that the first three volumes begin and end at notably formal dates, 1 January 1660–30 June 1661, 1 July 1661–30 June 1663, 1 July 1663–30 June 1665, it may fairly be guessed that in assembling his diary, Pepys worked to a general plan of its size and its shape.

The several volumes of the manuscript may be described as follows. The titles are given here in the form in which the binders stamped them on the spines:

IOVRNALL.
VOL. I: ·
1659. 1660.
1661.

1 January 1660 to 30 June 1661; 282 folios (7″ × 4⅜″). One paste-down and two blank leaves precede the bookplate and the diary entries. Blank pages occur between 30 June and 1 July 1660 (1);[14] between 31 August and 1 September 1660 (16); six blank leaves and a paste-down follow the diary entries. There are ink blots at 20 and 21 July and reddish

12. The photograph of the last page of the diary shows the large symbols and wide spacing of these later entries.

13. Jeremiah Rich, *The whole Book of Psalms in meter* (c. 1660). This may be the works that Pepys saw Coventry reading on 16 April 1661.

14. All blank pages are noted in the textual footnotes.

spots (? red ink) at 9 October. In 10 January 1660 a blank half-line (between 'I went' and 'home' beginning the next line) seems to indicate a new start in entering the diary. A similar break occurs in 23 March. On the top of the spine are traces of a rectangular gilt patch used for a shelfmark.

IOVRNAL.

VOL.

II.

1661.

1662.

1663.

1 July 1661 to 30 June 1663; 240 folios ($8\frac{1}{2}''\times 6\frac{2}{5}''$). A paste-down, two stubs and one blank page precede the bookplate and the diary entries. Blank pages occur between 31 December 1661 and 1 January 1662 (1); between 31 December 1662 and 1 January 1663 (3), and between 28 February and 1 March 1663 (2). In each of the entries for 23 August 1662 and 9 January 1663 are two blank pages pasted together, indicating points at which Pepys accidentally turned over two leaves while writing. Fifteen blank pages and a paste-down follow the diary entries.

IOVRNAL.

VOL.

III: ·

1663.

1664.

1665.

1 July 1663 to 30 June 1665; 286 folios ($8\frac{7}{10}''\times 6\frac{1}{2}''$). A paste-down and one blank page precede the bookplate and the diary entries. Single blank pages occur between 31 July and 1 August 1663, 31 October and 1 November 1663, 31 December 1663 and 1 January 1664, 29 February and 1 March 1664, and 31 March and 1 April 1664. At 28 May 1664 a leaf has been cut out. The diary entries finish on the paste-down at the back. At 14 July 1664 the margin occurs on the wrong side of the page. There are four ink blots on the edges of the pages, one covering about 200, the others about thirty pages. Three pieces of paper are pasted in at three points in this volume; at 13 October 1663 (two medical prescriptions, partly in an (?) apothecary's hand and partly in a mixture of Pepys's shorthand and longhand); at 17 November 1663 (a letter to the Earl of Sandwich dated 17 November 1663, again

written in Pepys's mixture of shorthand and longhand); and at 2–3 July 1664 ('*Dr. Burnetts advice to mee*', in Pepys's longhand). Between 31 December 1664 and 1 January 1665 an uncompleted page is filled out by two lists entitled '*Age of my Grandfather's Children*' and '*Theyr Children's ages*', and the following page is occupied by a series of '*Charmes*'.

IOVRNAL.

VOL.

IV.

1665.

1666.

⸭

1 July 1665 to 28 February 1667; 278 folios ($8\frac{7}{8}''\times6\frac{9}{10}''$). A marbled paste-down and five blank pages precede the bookplate and the diary entries. Blank pages occur between 31 December 1665 and 1 January 1666 (1), 31 January and 1 February 1666 (1), 28 February and 1 March 1666 (1), 30 April and 1 May 1666 (1), 31 August and 1 September 1666 (2), 31 October and 1 November 1666 (1), and 31 December 1666 and 1 January 1667 (1). In each of the entries for 10 July 1665 and 7 August 1666 are two blank pages, indicating points at which Pepys accidentally turned over two leaves while writing. At 11–12 December 1665 a small paper is pasted in containing a shorthand memorandum concerning the amount of coin in England. There are ink blots at 2 June 1666. One blank endleaf and a marbled paste-down follow the diary entries.

IOVRNAL.

VOL.

V.

1666.

1667.

1668.

1 March 1667 to 30 April 1668; 268 folios ($9\frac{1}{8}''\times6\frac{8}{10}''$). A marbled paste-down and five blank pages precede the bookplate and the diary entries. Single blank pages occur between 31 July and 1 August 1667, 30 September and 1 October 1667, 30 November and 1 December 1667, 31 December 1667 and 1 January 1668, and 31 March and 1 April 1668. One blank page, five blank leaves and a marbled paste-down follow the diary entries. Eight pages are blank for the period 10–19 April 1668. No diary entries are written in for these days, but pasted in after 9 April 1668 are three folded foolscap sheets of notes.

The pages they form are numbered 1–6, two of them in the wrong order.   On both sides of these sheets are rough shorthand notes and expense accounts for the period which is blank in the diary itself.   A leaf has been cut out between 30 April and 1 May 1667 and also between 21 and 22 June 1667.

IOVRNAL

VOL.

VI.

1668.

1669.

∵

1 May 1668 to 30 May 1669; 241 folios ($9\frac{1}{8}'' \times 6\frac{7}{10}''$). A marbled paste-down and three blank pages precede the bookplate and the diary entries. Blank pages occur between 31 May and 1 June 1668 (1), 14 and 15 September 1668 (2), and 31 January and 1 February 1669 (1). Thirty blank leaves and a marbled paste-down follow the diary entries. Ten pages are blank for the period 5–17 June 1668. No diary entries are written in for these days, but pasted in after 4 June are five folded foolscap sheets (the fifth a half-sheet). The sheets are occupied by rough shorthand notes and expense accounts for these days, together with the draft of a letter in shorthand and longhand. For the period 29 September–10 October 1668, 12 pages are left blank, but there are no sheets of rough notes representing those days. The penmanship in this volume, particularly in the last months, reflects the diarist's eye-trouble: symbols are larger and sometimes stumbling, and lines widely spaced.[15]

☆ ☆ ☆

(b) The Shorthand

Except for its scattering of names and words in longhand, the diary is written in the shorthand which was invented by Thomas Shelton (d. ?1650). Pepys developed a few idiosyncrasies in the course of using this shorthand during many years, but the forms he uses are essentially those prescribed in Shelton's *Short Writing* and *Tachygraphy*.[1]

15. See especially most of the entries from 19 April 1669 to the end of the diary. Nevertheless, much of the writing during the period of eye-trouble is clear and neat, even in the five or six days which he wrote on 16 February 1669 with the help of his optical tube.

1. See W. J. Carlton, *Biblioth. Pepysiana*, pt iv, *Shorthand Books*, pp. 29–46.

Methods of writing swiftly had been published in England for thirty-eight years before Shelton's first system, *Short Writing*, was published in London in 1626. Like most shorthand systems, it leaned heavily on its predecessors: much of it was adopted from Edmond Willis's *An abbreviation of writing by character*, which had been published only eight years before. Shelton took over the alphabet of simple straight lines and curves that Edmond Willis had devised, varying it with two symbols taken from the still earlier system of his namesake John Willis and also with a new-shaped *e* which was imitated from the secretary hand. He also adopted Edmond Willis's novel method of representing internal vowels. His own improvements were to simplify the method of representing diphthongs (or digraphs), to exclude the *e* in the representation of *em-*, *en-*, *es-* and *ex-*, and to reduce to about 300 the arbitrary symbols for oft-used words and suffixes – symbols which a learner needed to learn by rote.[2]

Shelton's system in his *Short Writing* was new, but by no means radical therefore. Nevertheless, it proved practical and in time extraordinarily popular. A second edition came out in 1630, and in 1635 it was published again, this time under the name of *Tachygraphy*, which it bore in Pepys's day.

Shorthand, a humble art at the present day, was in Pepys's time a device both novel and admirable. As such it was used by such scholars as Hartlib, Tillotson, Hooke, Locke and Newton, and Wilkins was to incorporate it in his philosophical language. It is therefore character-istic that the 1635 edition of Shelton's work was printed by the University Press at Cambridge. Its title-page bears the statement that the book was 'approoued by both Vnyuersities' – and to this the seventeenth-century owner of one copy has added his own observation, 'espesially by Cambridge'.[3] And that the system may have continued to be popular there even into Pepys's student days in 1651–4 is indicated by the facts that further editions of *Tachygraphy* were printed by the University Press in 1641 and 1647 and that introducing the system are encomiastic poems by several recent graduates of the university. Among these are the verses, 'To the Authour his friend', which were composed by Edward Rainbowe, Master of Magdalene in 1642–51.[4] Although we have no shorthand from his hand before 1660, Pepys, ever a man of fashion and an enthusiast for modern devices, may well

2. Ib., pp. 42–43.   3. Ib., p. vii.
4. Rainbowe was also a friend of Pepys's schoolmaster, John Langley.

have learned the art while he was at Magdalene, for when he began his diary on 1 January 1660 his expertness with the system shows that he must have been using it for some time.   There may indeed have been shorthand materials among the papers he destroyed at Christmas 1664 as being boyish or worthless.[5]

The skill he thus acquired came to serve him for many purposes.   He put it to use most frequently in his daily work, for making notes on navy affairs and for copying and drafting letters.   He also employed it for several diaries: not only for the great diary but also for the business journal (1663–72) which he called his 'Navy White Book', the parliamentary journal of 1677 and the journal of his journey to Tangier in 1683–4.[6]   And it also served him on special occasions, most notably in October 1680 when he took down from Charles II's dictation the story of the King's escape after the battle of Worcester.[7]

This practical application of shorthand was accompanied by a scholarly interest in stenography.   Pepys became one of the first great collectors of shorthand text-books, his chief rival being Elisha Coles, whose collection, mentioned in 1674, is now lost.[8]   The five volumes of shorthand pamphlets which Pepys had bound up about 1695 contains thirty-two items, from Timothy Bright's *Characterie* of 1588 to Abraham Nicholas's *Thoographia* of 1692: some of them are rare, and the copy of Thomas Heath's *Stenographie*, 1644, is apparently unique. Several are late editions, however, and it is possible that in accordance with his habit of discarding old editions of books in favour of new ones, Pepys had replaced some earlier editions when he closed his collection on 25 March 1695.[9]

Included in the collection are four of Thomas Shelton's books: *A tutor to tachygraphy* (1642), the Latin version of the system entitled *Tachy-graphia* (1671), *Tachygraphy* (1691), and *Zeiglographia* (1685). The first is a companion book to *Tachygraphy*, and although in 1642 it was published separately, usually the two works were issued as a single volume.   Pepys must have learned Shelton's shorthand from one of the several editions published before 1660 (there were at least eleven),

5. See 31 December 1664.
6. See below, p. lxix, n. 6; above, p. xxxvii, n. 41.
7. PL 2141 (MS. and Pepys's transcription); see below, p. 155, n. 1.
8. Elisha Coles (?1640–?1680), a schoolmaster, published *The newest, plainest, and the shortest short-hand* in 1674 and therein listed some thirty shorthand treatises which he apparently owned.
9. PL 13, 401, 402, 860, 1111.   For date of closing of collection, see Carlton, op. cit., p. xi.

and in fact the copy of the 1642 *Tutor* now in the Pepys Library[10] contains some annotations in ink by the diarist: brief notations on some of the principal symbols and a phrase or two in longhand.

Under its two titles, *Short Writing* and *Tachygraphy*, Shelton's system went into at least twenty-two editions between 1626 and 1710.[11] In 1649, near the end of his life, he also published a radically revised version of the system entitled *Zeiglographia*, which went into at least fourteen editions or reprints by 1711. One system with the other, Shelton's was among the most popular stenographies of the seventeenth century.[12] Its rivals were the *Stenography* or *Short Writing* first published by Theophilus Metcalfe (d. ?1646) in 1633, which went into a '55th edition' in 1721, and the system published by Jeremiah Rich (d. ?1677) in 1654, which under the titles *Charactery* (1646), *The penns dexterity* (1659) and *The pens dexterity compleated* (1669) went into some twenty-five editions and reprints. Rich's system was published at Leeds as late as 1792, and in 1736 Philip Gibbs declared in his *Historical account of compendious and swift writing* that Shelton's books (and Metcalfe's) might easily be come by and that his method was still well known and practised. All three systems were constructed on the same principles, their variations being chiefly in the shapes and values of certain symbols.

Compared with the well-known shorthands of our own day, the shorthand that Pepys used is simple, almost naïve. That, in fact, may have been one ground of its popularity, for it could have taken no one very long to learn it. Its essence is a brief way of representing the letters of the ordinary alphabet. For the cumbrous, time-consuming symbols that we have inherited from Egyptians, Phoenicians, Greeks and Latins, the shorthand substitutes a set of brief signs, a few of them cut-down forms of the ordinary letters, but the majority straight lines and simple curves. These symbols serve for consonants in all positions and for vowels that occur at the beginning of words. For vowels in the middle or at the end of words, two devices are employed. A medial vowel is represented by placing the following consonant (disjoined and written small) in five positions about the preceding consonant. These five positions represent *a, e, i, o, u,* and these serve for both long and short vowels and also for diphthongs. The following

---

10. PL 402 (11).

11. For editions, see Carlton, op. cit., pp. 29–36.

12. See J. Westby-Gibson, *Bibliography of shorthand* (1887), and K. Brown and D. C. Haskell, *The shorthand collection in the New York public library* (1935).

examples will illustrate the method in its simplest form. The consonant *b* is represented by a vertical straight stroke, the consonant *t* by an oblique straight stroke running down from right to left. If a small form of *t* is placed on top of *b*, slightly separated, the total symbol represents *b-a-t*; if it is placed on the right side of *b*, near the top, the symbol represents *b-e-t*; if right-centre it represents *b-i-t*; if right-bottom it represents *b-o-t*; if below *b* it represents *b-u-t*. Final vowels are symbolised by dots placed in the same five positions (and their values are the same). Since the five vowels serve for long and short forms and also for the related diphthongs, the word-symbols obviously have several possible meanings: *b-a-t* can mean 'bat', 'bate', 'bait'; *b-e-t* can mean 'bet', 'beet', 'beat'; *b-i-t* can mean 'bit', 'bite' and (since the spelling is quasi-phonetic) 'bight'; *b-o-t* can mean 'bott', 'bout', 'boat', 'boot' and 'bought'; and *b-u-t* can mean 'butt', 'butte' and 'Bute'. In addition to these basic devices, there are several further ways to facilitate speedy writing. Some consonant clusters, particularly *wr*, *br*, *mr*, *sk*, *sh*, are represented as short fusions of the basic consonant symbols. An *-s* inflection is represented by a dot usually placed before the symbol. Some three hundred brief arbitrary symbols are provided for words and affixes (i.e. prefixes and suffixes) in common use. Thus, a small upright cross stands for 'Christ' or '-ture', a small circle with a horizontal bar represents 'which' or '-ternal', and a dot represents 'I' or 'eye'.

Despite the long record of tachygraphy's popularity, it is far from being a perfect system. Edwin Chappell has pointed out some of its defects.[13] It presents long lists of arbitrary symbols which the learner must commit to memory and which occasionally present alternative meanings: the symbols which when joined represent *kl* also form an arbitrary symbol for 'it' and the suffix '-fication'. The same characters will represent such arbitrary meanings as 'mess-' and 'what'. Since the system makes only five distinctions for vowels and diphthongs, one symbol may frequently represent several words, such as 'on', 'one', 'own', or 'stripped', 'striped', or 'sit', 'site', 'sight', or 'sell', 'seal', 'seel' and so on. Symbols for different words are sometimes so much alike as to be almost indistinguishable; thus, 'your' and 'great', 'go' and 'give', 'work' and 'word', 'will' and 'answer', 'breadth' and 'width', 'they' and 'not', 'present' and 'promise', 'though', 'thou', 'through' and 'thought' are given symbols that are either the same for both words or so similar as to present the possibility of confusion in transcription. Finally, the

13. *Shorthand Letters*, pp. xi–xiii.

shorthand for some words, 'carpenter', 'congratulate', 'reimbursed', for example, are so long and cumbrous that it might be simpler and quicker to write them in longhand – as Pepys sometimes does in fact. Chappell advanced these defects in the system to justify his explanation that no claim for finality could be made for the transcription of the shorthand letters that he was publishing in 1933. A century or so before, John Smith, first transcriber of the diary, had complained of the burden that the system imposed on the memory, and the strain on the eyes that was caused by the smallness of the characters and the transparency of some of Pepys's pages.

It would be wrong to stress the defects of Shelton's system, however. It cannot be written so speedily as such modern systems as Pitman's or Gregg's; but neither does it take so much time to learn. In its day, it was used for reporting sermons and speeches, and it may be estimated that a tachygrapher in good practice might have been able to write at a hundred words per minute. That would not be enough to justify the claim of the rhetorical Cambridge poet who in verses prefixed to the early editions of *Tachygraphy* declared that the system enabled men to write as fast as they spoke. But it is a speed serviceable for many occasions, and certainly for the occasions of Pepys, who in this diary at least seems to have composed at a slow rate – the entry for 17 January 1668, which is said in the diary to have taken almost an hour, runs to less than 700 words. And any suggestion that Shelton's shorthand, when written in the careful way that Pepys uses in the diary, presents continual difficulties to the transcriber is simply not true. The difficulties mentioned in our last paragraph are more theoretical than real. Forms that may mean two, three, even four different words may seem disastrously ambiguous in a list or an example. But in any ordinary English context it is normally quite obvious which of the possible readings is intended; no one is likely to hesitate long in choices between 'great' and 'your', 'bat', 'bait' and 'bate', 'through', 'thou' and 'thought', or 'rod', 'rood', 'rode' and 'road'. Carelessness or error on the part of the stenographer is another matter; and there are occasions, despite the astonishing care that went into the manuscript, when Pepys writes a slovenly or incorrect form. Fortunately, the context nearly always makes clear what the correct reading (and writing) should be. There are also a few genuine ambiguities. It is impossible to be sure whether Pepys had a 'bit' to eat or a 'bite'.[14] It is equally impossible to be sure which of the several allomorphs of 'have' – 'has', 'hath', 'have',

14. See below, p. lix.

'had' – is represented by the *h*-symbol which stands for them all. In such cases of ambiguity, fortunately, a lead from Pepys's longhand writing of the diary period is sometimes available.[15] Difficulties may also arise when the stenographer writes a symbol slightly inaccurately, as when Pepys writes an extra curve at the beginning of the symbol for 'would' and so converts it into 'could'; sometimes either word fits the context. A further source of possible error in transcription lies in the transcriber and arises from a combination of shorthand and unfamiliarity on the transcriber's part with words or things familiar in the time the shorthand was written. It is this that explains, for example, the rum and bread which appears in earlier editions of the diary; *r* and *br* and *w* are very similar to one another in Shelton's shorthand, but it seems most likely that it was ignorance of the broom-and-reed men who served the navy in Pepys's day that led to the wrong choice.[16] Such occasions are fortunately not very numerous.

Occasionally the shorthand has proved puzzling; but that has usually been because it represents some unusual word or unusual meaning rather than because of the defects of the shorthand or any carelessness on Pepys's part. More potent sources of possible error in transcription are the seventeenth-century linguistic variants which may be represented by the same shorthand symbol (e.g. 'keep', 'kept') and the difficulty of being entirely consistent in interpreting so long a stretch of minutiae. The measures that have been taken to deal with these problems are set out in the following sub-section.

(c) The Text

The diary is one of the principal source-books for many aspects of the history of its period. It is also a repertory of the familiar language of its time, and therefore an important source for historians of the English language. Most importantly, it is one of the great classics of literature. These are the facts that have been weighed in preparing the text for this edition. No text which satisfied simply one group

15. See below, p. lx.
16. For examples of errors made by previous transcribers, see below, pp. xxix, nn. 61, 62, lxxxviii–lxxxix, n. 97.

among Pepys's readers would do; to be satisfactory, a text must meet the legitimate demands of many types of reader.

The text is here presented complete, and with a minimum of editorial tampering. But since a printed text cannot be quite the same as a manuscript, especially a manuscript largely in shorthand and abbreviated longhand, the preparation of this text presented a series of serious problems, some affecting the whole text, some relevant only to occasional details. This part of the Introduction is devoted to setting out these problems, the methods used to resolve them and the resolutions that have been applied to the text.

To adopt all the textual methods sometimes appropriate for historical documents, involving normalisation of spelling, capitalisation and punctuation, would rob the text of details highly significant to a student of literature and language. In particular, it would obscure the abundant small details that suggest how the diary was written and how Pepys may have read it aloud.[1] On the other hand, rigid adherence to certain fine details of the manuscript, such as its superscript letters, its ampersands, its many abbreviations and its limited and sometimes random punctuation, would make the edition a delight simply for a few students, whose legitimate interests would be better served by a facsimile. For all other readers, even the most scholarly, it would make reading the diary like walking on stones.

If the historian's normalising was unacceptable, therefore, so, too, was a rigorously diplomatic transcription. A compromise was called for. The response in the present edition is a text that with stated exceptions presents the diary as closely as possible as it appears in the manuscript. The main exceptions are certain normalisations, set out later in this sub-section, which were adopted mainly for the ease of the reader.

The implementation of these general principles was complicated by the shorthand in which the diary is written.[2] The system raises many problems of transcription, particularly as regards spelling, punctuation and the inflections to be used with certain oft-used verbs.

Resolutions for these problems were sought in Pepys's own usage, so far as that can be determined exactly. A sample of 100 scattered pages of the diary was first examined, with the sole purpose of discovering all shorthand forms and longhand words which might make for difficulty. These problem-forms were then categorised and listed.

1. See below, p. xcix.
2. See above, pp. xlviii+.

To the same end, Shelton's textbook[3] was examined, and all forms in it that were ambiguous or likely to cause difficulty were categorised and listed.   Since the objective was to come in these matters as close as possible to what Pepys might have done had he himself put the diary into longhand, these lists of problem forms were then compared with Pepys's own usages in ordinary writing.   For this purpose, all available documents he wrote in longhand during the years 1660–9 were examined:[4] namely, the many longhand words in the diary itself, the lengthy longhand sections of his 'Navy White Book', his letters in the collections of the Public Record Office, the British Museum, the Bodleian, the National Maritime Museum and in Heath's edition of his family letters, and Howarth's edition of *Letters and second diary*.   Detailed comparison of the problem-lists with Pepys's normal usages showed that the latter were commonly variable: that he would sometimes write 'he doth', for example, and sometimes 'he does'.   But in most instances, the examination revealed that at the diary period he had a clear preference: that he wrote 'he hath', for example, far more often than he wrote 'he has'.   In these circumstances, it was decided to adopt for the present text the variant that Pepys himself then preferred. When there was no clear preference, the usage now most familiar was adopted.

On the basis of these preliminary surveys, the following detailed principles were adopted before the preparation of the text was begun.

1. *Longhand*.   The diary employs a great deal of longhand, mostly for personal names, place names, names of ships, days, months and festivals, and titles of rank.   Titles of plays, songs and books are also often so distinguished, in whole or in part.   Additionally, scattered throughout the diary are a great many other words in longhand, some of them covering up shorthand symbols (and occasionally longhand), others apparently so written for the sake of emphasis, or out of hesitation in composition, or from some difficulty in the shorthand symbol, or for a variety of other reasons that can only be guessed at.   A large proportion of these longhand forms are abbreviated, many of them by the use of superscripts.

To differentiate all this longhand from the shorthand would make for an extremely ugly, uneasy type-page, and it has therefore been decided to represent longhand by italics only in certain cases: headings,

3. Thomas Shelton, *Tachygraphy* (1659).
4. This was done by the two Editors.

names of days and festivals that begin daily entries, titles of books, plays and music, names of ships, and foreign words other than those that occur in the erotic passages written in Pepys's *lingua franca*. Titles of books, etc., and entry-headings that Pepys writes in shorthand or in a mixed form are also italicised. The large formal hand he sometimes uses for headings and festivals is represented by larger italics.

Longhand words which Pepys spells in full are given with the spelling and capitalisation used in the diary, except that the archaic *v, u, y, i,* and *ff* have been replaced by *u, v, th, j,* and *F*. Superscript letters have been lowered. Thus, 'vsuall' is represented by 'usuall', 'euer' by 'ever', 'iudge' by 'judge', 'ffrench' by 'French' and 'yᵉ' by 'the'. Words abbreviated by Pepys are expanded (see below, Section 5).

2. *Shorthand.* By far the greatest part of the diary is written in Pepys's form of Shelton's shorthand.[5] Although this edition adopts Pepys's own spelling of longhand words, as far as that can be done in view of his many abbreviations, the same procedure was not feasible for the shorthand. The shorthand symbols for 'few', 'road', 'laughter', 'thought', 'pressed', 'stayed', for example, if transposed into ordinary letters would appear as 'fu', 'rod', 'laftr', 'thot', 'prest', 'stad'. Moreover, as has already been shown, one Pepysian symbol can represent several words. The symbol for 'write', for example, is also the symbol for 'rite', 'right', 'wright', and 'writ'; the words 'sell', 'cell', 'seel', and 'seal' all employ the same symbol; and so do 'plate', 'plait', 'plat' and also 'cole', 'coal', 'caul', 'cool', 'coll', and 'cowl'. In context, fortunately, the proper alternative is seldom in doubt. But the choice is not always immediately apparent, so that ease and intelligibility of reading can be ensured only by adopting a conventional spelling.

The problem that presented itself, therefore, was whether the conventional spelling to be used for the shorthand in this text should be our own or something similar to the spelling used by Pepys and his contemporaries. The possible objection to the first alternative is that it conflicts with our decision to print, as far as the abbreviations allow, Pepys's longhand as he wrote it. It conflicts, moreover, with our decision to retain Pepys's grammar, to keep his 'you was', 'he begun', 'ill-writ' and so on, rather than to change them to 'you were', 'he began', 'ill-written'. Unless Pepys's grammar and longhand were also modernised, to represent his spelling entirely in modern fashion would obscure a lot of details important to many scholars. To spell in

5. See above, pp. xlviii–liv.

seventeenth-century style (where it can be said to exist) is, however, not only difficult, but also leads to scholarly tampering. This is what a previous editor, H. B. Wheatley, tried to do,[6] and the result is a free-hand-antique, in which nothing can be relied on. The trouble is that seventeenth-century spelling was extremely variable and very incon-sistent; the same words could be spelled in present-day fashion and also in one, often two or three, earlier styles. These are a few examples, taken from Pepys's own longhand: 'fair', 'faire', 'fayre'; 'stayed', 'stay'd'; 'aequall', 'equal', 'equall'; 'cloathes', 'clothes', 'cloths'; 'murder', 'murther'; 'selfs', 'selfes', 'selves'; 'bag', 'bagg', 'bagge'; 'gowne', 'gown', 'gownd'; 'oblige', 'oblidge', 'obleege'. There is no means of knowing, at least in most instances, which of these variants Pepys may have had in mind in any particular case, and therefore there is no guide as to which of the variants should be adopted. An antique spelling is always a possibility, but to give it without knowing whether Pepys would have used it is to mislead scholars who might wish to use such materials as evidence for the language of the diarist and his contem-poraries.

From these considerations, it was decided that the basis of the spelling of the shorthand in this text should be present-day British usage. The procedure, although necessary, is not free from defect. Even although Pepys's own variants include almost every modern spelling, uniform spelling is quite alien to his habit; to adopt it entirely would, more-over, be subject to objections we have already mentioned.

It is fortunate, therefore, that a desirable mixture, a moderate kind of seventeenth-century inconsistency, can be achieved in systematic fashion and with sufficient accuracy. This is made possible by the phonetic spelling used in Pepys's shorthand. There is no particular point in following the phonetic spellings of the shorthand when they reflect pronunciations still used, even though the spelling is non-phonetic – to write 'stopt', danst', 'stept', 'advize', 'surprize', for example, instead of 'stopped', 'danced', 'stepped', 'advise', surprise'. So our text uses modern spelling in such cases, except for the licence of 'a-clock'. But there are many hundreds of words in the diary of which Pepys's pronunciation was different from ours or represents a seventeenth-century variant. The longhand he wrote during the period of the diary is sprinkled with phonetic spellings, such as 'whither' (whether), 'chare' (chore), 'baly' (bailiff), 'ketch' (catch), 'sithe' (sigh) and 'sperrits' (spirits). The same and comparable variants are also

6. See below, p. xciv.

represented phonetically in his shorthand: 'landscape', 'follow', 'farthing', 'burden', 'show', 'yourselves', 'knives' are thus written in shorthand that might be literally transcribed as *lanskip, falo, farding, burthen, shu, yourselfs, knifs*. It seemed therefore both justifiable and sensible to represent these forms by spellings that Pepys himself uses in longhand: 'lanskip', 'fallow', 'farding', 'burthen', 'shew', 'yourselfs', 'knifes' and so on. Thus, the general principle adopted for spelling shorthand-forms in this edition was that ordinarily the spelling was to be in present-day British style, but that when the shorthand indicated a seventeenth-century variation in spelling, and when that spelling indicated both a seventeenth-century pronunciation and a spelling that Pepys himself used, it should be spelled in the appropriate non-modern style. This compromise has certain merits. The variant spellings, both of longhand and shorthand words, combine to give the text an appropriate seventeenth-century coloration. And since every one of the variants is authentic, it is to be hoped that the text provides historical linguists with evidence they may need.

The exceptions are few, although one is important. The shorthand spells many *oi*-words with *i*: *jin, pint, ister, bil* for 'join', 'point', 'oyster', 'boil'. These represent an [ΛI]- pronunciation which was in good standing in Pepys's day and even later, and it was a question whether to transcribe the words with *i*. The contrary decision, to adopt the modern standard spellings, was determined by the apparent consistency with which Pepys used *oi/oy* in his longhand. Two individual words also led to much thought, if only because Pepys uses them so often. The form '*bit*' represents either 'bit' or 'bite'. It is therefore quite uncertain whether Pepys said that he had a 'bit to eat' or a 'bite to eat'. It was decided to adopt 'bit', but the decision is not certainly correct. Similarly, the first syllable of Pepys's form for 'betimes' may represent either 'bi' or 'by': 'bitimes' or 'by times' are equally possible readings. The decision was to adopt 'betimes' on the score that we now pronounce it 'bitimes'.

Another set of problems arises from the fact that Shelton's stenography represents some three hundred frequently used words or affixes by brief, arbitrary symbols. These are not spelled phonetically, and some of them represent more than one word or affix, while some employ the same forms as words written by the regular method of the system. Thus, for each of the pairs in the following groups, the shorthand provides only one symbol: (a) *hear/here, heart/hurt, answer/will, ask/shall, on/one, our/hour, send/sent, there/their, then/than, though/thou, grace/three, men/man, to/two/too, last/lay, feast/fee, see/saw, come/came, answer/swear*;   (b) *mer-/mar-, ob-/ab-, op-/ap-*; *-full/-fall, -ler/-lar* – there are others besides, some of them representing spelling variants common at the time, such as *per-/par-, pre-/prae-, of-/off-*.

Which of the alternatives to adopt in this edition was sometimes a simple decision: context, for example, is the guide between the words in the first group.   With other words the matter was complicated by the linguistic usages of Pepys and his contemporaries.   For example, they often used 'hath' as an alternative to both 'has' and 'have'.   With them, 'he doth' and 'he does' were both in good usage.[7]   Their 'come' and 'see' were possible variants of 'came' and 'saw'; and they commonly employed 'then' where we use 'than' (and *vice versa*).   Since the shorthand provides only a single arbitrary form for each of these groups of variants, a guide for choosing between the variants was sought in Pepys's own longhand.   On the basis of his preferences, as there displayed, we have selected 'saw', 'came', 'then', 'perticular', for example, instead of 'see', 'come', 'than', 'particular'.   When the subjects are third-personal singular 'doth' and 'hath' are used, on the score that Pepys rarely uses 'does' and 'has' in his longhand at this period.

A few special problems should also be mentioned.   Such shorthand forms as *kep* and *slep* are ambiguous; they may represent 'keep' and 'sleep' as present-indicatives or historical-presents; they may also reflect the colloquial past tenses that we now represent as 'kep' ' and 'slep' '.   Again, *met* and *lit* may represent either present time or past, 'meet', 'met' and 'light', 'lit'.   None of these problems can be solved quite satisfactorily, and the resolutions adopted for this edition represent simply editorial preferences.   Because Pepys rarely omits final consonants elsewhere 'keep' and 'sleep' are used even when the sense indicates past time.   Because Pepys's ordinary writing does not employ 'meet' and 'lit' as preterites, our decision is to print 'met' and 'light', with the understanding that the reader may interpret them as either present-indicative or historical-present forms.   On the other hand, the text prints 'writ' or 'wrote', 'begin' or 'began' or 'begun', 'sing' or 'sung' just as the shorthand indicates: the shorthand is phonetically distinctive with these words, and either variant is sanctioned by the ordinary writing of Pepys and his contemporaries.   With 'have' and 'had', for which the shorthand commonly uses one symbol, the

7. In Pepys's letters of the 1680s and '90s, however, 'does' has replaced 'doth'.

text adopts the one or the other according to which seemed the more appropriate in its particular context.

One last difficulty may be mentioned, one that has beset all editors who have prepared texts from Pepys's shorthand. Shelton's stenography, although it is generally efficient, uses some arbitrary symbols which are so similar to others that they may be easily misread (and almost as easily miswritten). Thus, *sk* and *sh* are written alike, with the result that 'Scot' and 'shot', 'skin' and 'shin' are indistinguishable in Pepys's shorthand. The symbols for 'that' and 'the' differ only in length, and then only slightly, so that it is not always certain whether the diarist intended the emphatic or the unemphatic word. For similar good reasons, an editor may make a wrong choice between 'made' and 'other', 'these' and 'those', 'again' and 'just', 'little' and 'good', or 'what', 'when' and 'which'.

The present text is therefore mixed in its spelling, that being, in the judgement of the Editors, the only form which will meet the legitimate demands of literary and linguistic scholars as well as historians, and at the same time be as nearly as possible true to the diary as Pepys wrote it.

3. *Pepys's lingua franca.* In the second half of the diary a number of passages are written in a mixture of foreign languages. Most of these passages are erotic, and the *lingua franca* is presumably meant to conceal the content. A few passages, however, are quite innocent in subject, and there the language may be simply playful. This language is basically Spanish (of a dictionary kind, and therefore considerably ungrammatical); but into it are mixed words from several other languages: English, French, and occasionally Dutch, Italian, Latin and Greek. The passages are all written in shorthand; and to obscure the content still further, many words are complicated by inserting between syllables the shorthand symbols for *l*, *r*, *m* or *n*.

In printing these passages, an attempt has been made to stick as closely as possible to what Pepys wrote: their spelling, grammar and dialect have been neither modernised nor corrected. As a result, they appear in this text with older French spellings, such as 'allois', or with Spanish forms that are now non-standard, such as 'moher' for 'mujer'. Such details are good witness to the extent of Pepys's knowledge of foreign tongues, and also to the sources from which he may have learned them. On the other hand, for the reader's comfort, the insertions of *r*, *l*, *m*, *n* have been excluded. One literal transcription has been given in a footnote to the first use of this device;[8] elsewhere, its use is merely reported in the textual footnotes.

4. *Punctuation*. The normal marks of punctuation are seldom used in the manuscript, probably because some of them are used instead as arbitrary symbols for common words: the colon and full-stop are thus employed to represent 'owe'/'oh' and 'eye'/'I' respectively. Except for the extremely rare use of a comma (which is used a few times to separate words in series), the only normal punctuation marks found in the manuscript are parentheses (the practice with these is not always the same as ours), new lines for paragraphs (usually flush with the left-hand margin, but sometimes indented), hyphens in compound words and compound names (although hyphens are restricted to longhand and even there they are used only seldom), apostrophes for possession (these too are rarely used and only in longhand), colons and full-stops for some abbreviations, dashes and full-stops occasionally in sums of money, full-stops and oblique strokes after some title headings, etc., a rarely-used square bracket for marking off a quotation. Pepys's standard stops, however, are two devices for indicating a break in a statement or the completion of it.   These are pyramids of three dots (∴) used in the earlier part of the diary, and ticks(√) which Pepys begins to use at 8 March 1667.

To present the diary in the minimally punctuated form of the manuscript would often prove confusing to the reader. The present edition adopts all the punctuation of the manuscript, except that square brackets have been replaced by quotation marks and that stops indicating abbreviations that have been expanded are omitted.   It also adds a fairly light modern-style punctuation. Pepys's triangles of dots and ticks, which do not always represent the end of a complete statement, have been replaced by full-stops or dashes as seemed appropriate. Pepys's single and double hyphens are represented by double hyphens. Stops have been added after entry-dates where he has omitted them.

Punctuation involves interpretation, of course.   But a reader of the present text who may be puzzled by any particular reading may normally recover Pepys's own usage in the diary simply by omitting the editorial commas, semi-colons and quotation-marks.   The paragraphing is all Pepys's, and the full-stops and dashes that separate sentences

8. See 31 May 1667.

and phrases correspond almost without exception to pyramids of dots or ticks in the manuscript. The short lines with which Pepys very occasionally marks off paragraphs etc. are reproduced.

The possessive *-s* constituted a problem. The shorthand gives no means to distinguish the plural possessive from the singular. In his long-hand, both in the diary and elsewhere, Pepys sometimes employs an apostrophe, but more often does not. Forms lacking an apostrophe may in context often be either singular or plural. Since there is in such cases no authoritative reading, it was decided to use an apostrophe in this text only where it appears in the manuscript or when there can be no doubt as to where it should be placed.

Aphetic forms, such as 'Chequer' (Exchequer), 'light' (alight) and 'prentice' (apprentice), have not been apostrophised. Pepys rarely apostrophises them in his ordinary writing elsewhere, and the un-apostrophised forms do not give difficulty to the reader. Apostrophes that Pepys uses in longhand, however, are reproduced.

In the interests of clarity, quotation marks have been introduced to mark off direct speech, and also to indicate sermon-texts and phrases which Pepys marks off from the rest of the text by means of parentheses or large writing.

The shorthand and abbreviated longhand almost always represent as separate units the compound words which we now either join or hyphenate. Pepys's longhand elsewhere, however, usually joins or hyphenates such words (although his preference in joining or hyphenat-ing is not always the same as ours in individual words). In shorthand, however, he disjoins the two elements of words that we now scarcely regard even as compounds. Among many examples are: 'nowhere', 'anywhere', 'itself', 'betimes', 'ourselfs', 'today', 'tomorow', 'awhile', 'ado', 'sometimes', 'herein' and 'otherwise', each of which appears in the shorthand as two words. Pepys rarely does this in longhand, however. For consistency, because it represents Pepys's ordinary usage, for the comfort of the reader and to avoid suggesting emphases that Pepys may not have intended, it was decided to join or hyphenate all such words in accordance with present-day usage.

5. *Abbreviations and contractions.* Abbreviations and contractions in the manuscript are restricted to longhand forms, most of them being names of persons, titles, offices, places, days and months. The abbre-viations of the most frequently used personal names sometimes consist solely of initials, and the same practice is used with the first part of

some compound place names. Christian names are commonly represented either by initials or abbreviations.

Initials can be ambiguous. 'W H', for example, represents both Will Howe and Will Hewer, and 'W hall' sometimes stands for either Westminster Hall or Whitehall. In the interests of clarity therefore, this edition fills out most abbreviations of names. In the case of personal names, abbreviated surnames are always extended; Christian names are left in the form in which Pepys wrote them. Truncations, such as 'The' and 'Tom', are reproduced, since in many cases they probably represent familiar pronunciations.

In filling out abbreviations of surnames and place names, the spelling that is now standard has been adopted, unless the abbreviation suggests otherwise. This means that when a surname or place name appears in a non-standard spelling, it is because Pepys has written it so in longhand or has given it an abbreviation that indicates a spelling which is no longer current. Typical examples of abbreviations are: *Backe*/ 'Backewell', *Br*/'Brouncker', *WP*/'W. Penn', *TH*/'T. Hayter', *Wh. hall*/'White-hall', *W^r hall*/Westminster-hall'. Abbreviations of titles, names of ranks, days, months, festivals and ordinary words have been expanded into modern spellings, unless the abbreviations suggest a different form: thus, *S^r*/'Sir', *Q*/'Queen', *D*/'Duke', *L^p*/'Lordship', *C, Capt*/'Captain', *Jan.*/'January', *tav*/'tavern', *gent*/'gentleman'; but *L^{pp}*/'Lordshipp', *Coll. Col^{ll}*/'Collonell', *cos*/'cosen', *Com^r*/'Comissioner'. With *Tang^r* and *Cambr.*, which Pepys almost invariably spells 'Tanger' and 'Cambrige' when he uses full longhand forms, the older spellings have been retained. Ampersands have been represented by 'and'.

6. *Numerals.* Pepys uses numerals not only as we do now but also as a kind of shorthand in names and other cases where we would now spell out the word. Thus, he employs '$\frac{1}{4}$' and '$\frac{1}{2}$' for 'quarter' and 'half', and he also calls a well-known tavern 'the 3 Tuns'. Such usages are represented in this edition by present-day usages, and numerals are restricted to situations where they are normally employed in present-day writing. The only exception is that Pepys's practice with sums of money and large numbers is retained. Roman numerals are therefore sometimes used for the numbers of shillings; the monetary sign for pounds, here represented as *l*, is placed after the figure; and no comma is employed in figures of one thousand and over.

In dating his entries in the diary, Pepys habitually writes the number of the day in the margin. It proved typographically impracticable to follow this practice in the present edition. Instead, the numbers have been indented at the beginning of the text. In the few instances in which Pepys runs two or three days (sometimes more) together, his marginal date-numbers have been indented at appropriate places and enclosed in double angle-brackets.

7. *Mr.* and *Mrs.* These honorifics are normally represented by arbitrary symbols in Pepys's shorthand, although the manuscript occasionally also uses 'M^r' and 'M^r'. The same symbols and abbreviations are also used for the common nouns which Pepys usually spells 'maister' and 'mistress' in longhand. For convenience, however, and because Pepys also does so in his ordinary writing, it has been decided to represent the honorifics in this text as 'Mr.' and 'Mrs.' When the symbols represent common nouns, however, they are transcribed as 'maister' and 'mistress', except that shorthand symbols or non-arbitrary symbols which transliterate as 'mastr' are printed as 'master', a spelling which Pepys sometimes uses in longhand.

8. *Capitals and hyphens in place names.* The text adopts the capitalisation of the longhand in the manuscript, even when this involves beginning the initial word of a sentence with a small letter. The manuscript almost always capitalises certain titles and offices of individual persons: 'the King', 'the Duke', 'the Admirall' and so on, and more often than not it capitalises the names of particular places and bodies, e.g., 'Parliament', 'the City', 'the Board'. But Pepys's usage in longhand is generally far from consistent. In transcribing the shorthand, therefore, Pepys's capitals have been adopted only with those words where his longhand seems to be consistent; otherwise the rule has been to use modern practice in regard to capitals.

Compound names are represented variously in the manuscript, sometimes wholly in shorthand, sometimes wholly in longhand (with or without abbreviation), sometimes in a mixture of the two forms. Usually the two elements are separate and unhyphenated. Sometimes, however, longhand forms are joined or hyphenated, e.g., 'Fleetstreete' or 'Lords-day'. In the vast majority of cases the second element in the name, 'street', 'green', 'alley', 'hall', 'garden', 'gate', 'lane', 'yard', etc., begins with a small letter. The present text follows the manuscript exactly when a compound name is written wholly and fully in longhand. For the more numerous cases when it employs shorthand entirely, a mixture of shorthand and longhand, or abbreviated forms, a compromise is adopted that is based upon Pepys's longhand else-where, viz., to hyphenate compound names and to begin their second elements with small letters.

9. *Pepys's corrections.* On about 4000 occasions Pepys changes a shorthand form. At times he does this by striking out a word, a short phrase or even a sentence or section. Normally, crossed-out symbols are replaced by forms written immediately after those they amend, although occasionally the emendation is made above the line. Very often, too, longhand is superimposed upon a shorthand form, or, more rarely, replaces another longhand form. Fortunately nearly all the replaced forms are still legible. Since they provide basic evidence on the diarist's considerations while he was writing, and also on his manner of composing and revising his work, the changes are all re-ported in the present edition; the correction being given in the text itself and the original form in a textual footnote. Unless otherwise stated, the changes reported are replacements of one shorthand symbol by another (in the case of ordinary words), or of longhand by long-hand (in the case of names). Similarly, incorrect or doubtful forms reported in the textual footnotes are shorthand symbols unless other-wise indicated.

In addition, Pepys has often added words, phrases and sentences. These he inserts over a line or in the margins, though sometimes he crowds them into the spaces between paragraphs and daily entries. These additions are distinguished in the present edition as follows: marginal insertions are enclosed in double angle-brackets; others in single angle-brackets.

Other peculiarities of the manuscript reported in the textual footnotes are the sections that Pepys, for various reasons, writes in extremely small characters or in very large ones, and the occasional places where there are blots, smudges or sections of poor penmanship.

10. *Editorial emendations.* Editorial changes and additions have been restricted to a minimum. Occasionally Pepys misses out a letter. Or he omits a word or name, leaving a blank; sometimes he repeats a word or phrase without crossing out the repetitions; now and then, though rarely, he seems to make an error in English. In this edition, Pepys's accidental and conscious omissions have, whenever possible, been repaired by placing the appropriate name, word, or letter in square brackets. Blanks in the manuscript are reproduced in the text.

Accidental repetitions have been removed from the text, but are reported in the textual footnotes. Pepys's few errors, such as 'Lord' for 'King',[9] have been corrected, and the erroneous words recorded in footnotes. Error on Pepys's part, however, has been assumed only reluctantly. Whenever a strange usage in the diary could be justified from seventeenth-century usage it has been retained, even though it may seem quite incorrect to a modern reader.

11. *Obscurities.* Pepys's shorthand is almost always extraordinarily neat and clear; even the passages written in minute characters are all very distinct. Sections written when his eyes were very painful are larger and commonly less precise than elsewhere, but they, too, give little trouble to the editor. Nevertheless, a few shorthand forms are illegible, or almost so, because of blots or poor writing. His longhand, which is less clear than his shorthand, also contains a few doubtful readings. And there are occasions when the inefficiencies of Shelton's stenography make for ambiguity.[10] In all such cases – they are not very many – the probable reading is given in the text, the less probable reading in a textual footnote.

W.M.

9. See 31 March 1662.
10. See above, p. lii.

III Previous Editions: The History of the Manuscript and its Publication, 1660-1899

It appears from the evidence of the diary itself that during the period of its composition it was normally kept under lock and key in Pepys's study in his house, possibly in a drawer of his desk,[1] or at the office. From the shelfmarks which he wrote on the front endleaves (each series of which represents a new adjustment of his books), it is clear that the six diary volumes were incorporated into his library at the same time, probably in the mid-1670s.[2] The shelfmarks also show that at no time until Pepys's last catalogue (1700)[3] were the volumes shelved together as a set, although volumes V and VI (which both appear to have been bound at the same time)[4] were never separated. In all the dispositions of the library books made before 1700 the diary volumes were distributed by size in four different places. The decision to unite them seems to have been made during the process of cataloguing in 1700, since at each entry in the catalogue itself, though not in the catalogue index constructed afterwards, the new shelfmarks (showing the diary volumes arranged in an unbroken sequence for the first time) were superimposed on deletions of those of 1693.[5]

It is difficult to assess what use Pepys may have made of the diary, both during the time of its composition and afterwards. He may occasionally have read it for pleasure – though he never records having done so during the diary period, and in fact he may well have been deterred both then and later from straining his eyesight by a surfeit of shorthand. Certainly the pages bear few traces of handling, though

1. It was here that in 1680 he kept his copy of Rochester's *Poems*: *Letters*, p. 105.

2. Each of the volumes bears only one pencilled number, which usually denotes that they were incorporated shortly before 1677. Had they been placed in the library by 1670 they would almost certainly have had two or three. I owe this point to Mr H. M. Nixon, who has made a study of the shelfmarks, based on the publication dates of the books.

3. This is the catalogue still extant in the PL. None of the earlier ones **survive**.

4. See above, p. xlii.

5. PL, 'Supellex Literaria Samuelis Pepys', i, Cat., p. 93; ib., Alphabet, pp. 61, 180; ib., ii, App., p. 163.

this may mean little, since he was so meticulous in his care of books and papers. He never added an index to it, or any other means of ready reference, and his 'Navy White Book',[6] which included most of the personal memoranda he wanted to keep by him concerning the period of the war, and had both marginal rubrics and an index, was likely to be rather more useful for official business than the diary. Nevertheless, the diary was put to some use, and could easily have been used more if the need had arisen. On 3 September 1663 Pepys looked up a back-reference in order to check a gipsy's prophecy that he would refuse a request for a loan. (It proved to be true.) And after the completion of the diary he used it to prepare himself for inquisition by the parliamentary Commission of Accounts of 1667–70.[7] When it required him in June 1669 to disclose whether Warren's great timber contract of 1664 had been 'grounded on the King or Duke's order', he applied himself 'to the examining of my Journall and other helpes to my recollecting the full truth in this Particular point . . .'.[8] In January 1670 he assured the same committee that he could, if required, give an account on oath of 'the particular manner' of his employing every day from the moment he took office to the end of the war in 1667.[9]

It is certainly clear that he hardly once tampered with his manuscript after it was finished. In several instances he did not fill in the blanks he had left in the course of writing, or correct the mistakes which would have been obvious on a re-reading.[10] The only addition he inserted after 1669, as far as can be ascertained, was the word '*mort.*' written (some time between March 1677 and October 1680) after the name of his brother John in the list of his family at 31 December 1664.[11]

Pepys long nourished the intention – until 1699 – of composing a general history of the navy,[12] but in the prolegomena to that unwritten

6. PL 2581; see below, 7 April 1664, n. The occasional marginal rubrics inserted in the diary refer only to his health or other personal matters.

7. Cf. 19 October 1666 ('This I set down for my future justification, if need be . . .').

8. Longleat, Coventry MSS 97, f. 115r.

9. PL 2874, p. 577.

10. Some corrections were made in the course of composition: above, p. xliv, below, p. ciii. The name 'Armourer' seems to have been added by Pepys later at 23 September 1667.

11. Some of the marginal rubrics may have been written by Pepys shortly after the completion of the diary. Two words in another hand have been interlineated at 1 December 1662. For the date of the insertion '*mort.*', see below, 31 December 1664, n.

12. 13 June 1664, 16 January 1668; *Priv. Corr.*, i. 15, 134, 201.

work (his volume of notes entitled 'Naval Minutes,' composed mostly in the 1680s),[13] there is not a single reference to the diary, although on some points, such as the controversy about the employment of gentle-men-captains, it contained a great deal of relevant material.

The diary was, however, carefully preserved in its entirety. On 31 December 1664 Pepys tore up all his papers 'not . . . fit to be seen if it should please God to take me away suddenly', but, confident in the secrecy of the shorthand, did not include the diary, although it con-tained much which he preferred to remain unknown. Similarly, he did not destroy it at the time of the Plague in the following year, while during the Great Fire he sent it for safe keeping to Sir William Rider's house at Bethnal Green, along with his money and his plate.[14] On 13 June 1667, when Dutch invaders lay in the river, the 'Journalls, which I value much' he delivered with other documents to a cousin in St Giles's, Cripplegate. In January 1673, when Pepys's house was burnt down, the diary volumes (in common, it appears, with his other books) escaped unscathed.[15] Whether he hid them later during the Popish Plot crisis of 1678–9 when he was held in the Tower under suspicion of treason, or in 1690 when arrested for alleged Jacobitism, we do not know. On either occasion his enemies, given knowledge of the diary's existence (as they had claimed to know in 1674 of a Popish crucifix in his house[16]), and given the means of reading its shorthand, would have been only too delighted to open to the world this Pandora's box.[17]

But Pepys kept the fact of its existence sufficiently secret. He probably mentioned it in none of his letters – certainly in none that have survived. Of his friends only Sir William Coventry appears to have been told of it,[18] and Coventry was given no details. The short-hand was known to no-one in his household except Hewer, who used

13. PL 2866; published by J. R. Tanner in 1926.
14. 3, 8 September 1666.
15. Cf. above, p. xxxvi, n. 39.
16. *CJ*, ix. 306; Grey, ii. 407+.
17. The diary contained, apart from his confessions of adultery, more generally dangerous material in his criticisms of colleagues and ministers, in his revelation of office secrets, above all in his bold words about the lechery and laziness of the King. It had been established in Peacham's case (1615) that the writing of sermon notes by a preacher could amount to treasonable publication. It is interesting to speculate whether this might have applied to Pepys's short-hand material.
18. 9 March 1669; cf. also 11 April 1660.

a different variety of Shelton.[19]   In the erotic passages he had gone to some pains to make transliteration difficult.   But once the diary was finished, he seems to have taken no special measures to conceal it.   The volumes, after admission to his library, were kept (like the rest of the books) in locked presses, but the title 'Journal' (discernible through the glazed doors) was printed on the spines, and the entries in his catalogues of 1693 and 1700 plainly recorded them several times (as 'My own Diary', 'Diary – Mr. Pepys's', etc.) in the longhand of an amanuensis.[20]

At Pepys's death in 1703 at Hewer's house in Clapham, his nephew and heir, John Jackson, was faced with the disposal of a lifetime's accumulation of books and manuscripts.   In York Buildings there remained, besides books 'design'd only for familiar use',[21] a great mass of personal and official papers.[22]   Some of these were to pass into the possession of Jackson's descendants; others were to go to the Bodleian as part of the bequest of Richard Rawlinson (d. 1755).   In the Clapham house were gathered, at Pepys's death or shortly afterwards, his particular treasures.   These were principally the bookcases containing not his everyday books but his 'library' – close on 3000 volumes, mostly printed books, but including also about 250 volumes of manuscripts (the diary among them), of music, and of prints and drawings. There was also a valuable collection of ship-models.   The library was the only collection specifically mentioned in his will, but he there made no reference to the diary itself or to any other of the library volumes. In the codicils of 12 and 13 May 1703 Pepys directed that the library should pass into the possession of his heir John Jackson, and after Jackson's death, into that of his old college, Magdalene, Cambridge, 'for the benefit of posterity'.[23]   By August 1705 Jackson had made a final recension of the library, renumbering the volumes, making fresh purchases in order to bring up the total to 3000, as required by Pepys's directions, and adjusting the catalogue accordingly.[24]   The six diary volumes were placed in the first of the twelve cases which now contained the collection.   The library, along with the other Pepys relics – the

---

19. See below, vii. 374, n. 1.   When Pepys and Hewer corresponded secretly in 1680 (during the Popish Plot scare) they used a code, not shorthand: Rawl. A 183, ff. 132, etc.   Cf. 17, 18 November 1666; 31 May 1669 & n.
20. Above, p. lxviii, n. 5.
21. PL, 'Supellex Literaria', i, Cat., p. 167.
22. See *Comp.*: 'The Diary and Related Manuscripts'.
23. PCC, Degg 97–8; see esp. quotation in *Pepysiana*, p. 264.
24. PL, 'Supellex Literaria', i, Cat., p. 165.

ship-models, the portraits, and the furniture ('an incomparable Musæum' as a friend of Pepys called it[25]) was now made accessible to the public in the house at Clapham until Jackson's death in 1723. Many saw it,[26] but no one, so far as is known, remarked on the diary. There were, of course, many items in the collection more easily appreciated.

When the library was moved to Cambridge in 1724 it was housed, in accordance with Pepys's wishes, in the 'New Building' at Magdalene (completed c. 1700), where it occupied a gallery constructed from rooms chosen by Jackson in 1704,[27] its presence being then, or shortly after, marked by an inscription painted on the outer wall over the colonnade: 'Bibliotheca. Pepysiana. 1724 Mens Cujusque is est Quisque.'[28] There it became one of the sights of Cambridge for the enquiring visitor.[29] But the books themselves, locked away and brought out only in the presence of the library-keeper or a fellow of the college, were more easily admired than studied. As for the diary, the fact that it was in shorthand must have frustrated any casual curiosity. On the other hand, the same fact might have attracted the interest of students and practitioners of shorthand, of whom there were several among the undergraduates and dons of Cambridge in the 1720s and '30s. In 1730 unofficial classes for the study of shorthand were being held in Trinity and in other colleges, including Magdalene itself. At the Hoop Inn in Jesus Lane a shorthand club held meetings.[30] Shelton's *Tachygraphy* was still current in the 1720s and probably later,[31] and a slight knowledge of that or of any similar method would have sufficed for the transcription of a brief passage of the diary if anyone so equipped had happened to look at it.

One of the stenographers who knew his Shelton and who was active in Cambridge at this time was John Byrom, the Jacobite poet (d. 1763). He had been a fellow of Trinity and was now devoting himself to the

25. Capt. Charles Hatton to Pepys, 28 September 1700: *Priv. Corr.*, ii. 75.

26. Cf. John Aubrey, *Nat. hist. and antiq. Surrey* (1719), App. v. 331–3; also a note on Pepys's collections (1708) in *Memoirs of the curious* (1710), ii. 178–9.

27. Magd. Coll., Master's Private Book, p. 103.

28. Cf. Magd. Coll., Register 1675–1814, p. 748. The motto is Pepys's. He seems to have adopted it after 1688: *Priv. Corr.*, i. 38, 112; *Pepysiana*, pp. 63+. It does not appear in the entry on Pepys in Guillim's *Heraldry* (1679).

29. Cf. John Nichols, *Lit. Anecdotes* (1812–15), vi. 532.

30. *Private journal ... of John Byrom* (ed. R. Parkinson), vol. ii, pt ii. 389, 394.

31. Byrom, op. cit., vol. i, pt i. 165; above. p. li.

teaching of his own method of shorthand in his native Lancashire, in London, and to a lesser extent in Cambridge. On 22 May 1728 his friend Peter Leycester wrote him a letter in which there occurs the first-known mention of the diary made by anyone other than Pepys himself.[32] 'I spent the last week at Cambridge. Whilst I was there, I went to see a curious collection of books bequeathed to Magdalen College by the late Mr. Pepys. In the catalogue I met with a book entitled *Shorthand Collection*, and would gladly have seen it, but the gentleman who showed us the library being a stranger, and unacquainted with the method of the catalogue, we could not find it. Mr. Haderton tells me it is a collection of shorthand books containing above a hundred and fifty[33] different methods. In searching for this book we found five [*sic*] large volumes quarto, being a journal of Mr. Pepys; I did not know the method, but they were writ very plain, and the proper names in common characters. If you think it worth your while to make Cambridge in your way to London, you will meet with these and I doubt not several other shorthand curiosities in the Magdalen library. I had not time, and was loath to be troublesome to the library keeper, otherwise I would have deciphered some of the journal . . .'.[34]

Byrom kept his own journal, which shows him staying at Cambridge, teaching shorthand and taking part in the meetings of the shorthand club, for several months in 1729–30 and again at intervals until 1748. He must have had opportunities of visiting the Pepys Library, but it is never mentioned in those parts of his journal which have survived. Byrom's classes were occasionally held in Magdalene College; on 4 November 1733 he went there and talked at Mr Scroop's 'about deciphering'.[35] On 22 January 1730 the club discussed '*Mens cujusque is est quisque*' – the motto painted on the outer wall of the Pepys Library.[36] How near Byrom came to the discovery of the diary itself, we shall never perhaps know.

Discoveries of some of the other riches in the library were made from time to time in the course of the eighteenth century. From its ballad

32. This is not counting the amanuensis who made the entries in the catalogue of Pepys's library.

33. *Recte* c. 30: W. J. Carlton, *Biblioth. Pepysiana*, pt iv, *Shorthand Books*, p. xvi. Samuel Hadderton was University Librarian, 1721–31.

34. Byrom, op. cit., vol. i, pt i. 301–2.

35. Ib., vol. i, pt ii. 523.

36. Ib., vol. i, pt ii. 411.

collection, one item ('The nutbrown maiden') had been published in 1707;[37] others appeared in Bishop Percy's *Reliques of ancient English poetry* (1765). Pepys's two volumes of prints and drawings of London and Westminster attracted the attention of John Bagford in 1715,[38] were known to Horace Walpole,[39] and were used by Richard Gough in the 1780 edition of his *British Topography*. Pepys's account of Charles II's escape after the battle of Worcester (taken down in shorthand at the King's dictation in 1680) was printed by Sir David Dalrymple in 1766.[40] Selections from two manuscripts of Scottish poetry were published by John Pinkerton in 1786 as *Ancient Scotish poems . . . from the MS. collections of Sir Richard Maitland*, the compiler describing the Pepys collections (vol. i, p. viii) as 'undoubtedly the most curious in England, those of the British Museum excepted; and . . . kept in excellent order'.

The first public reference to the diary (and the first known reference of any sort after Leycester's letter of 1728) was made by the Scottish writer, David Macpherson, in his *History of the European commerce with India* (1812). Writing about the trade in tea (pp. 130-1), he quoted from a 'curious memorandum in the diary of Mr. Pepys, the secretary of the Admiralty': 'Sept. 25, 1661' [*recte* 1660], 'I sent for a cup of tea (a Chinese drink) of which I had never drunk before'.[41] The transcriber had possibly been led to the passage by the words 'Cupp' and 'Tee' in longhand, but who he was remains a mystery.[42] At all events Macpherson or someone else with a knowledge of Shelton or of some cognate system had been the means of publishing the first extract from Pepys's diary ever printed.

The quotation and its source reached the notice of a wider public by

37. *Muses Mercury or Monthly Miscell.*, June 1707, p. 134.

38. PL 2972-3; John Leland, *Collectanea* (1770), vol. i, p. lxxxvi.

39. W. S. Lewis (ed.), *Corresp. of H. Walpole*, i. 89; ii. 253.

40. *An account of the preservation of King Charles II . . .*; printed from Pepys's longhand version, not from the original shorthand. Cf. above, p. l & n. 7.

41. For the correct transcription of the passage, see below, loc. cit. Macpherson's footnote adds little more: 'Mr. Pepys's curious and valuable manuscripts are preserved in the Pepysian Library in Cambridge.'

42. Macpherson had not cited the passage when writing on the same subject in his *Annals of commerce* (1805). Some reader admitted to the library may well have sent him the extract. In 1811 an unidentified copyist ('D. P.') had worked there on the books of prints, etc., of London and Westminster (PL 2972-3) in preparation for the *Londinia Illustrata* published by Robert Wilkinson in 1819: Bodl., MS. Top., London e. 2.

virtue of being repeated by the anonymous reviewer of Macpherson in the *Quarterly* of September 1812.[43] There followed shortly afterwards a series of events which led to the publication of the diary itself. In October 1813 the Rev. the Hon. George Neville (d. 1854), a young man of 24, was appointed Master of Magdalene. It may well be of significance that Thomas Grenville, the bibliophile (d. 1846), was an uncle and friend of the new Master. Conceivably Grenville or someone else may have examined the diary volumes as early as 1813–14, drawn by natural curiosity, by the quotation in Macpherson or the *Quarterly*, or by the entries in the library catalogue. But in April 1818 was published the diary of Pepys's contemporary and friend, John Evelyn, and according to the best available evidence[44] in a matter still in some respects obscure, it was this which led to the proposal to publish Pepys, though it may be that events preceding publication – news of the 'discovery' of the Evelyn manuscript in the autumn of 1814,[45] or news of the intention to publish it – may have created the first stirrings of a new interest in the Pepys.

What facts are certain are those stated in a letter written to the Master on 21 August 1818, four months after the appearance in print of Evelyn, by another of the Master's uncles, William Wyndham Grenville, 1st Baron Grenville (d. 1834), the Whig statesman, once Foreign Secretary.[46] Writing from Dropmore, his Buckinghamshire home, he reported that his brother, Thomas Grenville, the book collector, had brought him 'a MS. volume' which the Master had sent from Cambridge.[47] The book – though he did not say so – must have been volume I of the diary, and it is clear that Lord Grenville had been asked for information about the shorthand. The system, he wrote, was not dissimilar from the one he had learned as a law student, and he had been able to transcribe almost all the first three or four pages. He

43. *Quart. Review*, viii. 141.

44. A statement made in 1844 by William Upcott, who had helped William Bray to produce the first edition of Evelyn: qu. Evelyn (ed. de Beer), i. 54. This agrees with the implications of Lord Grenville's letter: below, p. lxxvi.

45. It had been known to the family before Bray and Upcott persuaded them in 1814 to allow it to be printed.

46. Original in PL; printed in, e.g., *Illust. London News*, 24 April 1858, p. 407; *Magd. Coll. Mag.* (1961–2), pp. 24–6. Thomas Grenville's correspondence now in the BM (Add. 28653, 41851–9) appears to contain nothing about the Pepys project.

47. Despite Pepys's will, which required that all the library volumes should be kept in the library itself, or, if on temporary loan, in the Master's Lodge.

was aware before starting on it, he said, that it would on many accounts be extremely interesting, and, proffering no further comment on the diary's contents, he went on to assure the Master that transcription was possible. 'Any man of ordinary talent', armed with the key to the shorthand which he (Lord Grenville) would supply, and fired by the 'lure of gain' could in 'a few months' dispatch the whole diary if he 'would set himself *sturdily* to it'. A professional shorthand writer would translate it in as many weeks as there were volumes,[48] but it would be better, he thought, to employ 'a Cambridge man, to work under your eye'. If published, it would form, he thought, an 'excellent accompaniment to Evelyn's delightful diary'. In a letter to the Master written four months later on 13 December 1818,[49] Lord Grenville made arrangements for returning the volume to the Master's keeping in London, and announced that from a reading of the first nine to ten pages he had constructed an alphabet of the symbols and a key to the arbitrary signs used in the system.

Lord Grenville was assuming in these letters that the Master himself, as the appointed guardian of the library under the terms of Pepys's will, would edit the diary. George Neville was a serious young man of antiquarian tastes and might well have done the work with credit. But being 'too much engrossed by more important duties'[50] – as Master and as Vice-Chancellor, 1818–19 – he passed on the task to his brother Richard (d. 1858), who was in 1825 to succeed to the Braybrooke title as the third Baron. The Master made some enquiries into the family history of the Pepyses, contributing a genealogical table to the first edition, but did little more beyond finding an amanuensis on whose work he later scribbled a few comments. By the spring of 1819, within a few months of the return to Cambridge of the volume which Lord Grenville had studied, the sturdy worker for whom he had asked had been found – John Smith (d. 1870), an undergraduate of St John's College, who in 1817, at the age of 19, had come up to Cambridge as a poor sizar, already cumbered with a wife and child. He was the son of a schoolmaster and writer of schoolbooks, the Rev. Thomas Smith, and (by his own account)[51] a descendant (presumably collateral) of the Jacobean adventurer, John Smith of Virginia.

Like his namesake, Smith explored largely in the dark. He met

48. These were wild underestimates of the size and difficulty of the task.
49. Original in PL; printed in *Magd. Coll. Mag.* (1961–2), p. 26.
50. Braybrooke (1825), vol. i, p. vi.
51. PL, Smith's transcript, vol. ii, pt i, f. 75*v*.

Lord Grenville only briefly, and never met the editor. He had no opportunity of discussing his difficulties with them. He found Lord Grenville's guide inaccurate and insufficient,[52] and was assured by three stenographers – one of them William Brodie Gurney, the best-known shorthand writer of the day, employed in the House of Commons – that his task was impossible.[53] The crux was that no one had yet identified Pepys's shorthand system as Shelton's. If that had been done – and it could easily have been done by any stenographical expert with the help of the collection of shorthand books in the Pepys Library – then Smith's task would have been greatly eased, for he could have used the library's copies of Shelton's *Tutor* (1642) and *Tachygraphy* (1691) as his guides. As it was, he seems to have availed himself of the help of the manuscript in the library which contains Pepys's two versions (one longhand, the other shorthand) of the narrative of the King's escape after Worcester fight.[54] Toiling for three years with great method, Smith finished his transcription in April 1822.[55]

Meanwhile, news of the project to publish Pepys had become known in literary circles in London. Stratford Canning, the diplomatist, wrote in his diary for 3 June 1820: 'I called on Gifford [editor of the *Quarterly*] . . . we talked of his Review. . . . He told me he had lately seen a curious journal, kept by a person named Pepys, who had been Secretary to the Admiralty in Charles II's time. Pepys, though most ably and usefully attentive to his official business, was in the habit of noting down all the occurrences of his life with the most singular minuteness. He employed shorthand for the purpose, the key to which it appears that some friend or other inquisitive person had discovered. . . . Gifford remarked that it afforded a picture of the times by no means unfavourable to the comparative morality of the present. Part of it will probably be published by Murray.'[56] John Murray in fact declined to publish it, and in 1823 a contract was concluded between Richard Neville and Henry Colburn, publisher of Evelyn. It came out in 1825.

The design for the Pepys was closely modelled on the plan adopted

52. Ib., vol. i, pt i, f. 14*v*.

53. *Illust. London News*, 27 March 1858, p. 311 (Smith to Editor, 23 March 1858).

54. PL, Smith's transcript, vol. i, pt ii, f. 274*v*. (Cf. above, p. l & n. 6.)

55. Ib., at last entry. He worked for twelve to fourteen hours a day according to his own statement in 1858: *Illust. London News*, loc. cit.

56. Qu. S. Lane Poole, *Life of . . . S. Canning*, i. 294.

by William Bray, editor of the Evelyn. Only a selection from the diary was printed, to which was added a number of the author's letters. In the case of the Pepys, the letters occupied just over one-third of the space allotted to the diary. The format (two quarto volumes) was the same in both cases. The Pepys was priced at six guineas the set.[57]

Over the making of this first edition Richard Neville (later Lord Braybrooke) had presided, and he seems to have taken most of the editorial decisions himself. He consulted his two Grenville uncles and, to a less extent, his brother the Master about the excisions from the diary text.[58] He employed a number of assistants in the writing of footnotes and the gathering and selection of the correspondence. He kept his own work to a minimum, and made no study either of the Pepys Library or of the Pepys manuscripts in the Rawlinson collection in the Bodleian Library.[59]

Braybrooke's main problem was the treatment of the text. In his Preface he gave an account of his editorial methods. Because of the diary's length, he had curtailed and condensed the matter, but the greatest care, he wrote, had been taken to preserve the original meaning, without making a single addition except 'where, from the shorthand being defective, some alteration appeared absolutely necessary'. His aim was 'to omit nothing of public interest', and for the rest to select material 'so as to illustrate the manners and habits of the age', retaining, however, all the drama notices for the sake of their uniqueness. Braybrooke's methods are revealed in the fifty-four volumes of Smith's transcript which he now prepared for the press.[60] Smith had had his

57. The title-page ran: *Memoirs of Samuel Pepys, Esq. F.R.S., Secretary to the Admiralty in the reigns of Charles II and James II. Comprising his diary from 1659 to 1669, deciphered by the Rev. John Smith, A.B. of St. John's College, Cambridge, from the original short-hand MS. in the Pepysian Library, and a selection from his private correspondence. Edited by Richard, Lord Braybrooke.*

58. Braybrooke (1848), vol. i, p. vi; PL, Smith's transcript, vol. i, pt i, f. 155v.

59. He did not know of the existence of the letters in the Rawlinson MSS until the printing of the work was far advanced: vol. i, p. viii. William Upcott was then employed to transcribe some of them.

60. The transcript was given to the PL by Mr Neville Grenville in February 1892: Magd. Coll., Orders and Mem. 1781–1906, pp. 288–9. It is a fair copy, with Smith's transcription on the right-hand pages, his notes on the left. Braybrooke marked the text in black pencil for the first edition, scoring through the passages to be omitted and adding his own words to bridge the gaps. He entered comments on Smith's work and a few draft footnotes of his own. There are also notes by George Neville, by Lord Grenville, and by a third person, possibly Thomas Grenville.

limitations. He had misread an occasional word both in shorthand and in longhand – sometimes from an ignorance, either of history or of language, for which it would be unreasonable to blame him.[61] But he had worked carefully, and on the whole made a remarkably accurate transcription.[62] If Braybrooke had printed Smith as faithfully as Smith had transcribed Pepys, the result would have been an excellent text.

Braybrooke produced, however, what was in many ways a travesty of the original. He gave no information about the manuscript beyond saying that it was contained in six volumes, and beyond printing in facsimile four lines from the first page. There was no explanation of the editorial problems created by the mixture of shorthand and long-hand and by the absence of punctuation. Apart from a few vague

61. The following are among his mistaken readings of the longhand (or short longhand) of the manuscript: 'nasty Dutchmen' ('masty Duch-men', 14 May 1660), 'Dr. F. Jones' (Dr. Foxe', 15 May 1660), 'Rooker' ('Booker', 24 October 1660), 'Ambassador Montagu' ('Abbot Montagu', 7 February 1661), 'Mr. George' ('Mr. Gouge', 10 August 1662), 'department-treasurers' ('Deputy Treasurers', 8 January 1664). Misreading the shorthand, he referred to Har-rington's theory of the balance of 'propriety' (i.e. property) as the 'balance of prosperity' (17 January 1660); to Pepys's half-shirts as his 'half-skirts' (13 October 1661); and to Albemarle's wood at Newhall as his 'wound' (28 December 1663). At 12 October 1667 he misread the shorthand form of 'gracious' for the numeral 36, so that the Lord Keeper was made to refer to the King's '36 acts'. Since Smith knew no Spanish, the few transcriptions he made of the erotic passages were inaccurate. He had deliberately omitted most of them, marking them 'Obj.' (objectionable). His attempt at the difficult note-form section at 5–12 June 1668 was full of errors.

62. Professor Matthews writes: 'His system of transcription had its faults. He ignored paragraphing, and the scribal changes – often significant – made by Pepys in the course of composition. He rendered the shorthand into modern spelling, as a general rule, but also adopted a few seventeenth-century conventions: e.g. "staid", "stopt", "publickly". He did not distinguish long-hand from shorthand, but usually retained longhand spellings. He normally filled out initials and abbreviations, but was inconsistent in this respect, especi-ally with Christian names. He generally adjusted Pepys's capitalisation to his own usage and spelled out small numerals. Otherwise he showed great re-spect for his text. He noted such features of the diary as erasures, marginalia, *lacunae*, blank pages and possible errors, but he made no editorial changes in the text given to Braybrooke, preferring to report these matters, together with doubtful readings, in the form of notes. The following is the full count of errors for the period 24 November–6 December 1665: "frost" (for frosty), "the" (but), "stole" (stolen), "afraid" (afeared), "soon as" (as soon as), "I did agree" (I agree), "surveyours" (Surveyors), "ashamed" (shamed), "afresh upon" (up[on]), "pearl" (pearls). Perhaps his rendering as "do" of a form best rendered "doth" should also be included.'

words in his preface, there was no account of his methods of work. All this was in the manner of his time; few editors, except those of classical texts, paid much regard to such matters in those days. And Braybrooke should not be blamed out of hand for omitting so much – almost three-quarters in fact – of the original. Even shorn of the passages which contemporary reticence certainly required to be excluded, the manuscript was far too long for the design of an edition which was also to include 241 letters.

But Braybrooke's methods had the effect of obscuring the differences between the manuscript and the printed version. His omissions (of whole entries, passages, phrases and words) were almost never marked for the reader's information.[63] He added or altered words or phrases in order to bridge the gaps made by his deletions, or in order to make an explanation without adding a footnote (e.g. 'Sandwich' after 'my lord'), but never made it clear that these were intrusions. He silently converted all Pepys's entry-dates into his own style ('9th January' where Pepys had written '9', etc.), thereby committing the anachronism of printing '22nd' for the seventeenth-century '22th' (two-and-twentieth). He or his assistants occasionally corrected a Smith mistake[64] but more often misread Smith's correct version.[65] On the whole, his work was amateurish compared with the professional quality of Smith's.[66]

63. He did once reproduce one of Pepys's blanks: vol. ii, p. 1.
64. At 19 October 1663 the 'poggins' put to the Queen's feet in a fever were corrected to 'pidgeons'; at 1 March 1666 'voice' was corrected to 'vows'. (This latter entry was not printed.)
65. E.g. 'coz. Stradwick' (1 January 1661) became 'coz. Hardwick'.
66. Professor Matthews writes: 'The following are examples of the changes Braybrooke made in the Smith text, taken from a sample check of the entries for 24 November–6 December 1665. At points where cuts were made, connective words were altered or added. A phrase was occasionally transferred into retained material to represent an essential detail in a passage that had been omitted. The sentence patterns were often changed by substituting lesser stops, even commas, for the full-stops that Smith used to represent Pepys's period-devices, and sometimes "and" was inserted. The effect was to change Pepys's sentences into longer and more rambling structures. Several small errors increased the number that Smith had made: thus "and" replaced "but", "where" (whom), "drunk" (drank), "Then home" (And to home), "Miss Tooker" (Mis Tooker), "those" (these), "recommendation" (recommending), "his presently" (presently) etc. Omissions ranged from complete entries to single words, and some of them pointlessly changed Pepys's meaning: for example, from Pepys's (and Smith's) "I sat near Mr. Laneare with whom I spoke, and in sight by chance and very near my fat brown beauty of our own Parish" (3 December), Braybrooke chose to omit "in sight by chance and very near".'

His favourite device – used countless times – was compression by omission. Pepys's phrase 'To my office and drank at Will's with Mr. Moore who told me . . .' (29 February 1660) became 'To my office. Mr. Moore told me . . .'. Often much lengthier omissions were made. For example, at 1 January 1664 Smith's version ran: 'I went to the Coffee House, sending my wife by Will and there stayed talking an hour with Colonel Middleton and others and among other things about a very rich widow, young and handsome, of one Sir Nicholas Gold's, a merchant, lately fallen, and of great courtiers that already look after her; her husband not dead a week yet. She is reckoned worth £80,000.' In Braybrooke, the first sentence was altered to: 'At the Coffee House where much talking about a very rich widow' and so on. Braybrooke would add or change the wording where he thought that clarity or his notions of good English required it. 'Satisfied' (6 April 1668) became 'satisfied with'; 'I did the office and myself right' (18 March 1668) became 'I did set the office and myself right'; 'and so home straight and to work' (19 September 1668) became 'and so home straight and to write' (presumably because Pepys had at that point mentioned the composition of a letter). Braybrooke omitted all indelicate passages of whatever sort, and converted objectionable words (pox, bawdy-house, codpiece, etc.) into more acceptable ones. In the last entry of the diary he quite suppressed Pepys's moving reference to his 'amours to Deb'. 'Young Mr. Whore' was converted to 'young Mr. Where' (9 January 1669), although the name was plain to read both in Pepys's longhand and in Smith's transcript. But that was perhaps a misprint.

In the footnotes to the edition Braybrooke sought 'to elucidate obscure passages' (though the really obscure ones he rarely printed at all), and here and there inserted 'short Biographical Sketches of the principal persons who are named, accompanied by such references as will enable the curious reader to inform himself more fully respecting them'. The notes were few, brief, and not always correct. A small number were derived from notes which Smith had added to his transcription.[67] That Braybrooke's work was thin and inadequate by the standards of modern scholarship goes without saying. But he provided rather more help to the reader than did William Bray

---

67. Some of these notes were much too elementary. After his definition of the meaning of 'courtesy' (at 9 March 1660), there was added (in ? Thomas Grenville's hand): 'These explanatory notes are so silly that they should every one of them be struck out. They would shame a child's Primer.'

in his Evelyn; he had taken some care over his biographies, and he or his assistants had identified most of the plays mentioned. On the other hand, he had not investigated the history of the navy and its organisation – he did not always know how to distinguish between the Navy Office and the Admiralty[68] – and he made no use of obvious literary sources (e.g. Marvell and Dryden), and next to no use of the historical sources then available – the parliamentary *Journals*, Cobbett's *Parliamentary History*, Clarendon, Burnet, Gramont, etc. He ignored the contents of the Pepys Library, apart from a few references to a small number of the prints and books in it.

The *Memoirs* received an enthusiastic welcome. Pepys was already known (though not widely) as a bibliophile and as a naval administrator. But here was a new Pepys: the diarist, and the man himself – or at least as much of the diarist and the man as was not concealed by the editor's monumental discretion. The anonymous reviewer in *The Times* (20 June 1825) made a forecast: 'Notwithstanding the extensive popularity of the Memoirs of Gramont and the still greater attractions of those of Evelyn, we have no hesitation in stating our opinion that these volumes will outstrip them both in public estimation.' 'For ourselves,' he added, 'we are delighted with them; they reach the *beau idéal* of what we desire from such records.' Pepys's account of everyday life was in fact of special value to the school of romantic historians and novelists then becoming fashionable. Scott, in the *Quarterly Review*,[69] thought that on the whole it offered no important new evidence about weighty affairs of state, but that it provided a richness of detail about the manners of its age which was unmatched, and that although inferior to Evelyn in 'its tone of sentiment and feeling', it was superior 'in variety and general amusement'. Jeffrey, in the *Edinburgh Review*, wrote of the diarist as having the most 'indiscriminating, insatiable and miscellaneous curiosity that ever prompted the researches, or supplied the pen, of a daily chronicler'.[70] Piquant, gossipy, lively, a treasure-box of new detail – this was the reviewers' general impression.[71] But

68. See vol. ii, App., p. 29.

69. Vol. 33/281+ (March 1826).

70. Vol. 43/26 (November 1825). The identification of the anonymous reviewer as Francis Jeffrey is made by *The Wellesley index to Victorian periodicals, 1824–1900* (ed. W. E. Houghton), i. 467.

71. Macaulay, in 1831, remarked that it 'formed almost inexhaustible food for my fancy. I seem to know every inch of Whitehall. I go in at Hans Holbein's gate, and come out through the matted gallery' : qu. G. O. Trevelyan, *Life and letters of Macaulay* (1880 ed.), i. 189.

not all comment was so friendly. To Sydney Smith the diary was 'nonsense'; to Creevey it appeared to be 'almost trash' when compared with the rest of the Pepys Library.[72] At any rate the publishers and most of the public were pleased, and Colburn brought out two reprints, in quarto and octavo forms, in 1828.

John Smith, the transcriber, had little share in the general rejoicing. He had been rewarded with a fee of £200,[73] a mention on the title page and a word of thanks in Braybrooke's Preface (almost in the manner of a grudging afterthought): 'In justice to the Reverend John Smith, (with whom I am not personally acquainted,) it may be added, that he appears to have performed the task allotted to him ... with diligence and fidelity, and to have spared neither time nor trouble in the undertaking'. The reviewers and the world of letters (and perhaps the editor himself) paid no attention to the young man who had slaved to make the shorthand intelligible to them. By the time the book was out, Smith had lost his minor university post as Deputy Esquire Bedell at Cambridge, and had become in his own words a 'poor and extremely oppressed curate' in Norfolk.[74] Some of his troubles were of his own making, for by the evidence of his own letters as well as by the witness of his critics,[75] he appears to have been self-assertive and tactless. Appointed to a rectory by Lord Chancellor Brougham in 1832 (perhaps in return for a radical pamphlet of 1828 on the state of the curates), he ventured further in his studies of Pepys by transcribing in 1836 some of the material preserved in the Rawlinson manuscripts: the shorthand diary of the visit to Tangier (1682–3) and a number of Pepys's letters. These, together with a biography, were published by Richard Bentley as *The life, journals and correspondence of Samuel Pepys* (2 volumes, 1841).[76]

Some time in the 1840s Colburn decided to bring out a third edition

---

72. Nowell C. Smith (ed.), *Letters of S. Smith*, i. 449 (Smith to Lady Holland, 20 June 1826); Sir H. Maxwell (ed.), *Creevey Papers*, ii. 280 (a comment made in 1834). The reviewer in *The Gentleman's Magazine* (1825, 95/233) wrote: 'Of their historical importance we think little . . . .'.

73. PL, MS. memo. by Smith, 5 October 1832. Scott was given just half this sum for his review of the book: Scott, *Journal* (ed. Lockhart, 1890), i. 65, 179.

74. PL, Smith to Lord Chancellor Brougham, 8 August 1832 (copy).

75. Cf. H. Gunning, *Reminiscences*, ii. 333+.

76. 'With the editing of these volumes I had no concern': Smith in *Illust. London News*, 27 March 1858, p. 311. The transcriptions in them were faulty, and the biography of Pepys full of errors.

of the original *Memoirs*, copies of the first two editions of 1825 and 1828 being exhausted. It appeared in five octavo volumes in 1848–9 (at two and a half guineas the set), and proclaimed itself on the title page as '*Considerably Enlarged*' – the correspondence having been reduced so that the diary could be printed more fully. In his Preface, Braybrooke admitted that 'a very general notion prevailed' that in the earlier editions he 'had used the pruning-knife with too much freedom'. 'Some persons even assumed,' he added, 'that the most entertaining passages had been excluded. . . . I determined, therefore, . . . to insert in its proper place every passage that had been omitted, with the exception only of such entries as were devoid of the slightest interest, and many others of so indelicate a character, that no-one with a well-regulated mind will regret their loss. . . . The *ipsissima verba* of the author are studiously retained, a few words only being occasionally introduced between brackets, where the sense was obscure or doubtful.' And for the first time the editor ventured a statement (not a very accurate one) about the shorthand: that it 'greatly resembled' Rich's system.[77]

Braybrooke now expanded the text, but only by introducing previously unprinted passages. He did not take the opportunity of restoring to their original length the telescoped parts of the 1825 text. All told, he printed some two-fifths of the diary, instead of the quarter or so published in 1825.[78] He now revised a small number of his 1825 readings, but only by correcting the punctuation. At 20 February 1667, for instance, the 1825 edition had: 'They talk how the King's viallin, Bannister, is mad; that the King hath a Frenchman come to be chief of some part of the King's musique.' Braybrooke now omitted the semi-colon so that the meaning of the sentence was entirely altered.[79] But apart from introducing square brackets for editorial interpolations (and those for explanatory interpolations only), he did not change his methods. In the newly printed sections as in the old, he compressed, paraphrased and bowdlerised as freely as ever – and again without giving notice in the text to the reader.[80] At 20 October 1663

77. Vol. i, pp. xiii–iv.

78. He now marked the Smith transcript in red pencil. On the endleaves was noted the number of extra pages to be printed.

79. This was pointed out by the anonymous reviewer in *The Athenaeum* (1848), p. 902: cf. ib., p. 1323.

80. Professor Matthews writes: 'E.g. at 5 April 1660 Smith's correct reading "We ready to set sail which we did about noon" became "We set sail at noon".'

(by misplacing an entry-date which both Pepys and Smith had placed correctly), Braybrooke conflated the events of two successive days, and in a footnote coped with the effect by the comment: 'Pepys seems to have dined twice in the same day.'

In the Preface Braybrooke wrote of his 'once more carefully reading over the whole of the MS.'. The reader was not however told that this manuscript was not that of the diary, but that of John Smith's transcription. Many traces of the debt which Braybrooke owed to Smith were removed from this edition. The tepid words of thanks from Braybrooke to Smith which had appeared in the 1825 Preface were omitted, and the whole history of the transcription left un-mentioned on the ground that it was sufficiently well known.[81] Braybrooke made a passing reference to the Tangier Journal, published in 1841,[82] but refrained from pointing out that that, too, had been transcribed by Smith.

Braybrooke's new commentary, while still consisting mainly of brief biographies, now included a few useful notes on antiquarian topics, most of them contributed by correspondents or assistants. Certain mistakes in the 1825 notes were corrected, but many remained. A few more sources were used – Clarendon, Baxter, the *Somers Tracts*, the *State Trials* – though very lightly. There was one new reference to a book in the Pepys Library.[83] The 'Life' of Pepys prefacing the diary was extended, but not greatly improved.

The publishers had, however, underestimated the hunger of the reading public. This was much the same public as was now greedily reading Macaulay's *History*, whose first volume, appearing at the close of 1848, had sold in tens of thousands like a popular novel. The new Pepys was re-issued in 1851 at 30*s*. the set, but was soon sold out, and Braybrooke undertook yet another new edition. This, the fourth ('*Revised and Corrected*'), appeared under the imprint both of Colburn

81. 'The history of Pepys's shorthand Diary being well known, the Preface has not been reprinted': vol. i, p. viii. In most copies I have seen, Smith's name is omitted from the title-page of volume I. The fact that it was included in those of the second and succeeding volumes suggests that this was an over-sight. Moreover, there are some copies (presumably of another issue) in which Smith's name appears on the title-pages of all volumes. After Braybrooke's death Smith announced (*Illust. London News*, 27 March 1858, p. 311) that he had prepared 'a History of the Diary, which may one day see the light'. Nothing appears to be known of this MS.

82. Vol. i, p. xxvi; cf. above, p. lxxxiii.

83. Vol. ii, p. 290, n.

and of his successors, Hurst and Blackett, in 1854. It was the last recension by Braybrooke, who died four years later at the age of 75. The 1848–9 edition, he explained, 'had found more general favour than its predecessors and was already out of print.... There appeared, indeed, no necessity to amplify, or in any way to alter the text of the Diary.' The text was therefore not expanded or altered 'beyond the correction of a few verbal errors and corrupt passages hitherto over-looked'.[84] But, stung perhaps by a reviewer's charge that his previous edition in 1848–9 was 'a book ... not edited at all',[85] Braybrooke gathered more assistants.

With their help new letters were printed. James Yeowell (sub-editor of *Notes and Queries*) distributed in their appropriate places under the printed text the notes which had lain in an *Addenda* section in the previous edition, revised the Index, and made extracts from 'such MS. materials as he discovered in the British Museum and the Bodleian Library'. John Holmes of the British Museum wrote some notes, verified others, and corrected proofs. Peter Cunningham, an authority on London topography, contributed notes during the course of printing. Braybrooke himself made some use of a copy of Rugge's 'Diurnall', a manuscript chronicle of public events (1659–70) written by a London barber and mainly constructed from newspapers. 'We may assume,' wrote Lord Braybrooke, with an unjustified complacency, 'that, considering the multiplicity of subjects occurring throughout the Diary, very few passages are now left unexplained.'

Braybrooke's successive concessions to the demand for yet more revelations had had the effect of leaving public interest only half-satisfied. What was there still left to reveal? What of the passages omitted in 1848–9 and 1854 because they were 'devoid of the slightest interest'?[86] It was difficult to believe that with a diarist such as Pepys there could be anything as dull as that. And did the 'indelicate' passages which Braybrooke had mentioned[87] relate to Pepys himself or to the King or to others? There could be no answers without a fresh transcription. In 1868 the Rev. J. Rawson Lumby, an ex-Fellow of Magdalene who knew the shorthand, was approached by Messrs Bell

84. E.g. 'morena' was substituted for the meaningless 'morma' at 22 October 1662 (Smith had transcribed it correctly though not very legibly), and 'Mr. Gouge' for 'Mr. George' at 10 August 1662.
85. *The Athenaeum* (1848), p. 902 (anon.).
86. Braybrooke (1848–9), vol. i, p. vi.
87. Ib., loc. cit.

and Daldy for a new transcription to be published in four volumes at 24s. The Master of the college had, however, first to give his consent, and the Master was the Rev. the Hon. Latimer Neville, son of the first editor. His reply came quickly: within three days of receiving Lumby's application he wrote requiring proof that his father's last edition was erroneous in all four volumes before the proposal could be considered, and even then would make no promises.[88]

But a few years later a senior Fellow of the college, the Rev. Mynors Bright, was given permission to start work on a new transcription.[89] He was a classical scholar who in his fifties had been forced to retire to a life of semi-invalidism. When it became clear in 1872 that he would have to leave Cambridge he learned the Shelton shorthand from the 1691 edition of the *Tachygraphy* in the Pepys Library. He also equipped himself with a key provided by the Cambridge polymath, John Couch Adams (d. 1892), Lowndean Professor of Astronomy and Geometry, whose work on the manuscripts of Isaac Newton in Cambridge had led him to a study of Shelton's shorthand.[90] This was the first time in the history of the work on Pepys's diary that the shorthand had been identified as Shelton's, but whether the discovery had been made by Lumby, Bright, Adams or someone else it is now impossible to say.[91]

Bright began work in November 1872 while he was still in Cambridge and finished the transcription in 1874 at his home in London.[92] By March 1875, after negotiating with John Murray, who again declined a chance of publishing the diary, he had concluded an agreement with Messrs George Bickers. His six volumes came out one by one between 1875 and 1879 in their series of 'Standard Authors'.[93] Bright almost abandoned the project when his first volume was greeted

88. PL, MS. 24B, Lumby to the Master, 21 November 1868; Master's reply (copy), 24 November.

89. Most of the following account is based on Bright's papers (February 1875–anuary 1882) now in the PL, and on the correspondence in the college archives.

90. Magd. Coll., College Letters 1854–94, p. 48. Cf. Notes & Rec. R. Soc., 18/10+.

91. Bright had used the Shelton textbook since 1872. J. E. Bailey, the antiquary and stenographer, wrote to him on 2 November 1875 informing him that Pepys's letters in the Bodleian were in Shelton, not Rich, and asking him to check some of his (Bailey's) transcriptions.

92. The diary was carried away from Cambridge for a second time (cf. above, p. lxxv & n. 47), but this time more excusably.

93. *Diary and correspondence of Samuel Pepys, Esq., F.R.S. From his MS. cypher in the Pepysian Library, with a life and notes by Richard Lord Braybrooke. Deciphered, with additional notes, by Rev. Mynors Bright.*

by a hostile anonymous review in *The Athenaeum* of 29 January 1876, and he went on to quarrel with his publisher over the question of re-issues. In the end, at Bright's insistence, only 1000 copies were printed and no re-issue was produced.

Bright stated in his Preface that he had published 'the whole of the Diary, with the exception of such parts as I thought would be tedious to the reader, or that are unfit for publication'.[94] According to his own claim, he had added 'about one third of matter never yet published'. In all, he had printed about four-fifths of the whole.[95]

As a transcriber, Bright was a careful worker (reading the whole manuscript twice over), but not so accurate as Smith. He entered his emendations and additions in an interleaved copy of the Braybrooke text of 1854 and in a notebook.[96] Many of the Braybrooke conventions (e.g. in date-styles and paragraphing) were thus carried over into Bright's text. He nowhere gave any detailed description of the manuscript or of his methods. He had not used Smith's transcript, which was still in the possession of the Braybrookes.

In his printed text Bright did not mark his omissions, nor did he indicate (either in the text or in general terms in the Preface) the fact that he had made many bowdlerisations. He refrained, however, from compressing Pepys's language, and from introducing his own (bowdlerisations apart). The punctuation he redesigned to his own taste. There were many inaccuracies and other blemishes in his readings of both the shorthand and the longhand.[97] Some mistakes could have been avoided by a better general knowledge of history.

94. Vol. i, p. viii.

95. Professor Matthews writes: 'The cuts ranged from complete entries to single words and small phrases; the omissions were largely of official business and the minor details of Pepys's personal and social life.'

96. These materials were bequeathed to Magdalene on his death in 1883. The notebook (referred to both in his interleaved Braybrooke and in his letters and papers) has disappeared; it seems to have contained simply transcriptions of those passages for which he could find no room in his interleaved copy. Wheatley, who succeeded him as editor, was unable to use it because it had by then been mislaid and was not sent to Magdalene by the Bright family until 1899. See the letters of 27 April 1888, 16 February, 12, 23 November 1899 (now in the PL).

97. Professor Matthews writes: 'In the case of the longhand he sometimes kept the original spelling and sometimes modernised it. For shorthand words he occasionally introduced antique spellings. He made no record of the scribal features of the Pepys MS. It is clear from a comparison of Bright's MS. with his printed text that in the course of printing and proofing many further

Col. Philip Jones (the Cromwellian soldier and politician: 'my late Lord Jones' of 9 February 1661) ought not to have been diminished into 'my late landlord Jones'; nor should 'the Queene of Sweden' (Christina: 11 April 1667) have been transmogrified into 'the Queen of Sheba'.[98] A brief enquiry into naval history might have told Bright that the Navy Treasurer's poundage ('3d': 8 September 1663) consisted of threepences, not 'thirds'; [99] and that the navy purveyor at 19 October 1666 dealt in broom and reed, as Smith rightly has it, not in 'bread and rum'. The 'gallant knights' whom Smith (and Braybrooke) had had Pepys observe in a garden at The Hague (18 May 1660: they were in fact 'knots' of flower-beds) were altered by Bright to 'gallant nuts' (in May !).

Bright had thought of his work as principally that of a transcriber of the text. His commentary was unambitious and did not amount to much more than a simple adaptation of that of Braybrooke. Braybrooke's 1828 'Life' of Pepys was reproduced, with the addition of a few details from college records. Braybrooke's 1854 selection of the correspondence was reprinted as it stood. There was only the briefest

---

textual errors were introduced. He printed in each volume lists of the relevant principal errors in and additions to previous editions. The errors were mostly Braybrooke's, not Smith's. I have set out some of Bright's errors in detail in *Journ. Engl. & Germ. Philol.*, 34/213+. Others may be cited here. Bright corrected Braybrooke's "brought" and "another abatement" to "bought" and "an abatement"; but he failed to correct such errors in the print as chapel (correctly "church"), barrels (barrel), Ledger (Liedger), where (whom), to do so (to do), and I unable (and unable), living (lying), the way (but way), those (these), recommendation (recommending). Among his own errors in the independent additions, these may be cited: he (who), scholar (skimmer), were (are), confidence (countenance), tried (wooed), the addition of a few subject-pronouns, and such normalisations of Pepys's grammar as eaten (eat) and wrote (writ). In his attempts to put into longhand the shorthand of Pepys's *lingua franca*, Bright, like Smith, was handicapped by the belief (as Wheatley reports) that the main element was French, whereas it is Spanish, with which Bright was obviously unfamiliar. Sometimes, in these passages, he merely copied the shorthand; occasionally he replaced a foreign word with an English one; frequently he wrenched Spanish words into French. The consequence, sometimes extraordinary and even nonsensical, was such errors as: sans toucher (sino tocar), Jason's women (hermosa mohers), mari (marido), my chose (my cosa), aller (andar), peu (poco), I might have had all else (I might have hecho algo else). Despite all these blemishes, the bulk of Bright's transcription is unexceptionable. It is solid, even laudable work.'

98. The latter mistake was put right in the *Corrigenda*: vol. vi, p. [v].

99. Smith made the same mistake at that point.

attempt at a history of previous editions, and a mere mention (without analysis) of John Smith's work. The principal footnotes to the diary were those of the Braybrooke editions of 1828 and 1854.[100] As for his own notes, about them the reviewer of volume I in *The Athenaeum* wrote, succinctly, 'there is nothing to be said'.[101] They were few and meagre, and were added, as Bright wrote, 'especially in explanation of any old custom or obsolete word'. He did not, in the Braybrooke manner, employ assistants, but a few friends and correspondents contributed information.[102] It would be easy to compile a list of Bright's shortcomings as a commentator. He was ignorant of naval affairs, referring to Pepys as Secretary to the Admiralty in the diary period.[103] He failed to use the books and papers in the Pepys Library and to consult the Rawlinson MSS in the Bodleian (which since 1862 had been made in large measure available in print by W. Dunn Macray's descriptive catalogue).[104] He neglected obvious and important sources such as the *Calendars of State Papers Domestic*, which, with their wealth of Navy Office papers, had been published (for the period 1660–7) several years before Bright's first volume came out.[105] He was capable, too, of giving a reference of sublime vagueness; at 25 February 1660, for instance: 'See *Notes and Queries*.' But in view of the fact that he never claimed to have attempted any serious independent commentary, perhaps the most appropriate criticism of Bright's work as a commentator is rather that he did next to nothing to enlighten his readers on the subject about which he had important new information – the shorthand. There was a brief footnote in volume I (p. xiv) which identified the system as Shelton's, instead of Rich's, which had been Braybrooke's guess; and a few sentences in the Preface to volume II – beyond that nothing to explain the Shelton method and Pepys's use of it. On the title page in fact Bright introduced a new and almost ineradicable confusion by referring to the shorthand as a 'cypher'. This encouraged the long-lived fallacy that Pepys had used a system of his own invention.

The first volume of Bright's edition had been reviewed in *The*

100. A licence to use the latter (still in copyright) was purchased by Bright from Bell's.

101. No. 2518 (29 January 1876) p. 158.

102. E.g. Hilton Price on banking.

103. Vol. i, p. viii.

104. *Catalogi codicum manuscriptorum biblioth. Bodleianae*, pt v, fasc. i, ii (1862, 1878).

105. They had appeared during 1860–6.

Academy[106] by an accomplished London antiquary and bibliophile, Henry Benjamin Wheatley (d. 1917). He had played some part in interesting Bickers in Bright's work; he had stood by, ready to take over, when Bright had quailed before other reviewers of the first volume, and, as an expert who had written books on the science of indexing, he had been engaged to construct the index to Bright's six volumes. After finishing it, being 'so impressed with the want of annotation', he published his *Samuel Pepys and the world he lived in* (1880) – the first book ever written about the diary. It was a gathering of diary material, presented with some explanations, under topical headings ('London', 'The Navy', 'Manners', Amusements', etc.). It did not, however, attempt any critical evaluation of the document or any serious account of the methods and circumstances of its composition.

Bright died in 1883, bequeathing to Magdalene all his Pepys materials, together with the copyright in his edition and in his transcription, and directing that the opportunity of publishing any fresh edition based on his work – his own edition being sold out by the time he made a will – should be offered first to Messrs George Bell.[107] By November 1885 Bell's had reached agreement with the college for a new edition, and had appointed Wheatley as editor.[108] The interleaved copy of the 1854 Braybrooke, which contained most (though not all)[109] of the Bright transcription, was in 1886 lent by the college to Bell's. The aim was now to produce a full, if not an absolutely complete, edition of the diary – omitting the correspondence altogether.[110] The methods used are obscure. Wheatley seems to

106. Vol. viii (November 1875), pp. 517–18.

107. Bell's owned the copyright of the Braybrooke editions of 1848 and 1854 which they had acquired by purchase from H. G. Bohn in 1864. Bohn had bought it in 1857 from the executor of Henry Colburn, publisher of the first edition.

108. In the account of the Wheatley edition which follows, correspondence and papers in the possession of Magdalene College and of Bell's have been used. None of Wheatley's letters, however, have survived in either place.

109. See above, p. lxxxviii, n. 96.

110. The agreement of November 1885 between Bell's and Wheatley specified an edition which would include both the diary and a selection from the correspondence. It is not known when or by whom this decision was altered. R. L. Stevenson had in 1881 published a perceptive essay on Pepys, in which he had asked for a complete edition of the diary. It was 'an established classic', 'an historical document' and its readers were 'entitled to be treated

have checked some at any rate of Bright's transcription of the longhand by reference to the original. There was much to regularise, in view of the inconsistencies in Bright's methods. As for the far more important matter of the shorthand, Wheatley had no knowledge of the subject, and the Smith transcript was inaccessible until 1892, when it came to Magdalene from the Braybrooke family.[III] An expert was therefore engaged: Hugh Callendar, Fellow of Trinity College, Cambridge, a young physicist and stenographer who was to write several books on shorthand and to invent a system of his own. In March 1890 he was invited by Bell's to examine select passages both of the diary manuscript and of Bright's transcription. Reporting his conclusions in the following June, he wrote that Bright had been guilty of a few scattered errors and omissions, that he had not consistently followed Pepys's longhand spellings, and that he had ignored the original paragraphing. He offered to carry out a complete revision, and estimated that it would take at least six months. The offer was not accepted, and exactly what of Callendar's work was published by Wheatley is not clear. In the few weeks he had spent on the task Callendar cannot have carried out any very extensive revision. Wheatley in his edition never described how the work on the text had been done; Callendar's share was referred to only by an ambiguous word of thanks in the Preface, and Wheatley nowhere gave any systematic explanation of the relation between the text which he printed and the Bright text which he had used as its basis. Callendar's function appears in the end (judging from his correspondence with Bell's) to have been simply to transcribe the erotic passages which Bright had copied in shorthand, together with those passages Bright had marked as not copied because of their 'unimportance'. At certain points he checked Bright's reading, but how these passages were chosen is not known. Some may have been those in which Bright's printed text differed from his manuscript transcription; others may have been

---

rather more like scholars and rather less like children': *Cornhill Mag.*, July 1881, pp. 31+ (repr. Stevenson, *Familiar Studies*, 1882, pp. 290+).

III. Above, p. lxxviii, n. 60. It is possible that Wheatley consulted it while his text was in course of printing, but he does not say so. His version of the last entry of the diary, although closer to Smith's reading than to Bright's, corresponds to neither of them exactly. He may have been following a reading by Callendar (q.v. above). There are innumerable points at which Smith was more accurate than Bright, but was not followed by Wheatley.

those listed in Bright's edition as mistakes in Braybrooke; others appear to have been chosen at random.

Wheatley's text was published in eight volumes during 1893–6 (followed by two volumes, *Index* and *Pepysiana*, in 1899),[112] and immediately established itself as the standard edition. It included almost the entire diary and was the first text to indicate suppressions by means of marks of omission (dots). Professor Matthews writes of Wheatley's text as follows: 'That he should have refrained from printing most of the erotic and scatological passages (close on 90 in all) is scarcely surprising in a Victorian editor, and in fact it is remarkable that he should have included so much, especially in the later volumes.[113] But he did not always mark omissions, and sometimes he was guilty of bowdlerisation, choosing to replace offensive words with synonyms more acceptable: thus "pissed" gave way to "dirtied".[114] To a scholarly taste, this was the least offensive of Wheatley's procedures. More serious lapses are far too numerous to be exemplified in detail: they may be found in abundance on every page, more in the early years of the diary than later. He omitted, apparently by oversight, substantial passages of the diary, sometimes complete days.[115] He omitted isolated words and phrases throughout the text, even when the words were completely innocent and necessary to the meaning. On the other hand, words, names and even phrases were frequently added. Phrases, sometimes even sentences and paragraphs, were at times printed in an order different from that of either Bright's manuscript or Pepys's, and the only explanations seem to be that the printer may have been confused by Bright's many insertions and that Wheatley did not proof-read with care. Bright's errors were increased by abundant editorial substitutions, made without reference to the manuscripts. The symbol for "pound" ("*l*" or "*li*" after the numeral) was

112. *The diary of Samuel Pepys M.A. F.R.S., Clerk of the Acts and Secretary to the Admiralty, transcribed from the shorthand manuscript in the Pepysian Library Magdalene College Cambridge by the Rev. Mynors Bright M.A., late fellow and President of the college. With Lord Braybrooke's notes. Edited with additions by Henry B. Wheatley F.S.A.*

113. The Master and Fellows of Magdalene protested to Bell's about the inclusion of objectionable passages; cf. Bell's reply, 16 January 1895: PL, MS. 24B.

114. 12 February 1660.

115. The entries for 26 November 1661, 25 March, 13 May, 19 November 1662 and 30 August 1663 were omitted, although there was nothing objectionable in them. All were transcribed, but none printed, by Bright.

converted to the modern-style "£" before the numeral. Punctuation was vastly increased, often by replacing full-stops with lesser stops or "and", sometimes by using full-stops where Pepys had none. Faulty readings were amended without notice, and some words were amended that needed no such charity. A multitude of variations from Pepys's *ipsissima verba* seems to have been the result of two conflicting principles: that the language should be given in seventeenth-century form, and that the language should be grammatically correct. These principles were not followed consistently, however; in many places Pepys's spelling and grammar were normalised; in far more places orthographical and grammatical antiquity was introduced. Such changes, applied to Pepys's longhand and shorthand alike, were done by no authority: there is no evidence at all that Wheatley consulted Pepys's text on such matters, or even Bright's. Wheatley's is the fullest edition of Pepys's text, but it is otherwise hardly the best. Few of its pages are totally free of errors; many are marred by a great number, some minor in significance but others affecting the style and the very meaning of the diary.'

As for the commentary, it was the work of a man knowledgeable and accurate as an antiquary, but working in a hurry. He commented on those matters about which he already knew something or about which he could easily inform himself (usually, it appears, from the reference books on the open shelves of the Reading Room of the British Museum).[116] He had no far-reaching ambitions or indeed any considered policy as a commentator. His work is greatly inferior, for example, to the work done by his contemporary Birkbeck Hill for Boswell. He did not look closely at his text to see what most needed elucidation; he made no study of Pepys's papers or books; he made only a cursory use of the Rawlinson and Carte manuscripts; he made no serious examination of the history of the period.[117] Most of the time (like his predecessors all the time) he interpreted the editor's role as a double one: that of a biographer or miniaturist (writing thumb-nail sketches), combined with that of a museum guide, pointing out items of quaint antiquarian interest – clothes, coins and so on.[118]

116. This is clear enough because most of them are still there.

117. Hence some of the textual errors (repeated from Bright): '1628' for '1618' (6 April 1663), 'King' for 'Prince' of Denmark (23 April 1663), 'the house where Mildmay died', for '. . . did [live]' (14 May 1665), etc.

118. He reproduced (with acknowledgements but unaltered) a number of notes from the Braybrooke and Bright editions.

Readers with an innocent taste for monumental inscriptions and the hall-marks of old silver were well enough served, and this was a public which Wheatley knew well.

But he did in addition achieve some substantial improvements. His notes on London topography were excellent – it was a subject on which he was an authority. He was the first of Pepys's editors to see the value of the entries on scientific subjects, and he related much of Pepys's information to Birch's edition of the minutes of the Royal Society.[119] With the help of experts, he made an attempt (much less successful) to deal with the musical entries. He used good sources for the theatrical notes. It must be owned too that, for all his antiquarianism, he went a little way towards treating the text in the manner of an historian. He (very occasionally) put other evidence alongside that of the diary; he ventured (though incompletely and inadequately) some explanation of Pepys's information (most of it printed for the first time) on naval administration; he did not entirely neglect public affairs. He knew the relevance of several of the more important historical sources. From volume IV onwards reference was here and there made to the *Calendars of State Papers Domestic.*[120] What he failed to do was to comment in the light of a consistent policy on matters of historical interest, and to make full and systematic use of the available historical sources. His edition, for all its value, was therefore of only limited use to scholars.

He was a worker of random habits – he might or might not identify a book as being in the Pepys Library; he might or might not give chapter and verse for a sermon text. His footnotes strayed on occasion far beyond the diary. Pepys's mention of Hole Haven, used as a harbour for quarantine, reminded him (at 26 November 1663) of lobsters; the appearance of the engineer de Gomme (at 24 March 1667) was the excuse for holding the reader with a story about 'a curious carved desk with Cromwell's arms upon it' in the possession of de Gomme's Victorian descendants. His Index (constructed by A. W. Cowdroy under his supervision) occupied an entire volume and was an improvement on its predecessors. Its biographical entries were full (though crudely subdivided), but, significantly, the subject entries (particularly on general subjects such as Church, Parliament, Science,

119. Thomas Birch, *Hist. Royal Soc.* . . . (1756–7).

120. There is one earlier reference in a note at 12 December 1663. It was from about this point in the diary that Wheatley also began to make a slight use of the Pepys papers in the Bodleian.

Music) were poorly designed and executed.   It suffered from faults in
structure, from inaccuracies, and from errors of identification and
omissions.   With the Index volume (1899), there appeared a volume
entitled *Pepysiana* – a ragbag of material, important and unimportant,
which Wheatley had collected himself or received from correspondents,
but had been unable to fit into his footnotes.   In chapter iv of that
volume he gave an account of the diary text.   (In the introductory
material to volume I of the edition, where the reader might well have
looked for this information, he had said nothing on the subject, though
he found room for a list of the people to whom mourning rings had
been distributed at Pepys's funeral.)   *Pepysiana* was not confined to the
diary period but ranged across the whole of Pepys's life and into all
manner of subjects, from 'Books dedicated to Pepys' to Pepys's notes
(1698) on Meheux's 'singular memory'.   The book was thrown together haphazard, so that it could not easily serve for reference, and
ended by being neither a commentary on the diary nor a satisfying
book in its own right.

                                                                    R.L.

IV THE DIARY AS LITERATURE

On 16 October 1665 Pepys reports entering his journal for eight days past and expresses the hope that thereafter he will be able to fall into his old way of doing it daily. Frequent notes throughout the diary, even in its first year, that two, three, four, up to ten, twelve, fourteen days were entered at one time[1] indicate, however, that the practice of day-by-day entry was seldom consistent. The phrase 'And so to bed', when it concludes a daily entry, shows that many entries were made late at night, just before Pepys turned in; but this practice, too, was in nowise consistent, for many entries were made during mornings and after-noons, as Pepys himself testifies. Nor does his 'And so to bed' always prove that the entry was made on the day it describes, since many such entries go on, with no break in style, to describe matters that occurred after the diarist was abed or asleep.[2] Much of the diary was written at Pepys's office, for secrecy as some have thought; but the diarist some-times preferred to work on it in his home, and sometimes he did so elsewhere, aboard ship, in lodgings, in several places in the country. Where he wrote seems to have been as much a matter of convenience as of secrecy; sometimes he worked in the office simply because his wife was away in the country, rain was coming into the house, or his home was being renovated.

Pepys uses many terms to describe his work on the diary. Some have an air reminiscent of accountancy, and a few imply that the com-position may have been more complicated than is usually thought: 'to set right', 'to make good', 'to put in order' and 'to perfect'. The last term[3] is particularly suggestive, for elsewhere Pepys uses it to

1. See, for example, 17 May 1660, 9 March 1661; 26 July, 24 September, 16 October 1665; 27 September, 19 October, 15 and 22 November 1668. That there were more such block entries than Pepys mentions seems evident from other details: such changes as 'a night before' from 'two nights before' (e.g. 12 July 1665), various series of days which were numbered incorrectly and then later corrected (e.g. 12–16 December 1660), series of days where all the material is run together without indentation for each day; entries where the sentence structure of the last entry on one day is carried through to the next day, etc.

2. See, for example, 13 and 17 January, 26 February, 8 March, 4 May 1661.

3. See 10 August 1662, 1 and 22 November 1668.

mean making a fair copy and bringing a draft into publishable form. The appearance of most of the manuscript, the regularity and even spacing of the symbols and lines, the straightness of the lines, the even colour of the ink over large sections, the neat disposition of the daily entries on the pages, all suggest that this is in fact largely a fair copy. And this general visual impression is supported by details in the manuscript itself.

The manuscript provides clear evidence that some parts of the diary were first written as rough notes. That some of the rest once existed in an earlier form (presumably a rough copy or draft) also seems to follow from the fact that in many entries a note on the act of making the entry is followed by notes on activities that happened after the entry was made. These are typical examples:

> I returned home and to my office, setting down this day's passages; and having a letter that all is well in the country, I went home to supper; then a Latin Chapter of Will and to bed.

> ... to the office, there set down my Journall, and so home to supper and to bed – a little troubled to see how my family is out of order by Wills being there, and also to hear that Jane doth not please my wife as I expected and could have wished.[4]

The later material has been added; but that the text as we have it represents a second copy is suggested by various details: the syntax for one thing, and the uniformity of ink and penmanship which characterises the added material and the material which precedes it.

Another kind of evidence that parts of the diary once existed in another form is afforded by the fact that during times of danger Pepys twice mentions entrusting his diary ('which I value much') to other people for safekeeping[5] – for during its absence he continued to keep up the diary, later copying it into the final manuscript. A similar procedure must also have been adopted during his period aboard ship in 1660 or his many trips to Brampton, Portsmouth and elsewhere, for it is highly unlikely he carried his diary-book with him.

Still further support comes from details of the manuscript. Considered as a whole, these details indicate that the composition of the diary was quite complicated.

4. See 22 June and 5 November 1663. For other examples, see 21 February, 6 March, 29 May, 14 July, 26 and 29 October, 21 December 1663, 15 and 26 June 1666, etc.

5. To Sir William Rider on 3 September 1666 (cf. 9 September 1666) and to his cousin Sarah on 13 June 1667.

Differences in ink and penmanship are striking. The ink varies between black and light brown, the shorthand symbols differ from section to section in size, sharpness, and angling, and the lines are spaced differently. These differences often run in blocks, and they tend to suggest that the entries were commonly made by series of days. These series sometimes agree with the blocks of entries mentioned by the diarist himself, but very often they disagree,[6] and the discrepancies seem to indicate that much of the diary may once have existed in two versions: one, a rough copy that Pepys destroyed, possibly section by section as he entered it into the diary-books; the other, the final manuscript.

The case for this hypothesis may be reinforced by several types of error in the manuscript. First, several words, such as 'love' (*recte* 'home') or 'made' (*recte* 'good'), which make nonsense and can best be explained as results of copying from slightly imperfect shorthand.[7] Second, numerous mistakes in pronouns and tenses (e.g. 'his' for 'my' and 'told' for 'tells') which suggest that Pepys was confusing direct and reported forms of speech, which is something very unlikely in a first copy but feasible enough in a second.[8] Third, numerous omissions or *homoeoteleuta*, most of them incipient and corrected but some not, which would not be likely to occur in an original text but are mistakes natural to a second copy, especially when the eye jumps from one instance of a word to a second, in the next line perhaps.[9] Fourth, many errors, such as 'mother' for 'murder' or 'is' for 'his' or 'state' for 'stayed', of representing one word by another of nearly the same sound.[10] Usually in these pairs the shorthand forms are substantially different, and the only explanation seems to be that the diarist spoke,

6. For example, the same small symbols and ink and writing-style are used from 23 December 1665 to 11 February 1666, yet on 14 and 26 January and 4 February Pepys writes of entering up blocks of days with which he was behindhand. Similar notes of entering series of days may be found in the Great Fire section of 1 September–10 October 1666, although Pepys himself states that the section was entered into the diary-book from loose papers three months later – and the ink and writing style show that it was done in blocks on several occasions.

7. See 15 May 1665 and 20 October 1666. If the original forms of these symbols were angled somewhat incorrectly they might be understood in a rapid reading as the words found in the manuscript.

8. See 26 January 1663, 11 December 1665.

9. See, for example, 30 April 1662, 4 March 1667, 25 February 1668, 14 September 1668.

10. See 27 June and 17 November 1662, 10 January 1661.

perhaps in a mutter, as he entered the matter into the manuscript – a practice that is more likely to have resulted from reading from another copy than from original composition.   Fifth, a number of statements that Pepys could not see what he was writing or that his writing was slubbering or his hand shaking, which are usually so graphically contradicted by the straight lines and neat penmanship of the entries themselves that it seems evident that the statements must relate to a prior copy.[11]   Sixth, many pages in which the symbols are tiny and the lines crowded, in striking contrast with pages that precede or follow.[12] These crowdings suggest that some series of days may have been squeezed into the manuscript later than entries which bear later dates, a practice for which there is direct evidence elsewhere in the manuscript.

Of most of these types of detail the manuscript yields many examples, scattered throughout the diary.   Their apparent testimony is that the manuscript at Magdalene must, in part at least, be a fair copy made from a rougher form.   And that this was indeed a Pepysian practice is made certain by what the diarist himself tells us about the famous section of the diary that describes the Great Fire.   On 11 October 1666 he squeezes in a memorandum that he had taken his journal during the fire and the disorders following (1 September–10 October) in loose papers 'until this very day' and could not get time to enter them in his book until the morning of 18 January.[13]

Further record of the practice, and evidence as to what the earlier copy was like, is afforded by two sets of notes for 10–19 April (at home) and 5–17 June 1668 (in the country).[14]   Blank pages are left in the manuscript at these points, and foolscap sheets of shorthand notes, organised by days, are bound in.   For 29 September–10 October of the same year there are also blank pages; but here there are no inserted sheets.

The shorthand on these sheets begins with accounts, and the accounting items are struck through and check-marked.   In addition to short annotations written on the lines of the accounting items, general observations on the day's activities are appended.   These general notes, and also the annotations in the accounts, are cryptic in style, even

---

11. See, for example, 5 August 1662, 26 October 1662, 10 May 1667.

12. Among the many examples are: 15-17 March and 28 November– 3 December 1662;   23-27 March, 7 May, 19 May 1663.

13. See example below, p. 204.

14. See 8-17 June 1660, and below, p. 172, n. 1.

though they have been copiously revised by excisions and insertions. Very clearly, these are rough notes, first revised, which Pepys meant to enter in his diary-book more meticulously, and perhaps more amply. It is to these materials, possibly, that he refers on 22 November 1668 when he writes of having left his journal for some days 'imperfect'. Taken with the details cited in our foregoing discussion, they suggest that similar rough notes may once have existed for much of the diary.

That may not be the whole story of how Pepys composed his diary, however. During the diary period Pepys kept several manuscript books: among them, a by-book, a 'book of tales', an account-book or books and a 'Brampton book', all of which have been lost;[15] the business journal he called his 'Navy White-Book',[16] which was largely in shorthand, and the great diary itself. The two series of rough notes, and possibly the many terms in the diary which seem to associate it with accounting,[17] suggest that the diary and accounts may have been products of a single process. A similar relationship may also have existed for the other three books, for sometimes the diary refers to entering a *bon mot* in the 'book of tales', occasionally it refers briefly to matters that are set out at length in the Navy White-Book, and once it mentions entering a journal-book out of a by-book.[18] All these records cannot have been composed simply from memory. For the accounts and business records, Pepys must have used invoices and minutes; and the characteristic formulae of the account may be seen here and there throughout the diary. For general observations, Pepys must often have drawn from notes. He speaks of his pocket-papers and of old broken office-notes in shorthand.[19] He also mentions a blacklead pencil he carried with him[20] and the silver fountain-pen that Sir William Coventry gave him:[21] with these, as he states, he reported sermons,[22] took down the very words of conversations[23] and copied in the theatre the echo-song in *The Tempest*.[24] It may therefore be assumed that his rough draft was partly assembled from bills, pocket-papers, minutes and similar basic materials relevant to the various manuscript books. Indeed, on one occasion the diarist refers to this practice when he mentions the difficulty of writing his diary during a

15. See 24 January 1664, 24 October 1663, 31 May 1666.   16. PL 2581.
17. Pepys applies the terms 'even' and 'enter' to the process of writing up both his diary and his accounts.
18. 24 January 1664.   19. 29 September 1665, 8 June 1664.
20. 11 May 1668.   21. 5 August 1663.
22. 19 August 1663.   23. 19 October 1666.   24. 11 May 1668.

time he was kept several days from his lodging, 'where my books and papers are'.[25]　Much has been written of Pepys's prodigious memory for detail.　But Pepys once consulted his physician about the decay of his memory,[26] and once he speaks of entering a series of days from memory but adds that it troubled him to remember it and that he was forced into doing so by the absence of his papers.[27]　It accords better with the evidence, therefore, and takes little away from Pepys's reputation, to assume that some of the diary's fine detail came ultimately from documents and notes.

At the other end there is also abundant witness that Pepys sometimes read over entries he had recently made in the diary-book and revised them.　The evidence is the hundreds of instances where longhand has been superimposed upon shorthand, sometimes in ink of different density and colour, and also the many notes that are squeezed into blank spaces at the ends of paragraphs or written in the margin. Except for one occasion apparently,[28] Pepys did not fill in the occasional blanks he left in his manuscript, mostly of names; but for part of the diary at least, one of his processes was a revision of the manuscript itself.

The logic of these details suggests five possible stages in the composition of the diary.　First, the accumulation of bills, minutes, official papers, news-books and rough notes on a day's proceedings.　Second, the gathering of these into a form which combined accounts with diary-style notes.　This process may at times have been skipped, and often it was done in a series of days.　Third, the entering of the accounts and business matters into the appropriate manuscript-books, and the first revision of the general entries which were intended for the final manuscript of the diary.　Fourth, entry of these general notes into the diary-book.　This process must have been slow; the available evidence indicates an average pace of less than twenty words per minute.　Pepys seems to have read in a mutter at times as he worked on this stage, and he certainly worked with extreme care, aiming at neatness and evenness comparable with that of a printed book.　The process may also be assumed to have entailed selection, occasional expansion and condensation, and a measure of polishing.　It was done, judging by writing style and ink, either by days or in blocks of days, and the crowding of certain entries seems to suggest that some blocks may have been entered later than entries that bear later date.　The two sections of

25. 10 November 1665.　26. 18 January 1661.　27. 10 November 1665.
28. 'Armourer': 23 September 1667.

rough notes bear witness to this procedure, and so does the Great Fire sequence, which, as Pepys states,[30] was entered at various times three months and more after the events, blank pages having been left for it – too few, to judge from the many entries in tiny characters. Judging by his practice of ending a day neatly at the bottom of a page and by the fact that each of the first three volumes ends on the last day of June, it is also likely that Pepys adapted many entries to the available space. The fifth and final process was reading over the entries that had been made shortly before, making small corrections and stylistic improvements, and inserting some further details at the ends of paragraphs and entries.

This series of five stages represents the most extreme form that Pepys's method of composition might take. The cryptic style of some entries suggests that there were at times no rough notes, and the evidence for late changes suggests that any final revision was done somewhat fitfully. Nevertheless, the manuscript makes it fairly certain that Pepys's way of writing was more complex than is usually assumed, and consequently that his great diary is no simple product of nature, thrown together at the end of each succeeding day. In part at least, it is a product fashioned with some care, both in its matter and its style.

This arduous procedure is something one might have expected from the diarist, for it may be doubted that Pepys ever did anything casually. It is a procedure, moreover, that explains many features of the diary. It explains, for example, the unevenness in manner and fullness; bare, notelike entries at one extreme and full, sweeping passages at the other, presumably as Pepys had less or more time or inclination to develop and refine from his basic notes and recollections.[31] It could explain also his remarkable skill in inserting long parenthetical statements into his sentences and still coming out with clean syntax. Impressive as it is, it may be simply a result of combining into one sentence two, sometimes three or more, separate entries from his rough notes. The procedure of composition could also explain Pepys's apparent prodigies of memory and much of the extraordinary detail of the diary; and, taken with his use of shorthand, it might also partly account for the peculiar happiness of his normal diary-style. In letters and in reports, Pepys tends to the extended sentences and rotund utterance of the public

30. Memorandum to 11 October 1666, 18 January 1667.
31. Compare 28–30 September 1660 with 2 September 1666, for example.

man. Thus, the letter to Sir George Carteret to which he refers in the diary at 14 November 1663 sets out in this way:

> The occasion of this morning's dispute at the Board was not more unwelcome to us all than your frequent mention of Sir William Warren's masts was particularly to me, for that I fear your dissatisfaction in that contract yet remains to my prejudice. The truth is, I blame myself for not giving you long since the account you demanded relating thereunto. But such is my unaptness to encourage any occasion of discontent, that notwithstanding that contract hath received so high a censure, and the compassing of it charged as a particular practice of mine (and that not only in the Office but in other places, where I am concerned to have my actions better understood), yet I have chosen rather to expect the issue of all this than be thought to design reproach to another more than right to myself by seeking justification in a matter little needing any. But since I find you still dissatisfied, and being doubtful how my silence may be interpreted, I have made it my afternoon's work to state the whole matter to you, and thus it is.[32]

Even in private letters to scholarly friends he sometimes speaks like a whale. And every now and then in the diary, especially when it is dealing with important public affairs, there are stretches of this ample manner.[33] But most of it is written in rapid, even impetuous language, simple and limited in its sentence patterns, familiar in its vocabulary, innocent of ornament or rhetoric, a diary-style which is close to ordinary speech, although it is more economical, denser with facts and more elliptical than most men's speaking:

> Then to the Dolphin to a dinner of Mr. Harris's, where Sir Wms. both and my Lady Batten and her two daughters and other company – where a great deal of mirth. And there stayed till 11 a-clock at night. And in our mirth, I sang and sometimes fiddled (there being a noise of fiddlers there) and at last we fell to dancing – the first time that ever I did in my life – which I did wonder to see myself to do. At last we made Mingo, Sir W. Battens black, and Jack, Sir W. Pens, dance; and it was strange how the first did dance with a great deal of seeming skill.[34]

Such a style might proceed naturally from notes; but so might a style heavy and ornate. And since Pepys publicly used the Ciceronian mode, his use of a simple quasi-conversational manner for the diary is a clear sign of either his instinctive or conscious response to what was

32. *Further Corr.*, p. 6. 33. 29 April 1663, for example. 34. See 27 March 1661.

proper for a private record. And flecking the pattern of the diary throughout are the traits of actual speech: the rhythms, the verbal usages, the idioms and linguistic fashions of Pepys himself and the people he heard and talked with. This prevailing style, endless detail in the matter, speaking quality in the manner, ellipses of verbs and pronouns appropriate to diary notation, is one of the most extraordinary features of Pepys's diary; and the symbol of its effectiveness is that Pepys is probably the only diarist who has contributed verbal formulae to the blood-stream of English. Most of this success must be attributed to Pepys's feeling for language and occasions and to his sensitivity to the patterns of conversation. But something must also be credited to the rapid composition made possible by the rough notes, written soon after the events, and to the continued use of shorthand which, however slowly it was written, permitted an easy flow into a final form and may also have sanctioned for Pepys a style different from that which he normally used in his longhand.

The procedure may also have facilitated one unusual and brilliant quality of Pepys's style, its peculiar sensitivity to the moment. 'Immediacy' is a word often used in connection with diaries; and it is a fact that among historical chronicles, diaries are valuable because of the shortness of the interval dividing event from record. But this is historical immediacy. Literary immediacy is something quite different: it is an effect of language and imagination. Most diaries, although they may record events only a few hours after they happened, are very far from giving the sense of the living moment that is so frequent in Pepys. In fact, Pepys himself does not always give it. The Tangier journal of 1683, written long after his inspiration had passed, hardly ever makes a reader feel he is present at what is described. Even in the great diary there are stretches that fail to do so. The two sections of rough notes[35] are historically immediate; but they have almost no sense of the moment. On the other hand, what is seemingly the most spontaneous and living series of entries in the diary, the long account of the Great Fire, was, as Pepys himself states, entered into the diary-book three months and more after the events.

There is paradox in the literary immediacy of the diary, and the explanation may lie in the two forms. The rough form provided the immediacy of history. Rewriting from it, Pepys had alternatives. He could simply abstract what he wanted; he could introduce pattern into the material; he could use the notes as a point of departure and go

35. See above, p. c.

on to maturer reflection and the more solemn manner of a chronicle of
the state and himself. Quite often he seems to have transferred
mechanically, and the entries are lacklustre, wanting both emotion and
variety in pattern. On several occasions he boiled down the material
for several days into single entries.[36] And sometimes he expatiated at
length as though he were writing a formal chronicle of *res gestae*. But
over an astonishingly large part of these nine and more years, Pepys
seems to have treated the rewriting as an opportunity for imaginative
re-entry into the recent past represented by his rough notes, and also
for making all those changes that contribute to immediacy in the
literary sense – the selection and combination of details, the effects of
conversation, the injection of judgement words, the retention of some
details that were reported while he was in the very act of writing the
rough notes and the addition of others that occurred while he wrote the
fair form.

From composition we may turn to motive. Pepys is rightly
regarded as a great civil servant, a remarkable administrator and
reformer, the 'Saviour of the Navy' as Bryant styles him. He would
not have disputed these praises. But he was disposed to explain his
superiority by talents that may strike us as less than heroic: a capacity
for mastering his business, attention to detail and zeal in taking pains,
punctiliousness and accuracy in minute-taking and book-keeping.
The last in particular is one ground for his contempt for his colleague
Povey and one cause of disputes in his household.[37]

The diary is a concomitant of Pepys's delight in book-keeping.
The rough notes from which the existing version may have been
written were, as we have seen, partly accounts, and the diary manuscript bears some of the marks of a book-keeper's hand, in its precise
spacing and lining, its almost complete freedom from blots. These are
externals and they partly reflect the ordinary neatness of the government clerk; but in the matter itself not a little reflects the mind of a
man who believes there is a vital correspondence between values and
dates. At the end of certain months, and more fully at the end of each
year, Pepys presents a balance-sheet for himself and the nation, a
concise statement that sets out the debits and credits in politics, morality
and finance, particularly in his own finance. This is a procedure which
loses distinctiveness in the body of the diary; but it is significant, and

36. For example, 14–15 May 1660, 8–13 and 16–19 July 1661, 9–10 February
1663, 12–13 September 1663.
37. See 8 February 1665 and 29 September 1664.

it reveals that one of Pepys's chief motives was one that explains the origin of many diaries of his time and later.

This was not his only motivation of course. Many diaries are the product of a puritanical urge to record (and so to correct) the writers' moral backslidings. There may well be an element of this motivation in Pepys, for certainly he was a puritan of a sort. Despite his fondness for pleasures of the flesh, he was a man divided, given to acting as recorder and punitive magistrate over his own inclinations. In his accounts of his amours, in his reports of quarrels with his wife, he is ready to report and condemn his own failings. He imposed on himself a system of fines (to be given to the poor) for going to the theatre, etc., beyond certain limits. With occasional lapses, he steadily fought the battle of labour against pleasure. But it may be doubted whether this puritanism was what motivated Pepys to become a diarist. More likely, it was his taste for history that set him out on his journey and sustained him for over nine years. The urge to be a chronicler of the times is probably the commonest reason for writing diaries. Not least among Pepys's many contributions to scholarship are his several great collections of documents on particular historical subjects: the history of the navy, the adventures of Charles II after his escape from the battle of Worcester, the activities of Captain John Scott, his accuser at the time of the Popish Plot, the development of handwriting and engraving and so on. Much of his collecting was solely for his own pleasure or use, but for some of it Pepys seemed to envisage publication (e.g. for the account of Charles II's escape from Worcester)[38] and one of Pepys's frustrations was not having time to write a history of the Second Dutch War – although in a period of leisure later in his life he did manage to publish a self-vindicating account of naval administration between 1679 and 1688.[39] It is often affirmed that the diary was secret, meant only for Pepys's own eyes. That was probably true for his lifetime. But some things suggest that he may have intended it to be read by future scholars of historical taste. He carefully guarded it, catalogued it in detail and set it in the library that he bequeathed to Magdalene specifically for the benefit of scholars. The diary *ab initio* was a history of the times:[40] a history of naval and public affairs; a history in which Pepys, though no angel, was clearly on the angels' side.

To the motivations of the accountant, the puritan and the historian might be added an inspiration even more basic. Pepys was a character-

38. See below, p. 155, n. 1. 39. See above, p. xxxviii. 40. See below, pp. cxiv+.

istic product of his day, a virtuoso, a man sympathetic to every new trend in science and scholarship.   In the diary period he was a friend or acquaintance of some of the chief scholars of that remarkable time – Hooke, Boyle, Wilkins, Petty, Evelyn – and later he was to add others. He displayed a lively interest in the scientific work that was being done at Gresham College; in 1665 he was elected a fellow of the Royal Society, and before then had attended its lectures and demonstrations. Nineteen years later he was honoured by being made the society's president, and it is his name that in 1687 authorises the imprimatur for what may well be the society's most famous publication, Newton's *Principia Mathematica*.   Yet for all his curiosity about the new experiments, for all his fondness for new technical devices and his belief that a good general scholar should know optics and mathematics,[41] in the presence of such giants as Boyle and Hooke, Pepys seems simply a curious tyro.   He bought and read scientific books as soon as they came off the press and made them a mainstay of his remarkable library. But sometimes he confesses his inability to understand them.[42]   The paradox, however, is more apparent than real.   The scope of natural philosophy was then broad enough to include interests that now form no part of natural science: shorthand, for example, or dialects, or the right way of writing.   Bacon himself had envisaged the advancement of the new learning by the collection of materials in a great many subjects, and in his *Essay on projects* he called for particular 'histories' of many human activities and of the natural conditions that motivated and shaped them.   Pepys's own collections, largely the product of later years but some just begun in the diary period, were to be directed to a remarkably large number of Bacon's specific recommendations: a history of music; a history of painting, sculpture, modelling, etc. (including collections of prints); a history of the printing of books, of writing, of sealing; a history of the art of war and the arts thereto belonging; a history of the art of navigation and of the crafts and arts thereto belonging.   Like his friend Evelyn, Pepys was a modern man, and so a Baconian.   No work is mentioned more often in the diary than Bacon's *Faber Fortunae*, an essay on self-help that he never tired of reading.[43]   His several collections of documents are witness to one phase of his later Baconian zeal; but the diary, too, is moulded in part by Baconian attitudes.   The prevalence of facts and details in its

41. See 17 October 1666.
42. 28 April 1667.
43. See 18 May 1661 & n.

history has a Baconian air; and so do many of its preoccupations with science and technology – it might even be argued that the shorthand itself is witness to Pepys's disposition towards the products of the new technology. Even more Baconian is its depiction of the diarist himself.

The most astonishing feature of the whole diary is the fullness and variety of its portrait of the writer, and its almost incredible honesty. No other diarist, not even the puritans or Boswell or Barbellion, lays himself so bare as Pepys does. Something of this may be attributed to Pepys's confidence in the obscurity of his shorthand, something to his egocentricity, something to puritanism, something perhaps to a book-keeper's ordinary honesty. But far more important as a motive than all these is Pepys's passion for microscopic observation of himself as he actually was. Egocentric and charged with feeling as the diary is, it often reads as though it had been written by an *alter ego*, by another man in the same skin, one who watched understandingly but rather detachedly the behaviour and motives of his fellow-lodger. The diary-form lends itself to this kind of duality, since the diarist is at once performer, recorder and audience. But it is some kind of commentary on human nature that very few diarists are able or willing to avail themselves of its opportunity: some throw themselves on their diaries as if in confession; most present themselves at their best, or rationalise, or fit themselves to a pattern, or talk about other matters than themselves. Through large areas of Pepys's diary, however, the diarist is both the observer and the observed, the penitent and the priest, the patient on the couch and the psychiatrist too, the man in the street and the behavioural sociologist. At one place or another almost every variation of his being is represented: waking, dreaming, acting, thinking, feeling, day-dreaming, rejoicing confidently, torturing himself with doubt and self-accusation. In those marvellous long records of quarrels with his wife he is always present as a third party, understanding both sides, but shrewd about both. His long-drawn-out and fascinating account of his successful siege of Deb Willet's virtue, a story that has the makings for a sentimental novelette, is converted into something that a major novelist might envy, a transformation made possible largely by the diarist-clinician's observation of the obsession that grew upon him and by his sociological recording of the degradation that slowly came upon Deb and the near-tragedy that developed in his own home. Much of the matter that is printed for the first time in the present edition might be labelled pornographic and scatological.

Since most of it is written in Pepys's own *lingua franca* and hedged with shorthand and dog-Latin devices, it may be judged to deal with behaviour that Pepys himself thought shameful.   Yet his presentation of this record of his moral deviations is clinical rather than moral or erotic; much of it reads like material for a scientific report on sexual behaviour in the human male.   That Pepys included it, although ashamed, is the most evident testimony to the full objective reporting, the scientific outlook, the Baconianism that went into the diary and the manner in which it was reported.

These are some of Pepys's motives in writing his diary, but although they explain some of its contents and qualities, they do not explain all. Nor do they explain why Pepys's diary is so much more interesting than others.   That it is possible for a diarist to be historically minded, scientific, honest, accurate, careful, copious, even to write in shorthand, and yet to be considerably dull, is evident from the diary (1709–12) of an eminent American colonist, William Byrd of Westover, Virginia.   And even John Byrom's (1722–44), although it is more varied and humane than Byrd's, is not precisely lively.   One essential difference was that Pepys was a typical seventeenth-century virtuoso, a man who justified himself by the diversity of his interests.   In Pepys, perhaps, they proceed from one single comprehensive quality, vitality; but if so, its manifestations relate to almost all aspects of his life and most features of his times: work, pleasure, friendship, business, public life and private, almost the whole range of society.   In his own mild way, John Evelyn touched on a few of them in his words at Pepys's death.[44]   But although Evelyn could appreciate his friend's industry and love of learning and music, he was, partly because of the nature of their friendship, partly because of his own nature, not fully cognisant of the intensity of Pepys's nature or the full range and quality of his talents and interests.

There is, for example, Pepys's intense attraction to beauty: that 'strange slavery that I stand in to beauty, that I value nothing near it'. An example is the occasion when he went to church 'and there stood wholly privately at the great doors, to gaze upon a pretty lady;   and from church dogged her home, whither she went to a house near Tower-hill;   and I think her to be one of the prettiest women I ever saw'.   Despite his lechery on other occasions, that represents a passion of platonic kind, and it is one that he also brings to painting, to music and to the remembrance of things past.   Housman himself is not more

44. See above, p. xl.

effective in describing the effect of a complete submission to beauty than is Pepys: 'but that which did please me beyond anything in the whole world was the wind-musique when the Angell comes down, which is so sweet that it ravished me; and endeed, in a word, did wrap up my soul so that it made me really sick, just as I have formerly been when in love with my wife; that neither then, nor all the evening going home and at home, I was able to think of anything, but remained all night transported, so as I could not believe that ever any music hath that real command over the soul of a man as this did upon me; and makes me resolve to practice wind-music and to make my wife do the like'.[45] Almost as much delight goes into his recall of his boyhood pleasures during his visit to Ashtead in 1663.[46] With matters intellectual and social, even with business it was much the same: all readers of the diary will surely remember Pepys's delight with the youngster whom he recognised to be so much like himself, 'with child to see any strange thing'.[47]

This zest and energy, this ready delight in things new as well as in old things, are vital in making Pepys the diarist he is. Of all English writers, perhaps the only one who is his equal in gusto is Chaucer. It is therefore no accident that Pepys should have collected Chaucer and admired him warmly as a poet.[48] Who else among English writers has Pepys's enthusiasm for everyday people, everyday life, or his habit of judging everything he liked the best that ever there was? Who else, even among Elizabethans, is so spontaneous with 'fine', 'rare', 'brave', 'mighty pleasant', 'exceeding good'.

The quality of a man and the quality of his book are not necessarily parallel, however, and when it comes down to bedrock, Pepys's supreme gift was that he was a fine writer. It is our habit when reading diaries to regard them as products of nature rather than of art. And in most cases the preconception is valid. Diaries *en masse* might well be regarded as natural products, and their commonly lumpish matters and styles witness the artlessness of their writers. But it is also true that almost all diaries that give genuine and protracted pleasure to an ordinary reader do so because the diarists possessed, instinctively or by training, some of the verbal, intellectual and emotional talents that characterise the novelist. Diaries are not novels; they are bound to reality, with its deplorable habit of providing excellent story situations and no artistically satisfactory ends. Nevertheless, it is not hard

45. 27 February 1668.   46. 25–27 July 1663.   47. 14 May 1660.
48. See 14 June 1663, 8 and 9 July and 10 August 1664, 21 November 1666.

to think of the best diarists as novelists tied for the occasion to reality
and the daily round.

This is particularly true of Pepys. His diary, as we have seen, was
composed slowly and carefully, and subjected to revisions. The
textual footnotes to this edition reveal abundant occasions when Pepys
has substituted words more precise, picturesque or tuneful. Far more,
one may assume, may have occurred in revision of the rough notes and
entering them into the final manuscript. And that Pepys had some
bent towards the art of the novelist, albeit of a romance kind, may be
argued from an entry for 30 January 1664:

> This evening, being in an humour of making all things even and clear
> in the world, I tore some old papers; among others, a Romance which
> (under the title of *Love a Cheate*) I begun ten year ago at Cambrige;
> and at this time, reading it over tonight, I liked it very well and
> wondered a little at myself at my vein at that time when I wrote it,
> doubting that I cannot do so well now if I would try.

That unfortunate victim to Pepys's passion for neatness was, judging
from its title, akin to the contemporary French romance. The
novelistic qualities that contribute to the delight of the diary are less
mannered, more realistic. They are numerous, and it will be enough
to list some of the more striking. The great crowd of characters,
many sketched by a phrase, an action, a comment, others appearing
through long stretches of the diary, growing in depth and variety as
detail follows detail and as Pepys's attitude to them hardens – or
changes. The abundance and variety of the conversation: some of it
bursting in as direct speech, most reported in Pepys's own words but
tinged with the tones and idioms of the speakers themselves. The
habit of presenting the weather, sometimes even the physical scene, not
as a discrete item, as is customary in diaries, but in emotional relationship with people and happenings. The passages of genre-painting:
the well-known and delightful pastoral scene on Epsom Downs, 'the
most pleasant and innocent sight that ever I saw in my life', for
example,[49] or the entries that describe his visit to his poor relations in
the Fens, a vivid series of Dutch portraits and landscapes in words.[50]
The instinctive habit of recalling fond memories of his boyhood and
youth at Durdans, Kingsland and Cambridge.[51] The selection of con-
crete details which are both vivid and symbolic, a remarkable skill
which is shown particularly well in the description of the Great Fire

49. See 14 July 1667.   50. See 17–18 September 1663.
51. See 25 July 1663, 12 May 1667, 25 May 1668.

and the Plague but is also evident throughout.   The practice of presenting quarrels with his wife as balanced digests of dialogues, and of
slipping into the reports small details about dress or the state of the sky.
The description of day-by-day happenings in affairs of long duration
in such a way as to lose nothing of any accumulating excitement, irony,
suspense or climax they may have offered.   The long, fascinating story
of Deb Willet's seduction and degradation has already been mentioned,
and there are shorter sequences of similar kind throughout the diary,
among them the story of the shocking illness, the sudden death and the
grimly comic burial of Pepys's brother, Tom, the strange infatuation
that William Wight the fishmonger, Pepys's uncle, developed for
Elizabeth Pepys, and the long defence of the navy that reaches its
climax in the diarist's great speech in the Commons.[52]

These practices and habits have been called novelistic.   Perhaps it
might be better to say that his zest and his literary instinct led Pepys to
relate a story excitingly whenever the material gave him a chance.
Whatever it is called, however, in the diary it is essentially an artistic
gift, and one that few diarists have possessed.   It is probably the lack
of that essential gift of art rather than any lack of opportunity that
causes diaries in general to be rated low in the literary scale.   Diaries,
even dull ones, have many virtues: for one thing, they probably bring
a reader closer to human actuality than any other form of writing.
As life-records they present a natural disorder and emphasis which is
artfully rearranged in biography, and so somewhat corrupted.   As self-
delineations they deal directly with people and events which in the
novel are subjected to the stresses and conventions of art and design.
And in many ways they are the most natural and instinctive product of
the art of writing.   But although tens of thousands are called to be
diarists, few are chosen to be really good ones.   Most diarists do not do
any of these things at all well.   The uniqueness of Pepys is that for
reasons that have been stated and for others that escape definition, he
does them all superbly.   In his own bailiwick, and at his best, he is as
much a nonpareil as are Chaucer and Shakespeare.   And in one
matter he is unique.   No one else has ever composed so brilliant and
so full an account of an actual man as he actually was.   And that must
be because he was not only a great man but because he was also a great
writer.

W. M.

52. See 5 March 1668.

V The Diary as History

The diary, although primarily a personal journal, was designed to serve also as a chronicle of public affairs. This dual purpose declares itself in the opening entry, which begins: 'Blessed be God, at the end of the last year I was in very good health . . .', and continues: 'The condition of the State was thus . . .'. The two subjects – the history of the man and the history of his country – become fused to a certain extent (or at least the boundaries between them become blurred) with the growth of Pepys's involvement in public life. But they still remain separable, and whenever the diarist breaks into the succession of daily entries in order to sum up – at the end of a volume or of a year – he makes a statement, balanced, like the opening entry, between personal and national affairs.

He was an extrovert, and the public and private themes are both stated in the same key, as it were – are both treated as objective events, with very few passages of introspection and of reminiscence to mark the differences between them or to hold up the flow of narrative development. The diary material was shaped simply by the fall of events, as in all good diaries. Now one history, now the other, moved to the forefront as its partner moved back. The long war crisis of 1667 left small room for private affairs, just as a domestic crisis (like his brother Tom's illness in 1664, or his affair with Deb Willet in 1668) crowded out public affairs.

It is this mingling of two varieties of record, in a diary executed on a large scale and in minute detail, which is the principal explanation of its character and value as an historical source. By reason of its detail and its length (it is roughly as long as Gibbon), it yields a great mass of information. By reason of the duality of its structure, it is free from some of the limitations of autobiography on the one hand, and of generalised national history on the other. Pepys's concern with the large events of the world outside himself makes it impossible for him to indulge for too long in personal *trivia*, while his concern with himself and the small events of everyday living always gives a human dimension to his account of public affairs. The diary serves therefore not only as a mirror but also as a private window giving on to a broad and varied external view – on to court politics and naval administration, or (at the other extreme) on to the simple domesticities of a London household. There is much else too – in particular, glimpses of the religious and cultural life of London. The view has one obvious drawback – it is impossible to see much of the countryside[1] – but a very large part of his contemporary England is displayed by Pepys. If all records of his period, except this one, were to disappear, it would still be possible to reconstruct much of Pepys's world from the diary alone.

Pepys's interest in public events was a natural one, and it would have been difficult for him to have thought of his life in any other way than in the context of political history. Born nine years before the outbreak of civil war, he had grown up not into the sort of world which could have been predicted at his birth but into the chaos and catastrophes of revolution. Londoners, as front-line witnesses of the upheaval, felt the force of events with particular sharpness. As a boy of sixteen Pepys had stood outside Whitehall Palace and watched – with approval – the execution of his King.[2] Moreover, it was in the political world that he had made his career, serving in the 1650s both Mountagu and the Exchequer. When the diary opens in 1660 it reveals a young man whose mind had already acquired the habit of political reflection. He was hunting out political news, observing parties and interests, making political judgements, concerning himself more and more in the 1660s to discover what good or evil had come out of the 'late times'. It was on politics that his career and livelihood, his social position and a large part of his happiness, all ultimately rested.

The result is that the diary contains both an individual's experience and the multiple experiences of his society. To historians this is a piece of particularly good fortune. Moreover, a good diary – whatever its design – can have a special usefulness to the study of history. It can be – and often is – more honest than letters;[3] more true to events than memoirs composed afterwards; less limited and less uncommuni-

1. The diary has no substantial information about agriculture, the principal industry of Pepys's England, and very little about life in the country or the country town. But presumably if it had, it would have been the work of a comparatively isolated person, and the less valuable.

2. Below, 1 November 1660.

3. Cf. the passages in which Pepys's diary gives the lie to Pepys's letters: below iii. 134 & n. 1; 16 December 1665 & n.; 20 July 1667 & n.

cative than institutional records.   At its best it may amount to something approaching a total transcript of experience, and if its author is a
man of significant experience, and has the right diary technique, then
its value is considerable.

To the historian, the cardinal value of the good diary is perhaps its
realism.   It will register the impression of events at the moment of
their impact, and not as they later appear by hindsight.   It will not
conceal the author's mistakes or bad judgements.   It will repeat itself,
contradict itself;   it will follow rumours and false clues.   It will move
not in large sweeps of time, like a history or an autobiography, but at
the pace of natural life, set by the rhythm of waking and sleeping.   Its
diurnal form will mean that its treatment of some events will be spasmodic and episodic, but this is the way in which many events – even
processes – happen.   Its sole principle of arrangement will be that of
chronology.   All that the diarist observes he will hold suspended in the
same stream of time which carries him and everything else along with
it – the large matters with the small, the distant with the intimate.
The diarist, although he will comment on events and may well relate
some events to others, will not attempt (if he is a good diarist) to isolate
them or rearrange them: he will merely mark their passing in the
stream.   His function is to register the daily flux of change – the
weather rather than the climate of his age.   And, more than that, if
he keeps his diary with a proper fullness, he will recall those things –
apparently slight but significant – which no other form of record is
so well designed to preserve, and which are often irrecoverable – a
dream or a mood, an impulse, a half-suppressed thought, intonations
of voices, the gestures and the silences that sometimes do service for
speech.[4]

So much for the ideal.   Pepys comes as close as anyone to it.   His
methods are models for the diarist.   His narrative, composed from
notes a few days after the event, and substantially unaltered thereafter,[5]
never suffers from the silent distortions and insidious afterthoughts (all
the effect of rewriting long after) which disfigure so much of the diary
of his friend Evelyn.   He wrote regularly and with a technique

---

4. Cf. (in Pepys's case) 6 November 1662 (a political dream);   7 August 1661,
27 January 1667 (suppressed impulses to steal);   5 April 1664 (the King's poor
elocution);   19 June 1667 (smiles and salutes bestowed by Pepys on bystanders
at Whitehall to make it clear he was not in disgrace);   25 March 1663 (hints,
mainly by silence, to a government contractor offering a gift).

5. See above, p. lxix & n. 10.

which seems assured and fully developed when he starts the diary and rarely flags to its end – cramming it with detail, spending hundreds of words, if necessary, on a single event or conversation. He could never have written, in the manner typical of Evelyn: 'I had discourse with the Dutch Ambassador concerning the present state of Flanders'[6] – and have left it at that – a note as dry and dead as a pressed leaf in the pages of a herbarium. Pepys would have caught and preserved the incident alive. He would have given not only the substance of the conversation but also the chance details – the diarist's clothes or the ambassador's mannerisms – which re-create atmosphere. The men and their encounter (and very likely the state of Flanders) would have been made vivid and memorable.

He never obtruded his views, though he often expressed them. He wrote honestly, concealing nothing. He wrote voluminously, and he dealt mainly in facts. His fondness for statistics is noticeable – not only in his references to public finance and the currency but in his account of naval engagements or of epidemics. The result is a diary which has a high density of hard factual information and an almost absolute freedom from cant and self-deceit. There is much, of course, that is missed from it, even within its own limits, and in some matters Pepys was wrong. But omissions and mistakes are few and on balance unimportant. His version of the daily round of living obviously excluded much that was routine. He often, for instance, wrote about composing the finished version of his diary (an irregular event), but never (as far as may be judged from some cryptic material) about the more regular event of making the preparatory notes.[7] He did not usually mention the prices of purchases, since these went into the account-books which were entered up from the same set of rough notes as the diary itself.[8] He did not normally report sermons at any length – as did Evelyn and other diarists of the period – but dismissed

6. Evelyn, 11 December 1667. This was Evelyn's normal way of reporting (cf. 27 April 1667: 'I had a greate deale of discourse with his Majestie at dinner'). He never gives details of the conversations which he had with Pepys himself and which are usually reported in some detail in Pepys.

7. Similarly, he often entered the fact that he shaved, but hardly ever that he washed his face – presumably because he shaved every few days, but washed more often.

8. Cf. above, p. ci. He recorded the successive rises in the cost of coal during the Dutch war because, like the enemy's threats to the Newcastle colliers which caused them, they were of professional concern to him.

them with a brief phrase or sentence.[9]   The only sermon reported
fully is the farewell sermon preached by the Presbyterian Dr Bates of
St Dunstan-in-the-West on 10 August 1662, shortly before his extrusion a fortnight later, and in that case the diarist's interest was in the
public event of the extrusion rather than in the sermon.

It is remarkable how often he misreported, just slightly, the words of
the sermon's text.   He had a faulty verbal memory, and did not trouble
to look up his Bible.   He made other verbal slips: 'my lord Chancellor'
for 'my lord Chamberlain', 'parliament' for 'House of Commons' are
typical examples.[10]   He very occasionally gave wrong dates; for
example, of a proclamation he had misread, or of parliamentary proceedings he knew of only from hearsay.[11]   Writing on 23 April 1669,
he misdated the council proceedings of the 21st, probably because he
was then catching up with twelve days' arrears.   At 12 October 1667
his summary of the Lord Keeper's speech at the opening of the parliamentary session is misleading because he had gleaned his news from
four informants two days after its delivery.   On other occasions his
attempts to compress complicated news items could lead to garbling.[12]
But, all told, his accuracy is remarkable.

Of his sources of information, some were commonplace at the time
and have often been used since – pamphlets and broadsheets for
domestic politics, or newspapers for news of distant parts and of naval
engagements.   In his hundred or so entries about the Plague he
regularly reproduced the figures of deaths published in the weekly
bills of mortality.   But with these materials he often combined information which is peculiarly his own.   For English news, the newspapers were dependent on him rather than he on them.   On naval
news he was himself a prime authority.   He also had access to the
manuscript newsletters from Holland or Flanders which reached the
Secretary of State giving foreign intelligence, and to which Pepys
could add the overseas news he heard from seamen and shippers.
As for the Plague, he knew enough about the methods of parish clerks
to correct the figures they submitted to the compilers of the official
bills of mortality.[13]

The validity of Pepys's information varies with its subject, and

9. Cf. 9 August 1663 (a reference to his intention to note the 'heads' of
sermons).

10. Below, p. 272 & n. 1; ii. 107 & n. 1.

11. Below, p. 286 & n. 1; p. 243 & n. 5.

12. E.g. below, p. 86 & nn. 3, 4.   13. 30, 31 August 1665.

general judgements of it ought to be few and guarded. On the daily detail of his own life, he is, of course, the unique authority, and he gives us an account which has certain distinct levels of interest. As a source of facts about everyday affairs, it yields fine detail not easily found elsewhere. As a variety of sub-history (if we may call it so), it may illuminate larger themes: as in early 1660, when Pepys's observation that M.P.'s were stockpiling their firewood[14] reminds us of the Rump's stubborn refusal to dissolve. More generally, this flow of prosaic information exerts, paradoxically, a powerful effect on the imagination. We are never in danger of forgetting that Pepys was in so many ways like ourselves: we can easily imagine ourselves in his situation. We make therefore the more effort to understand what is strange to us in him and his world. We are more interested in a man's politics or religion if we know what he had for dinner.

To the historian, one of the most interesting features of these private and domestic revelations is perhaps the information they give about Pepys's religion – to many of Pepys's contemporaries the most vital of all issues. We know from his letters that his High Anglicanism in his last years, after 1688, was a facet of his political convictions: a form taken by his loyalty to his old master James II. He had grown up under strong puritan influences, though never becoming in any strict or formal sense a Puritan. These were influences which no one alive in Interregnum England could escape, and Pepys had been directly subjected to them from his mother, his school and his university. There are clear traces of puritanism in Pepys – in his habit of attempting to control his behaviour by taking vows, perhaps also in his dislike of gaming and of swearing.[15] But his ecclesiastical position, clear enough by the time the diary opens, was by then that of a middle-of-the-road Erastian, distrustful of both ritualists and precisians, a loyal son of the Church of England but a strong critic of its clergy, staunchly anti-Roman but at the same time only amused by talk of the Pope as anti-Christ.[16] He attended both Presbyterian and Anglican services during the Interregnum, but preferred the Anglican. After the Restoration he went to his parish church with respectable frequency rather than with devout regularity; and if he slept during the sermon he usually had the excuse that it was during the afternoon service. In the whole of the diary period, he apparently never made his communion,

14. 17 February 1660.
15. Cf. 11 November 1661; 21 May 1663.
16. Cf. 28 August 1664.

at the monthly celebrations at his parish church or elsewhere.[17]   His
Lents were kept sketchily, and he observed Sunday as best he could,
which was sometimes not very well.   He read his Bible only a little,
and (probably in common with many other householders) regarded
family prayers mainly as a method of household management.   He
was at bottom, in the diary period, a worldling.   Yet there can be no
doubt of the sincerity of his religious feelings.   He turned naturally to
God, when alone, to express thanks or to ask for protection and help.
His Anglicanism may have been loosely formulated in so far as it was
a creed, but as a social discipline it was a cause to which his loyalty was
firm.   Just as his patriotism led him to support any stable government,
republican or monarchical, his Anglicanism was an expression of his
attachment to any church which could command the devotion of the
nation at large.   Living in times of ecclesiastical strife, he looked to
statesmen and church leaders to work out the terms of an ecclesiastical
peace.   He welcomed the proposals made for union between Presbyterians and Anglicans, particularly those of 1667–8, and at all times
he favoured toleration.   Seeing conventiclers carried off to prison, on
7 August 1664, he wrote: 'They go like lambs, without any resistance.
I would to God they would either conform, or be more wise and not be
ketched.'   Perhaps he was less religious than most men of his class and
generation, but his views on toleration – or something like them –
were widespread among the educated laity, and it was on ecclesiastical
pragmatism of this sort – on the layman's common sense – that the
solutions of these problems reached at the Revolution of 1688–9 were
largely to rest.   The evidence of the diary has at any rate the virtue of
offsetting the testimony of the clergy which tends to bulk too large in
the minds of most ecclesiastical historians.

Another subject on which the diary has special information is Pepys's
career during these years in the service of the state – in the Navy
Office primarily, but also in the Exchequer, the Privy Seal Office, the
Tangier Committee, and the Royal Fishery.   No other civil servant of
the seventeenth century kept a diary on such a scale, and its material,
particularly that concerning the Navy Office, may be used both to
supplement official records[18] and, occasionally, to correct them.

17. Cf. below, iii. 54, n. 1.
18. The date at which a civil servant began his duties, for instance, is not at
this period established (except roughly) by the date of his formal appointment
or the date at which he was first paid.   But in several cases (e.g. below, p. 191
& n. 2; ii. 206 & n. 4) Pepys gives it in the course of describing office events.

Some official naval papers covering the diary period have disappeared since Pepys's day (e.g. the Navy Office's day-books and minute-books), but many remain – a large body of correspondence (in most of which Pepys was involved), a complete series of contract books, warrant books and Navy Treasury ledgers, an office memorandum book (1660–8), and many miscellaneous papers.[19] Pepys himself kept (mostly in shorthand) a personal memorandum book (his 'Navy White Book', 1663–8),[20] as a memorial of all business which had gone wrong through the shortcomings of his colleagues, and as a means of self-protection against criticism in parliament or elsewhere. At several points it covers the same ground as the diary, but in greater detail.[21] All these official and semi-official records, together with those of the Lord High Admiral, and other government records, form the basis for a study of the work of Pepys's Navy Office, and to them the diary kept by the Clerk of the Acts serves only as an interesting supplement. By itself, it is a wayward, incomplete and prejudiced source for administrative history. It sometimes spends itself on the small transactions which had a special importance to Pepys himself, rather than on the larger matters which had less impact on him personally. But its value is that it can add unique detail, and that in general it provides administrative history with a personal dimension not provided by other sources. It gives an impression of the officials in action – of their daily routines; of their conversations together; of their anxiety to enlarge their functions so that they and their personal clerks could enjoy more fees; of their bargaining with merchants, their comings and goings between Seething Lane and the dockyards. Pepys's version of what happened is partial (in both senses of the word), but it is a vivid and on the whole credible picture of the human scene in which the play of administrative action took place. Pepys's judgements of his colleagues have the reputation of being over-severe. He may well have been a little self-righteous, and prone to the censoriousness which comes from an inflexible regard for professional standards. However, Batten, his principal *bête-noire*, had a poor reputation with

He describes the methods used by pursers to gain profits at 5 March 1667. Quite casually, at 29 April 1666, he makes clear one of the methods of consultation used in the nomination of J.P.'s.

19. For further information about these papers, see *Comp.*: 'Navy'; 'Navy Board'.

20. See above, p. ci & n.16.

21. Its material was not used in previous editions of the diary.

Coventry as well as with Pepys,[22] and is known to have left his office papers in disorder;[23] and Penn (another of Pepys's butts) was also criticised by Sandwich and by Gauden.[24]

There are certain office matters on which the diary is particularly useful. It is perhaps at its best in registering the successive stages of an extended event – the process of negotiating a contract, the composition of a long report, the story of a protracted piece of litigation. The crucial subject of naval finance is nowhere better treated in general terms, and although here the diary's statistical material is sparse, this is a weakness fairly easily remedied from other sources. In no other contemporary account are displayed so precisely the practical difficulties of trying to run the navy on inadequate grants and poor credit. In 1665 an experiment was tried which was to provide a solution. A sum of £1¼m. was granted by parliament, and was appropriated to the navy alone. The diary shows in detail how merchants and bankers reacted. The scheme was at first distrusted, by Pepys himself not least, but proved its value and was repeated (with certain changes) in the grants of 1666 and 1667. (Pepys's old master in the Exchequer, Sir George Downing, had much to do with its inception and success.) There is also some information in the diary about the beginnings of Treasury control over government spending, which started with the establishment of the Treasury commission of 1667 of which, Downing, as secretary, was the leading spirit. Pepys's references to his own dealings with the commission, both as Clerk of the Acts and as Treasurer for Tangier, illustrate the beginnings of the story. It was significant of another important constitutional trend of the time, too, that certain controls were also exercised over the Navy Board and Admiralty by parliament. Pepys gives a good account of the enquiries made by parliamentary committees appointed in 1667–8 into the management and conduct of the Second Dutch War, because he was himself in many respects closely involved, and took the lead (as 'the chief mover among them'[25]) in the defence of the Navy officials.

On several aspects of administrative history, the diary has the virtue of speaking indiscreetly where other sources are often silent. It can, in a few frank words, make plain the reasons for the appointment of naval commanders[26] or of Navy Board officials.[27] It reveals the lies

22. 19 January 1663.   23. NWB, p. 172.
24. 18 September, 6 October 1665.   25. 7 May 1667.
26. 31 May 1664; 16 December 1666.
27. 25 August 1663; 18, 21 November 1664; 13 October 1668.

with which Pepys protected everyone involved in the prize-goods
scandal of 1665 – including himself and his patron Sandwich.   It shows
how (with rather better justification) he and Warwick in November
1664 conspired to inflate their estimates of the costs of a naval war
against the Dutch as 'a scare to the Parliament, to make them give the
more money'.[28]   It gives instances of the suppression of evidence by
Pepys when under parliamentary scrutiny – e.g. about Warren's timber
contract of 1664, or the payment of seamen by tickets.[29]   Pepys sinned
cheerfully in all these cases, believing that he was acting in the public
interest.   There were also occasions, as with many other public
servants, when private advantage bulked large in his calculations.   At
least once he disobeyed office rules by trading with the navy on his
own account, supplying calico for flags,[30] and time and again he
accepted gifts of money and goods for services rendered.   In an age
when salaries (unaltered for generations) were artificially low, officials
were not expected to refuse all gifts, but the practice had its dangers
('so hard it is,' as Pepys reflected, 'for a man not to be warped against
his duty'[31]), and it is difficult for the historian to judge of its effects.
Pepys's own attitude is made clear enough in the diary.   There were
some gifts which obviously operated against the public interest, as in
Pepys's view did the frequent tributes of cash and goods which Batten
took from merchants quite indiscriminately.[32]   Such practices Pepys
condemned.   But he could not see anything wrong in a gift made
merely to expedite business or to establish good personal relations.
The test, perhaps a more elastic one than he was willing to admit, was
that the public service should also benefit.   He would never himself
'by anything be bribed to be unjust', but he 'was not so squeemish as
not to take people's acknowledgement where I have the good fortune
by my pains to do them good and just offices'.[33]   The wealth which
Pepys accumulated during the diary period (rising from £25 in liquid
capital in 1660 to £7000 in 1667) was built up not only from such gifts
but also (and perhaps principally) from fees and poundage income

---

28. 25 November 1664.   29. 2 March 1668; 29 October 1667.
   30. 8 October 1664.   He tampered with the records of the transaction,
scraping out his own name and substituting another (see 24 September 1666),
but had later to admit responsibility: HMC, *Rep.*, 8/1/133.   The total amount
involved was c. £750. Cf. also 21 April, 30 May 1662.
   31. 10 December 1663.   32. Cf. 27 June 1663; 3 May 1664.
   33. 12 December 1663.

from his Tangier post as well as his office in the navy. Nevertheless, proceeds from gifts were not inconsiderable: large sums of hundreds of pounds from big merchants such as Sir William Warren, £500 p.a. from Sir Denis Gauden as victualler of Tangier, and a succession of presents – silver flagons, 'an excellent Mastiffe, his name Towzer', 'a case of very pretty knifes with agate hafts',[34] and so on. This may not have harmed the Crown, but the gifts were often meant to influence decisions (it is noticeable how often the presents arrived in the midst of negotiations for a contract), and would have been awkward to explain to a critical House of Commons.[35] Some civil servants could joke about it. Cooling, secretary to the Lord Chamberlain, told Pepys that 'his horse was a Bribe, and his boots a bribe; . . . and invited me home to his house to taste of his bribe-wine'.[36] But Pepys had to be more careful. Receiving a letter from Capt. Grove on 3 April 1663, he closed his eyes before opening it, discerning money to be in it – 'not looking into it till all the money was out, that I might say I saw no money in the paper, if ever I should be Questioned about it'. The best defence of Pepys is that, surrounded as he was by the calculated generosity of merchants, he preserved his independence. He worked hard when there was no prospect of 'bribes' and at matters which brought no profit. He refused gifts if he thought fit, and he returned them to the donors if the service had not been performed. He upheld the criticisms made by an officer of Woolwich yard of the hemp served in by Sir Richard Ford, even though the latter was an influential merchant (and a neighbour of the Navy Office), because he 'would not have the King's workmen discouraged (as Sir W. Batten doth most basely do) from representing the faults of merchants goods, when there is any'.[37] He did not allow his understandings with Warren and others to deter him from criticising them before the Board, or from holding them to severe terms in the King's interest.[38] Pepys, like many other public servants, had mastered the useful art of receiving gifts without becoming corrupt – an art he shared with his King and with many contemporary politicians.

34. 17, 23 February 1664.
35. Cf. 2 March 1668. Moorcock, a timber merchant, once sent in a tender to the Board and a cake to Mrs Pepys on the same day: see 1 September 1664.
36. 30 July 1667.
37. 4 June 1662.
38. 16 July, 12 August 1664.

The political world in which Pepys's career was set is in many ways difficult to understand. It is full of contradictions which derive mainly from contradictory elements within the monarchy. It had great reserves of independent power, and yet it was to some extent and in some circumstances forced to accommodate itself to parliament, to a semi-independent local magistracy, and to national feelings. In this situation public opinion was of importance, and perhaps the greatest contribution which Pepys's diary makes to an understanding of political history is that it gives the best available single account of public opinion in the early years of the Restoration. It covers or touches on most topics of significance; its news is often unique and almost always accurate;[39] and it registers spoken rather than written or printed opinion – i.e. the opinion which, being evanescent, easily disappears from the record. Pepys may be said (though admittedly with some exaggeration) to have transcribed the political conversation of London. The town talked; Pepys listened.

Like Paris in the nineteenth century, London in the late seventeenth was a city alive with political excitement. The English then, like the French later, were known for political instability. They had strong views and lived in critical times. Moreover, the physical size of the political community was small. High politics were mostly conducted in a limited area – the capital – by a limited number of people. They concerned decisions made by an *élite* in Whitehall and Westminster whose members it was often possible for the London public to know, or to know of, as persons. The slowness of communications enlarged distances. Only occasionally (at times of great crisis or in the very infrequent general elections) did the provinces take an important part in political life; Europe and the rest of the world were days, weeks, months away. The scale of the political world, that is to say, did not dwarf the human beings inhabiting it. Issues of the most general sort could be discussed in terms of personalities. Another condition made for the intensity of political interest among Londoners – the fact that

---

39. The newsletter writers of the period also give public news similar to Pepys's, but there is no extant series of newsletters for the 1660s comparable in value with the diary. The letters written during 1677–86 from London by another knowledgeable public servant, Sir Robert Southwell (he wrote to Ormond, Lord-Lieutenant of Ireland, by almost every post) are the nearest equivalent to the diary accounts in this respect. See HMC, *Ormonde*, n. s., iv. 374+.

conversation was then the commonest mode of communicating political news and opinion. Newspapers, later to be the main carriers of this traffic, were then virtually forbidden to trade in it – they were official publications and by official policy were kept very brief and reticent. There was thus a premium on political talk.[40] On 6 June 1666, when the public learned that the battle fleets of Holland and England had met, forty enquirers flocked to Pepys's office to hear the result. Obviously this method of news-gathering was unsystematic and open only to Londoners, but it worked, and news by this means could travel quickly. Word of the Anglo-Dutch peace of 1667, which arrived at Whitehall at noon on 6 July, had travelled across town to Pepys's house in the city before he could sit down to his midday dinner. There were, of course, dangers in the oral transmission of news. Falsification of facts was easy, and false news could spread as easily as true, or more easily. Pressures of feeling could build up quickly, and were difficult to control in a large crowded city which had no effective police. The two great public panics of Pepys's lifetime were produced in these conditions – the revolutionary riots of 1641 and the Popish Plot scare of 1678–9. On the other hand, the virtue of these conditions was that they stimulated individuals to take an interest in politics. Modern democracies, which endow the citizen with so much more political power than he had in Pepys's day, also involve him in a type of political life so much more complex and impersonal that he may find some difficulty in participating in it.

It is therefore not surprising to find in the diary a great deal of solid political news in the form of what appears to be personal gossip. Pepys by great good fortune happened to be well placed as an eaves-dropper. He had the entry to the royal palace, to government offices, and to parliamentary committees; and the range of his acquaintance comprised almost all types of person from royalty downwards. Of those who governed England, in fact, only the leaders of the established church were unknown to Pepys. He attracted confidences. States-men and city councillors alike would divulge their secrets to him, and from a host of informants he would extract political news of varying interest. In those days of a very small civil service even minor civil

40. Broadsheets and pamphlets to some extent filled the role of modern newspapers. Pepys often read them, particularly at times of crisis. His dating here can be useful; e.g. on 14 February 1660 he read a broadsheet which in the Thomason Collection in the British Museum is dated the 16th: below, p. 55 & n. 4.

servants, being close to the heart of government, could tell Pepys the business methods of the Lord Treasurer, or of secret council proceedings.[41] And beyond the governing circles, Pepys went through London spreading a close-meshed net for his daily haul of news. It might be good fish or it might be red herring – but a day without a catch was to Pepys a day lost.[42]   He was regarded by Sandwich (and no doubt by others) as an authority on London opinion.[43]   He talked with merchants and financiers; with sailors and shopmen, drabs and dons.   Thanks to his gift for hobnobbing, he came near to hearing the talk of the whole town.

His diary technique was well suited to the purpose of recording oral news.   Despite his reputation among later commentators, he spent at least as much space on important news as on *trivia*.   He summarised each item, dated it, and gave its attribution.   He went out of his way to cultivate acquaintances he loathed (religious fanatics in particular) if he thought that their opinion might be of political interest.[44]   In listening, he would not interrupt an informant, even if he had heard his story before, in case he might pick up a new detail.   In reporting a conversation he would suppress his own opinions, with the result that his account of a talk which lasted for two hours – that with Robert Blackborne on 9 November 1663 – reads like a monologue.[45]

It is conceivable that he was led by his own interests to exaggerate the amount of political talk, but any exaggeration was not serious, because there are other witnesses to the same phenomenon.   De Cominges, the French ambassador, observed in 1665 that in London even the watermen spoke of state affairs to the milords as they rowed them to parliament.[46]   De Cominges himself, and most other envoys, thought it worthwhile to relay their impressions of London opinion regularly to their home governments.   Their despatches often cover the same ground as Pepys's diary entries, and (although usually inferior in detail and precision in their treatment of opinion) often confirm them. Clarendon's government itself paid coffee-house politicians the compliment in 1666 of attempting to shut down the coffee-houses 'with their calumnies and scandals'.[47]   It is also likely that Pepys over-emphasised

41. 29 December 1662; 2 March 1664.
42. Cf. 19 June 1661.
43. 9 March 1661.
44. 5 December 1662; 13 October 1663.
45. Cf. also 22 February 1664.
46. Qu. J. J. Jusserand, *French Ambassador*, p. 237.
47. Clarendon, *Life*, iii. 104.   The attempt was repeated in 1675.

those views he agreed with. He tended to find in public opinion what he had set out to find – criticism of the court's wastefulness, of parliament's ignorance and so on. He may well have exaggerated also the strength of Presbyterianism, which was not as important in church or state affairs as Pepys and many of his contemporaries thought.[48]

But on the whole Pepys's accounts of news and public opinion bear the stamp of an accurate record, if not always of an exact judgement. There were available to him three principal broadcasting centres of political news: the royal palaces at Whitehall and St James's, for news of court and government; Westminster Hall, for news of parliament; and, for overseas news, the Royal Exchange in the city. Pepys, besides frequenting all these places himself, had in each of them a number of well-placed informants.

His work for the Navy and Tangier took him often to court. Every Monday, with his colleagues of the Navy Board, he waited on the Lord High Admiral, the Duke of York, in his chambers in Whitehall or, in summer, in St James's.[49] He frequently visited government departments (particularly the Treasury) or attended council committees. During the war his visits multiplied, and involved occasionally attendance at the cabinet itself (which appears to have been the Navy Committee too during wartime), and at the meetings of ministers held a few days before the meetings of the cabinet in order to prepare business. Most of these visits he would prolong by gossiping in the galleries and ante-chambers, or in the highly political taverns near the

48. Not even in the Revolution had it been as strong or united a movement (or, to use the word in its exact ecclesiastical sense, as Presbyterian a movement) as it appeared to be. Its name and cause had covered a variety of political and ecclesiastical beliefs of the centre, and most lay Presbyterians quickly and easily moved rightwards at the Restoration. But it was Presbyterian clerics who had been the dominant influence in the Cambridge of Pepys's student days; it was with the Presbyterian political interest that the Mountagus had allied, and it was among Presbyterian merchants and shopkeepers of the city that Pepys had come to spend his working life. He was thus easily prompted, by the catchwords of the time and by the accident of his acquaintance, to mistake the nature of the movement. Clarendon himself was in similar case. In the early years of the Restoration he treated the Presbyterians gently and sympathetically, since they were then a force to be reckoned with. Composing his memoirs a decade later, he could write them off as a faction.

49. The meetings with the Admiral are rarely given much space in the diary. More attention is usually given to the proceedings of the Tangier Committee and later the Treasury Commission.

palace.   The King and Prince Rupert knew him, though not as well as did the Duke of York.   Albemarle would hand to him, unopened, naval despatches addressed to him as commander.[50]   To Clarendon and Arlington, with whom his dealings were rather less frequent, he was known as a prominent and industrious functionary.   Pepys knew intimately two officers of state who were often in the inner confidence of the government – Sir George Carteret (Treasurer of the Navy and Vice-Chamberlain of the King's Household), and Sir William Coventry (secretary to the Duke of York).   He also learned much from men less eminent but nevertheless well informed, such as Sir Hugh Cholmley, a courtier.   His spies for backstairs news were James Pearse (who had a place in the Queen's Household and was Surgeon to the Household of the Duke of York); Sarah, housekeeper to Sandwich, whose official lodgings were next door to Lady Castlemaine's house in King Street; and the courtiers Bab May and Tom Chiffinch.

It was from these palace sources that Pepys gained most of what he knew about the rise and fall of the King's ministers.   His material on the subject before 1667 is usually slight or incidental.   From time to time he names the 'cabal' – the inner circle of ministers – but the names (given at secondhand) have to be checked carefully.   He has some detail about the resignation of Secretary Nicholas in October 1662, which was to lead to Bennet's (Arlington's) appointment as his successor, and to the undermining of Clarendon's position.   His information (at 23 December 1662) that Clarendon was (according to James Pearse) 'as great . . . as ever he was with the King' is interesting in view of the controversies that have gathered around the question of Clarendon's responsibility for the royal declaration of 26 December which promised an indulgence to the Dissenters.[51]   But it is with the ministerial changes of 1667–8, in which Coventry was involved, that Pepys's evidence attains its greatest authority.   Clarendon's fall in the autumn of 1667, for which Coventry was in large part responsible, is fully described in a series of conversations which Pepys had with Coventry himself.   It is an account greatly superior to those written afterwards in the memoirs of Clarendon and the Duke of York, and one which later studies have vindicated without material alteration. The collapse in October–November 1668 of the York–Coventry influence and its replacement by that of the Buckingham–Arlington connection (assisted by Lady Castlemaine) can also be traced in Pepys

50. E.g. 10 January 1666.
51. Below, iii. 290, n. 2.

in a detail which is at all major points confirmed by the surviving correspondence.[52]

The history of the Privy Council is another theme illuminated by the diary. The official register of council proceedings gives only the results of debates, not the debates themselves, and has almost no evidence about the committees or informal groups which made the most important decisions. Pepys gives occasional accounts of what was said, or alleged to have been said, in meetings of full council[53] (some of them 'close' meetings from which Council clerks were excluded), and many accounts of committees[54] – all of which add to the official record. He throws some light on the dark matter of how council committees were composed and organised.[55] Characteristically, too, he can quite casually provide a piece of information (probably otherwise unrecorded) which is revealing. At a meeting on 3 July 1667, for instance, at the height of the invasion scare, when news of a landing by the Dutch at Harwich had just reached London, naval business was held up for 'near two hours' while 'the King and the whole tableful of Lords' discussed a private law dispute between an old man 'with a great gray beard' and his son 'for not allowing himself something to live on'. Albemarle was fast asleep before the case had ended.

The diary contains no studied portraits of individuals, but is rich in such snapshots as that of the sleeping Albemarle. There are the King and the Duke of York winking at each other at the council board;[56] Rupert, who at meetings 'doth nothing but swear and laugh a little, with an oath or two';[57] the slatternly and avaricious Duchess of Albemarle ('Dirty Besse'[58]) – a comic figure who might easily have

52. Pepys never exaggerated feminine influence in politics, for all his love of a good story. Clarendon, in his memoirs, had no doubt of the power of 'the Lady' (Castlemaine), and it is noticeable that Pepys was never inclined to attribute any political importance to the unpolitical Nell Gwyn.

53. Pepys's hearsay account (3 September 1662) of the meeting of 28 August 1662 at which Sheldon repulsed Clarendon's attempt to soften the execution of the act of uniformity is interesting. It includes one statement (that Albemarle supported Clarendon) which has not been traced in any other contemporary account, and may well be true.

54. That the 'cabinet' and the Council's Committee of Foreign Affairs were often the same body of men is clear from the entry at 8 February 1669.

55. E.g. 21 March 1669.

56. 14 February 1668.

57. 3 June 1664.   58. 4 November 1666.

been invented by a satirist. From a succession of small observations a picture often emerges. The King himself appears as lazy and self-indulgent, but also as intelligent, witty, genuinely interested in the navy, and if not himself an administrator, at least capable of galvanising others into efficiency. About the Duke of York, later James II, Pepys gives perhaps the most valuable information of all, since he knew him better than he knew any other great person. In 1661 – well before his reception into the Catholic church – James was known as 'a professed friend to the Catholiques',[59] affecting in his worship a height of ceremony which alarmed Pepys, and so unpopular that the news of the death of his only son in May of that year was said to 'please everybody'.[60] He had a penchant for French and Irish favourites; he was a militarist, and reputedly an enemy to parliament. On the other hand, his work as Lord High Admiral in the 1660s appears, according to Pepys's evidence, to have been done well and to have held his interest, though it had to give way sometimes to the stronger attractions of hunting and woman-ising. Moreover, he showed some capacity for sound judgement. When Pepys's clerk, Thomas Hayter, in 1663, confessed to having been discovered at a conventicle, word came from his Highness, who had been brought up in army camps to value loyalty above religious conformity, that 'he found he had a good servant, an Anabaptist; and unless he did carry himself more to the scandall of the office, he would bear with his opinion till he heard further'.[61] James's concern for religious toleration – hypocritical later when it was meant to lead to Catholic domination – seems to have been in these circumstances quite genuine. James could, also, be judicious in settling pay disputes, and it would be unsafe to assume that he was in these matters merely voicing the views of advisers.[62] Of course, the epoch-making mistakes he later committed as King arose from his interpretation of his functions as an anointed ruler, and the light thrown on them by evidence from the 1660s can only be indirect. But some of his failings and virtues are clear enough in the diary, and Pepys at any rate gives the lie to Macaulay's famous gibe that James was fit only to be a dockyard clerk.

Pepys's parliamentary news from Westminster Hall, being less picturesque, is less well known than his political news from the court. It has sometimes escaped the notice even of serious students of the

59. 18 February 1661.   60. 6 May 1661.   61. 15 May 1663.
    62. 8 April 1666. Cf. Cat., i. 30, n. 2; 32. For the Duke's independence of mind, see below, iv. 116.

subject, although it has been in print since Wheatley's edition of the 1890s. The diary covers a period in which facts about parliamentary debates are hard to come by. Of unofficial parliamentary diaries kept by members or officers of the Houses (on which the historian has mostly to rely), there are very few known examples – none at all for the Lords, and none for the Commons during the four sessions of 1663–5. Pepys offers parliamentary notes which are scattered and brief, but none the less very welcome.[63] He would make a point of learning, from members or from hearsay, about important debates, and although both houses debated in secret and forbade publication of votes and proceedings, news of their transactions was soon bruited around by word of mouth. Close by the parliamentary chambers themselves was Westminster Hall – with its shops and lawcourts and crowds, one of the most frequented of London's public places. Pepys had only to go and gossip there – walking 'from one man to another'[64] – to pick up the latest news of parliament. He more than once penetrated into the chambers themselves, although he was not a member of the Commons until 1673. As an official, he waited on parliamentary committees; as a member of the public, he attended trials held before the Lords; and he was not above gatecrashing large gatherings such as conferences between the Houses and end-of-session meetings, when in the press of people it was possible for strangers to gain admittance. Moreover, he had useful contacts among members of both Houses. Several of his colleagues on the Navy Board sat in the Commons[65] for most of the diary period; so did his relatives, Roger Pepys and Sir Thomas Crew. His colleagues usually expressed the views of the government; his relatives (by a happy chance) those of the opposition groups. He heard about debates in the Lords from Sandwich and from Sandwich's father-in-law, Lord Crew. His entries about parliamentary proceedings, culled from these sources, are far from constituting a running summary for all or even most sessions. They are occasional and disjointed notes about what was relevant to his work, or what seemed important or interesting. The most extended and significant series is the run of entries in October–December 1666 dealing with the Commons' debates on finance. Here, and elsewhere, Pepys's accounts

63. See, e.g., 26, 28 March 1664 (repeal of the Triennial Act).

64. 22 June 1663.

65. In the parliament elected in 1661 Carteret sat for Portsmouth, Coventry for Great Yarmouth, Batten for Rochester and Penn for Weymouth and Melcombe Regis.

of Commons' debates can sometimes be both fuller and more accurate than those of members who were present.[66] They sometimes tell of the unspoken feelings of members;[67] they report a debate, or committee proceedings, not covered by the official journal.[68] Those occasions when Pepys himself appeared before a parliamentary committee are (with the exception of the entry at 22 October 1667) given disappointingly brief reports.[69] The most interesting of the Lords' proceedings treated by Pepys are probably Clarendon's proposal to add a liberal proviso to the bill of uniformity (21 March 1662); Bristol's attempt to impeach Clarendon in 1663 (1, 2 July 1663; 23 September 1667); and the debates (4 January 1668) on the bill for establishing a parliamentary commission to examine accounts.

Pepys was also a chronicler of the views held by the general public of London on political matters. The two movements of opinion which receive his greatest attention are that which preceded the Restoration and that which followed the Dutch War. In reporting the former (during January–March 1660), Pepys wrote from a prejudice in the King's favour: his views were those of the civil servants and moderate politicians anxious to be rid of the republic. But he observed the unfolding of events coolly, noting the alternative schemes put about by rival groups – a republic, a monarchy, a new protectorate under Richard Cromwell, or a military *régime* under Monck. At 6 March he repeated, with approval, Mountagu's cautionary remark that the King if restored, 'would not last long . . . unless he carry himself very soberly and well'. On the same day Pepys noted that 'everybody now drink the King's health without any fear, whereas before it was very private that a man dare do it'. This alehouse report is as good a definition as any of the moment at which there was an open change in the public attitude to Charles in London. It happens that the city of London and its government played a critical part in the political revolution of early 1660. It was the resistance of the Common Council of the city to taxation which started the movement. Monck and his army arrived in the capital on 3 February; threw in their lot with the city on the 11th and with their support secured on the

66. See 24 June, 26 November 1666; 2 January, 25 July 1667; 14, 17, 28 February, 17 March 1668, etc.

67. 26 March 1664; 6 November 1665.

68. E.g. 6 November 1665; 26 November 1666; 2 January 1667, etc.

69. He reports the acclaim which greeted his long speech of 5 March 1668, but not the speech itself.

21st the return to the Rump of the surviving members excluded by force in 1648. These last – the 'secluded members' – outvoted the Rumpers, put in a new Council of State of moderates like themselves who then went on to call a new, freely elected parliament. The combination of military force with civic protest and parliamentary authority proved decisive: for the first time since 1641, law and the power to maintain order were on the same side in politics. Pepys's history of London in early 1660 is the best contemporary account we have. He noted both events and opinion; he knew Mountagu and his associates who were in power after the *coup* of 21 February; he lived in Westminster and regularly heard parliamentary news; he learned of the city's moves from Valentyne Fyge, a common-councilman who was also his family apothecary. Clarendon's later account of these months in his memoirs is much inferior to Pepys's: it is secondhand and includes only a single reference to public opinion.[70] Other authorities – the letters of royalist agents (on which Clarendon's account was based), or the despatches of the French envoy – do not have the wide range or the daily detail and continuity of Pepys's reports. If one thinks of Pepys as an historian of London one thinks immediately of his eyewitness stories of the Plague and the Fire – and rightly, if the criterion is vividness and artistic effect. But judged by the test of their contributions to knowledge, those famous passages are equalled and perhaps surpassed by this story of London's political revolution in the early months of 1660.

The Dutch War constitutes the central drama of the diary, just as the Restoration constitutes its opening scene and the Plague and Fire its spectacular interludes. In 1664–5 war was not only welcomed but demanded by many politicians, by great numbers of the public and, above all, by those merchants who stood to gain by it. The King appears to have been anxious to avoid it; his ministers were either vehemently against it or ruefully nervous. So were the naval experts, like Pepys and Coventry, who best knew the practical difficulties. Pepys's account of the war forms a large part of the diary and has many points of interest. It includes careful accounts of naval engagements which took place a long way from his desk in Seething Lane.[71]   More

70. *Hist.*, vi. 178.

71. These are usually constructed from the same sources as were used by the government's printed accounts of engagements. But Pepys uses important sources of his own in the accounts of the Bergen affair (1665) and the division of the fleet (1666).

predictably, it gives, at large, an administrator's view of the war effort, blaming wasteful courtiers and distrustful M.P.'s for the fatal shortage of money.   But the diary's special value is in its record of the public mood in the later part of the war, and particularly in the months which followed the Dutch raid up the Medway of June 1667 and the un-popular peace of July.   There is no other source which offers such a continuous run of evidence about the effects of the war on public opinion.   There had been defeats (which led men to commend Oliver Cromwell, 'so brave things he did and made all the neighbour-princes fear him'[72]); constant fears of invasion from both Holland and France;[73] rumours of peculation; mutinous crowds of starving seamen in the streets – and to all these the Plague and the Fire had added apocalyptic touches of doom.   Clarendon was brought down in disgrace in September–October 1667; other ministers took his place; but Pepys gives the impression that to many Londoners it seemed that monarchy itself stood in danger.   In August and November Pepys heard prophecies from three sources[74] that a commonwealth, in which 'men . . . minded their business'[75] would soon come in again.   This was wild talk, but it is clear that a new attitude towards the puritans was setting in.   Previously they had been marked down as rebels and regicides – even the Presbyterians had been tarred with the same brush and their services to the King in 1659–60 forgotten.   Now a few Presbyterians returned to public office; the Presbyterian group in the Commons was in 1668 courted by Buckingham; and in the winter of 1667–8 proposals were set on foot for ecclesiastical concessions to the Dissenters.[76]   The number of Pepys's references to this new situation is striking.   On 17 June 1667 he wrote: 'nothing but the reconciling of the presbyterian party will save us'.   Over a year later, when Jonson's *Bartholomew Fair* was staged, Pepys observed that the audience no longer had any stomach for its gibes against puritans.[77]   This attitude (which was real, although Pepys exaggerated it) was the first

72. 12 July 1667.

73. Even at the height of the Dutch attacks, it was invasion from France which was most feared: see, e.g., 18 June 1667.

74. 9, 20 August, 30 November 1667.

75. 3 June 1667.   There were riots in London for 'Reformation and Reduce-ment 'in March 1668.

76. The scheme for including moderate Presbyterians in the Anglican church was, Pepys reported on 10 February 1668, 'so much desired by much the greater part of the nation'.

77. 4 September 1668.

sign since the Restoration of an *entente* between Anglicans and Puritans, which, though it had still to pass through many vicissitudes and fluctuations, was one of the most important political re-alignments of the reigns of Charles II and James II.

The vast amount of scattered political news in the diary reflects the character of Pepys's friendships. He was an intimate of many men who like himself were enthralled by politics. The most interesting of them was Sir William Coventry, secretary to the Duke of York as Admiral. He saw Pepys so often and entrusted him with so many of his confidences – we have already noticed those about the fall of Clarendon – that Pepys's diary is the best single source we have for Coventry's views. He admitted to Pepys his selling of offices and commissions in the navy;[78] his views on parliamentary management;[79] his preference for commissions rather than individual ministers for certain government offices[80] (a contemporary innovation in the Treasury and elsewhere). He told Pepys in full the story of his part in the division of the fleet in June 1666 which led to its defeat in the Four Days Battle – an account much fuller and franker (especially in its criticisms of Albemarle) than the one he thought it prudent to give to parliament or to commit to paper.[81] Another intelligent public servant, Sir Philip Warwick, secretary to the Lord Treasurer, left little in print or manuscript behind him about this period, but some of his opinions on fiscal affairs are preserved in Pepys. In a conversation with Pepys (29 February 1664) he argued (as would most seventeenth-century officials) in favour of the excise as the best of all taxes, and defended the King's management of finances, blaming the deficit on the ignorance and niggardliness of parliament. In its essentials this last contention has been confirmed by historians.[82]

Whitehall and Westminster, where Pepys could pick up the best of his political news, were his principal listening-posts, but he also used a third – the Royal Exchange in the city, frequented by merchants and shippers in touch with many parts of the world. Here (or from his

78. 25 May 1663; 23 February 1668.
79. 'By bringing over one discontented man you raise up three in his room': 6 October 1666.
80. 28 October 1667.
81. 24 June 1666.
82. Similarly revealing are Pepys's reports from Sir Stephen Fox (Paymaster of the Army) and Sir George Carteret (Treasurer of the Navy) of how they used their private credit (to their own and the state's advantage) to meet official debts: 16 January, 12 April, 25 June 1667.

other contacts with the mercantile community) Pepys gathered his overseas news (much distorted when it concerned states with which England was at war), his news of ship movements (usually accurate), and his travellers' tales (usually picturesque).[83] For news of a more political nature from Europe, Pepys relied rather on Whitehall. Among his city acquaintances, Capt. George Cocke, hemp merchant, had a ready fund of political news, but it was usually on domestic politics.

In the end, however, the historian's debt to the diary will not be calculated simply by adding up the subjects on which it can yield significant information. Its total value is something greater than the sum of the value of its parts, and can best be stated by recalling the point with which this section started – the diary's dual structure; its combination of public chronicle and private journal. Because the diary tells an historical story in terms of an individual life, the reader is given not only an intellectual understanding of the period but also the means of achieving an imaginative sympathy with it. Reader and subject are united by a common humanity. This is not only one man's version of the history of a decade – this is what it felt like to be alive.

R.L.

83. For the last, see 11, 16 January, 30 December 1662; 11 December 1663; 16 September 1664; 17 August 1666, etc.

EDITORIAL ABBREVIATIONS[1]

AHR: *American Historical Review*

Allin: *The Journals of Sir Thomas Allin, 1660–1678* (ed. R. C. Anderson), 2 vols, London, Navy Records Soc., vols 79, 80; 1939, 1940

Aubrey: Aubrey, John, *Brief Lives* (ed. A. Clark), 2 vols, Oxford, 1898

Bell, *Fire*: Bell, Walter G., *The Great Fire of London in 1666 . . .*, London, 1923

Bell, *Plague*: Bell, Walter G., *The Great Plague in London in 1665*, London, 1951

Birch: Birch, Thomas, *The history of the Royal Society of London . . .*, 4 vols, London, 1756, 1757

BM: British Museum

Bodl.: Bodleian Library

Boyne: Boyne, W., *Trade tokens issued in the seventeenth century . . .* (ed. and rev. George C. Williamson), 2 vols, London, 1889, 1891

Braybrooke (1825)[2]: *Memoirs of Samuel Pepys . . .* (ed. Richard, Lord Braybrooke), 2 vols, London, 1825

Bryant, i, ii, iii: Bryant, Sir Arthur, *Samuel Pepys*
[vol. i] *The man in the making*, London, 1948 ed.
[vol. ii] *The years of peril*, London, 1947 ed.
[vol. iii] *The saviour of the navy*, London, 1949 ed.

Burnet: Burnet, Gilbert, *History of my own time* (pt i, *The reign of Charles II*, ed. O. Airy), Oxford, 1890

Carte: Carte MSS, Bodleian Library

Cat.: Tanner, J. R., *A descriptive catalogue of the naval manuscripts in the Pepysian Library at Magdalene College, Cambridge*, 4 vols, London, Navy Records Soc., vols 26, 27, 36, [57]; 1903–23

CJ: *Journals of the House of Commons*

Clarendon, *Hist.*: Edward, Earl of Clarendon, *The history of the rebellion . . .* (ed. W. Dunn Macray), 6 vols, Oxford, 1888

Clarendon, *Life*: *The life of Edward Earl of Clarendon . . . in which is included a continuation of his History of the Great Rebellion*, 3 vols, Oxford, 1827

1. This list gives extensions of the principal editorial abbreviations used in vols I–IX. Other lists will be found in vol. X.

2. Other editions of the diary by Braybrooke are similarly denoted by date.

Clowes: Clowes, Sir W. L., *The Royal Navy* . . . 7 vols, London, 1897–1903

Colenbrander: Colenbrander, H.T. (ed.), *Bescheiden uit vreemde archieven omtrent de groote Nederlandsche zeeoorlogen, 1652–76*, 2 vols, The Hague, *Rijks Geschiedkundige Publicatiën, Kleine serie, nos 18, 19;* 1919

Comp.: *Companion to the Diary* (vol. X of the present edition)

CSPClar.: *Calendar of the Clarendon State Papers* . . . (ed. O. Ogle *et al.*), Oxford, 1872–

CSPD: *Calendar of State Papers, Domestic Series*

CSPVen.: *Calendar of State Papers* . . . *relating to English affairs* . . . *in the archives* . . . *of Venice* . . .

CTB: *Calendar of Treasury Books* . . . *preserved in the Public Record Office*

Cunnington: Cunnington, C. W. and P., *Handbook of English costume in the seventeenth century*, London, 1955

Day and Murrie: Day, C. L. and Murrie, E., *English Song-Books, 1651–1702*, London, Bibliog. Soc., 1940 (for 1937)

DNB: *Dictionary of National Biography*

Downes: Downes, John, *Roscius Anglicanus* . . ., London, 1708

Duke of York, *Mem.* (naval): James, Duke of York, *Memoirs of the English affairs, chiefly naval, from* . . . *1660 to 1673* . . ., London, 1729

EHR: *English Historical Review*

Ehrman: Ehrman, John, *The navy in the war of William III, 1689–1697* . . ., Cambridge, 1953

ELH: *English Literary History*

Evelyn: *The diary of John Evelyn* (ed. E. S. de Beer), 6 vols, Oxford, 1955

Family Letters: Heath, Helen T. (ed.), *The letters of Samuel Pepys and his family circle*, Oxford, 1955

Feiling: Feiling, K., *British foreign policy, 1660–1672*, London, 1930

Firth and Rait: Firth, C. H. and Rait, R. S. (eds), *Acts and ordinances of the Interregnum, 1642–1660*, 3 vols, London, 1911

Further Corr.: *Further correspondence of Samuel Pepys, 1662–1679* . . . (ed. J. R. Tanner), London, 1929

GEC: G.E.C[okayne], *The complete peerage* . . . (ed. V. Gibbs *et al.*), London, 1910–

Genest: G[enest], J[ohn], *Some account of the English stage from* . . . *1660 to 1830*, 10 vols, Bath, 1832

GL: Guildhall Library, London

Gramont: Hamilton, Anthony, *Memoirs of the Comte de Gramont* (trans. P. Quennell, ed. C. H. Hartmann), London, 1930

Grey: Grey, Anchitell, *Debates of the House of Commons from . . . 1667 to . . . 1694 . . .*, 10 vols, London, 1769

Guizot: Guizot, F. P. G., *History of Richard Cromwell and the Restoration of Charles II* (trans. A. R. Scoble), 2 vols, London, 1856

Gunther: Gunther, R. W. T., *Early science in Oxford*, 14 vols, Oxford, 1923–45

Harl. Soc. Reg.: Publications of the Harleian Society, Register Section

Harris: Harris, F. R., *The life of Edward Mountagu, K. G., first Earl of Sandwich*, 2 vols, London, 1912

HMC: Historical Manuscripts Commission[1]

Kingd. Intell.: *The Kingdom(e)s Intelligencer*

Letters: Howarth, R. G. (ed.), *Letters and the Second Diary of Samuel Pepys*, London, 1933

l.h.: longhand

LIF: Lincoln's Inn Fields Theatre, Portugal Row (The Duke's House or The Opera)

Lister: Lister, T. H., *Life and administration of Edward, first Earl of Clarendon . . .*, 3 vols, London, 1838, 1837

LJ: *Journals of the House of Lords*

LRO: Corporation of London Records Office

Magalotti: Magalotti, Lorenzo, *Travels of Cosmo the Third, Grand Duke of Tuscany, through England . . . [1669]*, London, 1821

Marvell: Margoliouth, H. M. (ed.), *The poems and letters of Andrew Marvell*, 2 vols, Oxford, 1952

Mdx R. O.: Middlesex County Record Office

Merc. Pub.: *Mercurius Publicus*

Milward: *The diary of John Milward, Esq., Member of Parliament for Derbyshire, September 1666 to May 1668* (ed. C. Robbins), Cambridge, 1938

Monconys: Monconys, B. de, *Journal des voyages . . .*, Lyon, 1665–6

Mundy: *The travels of Peter Mundy in Europe and Asia, 1608–1667* (ed. Sir R. C. Temple), 5 vols, Cambridge, Hakluyt Soc., 1907–36; vol. v, *Travels in South-west England, with a diary of events in London, 1658–1663 . . .*, (ed. Temple and L. M. Anstey), ser. 2, no. lxxviii, 1936

1. References, where possible, cite the name of the owner of the collection. Elsewhere they cite report-number, volume-number and page-number in the following form: HMC, *Rep.*, 12/7/25.

N. & Q.: *Notes and Queries*

Naval Minutes: *Samuel Pepys's naval minutes* (ed. J. R. Tanner), London, Navy Records Soc., vol. 40, 1926

Nicoll: Nicoll, Allardyce, *A history of English drama, 1600–1900*, 6 vols, Cambridge, 1952–9

NMM: National Maritime Museum, Greenwich

North (ed. Rimbault): North, Roger, *Memoirs of musick* . . . (ed. E. F. Rimbault), London, 1846

North (ed. Wilson): Wilson, John, *Roger North on music*. . ., London, 1959

NWB: Pepys's 'Navy White Book' (PL 2581)

OED: *The Oxford English Dictionary*

Oppenheim: Oppenheim, M., *A history of the administration of the royal navy* . . . [*1509–1660*], London and New York, 1896

Parl. Hist.: *Cobbett's Parliamentary History of England*, 36 vols, London, 1806–20

Parl. Intell.: *The Parliamentary Intelligencer*

PCC: Prerogative Court of Canterbury

Penn: Penn, Granville, *Memorials of* . . . *Sir William Penn* . . . 2 vols, London, 1833

Pepysiana: Wheatley, H. B., *Pepysiana* (*The diary of Samuel Pepys*, ed. Wheatley, vol. X), London, 1899

PL: Pepys Library, Magdalene College, Cambridge

Priv. Corr.: *Private correspondence and miscellaneous papers of Samuel Pepys, 1679–1703* . . . (ed. J. R. Tanner), 2 vols, London, 1926

PRO: Public Record Office, London

Rawl.: Rawlinson MSS, Bodleian Library

Rep.: *Report*

Repert.: Repertories

repl.: replacing

RES: *Review of English Studies*

Routh: Routh, E. M. G., *Tangier: England's lost Atlantic outpost, 1661–1684*, London, 1912

Rugge: Rugge, Thomas, 'Mercurius Politicus Redivivus, or a Collection of the Most Materiall Occurances and Transactions in Publick Affaires since Anno Domini 1659' (BM, Add. 10116–17)

Sandwich: *The journal of Edward Mountagu, first Earl of Sandwich* . . ., *1659–1665* (ed. R. C. Anderson), London, Navy Records Soc., vol. 64, 1929

Sandwich MSS: Sandwich family papers preserved at Mapperton, Dorset

S.Ct: Salisbury Court Theatre

s.d.: *sub die*

s.h.: shorthand

Sharpe: Sharpe, R. R., *London and the kingdom* . . ., 3 vols, London, 1894–5

Shorthand Letters: *Shorthand Letters of Samuel Pepys* (ed. E. Chappell), Cambridge, 1933

Smith: Smith, John, *The life, journals and correspondence of Samuel Pepys* . . ., 2 vols, London, 1841

s.n.: *sub nomine*

Steele: Steele, R. R. (ed.), *Bibliotheca Lindesiana. A bibliography of proclamations of the Tudor and Stuart sovereigns* . . ., 2 vols, Oxford, 1910

Tangier Papers: *The Tangier papers of Samuel Pepys* (ed. E. Chappell), London, Navy Records Soc., vol. 73, 1935

Tanner: Tanner MSS, Bodleian Library

Tedder: Tedder, A. R., *The navy of the Restoration*, Cambridge, 1916

TR: Theatre Royal (The King's House: in Vere Street, Clare Market, until 7 May 1663; in Drury Lane thereafter)

Trans. Stat. Reg.: *A transcript of the registers of the worshipful Company of Stationers; from 1640–1708 A.D.* (ed. G. E. Briscoe Eyre, transcr. H. R. Plomer), 3 vols, London, Roxburghe Club, 1913–14

TRHS: *Transactions of the Royal Historical Society*

VCH: *The Victoria History of the Counties of England*

Verney Mem.: Verney, F. P. and M. M., *Memoirs of the Verney family during the seventeenth century*, 2 vols, London, 3rd ed., 1925

Wheatley: *The diary of Samuel Pepys* . . . (ed. H. B. Wheatley), 10 vols, London, 1893–9

Whinney and Millar: Whinney, M. and Millar, O., *English Art, 1625–1714*, Oxford, 1957

Whitear: Whitear, W. H., *More Pepysiana* . . ., London, 1927

Wing: Wing, Donald, *Short-title Catalogue*, 3 vols, New York, 1945–51

Wood, *L. & T.*: *The life and times of Anthony Wood* . . . (ed. A. Clark), 5 vols, Oxford, Oxf. Hist. Soc., vols 19, 21, 26, 30, 40; 1891–1900

METHODS OF THE COMMENTARY

Something more than a single series of footnotes was called for by a document so long, so detailed and so complex. The diary contains 1¼ million words; it is dense with facts; it is populated by over 3000 individuals, many of them hard to trace. In manner, it is often allusive and repetitive; because of its diurnal structure, it often pays out its account of a single transaction in several isolated instalments. In addition, its language is sometimes obscure. As well as being written (for the most part) in a seventeenth-century form of English which can present occasional problems to the modern reader (especially in the case of technical or familiar terms), it also uses a private vocabulary of foreign words (sometimes in a scrambled form) in the erotic passages.

From these characteristics alone, it followed that a fairly elaborate commentary was needed. Moreover, the diary's importance as an historical source for many subjects demanded that it should be collated with a variety of other evidence. It was particularly important to relate it to Pepys's other manuscripts of the period[1] – to the great collections of his papers which survive in the Pepys Library, in the Rawlinson MSS at the Bodleian and in the state papers in the Public Record Office and elsewhere – as well as to the papers of his family, friends, colleagues and correspondents, wherever they might be found. Beyond that, it was necessary to draw on as much as possible of the whole body of relevant source-material – national and local, official and unofficial, printed and unprinted. Only in that way could the editorial work of elucidation, explanation, evaluation and correction be attempted seriously. But if footnotes alone had been used for all these purposes they would have obscured the text they were meant to serve, and Pepys himself would have been almost invisible behind them.

The commentary has therefore been distributed in four places – in a supplementary volume (the *Companion*, vol. X of this edition) consisting entirely of editorial material; in notes which appear beneath the text; in a Select List of Persons, and in a Select Glossary. Both of

1. See 'The Diary and Related Manuscripts' in the *Companion*.

the latter are printed (without alteration) at the end of each volume of text. The methods used in the distribution are set out in this section and (briefly) in a Reader's Guide, which also appears in each volume of text. In this way, at the cost of some repetition, the text volumes are so equipped that each of them can be read, for many purposes, independently of the others.

The *Companion* is meant for occasional consultation. In it is gathered the information which the reader may well find it necessary or desirable to have, but which (in the judgement of the editors) he does not need to have immediately under his eye as he reads the pages of the diary. The volume consists of a single series of articles of varying length, equipped, where appropriate, with bibliographies, together with maps, and genealogical tables. Only a few references to the *Companion* are provided in the footnotes in the text volumes. Its contents include biographical articles on the persons mentioned by Pepys; topographical information about places in London (streets, buildings, etc.); essays on Pepys's health, on his intellectual interests ('Books', 'Music', 'Plays', 'Science'. 'Theatre', etc.), on his wealth and so on. Other matters which recur many times in the diary – events such as the Plague and the Fire, subjects such as clothes, food,[2] festival seasons (e.g. Christmas), social events (e.g. weddings), etc – are also given similar extended treatment. There the reader must look for the editors' views on the significance and value of the diary entries on several subjects not treated in the Introduction. There, too, will be found the editors' exposition of the evidence on which they have sometimes based what are necessarily brief and unsupported statements in the footnotes.

The *Companion* is a standing reservoir of comment; the footnotes, as it were, a running stream. They are kept to a minimum,[3] and are designed to deal with what is unique to each page. For the most part, they have three functions: (1) the elucidation of what is obscure (by reason of Pepys's spelling or syntax or whatever other reason), and the correction of what is inaccurate or misleading; (2) the explanation of

2. In the article on food contemporary recipes for some of the dishes which Pepys mentions are printed.

3. This rule is relaxed for the first month of the diary in order to introduce the reader as easily as possible to the text. There and elsewhere, several distinct points are often dealt with in a single footnote, provided that they occur close to each other in the text. For this reason it has been impossible to adopt uniform syntactical forms for the various types of footnote.

events and situations; and (3) the identification of manuscripts, books, plays, quotations, etc., and the selective identification of persons and places. Used with the Select Glossary (which covers technical and difficult words together with some place names which occur frequently), and with the Select List of Persons, the footnotes should make the diary intelligible in a way which will satisfy most readers for most purposes. They are composed in as brief a form as possible, and are designed to carry no more information than is required by their specific functions. They do not usually, for instance, give much biographical information. Biographies are to be found in the *Companion* and brief identification in the *Index*. A person who appears on Pepys's page only in passing, or whose identity is clear enough from the text (e.g. 'Aunt Wight', 'Mr. Secretary Bennet', 'Pierce the purser'), or from a nearby footnote, is not given any footnote of identification. But there are persons about whom a minimum of biographical information has to be given on the page itself – e.g. those who cannot be identified with certainty and yet whose identity is important for an understanding of the text. In such cases footnotes have been added, recording the fact of the doubt, but leaving discussion of the evidence to the *Companion* article. ('Probably' or 'possibly' or '?' used by the editor in these circumstances is usually an invitation to the reader to consult the *Companion*.) If either Pepys's spelling of a name[4] or his manner of reference to a person leads to obscurity, or if there is more than one person of the same name, an identification has been added (again, provided that the matter has contextual importance) in a footnote, or (in certain frequently recurring cases)[5] in the Select List of Persons. In addition to supplying identifications, biographical footnotes, where they occur, may also provide information about the individual's office, trade, age or family, etc.[6] Only the specific information relevant to Pepys's state-

4. Pepys spells the surname of his clerk Will Hewer in several different ways, and it might be difficult, for instance, to recognise 'Kerneeguy' (at 19 March 1665) as 'Carnegie'. In the editorial matter personal names are spelt according to modern standard usage (where it exists), or in the form used by modern works of reference (e.g. the *DNB*), or (in certain cases) in the form used by their owners.

5. E.g. those of 'my Lord', 'the General', 'the child', 'the Attorney-General', etc. Lord Mayors of London, on the other hand, are identified in footnotes, since they change annually.

6. The office is frequently given – sometimes because it is the best short explanation of an individual's activities and social status, sometimes because it is the best short guide to his reliability as a purveyor of news. The number of

ment in the text is given,[7] and in a summary form (e.g. 'relative by marriage') which is normally expanded in the *Companion*. These *personalia* are repeated at each recurrence if necessary; otherwise the number of cross-references would get out of hand. The common modern editorial convention of giving a main note at the first occurrence of a name, and thereafter supplying cross-references, is inappropriate to the treatment of this problem in a text that is so crowded with persons.

Similarly with other matters. To avoid cluttering up the pages of the text volumes, there are not many topographical footnotes. Places in the London area are dealt with in the *Companion*, under their names. Place names which recur frequently are given in the Select Glossary. A footnote is used if Pepys's reference to a place is obscure, or if the context demands it – if it will help the reader, for instance, to follow the wartime movements of ships. Matters of topographical interest outside the London area are usually dealt with in footnotes because they are non-recurrent, or almost so. Thus Hatfield House is described in a footnote, but Whitehall Palace in the *Companion*. Reference is made (where possible) to contemporary drawings, etc., of buildings only if Pepys in the text has remarked on their appearance.

The weather (about which Pepys's information is unsystematic) is not normally commented on in the footnotes, since it is best dealt with in the *Index* and *Companion* article, where it is summarised year by year and collated with other evidence. Abnormal or striking events, however, such as storms, gales and comets, receive footnotes.

The question of how to deal with semantic problems has given special difficulty. It is important to define every word and phrase that calls for definition (having regard to the needs of both British and American readers), but it is equally important not to litter the pages with repetitive footnotes. The solution has been to gather difficult words, phrases and proverbs (English and foreign) into a Large

---

hearths in a house is given (from the Hearth-Tax returns of 1663 onwards) as an indication of the householder's wealth and style of living, but usually in the *Companion* article.

7. E.g. at 22 December 1660 (i. 321, n. 2) the information given about the members of a dinner-party concerns only their common interest in Algiers, which was probably the reason for their being together at that place at that time.

Glossary which appears at the end of the *Companion* volume. This glossary contains comments as well as definitions, and records the extent (in fact slight) to which Pepys's material has been used by the *Oxford English Dictionary* and similar works. In addition, for the convenience of the reader whose interest is confined to discovering or reminding himself of meanings as he reads, a selection from the Large Glossary, containing words and phrases frequently used (but excluding most foreign words) is given as the Select Glossary at the end of each volume of text. Words which may give difficulty because they look easy (their meaning having changed since the seventeenth century, e.g. 'painful', 'impertinent', 'friends', 'curious', 'noise', 'amused') are marked with a light asterisk in the text to warn the reader who does not know the history of the word to look it up. They are all in the Select Glossary, as well as in the large one. A few definitions are given in the footnotes where it seemed obviously convenient to break the general rule.

Manuscripts have been identified in the footnotes wherever identification is possible. In the case of Pepys's own letters and papers mentioned in the text, an attempt has been made in the footnotes to list all known manuscript copies and all reliable printed copies.[8] Manuscript copies by certain of Pepys's clerks (Hewer, Hayter and Gibson) have been attributed to the copyists from the evidence of the handwriting. Other manuscripts than those written by Pepys himself and his clerks have been dealt with more summarily, but dates of letters are never omitted if known, since they establish the sequence of a correspondence, and may also illustrate both the currency of oral news and the speed of postal carriage.

As for printed works, a full list of those mentioned in the text or referred to in footnotes is given (with bibliographical details) in the *Index* Volume: 'Bibliography of Works Cited'.[9] Pepys's reading and book-collecting habits are dealt with in the articles 'Books',

8. The omissions are those of the letters printed by Braybrooke and Mynors Bright in their editions of the diary, and by John Smith in his *Life . . . and correspondence of S. Pepys*. Where extracts from Pepys's letters and papers are printed in the present work, the conventions here used in the presentation of the diary text are employed if he has used shorthand.

9. The footnotes give a bare minimum of information about the books which are mentioned only by the editors and not by Pepys. In these cases names of publishers and places of publication are omitted, and publication dates are given only if it is necessary to distinguish between editions or if the books were published before 1850.

'Science' etc. The footnote material provided on books, pamphlets and newspapers mentioned in the text of the diary may be characterised as follows. They have been identified, though a few inadequately described there (mostly pamphlets) have defied identification.[10] A book or pamphlet is given a full (or virtually full) title in the footnote if it was purchased by Pepys or if the title is the best and shortest guide to its contents. The year-date of publication is always given,[11] and the size (folio, duodecimo, etc.) is added if it is helpful in identifying the edition, or if it is in any other way significant – e.g. if Pepys reads it in the open air. Its presence in the Pepys Library (or absence from it) has been usually recorded (even for books which are not mentioned as purchases), and in those cases where a copy survives in the Library the official catalogue-number (that of John Jackson, still in use) is added, although occasionally (because Pepys habitually replaced older editions as new ones came out) the catalogue refers to a later edition. The place of publication is given only for books which are in the Pepys Library, and in these cases only if it is somewhere else than London. The record in the Stationers' Register of the licensing of a book is occasionally noted where that seems relevant. Where the diary has a significantly early reference to a book (i.e. usually one earlier than that given by the bookseller Thomason in his collection now in the British Library), attention is drawn to the fact in the footnote. References to newspapers are given by a single date – that of the last day they cover.

Music has needed only summary treatment in the footnotes and Select Glossary, where brief identifications of musicians, instruments and compositions have been provided. The notes on compositions include references to the manuscripts in the Pepys Library, and select references to contemporary publications. The *Companion* article 'Music' carries the main commentary on this subject and deals with Pepys's taste and knowledge as a musician.

Plays receive fuller treatment than music at the foot of the page, since performances so often appear in the diary as unique or discrete events for which the footnote is the appropriate form of comment. Within the limits of the evidence, plays and authors are identified.

---

10. Several gave difficulty, e.g. the book of tales referred to (at 12 May 1660, etc.) by the title of the second in the collection.

11. New books first put on the market in November or December were frequently given in the imprint the year-date of the following year: e.g. below, ii. 294 and n. 2.

The theatres are identified in both footnotes and the Select Glossary for the period 1660–6, where the problem of identification is complicated by changes of buildings and titles; in and after 1667, when only two companies were operating in two houses, it is sufficient to leave the reader to consult the entries 'King's House' and 'Duke's House' in the Select Glossary. Fuller treatment of Pepys's theatrical interests, of the plays he saw in the diary period and of the playhouses and players is left to the *Companion* (under 'Plays' and 'Theatre'; and in the biographical articles).

Pepys's items of public news – a prominent and important feature of the diary – are mostly dealt with in the footnotes. The notes comment on their validity and completeness, and sometimes on their origin and currency, and therefore refer to other evidence corroborating, contradicting or supplementing the diary. In all cases the references are selective: a single piece of additional evidence is often enough.

R.L.

READER'S GUIDE

This section is meant for quick reference. More detailed information about the editorial methods used in this edition will be found in the Introduction and in the section 'Methods of the Commentary' in vol I, and also in the statements preceding the Select Glossary at the end of each text volume and the Large Glossary in the *Companion*.

I. THE TEXT

The fact that the MS. is mostly in shorthand makes exact reproduction (e.g. of spelling, capitalisation and punctuation) impossible.

Spelling is in modern British style, except for those longhand words which Pepys spelt differently, and words for which the shorthand indicates a variant pronunciation which is also shown by Pepys's longhand elsewhere. These latter are given in spellings which reflect Pepys's pronunciations.

Pepys's capitalisation is indicated only in his longhand.

Punctuation is almost all editorial, except for certain full-stops, colons, dashes and parentheses. Punctuation is almost non-existent in the original since the marks could be confused with shorthand.

Italics are all editorial, but (in e.g. headings to entries) often follow indications given in the MS. (by e.g. the use of larger writing).

The **paragraphing** is that of the MS.

Abbreviations of surnames, titles, place names and ordinary words are expanded.

Single **hyphens** are editorial, and represent Pepys's habit of disjoining the elements of compound words (e.g. Wh. hall/White-hall). Double hyphens represent Pepys's hyphens.

Single **angle-brackets** mark additions made by Pepys in the body of the MS.; double angle-brackets those made in the margins.

Light **asterisks** are editorial (see below, Section II); heavy asterisks are Pepys's own.

Pepys's **alterations** are indicated by the word 'replacing' ('repl.') in the textual footnotes.

II. THE COMMENTARY

1. **Footnotes** deal mainly with events and transactions. They also

identify MSS, books, plays, music and quotations, but give only occasional and minimal information about persons and places, words and phrases. The initials which follow certain notes indicate the work of the contributing editors. Light asterisks in the text direct the reader to the Select Glossary for the definition of words whose meanings have changed since the time of the diary. References to the diary are given by volume and page where the text is in page-proof at the time of going to press; in other cases, by entry-dates. In notes to the Introduction, since almost all the references there are to the text, a simpler form of reference (by entry-date only) is used.

2. The **Select List of Persons** is printed unchanged in each text volume. It covers the whole diary and identifies the principal persons, together with those who are described in the MS. by titles or in other ways that make for obscurity.

3. The **Select Glossary** is printed unchanged at the end of each text volume. It covers the whole diary and gives definitions of most recurrent English words and phrases, and identifications of certain recurrent places.

4. The **Companion** (vol. X) is a collection of reference material. It contains maps, genealogical tables, and a Large Glossary, but consists mainly of articles printed for ease of reference in a single alphabetical series. These give information about matters which are dealt with briefly or not at all in the footnotes and the Select Glossary: i.e. persons, places, words and phrases, food, drink, dress, the weather etc. They also treat more systematically than footnotes can the principal subjects with which the diary is concerned: Pepys's work, interests, health etc. References to the *Companion* are given only rarely in the footnotes.

III. DATES

In Pepys's time two reckonings of the calendar year were in use in Western Europe. Most countries had adopted the New Style – the revised calendar of Gregory XIII (1582); Britain until 1752 retained the Old Style – the ancient Roman, or Julian, calendar, which meant that its dates were ten days behind those of the rest of Western Europe in the seventeenth century. 1 January in England was therefore 11 January by the New Style abroad. On the single occasion during the period of the diary when Pepys was abroad (in Holland in May 1660) he continued to use the Old Style, thus avoiding a break in the run of his dates. In the editorial material of the present work dates relating to countries which had adopted the new reckoning are given in both styles (e.g. '1/11 January') in order to prevent confusion.

It will be noticed that the shortest and longest days of the year occur in the diary ten days earlier than in the modern calendar. So, too, does Lord Mayor's Day in London – on 29 October instead of 9 November.

For most legal purposes (from medieval times until 1752) the new year in England was held to begin on Lady Day, 25 March. But in accordance with the general custom, Pepys took it to begin on 1 January, as in the Julian calendar. He gives to all dates within the overlapping period between 1 January and 24 March a year-date which comprehends both styles – e.g. 'January 1 $16\frac{59}{60}$.' In the present commentary a single year-date, that of the New Style, has been used: e.g. '1 January 1660'.

THE DIARY
1660

'The condition of the State was thus' (below, p. 1)

The Rump Parliament which had taken control of government after the fall of Richard Cromwell in May 1659 had on 13 October been dismissed by the army officers under Maj.-Gen. John Lambert. The officers' rule collapsed in December, and on Boxing Day the Rump was restored with the consent of most of the army leaders. But Lambert, most active and ambitious of them all, now stationed in the north country around Newcastle-upon-Tyne, had not been consulted. On the 27th the Rump had ordered him to disband his troops, but he was not likely to obey. Vice-Adm. John Lawson was the naval commander who had declared for the Rump on 13 December, and had thereupon brought the fleet into the Thames, where it lay off Gravesend. Gen. George Monck, as commander in Scotland, led the most highly disciplined army in the three nations, and from the beginning had made no secret of his disapproval of the officers' rebellion. Since November he had been moving slowly southwards, and was now around Coldstream, just north of the border. Lambert's troops in Northumberland lay across the line of his advance. On 1 January Monck began to cross into England, and it was soon clear that Lambert was too weak to oppose him. The main issue was now the question of Monck's intentions. Would he support the unpopular Rump, which consisted of no more than about 50 M.P.'s and left the greater part of the nation without representatives? Would he go further and insist on re-admission of the 'secluded members' – the 154 survivors of the moderates excluded in Pride's Purge of December 1648? Or further still, and declare for a 'free parliament' – i.e. for elections untrammelled by qualifications for the candidates? Everyone knew that a free and full Parliament meant restoration of the monarchy, but it was not yet prudent to say so too openly. London was strongly in favour of the admission of the secluded members, as a first step towards a free parliament, and the city government, in this crisis, tended to assume the *rôle* almost of a national authority. Hence the importance of the elections to the Common Council, on 21 December, which proved a great victory for the enemies of the army and of the Rump. Pepys's own views are those of the majority of the citizens.

Blessed be God, at the end of the last year I was in very good health, without any sense of my old pain[1] but upon taking of cold.

I lived in Axe=yard, having my wife and servant Jane, and no more in family then us three.[2]

My wife,[a] after the absence of her terms for seven weeks, gave me hopes of her being with child, but on the last day of the year she hath them again. The condition of the State was thus.[3] *Viz.* the Rump, after being disturbed by my Lord Lambert, was lately returned to sit again.[4] The officers of the army all forced to yield. Lawson lie[s] still in the River and Monke is with his[b] army in Scotland. Only my Lord Lambert is not yet come in to the Parliament; nor is it expected that he will, without being forced to it.

The new Common Council of the City doth speak very high; and hath sent to Monke their sword-bearer, to acquaint him with their desires for a free and full Parliament,[5] which is at present the desires and the hopes and expectation of all – 22 of the old secluded members having been at the House door the last week to demand entrance;[6] but it was denied them, and it is believed that they nor the people will not be satisfied till the House be filled.

a repl. 'after'   *b* repl. 'is'

---

1. Pepys had had an operation for stone on 26 March 1658.

2. Axe Yard was on the w. side of King St, Westminster. The Pepyses had lived in the house there since at least 26 August 1658: below, ii. 162. Jane Birch, their first servant, had been with them since about the same time.

3. See 'Preliminary Note', opp.

4. Lambert was not a peer, either of royal or Cromwellian creation, but was a Councillor of State and a general. The title 'Lord' was often used in such cases.

5. They had begun to organise their own militia, and proposed to present a petition to parliament for the admission of the secluded members. On 29 December they replied to a letter of Monck's (originally addressed to their predecessors on 12 November) and asked for his support: LRO, Journals 41x, ff. 214–17. Their swordbearer was William Man.

6. This was on the morning of 27 December. The 22 included John Crew, father-in-law of Pepys's patron, Edward Mountagu.

My own private condition very handsome; and esteemed rich, but endeed very poor, besides my goods of my house and my office, which at present is somewhat uncertain. Mr Downing master of my office.[1]

1. George Downing had been one of the four Tellers of the Receipt of the Exchequer since 1656. Pepys had served as a clerk there since 1654 or 1655.

JANUARY 1. 16$\frac{59}{60}$. *Lords=day.*

This morning (we lying lately in the garret) I rose, put on my suit with great skirts, having not lately worn any other clothes but them.

Went to Mr. Gunnings church at Exeter-house, where he made a very good sermon[a] upon these words: That in the fullness of time God sent his Son, made of a woman, &c., shewing that by "made under the law," is meant his circumcision, which is solemnised this day.[1]

Dined at home in the garret, where my wife dressed the remains of a turkey, and in the doing of it she burned her hand.

I stayed at home all the afternoon, looking over my accounts.

Then went with my wife to my father's; and in going, observed the great posts which the City hath set up at the Conduit in Fleet-street.[2]

Supped at my father's, where in came Mrs. The. Turner and Madam Morris[3] and supped with us. After that, my wife and I went home with them, and so to our own home.

a repl. incorrect symbol for 'sermon'

---

1. Peter Gunning (later Bishop of Chichester) had since c. 1656 made Exeter House Chapel in the Strand an important centre of illegal Anglicanism. For Pepys's Anglicanism, see below, p. 76 & n. 3. The text given here is a loose recollection of Gal., iv. 4. This and many later instances in the diary suggest that his verbal memory for biblical texts was often faulty.

2. John Pepys, a tailor, occupied a house and shop in Salisbury Court (abutting into St Bride's Churchyard) off the s. side of Fleet St. The posts were part of the city's defences which parliament was now trying to dismantle; on the following day the city agreed to remove them. LRO, Journals 41x, ff. 214–15; Common Hall Bks, v, f.437r.

3. Theophila (eight - year - old daughter of John and Jane Turner, who lived close by in Salisbury Court) was a relative of Pepys, her mother being daughter of John Pepys of Ashtead, Surrey. Madam Morris has not been identified. Spinsters, as well as married women, were commonly addressed or referred to by the prefix 'Mistress' ('Mrs')–'Miss' being a word of opprobrium. 'Madam' denoted an older person (usually a widow) as well as a Frenchwoman.

2. In the morning, before I went forth, old East brought me a dozen of bottles of sack and I gave him a shilling for his pains.[1]

Then I went to Mr. Sheply, who was drawing of sack in the wine-cellar to send to other places as a gift from my Lord,[2] and told me that my Lord hath given him order to give me the dozen of bottles.

Thence I went to the Temple to speak with Mr. Calthropp about the 60*l*: due to my Lord;[3] but missed of him, he being abroad. Then I went to Mr. Crew's and borrowed 10*l*: of Mr. Andrewes for my own use;[4] and so went to my office, where there was nothing to do. Then I walked a great while in Westminster-hall, where I heard that Lambert was coming up to London. That my Lord Fairfax was in the head of the Irish brigades but it was not certain what he would declare for.[5] The House was today upon finishing the act for the Council of State, which they did, and for the indemnity to the soldiers, and were

---

1. East was a servant of Pepys's master, Mountagu, whose London lodgings were in Whitehall Palace. The wine would be a New Year's gift.

2. Edward Mountagu; Pepys's first cousin once removed, whom he had served as secretary since c. 1654; 'my Lord' by virtue of having been a member of Cromwell's Council of State and Upper House, as well as a naval commander. Out of favour with the government since September 1659, he was now at Hinchingbrooke, his home near Huntingdon. Edward Shipley was his steward.

3. See below, p. 6 & n. 3.

4. John Crew (Mountagu's rich father-in-law) lived in Lincoln's Inn Fields; John Andrews was his steward.

5. Cf. the French ambassador's report (2 January) that Lambert, on hearing of the reassembly of the Rump, had set out from Newcastle to march on the capital at the head of an army of sectaries: Guizot, ii. 325–6.

Fairfax (Commander-in-Chief of the parliamentary army, 1645–50) had, in collusion with Monck, raised a rebellion in Yorkshire against Lambert on 30 December. The Irish Brigade (not 'brigades') consisted of troops brought over from Ireland to suppress Booth's rising in August 1659: they had served under Lambert unwillingly, and now deserted him in great numbers to join their old master Fairfax. Fairfax's intentions were unknown, because he had been out of politics for the past ten years. In fact, he and most of his followers among the gentry were secretly for a restoration: but at the moment they had to temporise, the Irish Brigade being firmly for the Rump. The rebels took York on 1 January, and a discreetly ambiguous manifesto announcing their aims arrived in London on the 4th: *A declaration of the Rt Honourable Thomas Lord Fairfax . . .* (BM, 1093 c. 33). See A. H. Woolrych in *Yorks. Arch. Journ.*, 39/483+.

to set again thereupon in the afternoon.[1]   Great talk that many
places have declared for a free Parliament;[2] and it is believed that
they will be forced to fill up the House with the old members.
From the Hall I called at home, and so went to Mr. Crew's (my
wife, she was to go to her father's),[3] thinking to have dined; but
I came too late.   So Mr. Moore and I and another Gentleman
went out and drank a cup of ale together in the new market,[4] and
there I eat some bread and cheese for my dinner.   After that, Mr.
Moore and I went as far as Fleet-street together and parted, he
going into the City, I to find Mr. Calthrop, but failed again of
finding him: so returned to Mr. Crews again, and from thence
went along with Mrs. Jemimah[5] home and there she taught me
how to play at Cribbige.   Then I went home, and finding my
wife gone to see Mrs. Hunt, I went to Will's and there sat with
Mr. Ashwell talking and singing till 9 a-clock, and so home.[6]
There, having not eat anything but bread and cheese, my wife
cut me a slice of brawn which I received from my Lady,[7] which
proves as good as ever I had any.   So to bed, and my [wife] had
a very bad night of it through wind and cold.

1. Parliament this day appointed 11
members of the Council of State and
passed an act defining their powers.
They also voted the terms on which
the army could be indemnified for
their 'interruption' of the Rump in
the previous October. CJ, vii. 801,
802.

2. Cf. Rugge's similar report of
about a week later: i, f.48v. But cf.
newspaper reports of declarations for
parliament (not for a free one): e.g.
Occurrences from foreign parts, 3 January,
p. 568; Merc. Pol., 5 January, p. 998;
and royalist reports of 2, 6 January in
CSPClar., iv. 508, 511, 513. Open
declarations for a free parliament (in
the sense of declarations for elections)
were not made until the end of January: Merc. Pol., 19 January, pp. 1035–
6; J. Latimer, Annals Bristol 17th cent.,
pp. 290–1; below, p. 55 & n. 4.

3. Alexander St Michel; he
appears to have lived at this time in
Hind Court, Fleet St: below, p. 199.

4. Henry Moore, lawyer, was a
member of John Crew's household.
The 'new market' was Clare Market,
Lincoln's Inn Fields.

5. Jemima, Edward Mountagu's
eldest child; at this time living in the
house of Scott, a surgeon or practitioner, where she was receiving treatment for malformation of the neck.
One of Pepys's duties was to look
after her.

6. John and Eliza Hunt were
neighbours and friends of the Pepyses;
'Will's' was an alehouse near Westminster Hall; Ashwell a colleague at
the Exchequer.

7. Jemima Mountagu, wife of
'my Lord'.

3. I went out in the morning, it being a great frost, and walked to Mrs. Turner's to stop her from coming to see me today, because of Mrs. Jem's coming. Thence I went to the Temple to speak with Mr. Calthrop, and walked in his chamber an hour but could not see him; so went to Westminster, where I found soldiers in my office to receive money, and paid it them.[1] At noon went home, where Mrs. Jem. Her maid. Mr. Sheply, Hawly[2] and Moore dined with me on a piece of beef and cabbage, and a collar of brawn. We then fell to cards till dark, and then I went home with Mrs.*a* Jem; and meeting Mr. Hawly, got him to bear me company to Chancery-lane; where I spoke with Mr. Calthrop, who told me that Sir James Calthrop was lately dead, but that he would write to his Lady that the money may be speedily paid.[3] Thence back to White-hall, where I understood that the Parliament have passed the Act for Indemnity to the soldiers and officers that would come in in so many days, and that my Lord Lambert should have benefit of the said Act. They have also voted that all vacancy in the House by the death of any of the old members shall be filled up; but those that are living shall not be called in.[4] Thence I went home; and there found Mr. Hunt and his wife and Mr. Hawly, who sat with me till 10 at night at cards, and so broke up. And to bed.

4. Early came Mr. Vanly to me for his half-year's rent, which I had not in the house, but took his man to my office and there paid him.[5] Then I went down into the Hall and to Will's, where Hawly brought a piece of his Cheshire cheese, and we were merry

a The symbol here is unusual in that it represents 'Mistress' in full.

---

1. Parliament had ordered the army a month's pay: *CJ*, vii. 797.

2. John Hawley, a colleague at the Exchequer.

3. This was a debt of £2000, still outstanding at Mountagu's death in 1672, contracted in the name of Sir Henry Wright, Mountagu's brother-in-law, who may have been either Mountagu's agent or his partner in the matter. Pepys collected £60 (probably interest charge) on 2 Febru-

ary. Cf. Wright to Mountagu, 4 May 1660: Carte 223, f. 198r. Sir James Calthorpe, of Ampton, Suff., held lands in E. Anglia and in Ireland. His cousin Lestrange Calthorpe (of the Middle Temple) was his executor and man of business.

4. *CJ*, vii. 798, 800, 802, 803, 805.

5. Pepys leased his house from Valentine Wanley, an alien living at Lambeth: cf. below, p. 245.

with it. Then into the Hall again, where I met with the Clerk and quartermaster of my Lord's troop,[1] and took them to the Swan and gave them their morning's draught, they being just come to town. Mr. Jenkings[2] showed me two bills of exchange for money to receive upon my Lord's and my pay. It snowed hard all this morning and was very cold, and my nose was much swelled with cold. Strange, the difference of men's talk: some say that Lambert must of necessity yield up; others, that he is very strong, and that the Fifth-monarchy men will stick to him if he declares for a free Parliament.[3] Chillington was sent yesterday to him with the vote of pardon and indemnity from the Parliament.[4]

From the Hall I came home, where I found letters from Hinchingbrooke[5] and news of Mr. Sheply's going[a] thither the next week. I dined at home, and from thence went to Wills to Shaw, who promised me to go along with me to Atkinson about some money; but I found him at cards with Spicer and D. Vines, and could[b] not get him along with me.[6] I was vexed at this and went and walked in the Hall, where I heard that the Parliament

a repl. 'coming'   b MS. 'would'

1. Appointed to the command of a regiment of horse in September 1658, Mountagu had been dismissed on the fall of Richard Cromwell in the following spring. His men were now commanded by Col. Matthew Alured, but Pepys (who had been taken on as colonel's secretary without performing any functions – a fairly common practice: cf. HMC, *Leyborne-Popham*, pp. 104, 105) still referred to the regiment as 'my Lord's'. The command was remodelled on 12 January, and Mountagu became colonel again on 20 April. In November the troop was disbanded: below, p. 304.

2. Quarter-master's clerk.

3. Cf. *A declaration of the Rt Honorable Thomas Lord Fairfax* (BM, 1093 c. 33), and *An extract of a letter from York, dated the 31 of Decemb. 1659 concerning the Lord Fairfax's raising that*

county in arms (BM, 669 f. 22/52). The latter reported that Lambert was marching south from Newcastle to join the Quakers in Yorkshire, but that, according to some accounts, he had not enough troops and would declare for re-admission of the secluded members. The Fifth-Monarchists were violent millenarians. On 6 January news of Lambert's submission arrived in parliament: *CJ*, vii. 804.

4. Capt. Edmund Chillenden was a prominent sectary and an old acquaintance of Lambert.

5. Edward Mountagu's house near Huntingdon.

6. Robin Shaw, Jack Spicer and Dick Vines were colleagues at the Exchequer; Thomas Atkinson a goldsmith of St Mary Woolnoth.

spent this day in fast and prayer;[1] and in the afternoon came letter[s] from the North, that brought certain news that my Lord Lambert his forces were all forsaking him and that he was left with only 50 horse and that he did now declare for the Parliament himself.[2] And that my Lord Fairfax did also rest satisfied and had laid down his arms, and that what he had done was only to secure the country again my Lord Lambert his raising of money, and free Quarter.

I went to Will's again, where I found them still at cards and Spicer had won 14s of Shaw and Vines.

Then I spent a little time with G. Vines and Maylard at Vines's at our vials.[3]

So home, and from thence to Mr. Hunt's and sat with them and Mr. Hawly at cards till 10 at night, and were much made of by them.

Home and so to bed; but much troubled with my nose, which was much swelled.

5. I went to my office, where the money was again expected from the Excise office, but none brought; but was promised to be sent this afternoon. I dined with Mr. Sheply at my Lord's lodgings upon his turkey-pie; and so to my office again, where the Excise money was brought and some of it told to soldiers till it was dark.

Then I went home, and after writing a letter to my Lord, and told him the news that the Parliament hath this night voted that the members that was discharged from setting in the years 1648 and 49 was duly discharged, and that there should be writs issued presently for the calling of others in their places.[4] And that Monke and Fairfax were commanded up to town, and that the Prince's lodgings were to be provided for Monke at White-hall.[5]

---

1. *CJ*, vii. 799, 803.

2. The letters were read in parliament in the afternoon: *CJ*, vii. 803. Summaries in *CSPD 1659–60*, pp. 293–6.

3. George Vines, like his brother Dick, worked at the Exchequer. They lived in a house at the corner of New Palace Yard and St Margaret's Lane. Maylard (Mallard) was a professional musician.

4. *CJ*, vii. 804; cf. ib., p. 846.

5. See order of Council of State (6 January): *CSPD 1659–60*, p. 302. For the Prince's Lodgings, see *Comp.*: 'Whitehall Palace'.

Then my wife and I, it being a great frost, went to Mrs. Jem, in expectation to eat a sack-posset; but Mr. Edwd.[1] not coming, it was put off; and so I left my wife playing at cards with her, and went myself with my lanthorn to Mr. Fage to consult concerning my nose, who told me that it was nothing but cold; and after that, we did discourse concerning public business,[2] and he told me that it is true the City hath not time enough to do much, but they are resolved to shake off the soldier[s];[3] and that unless there be a free Parliament chosen, he doth believe there are half the Common Council will not levy any money by order of this Parliament. From thence I went to my father's, where I found Mrs. Ramsey and her grandchild, a pretty girl, and stayed a while and talked with them and my mother and then took my leave; only, heard of an invitation to go to dinner tomorrow to my Cosen Tho. Pepys.[4]

I went back to Mrs. Jem, and took my wife and Mr. Sheply and went home.

6. This morning Mr. Sheply and I did eat our breakfasts at Mrs. Harpers, my brother John being with me, upon a cold turkey-pie and a goose;[5] from whence I went to my office, where we paid money to the soldiers till one of the clock, at which time we made an[a] end; and I went home and took my wife and went to my Cosen Tho Pepys's and found them just sat down to dinner, which was very good; only the venison pasty was palpable beef, which was not handsome.[6] After dinner I took my leave,

a MS. 'and'

---

1. Edward Mountagu, eldest son of 'my Lord'.

2. Valentine Fage (Fyge), apothecary, was a Common-Councilman for the St Bride's precinct of the ward of Farringdon Without, where Pepys's father lived. He was a Presbyterian.

3. Troops had occupied the city since the apprentices' riot of 5 December 1659 in favour of a free parliament.

4. A well-to-do merchant living in Newport St, Covent Garden; a Commissioner of Assessment and of the Militia for Westminster. After 1661 referred to in the diary as Thomas Pepys 'the executor'; after 1663, as 'Hatcham Pepys'. He and Pepys had a common ancestor, William Pepys of Cottenham (d. 1519).

5. Harper's was a tavern in King St, Westminster. John Pepys, aged 19, had just left St Paul's School; he went up to Cambridge in the following month.

6. Venison was often simulated.

leaving my wife with my cousin Stradwick,[1] and went to Westminster to Mr. Vines, where George and I fiddled a good while,[2] Dick and his wife (who was lately brought to bed) and her sister being there; but Mr. Hudson not coming according to his promise, I went away; and calling at my house on the wench, I took her and the lanthorn with me to my cousin Stradwick. Where, after a good supper, there being there my father, mother, brothers, and sister, my cousin Scot and his wife, Mr. Drawwater and his wife and her brother, Mr. Stradwick, we had a brave cake brought us, and in the choosing, Pall was queen and Mr. Stradwick was king.[3]   After that, my wife and I bid Adieu and came home, it being still a great frost.

7.   At my office, as I was receiving money of the probate of Wills,[4] in came Mrs. Turner, Theoph., Madam Morrice, and Joyce;[5] and after I had done I took them home to my house and Mr. Hawly came after, and I got a dish of steaks and a rabbit for them[6] while they were playing a game or two at cards.   In the middle of our dinner, a messenger from Mr. Downing came to fetch me to him.   So leaving Mr. Hawly there, I went and was forced[a] to stay till night in expectation of the French Embassador.[7] Who at last came, and I had a great deal of good discourse with one of his gentlemen concerning the reason of the difference between the zeal of the French and the Spaniard.   After he was gone, I went home and found my friends still at cards; and after that, I went along with them to Dr. Whores (sending my wife to Mrs. Jem's to a sack-posset), where I heard some symphony* and songs of his own making performed by Mr. Mage,[b] Harding, and

a   blot over symbol   b   MS. 'Maye'

---

1. Thomas Stradwick (Strudwick), a provision dealer in Turnagain Lane, west of Snow Hill, near Holborn Cross.

2. Probably on viols: cf. above, p. 8; below, ii. 71.   (E).

3. This was a Twelfth Night party. The cake served at supper usually contained a bean and a pea, the recipients of which were King and Queen respectively.   Pall (Paulina) was Pepys's unmarried sister, aged 20.

4. Fees were charged by the clerks for recording in the assignment books of the Exchequer the probate of all wills which affected government revenue.

5. Joyce Norton, cousin of Jane Turner and of Pepys.

6. Sc. from a cookshop: cf. below, p. 195 & n. 3.

7. Antoine de Bordeaux, accredited to England since 1652.

Mallard.[1] Afterwards, I put my friends into a coach and I went to Mrs. Jem – where I writ a letter to my Lord by the post and had my part of the posset, which was saved for me; and so we went home and put in at my Lord's lodgings, where we stayed late, eating of part of his turkey-pie and reading of Quarles *Emb[l]em.*[2] So home and to bed.

8. *Sunday.* In the morning I went to Mr. Gunings, where a good sermon, wherein he showed the life of Christ and told us good authority for us to believe that Christ did fallow his father's trade, and was a carpenter till 30 years of age. From thence to my father's to dinner; where I found my wife, who was forced to dine there, we not having one coal of fire in the house and it being very hard frosty weather. In the afternoon, my father, he going to a man's to demand some money due to my aunt Bell, my wife and I went to Mr. Messum's,[3] where a strange Doctor made a very good sermon. From thence, sending[a] my wife to my father's, I went to Mrs. Turners and stayed a little while; and then to my father's, where I found Mr. Sheply. And after supper went home together. Here I heard of the death of Mr. Palmer, and that he was to be buried at Westminster tomorrow.[4]

9. For these two or three days, I have been much troubled with thoughts how to get money to pay them that I have borrowed money of, by reason of my money being in my Uncles hands.[5]

I rose early this morning, and looked over and corrected my

a   blot over symbol

---

1. William Hoare was a physician living in Cannon Row, Westminster; Humphrey Mage, John Harding and Thomas Mallard were professional musicians. (E).

2. Francis Quarles, *Emblemes, divine and moral* (first published in 1635; not in the PL), most popular of contemporary emblem books (books of moralising verses etc). The editions of 1658 and 1660 had sold in phenomenal numbers: J. Horden, *F. Quarles, a bibliography.*

3. Probably Robert Mossom, an extruded minister who used the Anglican rites and prayer-book during the Interregnum, and who at this time conducted services at Carey House in the Savoy.

4. James Palmer had been Vicar of St Bride's, Fleet St, 1616–45, and had baptised Pepys there in 1633. He had died on 5 January, and was buried at St Margaret's, Westminster.

5. See below, p. 30; the uncle was Robert Pepys of Brampton, Hunts.

brother John's speech which he is to make the next Apposition;[1]
and after that I went towards my office and in my way met with
W. Simons, Muddiman, and Jack Price[2] and went with them to
Harpers, and in many sorts of talk I stayed till 2 of the clock in*a* the
afternoon.   I found Muddiman a good scholar – an arch rogue –
and one that, though he writes new[s]-books for the Parliament,
yet he did declare that he did it only to get money; and did talk
very basely of many of them.[3]   Among other things, W. Simons
told me how his uncle Scobell was on Saturday last called to the
bar for*b* entering in the journal of the House, for the year 1653,
these words – "This day his Excellence the Lord Generall Cromwell dissolved this House."[4]   Which words the Parliament voted
a forgery, and demanded of him how they came to be entered: he
answered that they were his own handwriting and that he did it
by virtue of his office and the practice of his predecessors;[5] and
that the intent of the practice was to let posterity know how such
and such a Parliament was dissolved, whether by the command
of the King or by their own neglect, as the last House of Lords
was;[6] and that to this end he had said and writ that it was dissolved by his Excellence the Lord Generall.   And that for the

a repl. 'and'   *b* MS. 'from'

---

1. On Apposition (Opposition)
Day at St Paul's School the pupils
performed exercises in the presence
of visiting examiners. Senior pupils,
like John Pepys, delivered orations
in competition for the 15 exhibitions
awarded to those going on to
Oxford or Cambridge. For John's
success, see below, p. 46.

2. Simons and Price were underclerks to the Council; Henry Muddiman a journalist.

3. The newsbooks were the weekly
newspapers *Parliamentary Intelligencer*
and its Thursday edition *Mercurius
Publicus*, both written by Muddiman and Giles Dury. They were
now written not on the Rump's behalf, but on Monck's, and soon came
to support the cause of a free parlia-

ment: J. B. Williams (J. B. Muddiman), *Hist. Engl. journalism*, pp.
174-5; *EHR*, 23/255+.

4. See *CJ*, vii. 804, 813. The
words written (under 20 April 1653)
were: 'This Day his Excellency the
Lord Generall dissolved this Parliament': House of Commons MSS,
Journal Dec. 24th 1652 – April 19th
1653, p. 664. Henry Scobell was
Clerk of the House.

5. Before 1640 there seems to have
been no regular usage requiring the
clerk to record a dissolution.

6. At the time of Charles I's execution the House of Lords had dwindled
to about six members.   It never met
after 6 February 1649 and was
abolished by an act of 19 March 1649.

word "dissolved," he never at that time did hear of any other term; and desired pardon if he would not dare to make a word himself, which it was six years after before they came themselfs to call it an Interrupcion.[1] But they were so little satisfied with this answer, that they did choose a committee to report to the House whether this crime*a* of Mr. Scobells did come within the Act of Indemnity or no.[2]

Thence I went with Muddiman to the Coffee-house, and gave 18*d* to be entered of the Club.[3] Thence into the Hall, where I heard for certain that Monke was coming to London, and that Bradshaw's lodgings[4] were preparing for him.

Thence to Mrs. Jem and found her in bed, and some was afraid that it would prove the small-pox. Thence back to Westminster-hall, where I heard how Sir H. Vane was this day voted out of the House and to sit no more there; and that he would retire himself to his house at Raby, as also all the rest of the nine officers that had their commissions formerly taken away from them were com-manded to their farthest houses from London during the pleasure of the Parliament.[5] Here I met with Quarter Maister of my Lord's troop and his clerk Mr. Jenings, and took them home and gave a bottle of wine and the remainder of my collar of brawn, and so good-night. After that, came in Mr. Hawly, who told

a repl. 'vote'

---

1. When Lambert prevented mem-bers from meeting on 13 October 1659, he was reported in the Journal to have 'interrupted' the session: *CJ*, vii. 797.

2. He appears to have been ac-quitted. The offending entry was expunged from the Journal.

3. The 'Rota club', recently estab-lished, for political debate, by the republican James Harrington at Miles's coffee-house (the Turk's Head), New Palace Yard: Aubrey, i. 289–90. Pepys attended several times before it broke up on 21 February, when it had become clear that republicanism was doomed.

4. John Bradshaw (president of the regicide tribunal) had occupied the

Deanery, Westminster, from 1649 until his death in October 1659. In fact, it was the Prince's Lodgings in Whitehall which were prepared for Monck: above, p. 8 & n. 5.

5. *CJ*, vii. 806. Sir Harry Vane, jun., of Raby Castle, co. Durham, a leading republican, was now under parliament's displeasure because of his association with the army during the 'interruption' of the Rump. 'The rest of' is misleading; Vane was not one of the officers. The latter, chief of whom was Lambert, had had their commissions withdrawn in October 1659, and had thereupon suspended the Rump. These orders of banish-ment proved ineffective.

me that I was missed this day at my office and that tomorrow I must pay all the money that I have, at which I was put to a great loss how I should get money to make up my cash,[1] and so went to bed in great trouble.

10.   Went out[a] early, and in my way met with Greatorex, and at an alehouse he showed me the first sphere of wire[2] that ever he made, and indeed it was very pleasant.   Whence to Mr. Crews and borrowed 10*l*; and so to my office and was able to pay my money.   Thence into the Hall; and meeting the Quarter Maister, Jenings and Captain Rider, we four went to a cook's to dinner.   Thence Jenings and I into London, it being through heat of the sun a great thaw and dirty, to show our bills of return; and coming back, drank a pint of wine at the Star in Cheapside.   So to Westminster, overtaking Captain Okeshott in his silk cloak, whose sword got hold of many people in walking.

Thence to the Coffee-house, where were a great confluence of gentlemen; *viz.* Mr. Harrington, Poultny cheareman, Gold, Dr. Petty, &[c].,[3] where admirable discourse till 9 at night.   Thence with Doling to Mother Lam's, who told me how this day Scott was made Intelligencer,[4] and that the rest of the members that were objected against[b] last night, their businesses were to be heard this day sennit.[5]   Thence I went[c] home and wrote a letter, and went to Harpers and stayed there till Tom carried it to the postboy at White-hall.   So home to bed.

11.   Being at Will's with Captain Barker,[6] who hath paid me

    a MS. 'home'   *b* repl. symbol rendered illegible
                c followed by blank half-line

---

1. On 4 January Pepys had borrowed money from the office to pay his rent.

2. Probably an armillary sphere. Ralph Greatorex was an inventor and mathematical instrument maker.

3. Harrington, founder of the club; William Pulteney of Masterton, Leics. (d. 1691), grandfather of the 18th-century statesman; Nicholas Gold, London merchant and politician; and William Petty, physician and pioneer social statistician.

4. Thomas Scott, republican and regicide, was now given (for the third time) control of the intelligence service, and a week later made Secretary of State.   Thomas Doling was a Council messenger and an old friend of Pepys.

5. These were associates of Vane who, like him, had collaborated with the army.   Two were expelled on the 17th.   *CJ*, vii. 806, 813–14, 837.

6. Probably Richard Baker, Commissioner of Customs and Excise.

300*l* this morning at my office, in comes my father; and with him I walked, and left him at W. Joyces[1] and went myself to Mr. Crews but came too late to dine; and therefore, after a game at shittle-cock with Mr. Walgrave and Mr. Edwd, I returned to my father; and taking him from W. Joyces, who was now*ᵃ* abroad himself, we inquired of a porter and by his direction went to an alehouse, where after a cup or two we parted. I went towards London and in my way went in to see Crowly, who was now grown a very great lion and very tame.[2] Thence to Mr. Stevens's with a pair of silver snuffers; and bought a pair of shears to cut silver and so homewards again.

From home I went to see Mrs. Jem, who was in bed and now granted to have the small-pox.[3]

Back again, and went to the Coffee-house but tarried not, and so home.

12. I drink my morning [draught] at Harpers with Mr. Sheply and a seaman; and so to my office, where Captain Holland[4] came to see me and appointed a meeting in the afternoon. Then I wrote letters to Hinchingbrooke[5] and sealed them at Wills, and after that went home; and thence to the Half Moon, where I found the Captain and Mr. Billingsly and Newman, a barber; where we were very merry and had the young man that plays so well on the Welch harp. Billingsly paid for all. Thence home, and finding my letters this day not gone by the carrier, I new-sealed them; but my Brother Tom[6] coming, we fell into dis-

a MS. 'not'

---

1. William Joyce had married Mary Fenner, Pepys's cousin, and was a tallow chandler in Russell St, Covent Garden.

2. Possibly a lion in the menagerie at the Tower, though Pepys's direct route from Covent Garden to the city would not have taken him there. He kept a tame lion-cub in the 1670's: Bryant, ii. 135.

3. It turned out to be chicken-pox, with which smallpox in its early stages was often confused. See below, p. 17; Carte 73, f. 212*r*.

4. Philip Holland, Captain of the *Assurance*, in which Mountagu had flown his flag in the Baltic expedition of 1659.

5. Pepys to Edward Mountagu: Carte 73, f. 212*r*; printed in *Letters*, p. 19.

6. Pepys's younger brother, aged 25; a tailor, living in his father's house in Salisbury Court. From 1661 he carried on the family business. He died unmarried in 1664.

course about my intention to feast the Joyces: I sent for a bit of meat for him from the cook's, and forgot to send my letters this night. So I went to bed and in discourse broke to my wife what my thoughts were concerning my design of getting money by, &c.

13. Coming in the morning to my office, I met with Mr. Fage and took him to the Swan. He told me how high Haslerigg and Morly the last night began at my Lord Mayor's to exclaim against the City of London, saying that they have forfeited their charter.[1] And how the Chamberlain of the City[2] did take them down, letting them know how much they were formerly beholding to the City, &c; he also told me that Monke's letter that came to them by the sword-bearer was a cunning piece, and that which they did not much trust to;[3] but they were resolved to make no more applications to the Parliament, nor to pay any money, unless the secluded members be brought in or a free Parliament chosen.

Thence to my office, where nothing to do. So to Will's with Mr. Pinkny, who invited me to their feast at his Hall the next Monday.[4] Thence I went home and took my wife and dined at Mr. Wade's.[5] And after that we went and visited Catau.[6] From thence home again, and my wife was very unwilling to let me go forth; but with some discontent, would go out[a] if I did; and I

---

a repl. 'home'

---

1. By their recent votes in favour of a free parliament; see above, p. 1, n. 5. Sir Arthur Hesilrige (principal leader of the Rump) and Col. Herbert Morley (recently appointed Lieutenant of the Tower) were members of the committee appointed to deal with the city: *CJ*, vii. 807. The Mayor was Thomas Aleyn, of Leadenhall St.

2. Thomas Player, sen.

3. Monck's reply, of 6 January 1660, to the city's letter of 29 December 1659. It was not clear from its wording whether Monck stood for the Rump or for a free parliament, and on its arrival the Common

Council forbore to debate it because 'they had not been able to discover what his sentiments were'. Guizot, ii. 330; *Two letters; the one sent by the Lord Mayor, aldermen and common council of London to his Excellency the Lord General Monck . . . the other, his Excellency's answer thereunto* (1659/60).

4. George Pinckney was parish clerk of St Benet's, Paul's Wharf. His Hall was that of the Company of Parish Clerks, of which he was this year Under-Warden.

5. A neighbour in Axe Yard.

6. 'Catau' (Kate) Sterpin, a maidservant to Elizabeth Pye of New Palace Yard.

going forth towards White-hall, I saw she fallowed me, and so I stayed and took her round through White-hall, and so carried her home angry. Thence I went to Mrs. Jem. And found her up and merry, and that it did not prove the small-pox but only the swine-pox; so I played a game or two at cards with her and so to Mr. Vines, where he and I and Mr. Hudson played half-a-dozen things, there being there Dick's wife and her sister. After that I went home and found my wife gone abroad to Mr. Hunt's, and came in a little after me. So to bed.

14. Nothing to do at our office. Thence into the Hall, and just as I was going to dinner from Westminster-hall with Mr. Moore (with whom I had been in the lobby to hear news, and had spoke with Sir Ant. Ashl. Cooper about my Lord's lodgings)¹ to his house, I met with Captain Holland, who told me that he had brought his wife to my house, so I posted home and got a dish of meat for them. They stayed with me all the afternoon and went hence in the evening.

Then I went with my wife and left her at market, and went myself to the Coffee-house and heard exceeding good argument against Mr. Harrington's assertion that overbalance of propriety* was the foundation of government.²

Home and wrote to Hinchingbrooke, and sent that and my other letters that missed of going on Thursday last. So to bed.

15. Having been exceedingly disturbed in the night with the barking of a dog of one of our neighbours, that I could not sleep

---

1. Cooper had been elected to the Council of State and given the apartments in Whitehall previously allotted to Mountagu, now out of employment. But, by friendly arrangement, the lodgings did not change hands. Below, p. 23; Pepys to Mountagu (12 January, in *Letters*, p. 19); *CSPD 1659–60*, p. 306.

2. A series of debates on the structure of the ideal republic had begun in the club on 20 December 1659 and ended sometime before 9 January.

They had involved discussion of Harrington's proposition that 'all Government is Founded upon over-balance in Propriety': *The Rota; or A model of a free-state, or equall Common-wealth . . . debated by a free and open society of ingenious gentlemen* (1660; received by Thomason, 9 January: BM, E 1013 (7)), p. 3. It was one of Harrington's favourite theses that no government is secure unless the governing classes possess a preponderance of landed wealth.

for an hour or two, I slept*a* late; and then in the morning took physic, and so stayed within all day.

At noon my Brother John came to me, and I corrected as well as I could his Greek speech against the Apposition,[1] though I believe he himself was as well able to do it as myself. After that, we went to read in the great Officiale about the blessing of bells in the Church of Rome.[2]

After that, my wife and I in pleasant discourse till night that I went to supper, and after that to make an end of this week's notes in this book, and so to bed.

It being a cold day and a great snow, my physic did not work so well as it should have done.

16. In the morning I went up to Mr. Crews, and at his bed-side he gave me direction to go tomorrow with Mr. Edwd. to Twickenham,[3] and likewise did talk to me concerning things of state and expressed his mind how just it was that the secluded members should come to sit again.[4] I went from thence, and in my way went into an alehouse and drank*b* my morning draught with Matt Andrews[5] and two or three more of his friends, coachmen. And of one of them I did hire a coach to carry us tomorrow to Twickenham.

From thence to my office, where nothing to do; but Mr. Downing, he came and found me all alone; and did mention to me his going back into Holland,[6] and did ask me whether I would go or no; but gave me little encouragement but bid me consider of it and asked me whether I did not think that Mr. Hawly could perform the work of the office alone or no. I confess I was at a great loss all the day after to bethink myself how to carry this business.

    a or 'sleep'   *b* repl. ill-formed symbol for 'drank'

---

1. See above, p. 12 & n. 1.

2. The service *De benedictione signi, vel campanae*, in pt ii of *Pontificale romanum Clementis VIII* . . ., of which several editions had been published. Pepys retained the Paris edition of 1664: PL 2814.

3. Edward Mountagu, jun. (aged 12) was to be put to school there.

4. John Crew (M.P. for Brackley, Northants.) was a leader of the secluded members.

5. Servant of John Crew.

6. The Council had ordered him on the 14th to return: *CSPD 1659-60*, p. 310. He was ambassador there as well as Pepys's employer in the Exchequer.

At noon Harry Ethell came to me and went along with Mr.
Maylard by coach as far as Salsbury Court; and there we set him
down and we went to the Clerkes,[1] where we came a little too
late; but in a closet we had a very good dinner by Mr. Pinkny's
courtesy. And after dinner we had pretty good singing and one
Hazard sung alone after the old fashion;[2] which was very much
cried up, but I did not like it.

Thence we went to the Greene Dragon on Lambeth hill, both
the Mr. Pinknys, Smith, Harrison, Morrice that sang the bass,
Sheply and I,[3] and there we sang of all sorts of things and I
ventured with good success upon things at first sight and after that
played on my flagelette; and stayed there till 9 a-clock, very merry
and drawn on with one song after another till it came to be so late.

After that, Sheply, Harrison[a] and myself, we went towards
Westminster on foot, and at the Golden Lion, near Charing-cross,
we went in and drank a pint of wine, and so parted; and thence
home, where I found my wife and maid a-washing.

I sat up till the bell-man came by with his bell, just under my
window as I was writing of this very line, and cried, "Past one of
the clock, and a cold, frosty, windy morning." I then went to
bed and left my wife and the maid a-washing still.[4]

17. Early, I went to Mr. Crew's; and having given Mr.
Edwd: money to give the servants, I took him into the coach[b]
that waited for us and carried him to my house, where the coach
waited for me while I and the child went to Westminster-hall and
bought him some pictures. In the Hall, I met Mr. Woodfine and

a repl. 'Harringto'-   b repl. 'ketch'

1. The Parish Clerks' Hall: see
above, p. 16, n. 4.
2. Perhaps a lutenist ayre as con-
trasted with later declamatory song-
forms. Hazard was probably Thomas
Hazard, later of the Chapel Royal.
(E).
3. Pepys sang bass, as is shown by
his music MSS in the PL. (E).
4. The household wash at this
period was a long and complicated
affair. John Houghton, the econo-

mist, wrote in 1695: 'I find upon
Enquiry that in good Citizens'
Houses, they wash once a Month, and
they use, if they wash all the Clothes
at home, about as many Pounds of
Soap as there be Heads in the Family,
and the higher the People be, the
oftner they change, the less pains the
Washers are willing to take, and the
more *Soap* is used . . .': *Coll. for
improvement of husbandry and trade*, 15
February 1695.

took him to Will's and drank with him.   Thence the child and I
to the coach, where my wife was ready, and so we went towards
Twickenham.   In our way, at Kinsington, we understood how
that my Lord Chesterfield had killed another gentleman about
half an hour before and was fled.[1]   We went forward and came
about one of the clock to Mr. Fuller's,[2] but he was out of town;
so we had a dinner there and I gave the child 40*s* to give to the two
Ushers.[3]

After that we parted and went homewards, it being market-day
at Brainford.   I set my wife down and went with the coach to
Mr. Crews, thinking to have spoke with Mr. Moore and Mrs.
Jane, he having told me the reason of his melancholy was some
unkindness from her after*a* so great expressions of love, and how he
had spoke to her friends* and had their consents.   And that he
would desire me to take an occasion of speaking with her, but by
no means not to heighten her discontent or distaste whatever it
be, but to make it up if I can.

But he being out of doors, I went away and went to see Mrs.
Jem, who was now very well again.   And after a game or two at
cards, I left her.   So I went to the Coffee club and heard very good
discourse; it was in answer to Mr. Harrington's answer, who said
that the state of the Roman government was not a settled government, and so it was no wonder that the balance of propriety was
in one hand and the command in another, it being therefore
always in a posture*b* of war; but it was carried by Ballat that it was
a steady government; though, it is true by the voices, it had been

a repl. 'so'   *b* repl.? 'unsteadiness'

---

1. The duellists were the 2nd Earl
of Chesterfield (who had already been
involved in two other duels) and
Francis Wolley, son of a Hammersmith doctor. They had quarrelled
about the price of a mare. Chesterfield took boat at Chelsea and later
fled to Holland where he obtained the
King's pardon. *The occasion and
manner of Mr Francis Wolley's death*
(1659/60); *Letters of Philip, 2nd Earl of
Chesterfield* . . . (1829), pp. 105–07;
CSPD 1657–8, p. 290; Rugge, i, f. 50r.
For duels, see below, iii. 171, n. 2.

2. William Fuller; Pepys's 'dear
friend' (below, p. 181). Now a
schoolmaster at Twickenham; after
the Restoration, Dean of St Patrick's
(1660), Bishop of Limerick (1663),
and of Lincoln (1667).

3. These were probably gratuities,
not fees; the custom of tipping
schoolmasters did not quite disappear
until the Public Schools Act of 1868:
Sir M. McDonnell, *Annals St Paul's
School*, p. 199.

carried before that it was an unsteady government.[1] So to-morrow it is to be proved by the opponents that the balance lie in one hand and the government in another.

Thence I went to Westminster and met Shaw and Washington, who told me how this day Sydenham was voted out of the House for setting any more this Parliament, and that Salloway was voted out likewise and sent to the Tower during the pleasure of the House.[2]

Home, and wrote by the post and carried [it] to White-hall; and coming back, turned in at Harper's, where Jack Price was, and I drank with him and he told me, among other things, how much the Protector[3] is altered; though he would seem to bear out his trouble very well, yet he is scarce able to talk sense with a man. And how he will say that "Who should a man trust, if he may not trust to a brother and an Uncle;"[4] and how much those men have to answer before God Almighty for their playing each the knaves with him as they did. He told me also that there was 100000*l* offered, and would have been taken, for his restitution, had not the Parliament come in as they did again. And that he doth believe that the Protector will live to give a testimony of his valour and revenge yet before he dies, and that the Protector will say so himself sometimes.

Thence I went home, it being late and my wife in bed.

18. To my office and from thence to Will's; and there Mr. Sheply brought me letters from the carrier and so I went home. After that to Wilkinson's, where we had a dinner for Mr. Talbot, Adams, Pinkny and his son, but his son did not come. Here we were very merry, and while I was here Mr. Fuller came thither and stayed a little while. After that we all went to my Lord's, whither came afterwards Mr. Harrison; and by chance seeing

---

1. For the use of ballot-boxes in the Rota club, see Aubrey, i. 290. Inter-regnum parliaments also used them for the election of councillors of state.

2. Col. William Sydenham and Maj. Richard Salwey had collaborated with the army in October–December 1659. The latter was suspended, not expelled: *CJ*, vii. 813–14. Robert

Shaw and Washington were colleagues of Pepys at the Exchequer.

3. Richard Cromwell; out of power since May 1659. Price was an underclerk of the Council.

4. The brother(-in-law) was Fleetwood and the uncle Desborough; both were leaders of the movement which had led to Richard Cromwell's fall.

Mr. Butler[1] coming by, I called him in and so we sat drinking a bottle of wine till night. At which time Mrs. Ann[2] came with the key of my Lord's study for some things, and so we all broke up; and after I had gone to my house and interpreted my Lord's letter by his Character,[3] I came to her again and went with her to[a] her lodging, and from thence to Mr. Crew's, where I advised with him what to do about my Lord's lodgings and what answer to give to Sir Ant: Cooper; and so I came home and to bed.

All the world is now[b] at a loss to think what Monke will do: the City saying that he will be for them, and the Parliament saying he will be for them.[4]

19. This morning I was sent for to Mr. Downing, and at his bedside he told me that he hath a kindness for me, and that he thought that he hath done me one; and that was, that he hath got me to be one of the Clerks of the Council; at which I was a little stumbled and could not tell what to do, whether to thank him or no; but I by and by did, but not very heartily, for I feared that his doing of it was but only to ease himself of the salary which he give me.[5]

a repl. 'again'   *b* MS. 'not'

---

1. A friend; usually referred to as 'Monsieur L'impertinent' because of his garrulity; 'cousin' of Pepys's Exchequer friends, the Bowyers. Not identified with certainty, but possibly Daniel Butler, of St Paul's School and Magdalen, Oxford (B.A. 1658); Vicar of Godmersham, Kent, in 1663. He disappears from the diary after December 1660 when he goes to Ireland.

2. Maid to Mountagu's daughter, Jemima.

3. Possibly the cipher used by Mountagu on his Baltic voyage of 1659. Pepys retained all his life an interest in ciphers and shorthands: see, e.g., *Letters*, pp. 145–9; *Priv. Corr.*, i. 152; W. J. Carlton, *Biblioth. Pep.* (pt iv: *Shorthand Books*).

4. Cf. the French ambassador's despatch (16 January): 'All parties now cast their eyes upon him, and each fancies that he is favourable to it': Guizot, ii. 330. Monck was now in Nottinghamshire; his chaplain, Gumble, had been in London from the 12th to the 16th, charged with messages to both parliament and the city.

5. He paid Pepys £50 p.a. as his personal clerk. The clerkship he now mentioned was probably a minor one. Four underclerks to the Council of State had been appointed on 16 January; on 1 February each was allowed an assistant: *CSPD 1659–60*, pp. 310, 314, 342. Cook, an underclerk, was given the impression that Pepys was to replace him: below, p. 25. Nothing came of the proposal. Downing's stinginess was notorious.

After that, Mr. Sheply staying below all this while for me, we went thence and met Mr. Pierce; so at the Harp and Ball drank our morning draught.   And so to White-hall, where I met with Sir Ant. Cooper and did give him some answer from my Lord and he did give us leave to keep the lodgings still.   And so we did determine thereupon that Mr. Sheply might now go into the country[1] and would do so tomorrow.

Back I went by Mr. Downing's order, and stayed there till 12 a-clock in expectation of one to come to read some writings; but he came not, so I stayed all alone reading the answer of the Dutch Embassador to our State, in answer to the reasons of my Lord's coming home which he gave for his coming, and did labour herein to contradict my Lord's arguments for his coming home.[2]   Thence to my office, and so with Mr. Sheply and Moore to dine upon a turkey with Mrs. Jem; and after that, Mr. Moore and I went to the French ordinary, where Mr. Downing this day feasted Sir Arth. Haslerig and a great many more of the Parliament; and did stay to put him in mind of me.   Here he gave me a note to go and invite some other members to dinner tomorrow.   So I went to White-hall, and did stay at Marshes with Simons, Luellin and all the rest of the Clerks of the Council, who I hear are all turned out, only the two Leighs; and they do all tell me that my name was mentioned the last night, but that nothing was done in it.

Hence I went and did leave some of my notes at the lodgings of the members, and so home.   To bed.

20.   In the morning I went to Mr. Downing's bedside and gave him an account what I had done as to his guests; and I went thence to my Lord Widdrington, who I met in the street going to seal the patents for the Judges today, and so could not come to

---

1. To Hinchingbrooke, Hunts.
2. In August 1659 Mountagu had brought home most of the English fleet from the Sound, contrary (it was alleged) to an agreement made in July with the Dutch.   His report and the protest made by the Dutch ambassador (Nieupoort) were both read in parliament on 16 September 1659: *CJ*, vii. 779.   They are printed (the latter in summary) in *Sandwich*, pp. 47–69.   Pepys had already made a copy for Mountagu's use: ib., p. 67. See Harris, i. 145+; cf. below, p. 141 & n. 2.

dinner.¹ I called upon Mr. Calthrop about the money due to my Lord. Here I met with Mr. Woodfine and drank with him at the Sun in Chancery-lane; and so to Westminster-hall, where at the lobby I spoke with the rest of my guests; and so to my office. At noon went by water with Mr. Maylard and Hales to the Swan in Fishstreete² at our colly-feast, where we were very merry at our Jole of ling. And from thence, after a great and good dinner of fish, Mr. Fauconbridge would go drink a cup of ale at a place where I had like to have shit in a skimmer that lay over the house of office.

Thence, calling on Mr. Stephens and Wooton³ (with whom I drank) about business of my Lord's, I went to the Coffee club, where there was nothing done but choosing of a committee for orders. Thence to Westminster-hall, where Mrs. Lane⁴ and the rest of the maids have their white scarfs, all having been at the burial of a young bookseller in the Hall.⁵ Thence to Mr. Sheply and took him to my house and drank with him, in order to his going tomorrow. So parted, and I sat up late making up my accounts before he go.

This day, three citizens of London went to meet Monke from the Common Council.⁶

21. Up early in finishing my accounts and writing to my Lord; and from thence to my Lord's and took leave of Mr. Sheply and possession of all the keys and the house.⁷ Thence to

---

1. On 18 January judges had been nominated by parliament, and Sir Thomas Widdrington had been appointed one of the three commissioners for the custody of the Great Seal: *CJ*, vii. 814–15.

2. Old Fish St.

3. A silversmith and a shoemaker respectively.

4. Betty Lane, who worked at a haberdasher's stall in Westminster Hall; she married Samuel Martin c. 1664. Throughout the period of the diary she and Pepys maintained a casual liaison. From October 1666 Pepys also had a similar affair with her sister Doll.

5. The scarves, hatbands and gloves worn at the funerals of unmarried persons were white. They were often distributed as gifts to the mourners.

6. Ald. John Fowke, Ald. William Vincent and Col. Bromfield were appointed for this purpose on the 19th: LRO, Journals 41x, f. 219r. They met Monck at Market Harborough, Leics.: T. Gumble, *Life of Gen. Monck* (1671), p. 222.

7. Mountagu's official lodgings in Whitehall Palace.

my office for some money to pay Mr. Sheply, and sent it him by the old man.[1] I then went to Mr. Downing, who chid me because I did not give him notice of some of his guests failed him; but I told him that I sent our porter to tell him and he was not within, but he told me that he was within till past 12 a-clock. So the porter or he lied. Thence to my office, where nothing to do. Then with Mr. Hawly, he and I went to Mr. Crews and dined there. Thence into London to Mr. Vernon's and I received my 25*l* due by bill for my trooper's pay.[2] Then back again to Steadman's at the Mitre in Fleetstreete, in our way calling on Mr. Fage, who told me how the City have some hopes of Monke.[3] Thence to the Mitre, where I drank a pint of wine, the house being in fitting for Banister to come thither from Pagets.[4] Thence to Mrs. Jem and gave her 5*l*. So home and left my money; and to White-hall, where Luellin and I drank and talked together an hour at Marshes, and so up to the clerks' room, where poor Mr. Cooke, a black* man that is like to be put out of his clerk's place, came and railed at me for indeavouring to put him out and get myself in, when I was already in a good condition. But I satisfied him; and after I had writ a letter there to my Lord, wherein I gave him an account how this day Lentall took his chair again and resolved a declaration, to be brought in on Monday, to satisfy the world what they entend to do.[5] So home and to bed.

22. I went in the morning to Mr. Messum's, where I met with W. Thurburne and sat with him in his pew. A very eloquent sermon about the duty of all to give good example in our lives and conversation, which I fear he himself was most guilty of not doing. After sermon, at the door by appointment my wife met me; and so to my father's to dinner, where we have not been, to my shame, in a fortnight before. After dinner my father showed

---

1. East, a servant.

2. See above, p. 7 & n. 1. The bill was an inland bill of exchange.

3. On the 19th Common Council had voted thanks to Monck for his letter of 6 January: LRO, Journals 41x, f. 219*r*.

4. Probably John Banister, composer and violinist; leader of the

King's band in 1663. A music-room was being made for him: below, p. 59. William Paget was an innkeeper. (E).

5. *CJ*, vii. 818, 819. William Lenthall, Speaker of Parliament, had on 13 January been granted leave of absence on grounds of ill-health: ib., p. 811.

me a letter from Mr. Widdrington of Christ's College in Cambrige – wherein he doth express very great kindness for my brother, and my father entends that my brother shall go to him.

To church in the afternoon to Mr. Herring, where a lazy poor sermon;¹ and so home with Mrs. Turner and setting with her a while, we went to my father's, where we supped very merry; and so by [coach] home. This day I began to put on buckles² to my shoes, which I had bought yesterday of Mr. Wotton.

23. In the morning called out to carry 20*l* to Mr. Downing, which I did and came back; and finding Mr. Pierce the surgeon, I took him to the Axe and gave him his morning draught. Thence to my office and there did nothing but make up my balance.   Came home and found my wife dressing of the girl's head, by which she was made to look very pretty.   I went out and paid Wilkinson what I did owe him, and brought a piece of beef home for dinner.   Thence I went out and paid Waters the Vintner, and went to see Mrs. Jem, where I found my Lady Wright; but Scott was so drunk that he would not be seen.   Here I stayed and made up Mrs. Anns bills and played a game or two at cards; and thence to Westminster-hall, it being very dark.   I pay Mrs. Michell my bookseller, and back to White-hall, and in the garden, going through to the Stone Gallery, I fell in a ditch, it being very dark.   At the Clerks' chamber I met with Simons and Luellin and went with them to Mr. Mounts chamber at the Cockpit,³ where we had some rare pot venison and Ale to abundance till almost 12 at night; and after a song round, we went home.   This day the Parliament sat late, and resolved of the declaration to be printed for the people's satisfaction, promising them a great many good things.⁴

24. In the morning to my office; where after I had drank my morning draught at Will's with Ethell and Mr. Stevens, I went and told part of the excise money till 12 a-clock.   And then called

---

1. John Herring, Vicar of St Bride's, Fleet St, was a Presbyterian ejected in 1662. Robert Mossom, whom Pepys had heard in the morning, was a High Anglican.

2. A new fashion: Cunnington, p. 156.

3. See *Comp.*: 'Whitehall Palace'.

4. *CJ*, vii. 819; see below, p. 27 & n. 4.

on my wife and took her to Mr. Pierce's, she in the way being exceedingly troubled with a pair of new pattens, and I vexed to go so slow, it being late. There when we came, we found Mrs. Carrick very fine, and one*a* Mr. Lucy, who called one another husband and wife;[1] and after dinner, a great deal of mad stir; there was pulling off Mrs. Bride's and Mr. Bridegroom's ribbons,[2] with a great deal of fooling among them that I and my wife did not like; Mr. Lucy and several other gentlemen coming in after dinner, swearing and singing as if they were mad; only, he singing very handsomely. There came in afterwards Mr. Southorne, clerk to Mr. Blackburne,[3] and with him Lieutenant Lambert, Lieutenant of my Lord's ship; and brought with them the declaration that came out today from the Parliament, wherein they declare for law and gospel, and for tithes;[4] but I do not find people apt to believe them.

After this, taking leave, I went to my father's; and my wife staying there, he and I went to speak with Mr. Crumlum[5] (in the meantime, while it was 5 a-clock, he being in the school, we went to my cousin Tom Pepy's shop, the turner in Paul's churchyard, and drank with him a pot of ale); he gave my father directions what to do about getting my brother an exhibition, and spoke very well of my brother.

Thence back with my father home, where he and I spoke privately in the little room to my sister Pall about her stealing of things, as my wife's scissors and my maid's book, at which my father was much troubled.

Hence home with my wife and so to White-hall, where I met with Mr. Hunt and Luellin and drank with them at Marshes, and afterwards went up and writ to my Lord by the post.

This day the Parliament gave order that the late Committee of Safety should come before them this day sennit, and all their

a symbol smudged

---

1. For mock-weddings, see *Comp.*: 'Weddings'.

2. Thus (symbolically) freeing them to perform as husband and wife.

3. Robert Blackborne, Secretary to the Navy Commissioners, c. 1653–60.

4. Printed in *Parl. or const. hist. Engl.* (1760), xxii. 58–62; declaring for impartial administration of justice, for a 'learned and pious Gospel Ministry' and for tithes – but also for a commonwealth.

5. Samuel Cromleholme, High Master of St Paul's School, 1657–72.

papers and their model of Government that they had made to be brought in with them.¹ So home and talked with my wife about our dinner on Thursday.

25. Called up*ᵃ* early to Mr. Downing; he gave me a Character, such a one as my Lord's, to make perfect. And likewise gave me his order for 500*l*: to carry to Mr. Frost; which I did, and so to my office.² Where I did do something about the character till 12 a-clock. Then home and found my wife and the maid at my Lord's, getting things ready against tomorrow. I went by water to my Uncle Whites³ to dinner, where I met my father; where we alone had a fine pole of ling to dinner. After dinner I took leave; and coming home, heard that in Cheapside there had been but a little before a Gibbett set up, and the picture of Huson⁴ hung upon [it] in the middle of the street. I called at Paul's churchyard, where I bought Buxtorfes Hebrew Grammar⁵ and read a declaration of the gentlemen of Northamptonshire—which came out this afternoon.⁶ Hence to my father's, where I stayed with my mother a while and then to Mr. Crews about a picture to be sent

a repl. 'home'

1. *CJ*, vii. 820. The Committee of Safety (composed mostly of military officers) ruled during the 'interruption' of the Rump, October–December 1659.

2. Downing needed a cipher as envoy to the United Provinces. He had been granted £500 of his pay on the day before: *CSPD 1659–60*, p. 591. Gualter Frost was Treasurer of the Council's contingencies.

3. William Wight, half-brother of Pepys's father; a fishmonger living in Aldgate Ward.

4. Col. John Hewson, regicide; particularly unpopular in the city because of his suppression of the rising of 5 December 1659; usually represented in lampoons as a one-eyed cobbler.

5. *Johannis Buxtorfii thesaurus grammaticus linguae sanctae Hebraeae* (Basle, 1651); PL 779.

6. *The humble address and hearty desires of the gentlemen, ministers and free-holders of the county of Northampton, presented to his Excellency the Lord General Monck, at his arrival at Northampton January 24, 1659*; a broadsheet calling for a full and free parliament. Pepys would perhaps be particularly interested because of the Crews' connection with Northamptonshire. The publication was premature, for the declaration was not presented until the 25th. It was printed in proper form on the 27th.

into the country, of Mr. Tho. Crew, to my Lord.[1]   So [to] my
Lady Wright to speak with her, but she was abroad; so Mr.
Evans, her butler, had me into his buttery and gave me sack and a
lesson * on his lute, on which he played very well.   Hence I went
to my Lord's and got most things ready against tomorrow, as fires
and laying the cloth, and my wife was making of her tarts and
larding of her pullets till 11 a-clock.   This evening Mr. Downing
sent for me and gave me order to go to Mr. Jessop[2] for his papers
concerning his despatch to Holland; which were not ready, only
his order for a ship to transport him he gave me.   To my Lord's
again and so home with my wife, tired with this day's work.

26.   To my office for 20*l*. to carry to Mr. Downing; which I
did and back again.   Then came Mr. Frost to pay Mr. Downing
his 500*l*., and I went to him for the warrant and brought it Mr.
Frost.   And called for some papers at White-hall for Mr. Downing,
one of which was an order of the Council for 1800*l* per annum,
to be paid monthly every month.[3]   And the other two, orders to
the Commissioners of the Customs to let his goods pass free.[4]
Home from my office to my Lord's lodgings, where my wife had
got ready a very fine dinner: *viz.* a dish of marrow-bones.   A
leg of mutton.   A loin of veal.   A dish of fowl, three pullets,
and two dozen of larks, all in a dish.   A great tart.   A neat's
tongue.   A dish of anchoves.   A dish of prawns;*a* and cheese.

My company was my father, my uncle Fenner, his two sons,[5]
Mr. Pierce, and all their wifes, and my brother Tom.   We were
as merry as I could frame myself to be in that company.   W.
Joyce, talking after the old rate and drinking hard, vexed his
father and mother and wife.   And I did perceive that Mrs. Pierce
her coming so gallant, that it put the two young women quite out
of courage.   When it became dark, they all went away but Mr.

a repl. 'live'

---

1. Probably the portrait by Lely
which was one of the set of portraits
by him of the Crew family, painted
at this period. The set, now dis-
persed, was formerly at Hinchingbrooke: R. B. Beckett, *Lely*, p. 42.
(OM).

2. William Jessop, underclerk to
the Council of State.
3. *CSPD 1659-60*, p. 591 (25
January).
4. Ib., p. 569 (25 January).
5. Sons-in-law, William and Anthony Joyce.

Pierce and W. Joyce and their wifes and Tom, and drank a bottle of wine afterwards, so that Will did heartily anger his father and mother by staying. At which I and my wife were very much pleased. Then they all went and I fell to writing of two Characters for Mr. Downing, and carried them to him at 9 a[a]-clock at night; and he did not like them but corrected them, so that tomorrow I am to do them anew.

To my Lord's lodging again and sat by the great log, it being now a very good fire, with my wife; and eat a bit and so home.

The news this day is a letter that speaks absolutely Monkes concurrence with this Parliament and nothing else, which yet I hardly believe.[1]

After dinner today, my father showed me a letter from my Uncle Rob. in answer to my last concerning my money, which I would have out of my Cozen Beck's hand, wherein Beck desires it four months longer, which I know not how to spare.

27. Going to my office, I met with Tom. Newton, my old comrade, and took him to the Crowne in the Palace[2] and gave him his morning draught. And as he alway did, did talk very high what he would[b] do with the Parliament; that he would[b] have what place he would, and that he might be one of the Clerks to the Council if he would. Here I stayed talking with him till the offices were all shut; and then I walked in the Hall and was told by my bookseller, Mrs. Michel, that Mr. G. Mountagu[3] had enquired there for me: so I went to his house and was forced by him to dine with him; and had a plenteous brave dinner and the greatest civility that I could have from any man. Thence home and so to Mrs. Jem and played with her at cards; and coming home again, my wife told me that Mr. Hawly had been there to speak with me and seemed angry that I had not been in the office that day; and she told me she was afraid that Mr. Downing may[c]

a   MS. 'and'   *b*   or 'could' (same symbol)   *c*   MS. 'my'

---

1. Three letters from Monck were read this afternoon in parliament: *CJ*, vii. 802. This was probably the one published on the 27th as *A letter of General George Monck's, dated at Leicester 23 January.*

2. New Palace Yard, Westminster. (R).

3. George Mountagu, 'my Lord's' cousin; fifth son of the 1st Earl of Manchester; he lived in Cannon Row, Westminster.

have a mind to pick some hole in my coat. So I made haste to
him, but found no such thing from him; but he sent me to Mr.
Sherwins about getting Mr. Squib to come to him tomorrow,
and I carried him an answer.[1] So home and fell a-writing the
Characters for Mr. Downing, and about 9 at night Mr. Hawly
came and sat with me; and after he was gone, I*a* sat up till almost
12 writing, and wrote two of them. In the morning, up early
and wrote another, my wife lying in bed and reading to me.

28. I went to Mr. Downing and carried him three Characters,
and then to my office and wrote another while Mr. Frost stood
telling money. And after I had done it, Mr. Hawly came into
the office and I left him and carried it to Mr. Downing, who then
told me that he was resolved to be gone for Holland this morning.
So I to my office again and despatch my business there; and came
with Mr. Hawly to Mr. Downing's lodging and took Mr. Squib
from Westminster-hall in a coach thither with me; and there we
waited in his chamber a great while till he came in; and in the
meantime sent all his things to the barge that lay at Charing-cross
stairs. Then came he in and took a very civil leave of me, beyond
my expectation, for I was fraid that he would have told me something of removing me from the office; but he did not, but that he
would do me any service that lay in his power. So I went down
and sent a porter to my house for my best fur cap; but he coming
too late with it, I did not present it to him. Thence I went to
Westminster-hall and bound up my cap at Mrs. Michell's, who
was much taken with my cap and endeavoured to overtake the
coach at the Exchange and to give it him there; but I met with
one that told me that he was gone, and so I returned and went to
Heaven;[2] where Luellin and I dined on a breast of mutton all
alone, discoursing of the changes that we have seen and the
happiness of them that have estates of their own. And so parted,
and I went by appointment to my office and paid young Mr.

a MS. 'and'

1. Downing was in dispute with
Arthur Squibb, jun., about a teller-
ship of the Exchequer: below, pp. 34,
49. Richard Sherwyn was clerk
to the Auditor of the Receipt in the
Exchequer.

2. An eating-place by Westminster
Hall. See *Comp.*: 'Taverns'. (R).

Walton[1] 500*l*; it being very dark, he took 300*l* by content.   He
gave me half a piece and carried me in his coach to St. Clemens,
from whence I went to Mr. Crews and made even with Mr.
Andrews and took in all my notes and gave him one for all.
Then to my Lady Wright and gave her my Lord's letter which he
bade me give her privately.   So home and then to Wills for a
little news; then came home[a] again and wrote to my Lord, and so
to White-hall and gave them to the post-boy.   Back again home
and to bed.

29.   In the morning I went to Mr. Guning's, where he made
an excellent[b] sermon upon the 2 of the *Galatians*, about the
difference that fell between St. Paul and Peter (the feast-day of St.
Paul being but a day or two ago);[2] whereby he did prove that
contrary to the doctrine of the Roman Church, St. Paul did never
own any dependence or that he was inferior to St. Peter, but that
they were equal; only, one a perticular charge of preaching to the
Jews and the other to the Gentiles.

Here I met with Mr. Moore and went home with him to dinner
to Mr. Crews, where Mr. Spurrier being in town did dine with us.
From thence I went home and spent the afternoon in casting up of
my accounts; and do find myself to be worth[c] 40*l* and more, which
I did not think, but am afraid that I have forgot something.

To my father's to supper, where I heard by my Brother Tom
how W. Joyce would the other day have Mr. Pierce and his wife
to the tavern after they were gone from my house, and that he
had so little manners as to make Tom pay his share, notwithstanding that he went upon his account.   And by my father I
understand that my uncle Fenner and my aunt was much pleased
with our entertaining them.

After supper home, without going to see Mrs. Turner.

30.   This morning, before I was up, I fell a-singing of my song

a   repl. 'in'   b   repl. 'extent'   c   repl. 'w'-

---

1. Presumably son of Robert Walton, draper of London, who had
supplied clothes to the army: orders
for payment are in *CSPD 1659-60*,
pp. 118 etc.; PRO, E 403/1757 (25
January).

2. The feast of the conversion of St
Paul, 25 January.

Great, good, and just, &c.[1] and put myself thereby in mind that this was the fatal day, now ten[2] year since, his Majesty died.

Scull the waterman came and brought me a note from the Hope, from Mr. Hawly with direction about his money, he tarrying there till his master be gone.

To my office, where I received money of the excise of Mr. Ruddyer; and after we had done, went to Will's and stayed there till 3 a-clock; and then, I taking my 12*l*-10*s*. 00*d* due to me for my last Quarter salary, I went with them by water to London, to the house where Signor Torriano used to be, and stayed there a while with Mr. Ashwell, Spicer and Ruddier. Then I went and paid 12*l*. 17*s*. 06*d* due from me to Captain Dick Mathews[3] according to his direction the last week in a letter. After that I came back by water, playing on my Flagelette; and not finding my wife come home yet from her father's, I went and sat a while and played at cards with Mrs. Jem, whose maid had newly got an ague and was ill thereupon.

So homewards again; have great need to do my business; and so pretending to meet Mr. Shott the wood-monger of Whitehall, I went and eased myself at the Harp and Ball. And thence home, where I sat reading till bed-time, and so to bed.

There seems now to be a general cease of talk, it being taken for granted that Monke doth resolve to stand to the Parliament and nothing else. I spent a little time this night in knocking up nails for my hats and cloaks in my chamber.

31. In the morning I fell to my lute till 9 a-clock. Then to my Lord's lodgings and set out a barrel of soap to be carried to Mrs. Ann. There I met with Nick Bartlet, one that had been a servant of my Lord's at sea, and at Harpers gave him his morning draught. So to my office, where I paid 1200*l* to Mr. Frost; and at noon went to Wills to give one of the Excise Office a pot of ale that came today to tell over a bag of his that wanted 7*l* in it, which he found over in another bag. Then home and dined with my wife, when in came Mr. Hawly, newly come from shipboard

1. Possibly John Wilson's setting of a version of the poem by Montrose: Bodl., MS. Mus. b. 1, f. 147*r*. (E).

2. *Recte* eleven.

3. An associate of Mountagu (cf. Sandwich, pp. 45, 148); possibly at this time an officer serving in his regiment.

from his master. And brought me a letter of direction what to do in his lawsuit with Squib about his house and office.[1] After dinner, to Westminster-hall, where all us clerks had order to wait upon the Committee at the Star Chamber that is to try Collonell Jones,[2] and was to give an account what money we had paid him; but the Committee did not sit today. Hence to Will's, where I sat an hour or two with Mr. Godfry Austin, a scrivener in King's-street.

Here I met, and afterwards bought, the answer to Generall Monkes letter; which is a very good one, and I keep it by me.[3]

Thence to Mrs. Jem, where I found her maid in bed in a fit of the ague. And Mrs. Jem among the people below, at work; and by and by she came up hot and merry, as if they had give her wine; at which I was troubled, but said nothing.

After a game at cards, I went home and wrote by the post and carried it to White-hall; and coming back, called in at Harper's and drank with Mr. Pulford, servant to Mr. Waterhouse,[4] who tells me that whereas my Lord Fleetwood should have answered to the Parliament today, he wrote a letter and desired a little more time, he being a great way out of town.[5] And how that he is quite ashamed of himself, and confesses how he had deserved

1. Hawley's master was Downing. Arthur Squibb claimed the reversion of one of the tellers' places in the Exchequer. For the lawsuit, see below, p. 49 & n. 1.

2. Col. John Jones (with two other members of the Committee of Safety) had been impeached on 19 January, and accused, *inter alia*, of having levied Irish customs and excise duties without parliament's authority: Ludlow, ii. 467–8. Another Col. Jones (Philip), Comptroller of the Household to Oliver Cromwell, had been impeached in May 1659 for embezzlement.

3. *To His Excellency General Monck. A letter from the gentlemen of Devon in answer to his Lordships of January 23* . . .; a broadsheet, published this day,

arguing for a free parliament, and (by implication) for monarchy; not in the PL.

4. Nathaniel Waterhouse, Master of the Green Cloth first to Oliver, then to Richard Cromwell.

5. Parliament was enquiring into the expenditure of public money during the 'interruption' of parliamentary government, October–December 1659. Lt-Gen. Charles Fleetwood, leading political figure of the army since Oliver Cromwell's death, was held primarily responsible, but appears to have escaped punishment: *CJ*, vii. 820. On 1 March he wrote to Mountagu from Feltwell, Norf., where, he said, he had gone for quietness' sake: Carte 73, f. 216r.

this for his baseness to his Brother.[1] And that he is like to pay part of the money, paid out of the Exchequer during the Committee of Safety, out of his own purse again, which I am glad on. Home and to bed, leaving my wife reading in *Polixandre*.[2] I could find nothing in Mr. Downing's letter, which Hawly brought me, concerning my office; but I could discern that Hawly had a mind that I would get to be Clerk of the Council, I suppose that he might have the greater salary; but I think it not safe yet to change this for a public imployment.[3]

1. In April–May 1659 Fleetwood had taken the lead in the *coup d'état* which overthrew the Protectorate of Richard Cromwell, his brother-in-law.

2. *Polexandre*; Marin le Roy de Gomberville's heroic romance, first published in 1632–9; not in the PL.

3. Pepys, although working in the Exchequer in the public service, was (like most junior clerks) employed privately by his chief, Downing.

FEBRUARY.

1. In the morning went to my office, where afterwards the old man[1] brought me my letters from the Carrier. At noon I went home and dined with my wife on pease porridge and nothing else. After that I went to the Hall and there met with Mr. Swan and went with him to Mr. Downing's counsellor; who did put me in very little hopes about the business between Mr. Downing and Squibb, and told me that Squibb would carry it against him. At which I was much troubled. And with him went to Lincolnes-Inn and there spoke with his Atturny, who told me the day that was appointed for the trial. From thence I went to Sir Harry Wright's and got him to give me his hand for the 60*l* which I am tomorrow to receive of Mr. Calthrop.[2] And from thence to Mrs. Jem: and spoke with Madam Scott and her husband, who did promise to have her thing for her neck done this week.[3] Thence home and took Gammer East and James the porter, a soldier, to my Lord's lodgings – who told me how they were drawn into the field today, and that they were ordered to march away tomorrow to make room for Generall Monke.[4] But they did shout their Collonell (Collonell Fich) and the rest of the officers out of the field, and swore they would not go without their money; and that if they would not give it them, they would go where they might have it, and that was the City.[5] So the Collonell went to the Parliament and commanded what money could be got, to be got against tomorrow, for them and all the rest of the soldiers in town, who in all places made a mutiny this

1. East, a servant of Mountagu: below, p. 57.

2. See above, p. 6 & n. 3.

3. Scott, the practitioner in charge of Jemima Mountagu's treatment for congenital malformation of the neck, was now fitting her with a collar (probably made of iron padded with leather). See *Letters*, pp. 12–13, 16.

4. At Monck's request all the troops in London, apart from two regiments he could trust, were ordered into country quarters to make room for his men. He was now at St Albans, and marched to Barnet on the 2nd. The 'field' was St James's Field, near St James's Palace.

5. According to Ludlow (ii. 214), some Presbyterians in the city sent money to the mutineers next day, but it had no effect in detaching them from the Rump's service.

day and do agree together.[1]   Here I took some bedding to send
to Mrs. Ann for her to lie in now she hath her fits of the ague.
Thence I went to Wills, and stayed like a fool there and played at
cards till 9 a-clock and so came home – where I found Mr. Hunt and
his wife, who stayed and sat with me till 10;   and so good-night.

2.   I drank at Harpers with Doling;   and so to my office, where
I found all the officers of the regiments in town waiting[a] to
receive money that their soldiers might go out of town;   and what
was in the exchequer they had.   At noon, after dining at home,
I called at Harpers for Doling, and he and I met with Luellin and
drank with him at the Chequer[b] at Charing-cross;   and thence he
and I went to the Temple to Mr. Calthrops chamber, and from
thence had his man by water to London-bridge to Mr. Calthrops,
a grocer, and received 60*l.* for my Lord.   In our way we talked
with our waterman, White, who told us how the watermen have
lately been abused by some that have a desire to get in to be
watermen to the State, and have lately presented an address of
9 or 10000 hands to stand by this Parliament;   when it was only
told them that it was to a petition against Hackny coaches.   And
that today they have put out another to undeceive the world and
to clear themselfs;   and that among the rest, Cropp, my waterman
and one of great practice, was one that did cheat them thus.[2]

a repl. 'stand'   *b* repl. 'Exchequer'

---

1. A month's pay was ordered for
them on the 2nd, but their arrears
amounted to very much more: *CJ*,
vii. 830.

2. See the account in Rugge, i,
f.53*r–v*. The bogus petition (organised
by William Wetton) had specifically
declared against a King and a House
of Lords.   It had been presented on
31 January and printed: *CJ*, vii. 828;
*The humble address and congratulation
of many thousand watermen belonging
to the river of Thames* (Bodl., Wood,
276 a, no. 194).   The reply (written
by Prynne) was presented this day:
CSPClar., iv. 543; *A declaration of all
the watermen in and about the city of
London, between Gravesend and Stanes,*

or, *A hue and cry after Col. Whitton and
his decoys* (Bodl., Wood, 276 a, no.
210); E. W. Kirby, *William Prynne*,
p. 131.   This repudiated the former
petition and in the name of 10,000
watermen demanded a full and free
parliament.   On the day before this
second address was presented the
Council of State had drawn up its list
of official watermen – places coveted
principally because they gave freedom
from impressment: *CSPD 1659–60*,
p. 343.   For the watermen's jealousy
of hackney coaches, see J. Parkes,
Travel in Engl. in 17th cent., p. 98.
Both Robert and William Crop
signed the bogus address.

After I had received the money, we went to the Bridge Taverne and drank a Quart of wine and so back by water, landing Mr. Calthrop's man at the Temple; and we went homewards, but over against Somerset-house, hearing the noise of guns, we landed and found the Strand full of soldiers.[1] So I took my money and went to Mrs. Johnson, my Lord's sempstress; and giving her my money to lay up, Doling and I went upstairs to a window, and looked out and saw the Foot face the Horse and beat them back, and stood bawling and calling in the street for a free Parliament and money. By and by a drum was heard to beat a march, coming towards them; and they got all ready again and faced them, and they proved to be of the same mind with them; and so they made a great deal of joy to see one another. After all this, I took my money and went home on foot and lay up my money; and changing my stockings and shoes, I this day having left off my great skirt-suit and put on my white suit with silver lace coat; and went over to Harpers, where I met with W. Simons, Doling, Luellin and three merchants; one of which had occasion to use a porter, and so they sent for one[2] and James, the soldier, came; who told us how they had been all day and night upon their guard at St. James's and that through the whole town they did resolve to stand to what they had began, and that to-morrow he did believe they would go into the City and be received there.

After all this, we went to a sport called Selling of a Horse for a Dish of Eggs and Herrings;[3] and sat talking there till almost 12 a-clock and then parted: they were to go as far as Allgate. Home and to bed.

3. Drank my morning draught at Harpers and was told there that the soldiers were all quiet, upon promise of pay. Thence into St. James's Park, and walked there to my place for my Flagelette[4] and there played a little, it being a most pleasant

---

1. Early in the afternoon the regiment of foot lately given to the Speaker's son, Col. Sir John Lenthall, had attacked some of their officers, and seized control of their headquarters in Somerset House: Rugge, i, f.54r–v.

2. For street porters, see W. M. Stern, *Porters of London*, esp. pp. 38+. They divided the territory among themselves.

3. Possibly a game of chance.

4. See below, p. 58 & n. 2.

morning and sunshine. Back to White-hall, where in the guard-chamber I saw about 30 or 40 prentices of the City who were taken at 12 a-clock last night and brought prisoner hither*a*.[1] Thence to my office, where I paid a little more money to some of the soldiers under Lieutenant-Collonell Miller (who held out the Tower against the Parliament after it was taken away from Fich by the Committee of Safety, and yet is continued in his office);[2] about noon Mrs. Turner came to speak with me and Joyce, and I took them and showed them the manner of the House's sitting, the doorkeeper very civilly opening the door for us. Thence with my Cosen Roger Pepys; it being term time, we took him out of the Hall to Priors, the Renish wine-house, and there had a pint or two of wine and a dish of Anchoves, and bespake three or four dozen of bottles of wine for him against his Wedding.[3] After this done, he went away and left me order to call and pay for all that Mrs. Turner would have. So we called for nothing more there, but went and bespoke a shoulder of mutton at Wilkinsons, to be dressed as well as it could be done, and sent a bottle of wine home to my house. In the meantime, she and I and Joyce went walking all over White-hall, whither Generall Monke was newly come and we saw all his forces march by in very good plight and stout officers.[4] Thence to my house, where we dined; but with a great deal of patience, for the mutton came in raw and so we were fain to stay the stewing of it. In the meantime, we sat studying of a posy for a ring for her, which

a MS. 'himself'

---

1. They had risen in Leadenhall St in support of the soldiers' mutiny on the evening of the 2nd; 38 were arrested. *Merc. Pol.*, 9 February, p. 1074; Rugge, i, f.55r.

2. On 12 December 1659 Lt-Col. John Miller, faithful to the Committee of Safety, had resisted an attempt made by Col. Thomas Fitch, his superior officer, to hand over the Tower to parliamentary agents. When parliament came in again at the end of December he had quickly made his peace with them, and was now lieutenant-colonel in Twistleton's regiment.

3. Roger Pepys, a barrister of the Middle Temple, was now about to marry his third wife, Parnell Duke, of Worlingham, Suff.

4. Cf. another eye-witness: 'Every second man of his horse had carbines by their sides besides their swords and a case of pistols. The foot had the best arms and were the likliest men that ever I saw ...': HMC, *Leyborne-Popham*, p. 144.

she is to have at Rog Pepys his wedding.   After dinner I left them
and went to hear news; but only found that the Parliament-house
was most of them with him[1] at White-hall, and that in his passage
through the town he had many cry to him for a free Parliament;[a]
but little other[b] welcome.[2]   I saw in the Palace-yard how unwilling some of the old soldiers were yet to go out of town without their money; and swore, if they[c] had it not in three days as
they were promised, they would do them more mischief in the
country then if they had stayed here; and that is very likely, the
country being all discontented.[3]   The town and guard are
already full of Monkes soldiers.   I returned, and it growing
dark, I and they went to take a turn in the park, where Theoph
(who was sent for to us to dinner) outrun my wife and another
poor woman, that laid a pot of ale with me that she would outrun
her.   After that, I set them as far as Charing-cross and there left
them and my wife; and I went to see Mrs. Ann, who begun very
high about a flock-bed I sent her, but I took her down.   Here I
played at cards till 9 a–clock.   So home and to bed.

4.   In the morning, at my lute an hour and so to my office;
where I stayed expecting to have Mr. Squibb come to me, but he
did not.   At noon, walking in the Hall, I found Mr. Swan and
got him and Captain Stone together, and there advised about
Mr. Downings business.   So to Wills, and sat there till 3 a–clock;
and then to Mr. Swans (where I found his wife in very genteel
mourning for her father) and took him out by water to the counsellor at the Temple, Mr. Stephens, and from thence to Grays
Inn, thinking to speak with Sollic[i]tor Ellis; but found him not, so
we met with an acquaintance of his in the walks and went and
drank; where I eat some bread and butter, having eat nothing all
day, while they were by chance discoursing of Marriot the great

a 'a free parliament' repeated but bracketed
b the symbol may also mean 'made'   c repl. 'that'

1. Monck.

2. Gumble, one of Monck's chaplains, observed: 'The *Scotch* forces did
not find the usual welcome of the
people, as they did in other places;
only they were gazed upon, and that
was all their entertainment': *Life of*

Gen. Monck (1671), p. 228.

3. The soldiers were to be quartered in Kent, where there was
already some resistance to taxation:
HMC, *Leyborne-Popham*, p. 144;
CSPD 1659–60, pp. 340–1.

eater;[1] so that I was, I remember, ashamed to eat what I would have done. Here Swan showed us a ballat to the tune of *Mardike*, which was most incomparably writ in a printed hand; which I borrowed of him, but the song proved but silly and so I did not write it out.[2] Hence we went, and leaving Swan at his master's, my Lord Widdrington, I met with Spicer, Washington, and D. Vines in Lincolnes-Inn court; and were buying of a hanging Jack to roast birds on, of a fellow that was there selling of some. I was fain to slip from these and went to Mr[s]. Crews; to her[a] and advised about a maid to come and be with Mrs. Jem: while her maid is sick, but she could spare none. Thence to Sir Harry Wrights; but my Lady not being within, I spoke to Mrs. Carter about it, who will get one against Monday. So with a link-boy to Scotts, where Mrs. Ann was in a fit; but I spoke not to her but told Mrs. Jem what I had done; and after that, went home and wrote letters into the country by the post. And then played a while on my lute, and so down to supper and then to bed.

All the news today is that the Parliament this morning voted the House to be made up 400 forthwith.[3]

This day my wife killed her turkey that Mr. ⟨Sheply⟩ gave her, that came out of Zeeland[4] with my Lord; and could not get her maid Jane by no means at any time to kill anything.

5. *Lord's day*. In the morning before church-time, Mr. Hawly, who hath for this day or two looked something sadly,

a MS. 'hear'

---

1. Ben Marriott, of Gray's Inn (d. 1653), a by-word for gluttony and the subject of several coarse pamphlets, e.g. *The great eater of Grayes-Inne, or The life of Mr Marriott the cormorant*, by G. F., Gent. (1652/3).

2. This tune is no. 20 in 'Select new tunes and jiggs for the treble violin', supplement to John Playford's *Dancing Master* (1665), and no. 27 in his *Musick's delight on the cithren* (1666). Verses about the capture of Mardyke in 1657 (q.v. below, p. 250, n. 2) and beginning 'When first Mardike was made a prey' are in *Merry Drollery* (1661); Thomas D'Urfey, *Wit and mirth* (1707), pp. 141-3; and *Songs compleat, pleasant and divertive* (1719), pp. 65-7. (E).

3. The full total of the house, elected by the constituencies of 1640, would have been 507. The Rump, in this vote (*CJ*, vii. 834), preferred the English and Welsh constituencies of the revolutionary constitution of 1653, which even Richard Cromwell had abandoned and which almost everybody wanted to forget.

4. In Denmark; Mountagu's fleet had returned from there in August 1659.

which methought did speak something in his breast concerning me, came to me, telling me that he was out 24*l*, which he could not tell what was become of, and that he doth remember that he had such a sum in a bag the other day, and could not tell what he did with it; at which I was very sorry but could not help him. In the morning to Mr. Guning, where a stranger, an old man, preached a good honest sermon upon "What manner of love is this that we should be called the sons of God."[1] After sermon I could not find my wife, who promised to be at the gate against my coming out, and waited there a great while; then went to my house and finding her gone, I returned and called at the Chequer, thinking to dine at the ordinary with Mr. Chetwind or Mr. Thomas; but they not being there, I went to my father and found her there, and there I dined. To their church[2] in the afternoon, and in Mrs. Turners pew my wife took up a good black hood and kept it. A stranger preached a poor sermon, and so I read over the whole book of the story of Tobit. After sermon, home with Mrs. Turner; stayed with her a little while; then she went into the Court to a christening[3] and we to my father's – where I writ some notes for my Brother John to give to the Mercers tomorrow, it being the day of their Apposition.[4] After supper, home; and before going to bed, I stood writing of this day its passages – while a drum came by, beating of a strange manner of beat, now and then a single stroke; which my wife and I wondered at, what the meaning of it should be.

1. A loose recollection of 1 John, iii. 1.

2. St Bride's, Fleet St.

3. I.e. to a private house in Salisbury Court. There is no baptism recorded for this day in St Bride's register. Baptism of infants in private houses (already fashionable in the early 17th century) had become widespread during the revolution, the Puritans encouraging it, and the Anglicans finding it preferable to the official public ceremonies. It now continued as a common practice, despite the protests of stricter churchmen. Pepys attended many such ceremonies (see esp. below, ii. 109), but unlike Evelyn, never expressed in his diary any disapproval. Evelyn, 12 April 1689, 31 December 1699: J. H. Overton, *Life in Engl. church, 1660–1714*, pp. 163–5; H. Maynard Smith, *Early life . . . of Evelyn*, pp. 17–18.

4. The Mercers' Company were trustees of St Paul's School; the letters were connected with his application for the exhibition granted him at the Apposition Court of the company on 8 February: cf. above, pp. 12, 27.

This afternoon at church I saw Dick Cumberland at church newly come out of the country from his living.[1] But did not speak to him.

6. Before I went to my office, I went to Mr. Crews and paid Mr. Andrewes the same 60*l.* that I[a] had received of Mr. Calthrop the last week. So back to Westminster and overtook Mr. Squibb and walked with him[b] thither; where we found the soldiers all set in the Palace-yard to make way for Generall Monke to come to the House. At the Hall we parted; and meeting Swan, he and I to the Swan and drank our morning draught; so back again to the Hall, where I stood upon the steps and saw Monke go by, he making observance to the judges as he went along.[2] At noon my father dined with me upon my turkey that was brought from Denmarke; and after dinner he and I to the Bull-head tavern, where we drank half a pint of wine and so parted. I to Mrs. Ann;[3] and Mrs. Jem being gone out of the chamber, she and I had a very high bout: I rattled her up, she being in her bed; but she becoming more coole, we parted pretty good friends. Thence I went to Wills, where I stayed at cards till 10 a-clock; lost half a crown and so home to bed.

7. In the morning, I went early to give Mr. Hawly notice of my being forced to go into London; but he having also business, we left our office business to Mr. Spicer and he and I walked as far as the Temple, where I halted a little and then went to Pauls schoole; but it being too soon, I went and drank my morning draught with my Cosen Tom. Pepys the turner, and saw his house

a. MS. 'he'   *b.* repl. 'then'

---

1. A lifelong friend; now Rector of Brampton, Northants.; later (1691) Bishop of Peterborough.
2. I.e. to the judges of the courts held in Westminster Hall. A small group of M.P.'s in procession, led by the Serjeant-at-Arms, accompanied Monck from the Court of Wards, where he had been waiting, to the House. Monck was equally careful in his demeanour towards parliament itself to convey his respect for civil authority. He received parliament's thanks and made a speech, but 'out of his great respects to the Parliament' declined to sit on the chair offered to him: *Merc. Pol.,* 9 February, p. 1081.
3. Maidservant.

and shop.   Thence to school, where he that made the speech for the seventh-form, in praise of the Founder, did show a book that Mr. Crumlum had lately got, which is believed to be of the Founder's own writing.[1]   After all the speeches, in which my Brother John came off as well as any of the rest, I went straight home and dined; then to the Hall, where in the Palace I saw Monk's soldiers abuse Billing and all the Quakers that were at a meeting-place there; and indeed, the soldiers did use them very roughly and were to blame.[2]   So after drinking with Mr. Spicer, who had received 600*l* for me this morning, I went to Captain Stone and with him by coach to the Temple-garden (all the way talking of the disease of the stone); where we met Mr. Squib, but could do nothing till tomorrow morning.   Thence back on foot home, where I found a letter from my Lord in Character, which I construed; and after my wife had shown me some ribbon and shoes that she had taken out of a box of Mr. Mountagus, which formerly Mr. Kipps had left her when[a] his master was at sea,[3] I went to Mr. Crew and advised with him about it, it being concerning my Lord's coming up to town, which he desires upon my advice the last week in my letter.   Thence, calling upon Mrs. Ann, I went home and wrote in Character to my Lord an answer to his letter.   This day Mr. Crew told me that my Lord St. John's is for a free Parliament, and that he is very great with

a   repl. 'where'

---

1. The book cannot now be identified, since the libraries of both Cromleholme and the school perished in the Great Fire of 1666. The founder was Dean Colet (d. 1519). The speeches made by the candidates for leaving exhibitions formed part of the Apposition proceedings.

2. The Scottish soldiers were, more than the English, unfriendly to Quakers. For this incident and its effects, see W. C. Braithwaite,

Beginnings of Quakerism, p. 471. On 9 March Monck issued an order forbidding his men to disturb Quaker meetings. Edward Billing (a Westminster brewer) was a prominent Friend; the meeting was probably that held at the house of Stephen Hart in New Palace Yard: Braithwaite, p. 379.

3. George Mountagu, cousin of 'my Lord', had accompanied him on the Baltic voyage of 1659.

Monke[1] - who hath now the absolute command and power to do anything that he hath a mind to do.

Mr. Moore told me of a picture hung up at the Exchange, of a great pair of buttocks shitting of a turd into Lawsons mouth, and over it was writ "The thanks of the House."[2]

Boys do now cry "Kiss my Parliament" instead of "Kiss my arse," so great and general a contempt is the Rump come to among all men, good and bad.

8. A little practice on my flagelette, and afterwards walking in my yard to see my stock of pigeons (which begin now with the spring to breed very fast), I was called on by Mr. Fossan, my fellow-pupil at Cambrige, and I took him to the Swan in the Palace-yard and drank together our morning draught. Thence to my office, where I received ,money; and afterwards, Mr. Carter, my old friend at Cambrige, meeting me as I was going out of my office, I took him to the Swan; and in the way I met with Captain Lidcott, and so we three went together and drank there, the Captain talking as high as ever he did and more, because of the fall of his brother Thurlow.[3] Hence I went to Captain Stone, who told me how Squibb had been with him and that he could do nothing with him; so I returned to Mr. Carter and with him to Wills, where I spent upon him and Monsieur L'impertinent aliàs Mr. Butler,[4] who I took thither with me; and thence to the Renish wine-house, and in our way met with Mr. Hoole, where I paid for my Cosen Rogr. Pepys his wine; and after drinking, we parted; so I home, in my way delivering a letter which among the rest I had from my Lord today to Sir W

1. Oliver St John, Lord Chief Justice of Common Pleas, was a leader of the Presbyterian politicians and of both Crew and Monck, and now in favour of something more than the mere admission of the secluded members. He was already in touch with royalist agents (*CSPClar.*, iv. 522), but was distrusted by them, and was usually counted an adherent of Richard Cromwell.

2. John Lawson (commanding the fleet) was a republican and a friend of the Rump.

3. John Thurloe, Oliver Cromwell's Secretary of State, out of power since the fall of Richard Cromwell in May 1659, had married Capt. Robert Lidcott's sister, Anne. Both Fossan and Carter were clergymen.

4. See above, p. 22 & n. 1.

Wheeler.[1]   At home, my wife's brother[2] brought her a pretty black dog which I liked very well, and went away again.   Hence, sending a porter with the hamper of bottles to the Temple, I called in my way upon Mrs. Jem, who was much frighted till I came to tell her that her mother was well.   So to the Temple, where I delivered the wine and received the money of my Cosen Rogr. that I laid out; and thence to my father's, where he showed me a base angry letter that he had newly received from my Uncle Robt. about my brother John; at which my father was very sad, but I comforted him and wrote an answer.   My brother John hath an exhibition granted him from the school.[3]   My father and I went down to his kitchen, and there we eat and drank; and about 9 a-clock I went away homewards, and in Fleetstreet received a great jostle from a man that had a mind to take the wall,[4] which I could not help.   I came home and to bed.   Went to bed with my head not well, by my too much drinking today.   And I had a boyle under my chin which troubled me cruelly.

9.   As soon as out of my bed, I wrote letters into the country to go by the carrier today.   Before I was out of my bed, I heard the soldiers very busy in the morning, getting their horses ready where they lay at Hiltons, but I knew not then their meaning in so doing.

After I had writ my letters, I went to Westminster up and down

1. Sir William Wheler, Cannon Row, Westminster, a merchant who sometimes acted as banker to Mountagu.

2. Balthasar St Michel.

3. Fifteen Pauline exhibitions of £10 p.a. each were awarded; the exhibitioners being required to be sizars at Cambridge or battelers at Oxford: Sir M. McDonnell, *Annals St Paul's School*, pp. 185, 220.

4. A constant source of dispute when pavements were narrow and roads filthy.   In 1684 a 'Blade of the Towne' ran through and killed a

waterman who took the wall of him: HMC, *Eliot Hodgkin*, p. 17. Dr Johnson said it was in the time of his own generation that the rule was established 'that every man keeps to the right; or, if one is taking the wall, another yields it, and it is never a dispute'.   But when his mother had lived in London, 'there were two sets of people, those who gave the wall, and those who took it; the peaceable and the quarrelsome': Boswell's *Life* (ed. Birkbeck Hill, rev. Powell), v. 230-1.

the Hall; and with Mr. Swan walked a little,*a* talking about Mr.
Downing's business. And went with him to Mr. Phelps's house,
where he had some business to solicit; where we met Mr. Rogers
my neighbour, who did solicit against him and talked very high,
saying that he would not for 1000*l* appear in a business that Swan
did. At which Swan was very angry, but I believe he might be
guilty enough. In the Hall, I understand how Monke is this
morning gone into London with his army; and met with Mr.
Fage, who told me that he doth believe that Monke is gone to
secure some of the Common Council of the City, who were very
high yesterday there and did vote that they would not pay any
taxes till the House was filled up.[1] Up I went to my office, where
I wrote to my Lord after I had been at the upper bench; where
Sir Robt. Pye this morning came to desire his discharge from the
Towre, but it could not be granted.[2] After that I went [to]
Mrs. Jem., who I had promised to go along with to her Aunt
Wrights; but she was gone, so I went thither and after drinking a
glass of sack, I went back to Westminster-wards, and meeting
with Mr. Pierce the surgeon, who would needs take me home
with him; where Mr. Lucy, Burrell, and others dined; and after

a MS. 'good', but the symbols for 'little' and 'good' are very similar.
Alternatively Pepys may have omitted e.g. 'while' after 'good'.

---

1. This quarrel between Parliament
and the city during 9–12 February
was the turning-point which led to
the Restoration. The city had not
in fact voted on the 8th against the
payment of taxes, but Common
Council had received with favour a
petition from householders and free-
men protesting against the tax: LRO,
Journals 41x, f.220r. Ever since the
re-assembly of the Rump, and especially since 26 January, when Parliament voted a tax, petitions had
poured into both city and Parliament
against the levy of public money
by an unrepresentative parliament.
(Pepys reported similar protests at 5
and 13 January.) On this day,
therefore, the Council of State and
Parliament acted with vigour, and
sent Monck's troops into the city
with orders to rase its defences to the
ground, and to arrest eleven leaders
of the resistance. But the decision
resulted in a union between army and
city which brought about the overthrow of the republicans in Parliament.
2. Pye (M.P. for Berkshire) had
been imprisoned on 25 January for
presenting a petition from the county
for the re-admission of the secluded
members. His application for release
was refused, although it does not
seem to have been strongly opposed
by government counsel: Ludlow, ii.
232–3. He was discharged on 21
February.

dinner I went home and to Westminster Hall; where meeting Swan, I went with him by water to the Temple to our Councell and did give him a fee to make a motion tomorrow in the Exchequer for Mr. Downing; and thence to the Hall, where I heard a cause very finely pleaded between my Lord Dorsett and some other noble persons, his Lady and other ladies of Quality being there; and it was about 330*l* per annum that was to be paid to a poor spital, which was given by some of his predecessors and given on his side.¹   Thence, Swan and I to a drinking-house near Temple-bar; where while he writ, I played of my flagelette till a dish of poached eggs was got ready for us; which we eat, and so by coach home.   I called at Mr. Harpers, who told me how Monke had this day clapped-up many of the Common Council,² and that the Parliament had voted that he should pull down their gates and portcullisses, their posts and their chains, which he doth entend to do, and doth lie in the City all night.³ I went home and got some Allum to my mouth, where I have the beginnings of a Cancre, and have also a plaster to my boyle underneath my chin.

10.   In the morning I went to Mr. Swan, who took me to the Court of Wards; where I saw the three Lords Commissioners setting upon some cause where Mr. Scobell was concerned, and my Lord Fountaine took him up very roughly about something that he said.⁴   After that, we went to the Exchequer, where the Barons were hearing of causes; and there I made affidavit that Mr. Downing was gone into Holland by order of the Council of State, and this affidavit I gave to Mr. Stevens our lawyer.   Thence

1. This was one of a long series of suits in Chancery concerning the income of Sackville College, East Grinstead, Sussex, a hospital (almsgrandfather, the 2nd Earl, in 1609. The 'other noble persons' involved were the 3rd Earl and Countess of Northampton, and the 2nd Earl and Countess of Thanet.   An injunction was issued in favour of the hospital in January 1661. [Frank Hill], *Sackville Coll.*, pp. 126–7.

2. He arrested nine of the eleven named by parliament.

3. This was in reply to a protest which Monck had addressed to parliament soon after he had started the unwelcome work of destruction. Parliament repeated the Council of State's orders, and sent two members to see that they were carried out.

4. This was a Chancery case; the Commissioners of the Great Seal sat in what had been until 1646 the Court of Wards, by Westminster Hall.

to my office, where I got money of Mr. Hawly to pay the lawyer; and there found Mr. Lenard, one of the Clerks of the Council, and took him to the Swan and gave him his morning draught.

Then home*a* to dinner, and after that to the Exchequer, where I heard all the afternoon a great many causes before the Barons; in the end came ours, and Squibb proved clearly by his patent that the houses and office did now belong to him.[1]   Our lawyer made some kind of opposition, but to no purpose; and so the cause was found against us and the foreman of the Jury brought in 10*l* damages; which the whole Court cried shame of, and so he cried 12*d*.   Thence I went home, vexed about this business; and there I found Mr. Moore, and with him went into London to Mr. Fage about the canker in my mouth, which begins to grow dangerous; who gave me something for it, and also told me what Monke had done in the City.   How he had pulled down the most part of the gates and chains that they could break down; and that he was now gone back to White-hall.[2]   The City look mighty blank and cannot tell what in the world to do, the Parliament having this day ordered that the Common Council sit no more, but that new ones be chosen according to what Qualificacions they shall give them.[3]   Thence I went and drank with Mr. Moore at the Sugar loafe by Temple-bar, where Swan and I was last night, and so we parted.   At home, I found Mr. Hunt, who sat talking with me a while; and so to bed.

11.   This morning I lay long abed; and then to my office, where I read all the morning my Spanish book of Rome.[4]   At

a accidental stroke below symbol

1. The case concerned possession of a house in Westminster owned by Arthur Squibb (once Teller of the Exchequer) and occupied by William Swan. William Beaver, Squibb's tenant, brought an action of trespass and ejection: PRO, E 13/637, m. 25; E 12/19, p. 21. Cf. above, p. 34 & n. 1.

2. He went back on the evening of this day, against parliament's wishes. His officers and men had refused to complete the work of destroying the city's defences.

3. This order was made not on the 10th, but on the afternoon of the 9th: CJ, vii. 838.

4. *Las cosas maravillosas della sancta ciudad de Roma* (Rome, 1651; PL 592): a Spanish version of the stock guide-book for pilgrims, *Mirabilia urbis Romae*. This must have been one of the earliest purchases of Spanish books which he made: S. Gaselee, *Span. books in lib. of S. Pepys* (Bibliog. Soc., Trans., Supp. no. 2, 1921), p. 6. Pepys was a fairly good Spanish scholar, and could both speak and read the language.

noon I walked in the Hall, where I heard the news of a letter from Monke, who was now gone into the City again and did resolve to stand for the sudden filling up of the House; and it was very strange how the countenance of men in the Hall was all changed with joy in half an hour's time. So I went up to the Lobby, where I saw the Speaker reading of the letter;[1] and after it was read, Sir A. Haslerig came out very angry; and Billing standing at the door, took him by the arm and cried, "Thou man, will thy beast carry thee no longer? thou must fall." The House presently after rose, and appointed to meet again at 3 a-clock. I went then down into the Hall, where I met with Mr. Chetwind, who had not dined no more then myself; and so we went towards London, in our way calling at two or three shops, and could have no dinner; at last, within Temple-bar, we found a pullet ready-roasted, and there we dined. After that, he went to his office in Chancery-lane, calling at the Rolles, where I saw the lawyers pleading;[2] then to his office, where I sat in his study singing while he was with his man (Mr. Powells son) looking after his business. Thence we took coach for the City to Guild-hall, where the hall was full of people expecting Monke and Lord Mayor to come thither, and all very joyful. Here we stayed a great while; and at last, meeting with a friend of his, we went to the Three Tun tavern[3] and drank half a pint of wine; and not liking the wine, we went to an alehouse,[a] where we met with company of this third man's acquaintance and there we drank a little: hence I went alone to Guild-hall to see whether Monke was come yet or no, and met him coming out of the chamber where he had been with the Mayor and Aldermen; but such a shout I never heard in all my life, crying out "God bless your Excellence."[4] Here I met with Mr. Lock, and took him to an

a repl. 'alea'-

1. Monck and his officers had decided on resistance to the Rump, and early this morning sent a letter requiring them to fill their vacancies by 17 February, and to dissolve by 6 May: *A letter from his Excellencie the Lord General Monck, and the officers under his command, to the Parliament*; CJ, vii. 841.

2. The court of the Master of the Rolls (part of Chancery) was held at his official residence in Chancery Lane.

3. In Guildhall Yard; Monck's headquarters, 9–10 February.

4. A special court had been summoned for 4 p.m. to deal with Monck's request for quarters: LRO, Repert. 67, f.43r.

alehouse and left him there to fetch Chetwind; when we were come together, Lock told us the substance of the letter that went from Monke to the Parliament.[1] Wherein, after complaints that he and his officers were put upon such offices against the City as they could not do with any content or honour. That there are many members now in the House that were of the late tyrannical Committee of Safety. That Lambert and Vane are now in town, contrary to the vote of Parliament.[2] That there was many in the House that do press for new oaths to be put upon men; whereas we have more cause to be sorry for the many others that we have already taken and broken.[a] That the late petition of the Fanatique people presented by Barebone, for the imposing of an oath upon all sort of people, was received by the House with thanks.[3] That therefore he doth desire that all writts for filling[b] up of the House be issued by Friday next, and that in the meantime he would retire into the City, only leave them guards for the security of the House and Council. The occasion of this was the order that he had last night to go into the City and disarm them and take away their charter;[4] whereby he and his officers see that the House had a mind to put them on[c] things that should make them odious; and so it would be in their power to do what they would with them. He told us that they had sent Scott and

a repl. 'brother'   *b* repl. 'for calling of a'
c MS. 'of' or 'off'

---

1. The letter sent earlier that day after the meeting of the council of officers. The summary which Pepys gives is accurate and substantial, but does not include Monck's declaration that he would oppose the admission of active royalists to any new parliament (a promise he never fulfilled). Matthew Lock was Monck's secretary.

2. Both had been ordered out of town on 9 January. Vane had been allowed to stay until the 14th on grounds of ill-health; Lambert had lain in hiding, but at the moment was under summons to appear before the Council on 13 February.

3. Praisegod Barebone presented a petition on 9 February on behalf of the 'well-affected' inhabitants of London, demanding the imposition of an oath of abjuration of monarchy: *CJ*, vii. 838. See below, p. 56 & n. 1.

4. There appears to be no direct proof of any attempt against the charter itself, but parliament had asked the Council of State on the 10th to consider further measures against the city, and on the same day the city Recorder had been summoned to the Council: *CJ*, vii. 840; *CSPD 1659-60*, p. 354.

Robinson to him this afternoon, but he would not hear them.[1]
And that the Mayor and Aldermen had offered him their own
houses for himself and his officers, and that his soldiers would
lack for nothing.[2]   And endeed I saw many people give the
soldiers drink and money, and all along in the streets cried, "God
bless them" and extraordinary good words.   Hence, we three
went to a merchant's house hard by, where Lock writ a note and
left; where I saw Sir Nich. Crisp and so we went to the Star
taverne (Monke being then at Bensons),[3] where we drank and I
wrote a letter to my Lord from thence.   In Cheapside there was
a great many bonefires, and Bow bells and all the bells in all the
churches as we went home were a-ringing.   Hence we went
homewards, it being about 10 a-clock.   But the common joy
that was everywhere to be seen!   The number of bonefires, there
being fourteen between St. Dunstan's and Temple-bar.   And at
Strand bridge I could at one view tell 31 fires.   In King-streete,
seven or eight; and all along burning and roasting and drinking
for rumps – there being rumps tied upon sticks and carried up and
down.   The buchers at the maypole in the Strand rang a peal
with their knifes when they were going to sacrifice their rump.
On Ludgate-hill there was one turning of the spit, that had a
rump tied upon it, and another basting of it.   Indeed, it was past
imagination, both the greatness and the suddenness of it.   At one
end of the street, you would think there was a whole lane of fire,
and so hot that we were fain to keep still on the further side merely
for heat.[4]   We came to the chequer at Charing-cross, where

1. Thomas Scott and Luke Robinson were the two M.P.'s sent to
attend Monck in his march towards
London, and it was they who had
introduced him to the House on the
6th.   They were now sent by Parliament with a conciliatory message.
Ludlow (who had the news from
Scott himself) says (ii. 222) that
Monck, after at first refusing to see
them, gave them a frigid reception.
2. The official minute of the
meeting simply records the aldermen's agreement to provide quarters
in inns and other public houses:
LRO, Repert. 67, f.43r.   Meantime.

the soldiers were drawn up in
Finsbury Fields, waiting.
3. Thomas Benson, vintner, kept
the Bull's Head Tavern on the n.
side of Cheapside, west of Lawrence
Lane.   There Monck spent the early
evening writing letters and arranging
billets for his men: HMC, *Leyborne-Popham*, p. 219; T. Gumble,
Life of Gen. Monck (1671), p. 255.
4. This night's celebrations passed
into history as the 'Burning of the
Rump'.   Cf. Aubrey, ii. 76; engraving in Butler's *Hudibras* (1710
ed.), pt 3, opp. p. 146.

Chetwind wrote a letter and I gave him an account of what I had writ for him to write. Thence home and sent my letter to the post-house in London, and my wife and I (after Mr. Hunt was gone whom I found waiting for me at my house) went out again to show her the fires; and after walking as far as the Exchange, we returned and to bed.

12. In the morning, it being Lords day, Mr. Pierce came to me to enquire how things go. We drank our morning draught together and thence to White-hall, where Dr. Homes[1] preached; but I stayed not to hear; but walking in the court, I heard that Sir Arth. Haslerig was newly gone into the City to Monke[2] and that Monkes wife removed from White-hall last night. Home again, where at noon came according to my invitation my Cosen Tho. Pepys and his partener,[3] came and dined with me; but before dinner we went and took a walk round the parke, it being a most pleasant day as ever I saw. After dinner we three went into London together, where I heard that Monke had been at Paul's in the morning[4] and the people had shouted much at his coming out of the church. In the afternoon he was at a church in Broad-street, whereabout he doth lodge.[a5] But not knowing how to see him, we went and walked half an hour in Moore-fields, which was full of people, it being so fine a day. Here I took leave of them, and so to Pauls; where I met with Mr. Kirtons apprentice, the crooked fellow, and walked up and down with him two hours, sometimes in the street looking for a tavern to drink at; but not

a repl. 'live'

1. Dr Nathaniel Holmes, Independent, preacher to the Council.

2. The Council of State was trying to persuade Monck to return to Westminster; no doubt Hesilrige's visit had this purpose: cf. John Price, *Mystery and method of his Majesty's happy restauration* (1680), p. 108. For an exchange of letters between the two men on this day, see *Clarke Papers* (ed. C. H. Firth), iv. 260–1; *Clar. State Papers* (1767–86), iii. 678; Ludlow, ii. 224, n. 1. Hesilrige was commonly thought to have more influence than anyone else with Monck: Clarendon, *Hist.*, vi. 192.

3. For Thomas Pepys, see above, p. 9, n. 4. The partner has not been identified.

4. With the Lord Mayor and Corporation.

5. He lodged at the Glasshouse, Broad St; the church was probably St Peter-le-Poer. This entry is more accurate than the account of Monck's movements given in the government newspapers: *Merc. Pol.* and *Pub. Intell.*, 16 February.

finding any open, we darst not knock[1] – other times in the
churchyard, where he told me that he had seen the letter printed.[2]
Hence to Mrs. Turner's, where I found my wife, Mr. Edw: Pepys,
and Roger[3] and Mr. Armiger being there, to whom I gave as
good an account of things as I could. And so to my father's,
where Ch. Glascocke was overjoyed to see how things are now;
who told me how the boys had last night broke Barebones
windows.[4] Hence home; and being near home, we missed our
maid and was at a great loss and went back a great way to find her;
but when we could not see her, we went homewards and found
her there, got before us, which we wondered at greatly. So to
bed, where my wife and I had some high words upon my telling
her that I would fling the dog which her brother gave her out at
the window if he pissed the house any more.

13. To my office till noon; thence home to dinner, my mouth
being very bad of the Canker and my left leg beginning to be sore
again. After dinner, I went to see Mrs. Jem, and in the way met
with Catau[5] on foot in the street and talked with her a little. So
home and took my wife to my father's. In my way I went to
Playfords; and for two books that I had and 6s. 6d to boot, I had
my great book of songs, which he sells always for 14s.[6] At my
father's I stayed a while, while my mother sent her maid Besse
to Cheapside for some herbs to make a water for my mouth.
Then I went to see Mr. Cumberland; and after a little stay with
him, I returned and took my wife home. Where, after supper,
to bed.

This day, Monke was invited to White-hall to dinner by my

1. Alehouse-keepers were forbidden, by the terms of their licences,
to serve drink during the hours of
divine service. But see below, p.
68. Joshua Kirton was a bookseller.

2. Monck's letter to parliament of
the day before. The copy in the
Thomason tracts in the BM is dated
13 February: BM, E 1015/17.

3. Roger Pepys; he and the others
mentioned here were relatives of the
diarist and of Mrs Turner.

4. Glascocke was a distant relative

of Pepys and lived, like Barebone,
in Fleet St. The incident has been
wrongly ascribed to the evening of
the 9th: Louise F. Brown, *Polit.
activities of Baptists* etc., p. 196.

5. See above, p. 16, n. 6.

6. John Playford almost mono-
polised the publishing of music at
this time. His shop was in the Inner
Temple. The 'great book of songs'
was possibly Playford's *Select ayres and
dialogues* (1659). (E).

Lord; not seeming willing, he would not come.[1]   I went to Mr.
Fage from my father's, who had been this afternoon with Monke,
who doth promise to live and die with the City and for the
honour of the City.[2]   And indeed, the City is very open-handed
to the soldiers, that they are most of them drunk all day, and have
money given them.   He did give me something for my mouth,
which I did use this night.

14.   Called out in the morning by Mr. Moore (whose voice
my wife hearing in my dressing-chamber with me, she got herself
ready and came down and challenged him for her Valentine, this
being that day);[3] to Westminster-hall, there being many new
Remonstrances and Declaracions from many county to Monke
and the City, and one coming from the North from Sir T. Fairfax.[4]
Hence I took him to the Swan and gave him his morning draught.
So to my office, where Mr. Hill of Worcestershire*a* came to see
me and my partener[5] at our office, with whom we went to

a repl. 'Shrops'-

1. Monck was anxious not to
associate himself too closely with the
Council of State in this crisis: cf.
CSPD 1659–60, pp. 358–9, 360; *Clarke
Papers* (ed. Firth), iv. 261–3.
2. A special court of aldermen,
with Monck in attendance, had been
held at Drapers' Hall: LRO, Repert.
67, f.43r. Possibly Monck's reply to
the Council of State was drawn up
after this meeting.
3. A common convention was that
women chose the first man they saw.
4. In these addresses – often the
product of secret royalist organisation – the country was protesting
against the imposition of taxes by an
unrepresentative parliament. Norfolk, e.g., had recently petitioned both
the Rump and Monck, and on this
day manifestoes from Oxfordshire
and Warwickshire appeared in print:
BM, 190 g. 13/148; 669 f.23/35, 45.

The 'one coming from the North' was
addressed to Monck from Yorkshire,
and was published both in York and
in London.   It declared against taxes
and demanded either the admission
of the secluded members or a free
parliament: BM, 669 f.23/48; cf.
CSPD 1659–60, p. 356.   In another
(spurious) version (13 February;
BM, 669 f.23/47) an armed rising
was threatened by the 'lords, knights,
esquires' *et al.* of the county and city
of York.   Both versions were acquired by Thomason on the 16th.
It is difficult to be sure which version
Pepys refers to: Fairfax's name
appears at the head of the signatories
to the pacific one, and in the title of
the militant one.   Despite his Scottish barony, Fairfax was still often
called 'Sir Thomas'.
5. John Hawley.

Wills to drink. At noon I went home and so to Mr. Crews; but they had dined and so I went to see Mrs. Jem, where I stayed a while; and home again, where I stayed an hour or two ⟨at my lute⟩, and so forth to Westminster-hall, where I heard that the Parliament hath now changed the oath so much talked to a promise;[1] and that among other Qualificacion for the members that are to be chosen, one is that no man, nor the son of any man, that hath been in arms during the life of the father shall be capable of being chosen to sit in Parliament.[2] To Wills, where like a fool I stayed and lost 6d at cards. So home and wrote a letter to my Lord by the post; and so after supper to bed.

This day, by an order of the House, Sir H. Vane was sent out of town to his house in Lincolnshire.[3]

15. Called up in the morning by Captain Holland – and Captain Cuttance, and with them to Harpers; thence to my office; thence with Mr. Hill of Worcester to Wills, where I gave him a letter to Nan Pepys, and some merry pamphlets against the Rump to carry to her into the country.[4] So to Mr. Crews; where the dining room being full, Mr. Walgrave and I dined below in the buttery by ourselfs, upon a good dish of buttered salmon. Thence to Hering the merchant about my Lord's Worcester money,[5] and back to Pauls churchyard, where I stayed reading in Fullers history of the Church of England[6] an

1. The oath of abjuration was to be replaced by a simple declaration of allegiance to the commonwealth. The bill was now at report stage, and passed on the 16th. *CJ*, vii. 842-3, 845.

2. This refers to another bill, passed on the 18th. All who had fought against parliament were to be excluded, and their sons also during their fathers' life-times; but an exception was made for sons who had borne arms for parliament: ib., p. 842.

3. At Belleau: ib., p. 841.

4. Anne Pepys was a cousin, now married to —— Hall of Worcestershire. For the many 'merry pamphlets' against the Rump, see the lists in

G. K. Fortescue, *Cat. Thomason tracts*, ii. 671; and Wing, R 2270-9. An order forbidding their publication only stimulated demand.

5. No Worcester property of Mountagu's has been traced; possibly this was a loan secured on excise revenue. As a Treasury commissioner, he had been in charge of some Worcestershire revenues: Carte 73, f.38*v*. See below, p. 80 & n. 3.

6. Thomas Fuller, *The church-history of Britain*; first published 1655; the liveliest of all church histories. It became one of Pepys's favourite books, especially for Sunday reading. See below, p. 261, n. 3.

hour or two; and so to my father's, where Mr. Hill came to me and I gave him direction what to do at Worcester about the money. Thence to my Lady Wrights and gave her a letter from my*ᵃ* Lord privately. So to Mrs. Jem and sat with her, who dined at Mr. Crews today and told me that there was at her coming away at least 40 gentlemen (I suppose members that were secluded, for Mr. Walgrave told me that there was about 30 met there the last night) came dropping in one after another thither.[1] Hence home and wrote into the country against tomorrow by the carrier; and so to bed.

At my father's I heard how my cousin Kate Joyce had a fall yesterday from her horse and had some hurt thereby.[2]

No news today, but all quiet to see what the Parliament will do about the issuing of the writs tomorrow for filling up of the House according to Monkes desire.

16. In the morning at my lute. Then came Shaw and Hawly, and I gave them their morning draught at my house. So to my office, where I writ by the carrier to my Lord; and sealed my letter at Wills and gave it old East to carry it to the carrier's – and to take up a box of China oranges and two little barrels of Scallops at my house, which Captain Cuttance sent to me for my Lord. Here I met with Osborne and with Shaw and Spicer, and then we went to the Sun tavern in expectation of a dinner, where we had sent us only two trencherfuls of meat, at which we were very merry, while in came Mr. Wade and his friend Captain Moyse (who told us of his hopes to get an estate merely for his name-sake)[3]; and here we stayed till 7 at night, I winning a Quart of sack of Shaw that one trencherful that was sent us was all lamb, and he that it was veale. I, by having but 3*d* in my pocket, made

a 'my' repeated

---

1. On the evening of the 14th Monck had held a conference at Drapers' Hall attended by secluded and sitting members: *Clarke Papers* (ed. Firth), iv. 264. John Crew was a leader of the secluded members.

2. She suffered from fits.

3. Capt. Moyse was Richard Moyses (hence the wordplay on Moses and the Promised Land); an army officer, regimental agent and farmer of recusants' estates.

shift to spend no more; whereas if I had had more I had spent more, as the rest did.   So that I see it is an advantage to a man to carry little in his pocket.

Home; and after supper and a little at my lute, I went to bed.

17.   In the morning, Tom, that was my Lord's foot-boy, came to see me and had 10s. of me of the money of his which I have to keep of his.   So that now I have but 35s more of his.   Then came Mr. Hill the instrument-maker, and I consulted with him about the altering of my lute and my viall.   After him, I went into my study and made up my accounts, and find that I am about 40l beforehand in the world.   And that is all.   So to my office and from thence brought Mr. Hawly home with me to dinner; and afterdinner wrote a letter to Mr. Downing about his business – and gave it Hawly; and so I went to Mr. Gunings to his weekly fast; and after sermon, meeting there with Mr. L'impertinent,[1] we went and walked in the park till it was dark.   I played on my pipe at the Echo,[2] and then drank a cup of ale at Jacob's.   So to Westminster-hall, and he with me; where I heard that some of the members of the House was gone to meet with some of the secluded members and Generall Monke in the City.[3]   Hence we went to White-hall, thinking to hear more news.   Where I met with Mr. Hunt, who told me how Monke had sent for all his goods that he had here into the City.   And yet again, he told me that some of the members of the House had this day laid in firing into their lodgings at White-hall for a good while.   So that we are at a great stand to think what will become of things, whether Monke will stand to the Parliament or no.   Hence, Monsieur Limpertinent and I to Harpers and there drank a cup or two to the King, and to his fair sister Frances[4] good health, of whom we had much discourse of her not being much the worse for the

1. (? Daniel) Butler; see above, p. 22 & n. 1.
2. Pepys's pipe was his flageolet (he did not start learning the recorder until 1668); the Echo was a place (? a grotto: cf. below, pp. 70, 147). (E).
3. This was the second of a series of meetings between these parties –

the first having been held on the 14th – which led to the re-admission of the secluded members on 21 February.   See Godfrey Davies, *Restoration*, pp. 287–8.
4. Frances Butler (Boteler): to Pepys the 'greatest beauty' of all the ladies he knew: below, ii. 125.

small-pox which she had this last summer. So home and to bed. ⟨This day we were invited to my uncle Fenners wedding feast, but went not, this being the 27th year.⟩*a*

———

18. A great while at my Viall and voice, learning to sing *Fly boy, fly boy* without book.[1] So to my office, where little to do. In the Hall I met with Mr. Eglin[2] and one Looker, a famous gardiner, servant to my Lord Salsbury; and among other things, the gardiner told a strange passage in good earnest: how formerly Mr. Eglin did in his company put his finger, which being sore had a black case over it, into a woman's belly, he named her Nan (which I guess who it is), and left his case within her; which Mr. Eglin blushed but did not deny it. Which truly I was sorry to hear and did think of it a good while afterward. Home to dinner; and then went to my Lord's lodgings to my turret there, and took away most of my books and sent them home by my maid. Hither came Captain Holland to me, who took me to the Half-Moone tavern and Mr. Southorne, Blackburnes clerk. Thence he took me to the Mitre in Fleet-street, where we heard (in a room over the music-room) very plainly through the ceiling. Here we parted, and I to Mr. Wottons[3] and with him to an alehouse and drank; where he told me a great many stories of comedies which he had formerly seen acted and the names of the principal actors, and gave me a very good account of it. Hence to White-hall, where I met with Luellin and at the Clerkes chamber wrote a letter to my Lord. So home and to bed. This day, two soldiers were hanged in the Strand for their late mutiny at Somerset-house.[4]

———

19. *Lords=day.*
Early in the morning, I set my books that I brought home yesterday up in order in my study. Thence, forth to Mr. Harpers to drink a draught of purle; whither by appointment

a addition crowded in between entries at end of line

———

1. Music by Simon Ives; source of words untraced. Printed in John Playford, *Select ayres and dialogues* (1659), p. 90. (E).

2. Samuel Edlin, who had entered Magdalene College in 1653; elected a fellow, 25 April 1660; deacon and priest, 1662.

3. Shoemaker.

4. See above, p. 38 & n. 1; *Pub. Intell.*, 20 February, p. 1019; Rugge, i, f.61r.

Monsieur L'impertinent who did intend too, upon my desire, to go along with me to St. Bartholomew's to hear one Mr. Sparkes; but it raining very hard, we went to Mr. Gunings and heard an excellent sermon. And speaking of the character that the Scripture gave of Ann the mother of the blessed Virgin, he did there speak largely in commendation of Widowhood, and not as we do to marry two or three wifes or husbands, one after another.[1] Here I met with Mr. Moore and went home with him to dinner, where he told me the discourse that happened between the secluded members and the members of the House before Monke last Friday. How the secluded said that they did not entend by coming in to express revenge upon these men, but only to meet and dissolve[a] themselfs, and only to issue writs for a free Parliament.[2]

He told me how Haslerigg was afraid to have the candle carried before him, for fear that the people seeing him should do him hurt. And that he is afeared to appear in the City. That there is great likelihood that the secluded members will come in, and so Mr. Crew and my Lord are likely to be great men, at which I was very glad.

After dinner there was many secluded members come in to Mr. Crew; which, it being the Lord's day, did make Mr. Moore believe that there was something extraordinary in the business.

Hence home and brought my wife to Mr. Messums to hear him. And indeed he made a very good sermon; but only, too eloquent for a pulpit. Here Mr. Limpertinent helped me to a seat. After sermon, to my father's and fell in discourse concerning our going to Cambrige the next week with my Brother John.

To Mrs. Turner, where her Brother, Mr. Edwd. Pepys, was there, and I sat a great while talking of public business of the times with him. So to supper to my father's, all supper talking of Johns going to Cambrige.

So home[b] and it raining, my wife got my mother's frieze-

a written over symbol now illegible   *b* repl. 'home'

---

1. Cf. Luke, ii. 25+. Anna was the holy woman (seven years married, 84 years a widow) who received the infant Jesus at the Temple, and who has been traditionally identified as the mother of the Virgin.

2. Presumably Moore got his news from John Crew, who attended the meeting. The conference failed to reach agreement.

mantle and my Brother Johns hat; and so we went all along home. And to bed.

20. In the morning at my lute. Then to my office, where my partener and I made even our balance. Took him home to dinner with me, where my Brother John came to dine with me. After dinner I took him to my study at home and at my Lord's, and gave him some books and other things against his going to Cambrige. After he was gone, I went forth to Westminster-hall, where I met with Chetwind, Simons and Gregory; and with them to Marshes at White-hall to drink, and stayed there a pretty while reading a pamphlet, well-writ and directed to Generall Monke in praise of the form of Monarchy which was settled here before the Warrs.[1]

They told me how that Speaker Lenthall doth refuse to sign the writs for choice of new members in the place of the excluded; and by that means the writs would not go out today.[2] In the evening Simons and I to the Coffee Clubb,[3] where nothing to do. Only, I heard Mr. Harrington and my Lord of Dorsett and another lord talking of getting another place, as the Cockpitt; and they did believe it would come to something. After a small debate upon the Question whether learned or unlearned subjects are the best, the club broke off very poorly, and I do not think they will meet any more.[4] Hence with Vines &c to Wills; and after a pot or two, home; and so to bed.

21.[a] In the morning, going out, I saw many soldiers going toward Westminster; and was tol[d] that they were going to admit the secluded members again. So I to Westminster-hall, and in Chancery-row I saw about 20 of them, who had been at

a small filled-in circle in upper margin

---

1. Probably [?Roger L'Estrange], *A plea for limited monarchy, as it was established in this nation, before the late war. In an humble addresse to his Excellency, General Monck.*

2. He had to sign, not the writs, but the warrant directing the Commissioners of the Great Seal to issue them. He refused on the ground that the

secluded members might have cause for action against him. The House thereupon empowered the Clerk to act in his stead: *Merc. Pol.*, 23 February, pp. 1114–17; Ludlow, ii. 233.

3. See above, p. 13 & n. 3.

4. No later meeting is known: Aubrey, i. 291.

White-hall with generall Monke, who came thither this morning and made a speech to them and recommended to them a commonwealth, and against Ch. Stuart.[1] They came to the House and went in one after another, and at last the Speaker came. But it is very strange that this could be carried so private, that the other members of the House heard nothing of all this till they found them in the House, insomuch that the soldiers that stood there to let in the secluded members, they took for such as they had ordered to stand there to hinder their coming in.[2] Mr. Prin came with an old basket-hilt sword on, and had a great many great shouts upon his going into the hall.[3] They sat till noon, and at their coming out Mr. Crew saw me and bid me come to his house; which I did, and he would have me dine with him, which I did, and he very joyful; told me that the House had made Generall Monke generall of all the forces in England, Scotland, and Ireland. And that upon Monkes desire, for the service that Lawson had lately done in pulling down the Committee of Safety, he had the command of the Sea for the time being.[4] He advised me to send for my Lord forthwith, and told me that there is no Question but, if he will, he may now be imployed again; and that the House doth entend to do nothing more then to issue writs and to settle a foundation for a free parliament. After

1. Monck read a statement defining the terms on which the secluded members were about to be restored to their places. They were to arrange for a new parliament to meet on 20 April. *The speech and declaration of . . . Monck delivered at Whitehall . . . Feb. 21. 1659 . . .* (1659/60); reprinted several times: e.g. *Somers Tracts* (ed. Scott), vi. 551+.

2. Ludlow (ii. 235) asserts that Monck had assured the Council of State on the night of 20 February that no such attempt would be made by the secluded members, and undertook to double the guard to satisfy them. On the other hand, Monck had already declared his intention at meetings held on 17 and 20 February which some Rumpers had attended (cf.

above, p. 60). Possibly a few of the Rumpers were in fact taken by surprise: the evidence is discussed in *CSPVen. 1659–61*, p. xxiii. There were 18 Rumpers to 73 secluded members at the meeting of 21 February: R. Wodrow, *Hist. sufferings Church of Scotland* (1828–30), i. 5–6.

3. William Prynne, lawyer and pamphleteer, a principal spokesman for the secluded members, had led two previous attempts to gain admittance. Aubrey remarks (ii. 175) that Prynne's sword, too long for ceremonial wear in a procession, ran between Sir William Waller's 'short legges, and threw him downe, which caused laughter'.

4. *CJ*, vii. 847.

dinner I back to Westminster-hall with him in his coach.*a*   Here
I met with Mr. Lock and Pursell, Maisters of Musique;[1] and with
them to the Coffee-house into a room next the Water by ourselfs;
where we spent an hour or two till Captain Taylor came to us,
who told us that the House had voted the gates of the City to be
made up again and the members of the City that are in prison to
be let at liberty; and that Sir G. Booth's case be brought into the
House tomorrow.[2]

Here we had variety of brave Italian and Spanish songs and a
Canon for 8 *Voc:*, which Mr. Lock had newly made on these
words: *Domine salvum fac Regem*, an admirable thing.[3]

Here also, Captain Taylor began a discourse of something that
he hath lately writ about Gavelkinde in answer to one that hath
writ a piece upon the same subject.[4]   And indeed, discovered a
great deal of study in antiquity in his discourse.   Here, out of the
window it was a most pleasant sight to see the City from [one] end
to the other with a glory about it, so high was the light of the
Bonefires and so thick round the City, and the bells rang everywhere.   Hence home and wrote to my Lord; afterward came
down and found Mr. Hunt (troubled at this change)[5] and Mr.
Spong, who stayed late with me, singing of a song or two, and
so parted.   My wife not very well, went to bed before.

This morning I met in the hall with Mr. Fuller of Christ's.
And told him of my design to go to Cambrige, and whether.[6]
He told me very freely the temper of Mr. Widdrington; how he
did oppose all the fellows in the college, and that there was a great

a blot in left-hand margin

---

1. Matthew Locke the composer
(to be distinguished from Monck's
secretary of the same name), and
either Thomas or the elder Henry
Purcell, uncle and father respectively
of the famous Purcell. (E).

2. *CJ*, vii. 847, 848. Sir George
Booth (M.P. for Cheshire) had led
the Presbyterian-Royalist rising of
August 1659, and was now a prisoner
in the Tower. He was released on
the 22nd. Silas Taylor was an
antiquary and musician. His patron

Edward Harley, was one of the most
prominent of the secluded members.

3. Untraced. (E).

4. Silas Taylor's *History of gavelkind* (1663) was written in answer to
William Somner's *A treatise of gavelkind* (1660). For gavelkind, see
below, ii. 17 & n. 1.

5. His wife was a relative of
Cromwell, and he seems to have
feared for his post in the Excise.

6. I.e. whither; to which college.

distance between him and the rest;[1] at which I was very sorry, for that he told me he feared it would be little to my Brothers advantage to be his pupil.

22. In the morning, entended to have gone to Mr. Crews to borrow some money; but it raining, I forbore and went to my Lord's lodging and look that all things were well there. Then home and sang a song to my vial; so to my office and to Wills, where Mr. Pierce found me out and told me that he would go with me to Cambridge, where Collonell Ayres's Regiment, to which he is surgeon, lieth. Walking in the hall, I saw Major-Generall Brown, who hath a long time been banished by the Rump; but now, with his beard overgrown, he comes abroad and sat in the House.[2]

To my father's to dinner, where nothing but a small dish of powdered beef and a dish of carrots, they being all busy to get things ready for my Brother John to go tomorrow.

After dinner, my wife staying there, I went to Mr. Crews and got 5*l* of Mr. Andrews; and so to Mrs. Jemim., who now hath her instrument about her neck; and endeed, is infinitely altered and holds her head upright.[3] I paid her maid 40*s*. of the money that I have received of Mr. Andrews.

Hence home to my study, where I only writ thus much of this day's passages to this ∴ and so out again. To White-hall, where I met with Will Simons and Mr. Mabbott at marshes, who

1. Cf. above, p. 26. Ralph Widdrington had quarrelled with his colleagues, particularly with the liberal theologians (the Latitude-men, or Cambridge Platonists) among them. Relying on his political influence (his brother was Sir Thomas Widdrington, late Speaker, now First Commissioner of the Great Seal), he had in 1659 tried to displace Ralph Cudworth from the mastership. He was ejected from his fellowship in 1661-2, but was restored on appeal to the Privy Council, and had his revenge by residing for the rest of his life.

2. Ald. and Maj.-Gen. Richard Browne, probably the most important of the city Presbyterians, had been proclaimed against for his royalism in June 1659, and had lain in hiding in the Stationers' Hall in London since Booth's rising of that summer: *CSPD 1659-60*, p. 52; James Heath, *Brief Chronicle* (1663), p. 753. The proclamation was annulled on this day and he was re-admitted to the House: *CJ*, vii. 848. He became Lord Mayor in October 1660.

3. See above, p. 36.

told me how the House had this day voted that the gates of the
City should be set up at the cost of the State. And that Major-
Generall Brown's being proclaimed a traitor be made void, and
several other things of that nature.[1]

Home for my lantern and so to my father's, where I directed
John what books to put [up] for Cambrige.

After that to supper, where my Uncle Fenner and my Aunt.
The. Turner and Joyce at a brave leg of veal roasted, and were
very merry against John going to Cambrige. I observed this
day how abominably Barebones windows are broke again last
night.[2] At past 9 a-clock my wife and I went home.

23. *Thursday.* My birthday: now 27 years.

A pretty fair morning; I rose and after writing a while in my
study, I went forth. To my office, where I told Mr. Hawly of
my thoughts to go out of town tomorrow. Hither Mr. Fuller
comes to me and my Uncle Thomas too; whence I took them to
drink, and so put off my uncle. So with Mr. Fuller home to my
house, where he dined with me; and he told my wife and I a great
many stories of his adversities since these troubles, in being forced
to travel in the Catholique countries, &c; he showed me his bills,
but I had not money to pay him.[3] We parted, and I to White-
hall, where I was to see my horse which Mr. Garthwayt lend me
tomorrow. So home, where Mr. Pierce comes to me about
appointing time and place where and when to meet tomorrow.
So to Westminster-hall, where after the House rose, I met with
Mr. Crew, who told me that my Lord was chosen by 73 voices to
be one of the Council of State. Mr. Pierpoint had the most, 101,
and himself next, 100.[4] He brought me in the coach home,

1. *CJ*, vii. 848.
2. He lived in Fleet St. Cf.
above, p. 54 & n. 4.
3. William Fuller (a friend of
Pepys, and now a schoolmaster at
Twickenham) had been expelled
from his studentship at Christ Church,
Oxford, during the revolution; his
sufferings were alluded to later when
he was rewarded with an Irish

deanery: Wood, *Ath. Oxon.* (ed.
Bliss), iv. 850. The bills were for the
schooling of Edward, Mountagu's
son.
4. The Journal of the House does
not give these figures, but establishes
that 114 M.P.'s were present and
voting: *CJ*, vii. 859. Monck was
chosen unanimously, the rest by
ballot.

he and Mr. Anslow[1] being in it.   I back to the Hall, and at Mrs.
Michalls shop stood talking a great while with her and my Chaplain, Mrs. Mumford,[2] and drank a pot or two of ale on a wager
that Mr. Prin is not of the Council.[3]   Home, and writ to my
Lord the news of the choice of the Council by the post; and so to
bed.

24. I rose very early; and taking horse at Scotland-yard at
Mr. Garthwayts stable, I rode to Mr. Pierces – who rose; and in
a Quarter of an hour, leaving his wife in bed (with whom Mr.
Lucy methought was very free as she lay in bed), we both
mounted and so set forth about 7 of the clock, the day and the
way very foul. About Ware we overtook Mr. Blayton,
brother-in-law to Dick Vines, who went thenceforward with us;
and at Puckrige we baited. Where we had a loin of mutton
fried and were very merry; but the way exceeding bad from
Ware thither. Then up again and as far as Foulmer, within six
mile of Cambrige, my mare being almost tired: here we lay at
the Chequer. Playing at cards till supper, which was a breast of
veal roasted. I lay with Mr. Pierce, who we left here the next
morning upon his going to Hinchingbrooke to speak with my
《25》 Lord before his going to London; and we two came to
Cambrige by 8 a-clock in the morning, to the Faulcon
in the Petty Cury.[4] Where we found my father and brother very
well. After dressing myself, about 10 a-clock, my father, brother
and I to Mr. Widdrington at Christ's College, who received us
very civilly and caused my brother to be admitted,[5] while my
father, he and I sat talking. After that done, we take leave. My
father and brother went to visit some friends, Pepys's, scholars in

1. Arthur Annesley, later 1st Earl
of Anglesey, himself elected this day
to the Council.

2. A shopkeeper. 'Chaplain' is
probably a joke-name (chap-lain=
sell-wool).   At 18 March 1666 Pepys
calls another of the Hall shopkeepers
his 'second wife'.

3. He was one of the committee
appointed to bring in the bill for
electing the Council, but was not
himself elected.

4. On the s. side of Petty Cury, on
the site now partly marked by Falcon
Yard; a large inn – probably the best
in Cambridge: *Cambridge . . . etched
by R. Farren*, p. 3, pl. vi; R. Comm.
Hist. Mon., *City of Cambridge*, ii. 329.

5. Ralph Widdrington was his
tutor. John Pepys jun. (as a sizar
paying reduced charges) now paid a
fee of 5s.: Christ's Coll., Admission
Bk 1622–75, f. 136v. He became a
scholar later: below, ii, 44.

Cambrige,[1] while I went to Magdalen College to Mr. Hill, with whom I found Mr. Zanchy, Burton, and Hollins, and was exceeding civilly received by them;[2] I took leave, on promise to sup with them, and to my Inn again, where I dined with some others that were there at an ordinary. After dinner, my brother to the college and my father and I to my Cosen Angiers to see them; where Mr. Fairbrother came to us. Here we sat a while talking. My father, he went to look after his things at the Carriers and my brother's chamber, while Mr. Fairbrother, my Cosen Angier and Mr. Zanchy, who I met at Mr. Mortons shop (where I bought *Elenchus Motuum*,[3] having given my former to Mr. Downing when he was here), to the Three tuns,[4] where we drank pretty hard and many healths to the King &c till it begin to be darkish; then we broke[a] up and I and Mr. Zanchy went to Magdalen College, where a very handsome supper at Mr. Hills chamber, I suppose upon a club among them; where in their discourse I could find that there was nothing at all left of the old preciseness in their discourse, specially on Saturday nights.[5] And Mr. Zanch[y] told me that there was no such thing nowadays among them at any time. After supper and some discourse, then to my Inn, where I found my father in his Chamber; and after some discourse and he well satisfied with this day's work, we went to bed, my brother lying with me, his things not being come by the carrier that he could not lie in the college.

a repl. 'brol'

---

1. Possibly Robert Pepys (of Cambridgeshire), Fellow of Queens' 1659–61; and Robert Pepys (son of Richard Pepys, mercer, of London), admitted pensioner of Christ's, June 1659.

2. All were Fellows of Magdalene, the college at which Pepys had been an undergraduate, 1651–4.

3. By George Bate, a defence (in Latin) of Charles I; first published in Edinburgh, 1650. PL 1055 is a copy of the 1661 reprint. In 1663 Bate published a second part which Pepys also bought: below, iv. 42 & n. 1. The bookshop was probably William Morden's: cf. PL 884, a book Pepys bought there in 1654.

4. On Market Hill, by St Edward's Passage; closed down in 1790. C. H. Cooper, *Memorials of Cambridge*, iii. 285; R. Comm. Hist. Mon., *City of Cambridge*, ii. 327.

5. It was in Hill's chamber on Friday 21 October 1653, in the presence of all the fellows then resident, that Pepys and a companion, Hind, had been solemnly admonished by Wood and Hill for having been 'scandalously overseene in drink the night before': Magd. Coll., Reg. ii, f.3*a*.

26. *Sunday*. My brother went to the college to Chappell.

My father and I went out in the morning and walk out in the fields behind King's College and in King's College chapel yard; and there we met with Mr. Fayrbrother. Who took us to Butolphes Church, where we heard Mr. Nicholas of Queen's College (who I knew in my time to be Tripos with great applause) upon this text: "For thy commandments are broad."[1]   Thence my father and I to Mr. Widdrington's chamber to dinner, where he used us very courteously again and had two fellow-commoners at table with him, and Mr. Pepper, a fellow of the college. After dinner, while we sat talking by the fire, Mr. Pierces man, to tell me that his master was come to town; so my father and I took leave and found Mr. Pierce at our Inn, who told us that he had lost his Journy, for my Lord was gone from Hinchingbrooke to London on Thursday last, at which I was a little put to a stand.   So after a cup of drink, I went to Magdalen College to get the Certificate of the college for my Brother's entrance there, that he might save his year.[2]   I met with Mr. Burton in the Court, who took me to[a] Mr. Pechells chamber, where he was and Mr. Zanchy; by and by, Mr. Pechell and Sanch[y] and I went out. Pechell to church – Sanch[y] and I to the Rose tavern, where we sat and drank till sermon done; and then Mr. Pechell came to us and we three sat drinking the King's and his whole family's health till it begin to be dark.   Then we parted; Sanch[y] and I went to my lodging, where we found my father and Mr. Pierce at the door, and I took them both and Mr. Blayton to the Rose tavern[3] and there gave them a quart or two of wine, not telling them that we

.*a*   MS. 'took me sent me to'

---

1. A loose recollection of Ps. cxix. 96. The Tripos was a bachelor of arts who made a comic disputation with the candidates for bachelors' degrees; on this occasion, he was Daniel Nichols, Fellow of Queens'.

2. John, admitted to Magdalene in June 1659, had transferred to Christ's before taking up residence. He would be allowed to count the term as part of his period of residence:

D. A. Winstanley, *Unreformed Cambridge*, p. 42.

3. This fronted on Market Hill, had its carriage entrance in Trinity St, and was next door to the Angel. It ceased to be an inn c. 1814. Nothing remains of its buildings, but the modern Rose Crescent marks the site of its yard and approaches. J. W. Clark and A. Gray, *Old plans . . . of Cambridge*, pl. vi; R. Comm. Hist. Mon., *City of Cambridge*, ii. 330.

had been there before.   After that we broke up; and my father, Mr. Zanch[y] and I to my Cosen Angiers to supper, where I caused two bottles of wine to be carried from the Rose tavern; but was drank up, and I had not the wit to let them know at table that it was I that paid for them, and so I lost my thanks for them.   After supper, Mr. Fayrbrother, who supped there with us, took me into a room by himself and showed me a pitiful copy of verses upon Mr. Prinn, which he esteemed very good and desired that I would get them given to Mr. Prin, in hopes that he would get him some place for it;[1] which I said I would do, but did laugh in my sleeve to think of his folly, though indeed a man that hath alway expressed great civility to me.   After that, we sat down and talked; I took leave of all my friends and so to my Inn.   Where, after I had wrote a note and enclosed the*a* certificate to Mr. Widdrington, I bade good-night to my father; and John went to bed but I stayed up a little while, playing the fool with the lass of the house at the door of the chamber; and so to bed.

27.   Up by 4 a–clock, and after I was ready, took my leave of my father, whom I left in bed; and the same of my Brother John to whom I gave 10s.   Mr. Blayton and I took horse and straight to Saffron Walden, where at the White Hart[2] we set up our horses and told the maister of the house to shew us Audly end house;[3] who took us on foot through the park and so to the house, where the housekeeper showed us all the house; in which the stateliness of the ceilings, chimney-pieces, and form of the

a   repl. 'Mr.'

---

1. The verses (presumably in MS.) have perished, and nothing attributable to their author survives in print. He was William Fairbrother, lawyer, Fellow of King's.

2. In King St; the town's most popular inn; now (1965) the Hoops. The innkeeper in 1656 was John Potter.   *Trans. Essex Arch. Soc.* (n.s.) 14/14.

3. Built by the 1st Earl of Suffolk in James I's reign; at this time the residence of James Howard, 3rd Earl;

sold to the King in 1669.   Contemporary descriptions by travellers remark on its size (it was reputedly the largest private house in England), on its mantelpieces and its ceilings.   See Evelyn, 1 September 1654; Magalotti, pp. 203+ [c. 1669]; R. Thoresby, *Diary* (ed. Hunter, 1830), i. 65 [1680]; HMC, *Rep.*, 13/2/264 [1681]; H. Winstanley, 'Plans of Audley End' (1688; BM, Maps, 25 c. 14); C. Fiennes, *Journeys* (ed. Morris), pp. 63–4 [1697].

whole was exceedingly worth seeing. He took us into the cellar, where we drank most admirable drink, a health to the King. Here I played on my Flagelette, there being an excellent Echo.[1] He showed us excellent pictures; two especially, those of the four Evangelistes and Henry 8th.[2] After that, I gave the man 2s for his trouble and went back again. In our going, my landlord carried us through a very old Hospital or Almeshouse, where 40 poor people was maintained;[3] a very old foundation, and over the chimney in the mantelpiece was an Inscripcion in brass: *Orate pro animâ Thomæ Bird* &c.;[4] and the poor's box also was in the same chimney-piece, with an Iron door and locks to it, into which I put sixpens: they brought me a draught of their drink in a brown bowl, tipped with silver, which I drank of; and at the bottom was a picture of the Virgen and the child in her arms, done in silver.[5] So we went to our Inn, and after eating of something and kissed the daughter of the house, she being very pretty, we took leave; and so that night, the road pretty good but the weather rainy, to Eping. Where we sat and played a game at draughts; and after supper and some merry talk with a plain bold maid of the house, we went to bed.

28. Up in the morning, and had some red Herrings to our breakfast while my boot-heel was a-mending; by the same token, the boy left the hole as big as it was before. Then to horse and for London through the Forrest, where we found the way good, but only in one path; which we kept as if we had rode through a kennel all the way.

We found the shops all shut, and the Militia of the red Regiment[6] in arms at the Old Exchange; among which I found and

---

1. 'Cellars very large & arched with stone, celars I never saw any so neate and well dispos'd': Evelyn, loc. cit. Pepys and his wife sang here on 8 October 1667. (E).

2. Untraced. (OM).

3. The King Edward VI almshouses in Abbey Lane, founded c. 1400. Description and illust. in R. Comm. Hist. Mon., *Essex*, i. 239–41.

4. '*Magistri*' should be supplied before '*Thomæ*', and '*Bird*' should read '*Bryd*'. The brass commemorates a 15th-century Rector of Great Munden, Herts.: illust. in *Trans. Essex Arch. Soc.* (n.s.) 6/166.

5. Description in *Archaeologia*, 50/163–4.

6. The six infantry regiments of the city militia (or trainbands) were known, from the colour of their standards, as the Red, Blue, Orange, White, Green and Yellow Regiments.

spoke to Nich. Osborne, who told me that it was a thanksgiving-
day through the City for the return of the Parliament.[1]   At Pauls
I light, Mr. Blayton holding my horse;   where I found Dr.
Reynolds in the pulpit and generall Monke there, who was to
have a great entertainment at Grocers hall.[2]   So home, where my
wife and all well.   Shifted myself, and so to Mr. Crews and then
to Sir Harry Wrights, where I found my Lord at dinner; who
called for me in and was glad to see me.   There was at dinner
also Mr. John Wright and his lady, a very pretty lady, Alderman
Allen's daughter.   I dined here with Will Howe, and after
dinner went out with him to buy a hat (calling in my way and
saw my mother), which we did at the Plough in Fleetstreete by
my Lord's direction, but not as for him.   Here we met with Mr.
Pierce a little before, and he took us as we were coming from my
mother's to the Greyhound tavern and gave us a pint of wine;
and, as the rest of the seamen do, talks very high again of my
Lord.   After we had done about the hat, we went homeward,
he to Mr. Crews and I to Mrs. Jem and sat with her a little.   Then
home, where I found Mr. Sheply, almost drunk, come to see me;
afterward, Mr. Spong comes, with whom I went up and played
with him a Duo or two,[3] and so good-night.

I was endeed a little vexed with Mr. Sheply, but said nothing,
about his breaking open of my study at my house merely to give
him the key of the stair-door at my Lord's, which lock he might
better have broke then mine.

29.   To my office, and drank at Wills with Mr. Moore, who
told me how my Lord is chosen generall at sea by the Council and
that it is thought that Monke will be joined with him therein.[4]

Home and dined;   after dinner, my wife and I by water to

1. *CJ*, vii. 850.
2. Cf. Rugge, i, f.67r. Monck was
now made free of all twelve city
livery companies in turn: cf. below,
p. 79 & n. 2.   The sermon at St Paul's
was by Dr Edward Reynolds, a
moderate Presbyterian (soon to become Bishop of Norwich), much in
demand at this juncture as a preacher
on state occasions.

3. Probably on flageolets: cf.
below, iii. 237.   (E).
4. These appointments were made
by parliament on 2 March, Mountagu and Monck becoming Generals
of the Fleet for the ensuing summer:
CJ, vii. 860.

London, and thence to Herrings, the merchant in Coleman-street, about 50*l* which he promises I shall have on Saturday next. So to my mother's and then to Mrs. Turner's, of whom I took leave and her company, because she was to go out of town tomorrow with Mr. Pepys[1] into Norfolke. Here my Cosen Norton gave me a brave cup of Metheglin, the first I ever drank. To my mother's and supped there; she showed me a letter to my father from my Uncle,[2] inviting him to come to Brampton while he is in the country. So home and to bed.

This day my Lord came to the House, the first time since he came to town; but he had been at the Council before.

1. Edward Pepys of Broomsthorpe, Norf.　　2. Robert Pepys of Brampton, Hunts.

MARCH.

1. In the morning went to my Lord's lodgings, thinking to have spoke with Mr. Sheply, having not been to visit him since my coming to town. But he being*a* not within, I went up, and out of the box where my Lord's pamphlets lay I chose as many as I had a mind to have for my own use and left the rest. Then to my office, where little to do; but Mr. Sheply comes to me, so at dinner time he and I went to Mr. Crews (whither Mr. Thomas was newly come to town, being sent with Sir H. Yelverton, my old School fellow at Paul's Schoole, to bring the thanks of the County to generall Monke for the return of the Parliament);[1] but old Mr. Crew and my Lord not coming home to dinner, we tarried late before we went to dinner. It being the day that John, Mr. John Crew's coachman, was to be buried in the afternoon, he being a day or two before killed with a blow of one of his horses that struck his skull into his brains. From thence Mr. Sheply and I went into London to Mr. Laxton's, my Lord's Apothecary; and so by water to Westminster, where at the Sun he and I spent two or three hours at a pint or two of wine, discoursing of matters in the country; among other things, telling me that my Uncle did to him make a very kind mention of me and what he would do for me.[2] Thence I went home, and went to bed betimes.

This day, the Parliament did vote that they would not sit longer then the 15th day of this month.[3]

2. This morning I went early*b* to my Lord at Mr. Crew's, where I spoke to him. Here were a great many too, come to see

a repl. 'before'   *b* symbol blotted

---

1. Thomas, eldest son of John Crew, today presented an address from a body of Northamptonshire gentry; later published as *The second addresse from the gentlemen of the county of Northampton to his Excellency the Lord Generall Monck* (BM, 669 f.24/13).

2. Robert Pepys of Brampton had in 1657 made a will giving to Pepys a reversionary interest in the greater part of his property.

3. *CJ*, vii. 857.

him, as Secretary Thurlow who is now by this Parliament chosen again Secretary of State. There was also generall Monkes trumpeters to give my Lord a sound of their trumpets this morning. Thence I went to my office and wrote a letter to Mr. Downing about the business of his house. Then going home, I met with Mr Eglin, Chetwind and Thomas, who took me to the Leg in King's-street, where we had two brave dishes of meat, one of fish, a carp and some other fishes, as well done as ever I eat any. After that to the Swan tavern, where we drank a Quart or two of wine, and so parted. So I to Mrs. Jem. and took Mr. Moore with me (who I met in the street), and there I met W. How and Sheply. After that to Westminster-hall, where I saw Sir G. Booth at liberty.[1] This day I hear the City Militia is put into a good posture, and it is thought that Monke will not be able to do any great matter against them now, if he have a mind.[2]

I understand that my Lord Lambert did yesterday send a letter to the Council, and that tonight he is to come and appear to the Council in person.[3] Sir Arth. Haslerigg doth not yet appear in the House.[4] Great is the talk of a single person, and that it would now*a* be Charles, George, or Richard again.[5] For the last of which, my Lord St. Johns is said to speak high.[6] Great also is the dispute now in the House in whose name the writs shall run for

a repl. 'not'

---

1. Cf. above, p. 63, n. 2.
2. Ten thousand foot had been raised, and the commissions filled by royalists. Companies had been standing guard every night since 26 February. Monck was still, to judge by his public statements, a republican. GL, MS. 186/1, pp. i–viii; T. Carte, *Orig. Letters* (1739), ii. 309–10; *Nicholas Papers* (ed. G. F. Warner), iv. 196–7.
3. The letter was read in parliament on the 1st. Lambert did not obey the order to appear on the 2nd.
4. He and a few republicans of the old guard had seceded on 21 February.

They were said to be secretly in touch with Lambert.
5. I.e. Charles II, George Monck or Richard Cromwell (late Lord Protector). These rumours persisted for some time: see the report of 23 March in Lister, iii. 93. A pamphlet published about a month earlier (*The pedigree and descent of his excellency Generall Monk*) had attempted to prove that Monck was of the blood royal.
6. Many royalist agents at about this time reported to this effect: *CSPClar.*, iv. 572, 586, 592; T. Carte, *Orig. Letters*, ii. 310, 331–2. With Thurloe, Oliver St John was the most prominent of the 'Protectorians'.

the next Parliament – and it is said that Mr. Prin in open House said, "In King Charles's."[1]

From Westminster-hall, home. Spent the evening in my study; and so after some talk with my wife, then to bed.

3. To Westminster-hall, where I found that my Lord was last night voted one of the generalls at sea, and Monke the other.[2] I met my Lord in the Hall, who bade me come to him at noon. I met with Mr. Pierce the purser, Lieutenant Lambert, Mr. Creed, and Will Howe, and went with them to the Sun Taverne.[3] Up to my office, but did nothing. At noon home to dinner to a sheep's head; my Brother Tom came and dined with me, and told me that my mother was not very well and that my Aunt Fenner was very ill too. After dinner, I to Warwick house in Holborne to my Lord, where he dined with my Lord of Manchester, Sir Dudly North, my Lord Fiennes, and my Lord Barkly.[4] I stayed in the great hall, talking with some gentlemen there till they all came out. Then I by coach with my Lord to Mr. Crews, in our way talking of public things and how I should look after getting of his Comission's despatch. He told me he feared there was new design hatching, as if Monke had a mind to get into the saddle.[5] Here I left him, and went by appointment to Hering the merchant but*a* missed of my money, at which I was much troubled but could not help myself. Returning, met with Mr. Gifford, who

a repl. 'again'

---

1. Prynne was in charge of the bill for the dissolution and on 1 March argued that this was the only valid form of summons and that the Long Parliament had been dissolved by the death of the King in 1649. He used language just as bold on the same issue a week later: T. Carte, op. cit., ii. 312–13.

2. *CJ*, vii. 858.

3. All had been with Mountagu to the Baltic in 1659, when John Creed had served as Secretary and Deputy-Treasurer of the fleet.

4. The 2nd Earl of Manchester, Mountagu's cousin (who lived at

Warwick House, having married the Earl of Warwick's widow); North, who had married a niece of Manchester; Nathaniel Fiennes ('Lord' by virtue of high legal and political office in the Protectorate); and Lord Berkeley (of Berkeley) were all political Presbyterians and active in plans for a restoration.

5. Some extreme republicans – to save themselves from something worse – were pressing Monck to become sole ruler. A few of his officers approved of the plan, but Monck himself certainly did not.

took me and gave me half a pint of wine and told me, as I this day hear from many, that things are in a very doubtful posture, some of the Parliament being willing to keep the power in their hands. After I had left him, I met with Tom Harper, who took me to a place in Drury lane, where we drank a great deal of strong water, more then ever I did in [my] life at one time before. He talked*a* hog-high that my Lord Protector would come in place again, which endeed is much discoursed of again, though I do not see it possible. Hence home and writ to my father at Brampton by the post; so to bed.

This day I am told that my Lord Generall Fleetwood told my Lord that he feared the King of Sweden is dead of a fever at Gottenburg.[1]

4. *Lords day.* Before I went to church I sang *Orpheus Hymne*[2] to my Viall. After that to Mr. Guning's; an excellent sermon upon Charity. Then to my mother to dinner, where my wife and the maid was come. After dinner, we three to Mr. Messum's, where we met Monsieur Limpertinent, who got us a seat and told me a ridiculous story; how that last week he had caused a simple citizen to spend 80*l* in entertainments of him and some friends of his, upon pretence of some service that he would do him in his suit after a widow. Then to my mother again; and after supper, she and I talked very high about Religion, I in defence of the Religion I was born in.[3] Then home.

5. Early in the morning, Mr. Hill comes to string my Theorbo, which we were about till past 10 a-clock, with a great deal of pleasure. Then to Westminster, where I met with Mr. Sheply and Mr. Pinkney at Wills, who took me by boat to Billingsgate at the Salutacion tavern; whither by and by Mr. Talbot and

a MS. 'talt'

---

1. Charles X had died on 3/13 February. Mountagu had met the King during his expedition to the Sound in 1659.

2. 'O king of heaven and hell' – Henry Lawes's setting of Sir John Birkenhead's words; headed 'Orpheus Hymn to God' in Lawes's *Second book of ayres and dialogues* (1655), pp. 47–8; not in the PL. (E).

3. I.e. orthodox Anglicanism. Possibly his mother had become a Puritan; but she was no sectary: see below, 18 March 1664.

Adams came and bring a great good meat, a ham of bacon, &c: here we stayed and drank till Mr. Adams begun to be overcome; then we parted, and so to Westminster by water, only seeing Mr. Pinkny at his own house, where he showed me how he hath alway kept the Lion and Unicorne in the back of his chimney bright, in expectation of the King's coming again. At home I found Mr. Hunt, who told me how the Parliament have voted that the Covenant be new-printed and hung in churches again.[1]

Great hopes of the King's coming again.

To bed.

6. *Shrove=tuesday.*

I called Mr. Sheply and we both went up to my Lord's lodgings at Mr. Crew's, where he bade us to go home again and get a fire against an hour after – which we did at White-hall, whither he came; and after talking with him and I about his going to sea, he called me by myself to go along with him into the garden, where he asked me how things were with me and what he hath endeavoured to do with my uncle to get him to do something for me; but that he would say nothing to. He likewise bade me look out now, at this turn, some good place; and he would use all his own and all the interest of his friends that he hath in England to do me good. And asked me whether I could without too much inconvenience go to sea as his Secretary, and bade me think of it. He also begin to talk of things of state, and told me that he should now want one in that capacity at sea that he might trust in. And therefore he would have me to go.[2]

He told me also that he did believe the King would come in, and did discourse with me about it and about the affection of the people and City – at which I was full glad. After he was gone, I waiting upon him through the garden till he came to the Hall, I*ᵃ* left him and went up to my office, where Mr. Hawly brought

a repl. 'where'

---

1. *CJ*, vii. 862. This was the oath of September 1643 providing for a limited monarchy – the original aim of the Revolution.

2. John Creed, who had served Mountagu in this post in the Baltic voyage of 1659, was perhaps too much of a Puritan: cf. above, p. xxx.

one to me, a seaman that had promised 10*l* to him if he gat*ᵃ* him
a purser's place, which I think to endeavour to do. Here comes
my uncle Thom., who I took to Wills and drank with: poor
man, he came to enquire about the Knights of Windsor,[1] of
which he desires to get to be one. While we were drinking,
in comes Mr. Day, a Carpenter in Westminster, to tell me that
it was Shrove-tuesday and that I must go with him to their yearly
club upon this day, which I confess I had quite forgot. So I
went to the Bell, where was Mr.'s Eglin, Veezy, Vincent a
butcher, one more, and Mr. Tanner, with whom I played upon
a viall and he the viallin after dinner, and were very merry, with
a special good dinner – a leg of veal and bacon, two capons and
sausages and fritters, with abundance of wine. After that I went
home, where I found Kate Sterpin who hath not been here a
great while before. She gone, I went to see Mrs. Jem, at whose
chamber-door I found a couple of ladies; but she not being
there, we hunted her out and found that she and another had
hid themselfs behind a door. Well, they all went down into
the dining-room, where it was full of tag, rag, and bobtail,
dancing, singing, and drinking, of which I was ashamed and so
after I had stayed a dance or two, I went away. Going home,
called at my Lord's for Mr. Sheply, but found him at the Lion
with a Pewterer that he had bought pewter today of: with them
I drank, and so home and wrote by the post by my Lord's
command, for J. Goods to come up presently – for my Lord
entends to go forthwith into the *Swiftsure* till the *Nazeby* be
ready.

This day I hear that the Lords do entend to sit, and great store
of them are now in town and I see in the Hall today.[2]

Overton at Hull doth stand out, but can it is thought do

a MS. 'gat get'

---

1. The Society of Poor Knights of
Windsor, today known as the Military Knights. Thomas Pepys was in
November granted an almsroom in
Winchester cathedral: *CSPD 1660-1*,
p. 359.
2. Since the admission of the secluded M.P.'s, some Presbyterians, led
by Manchester, had wanted to restore the House of Lords, which had
not met since February 1649. Monck
prevented them from sitting until the
new parliament met on 25 April.

nothing; and Lawson it is said is gone with some ships thither, but all that is nothing.[1]

My Lord told me that there was great endeavours to bring in the Protector again; but he told me too, that he did believe it would not last long if he were brought in; no, nor the King neither (though he seems to think that he will come in), unless he carry himself very soberly and well. Everybody now drink the King's health without any fear, whereas before it was very private that a man dare do it. Monke this day is feasted at Mercers-hall, and is invited one after another to all the twelve halls in London.[2]

Many think that he is honest yet, and some or more think him to be a fool that would raise himself, but think that he will undo himself by endeavouring it.

My mind, I must needs remember, hath been very much eased and joyed in my Lord's great expression of kindness this day; and in discourse thereupon, my wife and I lay awake an hour or two in our bed.

7. *Ash wednesday.* In the morning I went to my Lord at Mr. Crews; in my way, Washington overtook me and upon my question whether he know any place now void that I might have by power over friends, he told me that this day Mr. G. Mountagu was to be made *Custos Rotulorum* for Westminster, and that by friends I might get to be named by him Clerke of the Peace, with which I was, as I am at all new things, very much joyed;[3] so when I came to Mr. Crews, I[a] spoke to my

a repl. 'he'

---

1. Maj.-Gen. Robert Overton, Governor of Hull, was trying to organise a republican rising among the troops in Yorkshire. At the Council's orders he submitted, and resigned his government on the 12th. Lawson, also a republican, had just been displaced from command of the fleet. He submitted by the 10th.

2. Cf. above, p. 71 & n. 2. At these feasts in the halls of the twelve great livery companies, the entertainment – songs, pastorals etc. – became progressively bolder and more roya-

list. At the Mercers' feast a rump was passed round: *Nicholas Papers* (ed. Warner), iv. 199–200.

3. The Mountagus had a close connection with the city of Westminster, and the Earl of Manchester soon afterwards became High Steward. But George Mountagu's appointment seems never to have been made; the Earl of Clare became *custos* and Thomas Lewis his clerk of the peace. Mdx Rec. Off., Westminster Sess. Rolls, 1224/1 and 2; HMC, *Rep.*, 8/2/66.

Lord about it; who told me that he believed Mr. Mountagu had already promised it and that it was given him only that he might gratify one person with the place I look for. Here, among many that was here, I met with Mr. Lynes the Chyrurgeon, who promised me some seeds of the Sensible plant.[1]   I spoke too with Mr. Pierce the surgeon, who gave me great encouragement to go to sea with my Lord.   Hence going homeward, my Lord overtook me in his coach and called me in; and so I went with him to St. James's; and G. Montagu being gone to White-hall, we walked over the park thither, all the way he discoursing of the times and of the change of things since the last year and wondering how he could bear with so great disappointment as he did. He did give me the best advice that he could what was best for me, whether to stay or go with him, and offered all the ways that could be how he might do me good, with the greatest liberty and love that could be.   I left him at White-hall and myself went to Westminster to my office, whither nothing to do, but I did discourse with Mr. Faulconberg about Le Squires place, and have his consent to get it if I could.[2]   I afterwards in the Hall met with W. Simons, who put me in the best way how to get it done.   Thence by appointment to the Angell in Kingstreete, where Chetwind, Mr. Thomas and Doling was at oysters, and beginning Lent this day with a fish dinner.   After dinner Mr. Thomas and I by water to London, where I went to Herings and received the 50l of my Lord's upon Franks bill from Worcester;[3] I gave in the bill and set my hand to his book.   Thence I went to Popes-head-ally and called on Adam Chard and bought a Catt=call there; it cost me two groats.   Thence went and gave him a cup of ale.   After that to [the] Sun behind the Exchange; where meeting my Uncle Wight by the way, I took him with me thither, and after drinking a health or two round at the Cock (Mr. Thomas being gone thither) we parted, he and I home-

---

1. *Mimosa pudica* or *sensitiva*; so-called because its leaves contract when touched; introduced from Barbados (or Goa) in the 1630s. The King sent an enquiry about it to the Royal Society in July 1661: Birch, i. 34.

2. Scipio le Squire (d. 1659) had been Vice-Chamberlain of the Receipt in the Exchequer; Edward Falconberg was a Deputy-Chamberlain. John Todd succeeded to le Squire's place on 13 April: *Rep. Dep. Keeper*, 5/277.

3. See above, p. 56 & n. 5. Frank was possibly Ald. Francis Franke, Mayor of Worcester, 1651-2.

wards; parted at Fleetstreet, where I found my father newly come home from Brampton very well; who left my Uncle with his leg very dangerous, and he doth believe he cannot continue in that condition long. He tells me that my Uncle did acquaint him very largely what he did intend to do with his estate; to make me his Heire and to give my Brother Tom some things, and that my father and mother should have something likewise for to raise portions for Joh. and Pall: I pray God he may be as good as his word. Here I stayed and supped; and so home, there being Joyce Norton there and Ch. Glascock. Going home, I called at Wottons and took home a pair of shoes. At home, Mr. Sheply sat with me a little while; and so we all to bed.

This news and my Lord's great kindness make me very cheerful within; I pray God make me thankful.

This day, according to order, Sir Arthur appeared at the House; what was done I know not. But there was all the Rumpers almost come to the House today.[1]

My Lord did seem to wonder much why Lambert was so willing to be put into the Toure, and thinks he hath some design in it; but I think that he is so poor that he cannot use his liberty for debts if he were at liberty – and so it is as good and better for him to be there then anywhere else.[2]

8. To White-hall to bespeak some firing for my father at Shotts; and likewise to speak to Mr. Blackburne about Batters being Gunner in the *Wexford*. Then to Westminster-hall, where there was a general damp over men's minds and faces, upon some of the officers of the army being about making a Remonstrance again Ch. Stuart or any single person &c; but at noon it was told that the generall hath put a stop to it, and so all was

---

1. Overton's attempted rising led Parliament on the 6th to summon Sir Arthur Hesilrige before them, in order to deprive him of his military commands. His case was now referred to the Council. He and his associates had not attended Parliament since the admission of the secluded members on 21 February.

2. Lambert had so long evaded arrest that it was a surprise when he suddenly submitted and appeared before the Council on the 5th. But that he should have chosen to go to the Tower is sufficiently explained by the fact that the alternative was to provide a surety of £20,000 for good behaviour.

well again.[1]   Here I met with Jesper,[2] who was to look for me to
bring me to my Lord at the Lobby; whither, sending a note to
my Lord, he comes out to me and gave me direction to look
after getting some money for him from the Admiralty, saying
that things are so unsafe that he would not lay out a farthing for
the State till he had received some money of theirs.

Home about 2 a-clock and took my wife by land to Pater-
noster-row to buy some Paragon for a petticoat, and so home
again – in my way meeting Mr. Moore, who went home with
me while I eat a bit; and so back to White-hall again, both of
us.   He waited at the Councell for Mr. Crew; I to the Admiralty,
where I got the order for the money, and have taken care for
the getting of it assigned upon Mr. Huchinson, Treasurer for the
Navy, against tomorrow.[3]   Hence going home, I met with
Mr. King that belonged to the Treasurers at warr and took him
to Harpers; who told me how he and the rest of his fellows are
cast out of office by the new Treasurers.[4]

This afternoon some of the officers of the army and some of
the Parliament had a conference at White-hall to make all right
again, but I know not what is done.[5]

This noon I met with Captain Holland at the Dog Taverne,
with whom I advised how to make some advantage of my Lord's
going to sea, which he told me might be by having of five or
six servants entered on board, and I to give them what wages
I pleased, and so their pay to be mine.   He was also very urgent

1. At a general council at St James's
this morning Monck refused to allow
his officers to present this remonstrance to Parliament on the ground
that in no circumstances should the
civilian authority be constrained by
the military. In the afternoon he held
a conference with a select number of
officers and of M.P.'s at which he
pacified the military leaders. The
next day they were sent to their commands. Guizot, ii. 366–7; *CSPClar.*,
iv. 591, 593–4; *Nicholas Papers* (ed.
Warner), iv. 201.

2. Jasper, a negro footman of
Mountagu.

3. An imprest (8 March) for £500
'on account of his entertainment as
general at sea': *CSPD 1659–60*, p.
530.

4. Two new Receivers-General and
Treasurers-at-War had been appointed
on 2 February to administer (under
the Army Committee) the revenue
collected by the January assessment
for the payment of the armed forces:
Firth and Rait, ii. 1405. They employed county receivers and treasurers, but King was presumably a
servant in their central office.

5. See above, n. 1.

to have me take the Secretary place that my Lord doth proffer me.

At the same time, in comes Mr. Wade and Mr. Sterry, Secretary to the Plenepotentiary in Denmarke, who brought the news of the death of the King of Sweden at Gottenburgh the 3d of the last month. And told me what a great change he found when he came hither, the Secluded members being restored. He also spoke very freely of Mr. Wades profit, which he made while he was in Zeeland; and how he did believe that he cheated Mr. Powell,[1] and that he made above 500*l* on the voyage – which Mr. Wade did very angrily deny – though I believe he was guilty enough.

9. To my Lord at his lodging and came to Westminster with him in the coach, with Mr. Dudly with him; and he in the Painted chamber walked a good while; and I telling him that I was willing and ready to go with him to sea, he agreed that I should, and advised me what to write to Mr. Downing about it. Which I did at my office: that by my Lord's desire I offered that my place might for a while be supplied by Mr. Moore, and that I and my Security would be bound by the same bond for him.[2] I went and dined at Mr. Crews, where Mr. Hawly comes to me and I told him the business and showed him the letter, promising him 20*l*. a year, which he liked very well of. I did the same to Mr. Moore, which he also took for a courtesy. In the afternoon by coach, taking Mr. Butler with me, to the Navy Office about the 500*l* for my Lord, which I am promised to have tomorrow morning. Then by coach back again, and at White-hall at the Council chamber spoke with my Lord and got him to sign the acquittance for the 500*l*; and he also told me that he had spoke to Mr. Blackburne to put off Mr. Creed and that I should come to him for direction in that employment.

After this, Mr. Butler and I to Harpers, where we sat and drank for two hours till 10 at night; the old woman,[3] she was drunk, begun to talk foolishly in commendation of her son James.

---

1. John Powell was steward to the plenipotentiaries sent in 1659 to arrange the peace between Sweden and Denmark; Thomas Wade a navy victualling agent.

2. It was usual for Exchequer officials to enter into bonds.

3. Mrs Mary Harper.

Home and to bed.

All night troubled in my thoughts how to order my business upon this great change with me, that I could not sleep; and being overheated with drink, I made a promise the next morning to drink no strong drink this week, for I find that it makes me sweat in bed and puts me quite out of order. This day it was resolved that the Writts do go out in the name of the Keepers of the Liberty.[1] And I hear that it is resolved privately that a treaty be offered with the King.[2] And that Monke did check his soldiers highly for what they did yesterday.

10.   In the morning went to my father, whom I took in his cutting-house; and there I told him my resolution to go to sea with my Lord and consulted with him how to dispose of my wife; and at last resolved of letting her be at Mr. Bowyers.[3]   Thence to the Treasurer of the Navy, where I received 500*l* for my Lord; and having left 200 of it with Mr. Rawlinson at his house for Sheply, I went with the rest to the Sun taverne on Fish-street hill, where Mr. Hill, Stevens and Mr. Hater of the Navy Office had invited me; where we had good discourse and a fine breakfast of Mr. Hater.   Then by coach home, where I took occasion to tell my wife of my going to sea, who was much troubled thereat and was with some dispute at last willing to continue at Mr. Bowyers in my absence.   After that to see Mrs. Jemi: and paid her maid 7*l*:; and then to Mr. Blackburne, who told me what Mr. Creed did say upon the news of my coming into his place, and that he did propose to my Lord that there should be two Secretarys: which made me go to Sir H. Wright's where my Lord dined and spoke with him about it; but he seemed

1. The bill for the dissolution of parliament was given its second reading on this day: *CJ*, vii. 868. The writs were made out in the name of the 'keepers of the Liberty of England by authority of Parliament': *Pub. Intell.*, 20 February, p. 1124. For the debate on this matter, see above, p. 75 & n. 1.

2. Certain Councillors of State now attempted to extract from Charles the concessions granted by his father in 1648 in the Treaty of Newport – principally a temporary establishment of Presbyterianism. The overtures failed and the King was restored without conditions.

3. Robert Bowyer ('my father Bowyer'), Usher of the Receipt of the Exchequer; a close friend of Pepys. His country house was at Huntsmoor, Iver, Bucks.

not to agree to the motion.   Hither W. Howe comes to me and so to Westminster; in the way he told me what I was [to] provide and so forth against my going.   He went with me to my office, whither also Mr. Mage comes half-foxed and played the fool upon the viallin, that made me weary.   Then to Whitehall and so home and set many of my things in an order against my going.   My wife was up*a* making of caps for me, and the wench making an end of a pair of stockings that she was knitting of.   So to bed.

11.   *Sunday.*   All the day busy without my band on, putting up my books and things in order to my going to sea.   At night my wife and I went to my father's to supper, where J. Norton and Ch. Glascocke supped with us; and after supper home, where the wench had provided all things against tomorrow to wash.   And so to bed, where I much troubled with my cold and coughing.

12.   This day the wench ris at 2 in the morning to wash, and my wife and I lay talking a great while; I, by reason of my cold, could not tell how to sleep.   My wife and I to the Exchange, where we bought a great many things, where I left her and went into London; and at Bedells, the bookseller at the Temple gate, I paid 12*l* 10*s*. 6*d*. for Mr. Fuller by his direction.   So I went to do a great many things, in order to my going.   So came back and at Wilkinson's found Mr. Sheply and some sea people, as the cook of the *Nazeby* and others, at dinner.   Then to the White-horse in Kings-street, where I got Mr. Biddles horse to ride to Huntsmore to Mr. Bowyers; where I found him and all well and willing to have my wife come and board with them while I was at sea, which was the business I went about.   Here I lay and took a thing for my cold by Mrs. Bowyers direction, *viz.* a spoonful of honey and a nutmeg scraped into it and so take it into the mouth, which I found did do me much good.

13.   It rained hard and I got up early and got to London by 8 a-clock.   At my Lord's lodgings I spoke with him, who told me that I was to be Secretary and Creed to be Deputy-Treasurer

a   possibly 'late'

for the Fleet, at which I was troubled but I could not help it.[1] After that to my father's to look after things, and so at my shoe-maker and others. At night to White-hall, where I met with Simons and Luellin; drank[a] with them at Roberts's at White-hall. Then to the Admiralty, where I talked with Mr. Creed, both the Brothers,[2] and they were very seemingly willing and glad that I have the place since my Lord would dispose of it otherwise then to him. Home and to bed.

This day the Parliament voted all that had been done by the former Rump against the House of Lords be void.[3] And tonight, that the writs go out without any Qualificacion.[4] Things seem very doubtful[b] what will be the end of all; for the Parliament seems to be strong for the King, which the soldiers do all talk against.

14. To my Lord, where infinite of applications to him and to me, to my great trouble; my Lord he gave me all the papers that was given to him, to put in order and give him an account of them. Here I got half a piece of a person of Mr. Wrights recommending[c] to my Lord to be preacher in the *Speaker* frigate. I went hence to St. James, and Mr. Pierce the surgeon with me, to speak with Mr. Clerke, Monkes secretary, about getting some soldiers removed out of Huntington to Oundle; which my Lord told me he did to do a courtesy to the town, that he might have the greater interest in them in the choice of the next Parliament; not that he entends to be chosen himself, but that he might have Mr. G. Mountagu and my Lord Mandevill chose there in

a MS. 'at drank'   *b* preceded by blot   *c* repl. 'com'-

---

1. These posts were usually held by the same person.

2. John and Richard Creed, both of whom had served in the navy under Mountagu since c. 1657.

3. More correctly, a committee was appointed to report on what the Rump had done concerning the Lords: *CJ*, vii. 872.

4. More correctly, qualifications were imposed on candidates (similar to those voted a month earlier: see above, p. 56 & n. 2), but a motion to exclude royalists from the electorate was now defeated: *CJ*, vii. 874.

spite of the Bernards.[1]   This done (where I saw Generall Monke
and methought[a] he seemed a dull, heavy man),[2] he and I to White-
hall, where with Luellin we dined at Marshes.   Coming home,
telling my wife what we had to dinner, she had a mind to some
Cabbage, and I sent for some and she had it.   Went to the
Admiralty, where a strange thing how I was already courted by
the people.   This morning, among others that came to me, I
hired a boy of Jenkins of Westminster, and Burr to be my clerk.
This night I went to Mr. Creed's chamber, where he gave me
the former book of proceedings in the Fleete and the Seale.[3]
Then to Harpers, where old Beard was, and I took him by
coach to my Lord's but he was not at home, but afterwards I
found him out at Sir H. Wrights.   Thence by coach, it raining
hard, to Mrs. Jem:, where I stayed a while, and so home and
late at[b] night put up my things in a sea-chest that Mr. Sheply
lent me – and so to bed.

15.   Early, packing up my things and sending them to my
Lord's lodgings to be sent by cart with the rest of my Lord's.
So to Wills, where I took leave of some of my friends.   Here
I met with Ad: Chard and Tom Alcock, one that went to school
with me at Huntington,[4] but I have not seen him this sixteen
years.   So in the Hall paid and made even with Mrs. [and] Mr.
Michel.   Afterwards met with old Beale, and at the Axe paid
him this Quarter to Lady-day next.[5]   In the afternoon Dick

---

a first part of word corrected from ? 'men'   *b* 'at' repeated

---

1. John Bernard of Brampton and
his brother-in-law Nicholas Pedley
were in March the successful candidates for Huntingdon borough.   The
former had sat for the county in the
last three parliaments; Pedley for the
county in the last two.   For the elec-
toral rivalry between the Bernards
and the Mountagus, see VCH, *Hunts.*,
ii. 29–30.

2. Cf. the similar opinion of Burnet and others: Burnet, i. 161–2 & n.

3. Records of the Baltic voyages,
1659, and the Admiral's seal.

4. Some time during the Civil War

Pepys had been sent out of London to
stay with relatives in E. Anglia.   He
probably lived at the house of his
uncle, Robert Pepys of Brampton,
Hunts., and attended the grammar
school at Huntingdon (where Oliver
Cromwell had been a pupil thirty
years before), but the only evidence
on the matter is this entry.   He returned to London and entered St
Paul's School in c. 1646.   The Tom
Alcock here mentioned was probably
a relative.

5. This was rent for his house: see
below, p. 88.

Mathews comes to town and I went and drank with him at Harpers. So into London by water; and in Fish-street my wife and I bought a bit of salmon of 8*d.* and went to the Sun tavern and eat it, where I did promise to give her all that I have in the world but my books, in case I should die at sea. From thence homewards; in the way, my wife bought linen for three smocks and other things. I went to my Lord's and spoke with him; so home with Mrs. Jem by coach and then home to my own house. From thence to the Fox in King-streete to supper at a brave turkey of Mr. Hawlys, with some friends of his there, Will Bowyer, &c: after supper I went to Westminster-hall and the Parliament sat till 10 at night, thinking and being expected to dissolve themselfs today; but they did not. Great talk to-night that the discontented officers did think this night to make a stir; but prevented.[1] To the Fox again; home with my wife and to bed, extraordinary sleepy.

16. No sooner out of bed but troubled with abundance of Clients, seamen. My landlords, Vanly's, man came to me by my direction yesterday, for I was*[a]* there at his house as I was going to London by Water; and I paid him rent for my house for this Quarter ending at Ladyday, and took an acquittance that he brought me from his master. Then to Mr. Sheply to the Rhenish wine-house; where Mr. Pim the tailor was, and gave us a morning draught and a neat's tongue. Home, and with my wife to London. We dined at my father's, where Joyce Norton and Mr. Armiger dined also; after dinner my wife took leave of them in order to her going tomorrow to Huntsmore. In my way home I went to the Chappell in Chancery lane to bespeak paper of all sorts and other things belonging to writing,

a   repl. 'would'

---

1. The army officers objected particularly to the establishment of a new militia by parliament, and held a meeting at 9 p.m. Cf. the French ambassador's despatch (evening, 15 March): 'As hitherto the officers have never deferred to their other commanders when once they have been aroused, every one expects some great event before long': Guizot, ii. 380. Cf. also Ludlow, ii. 242–4.

against my voiage.[1] So home, where I spent an hour or two about my business in my study. Thence to the Admiralty and stayed a while; so home again, where Will Bowyer came to tell us that he would bear my wife company in the coach tomorrow. Then to Westminster-hall, where I heard how the Parliament had this day dissolved themselfs and did pass very cheerfully through the Hall and the Speaker without his Mace.[2] The whole Hall was joyful thereat, as well as themselfs; and now they begin to talk loud of the King. Tonight I am told that yesterday,[a] about 5 a-clock in the afternoon, one came with a ladder to the great Exchange and wiped with a brush the Inscripcion that was upon King Charles, and that there was a great bonefire made in the Exchange and people cried out "God bless King Charles the Second."[3] From the Hall I went home to bed, very sad in mind to part with my wife tomorrow, but God's will be done.

17. This morning bade Adieu in bed to the company of my wife. We rose and I gave my wife some money to serve her for a time, and what papers of consequence I had. Then I left her to get her ready and went to my Lord's with my boy Eliezer to my Lord's lodging at Mr. Crews. Here I had much business with my Lord; and papers, great store, given me by my Lord[b] to dispose of as of the rest. After that, with Mr. Moore home to my house and took my wife by[c] coach to the Chequer in Holborne; where after we had drunk &c., she took coach and

a repl. 'last'   *b* repl. 'Lord'   *c* repl. 'the'

---

1. The Rolls Chapel was a government office (in non-revolutionary times, the Crown Office) at which were kept certain chancery records. No other mention of its use as a store for official stationery has been traced.

2. *CJ*, vii. 880.

3. The French ambassador, who saw it happen, said the time was 7 p.m. (Guizot, ii. 382), but Pepys's 5 p.m. is more likely, for it was done during the afternoon Exchange. The gilded

inscription – *Exit tyrannus, regum ultimus* etc. – had been painted over the niche which had contained the statue of Charles I. The statue itself had been pulled down in 1650. The man who obliterated the words was later identified as Michael Darby, 'now painter to the Company of Mercers': *Merc. Pub.*, 23 August 1660, p. 534. Cf. Rugge, i, f.77r; *An exit to the exit tyrannus . . .* (1660); *The loyal subjects tears . . .* (1659/60).

so farewell. I stayed behind with Tom Alcock and Mr. Anderson my old chamber fellow at Cambrige his brother, and drank with them there, who were come to me thither about one that would have a place at sea. Thence with Mr. Hawly to dinner at Mr. Crews. After dinner, to my own house, where all things were put up into the dining-room and locked up, and my wife took the key along with her. This day, in the presence of Mr. Moore (who made it) and Mr. Hawly, I did (before I went out with my wife) seal my will to her, whereby I did give her all that I have in the world but my books, which I gave to my Brother John, excepting only French books, which my wife is to have.[1]

In the evening at the Admiralty: met my Lord there and got a Comission for*a* Williamson to be Captain of the *Harp* frigate, and afterwards went by coach, taking Mr. Crips with me, to my Lord and got him to sign it at table as he was at supper. And so to Westminster back again with him with me, who hath a great desire to go to sea; and my Lord this day told me that he would do him any favour. So I went home with him to his mother's house by me in Ax-yard, where I found Dr. Clodius's wife[2] and sat there talking and hearing of old Mrs. Crispe playing of her old lessons* upon the Harpsicon till it was time to go to bed. After that, to bed I went; and Laud her son lay with me in the best chamber in her house, which indeed was finely furnished.

18. 《This day was very rainy all day.》 I rose early and went to the Barber's (Jervas) in the Palace-yard and was trimmed by him; and afterward drank with him a cup or two of ale, and did begin to hire his man to go with me to sea. Then to my Lord's*b* lodging, where I found Captain Williamson and gave him his commission to be Captain of the *Harpe* and he gave me a piece of gold and 20*s.* in silver. So to my own house,

a repl. 'signed'   *b* repl. 'house

---

1. Of the five wills Pepys made in the period of the diary (this being the first), no trace apparently remains.
2. Mary, daughter of Samuel Hartlib, the writer on education and economic affairs, who had married Dr Frederick Clodius, physician and chemist; near neighbours of Pepys in Axe Yard.

where I stayed a while and then to dinner with Mr. Sheply at my Lord's lodgings. After that to Mr. Messum's, where he made a very gallant sermon upon "Pray for the life of the King, and the King's son." *Esra* 6. 10.

From thence to Mr. Crews, but my Lord not being within I did not stay; but went away and met with Mr. Woodfine, who took me to an ale=house in Drury-lane; and we sat and drank together and eat toasted cakes which were very good, and we had a great deal of mirth with the mistress of the house about them. From thence homewards, and called at Mr. Blagrave's,[1] where I took in my note that he hath of mine for 40*s*, which he two years ago did give me as a pawne while he had my lute; so that all things are even between him and I. So to Mrs. Cripse, where she and her daughter and son and I sat talking till 10 a-clock at night, I giving them the best advice that I could concerning their son, how he should go to sea; and so to bed.

19. Early to my*ᵃ* Lord, where infinite of business to do, which makes my head full; and indeed, for these two or three days I have not been without a great many cares and thoughts concerning them. After that to the Admiralty, where a good while with Mr. Blackborne, who told me that it was much to be feared that the King would come in, for all good men and good things were now discouraged. Thence to Wilkinsons, where Mr. Sheply and I dined; and while we were at dinner, my Lord Monkes lifeguard came by with the sergeant-at-armes before them, with two proclamations; that all Cavaliers do depart the town, and*ᵇ* the other that all officers that were lately disbanded should do the same.[2] The last of which Mr. R. Creed, I remember, said that he looked upon as if they had said that all God's people should depart the town. Thence with some Sea=officers to the Swan, where we drank wine till one came to me to pay

a blot over symbol   *b* MS. 'that'

1. Either Robert or Thomas Blagrave, both later royal musicians. (E).

2. Steele, nos 3166, 3170; 17 March. Disbanded officers, papists and malignants were to absent themselves between 25 March and 1 May, i.e. during the parliamentary elections and the first week of the new session.

me some money from Worcester, *viz.*, 25*l*;[1] his name is Wilday.
I sat in another room and took the money and drank with him
till the rest of my company was gone and so we parted.   I going
home, the water was high, and so I got Crockford to carry me
over it.[2]   So home and left my money there.

All the discourse nowaday is that the King will come again;
and for all I see, it is the wishes of all and all do believe that it
will be so.

My mind is still much troubled for my poor wife, but I hope
that this undertaking will be worth my pains.

To White-hall and stayed about business at the Admiralty late;
then to Tony Robins's, where Captain Stokes, Mr. Luddington
and others were, and I did solicit the Captain for Laud Crispe,
who gave me a promise that he would entertain him.

After that to Mrs. Crisps, where Dr. Clodius and his wife
were.   He very merry with drink.   We played at cards late.
And so to bed.   ⟨This day my Lord dined at my Lord Mayor;
and Jaspr: was made drunk there, which my Lord was very
angry at.⟩[a]

20.   ⟪The weather still very rainy.⟫   This morning I rose
early and went to my house to put things in a little order against
my going, which I conceive will be tomorrow.   After that to
my Lord, where I found very great deal of business, he giving
me all letters and papers whatever that comes to him about
business, for me to give him an account of when we come on
shipboard.   Hence with Captain Isham by coach to White-hall to
the Admiralty.   He and I and Chetwind, Doling and Luellin,
dined together at Marshes at White-hall.   So to the Bull-head,
whither W. Simons comes to us and I gave them my foy against
my going to sea.   And so we took leave one of another, they
promising me to write to me to sea.   Hither comes Pim's boy
by my direction, with two Monteeres for me to make my choice
of; and I chose the saddest colour and left the other for Mr.
Sheply.*   ⟪*I am in an error here: for I did not take leave of them

a addition crowded in between entries at end of line

1. See above, p. 56 & n. 5.   appears to have been one of the local
2. The river had overflowed its   porters.
banks at Westminster.   Crockford

till the*ª* next day after.》 Hence by coach to London, and took
a short melancholly leave of my father and mother, without
having time to drink or say anything of business one to another;
and endeed, I had a fear upon me that I should scarce ever see my
mother again, she having a great cold then upon her.   Then to
Westminster, where by reason of rain and an Easterly wind, the
water was so high that there was boats rowed in King-streete and
all our yard was drownded, that one could not go to my house,
so as no man hath seen the like almost.   Most houses full of
water.[1]   Then back by coach to my Lord's, where I met Mr.
Sheply, who stayed with me waiting for my Lord's coming in
till very late: then he and I and W. How went with our swords
to bring my Lord home from Sir H. Wrights.   He resolved to
go tomorrow if the wind ceased.   Sheply and I home by coach;
I to Mrs. Crisps, who had sat over a good supper long looking
for me.   So we sat talking and laughing till it was very late;
and so Lawd and I to bed.

21. To my Lord's; but the wind very high against us and
the*ᵇ* weather bad, we could not go today.   Here I did very
much business; and then to my Lord Widdrington from my
Lord, with his desire that he might have the disposal of the
Writts for the Cinqueports.[2]   My Lord was very civil to me, and
called for wine and writ a long letter in answer.   Thence I went
to a ⟨Taverne⟩ over against Mr. Pierce's with Judge-advocate

repl. 'today'   *b* repl. 'north'

---

1. Parts of Westminster were
notoriously subject to floods before
the Thames was embanked in the 19th
century.   For this flood, see Mundy,
v. 114-15; below, p. 95. Cf. also
Rugge, i, f.81r: 'In this month of
March the wind was very high and
caused great tides . . . great hurt was
don to the inhabantents of Westminster Kinge Street in the lower
houses and poor foukes cellars quit
drownd.'
2. As First Commissioner of the
Great Seal, Sir Thomas Widdrington

controlled the issue of parliamentary
writs.   The Lord Warden of the
Cinque Ports usually had the disposal
of those addressed to his ports, and
nominated one member in each.   But
the office was now vacant and its
powers vested in the Council of State:
Carte 73, f.362r; W. Boys, *Hist.
Sandwich* (1792), ii. 780; G. Wilks,
Barons of Cinque Ports, p. 87. Mountagu's request was successful: below,
p. 96. Perhaps as a result he chose
Sandwich as the title of the earldom
bestowed on him at the Restoration.

Fowler and Mr. Burr;[1] and sat and drank with them two or three pints of wine. After that to Mr. Crew's again and gave my Lord an account of what I had done; and so about my business to take leave of my father and mother, which by a mistake I have put down yesterday. Thence to Westminster to Crisps, where we were very merry; the old woman sent for a supper for me and gave me a Handkercher with strawberry buttons on it. So to bed.

22. Up very early and set things in order at my house, and so took leave of Mrs. Crispe and her daughter (who was in bed) and of Mrs. Hunt. Then to my Lord's lodging at the gate and did so there, where Mr. Hawly came to me and I gave him the key of my house to keep; and he went with me to Mr. Crews and there I took my last leave of him. But the weather continuing very bad, my Lord would not go today. My Lord spent this morning private in sealing of his last will and testament with Mr. Wm. Mountagu.[2] After that I went forth about my own business to buy a pair of riding gray serge Stockings – a sword and belt and shoes. And after that took Wotton and Brigden[3] to the Popes-head tavern in Chancery-lane, where Gilb. Holland and Shelston was; and we dined and drank a great deal of wine, and they paid all.

Strange how these people do now promise me anything; one a Rapier, the other a vessel of wine or a gown,*a* and offered me his silver hatband to [do] him a courtesy. I pray God keep me from being proud or too much lifted up hereby.

After that to Westminster and took leave of K. Sterpin, who was very sorry to part with me; and after that, of Mr. George Mountagu, and received my warrant of Mr. Blackburne to be Secretary to the two Generalls of the Fleete. Then to take my

a ? 'gun'

---

1. John Fowler was Judge-Advocate of Mountagu's fleet in 1659 and again in 1660. John Burr was Pepys's clerk for the present voyage.

2. William, second son of Edward, 1st Lord Mountagu of Boughton, and first cousin of 'my Lord'; barrister and 'my Lord's' principal legal adviser. This will does not appear to have survived.

3. The shoemaker and armourer respectively from whom Pepys had just bought these goods. Both had shops in Fleet St.

leave of the clerks of the Councell; and thence Doling and Luellin would have me go with them to Mount's chamber, where we sat and talked and drank and then I went away. So to my Lord (in my way meeting Chetwind and Swan and bid them farewell), where I lay all night with Mr. Andrews.

This day Mr. Shepley went away on board and I sent my boy with him; this day also Mrs. Jemim: went to Marrowbone, so that I could not see her.

Mr. Moore being out of town tonight, I could not take leave of him nor speak to him about business, which troubled me much.

I left my small keys therefore with Mr. Andrews for him.

23. Up early. Carried my Lord's Will in a black box to Mr. Wm. Mountagu for him to keep for him. Then to the Barbers and put on my Cravatt[a] there. So to my Lord again, who was almost ready to be gone and had stayed for me.

Hither came Gill. Holland, and brought me a Stick=rapier – and Shelston a sugar-loaf;[1] and had brought his wife, which he said was a very pretty woman, to the Ship tavern hard by for me to see, but I could not go. Young Reeve also brought me a little Perspective glasse which I bought for my Lord; it cost me 8s. So after that[b] my Lord in Sir H. Wrights coach with Captain Isham, and Mr. Tho. and John Crew with him. And I and W. Howe in a Hackny to the Towre, where the barges stayed for us.

My Lord and the Captain in one, and W. How and I and Mr. Ibbott and Mr. Burr in the other, to the Long Reach, where the *Swiftsure* lay at Anchor (in our way we saw the great breach which the late high water had made, to the loss of many 1000*l* to the people about Limehouse).[2] As soon as my Lord on board, the guns went off bravely from the Ships; and a little while after comes the Vice-admirall Lawson and seemed very respectful

---

a MS. l.h. 'Crasvatt'   b followed by blank half-line

---

1. Shelston (a grocer of Leadenhall St) later applied to Pepys for a job: below, p. 242.

2. The riverside was embanked here, but vulnerable to spring tides.

to my Lord, and so did the rest of the Comanders of the frigates that were thereabouts.

I to the Cabbin allotted for me, which was the best that any had that belonged to my Lord. I got out some things out of my chests for writing, and to work presently, Mr. Burr and I both. I supped at the Deck table with Mr. Sheply. We were late, writing of orders for the getting of ships ready, &c.; and also making of others to all the Seaports between Hastings and Yarmouth to stop all dangerous persons that are going or coming between Flanders and there.[1]

After that to bed in my cabin, which was but short; however, I made shift with it and slept very well; and the weather being good, I was not sick at all; yet I know not when I shall be.

24. At work hard all the day, writing letters to the Councill &c. This day Mr. Creed came on board and dined very boldly with my Lord, but he could not get a bed there.

At night Captain Isham, who had been at Gravesend all last night and today comes and brought Mr. Lucy (one acquainted with Mrs. Pierce, with whom I had been at her house); I drank with him in the Captain's cabbin, but by business could not stay with him. I despatch many letters today abroad – and it was late before we could get to bed. Mr. Sheply and How supped with me in my Cabbin and the boy Eliezr. flung down a can of beer upon my papers which made me give him a box of the eare, it having all spoiled my papers and cost me a great deal of work. So to bed.

25. About 2 a-clock in the morning, letters came from London by our Coxon; so they waked me, but I would not rise but bid him stay till morning, which he did; and then I rose and carried them in to my Lord, who read them a-bed. Among the rest, there was the Writt and Mandate for him to dispose to the Cinque Ports for choice of Parliament men.[2] There was also one for me from Mr. Blackburne, who with his own hand superscribes it to *S.P. Esqr.*, of which, God knows,

1. For the reply from Yarmouth to this order, see *CSPD 1659–60*, p. 400.   2. Carte 73, ff.234r, 235r: council order, 24 March.

I was not a little proud.[1]   After that, I wrote a letter to the clerk
of Dover=Castle to come to my Lord about Issuing of those writs.

About 10 a-clock Mr. Ibbotts at the end of the long table begin
to pray and preach and endeed made a very good sermon, upon
the duty of a Christian to be steadfast in the faith.[a]

After that the Captain Cuttance[2] and I have oysters, my Lord
being in his Cabbin, not entending to stir out today.   After that,
up into the great Cabbin above to dinner with the Captain,
where was Captain Isham and all the officers of the ship.   I took
place of all but the Captain.   After dinner I writ a great many
letters to my friends at London; and after that, the sermon begin
again, all which time I slept, God forgive me.

After that, it being a fair day, I walked with the Captain upon
the Deck talking.   At night I supped with him and after that
had orders from my Lord about some business to be done against
tomorrow, which I sat up late and did; and then to bed.

26.   This day it is two years since it pleased God that I was
cut of the stone at Mrs. Turner's in Salisbury-court.   And did
resolve while I live to keep it a festival, as I did the last year at
my house, and for ever to have Mrs. Turner and her company
with me.[3]   But now it pleases God that I am where I am and
so am prevented to do it openly;   only, within my soul I can and

a word uncertain

---

1. Esquires constituted the rank
above gentlemen. 'Any that are in
superiour Publick Office for King or
State are reputed Esquires or equal to
Esquires': E. Chamberlayne, *Angl.
Not.* (1669), p. 475. Pepys became
an indubitable esquire when in the
summer he was appointed Clerk of
the Acts to the Navy Board.   Most of
his colleagues on the Board were
knights, and the Clerk was often
known as 'Squire Peaps', e.g., to the
plumber who helped with the alterations in 1661 to the office: PRO, SP
29/81, no. 21. But he did not protest at the end of 1660 when under the
poll-tax he was rated as a mere
gentleman: below, p. 315.

2. Roger Cuttance, Captain of the
Naseby, now fitting out as the admiral's flagship: cf. above, p. 78;
below, p. 100.

3. The operation was a common
one, but dangerous and brutally painful. It was usual for operations to be
performed in private houses and inns;
only the rich went to hospital. Jane
Turner, a relative, wife of John
Turner, barrister, had provided accommodation. The surgeon was
Thomas Hollier (Holliard), of St
Thomas's Hospital, who continued to
attend Pepys for this trouble. Pepys's
annual 'festival' was regularly held
during the diary period.

do rejoice and bless God, being at this time, blessed be His holy name, in as good health as ever I was in my life.

This morning I rise early and went about making of an establishment of the whole fleet and a list of all the ships, with the number of men [and] guns: about an hour after that, we had a meeting of the principal commanders and seamen to proportion out the number of these things.[1] After that to dinner, there being very many commanders on board. All the afternoon very many orders were made, till*a* I was very weary.

At night Mr. Sheply and W. Howe came and brought some bottles of wine and something to eat at my Cabbin, where we were very merry, remembering the day of being cut of the stone. The Captain Cuttance came afterwards and sat drinking a bottle of wine till 11 a-clock at night, which is a kindness he doth not usually do to the greatest officer in the ship. After that to bed.

27. Early in the morning at making a fair new Establishment of the fleet to send to the Council.[2] This morning the wind came about and we fell into the Hope, and in our passing by the Vice=admirall, he and the rest of the frigates with him did give us abundance of guns and we them, so much that the report of them broke all my windows in my Cabbin and broke off the iron bar that was upon it to keep anybody from creeping in at the Scuttle. This noon I sat the first time with my Lord at table since my coming to sea. All the afternoon exceeding busy in writing of letters and orders. In the afternoon Sir Harry Wright came on board us about his business of being chosen Parliament man.[3] My Lord brought him to see my Cabbin, where I was hard a-writing. At night supped, with my Lord too, with the Captain. And after that to work again till it be very late. So to bed.

28. This morning and the whole day busy, and that the more because Mr. Burr was about his own business all the day at

a preceded by symbol rendered illegible

1. Mountagu's report of this meeting (sent to Blackborne, 27 March) is summarised in *CSPD 1659–60*, p. 538.
2. Cf. 'Accompt of the Conditions of the several Shipps recd. from the

Fleete in Aprill 1660': PRO, PRO 30/24/3, no. 95.
3. Wright (Mountagu's brother-in-law) was elected at Harwich on 3 April.

Gravesend. At night there was a gentleman very well bred, his name was Banes,[1] going for Flushing, who spoke French and Latin very well, brought by direction from Captain Clerke hither as a prisoner because he cried out of the vessel that he went in, "Where is your King? We have done our business; *Vive le Roy.*" He confessed himself a Cavalier in his heart and that he and his whole family had fought for the King; but that he was then drunk, having been all night taking his leave at Gravesend the night before, and so could not remember what it was that he said; but in his words and carriage showed much of a gentleman. My Lord had a great kindness for him, but did not think it safe to release him; but commanded him to be used civilly, so he was taken up to the Master's cabin and had a supper there. In the meantime I writ a letter to the Council about him and an order for the vessel to be sent for back that he was taken out of. But a while after, he sent a letter down to my Lord, which my Lord did like very well and did advise with me what was best to be done; so I put in something to my Lord and then to the Captain that the gentleman was to be released and the letter stopped, which was done. So I went up and sat and talked with him in Latin and French, and drank a bottle or two of wine with him; and about 11 a-clock at night he took boat again, and so God bless him. Thence I to my cabin and to bed. To-day we have news of the election at Huntington for Bernard and Pedly, at which my Lord was much troubled for his friends missing of it.[2]

29. We lie still a little below Gravesend.

At night Mr. Sheply returned from London and told us of several elections for the next Parliament. That the King's Effigies was new-making, to be set up in the Exchange again.[3]

This evening was a great whispering of some of the Vice-admiralls captains that they were dissatisfied and did intend to

---

1. Possibly the Robert Banes, of Hampshire, arrested in the autumn of 1659 for suspected complicity in Booth's rising.

2. See above, p. 87 & n. 1. But Mountagu's defeated friends were both, by his influence, elected elsewhere: George Mountagu for Dover and Viscount Mandeville for Huntingdonshire.

3. Charles I's statue was set up again on 7 May. Cf. above, p. 89 & n. 3.

fight*a* themselfs to oppose the Generall: but it was soon hushed'
and the Vice-admirall did wholly deny any such thing and
protested to stand by the Generall.¹

At night, Mr. Sheply, W. Howe, and I supped in my cabin.
So up to the Master's cabin, where we sat talking; and then
to bed.

30. I was saluted in the morning with two letters from some
that I had done a favour to, which brought me in each a piece
of gold. This day, while my Lord and we were at dinner, the
Nazeby came in sight toward us, and at last came to Anchor
close by us. After dinner my Lord and many others went on
board her, where everything was out of order; and a new
chimney made for my Lord in his bedchamber, which he was
much pleased with. My Lord in his discourse discovered a great
deal of love to this ship.²

31. This morning Captain Jowles of the *Wexford* came on
board, for whom I got commission from my Lord to be commander of that ship – upon the doing thereof he was to make the
20*s.* piece that he sent me yesterday up 5*l.*; wherefore he signed
me a bill that he did owe me 4*l* – which I sent my boy to Gravesend with him, and he did give the boy 4*l* for me, and the boy
gave him the bill under his hand. This morning, Mr. Hill that
lives in Axe=yard was here on board with the Vice-Admirall;
I did give him a bottle of wine, and was exceedingly satisfied
with the power that I have to make my friends welcome. Many
orders to make all the afternoon; at night, Mr. Sheply, Howe,
Ibbott and I supped in my cabin together.

a possibly 'fit'

---

1. But several were soon relieved
of their commissions: below, p. 109
& n. 2.

2. She had been his flagship in the
Baltic in 1659.

APRILL.

1. *Lords day.* Mr. Ibbott preached very well. After dinner my Lord did give me a private list of all the ships that were to be set out this summer, wherein I do discern that he hath made it his care to put by as much of the Anabaptists as he can. By reason of my Lord and my being busy to send away the Packet by Mr. Cooke of the *Nazeby*, it was 4 a-clock before we could begin sermon again. This day Captain Guy came on board from Dunkirke, who tells me that the King will come in and that the soldiers at Dunkirke do drink the King's health in the streets.[1] At night the Captain, Sir R. Stayner, Mr. Sheply, and I did sup together in the Captain's cabin. I made a commission tonight to Captain Wilgress of the *Beare*, which got me 30s. So after writing a while, I went to bed.

2. Up very early, and to get all my things and my boy's packed up. Great concourse of commanders here this morning to take leave of my Lord upon his going into the *Naseby*, so that the table was full; so there dined below many commanders and Mr. Creed, who was much troubled to hear that he could not go along with my Lord, for he had already got all his things thither, thinking to stay there; but W. Howe was very high against it, and he indeed did put him out, though everybody was glad of it. After dinner I went in one of the boats with my boy before my Lord, and made shift before night to get my cabin in pretty good order. It is but little; but very convenient, having one window to the sea and another to the Deck – and a good bed. This morning comes Mr. Edw. Pickering, like a coxcomb as he always was.[2] He tells me that the

1. Dunkirk, acquired in 1658 from Spain and sold to the French in 1662, now had a large and ill-paid garrison which was an important political force. It had been the centre of much royalist intrigue. Reports similar to Pepys's are in *CSPClar.*, iv. 611, 625 (22, 23 March). The garri-son finally declared for the King c. 7 May: Sir W. Lower, *Relation*, p. 13.

2. Pickering was Mountagu's nephew and a member of his household until 1663. Roger North's opinion of him was much the same as Pepys's: *Lives of Norths* (ed. A. Jessopp), i. 76.

King will come in, but that Monke did resolve to have the doing of it himself, or else to hinder it.

3. Late to bed. About 3 in the morning there was great knocking at my cabin, which with much difficulty (as they say) waked me and I rise; but it was only for a packet, so I went to my bed again. And in the morning gave it my Lord.

This morning Captain Isham comes on board to see my Lord and drink his wine before he went into the Downes; there likewise came many merchants to get convoy to the Baltique, which a course was taken for.

They dined with my Lord, and one of them, by name Alderman Wood,[1] talked much to my Lord of the hopes that we have now to be settled (under the King he meant); but my*a* Lord took no notice of it. After dinner, which was late, my Lord went on shore; and after him, I and Captain Sparling went in his boat; but the water being almost at low water, we could not stay for fear of not getting into our boats again. So back again. This day came the Lieutenant of the *Swiftsure* (who was sent by my Lord to Hastings, one of the Cinque ports, to have got Mr. Edwd. Mountagu to have been one of their burgesses); but could not, for they were all promised before.[2] After he had done his message, I took him and Mr. Pierce the surgeon (who this day came on board, and not before) to my cabin, where we drank a bottle of wine. At night busy a-writing, and so to bed. My heart exceeding heavy for not hearing of my dear wife; and indeed, I do not remember that ever my heart was so apprehensive of her absence as at this very time.

4. This morning I despatched many letters of my own private business to London. There come Collonell Tomson with the wooden leg and Generall Pen and dined with my Lord and Mr.

a MS. 'not'

---

1. ?William Wood, timber merchant, Wapping.
2. The lieutenant brought a letter from the Town Clerk of Hastings: Carte 73, f.372r. Edward Mountagu (eldest son of the 2nd Lord Mountagu of Boughton) failed also to get in at Weymouth, but in 1661 was elected to the following parliament for Sandwich.

Blackburne.[1] Who told me that it was certain now that the King must of necessity*a* come in; and that one of the Council told him that there [is] something doing in order to a treaty already among them.[2] And it was strange to hear how Mr. Blackburne did already begin to commend him for a sober man, and how quiet he would be under his government, &c.

I dined all alone to prevent company, which was exceeding great today, in my cabin.

After these two were gone, Sir W. Wheeler and Sir John Pettus came on board and stayed about two or three hours, and so went away.[3]

The Commissioners came today, only to consult about a further reducement of the fleet and to ⟨pay⟩ them off as fast as they can.

I did give Davis, their servant, 5*l*-10*s* to give to Mr. Moore from me, in part of the 7*l*: that I borrowed of him; and he is to discount*b* the rest out of the 36*s*. that he doth owe mee.

at night, my Lord resolved to send the Captain of our ship to Waymouth and promote his being chosen there, which he did put himself into a readiness to do the next morning.[4]

This evening the Lieutenant of our ship and the Doctor sat with Mr. Sheply and W. Howe and I, singing and talking till 12 at night: and so to bed.

5. Infinite of business all the morning of orders to make, that I was very much perplexed that Mr. Burr had failed me of coming back last night, and we ready to set sail. Which we did about noon, and came in the evening to Lee road and anchored.

a repl. 'nothing'   *b* repl. 'discontent'

---

1. George Thomson and William Penn, sen., were Admiralty Commissioners; Robert Blackborne was Secretary to the Admiralty Committee.

2. Cf. above, p. 84 & n. 2. On 3 April a report to the King warned him to be in readiness to receive overtures shortly: *CSPClar.*, iv. 634. The special measures which the Council took to ensure secrecy seem to have been of no avail: cf. ib., loc. cit.; T.

Carte, *Orig. Letters* (1739), ii. 317-18: Louise F. Brown, *Shaftesbury*, p. 96, n. 34.

3. Wheler was a Presbyterian merchant and a friend of Mountagu; Pettus a wealthy royalist who had supplied money from England to the King in exile.

4. Capt. Roger Cuttance was a native of Weymouth; for the result of the election, see below, p. 108.

At night Mr. Sheply overtook us, who had been at Grayes-market this morning. I spent all the afternoon upon the deck, it being very pleasant weather. This afternoon Sir Rich. Stayner and Mr. Creed, after we were come to anchor, did come on board us, and Creed brought me 30*l* which my Lord had ordered him to pay me upon account. And Captain Clerke brought me a knotted Cane.*a* At night, very sleepy, to bed.

6. This morning came my brother-in-law Balty to see me and to desire to be here with me as Reformado, which did much trouble me. But after dinner (my Lord using him very civilly at table), I spoke to my Lord and he promised me a letter to Captain Stokes for him, that he should be there. All the day with him, walking and talking; we under sail as far as the Spitts. In the afternoon, W. How and I to our Viallins, the first time since we came on board. This afternoon I made even with my Lord to this day, and did give him all the money remaining in my hand.

In the evening, it being fine moonshine, I stayed late, walking upon the Quarter-deck talking with Mr. Cuttance, learning of some sea terms; and so down to supper and to bed – having an hour before put Balty into Bur's cabin, he being out of*b* the ship.

7. This day, about 9 a-clock in the morning, the wind grew high; and we being among the sands, lay at anchor. I begin to be dizzy and squeamish. Before dinner, my Lord sent for me down to eat some oysters, the best my Lord said that ever he eat in his life, though I have eat as good at Bardsey. After dinner and all the afternoon I walked upon the deck to keep myself from being sick; and at last, about 5 a-clock, went to bed and got a caudle made me, and sleep upon it very well. This day Mr. Sheply went to Sheppy.

8. *Lords day.* Very calm again and I pretty well, but my head ached all day. About noon set sail; in our way I saw many wracks and masts, which are now the greatest guides for ships. We had a brave wind all the afternoon. And overtook

a l.h. uncertain   *b* MS. 'out of on'

two good merchantmen that overtook us yesterday, going to the East Indys,[1] and the lieutenant[2] and I lay out of his window with his glass, looking at the women that were on board them, being pretty handsome. This evening Major Willowby, who hath been here these three or four days on board with Mr. Pickering, went*a* on board a katch for Dunkirke. We continued sailing when I went to bed, being somewhat ill again. I and Will Howe, the surgeon, parson, and Balty supped in the Lieutenant's cabin and afterward sat disputing, the parson for and I against extemporary prayer very hot.

9. We having sailed all night, were come in sight of the North and South forelands in the morning, and so sailed all day. In the afternoon we had a very fresh gale, which I brooked better then I thought I should be able to do. 《*This afternoon I first saw France and Callis, with which I was much pleased, though it was at a distance.》 About 5 a-clock we came to the Goodwin; so to the castles about Deale,[3] where our fleet lay, among whom we anchored. Great was the shot of guns from the castles and ships and our answers, that I never heard yet so great rattling of guns. Nor could we see one another on board for the smoke that was among us, nor one ship from another. As soon as came to anchor, the captains came from on board their ships all to us on board. This night I writ letters for my Lord to the Council, &c.,[4] which Mr. Pickering was to carry, who took his leave this night of my Lord. And Balty, after I had writ two or three letters by him to my wife and Mr. Bowyer and had drank a bottle of wine with him in my cabin which J. Goods and W. Howe brought on purpose, he took leave of me too, to go away tomorrow morning with Mr. Pickering.

a repl. 'took'

---

1. The *Eagle, Richard and Martha* and *American* were now bound for Surat in India: *Cal. court mins E. India Co. 1660-3* (ed. E. B. Sainsbury), p. iii.

2. David Lambert, companion of Pepys on the Baltic voyage, 1659.

3. The 16th-century artillery forts of Walmer, Deal and Sandown.

4. E.g. Mountagu to Admiralty Commissioners, PRO, SP 18/224, nos 33, 34 (summary in *CSPD 1659-60*, p. 544); sending a list of ships and promising to enquire into the condition of the fleet.

I lent Balty 15s. which he was to pay to my wife. It was one a-clock in the morning before we parted. This evening Mr. Sheply came on*a* board, having escaped a very great danger upon a sand coming from Chattam.

10. This morning, many or most of the commanders in the fleet came on board and dined here – so that some of them and I dined together in the Roundhouse, where we were very merry. Hither came the Vice-admirall[1] to us, and sat and talked and seemed a very good-natured man. At night, as I was all alone in my cabin in a melancholy fit playing on my viallin, my Lord and Sir R. Stayner came into the coach and supped there, and called me out to supper with them. After that, up to the Lieutenants Cabbin, where he and I and Sir Rich: sat till 11 a-clock talking; and so to bed. ⟨This day my Lord Goring[2] returned from France and landed at Dover.⟩*b*

11. A gentleman came this morning from my Lord of Manchester to my Lord for a pass for Mr. Boyle,[3] which was made him. I eat a good breakfast by my Lord's order with him in the great cabin below. The wind all this day was very high – so that a gentleman that was at dinner with my Lord that came along with Sir John Bloys[4] (who seemed a fine man) was forced to rise from table. This afternoon came a great paquet of letters from London directed to me; among the rest, two from my dear wife, the first that I have since my coming away from London. All the news from London is that things go ever further toward a King. That the Skinners Company the other day at their entertaining of Generall Monke had took down the Parliament arms in their Hall and set up the Kings.[5]

    In the evening my Lord and I had a great deal of discourse

a repl. 'home'   *b* addition crowded in between entries at end of line

---

1. John Lawson.
2. Probably George (Goring), Earl of Norwich, royalist leader in the Second Civil War; abroad since 1650; still often called by the title of his barony, since his earldom was a civil war creation.
3. Probably Charles Boyle, second son of the 2nd Earl of Cork, a member

of one of the greatest of the royalist families of Ireland.
4. *Recte* Sir John Boys. He and Sir John Grenville carried news of Lambert's defeat to the King: Lower, *Relation* (1660), p. 6.
5. This was on 4 April: cf. *CSPClar.*, iv. 626.

about the several Captaines of the fleet and his interest among them, and had his mind clear to bring in the King. He confessed to me that he was not sure of his own Captain to be true to him,*a* and that he did not like Captain Stokes. At night W. Howe and I at our viallins in my cabin, where Mr. Ibbott and the Lieutenant were late. I stayed the Lieutenant late, showing him my manner of keeping a Journall.[1] After that, to bed.

It comes now in my mind to observe that I am sensible that I have been a little too free to make mirth with the Minister of our ship, he being a very sober and an upright man.

12. This day, the weather being very bad, we had no strangers aboard. In the afternoon came the Vice-admirall on board, with whom my Lord consulted and I sent a packet to London at night with several letters to my friends; as, to my wife about my getting of money*b* for her when she shall need it – to Mr. Bowyer, that he tell me when the masters of the offices be paid.[2] To Mr. Moore, about the business of my office and making even with him as to matter of money. At night, after I had despatch[ed] my letters, to bed.

13. This day very foul all day for rain and wind. In the afternoon set my own things in my cabin and chests in better order then hitherto and set my papers in order. At night sent another packet to London by the post; and after that was done, I went up to the Lieutenant's cabin and there we broached a vessel of ale that we had sent among us four from Deale today – there was the Minister and Doctor with us. After that, till one a-clock in the morning writing letters to Mr. Downing about my business of continuing my office to myself, only Mr. Moore

a MS. 'me' *b* MS. 'my'

---

1. Only twice in the diary does Pepys record having admitted to keeping a journal. The other occasion is on 9 March 1669, when he informed Coventry.

2. Robert Bowyer was an Exchequer official. The masters of the offices were the senior officials, such as Downing, Pepys's employer. Since Pepys received his salary from Downing himself and not from the Exchequer, his letter to Bowyer may have been an indirect way of getting to know when he himself would be paid.

to*a* execute it for me. I had also a very serious and effectuall letter from my Lord to him to that purpose. After that done, then to bed; and it being very rainy and the rain coming upon my bed, I went and lay with Joh. Goods in the great cabin below – the wind being so high that we were fain to lower some of the masts. I to bed; and what with the goodness of the bed ⟪14⟫ and the rocking of the ship, I slept till almost 10 a-clock – and then rise and drank a good morning draught there with Mr. Sheply, which occasioned my thinking upon the happy life that I live now, had I nothing to care for but myself. The sea was this morning very high; and looking out of the window, I saw our boat come with Mr. Pierce the purser in it, in great danger; who endeavouring to come on board us, had like to have been drowned had it not been for a rope.

This day I was informed that my Lord Lambert is got out of the Tower and that there is 100*l* proffered to whoever shall bring him forth to the Council of State.[1] My Lord is chosen at Waymouth this morning; my Lord had his freedom brought him by Captain Tiddiman of the port of Dover, by which he is capable of being elected for them.[2] This day I heard how the army have in general declared to stand by what the next Parliament shall do.[3] At night supped with my Lord.

15. *Lords=day.* Up early and was trimmed by the barber in the great cabin below; after that, to my closet*b* and then to sermon; then to dinner, where my Lord told us how the University of Cambrige have a mind to choose him for their burgess;

a   repl. 'only Mr.'
b   MS. 'closen'; possibly a confusion of 'cabin' and 'closet'

---

1. He escaped on the evening of the 10th, allegedly with the help of a maid who wore his nightcap and impersonated him in bed. He had almost a day's start of the proclamation ordering his arrest, issued on the 11th: Steele, no. 3178.

2. For correspondence to and from Mountagu concerning these elections, see Carte 73, ff. 357, 382, 384, 395.

Capt. Thomas Teddiman (a Dover man) acted as his agent there. Mountagu was chosen for both places, but on being raised to the peerage resigned both before taking his seat.

3. Monck had compelled his officers and men to sign an engagement to this effect on the 9th: Whitelocke, *Memorials,* iv. 406.

which he pleased himself with, to think that they do look upon him as a thriving man, and said so openly at table.[1] At dinner-time Mr. Cooke came back from London with a packet which caused my Lord to be full of thoughts all day; and at night bid me privately to get two commissions ready, one for Captain Robt. Blake to be Captain of the *Worcester* in the room of Captain Dekings, an Anabaptist and one that hath witnessed a great deal of discontent with the present proceedings.[2] The other for Captain Coppin to come out of the   [a] into the *Newbery* in the room of Blake, whereby I perceive that Generall Monke doth resolve to make a thorough change to make way for the King. From London I hear that the Phanatiques have held up their heads high since Lambert got out of the Tower, but I hope all that will come to nothing. Late a-writing of letters to London to get ready for Mr. Cooke. Then to bed.

《16》 And about 4 a-clock in the morning, Mr. Cooke waked me where I lay in the great cabin below, and I did give him his packet and directions for London. So to sleep again. All the morning giving out orders and tickets to the Commanders of the fleet to discharge all Supernumerarys that they have above the number that the Council hath set in their last establishment.[3]

    a 'Newbery' crossed out. Supply '*Langport*'.

---

1. Monck, elected both for Cambridge University and for Devonshire, had chosen to serve for the latter. This offer was thereupon transmitted to Mountagu: W. Hetley to Mountagu, Cambridge, 12 April; Carte 73, f.400*r*. But in the event Mountagu's cousin, William Mountagu, second son of Edward, 1st Baron Mountagu of Boughton, was returned. Cf. M. B. Rex, *University representation in Engl. 1604–90*, pp. 198–200, App. vi.

2. Writing to Monck on 12 April, Mountagu had complained against Deakins of the *Worcester* as an Anabaptist 'much discontented & busye in stirringe up others', and against Newberry of the *Plymouth* who had a method of governing his ship which was 'very discontentinge & wearisome to his men that are not of his way'. Mountagu asked that they should both be removed, but that he himself be spared the task of proposing their dismissal: Carte 73, f.399*r* (copy in Mountagu's hand). Deakins had been a favourite of Lawson's, who in fact had recently asked Mountagu to make him Rear-Admiral: ib., f.355*r*. He was now sent off to the Straits on convoy duty: Harris, i. 176.

3. The orders of the Admiralty Commissioners (11 April) are in Carte 73, f.391*r*; for Mountagu's reply of the 13th, see *CSPD 1659–60*, p. 413.

After dinner busy all the afternoon writing – and so till night; then to bed.

17.   All the morning getting ready commissions for the Vice-Admirall and Rear-Admirall,[1] wherein my Lord was very careful to express the utmost of his own power, commanding them to obey what orders they should receive from the Parliament &c., or both or either of the Generalls.   The Vice-Admirall dined with us; and in the afternoon my [Lord] called me to give him the commission for him; which I did, and he gave it him himself.
A very pleasant afternoon, and I upon the deck all the day. It was so clear that my Lord's glass showed us Calais very plain, and the Cliffes were as plain to be seen as Kent; nay, my Lord at first made me believe that it was Kent.   At night, after supper, my Lord called for the Rear-Admirall commission, which I brought him; and I sitting in my study, heard my Lord discourse with him concerning Dekings and Newberys being put out of commission.   And by the way I did observe that my Lord did speak more openly his mind to me afterwards at night then I could find that he did to the Rear-Admirall, though his great confidant – for I was with him an hour together, where he told me clearly his thoughts that the King would carry it, and that he did think himself very happy that he was now at sea, as well for his own sake as that he thought he might do his country some service in keeping things quiet.   To bed and shifted myself from top to toe – there being Joh. Goods and W. Howe sat late by my bedside talking.   So to sleep – every day bringing me a fresh sense of the great pleasure of my present life.

18.   This morning very early came Mr. Edwd. Mountagu on board, but what was the business of his coming again or before, without any servant and making no stay at all, I cannot guess.[2] This day Sir R. Stayner, Mr. Sheply, and as many of my Lord's

1. Lawson and Stayner; for the commissions, see *CSPD 1659–60*, p. 547.

2. Edward Mountagu (son of the 2nd Lord Mountagu of Boughton) had gone to Flanders from the fleet on 10 April and now returned with letters to Mountagu from the King

and the Duke of York: Sandwich, p. 74.   He had acted as intermediary between Mountagu and the court since the previous summer: Clarendon, *Hist.*, vi. 186–8; *CSPClar.*, iv. 246, 634–5. Cf. *Naval Minutes*, p. 387; Whitelocke, *Memorials*, iv. 408.

people as could be spared, went to Dover to get things ready against tomorrow for the election there.

I all the afternoon dictating in my cabin (my own head being troubled with multiplicity of business) to Burr, who writ for me above a dozen letters, by which I have made my mind more light and clear then I have had it yet since I came on board. At night sent a packet to London. And Mr. Cooke returned thence, bringing me this news: that the Sectarys do talk high what they will do; but I believe all to no purpose. That the Cavaliers are something unwise to talk so high on the other side as they do. That the Lords do meet every day at my [Lord] of Manchesters, and resolve to sit the first day of the Parliament.[1] That it is evident now that the Generall and the Council do resolve to make way for the King's coming. And it is now clear that either the Fanatiques must now be undone, or the Gentry and citizens throughout England and clergy must fall, in spite of their Militia and army, which is not at all possible*a* I think.[2] At night I supped with W. Howe and Mr. Luellin (being the first time that I have been so long with him) in the great cabin below.*b* ⟨After that to bed; and W. Howe sat by my bedside and he and I sang a psalm or two; and so I to sleep.⟩*c*

19. A great deal of business all this day; and Burr being gone to shore without my leave did vex me much.

At dinner news was brought us that my Lord was chosen at Dover. This afternoon came one Mr. Mansell on board as a Reformado, to whom my Lord did show exceeding great respect, but upon what account I do not yet know.[3] This day it hath rained much, so that when I came to go to bed I found it wet through; so I was fain to wrap myself up in a dry sheet and so lie all night.

a repl. 'at'   *b* repl. ? 'too'   *c* addition crowded into bottom of page

---

1. These were the Presbyterian peers, who aimed at imposing terms on the King. They held that the act of 1649 abolishing their House had been nullified by the recent act dissolving the Long Parliament, in which the rights of the Upper House (i.e. of the parliamentary peers of 1648) had been expressly reserved.

2. Both militia and army had been carefully remodelled since 21 February.

3. This was probably Francis Mansell, who had arranged the last stages of the King's escape to France in 1651; or (possibly) Rowland Mansell, a kinsman of Mountagu.

20.　All the morning I was busy to get my window altered and to have my table set as I would have it; which after it was done, I was infinitely pleased with it, and also to see what a command I have to have everyone ready to come and go at my command.　This evening came one Mr. Boyle[1] on board for whom I writ an order for a ship to transport him to Flushing, He supped with my Lord, my Lord using him as a person of Honour.　This evening too, came Mr. John Pickering on board us.　This evening my head ached exceedingly, which I impute to my sitting backwards in my cabin otherwise then I am used to do.　Tonight Mr. Sheply told me that he heard for certain at Dover that Mr. Edwd. Mountagu did go beyond sea when he was here first the other day, and I am apt to believe that he went to speak with the King.

This day one told me how that at the Eleccion at Cambrige for Knight of the shire, Wendby and Thornton, by declaring to stand for the Parliament and a King and the settlement of the Church, did carry it against all expectation against Sir Dudl. North and Sir Thom. Willis.[2]

I supped tonight with Mr. Sheply below at the half-deck table; and after that saw Mr. Pickering, whom my Lord brought down to his cabin; and so to bed.

———

21.　This day dined Sir John Boys and some other gentlemen, formerly great Cavaliers; and among the rest, one Mr. Norwood, for whom my Lord gave a convoy to carry him to the Brill;[3] but he is certainly going to the King – for my Lord commanded me that I should not enter his name in my book. My Lord doth show them and that sort of people great civility. All their discourse and others' are of the King's coming, and we

1. See above, p. 106 & n. 3.
2. Thomas Wendy and Isaac Thornton were inferior in quality and estate to North and Willys. They offered to withdraw if their opponents would declare for King and Church, but the offer was refused. When this was announced to the assembled freeholders, the cry went up for Thornton and Wendy: *CSPClar.*, iv. 657.

3. Boys was a leader of the Kent royalists, and had been recently imprisoned for demanding a free parliament (*CSPD 1659–60*, p. 330); Maj. Henry Norwood was a royalist agent. Both now carried letters from Mountagu to the King: *CSPClar.*, iv. 687; cf. below, p. 125.

begin to speak of it very freely. And heard how in many churches in London and upon many signs there and upon merchants' ships in the river they have set up the King's arms.[1]

In the afternoon the Captain would by all means have me up to his cabin; and there treated me huge nobly, giving me a barrel of pickled oysters, and opened another for me, and a bottle of wine, which was a very great favour.

At night late singing with W. Howe, and under the barber's hands in the coach. This night there came one with a letter from Mr. Edwd. Mountagu to my Lord, with command to deliver it to his own hand. I do believe that he doth carry some close business on for the King.[2]

This day I had a large letter from Mr. Moore, giving me an account of the present dispute at London that is like to be at the beginning of the Parliament, about the House of Lords, who do resolve to sit with the Commons, as not thinking themselfs dissolved yet – which, whether it be granted or no, or whether they will sit or no, it will bring a great many inconveniencys. His letter I keep,[3] it being a very well-writ one.

22. *Sunday. Easterday.*

Several Londoners, strangers, friends of the Captains, dined here; who, among other things, told us how the King's arms are every day set up in houses and churches, perticularly in All-hallows Church in Thames-street – John Simpson's church – which, being privately done, was a great eyesoare to his people when they came to church and saw it.[4] Also, they told us for certain that the King's statue is making by the Mercers Company (who are bound to do it) to set up in the Exchange.[5]

---

1. The meeting of the new parliament – fixed for 25 April – was now close at hand, and the elections had gone overwhelmingly against the die-hard republicans. For the past three weeks or so signs of a jubilant royalism had been openly displayed in London – pictures of the King in the windows of houses, the royal arms in churches and on ships, etc. *CSPClar.*, iv. 625, 630, 634; Rugge, i, f.87r.

Pepys has an earlier reference to the display of the King's arms at 11 April.

2. See above, p. 110, n. 2.

3. Untraced.

4. Simpson was notoriously anti-monarchical: cf. *CSPD 1660–1*, pp. 97, 162.

5. Cf. above, p. 99 & n. 3. The Mercers were made trustees of the Exchange by Sir Thomas Gresham, who founded it in 1566–8.

After sermon in the afternoon I fell to writing letters against tomorrow, to send to London.   And after supper to bed.

23.   All the morning very busy getting my packet ready for London, only for an hour or two had the Captain and Mr. Sheply at my Cabbin at the barrel of pickled oysters that the Captain did give me on Saturday last.   After dinner I sent Mr. Dunn to London with the packet.   This afternoon I had 40s: given me by Kaptain Cowes of the *Paradox*; in the evening, the first time that we have had any sport, among the seamen; and indeed, there was extraordinary good sport after my Lord had done, playing at nine-pins.   After that, W. Howe and I went to play two Trebles in the great Cabbin below; which my Lord hearing, after supper he called for our instruments and played a set of Lock's, two trebles and a bass.[1]   And that being done, he fell to singing of a song made*a* upon the Rump, with which he pleased himself well – to the tune of *The Blacksmith*.[2]

After all that done, then to bed.

24.   This morning I had Mr. Luellin and Mr. Sheply to the remainder of my oysters that were left yesterday.   After that, very busy all the morning.   While I was at dinner with my Lord, the Coxon of the Vice-Admirall came for me to the Vice-Admirall to dinner; so I told my Lord and he gave me leave to go.   I rise therefore from table and went, where there was very many commanders and very pleasant we were, on board the *London*, which hath a state-room much bigger then the *Nazeby* – but not so rich.   After that with the captain on board our own ship, where we were saluted with the news of Lamberts being taken, which news was brought to London on Sunday last: he

a symbol blotted

---

1. Presumably a group of viol pieces from Matthew Locke's *Little consort of three parts . . . the first 20 are for two trebles and a basse* (1656).   (E).

2. A traditional tune similar to 'Greensleeves': W. Chappell, *Old Engl. popular music* (rev. Wooldridge), i. 241.   It was often used as a setting for ballads, but the one here referred to has not been traced.   There are several collections of Rump songs: e.g. A. Brome, *Rump, or An exact collection of the choycest poems and songs relating to the late times* (1662); T. Wright (ed.), *Polit. ballads published in Engl. during Commonwealth* (1841).(E).

was taken in Northamptonshire by Collonell Ingolsby, in the head of a party, by which means their whole design is broke and things now very open and safe – and every man begins to be merry and full of hopes.[1]   In the afternoon my Lord gave me a great large Character to write out, so I spent all the day about it.   And after supper my Lord and we had some more very good Musique and singing of *Turne Ameryllis*, as it is printed in the Song-book,[2] with which my Lord was very much pleased. After that to bed.

25. All the morning about my Lord's Character. Dined today with Captain Clerke on board the *Speaker* (a very brave ship), where was the Vice-Admirall, Rear-Admirall, and many other commanders.

After dinner home, not a little contented to see how I am treated and with what respect made a fellow to the best commanders in the fleet.

All the afternoon finishing of the Character; which I did and gave it my Lord, it being very handsomely done and a very good one in itself, but that not truly Alphabeticall.

Supped with Mr. Sheply, W. Howe, &c. in Mr. Pierce the Purser his cabin, where very merry; and so to bed. Captain Isham came hither today.

26. This day came Mr. Donne back from London, who brought letters with him that signify the meeting of the Parliament yesterday. And in the afternoon, by other letters I hear that about twelve of the Lords met and have chosen my Lord of Manchester Speaker of the House of Lords (the young Lords that never sot yet, do forbear to sit for the present); and Sir

---

1. This was the last rising of the fanatics before the Restoration, and the last fling of their most dangerous leader. Col. Richard Ingoldsby, at the head of a detachment of regulars, reinforced by militia, came up with the rebels near Daventry on the 22nd. Lambert and his principal supporters were taken without a fight; the rest fled. The news was conveyed to

Mountagu in a letter from Sir Anthony Ashley Cooper, London, 23 April: Sandwich MSS, Letters from Ministers, i, f.23r.

2. Playford's *Select ayres and dialogues* (1659), pp. 112-13, has Thomas Brewer's new setting of James Shirley's lyric 'Turn Amaryllis to thy swain' (*Schoole of complement*, 1631, p. 37). (E).

Harbottle Grimstone Speaker of the House of Commons.[1]   The
House of Lords sent to have a concurrence with the House of
Commons; which after a little debate was granted.[2]

Dr. Renalds preached before the Commons before they sat.[3]

My Lord told me how Sir H. Yelverton (formerly my schoolfellow) was chosen in the first place for Northamptonshire and
Mr. Crew in the second.   And told me how he did believe that
the Cavaliers have now the upper hand clear of the Presbyterians.[4]

All the afternoon I was writing of letters; among the rest, one
to W. Simons, Peter Luellin and Tom Doling; which because
it is somewhat merry, I keep a copy of.[5]

After that done, Mr. Sheply, W. Howe and I down with Jo
Goods into my Lord's Storeroome of wine and other drink,
where it was very pleasant to observe the massy timbers that the
ship is made of.   We in the room were wholly under water
and yet a deck below that.

After that to supper, where Tom Guy supped with us and
we had very good laughing; and after that some Musique, where
Mr. Pickering, beginning to play a bass part upon my viall, did
it so like a fool that I[a] was ashamed of him.

After that to bed.

27.   This morning Burr was absent again from on board,
which I was troubled at and spoke to Mr. Pierce, purser, to speak
to him of it and tell him my mind.

This morning Pim[6] spent in my cabin, putting a great[b] many

a repl. 'he'   *b* repl. 'pr'-

---

1. Both Manchester and Grimston
were leading Presbyterians. The
'young Lords' were those who had
succeeded to their titles and come of
age since the House had ceased to
meet early in 1649. Monck persuaded them to bide their time: two
in fact went to the House but did not
enter. There was a total attendance
of ten at the Lords on 26 April. *LJ*,
xi. 3; Guizot, ii. 414.

2. *CJ*, viii. 1.   The Lords had sent
a message proposing the concurrence
of the Commons in keeping a fast on
the following Monday. By receiving the message the Commons recognised the legal existence of the Lords.

3. Ib., viii. 1.   The preacher was
the moderate Presbyterian, Dr Edward Reynolds, and the service held
in St Margaret's. The sermon was
printed as *The author and subject of
healing in the Church* (1660).

4. For the cavaliers' success in the
elections, see L. F. Brown in *EHR*,
22/52–3.

5. Untraced.

6. Mountagu's tailor.

ribbons to a suit.   After dinner, in the afternoon came on board Sir Tho. Hatton and Sir R. Maleverer, going for Flushing; but all the world know that they go where the rest of the many gentlemen in the [fleet] everyday flock, to the King at Bredagh.[1] They supped here, and my Lord treated them as he doth the rest that go thither, with a great deal of civility.   While we were at supper, a packet came; wherein much news from several friends. The chief is that that I have from Mr Moore, *viz.* that he fears the Cavaliers in the House will be so high that the others will be forced to leave the House and fall*ᵃ* in with the Generall Monke; and so offer things to the King so high on the Presbiterian account that he may refuse, and so they will endeavour some more mischief; but when I told my*ᵇ* Lord it, he shook his head and told me that the Presbyters are deceived, for the Generall is certainly for the King's interest, and so they will not be able to prevail that way with him.

After supper the two Knights went from on board on board the *Grantham* – that is to convey them to Flushing.   I am informed that the Exchequer is now so low, that there is not 20*l* there to give the messenger that brought the news of Lamberts being taken;[2] which story is very strange, that he should lose his reputation of being a man of courage now at one blow, for that he was not able to fight one stroke, but desired of Collonell Ingolsby several times for God's sake to let him escape.[3]

Late reading my letters, my mind being much troubled to think that after all our hopes we should have any cause to fear any more disappointments therein.

To bed.   This day I made even with Mr. Creed, by sending him my bill and he me my money by Burr, whom I sent for it.

a   repl. ? 'never'   *b*   repl. 'him it'

---

1. Charles had arrived at Breda from Brussels on 4/14 April, and the English government no longer attempted to prevent royalists like Hatton and Mauleverer from going there. Chancellor Hyde was expecting important news from Hatton. Lower, *Relation* (1660), p. 5; *CSPClar.*, iv. 652.

2. A council warrant was issued on 23 April for the payment of £20 to Thomas Wright for this service: *CSPD 1659–60*, p. 598.

3. Lambert was said to have prevented his officers from leading a charge: Whitelocke, *Memorials*, iv. 408.

28.   That morning sending a packet by Mr. Dunne to London. In the afternoon I played at nine-pins with Mr. Pickering, I and Mr. Pett against him and Ned Osgood, and won a crown apiece of him.   He had not money enough to pay me.   After supper, my Lord exceeding merry; and he and I and W. Howe to sing. And so to bed.

29.   *Sunday*.   This day I put on first my fine cloth suit, made[a] of a cloak that had like to have been beshit behind a year ago the very day that I put it on.

After sermon in the morning, Mr. Cooke came from London with a packet, bringing news how all the young lords that were not in arms against the Parliament do now sit.[1]   That a letter is come from the King to the House; which is locked up by the Council till next Tuesday, that it may be read in the open House when they meet again, they having adjourned till then to keep a fast tomorrow – and so the contents is not yet known.[2]

13000*l* of the 20000*l* given to Generall Monke is paid out of the Exchequer – he giving 12*l* among the teller-clerks of the Exchequer.[3]

My Lord called me into the great Cabbin below, where I opened my letters and he told me that the Presbyterians are quite mastered by the Cavaliers,[4] and that he fears Mr. Crew did go a little too far the other day in keeping out the young Lords from sitting.   That he doth expect that the King should be brought over suddenly, with[out] staying to make any terms at all, saying that the Presbyters did intend to have brought him in with such conditions as if he had been in chains.   But he shook his shoulders when he told me how Monke had betrayed them, for it was he that did put them upon standing to keep out the Lords and the other

a MS. 'mot'

1. Eight were admitted on the 27th: *LJ*, xi. 5.
2. *CJ*, viii. 3+. The letter conveyed the Declaration of Breda: see below, p. 123.
3. The sum was voted to him on 16 March in substitution for the gift of Hampton Court, which he refused. The warrant for the payment of £13,000 had been issued on 21 March, and the balance was to be paid in September: *CSPD 1659–60*, p. 594.
4. The cavaliers dominated the crucial Committee for Privilege and Elections, which scrutinised the returns and interpreted in their own interest the Act for Qualifications passed by the last parliament.

members that came not within the Qualificacions – which he[1]
did not like; but however, he hath done his business, though it be
with some kind of baseness.[2]

After dinner I walked a great while upon the deck with the
Chyrurgeon and Purser and other officers of the ship; and they
all pray for the King's coming, which I pray God send.

30. All the morning getting instructions ready for the
Squadron of ships that are going today to the Streights; among
others, Captain Teddiman, Curtis, and Captain Robt. Blake to
be commander of the whole Squadron.[3]

After dinner to nine-pins, W. Howe and I against Mr. Creed
and the Captain; we lost 5s apiece to them. After that, W. How,
Mr. Sheply and I, we got my Lord's leave to go to see Captain
Sparling: so we took boat and first went on shore, it being very
pleasant in the fields.[a] But a very pitiful town Deale is.[4] We
went to Fullers (the famous place for ale); but they had none
but what was in the fat. After that to Pooles, a tavern in the
town,[5] where we drank; and so to boat again and went to the
Assistance,[6] where we were treated very civilly by the Captain;
and he did give us such musique upon the harp by a fellow that
he keeps on board, that I never expect to hear the like again –
yet he a drunken simple fellow to look on as any I ever saw.
After that on board the *Nazeby*, where we found my Lord at
supper; so I sat down and very pleasant my Lord was with Mr.

a MS. 'fells' or 'fiels'

---

1. Mountagu.
2. Bordeaux, the French ambassador, wrote on the 30th: 'Those [of
the Lords] even who have borne
arms against the Parliament will take
their seats. He [Monck] has con-
sented to the admission of all the
members of the House of Commons
without regard to qualifications;
which leads the army to murmur, and
weakens the credit of the Presbyterian party, the leaders of which
accuse the general of having duped
them': Guizot, ii. 417.

3. A squadron of four sailed this
day to convoy a fleet of merchantmen
to the Mediterranean: Sandwich,
pp. 74–5.
4. Much new building had been
done by the time of Celia Fiennes's
visit in 1697, when she admired the
prosperous look of the 'neate brick-
work': *Journeys* (ed. Morris), p. 128.
5. Mountagu's letters were directed
to Poole's at this time: cf. Carte 73,
f.376r.
6. Sparling's ship.

Creed and Sheply, who he puzled about finding out the meaning of the three holes which my Lord hath cut over the Chrystall of his watch.[1]   After supper, some musique.   Then Mr. Sheply, W. Howe and I up to the Lieutenants Cabbin, where we drank, and I and Will Howe were very merry; and among other froliques, he pulls out the spiket of the little vessel of ale that was there in the Cabbin and drew some into his Mounteere; and after he had drunk, I endeavouring to dash it in his face, he got my velvett studying-cap and drew some into mine too, that we made ourselfs a great deal of mirth, but spoiled my clothes with the ale that we dash up and down; after that, to bed very late – with drink enough in my head.

1. A 'watch' at this period might be a pocket- or pendant-watch, or a non-striking clock.   Crystal was normally used for the face, and sometimes for the whole case.   The holes may have been the means of suspending it from cords in order to minimise the effects of the ship's motion.

1. This morning I was told how the people of Deale have set up two or three Maypooles and have hung up their flags upon the top of them, and do resolve to be very merry today, it being a very pleasant day. I wished myself in Hide parke.[1]

This day I do count myself to have had full two years of perfect cure for the stone, for which God of heaven be blessed. This day Captain Parker came on board; and without his expectation, I have a commission for him for the *Nonesuch* frigatt (he being now in the *Cheriton*), for which he gave me a French pistoll.[2] Captain Hen. Cuttance hath commission for the *Cheriton*. After dinner to nine-pins, and won something. The rest of the afternoon at my cabin, writing and piping.

While[a] we were at supper, we heard a great noise upon the Quarter Deck; so we all rise instantly, and found that it was to save the Coxon of the *Cheritons* boate; who dropping overboard, could not be saved, but was drowned. Today I put on my suit that was altered from the great skirts to little ones.

Today I hear they were very merry at Deale, setting up the Kings flag upon one of their Maypooles and drinking his health upon their knees in the streets and firing the guns – which the soldiers of the Castle threatened, but durst not oppose.

2. In the morning at a breakfast of Radyshes at the Pursers cabin. After that to writing – till dinner – at which time comes Dunne from London with letters that tell us the wellcome Newes

a repl. 'This'

---

1. This was the first May Day on which the erection of maypoles had been allowed since their suppression by the Puritans in 1644 and 1654. During the revolution, May Day had continued to be celebrated as a holiday, and Londoners had still gone in their finery to Hyde Park much as usual: cf. *The yellow book: or A serious letter sent by a private Christian to the Lady Consideration, the first day of May, 1656 . . .* (1656). The Park had been open to the public since the 1620's: James Shirley, *Hyde Park* (dedication).

2. *Pistole*; gold coin worth 17s. 6d.

of the Parliaments votes yesterday,[1] which will be remembered for the happiest May-day that hath been many a year to England.

The King's letter was read in the House, wherein he submits himself and all things to them – as to an act of Oblivion to all, unless they shall please to except any; – as to the confirming of the Sales of the King's and Church lands, if they see good.

The House, upon reading the letter, order 50000*l* to be forthwith provided to send to His Maiesty for his present supply. And a committee chosen to return an answer of thank[s] to His Majesty for his gracious Letter. And that the letter be kept among the Records of the Parliament. And in all this, not so much as one Noe. So that Luke Robinson himself stood up and made a recantation for what he hath done and promises to be a loyall subject to his Prince for the time to come.[2]

The City of London have put out a Declaracion, wherein they do disclaim their owning any other governments but that of a King, Lords, and Commons.[3] Thanks was given by the House to Sir Joh. Greenevill, one of the bedchamber to the King, who brought the letter; which they continued bare all the time it was reading.

Upon notice made from the Lords to the Commons of their desire that the Commons would join with them in their vote for King, Lords, and Commons, the Commons did concur and voted that all books whatever that are out against the government of King, Lords, and Commons should be brought into the House and burned.

Great joy all yesterday[a] at London; and at night more bonefires then ever and ringing of bells and drinking of the King's health upon their knees in the streets, which methinks is a little too much. But everybody seems to be very joyful in the business – insomuch that our sea-commanders now begin to say so too, which a week ago they would not do. And our

a repl. 'this'

---

1. Thurloe to Mountagu, 1 May: Sandwich MSS, Letters from Ministers, i, f.25*r*. Cf. *CJ*, viii. 4–8.

2. He was M.P. for Scarborough, and until this moment a vociferous republican. He spoke first after the reading of the letter, 'all bathed in tears': HMC, *Rep.*, 5/199.

3. *A declaration and vindication of the Lord Mayor, aldermen and commons of the city of London in common-councell assembled.*

seamen, as many as have money or credit for drink, did do nothing else this evening.

This day came Mr. North (Sir Dudly North's son) on board to spend a little time here, which my Lord was a little troubled at; but he seems to be a fine gentleman and at night did play his part exceeding well at first sight.[1]

After Musique I went up to the Captain's cabin with him and Lieutenant Ferrers, who came hither today from London to bring this news to my Lord; and after a bottle of wine, we all to bed.

3. This morning my Lord showed me the King's declaration and his letter to the two Generalls to be communicated to the fleet. The contents of the letter are his offer of grace to all that will come in within 40 days, only excepting them that the Parliament shall hereafter except. That the sales of lands during these troubles, and all other things, shall be left to the Parliament, by which he will stand. The letter dated at Breda, April $\frac{4}{14}$ 1660, in the 12th year of his Raigne.[2] Upon[a] the receipt of it this morning by an express, Mr. Phillips, one of the messengers of the Council from Generall Monke, my Lord summoned a council of war, and in the meantime did dictate to me how he would have the vote ordered which he would have pass this council. Which done, the commanders all came on board, and the council set in the coach (the first council of war that hath been in my time), where I read the letter and declaration; and while they were discoursing upon it, I seemed* to draw up a vote; which

a MS. 'My upon'

1. Charles, eldest son of Sir Dudley; later (1677) 4th Baron North. A relative of Mountagu by marriage, he came of a very musical family: cf. Roger North, *Lives of Norths*, passim.

2. The Declaration of Breda was also communicated to parliament, the city and the army. Mountagu's copy, together with the letter from the King, and copies (in Pepys's hand) of the letters exchanged between Monck and Mountagu are in Sandwich MSS, App., ff. 200–4. Cf. *CJ*, viii. 4–6. Charles II dated the beginning of his reign not from his restoration, but from the death of his father.

being offered, they passed.[1] Not one man seemed to say no to it, though I am confident many in their hearts were against it.

After this was done, I went up to the Quarter-deck with my Lord and the commanders, and there read both the papers and the vote; which done, and demanding their opinion, the seamen did all of them cry out "God bless King Charles" with the greatest joy imaginable.

That being done, Sir R. Stayner, who had invited us yesterday, took all the commanders and myself[a] on board him to dinner; where[b] dinner not being ready, I went with Captain Hayward to the *Plimouth* and *Essex*, and did what I had to do there and returned, where very merry at dinner. After dinner, to the rest of the ships (I stayed at the *Assistance* to hear the harper a good while) quite through the fleet. Which was a very brave sight, to visit all the ships and to be received with the respect and Honour that I was on board them all. And much more to see the great joy that I brought to all men; not one through the whole fleet showing the least dislike of the business. In the evening, as I was going on board the Vice-Admirall, the Generall begun to fire his guns, which he did all that he had in the ship; and so did all the rest of the commanders, which was very gallant, and to hear[c] the bullets go hissing over our heads as we were in the boat. This done and finished my Proclamation, I returned to the *Nazeby*, where my Lord was much pleased to hear how all the fleet took it; and in a transport of joy showed me a private letter of the King's to him and another from the Duke of Yorke in such familiar style as to their common friend, with all kindness imaginable. And I found by the letters, and so my Lord

a repl. 'the'   b repl. 'with'   c repl. 'see'

---

1. The vote ran: 'Resolved (*nemine contradicente*) that the Commanders and Officers of the Fleet do receive the gracious Declaration of his Majesty, as also the expressions of his gracious purposes towards them and the whole Fleet (communicated in a Letter to the Generals) with great joyfulness of heart; and for them do return unto his Majesty their most humble thanks, declaring and professing their exact loyalty and duty unto his Majesty, and desire the Generals of the Fleet humbly to represent the same unto him. *It was also resolved* That the said Letter, Declaration and Vote should be publickly read to the respective ships and Companies of the Fleet now in the Downs, to know their sense concerning the same.': *Faithfull Post*, 8 May, p. 415.

told me too, that there hath been many letters sped between them for a great while, and I perceive unknown to Monke. And among the rest that have carried these letters, Sir John Bois is one, and the Mr. Norwood which had a ship to carry him over the other day, which my Lord would not have me put down his name in the book.[1] The King speaks of his being courted to come to The Hague, but doth desire my Lord's advice whether to come to take ship. And the Duke offers to learn the seaman's trade of him, in such familiar words as if Jack Cole and I had writ them.[2] This was very strange to me, that my Lord should carry all things so wisely and prudently as he doth, and I was over-joyful to see him in so good condition; and he did not a little please himself to tell me how he had provided for himself so great a hold in the King.

4. After this to supper, and then to writing of letters till 12 at night and so up again at 3 in the morning. My Lord seemed to put great confidence in me and would take my advice in many things. I perceive his being willing to do all the Honour in the world to Monke and to let him have all the Honour of doing the business, though he will many times express his thoughts of him to be but a thick-skulled fellow; so that I do believe there is some agreement more then ordinary between the King and my Lord to let Monke carry on the business, for it is he that must do the business, or at least that can hinder the business if he be not flattered and observed. This my Lord will hint himself sometimes.

My Lord, I perceive by the King's letter, hath writ to him about his father Crew, and the King did speak well of him; but my Lord tells me that he is afeared that he hath too much con-

1. Correspondence between Mountagu and the King seems to have begun in the spring of 1659 while Mountagu was in the Baltic, but the earlier letters do not appear to have survived: Harris, i. 134–5, 144, 178. Pepys probably here refers to the correspondence of early 1660. It was later wrongly assumed (perhaps because of Pepys's close connection with James, Duke of York, and because of

his resignation from office in 1689) that Pepys himself had been an intermediary: cf. Abel Boyer, *Hist. Queen Anne* (1722), App., p. 36.

2. Cole was a schoolfellow of Pepys. The Duke had first been at sea in 1649, when he was 16. Pepys later (c. 1680) made a note in his *Naval Minutes* (pp. 233, 382): 'When began the Duke of York his seamanship?'

cerned himself with the Presbyterian[s] against the House of Lords
– which will do him a great discourtesy.

I wrote this morning many letters, and to all the copies of the
vote of the council of Warr I put my name; that if it should come
in print, my name may be at it.

I sent a copy of the vote to Doling, inclosed in this letter:

> "Sir,
>
> He that can fancy a fleet (like ours) in her pride, with
> pendants loose, guns roaring, caps flying, and the loud *Vive
> le Roy's*[1] echoed from one ship's company to another, he and
> he only can apprehend the joy this enclosed vote was re-
> ceived with, or the blessing he thought himself possessed of
> that bore it, and is
>
> Your humble servant."[2]

About 9 a-clock I got all my letters done, and sent them by
the messenger that came yesterday.

This morning came Captain Isham on board with a gentleman
going to the King, by whom very cunningly my Lord tells me
he intends to send an account of this day's and yesterday's actions
here,[3] notwithstanding that he hath writ to the Parliament to
have leave of them to send the King the answer of the Fleete.

Since my writing of the last Paragraph, my Lord called me to
him to read his letter to the King, to see whether I could find any
slips in it or no. And as much of the letter as I can remember
is thus:[4]

1. Clarendon (*Hist.*, vi. 229) describes how the King was 'received
by all the officers and seamen ... with
those exclamations which are peculiar to that people, and in which they
excel'. Was the phrase '*Vive le Roy*'
in common English use? Cf. Marvell: 'I will have a fine pond and a
pretty decoy,/Where the Ducks and
the Drakes may their freedomes
enjoy,/And Quack in their Language
still Vive le Roy': *The Kings vowes*,
ll. 52–4; and cf. Capt. Baines's '*Vive
le Roy*' on 28 March above.

2. See below, p. 131 & n. 2.
Some of the phrases in Pepys's letter
were used by the government newspapers: *Merc. Civ.*, 8 May, p. 31
(repeated in *Merc. Pub.*, 10 May,
pp. 295–6): 'The General fired the
first gun himself, and cried *God bless
his Majesty*. Then might you see the
Fleet in her pride, with pendants
loose, Guns roaring, Caps flying, and
loud *Vive le Roy's* ecchoed from one
Ships company to another ...'.

3. Printed in *LJ*, xi. 16. The
gentleman appears to have been Mr
Gery: Sandwich, p. 75.

4. Pepys's paraphrase is substantially complete; cf. the original (dated
this day) printed in Lister, iii. 104–6.

"May it please your Most Excellent Majesty; and so begins.

That he yesterday*a* received from Generall Monke his Majesty's letter and declaration; and that Generall Monke had desired him to write to the Parliament to have leave to send the vote of the Seamen before he did it send it to him. Which he hath done by writing to both Speakers; but for his private satisfaction he hath sent it thus privately (and so the copy of the proceedings yesterday was sent him), and that this came by a gentleman that came this day on board, entending to wait upon his Majesty. That he is my Lord's countryman, and one whose friends have suffered much on his Majesty's behalf.

That my Lord Pembrooke and Salisbury are put*b* out of the House of Lords.[1]

That my Lord is very joyful that other countries do pay him the civilities and respect due*c* to him; and that he doth much rejoice to see that the King doth resolve to receive none of their assistance, or some such words, from them, he having strength enough in the love and Loyalty of his own subjects to support him.

That his Majesty hath chosen the best place, Scheveling, for his imbarquing; and that there is nothing in the world of which he is more ambitious then to have the Honour of attending his Majesty, which he hoped would be speedy.

That he hath commanded the vessel to attend at Helversluce till this gentleman returns, that so, if his Majesty do not think it fit to command the fleet himself, yet that he may be there to receive his commands and bring [them] to his Lordshipp.

He ends his letter: that he is confounded with the thoughts of the high expressions of love to him in the King's letter; and concludes,

"Your most loyal, dutiful, faithful and obedient subject and servant, E.M."

a repl. 'hath' *b* repl. 'out' *c* repl. 'to'

1. Mountagu was wrong, for both can be shown from the *Lords' Journals* to have attended the House very soon after this date. But both were unpopular with their fellow peers, because Pembroke's father and Salisbury himself had sat in the Lower House after the abolition of the House of Lords in 1649.

The rest of the afternoon at nine-pins.   In the evening came a packet from London; among the rest, a letter from my wife which tells me that she hath not been well, which did exceedingly trouble me; but my Lord sending Mr. Cooke this night, I wrote to her and sent a piece of gold inclosed to her, and writ also to Mrs. Bowyer and enclosed a half-piece to her for a token.

After supper at the table in the coach, my Lord talking concerning the uncertainty of the places of the Exchequer to them that have them now, he did at last think of an office which doth belong to him in case the King doth restore every man to his places that ever have been patent, which is to be one of the clerks of the Signett,[1] which will be a fine imployment for one of his sons.

After all this discourse, we broke up and to bed.

In[a] the afternoon came a Minister on board, one Mr. Sharpe, who is going to the King; who tells me that Commissioners are chosen, both of Lords and Commons, to go to the King; and that Dr. Clarges is going to him from the Army and that he will be here tomorrow.[2]

My letters at night tell me that the House did deliver their letter to Sir John Greenville in answer to the King's standing, and that they gave him 500l for his pains, to buy him a Jewell.[3] And that besides the 50000l ordered to be borrowed of the City for the present use of the King, the twelve companies of the City do give every one of them to his Majesty, as a present, 1000l.[4]

5.   All the morning very busy, writing letters to London and

a   preceded by '5' crossed out

---

1. In fact, the office of which he held the reversion was that of a Clerk of the Privy Seal and Registrar of the Court of Requests, granted in March 1637: *CSPD 1636–7*, p. 534.

2. James Sharp, a leader of the moderate Presbyterians in Scotland, was sent by Monck to the King to help with the negotiations between the King and the Presbyterians of both kingdoms. The Lords chose their six commissioners on the 3rd: *LJ*, xi. 12.   The Commons appointed a committee on the same day to consider their choice.   The names were not announced until the 7th: *CJ*, viii. 11, 15.   Thomas Clarges (Monck's brother-in-law and confidential agent) was the Commissary-General.

3. On 2 May: *CJ*, viii. 8.

4. *CJ*, viii. 10 (3 May); resolution of Common Council (2 May): LRO, Common Hall Bks, v, ff.441v–2v.

a packet to Mr. Downing to acquaint him with what hath been done lately in the fleet. And this I did by my Lord's command, who, I thank him, did of himself think of doing it to do me a kindness, for he writ a letter himself to him, thanking him for his kindness to me.

All the afternoon at nine-pins. At night after supper, good Musique: My Lord, Mr. North, I and W. Howe. After that to bed.

This evening came Dr. Clarges to Deale, going to the King – where the Townes-people strowed the street with Herbes against his coming, for joy of his going. Never was there so general a content as there is now. I cannot but remember that our Parson did in his prayer tonight pray for the long life and happiness of our King and dread Soveraigne, that may last as long as the sun and Moone endureth.

6. *Lords day.*

This morning, while we were at sermon, comes in Dr. Clarges and a*ᵃ* Dozen gentlemen with him to see my Lord – who after sermon dined with him. I remember that last night, upon discourse concerning Clarges, my Lord told me that he was a man of small *entendimiento.*

This noon there was a gentleman with me, an officer of Dunkirke going over, who came to me for an order and told me that he was lately with my uncle and aunt Fenner and that Kate's fitts of the convulsion did hold her still.

It fell very well today; a stranger preached here today for Mr. Ibbott, one Mr. Stanly, who prayed for King Charles, by the grace of God, &c., which gave great contentment to the gentlemen that were on board here, and said they would talk of it when they came to Breda, as not having it done yet in London so publicly.¹

After they were gone from on board, my Lord writ a letter to the King² and gave it me [to] carry privately to Sir W.

a repl. ? 'about'

---

1. The parliamentary order en-
joining ministers to pray for the
King was not voted until the 9th.
The preacher was probably William
Stanley (d. 1680), Vicar of Walmer
and Rector of Ripple, Kent.
    2. Bodl., Clar. 72, ff. 240-1, 6
May; protesting his loyalty.

Compton on board the *Assistance*, which I did; and after a health to his Majesty on board there, I left them under sail for Breda: *a* back again and found them at sermon; I went up to my cabin and looked over my accounts, and found that all my debts paid and my preparation to sea paid for, I have above 40*l* clear in my purse.[1] After supper to bed.

7. This morning Captain Cuttance sent me a dozen of bottles of Margett ale – three of which I drank presently with some friends in the Coach: my Lord went this morning about the flag-ships in a boat, to see what alterations there must be as to the armes and flags. He did give me order also to write for silk*b* flags and Scarlett wastecloaths.[2] For a rich barge. For a noise of Trumpetts; and a set of Fidlers.

Very great deal of company came today; among others, Mr. Bellasses, Sir Tho. Lenthropp, Sir Henr. Chichly, Collonell Phill: Honiwood, and Captain Titus,[3] the last of whom my Lord showed all our Cabbins, and I suppose he is to take notice what room there will be for the King's entertainment.

Here was also all the Jurates of the town of Dover, come to give my Lord a visit. And after dinner all went away.

I could not but observe that the Vice-Admirall,[4] after dinner away, came into the great Cabbin below, where the Jurates and I and the commanders for want of room dined, and there told us

a repl. ? 'his'   *b* MS. 'silks'

---

1. The diary registers Pepys's rapid progress from these small beginnings. For details, see *Comp.*: 'Finances'. His cash capital (c. £25 in March 1660) rose to £6700 in April 1667, of which £3000 had been gained in 1665–6, during the height of the Dutch war. His personal accounts, often mentioned in the diary, have not survived.

2. To decorate the ship bringing home the King. The Council of State's instructions to this effect are in Sandwich MSS., App., ff. 208, 213,

222. The Admiralty Commissioners had in fact ordered silk flags for the *Naseby* on this day; the waistcloths were ordered on the 11th: *CSPD 1659–60*, pp. 431–2, 437.

3. All were active royalists. Leventhorpe ('Lenthropp') and Titus had recently been involved in Booth's rising: *CSPD 1659–60*, pp. 191, 396; *CSPClar.*, iv. 658. The latter was a Groom of the Bedchamber to the King.

4. John Lawson, the ex-republican.

we must drink a health to the King; and himself called for a bottle of wine, and begins his and the Duke of Yorkes. In the afternoon I lost 5s. at nine-pins.

After supper, Musique and to bed – having also among us at the coach-table wrote a letter to the French Embassador in French – about the release of a ship that we have taken.

After I was in bed, Mr. Sheply and W. Howe came and sat in my cabin, where I gave them three bottles of Marget ale, and sat laughing and very merry till almost one a-clock in the morning; and so good-night.

8. All the morning busy. After dinner there came several persons of Honour, as my Lord St. Johns and others, for convoy to Flushing, and great giving of them salutes. My Lord and we at nine-pins: I lost nine shillings. While we were in play, Mr. Cooke comes on board with letters from London, bringing me news of my wife: that he went to Huntsmore to see her, and brought her and my father Bowyer to London where he left her at my father's very well; and speaks very well of her love to me. My letters today tell me how it was entended that the King should be proclaimed today in London with a great deal of pomp.[1] I have also news who they are that are chosen of the Lords and Commons to attend the King.

And also the whole story of what we did the other day in the fleet at reading the King's declaration; and my name at the bottom of it.[2] After supper, some music and to bed – I resolving to rise betimes tomorrow to write letters to London.

9. Up very early, writing a letter to the King as from the two Generalls of the fleet in answer to his letter to them, wherein my Lord doth give most humble thanks for his gracious

1. Accounts of the proclamation are in Rugge, i, f.92r–v; *Parl. Intell.*, 14 May, pp. 308–10.

2. All the three foregoing items of news are in *Faithfull Post* (no. 53) which appeared this day. The fleet's declaration (q.v. above, p. 124 & n. 1) is at pp. 414–15, subscribed 'Samuel Pepys, Secretary'. Pepys

may be referring here to the publication of the declaration as a broadside or in another newsheet. It had been read in both houses of Parliament on 7 May. But no other printed version including Pepys's name has been traced; the larger official newsbooks (e.g. *Parl. Intell.*, 7 May, p. 304) omitted it.

letter and declaration.   And promises all duty and obedience to him.[1]

This letter was carried this morning to Sir Petr. Killigrew, who came hither this morning early to bring an order from the Lords' House to my Lord, giving him power to write an answer to the King.[2]   This morning my Lord St. John and other persons of Honour were here to see my Lord, and so away to Flushing.

After they were gone, my Lord and I to write letters to London, which we sent by Mr. Cooke, who was very desirous to go because of seeing my wife before she went out of town.

As we were sitting down to dinner, in comes Noble with a letter from the[a] House of Lords to my Lord, to desire him to provide ships to transport the Commissioners to the King, which are expected here this week.[3]   He brought us certain news that the King was proclaimed yesterday with great pomp, and brought down one of the proclamations, with great joy to us all; for which God be praised.

After dinner to nine-pins and lost 5s.

This morning came Mr. Saunderson, that writ the story of the King, hither, who is going over to the King.   He calls me Cozen and seems to be a very knowing man.[4]

After supper to bed betimes, leaving my Lord talking in the Coach with the Captain, &c.

10.   This morning came on board Mr. Pinkny and his son, going to the King[b] with a petition finely writ by Mr. Whore,

a   MS. 'my the'   b   MS. 'here'

---

1. Bodl., Clar. 72, ff. 280–1, 9 May; a draft of the King's reply (13/23 May) is in BM, Egerton 2537, f.39r.

2. Cf. above, p. 123.   The order to Mountagu is in LJ, xi. 61; the letters conveying it are in Sandwich MSS, App., ff. 209, 212, 214, 215.   Killigrew ('Peter the Post') was a King's messenger now carrying news to Charles of his proclamation in London.

3. Cf. LJ, xi. 18.

4. William Sanderson, courtier and historian, had published A complete history of the life and reign of King Charles . . . (1658).   Both his family and Pepys's derived from Cottenham, Cambs.

for to be the King's embroiderer[1] – for whom and Mr. Sanderson I got a ship. This morning came my Lord Winchelsea and a great deal of company and dined here.

In the afternoon, while my Lord and we were at Musique in the great cabin below, comes in a messenger to tell us that Mr. Edwd. Mountagu, my Lord's son, was come to Deale – who afterwards came on board with Mr. Edw. Pickering with him. The child was sick in the evening.

At night, while my Lord was at supper, in comes my Lord Lauderdale and Sir J. Greenville, who supped here and so went away. After they were gone, my Lord called me into his cabin and told me how he was commanded to set sail presently for the King, and was very glad thereof; and so put me to writing of letters and other work that night till it was very late, he going to bed.[2] I got him afterwards to sign things in bed. After I had done some more work, I to bed also.

11. Up very early in the morning. And so about a great deal of business, in order to our going hence today. Burr going on shore last night made me very angry, so that I sent for Mr. Pitts to come to me from the Vice-Admirall, entending not to have imployed Burr any more. But Burr by and by coming and desiring humbly that I would forgive him, and Pitts not coming, I did set him to work.

This morning we begun to pull down all the State's arms in

1. George Pinckney, sen., again petitioned for this office in (? March) 1661, recalling that he had been promised it the year before at The Hague, when he had presented to the King a book on whose cover he had embroidered the royal arms. He was then granted a moiety of the office; and in November 1663 his son Charles was also granted a moiety. Richard Hoare was in 1668 a clerk in the Prerogative Court of the Archbishop of Canterbury. Pepys kept, for its calligraphic interest, a petition in his hand: PL 2983, p. 250.

2. By a resolution of both Houses of the 9th, he was to await orders from the King. But Grenville urged on him the importance of going immediately; Mountagu therefore sent word to the King by Grenville that he would lose no time in sailing. *LJ*, xi. 21; Sandwich MSS, App., f.218r; Sandwich, p. 75; Harris, i. 182. Mountagu wrote to the President of the Council (11 May) announcing the fleet's departure for Scheveningen, 'the best place and nearest where his Majesty is for such great shipps as ours are to ride in': BM, Sloane 1519, f.208r (in Pepys's hand).

the fleet – having first sent to Dover for painters and others to come to set up the King's.[1]

The rest of the morning writing of letters to London, which I afterwards sent by Dunne.

I had this morning my first opportunity of discoursing with Dr. Clarke,[2] who I find to be a very pretty man and very knowing; he is now going in this ship to the King.

There dined here my Lord Crafford[3] and my Lord Cavendish[4] and other Scotchmen, who I afterwards ordered to be received on board the *Plimouth* and to go along with us.

After dinner we set sail from the Downes, I leaving my boy to go to Deale for my linen.

In the afternoon, overtook us three or four gentlemen; two of the Bertus[5] and one Mr. Dormerhoy,[6] a Scotch gentleman (who I found afterwards to be a very fine man); who telling my Lord that they heard that the Commissioners were come out of London today, my Lord dropped Anchor over against Dover Castle (which gave us about 30 guns in passing), and upon a high debate with the Vice and Rear-Admirall whether it were safe to go and not stay for the Commissioners, he did resolve to send Sir R. Stayner to Dover to inquire of my Lord Winchelsea[7] whether or no they are come out of London or no, and then to resolve tomorrow morning of going or not – which was done.

It blew very hard all this night, that I was afeared of my boy. About 11 at night came the boats from Deale with great store of provisions; by the same token John Goods told me that

1. See the vote of both Houses, 9 May: *LJ*, xi. 20. Four workmen, sent from Chatham, were kept busy at Dover until 24 May, and were paid £19 12s.: PRO, Adm. 20/1, p. 193.

2. Timothy Clark(e), later physician to the King, and soon to become a good friend of Pepys.

3. The 17th Earl of Crawford; recently (3 March) released from imprisonment for royalism; soon to be appointed Lord Treasurer of Scotland; with Lauderdale, the leader of the group of Scottish politicians on their way to Breda. J. Nicoll, *Diary* (1836), p. 285.

4. Later Earl and 1st Duke of Devonshire; not a Scot, and Pepys's words need not be read as implying that he was.

5. Robert and Edward Bertie, sons of the 1st Earl of Lindsey; through their mother related to Mountagu.

6. Probably Thomas Dalmahoy, who had married Elizabeth, widow of the 2nd Duke of Hamilton.

7. Governor of Dover Castle.

above 20 of the fowle are smothered.   But my boy was put on board the *Northwich*.   To bed.

12.   This morning I enquired for my boy whether he was come well or no, and it was told me that he was well in bed.

My [Lord] called me to his chamber,*a* he being in bed, and gave me many orders to make for direction for the ships that are left in the Downes.   Giving them the greatest charge in the world to bring no passengers with them when they come after us to Scheveling bay – excepting Mr. Edw. Montagu, Mr. Tho. Crew, and Sir H. Wright.

Sir R. Stayner hath been here early in the morning and told my Lord that my Lord Winchelsea understands by letters that the Commissioners are only to come to Dover to attend the coming over of the King.[1]   So my Lord did give order for weighing anchor;   which we did, and sailed all day.

In our way in the morning, coming in the midway between Dover and Callis, we could see both places very easily, and very pleasant it was to me but the farther we went the more we lost sight of both lands.

In the afternoon at cards with Mr. North and the Doctor. There meet*b* us in the *Lark* frigate, Sir R. Freeman and some others, going from the King to England, who came to see my Lord and so onwards of their voyage.

In the afternoon upon the Quarter-deck, the Doctor told Mr. North and me an admirable story called *The Fruitlesse præcaution*:[2] an exceeding pretty story and worth my getting without book when I can get the book.

a   blot above symbol   *b*   MS. 'me'

---

1. This was a misunderstanding. The commissioners had been instructed to make 'Speedy Repair to such Place where His Majesty shall be': *LJ*, xi. 22.   They took ship on the *Hampshire* and the *Yarmouth* and arrived off Scheveningen on the evening of the 14th: Sandwich, p. 76; cf. HMC, *Rep.*, 5/150.

2. One of the 'novels' of the French writer Paul Scarron (d. 1660).

It is clear from the entry at 16 October 1660 that Pepys is referring to an English version: three of the tales had been translated and published separately in 1657 by John Davies of Kidwelly.   For the editions, see *DNB*, 'Davies'; A. Esdaile, *List of Engl. tales ... pub. before 1740*, pp. 301–2; Wing, S 833–6.   Pepys did not retain any in the PL.

This evening came Mr. Sheply on board, whom we had left at Deale and Dover getting of provision and borrowing of money.

In the evening late, after discourse with the Doctor, &c., to bed.

13. *Lords. day.*

Trimmed in the morning; after that to the Cooke room with Mr. Sheply, the first time that I was there this voyage.

Then to the Quarter Deck, upon which the taylors and painters were at work cutting out of some pieces of yellow cloth into the fashion of a crown and *C.R.* and put it upon a fine sheet, and that into the flag instead of the State's arms; which, after dinner, was finished and set up – after it had been showed to my Lord, who took physic today and was in his chamber; and liked it so well as to bid me give the tailors 20s. among them for doing of it.

This morn Sir J. Bois and Captain Isham met us in the *Nonsuch*, the first of whom, after a word or two with my Lord, went forward; the other stayed.

I heard by them how Mr. Downing hath never made any address to the King, and for that was hated exceedingly by the Court, and that he was in a Duch ship which sailed by us then, going for England with disgrace.[1]

Also, how Mr. Morland was knighted by the King this week, and that the King did give the reason of it openly, that it was for his giving him intelligence all the time that he was clerk to Secretary Thurloe.[2]

In the afternoon a council of war, only to acquaint them that

1. Downing had in fact successfully approached a royalist agent on 25 March (T. Carte, *Orig. Letters*, 1739, ii. 319–22) and from then onwards had passed information to the King. His visit to England was hurried, for he was back in The Hague by midnight on 19 May with letters of recommendation from Monck: Lower, *Relation* (1660), pp. 72–3. See also below, p. 153.

2. Samuel Morland (diplomat, mathematician and mechanical engineer) had been Pepys's tutor at Magdalene. While assistant to Secretary Thurloe from 1654 he had supplied information to the royalists. He was knighted on 10 May 1660, and raised to the baronetage on the following 18 July.

the Harp must be taken out of all their flags, it being very offensive to the King.[1]

Mr. Cooke came after us in the *Yarmouth*, bringing me a letter from my wife and a Latin letter from my brother Jo:, with both which I was exceedingly pleased.

No sermon all day, we being under sail; only at night, prayers, wherein Mr. Ibbott prayed for all that were related to us in a spiritual and fleshly way.

We came within sight of Middleburg shore.

Late at night we writ letters to the King of the news of our coming, and Mr. Edwd Pickering carried them.

Captain Isham went on shore, nobody showing of him any respect; so the old man very fairly took leave of my Lord, and my Lord very coldly bid him God be with you. Which was very strange, but that I hear that he kept[a] a great deal of prating and talking on shore at[b] the King's Court what command he had with my Lord, &c.[2]

After letters was gone, then to bed.

14. In the morning, when I waked and rose, I saw myself out of the Scuttle close by the shore, which afterwards I was told to be the Duch shore. The Hague was clearly to be seen by us.

My Lord went up in his night gowne* into the Cuddy to see how to dispose thereof for himself and us that belong to him, to give order for our removall today.

a MS. 'keep'   *b* blot in left-hand margin

---

1. Earlier in the year the Rump had restored the Commonwealth standard of 1649–53, which had replaced the royal standard, and which consisted of the cross of St George together with the Irish harp. See W. G. Perrin, *Brit. Flags*, pl. vi. fig. 5, and pp. 62+. It was this which Mountagu himself was now flying from his flagship. The King objected to the use of the Irish emblem, since Ireland was regarded as a dependency. The harp did not reappear on flags until the parliamentary union of 1801. Orders of the Council of State and of the Admiralty committee (5, 7 May) had restored all standards, flags and jacks 'as were in use before 1648': *CSPD 1659–60*, pp. 431–2. Under Cromwell, in 1654–8, the union jack (i.e. the cross of St Andrew surmounted by that of St George) had been used, with the harp added, to symbolise the union of the three nations.

2. Henry Isham (now aged c. 67) was the brother of Mountagu's stepmother and had served Rupert and Maurice in Spain and Portugal during the royalist exile.

Some masty Duchmen came on board to proffer their boats to carry things from us on shore &c., to get money by us.

Before noon, some gentlemen came on board from the shore to kiss my Lords hands. And by and by Mr. North and Dr. Clerke went to kiss the Queen of Bohemia's[1] hands from my Lord, with a dozen of attendants from on board to wait on them; among which I sent my boy – who, like myself, is with child to see any strange thing.

After noon they came back again, having kissed the Queen of Bohemia's hand, and was sent again by my Lord to do the same to the Prince of Orange.[2] So I got the Captain to ask leave for me to go, which my Lord did give; and I, taking my boy and Judge Advocate with me, went in company with them. The weather bad; we were soundly washed when we came near the shore, it being very hard to land there.

The shore is, as all the country between that and The Hague, all sand. The rest of the company got a coach by themselfs. Mr. Creed and I went in the fore-part of a coach, wherein there was two very pretty ladies, very fashionable and with black paches, who very merrily sang all the way and that very well. And were very free to kiss the two[a] blades that were with them.[3]

I took out my Flagelette and piped, but in piping I dropped my rapier=stick; but when I came to The Hague, I sent my boy back again for it and he found it, for which I did give him 6*d*. but some horse had gone over it and broke the scabbard. The Hague is a most neat place in all respects. The houses so neat in all places and things as is possible.

Here we walked up and down a great while, the town being now very full of Englishmen, for that the Londoners[4] were come on shore today.

But going to see the Prince, he was gone forth with his

a   followed by small blot

---

1. Elizabeth, daughter of James I of England, and widow of Frederick, Elector Palatine, titular King of Bohemia.

2. The future William III of England, now nine years old, son of Mary, elder daughter of Charles I.

3. For the freedom with which unmarried Dutchwomen bestowed their kisses, see J. Ray, *Observations . . . made in a journey through part of the Low-Countries* (1673), p. 55.

4. Representatives of the city who had travelled in the *Norwich*: Sandwich, p. 76.

Governor;[1] and so we walked up and down the town and Court to see the place;[2] and by the help of a stranger, an Englishman, we saw a great many places and were made to understand many things, as the intention of the Maypoles which we saw there standing at every great man's door, of different greatness according to the Quality of the person.[3] About 10 at night the Prince comes home, and we found an easy admission. His attendance very inconsiderable as for a prince. But yet handsome, and his tutor a fine man and himself a very pretty boy. It was bright Mooneshine tonight. This done, we went to a place we had taken up to sup in – where a sallet and two or three bones of mutton were provided for a matter of ten of us, which was very strange. After supper the Judge and I to another house to bed, leaving them there; and he and I lying together in one of their press-beds, there being two more in the same room, but all very neat and handsome; and my boy sleeping upon a bench by me, we lay till past 3 a-clock; and then rise ⟪15⟫ and up and down the town to see it by daylight. Where we saw the soldiers of the Prince's guard, all very fine, and the Burgers of the town with their arms and musquets as bright as silver; I meeting this morning a Schoole-Master that spoke good English and French, he went along with us and showed us the whole town.[4] And indeed, I cannot speak enough of the gallantry of the town. Everybody of fashion speak French or Latin, or both. The women, many of them very pretty and in good habitt, fashionable, and black spots.

He went with me to buy a couple of basketts, one of them for Mrs. Pierce, the other for my wife.

1. Count Zuylestein (d. 1672), tutor and uncle of the Prince of Orange.

2. For The Hague, see Jacob de Riemer, *Beschrijving van 'sGraven-Hage* (Delft, 1730–9): view, i. 70. The 'Court' was the Binnenhof; view (c. 1729) in de Riemer, i. 108. Its gardens were reckoned by Evelyn to be among the finest he knew (J. Evelyn to Sir T. Browne, 28 January 1658, in Sir Thomas Browne, *Works*, ed. Keynes, vi. 305); a description

(1634) is in Sir W. Brereton, *Travels* (1844), p. 28.

3. For the customary planting of maypoles in Holland, see H. E. van Gelder, *'sGravenhage in zeven eeuwen*, p. 189; J. Hastings (ed.), *Encycl. religion and ethics*, x. 95.

4. Pepys surprisingly does not record Charles II's entry into The Hague at 11 a.m.: Lower, *Relation* (1660), pp. 33–6.

After he was gone (we having first drank with him at our lodging), the Judge and I to the *grand Salle*, where we were showed the place where the States-generall sit in council.¹ The hall is a great place, where the flags that they take from their enemies are all hung up. And things to be sold, as in Westminster-hall, and not much unlike it but that not so big – but much neater.

After this to a bookseller's and bought, for the love of the binding,² three books – the French Psalms in four parts³ – Bacon's *organon*,⁴ and Farnaby's *Rhetoric*.⁵

After that, the Judge, I, and my boy by coach to Scheveling again – where we went into a house of entertainment and drank there, the wind being very high; and we saw two boats overset there and the gallants forced to be pulled on shore by the heels – while their trunks, portmanteaus, hats, and feathers were swimming in the sea. Among others, I saw the Ministers that came along with the Commissioners sadly dipped – Mr. Case⁶ among the rest. So they came in where we was; and I being in haste, left my Copenhagen knife⁷ there and so lost it.

Having stayed here a great while, a Gentleman that was going to kiss my Lord's hand from*ᵃ* the Queen of Bohemia and I hired a Duch boat for four Rix Dollers to carry us on board. We were fain to wait a great while before we could get off from the shore. The sea being very rough.

a repl. 'for'

---

1. The Great Hall ('Zaal') of the Binnenhof. Cf. Evelyn (17 August 1641): 'a very stately Hall . . .; the sides . . . furnish'd with shopps'. See the picture by Dirck van Deelen (1651) in the Mauritshuis (no. 26).
2. Of the books now bought, the Farnaby is presumably PL 81: a plain white limp vellum of the sort which though common in Holland seems to have been unusual in England after 1650. (Inf. from H. M. Nixon.)
3. ? replaced in the PL by Henry du Mont's four-part setting of Anthoine Godeau's paraphrase (Paris, 1663: PL 1644-7): see below, iii. 99.

4. Probably either the Leyden edition of 1650 or the Amsterdam edition of 1660; not in the PL.
5. Thomas Farnaby, *Index Rhetoricus* (Amsterdam, 1648); ? PL 81.
6. Thomas Case, Presbyterian Rector of St Giles-in-the-Fields, one of the representatives of the London clergy: *CJ*, viii. 20. They had travelled with the commissioners sent by Parliament and the city of London.
7. Possibly a knife bought while Pepys was in the Baltic for a few days in the summer of 1659 delivering despatches to Mountagu.

The Duchman would fain have us all paid that came into our boat, besides us two and our company, there being many of our ship's company got in who were on shore. But some of them had no money to give them, having spent all on shore.

Coming on board, we found all the Commissioners of the House of Lords at dinner with my Lord; who after dinner went away for shore.

Mr. Morland, now Sir Samuel, was here on board, but I do not find that my Lord or*a* anybody did give him any respect, he being looked upon by him and all men as a knave. Among others, he betrayed Sir Rich: Willis that married Dr. Foxes daughter, that he had paid him 1000*l* at one time, by the Protector and Secretary Thurloes order, for intelligence that he sent concerning the King.[1]

In the afternoon my Lord called me on purpose to show me his fine clothes which are now come hither; and indeed, are very rich – as gold and silver can make them. Only his sword he and I do not like.

In the afternoon my Lord and I walked together in the Coach two houres, talking*b* together upon all sorts of discourse – as Religion, wherein he is I perceive wholly Scepticall, as well as I, saying that indeed the Protestants as to the Church of Rome are wholly fanatiques. He likes uniformity and form of prayer.

About State business, among other things he told me that his conversion to the King's cause (for so I was saying that I wondered from what time the King could look upon him to be become his friend), from his being in the Sound, when he found what usage he was likely to have from a Comonwealth.[2]

My Lord, the Captain, and I supped in my Lord's chamber – where I perceive that he did begin to show me much more respect then ever he did yet.

a repl. 'and'   *b* repl. 'he'

1. Morland claimed to have saved the King's life in 1659 by warning him of a treacherous plot of Willys's to inveigle him to England. Willys was then a member of the royalist underground movement, and Morland an official of the republican government, in the Secretary of State's office. For details, see *Comp.*: 'Willys, Sir Richard'.

2. In August 1659 in the Baltic, Mountagu found himself at odds with the civilian commissioners sent by the republican government, and withdrew most of the fleet.

After supper my Lord sent for me, entending to have me play at cards with him; but I not knowing Cribbige,[1] we fell into discourse of many things, till it was so rough sea and the ship seeled so much that I was not able to stand; and so he bid me go to bed.

16.   As soon as I was up, I went down to be trimmed below in the great cabin, but then come in some with visits; among the rest, one from Admirall Opdam[2] who spoke Latin well, but not French nor English – to whom my Lord made me to give his answers and to entertain.   He brought my Lord a tierce of wine and a barrel of butter as a present from the Admirall.

After that to finish my trimming; and while I was doing of it, in comes Mr. North very sea-sick from shore, and to bed he go.   After that to dinner, where Comissioner*a* Pett was come to take care to get all things ready for the King on board.[3]

My Lord in his best suit, this the first day, in expectation to wait upon the King.   But Mr. ⟨Ed.⟩ Pickering, coming from the King, brought word that the King would not put my Lord to the trouble of coming to him – but that he would come to the shore to look upon the fleet today; which we expected, and had our guns ready to fire and our Scarlett wastecloaths out and silk pendants; but he did not come.[4]

My Lord and we at nine-pins this afternoon upon the Quarter-deck, which is very pretty sport.

This evening came Mr. John Pickering on board like an asse, with his feathers and new suit that he had made at The Hague. My Lord very angry for his staying on shore, bidding me a little before to send for him, telling me that he was afeared that for his father's sake he might have some mischief done him – unless he used the Generalls name.[5]

a l.h. repl. s.h. 'com'-

---

1. At 2 January 1660 Pepys records having been taught the game by Jemima, 'my Lord's' daughter.

2. Mountagu's opponent in the Baltic, 1659.

3. Peter Pett had been Commissioner of the Navy at Chatham since 1648. The Council had on 5 May ordered him to join the fleet for this

purpose: *CSPD 1659–60*, pp. 431–2.

4. His day was over-busy with audiences and visits: Lower, *Relation* (1660), pp. 34–57.

5. Sir Gilbert Pickering, his father, was an unpopular republican, and brother-in-law of the General (Mountagu).

To supper; and after supper to cards; I stood by and looked on till 11 at night; and so to bed.

This afternoon Mr. ⟨Ed.⟩ Pickering told me in what a sad, poor condition for clothes and money the King was, and all his attendants, when he came to him first from my Lord – their clothes not being worth 40s, the best of them. And how over-joyed the King was when Sir J. Greenville brought him some money; so joyful, that he called the Princesse Royall and Duke of Yorke to look upon it as it lay in the Portmanteau before it was taken out.

My Lord told me too, that the Duke of Yorke is made High Admirall of England.[1]

17. Up early to write down my last two days observations. Then Dr. Clerke came to me to tell me that he heard this morning, by some Duch that are come on board already to see the ship, that there was a Portugese taken yesterday at The Hague that had a design to kill the King. But this I heard afterwards was only the mistake upon one being observed to walk with his sword naked, he having lost his scabbard.[2]

Before dinner, Mr. Edward and I, W. Howe – Pim and my boy, to Skeveling, where we took coach, and so to The Hague, where walking, intending to find one that might show us the King incognito, I met with Captain Whittington (that had formerly brought a letter to my Lord from the Mayor of London) and he did promise me to do it; but first we went and dined – at a French house, but paid 16s for our part of the club. At dinner, in came Dr. Cade, a merry mad parson of the King's. And they two after dinner got the child and me (the others not being able to crowd in) to see the King, who kissed the child very affectionately.[3] There we kissed his and the Duke of Yorkes

---

1. His patent of appointment was not issued until 29 January 1661.

2. Lower (*Relation*, 1660, pp. 61–3) recounts two such alarms on this day, neither agreeing with the details given by Pepys. What appears to be a third (concerning an attempt by a Frenchman) is given in *Diary of Henry*

Townshend (ed. Willis Bund), i. 43. The King's guards were strengthened.

3. The child was Edward Mountagu, 'my Lord's' son. The King was lodged at the Mauritshuis; Lower, p. 34.

and the Princesse Royalls[1] hands. The King seems to be a very sober man; and a very splendid Court he hath in the number of persons of Quality that are about him; English, very rich in habit. From the King to the Lord Chancellor,[2] who did lie bed-rid of the goute: he spoke very merrily to the child and me. After that, going to see the Queen of Bohemia, I met with Dr. Fuller,[3] who I sent to a tavern with Mr. Edwd. Pickering, while I and the rest went to see the Queen – who used us very respectfully. Her hand we all kissed. She seems a very debonaire, but plain lady.

After that to the Doctor, where we drank a while. And so, in a coach of a friend's of Dr. Cade, we went to see a house of the Princesse Dowagers in a parke about half a mile or a mile from The Hague, where there is one the most beautiful room[s] for pictures in the whole world.[4] She had her own picture upon the top, with this word, dedicating it to the memory of her husband:

Incomparabili marito inconsolabilis vidua.[5]

Here I met with Mr. Woodcock of Cambrige, Mr. Hardye and another. And Mr. Woodcock beginning, we had two or three fine songs, he and I and W. Howe, to the Echo, which was very pleasant, and the more because in a haven of pleasure and in a strange country – that I never was taken up more with a sense

1. Mary, Princess Dowager of Orange, sister of Charles II and widow of Prince William II of Orange.

2. Sir Edward Hyde; also accommodated in the Mauritshuis: Lower, *Relation*, p. 57.

3. Thomas Fuller (Anglican author and divine; friend of the Mountagus of Boughton), had come to The Hague as chaplain to Lord Berkeley (of Berkeley), one of the parliamentary commissioners sent to the King.

4. The Oranjezaal in the Huis ten Bosch. The house, begun by Prince Frederick Henry of Orange (d. 1647) to the design of van Campen, had

been completed by his widow, Amalia van Solms. She had decorated the central hall (lit by a roof-lantern) with canvases glorifying her husband's career. See D. F. Slouthower, *De paleizen van Frederik Hendrik*, pp. 178+; J. G. van Gelder in *Nederlandsch Kunsthistorisch Jaarboek* (1948–9), pp. 119+; J. Judson, *Gerrit van Honthorst*, p. 123. (OM).

5. A half-length by Gerrit van Honthorst (d. 1656), now in Berlin. The inscription was probably composed by Constantijn Huygens. (OM).

of pleasure in my life. After that we parted and back to The Hague and took a tour or two about the Forehault, where the ladies in the evening do as our ladies do in Hideparke.¹ But for my life I could not find one handsome; but their coaches very rich and themselfs so too.

From thence, taking leave of the Doctor, we took waggon to Skeveeling, where we had a fray with the Botswayne of the *Richmond*, who would not freely carry us on board; but at last he was willing to it; but then it was so late we durst not go; so we returned between 10 and 11 at night in the dark, with a waggon with one horse, to The Hague; where being come, we went to bed as well as we could be accommodated, and so to sleep.

18. Very early up; and hearing that the Duke of Yorke, our Lord High Admirall, would go on board today, Mr. Pickering and I took waggon for Scheveling, leaving the child in the Doctor's hands (Mr. Pierce) with direction to keep him within doors all day till he heard from me.

But wind being very high, that no boats could get off from shore, we returned to The Hague (having breakfasted with a gentleman of the Dukes and Commissioner Pett, sent on purpose to give my Lord notice of his coming), where I hear that the child is gone to Delfe to see the town;² so we all, and Mr. Ibbott the Minister, took a schuit and (very much pleased with the manner and conversation of the passengers, where most speak French) went after them, but met them by the way. But however, we went forward, making no stop – where when we were come, we got a smith's boy of the town to go along with us (but could speak nothing but Duch) and he showed us the church where Van Trump lies intombed with a very fine Monument: his epitaph concludes thus (*Tandem Bello Anglico tantum non victor certé invictus vivere et vincere desijt*). There is a sea-

<hr/>

1. For the 'tour' in Hyde Park, see below, iv. 95 & n. 3. The Voorhout was the principal street, a wide avenue lined with trees.

2. For Delft (c. five miles from The Hague), see Dirck van Bleyswijck, *Beschrivinge der stadt Delft* (Delft, 1667); Monconys, ii. 132–4, 143–4.

fight the best cut in Marble, with the Smoake the best expressed
that ever I saw in my life.[1]

From thence to the great church that stands in a fine great
Merket-place over against the Stathouse; and there I saw a stately
tomb of the old Prince of Orange, of Marble and brass. Wherein,
among other rarities, there is the angels with their trumpets,
expressed as it were calling.[2] Here were very fine organs in both
the churches. It is a most sweet town, with bridges and a river
in every street.

Observing that in every house[a] of entertainment there hangs
in every room a poor-man's box and desirous to know the
reason thereof, it was told me that it is their custom to confirm
all bargains by putting something into the poor people's box,[3]
and that that binds as fast as anything.

We saw likewise the Guesthouse,[4] where it was very pleasant
to see what neat preparation there is for the poor. We saw one
poor man a-dying there.

After we had seen all, we light by chance of an English house
to drink in, where we were very merry discoursing of the
town and the thing that hangs up like a bushell in the Stathouse,
which I was told is a sort of punishment for some sort of offenders
to carry through the streets of the town over his head, which is

a   repl. 'place'

---

1. The monument of Adm. Martin
Harpertszoon Tromp (d. 1653) is in
the Oude Kerk; engravings of the
church and of the monument are in
Bleyswijck, where the monument is
described and the inscription given in
full (pp. 182–6). Monconys (ii. 133)
describes it as '*fait comme un Autel de
Chapelle*'. In the original epitaph,
'*ac*' is used instead of '*et*', and the date
of his death and his age are inserted
between '*invictus*' and '*vivere*'.

2. William the Silent (d. 1584) is
buried in the Nieuwe Kerk. The

monument (c. 1622) is by Hendrik de
Keyser: descriptions and representa-
tions in Bleyswijck, pp. 190, 260–72;
Monconys, ii. 133–4 [1663]; James
Yonge, *Journal* (ed. Poynter), pp.
100–1 [1666].

3. The *armbus*. The Dutch were
generally held to be the most successful of all European nations in their
treatment of the poor. Cf. the
French poor-box: below, iii. 204.

4. The Oude Gasthuis (almshouse),
in the Cornmarket; description
[1634] in Brereton, *Travels*, pp. 21–2.

a great weight.[1] Back by water, where a pretty sober Duch lass sat reading all the way, and I could not fasten any discourse upon her.

At our landing we met with Comissioner Pett going down to the water-side with Major Harly, who is going upon a despatch into England.[2]

They having of a coach, I left the parson and my boy and went along with Comissioner*a* Pett, Mr. Ackworth and Mr. Daws, his friends, to the Princesse Dowagers house again. Whither also my Lord Fairfax and some other English lords did come to see it. And my pleasure was encreased by seeing of it again. Besides, we went into the garden, wherein is gallant knots, better then ever I saw, and a fine echo under the house in a vault made on purpose with pillers, where I played on my flagelette to great advantage.

Back to The Hague, where not finding Mr. Edward, I was much troubled, but went with the Parson to supper to Commissioner Pett, where we sat late. And among other mirth, Mr. Ackworth vyed wifes, each endeavouring to set his own wife out to the best advantage, he having as they said an extraordinary handsome wife[3] – but Mr. Daws could not be got to say anything of his.

After that to our lodging, where W. Howe and I exceeding

a   l.h. repl. s.h. 'them'

1. Probably as a punishment for drunkenness: William Andrews, *Bygone Punishments*, pp. 204–6. Evelyn (17 August 1641) wrote that it reminded him of a butter-churn, and that it was hung round the necks of unchaste women. According to Brereton (*Travels*, pp. 19–20), petty larceny and overcharging (by shippers) were also punished in this way.

2. Robert Harley, younger son of Sir Robert Harley of Brampton Bryan, Hereford, acted as intermediary between the court and the Presbyterians at this time: *Letter-book of Mordaunt* (ed. M. Coate), p. 10.

3. Ackworth was naval storekeeper at Woolwich; his wife was a sister of Commissioner Peter Pett. On meeting her for the first time a little later Pepys puts her down 'a very proper lovely woman' (below, ii. 13), but he apparently never got a chance to 'begin acquaintance' with her: see below, iv. 241.

troubled not to know what is become of our young gentleman.
So to bed.

19. Up early, hearing nothing of the child, and went to
Scheveling, where I found no getting on board, though the
Duke of Yorke sent[a] every day to see whether he could do it
or no.[1]

Here I met with Mr. Pinkny and his sons, and with them went
back to The Hague, in our way lighting and going to see a woman
that makes pretty rock-work[2] in shells &c., which could I have
carried safe, I would have bought some of.

At The Hague we went to buy some pictures, where I saw a
sort of painting done upon woollen cloth, drawn as if there was
a curtain over it, which was very pleasant but dear.

Another pretty piece of painting I saw, of which there was a
great wager laid by young Pinkny and I whether it was a principal or a copy: but not knowing how to decide, it was broke
off and I got the old man to lay out as much as my piece of gold
came to; and so saved my money, which had been 24*s* lost I
fear.

While we were here buying of pictures, we saw Mr. Edwd
and his company land – who told me they had been at Leyden
all night, at which I was very angry with Mr. Pierce and shall
not be friends, I believe, a good while.

To our lodging to dinner.   After that out to buy some linen
to wear against tomorrow, and so to the barber's.   After that
by waggon to Lausdune, where the 365 children were born.
We saw the hill where they say the house stood and sunk,
wherein the children were born.   The basins wherein the male
and female children were baptised do stand over a large table
that hangs upon a wall, with the whole story of the thing in

---

    a repl. 'went'   *b* l.h. repl. s.h. 'cloth'

---

1. The weather was so rough that
he did not get on board until 22 May.
2. Miniature grottoes: cf. *Phil.*
Trans., 24/1955; A. R. Wright,
Brit. cal. customs, Engl. (ed. T. E.
Lones), iii. 40.

Duch and Latin – beginning, *Margarita Herman Comitissa*, &c.: the thing was done about 200 year ago.[1]

The town is a little small village, which answers much to one of our small villages, such a one as Chesterton[2] in all respects; and one would have thought it in England but for the language of the people.

We went into a little drinking-house, where there was a great many Duch boores eating of fish [in] a boorish manner, but very merry in their way. But the houses here as neat as in the great places. From hence to The Hague again, playing at Crambo in the waggon, Mr. Edwd:, Mr. Ibbot, W. Howe, Mr. Pinkny, and I. When we were come thither, W. Howe and Mr. Ibbott and Mr. Pinckny went away for Scheveling – while I and the child to walk up and down the town – where I met my old chamber fellow Mr. Ch. Anderson and a friend of his (both Physicians), Mr. Wright, who took me to a Duch house where there was an exceeding pretty lass and right for the sport; but it being Saturday, we could not have much of her company; but however, I stayed with them (having left the child with his

1. This was a famous story and a visit to Loosduinen was almost compulsory for all sight-seers. Pepys later acquired a ballad on the subject: H. E. Rollins (ed.), *Pepysian Garland*, pp. 121+. Margaret, Countess of Henneberg, on being asked for alms by a poor woman carrying twins, is said to have refused and to have told the woman that her twins could not be the children of one father (it being a common superstition that twins were the fruit of adultery). The woman thereupon pronounced a curse that the Countess should have as many children at a birth as there were days in the year. As a result, she gave birth to 365 children on Good Friday 1277, half boys, half girls (the odd one over being a herma-phrodite). The boys were baptised John, the girls Elizabeth, but all of them died, with their mother, shortly afterwards. The basins which Pepys saw were in the church; the inscrip-tion is given in full in Rollins, loc. cit. The allegation that the Countess's house sank into the ground does not appear to occur in the printed ac-counts and may be an inspired addi-tion made by the local guides. Pepys's date (about 200 years out) is also given in 1623 by James Howell in *Epistolae Ho-Elianae* (ed. Jacobs), i. 113. Erasmus and Sir Thomas Browne were among the many who believed the tale. For the literature on the subject, see *N. & Q.*, 28 October 1922, pp. 351-4. The basins and inscription are still in the church.

2. Near Cambridge.

uncle Pickering, who I met in the streets) till 12 at night; by that time Charles was almost drunk; and then broke up, he resolving to go thither again (after he had seen me at my lodging) and lie with the girl, which he told me he had done in the morning.

Going to my lodging, we met with the bellman, who strikes upon a clapper, which I took in my hand and it is just like the clapper that our boys fright the birds away from the corn with in summer time in England. To bed.

20. Up early; and with Mr. Pickering and the child by waggon to Scheveling, where it not being yet fit to go off, I went to lie down in a chamber in the house, where in another bed there was a pretty Duch woman in bed alone; but though I had a month's-mind to her, I had not the boldness to go to her. So there I sleep an hour or two. At last she rise; and then I rise and walked up and down the chamber and saw her dress herself after the Duch dress,[1] and talked to her as much as I could; and took occasion, from her ring which she wore on her first finger, to kiss her hand; but had not the face to offer anything more. So at last I left her there and went to my company.

About 8 a-clock I went into the church at Scheveling, which was pretty handsome; and in the Chancell a very great upper part of the mouth of a whale; which indeed was of a prodigious bigness, bigger then one of our long-boats that belong to one of our ships.[2]

Commissioner Pett at last comes to our lodging, and caused the boats to go off; so some*a* in one boat, some in another, we all bid Adieu to the shore.

But through badness of weather we were in great danger, and a great while before we could get the ship; so that of all

a repl. 'one'

---

1. Bedrooms at inns (English as well as Dutch) were often occupied by several people of both sexes who were strangers to each other, and incidents of this sort were not uncommon: Lawrence Wright, *Warm and snug*, pp. 125–6, 128.

2. See Jacob de Riemer, *Beschrijving van 'sGraven-Hage*: for an engraving of the town, i. 36; for the church, i. 27–51; for the whale (caught in 1617), and its Latin inscription, i. 59–60.

the company not one but myself that was not sick – I keeping myself in the open ayre, though I was soundly wet for it. This hath not been known, four days together such weather at this time of year, a great while – endeed, our fleet was thought to be in great danger, but we found all well. And Mr. Tho: Crew came on board.

I having spoke a word or two with my Lord, being not very well settled, partly through last night's drinking and want of sleep, I lay down in my gown upon my bed and sleep till the 4 a-clock gun the next morning waked me, which I took for 8 at night that night; and rising to piss, mistook the sun-rising for the sun-setting on Sunday night.

《21》 So into my naked bed and sleep till 9 a-clock. Then John Goods waken[ed] me and by the Captaines boy brought me four barrels of Mallows oysters which Captain Tatnell had sent me from Murlace.

The weather foul all this day also.

After dinner, about writing one thing or another all day and setting my papers in order, having been so long absent.

At night, Mr. Pierce, Purser (the other Pierce[1] and I having not spoke to one another since we fell out about Mr. Edwd:) and Mr. Cooke sat with me in my Cabbin and supped with me, and then I went to bed.

By letter that came hither in my absence, I understand that the Parliament hath ordered all persons to be secured, in order to a trial, that did sit as judges in the late King's death; and all the officers, too, attending the Court.[2]

Sir John Lenthall moving in the House that all that had borne arms against the King should be exempted from pardon, he was called to the bar of the House; and after a severe reproof, he was degraded his Knighthoode.[3]   At Court I find that all things

---

1. James Pearse, ship's surgeon: above, p. 148.

2. *CJ*, viii. 25-6; *LJ*, xi. 33.

3. On 12 May, in a debate on the bill of indemnity, objection had been taken to Lenthall's argument that 'he that first drew his Sword against the King, committed as high an Offence, as he that cut off the King's Head'.

He was reprehended by the House, and on the 23rd lost his seat, the election having been the subject of a double return: *CJ*, viii. 24-5, 42. The House did not deprive him of his knighthood, which would have been beyond its powers. His title was a Cromwellian creation and lapsed with the Restoration.

grow high. The old Clergy talk as being sure of their lands again, and laugh at the presbitery; and it is believed that the Sales of the King and Bishops' lands will never be confirmed by Parliament, there being nothing now in any man's power to hinder them and the King from doing what they have a mind; but everybody willing to submit to anything.

We expect every day to have the King and Duke on board so soon as it is fair.

My Lord doth nothing now; but offers all things to the pleasure of the Duke as Lord High Admirall – so that I am at a loss what to do.

22. Up very early; and now beginning to be settled in my wits again. I went about setting down my last four days' observation this morning. After that, was trimmed by a barber that hath not trimmed me yet, my Spaniard being on shore.

News brought that the two Dukes are coming on board, which, by and by they did in a Duch boat, the Duke of Yorke in yellow trimming, the Duke of Glocester in gray and red.[1]

My Lord went in a boat to meet them, the Captain, myself, and others standing at the entering Port.

So soon as they were entered we shot the guns off round the fleet. After that, they went to view the ship all over and were most exceedingly pleased with it.

They seem to be both very fine Gentlemen.

After that done, upon the Quarter Deck table under the awning, the Duke of Yorke and my Lord, Mr. Coventree[2] and I spent an houre at allotting to every ship their service in their return to England;[a] which having done, they went to dinner, where the table was very full – the two Dukes at the upper end, my Lord Opdam next on one side, and my Lord on the other.

Two[b] guns given to every man while he was drinking the King's health, and so likewise[c] to the Dukes healths.

a   repl. 'London'   b   ? 'eleven'   c   ? 'less'

---

1. Lower (*Relation*, 1660, p. 86) gives the 21st as the date of this visit. Gloucester was York's younger brother.

2. William Coventry, the Duke of York's secretary, soon to become one of Pepys's closest associates in the work of the navy.

I took down Monsieur D'esquier to the*a* great Cabbin below and dined with him in state alone, with only one or two friends of his.

All dinner the Harper belonging to Captain Sparling played to the Dukes.

After dinner, the Dukes and my Lord to see the Vice and Rere-Admirall; and I in a boat after them.

After that done, they made to the shore in the Duch boat that brought them, and I got into the boat with them. But the shore was so full of people to expect their coming as that it was as black (which otherwise is white sand) as everyone would stand by another.

When we came near the shore, my Lord left them and came into his own boat, and Generall Pen and I with him – my Lord being very well pleased with this day's work.

By the time we came on board again, news is sent us that the King is on shore; so my Lord fired all his guns round twice, and all the fleet after him; which in the end fell into disorder, which seemed very handsome.

The gun over against my Cabbin I fired myself to the King, which was the first time that he hath been saluted by his own ships since this change. But holding my head too much over the gun, I have almost spoiled my right eye.

Nothing in the world but going of guns almost all this day. In the evening we begun to remove Cabbins; I to the Carpenters Cabbin and Dr. Clerke with me – who came on board this afternoon, having been twice duckt in the sea today coming from shore, and Mr. North and John Pickering the like. Many of the King's servants came on board tonight; and so many Duch of all sorts came to see the ship till it was quite dark that we could not pass one by another, which was a great trouble to us all.

This afternoon Mr. Downing (who was knighted yesterday by the King) was here on board and had a ship for his passage into England with his lady and servants. By the same token, he called me to him when I was going to write the order to tell me that I must write him *Sir G. Downing.*

My Lord lay in the Roundhouse tonight.

This evening I was late, writing a French letter myself by my Lord's order to *Monsieur Kragh, Embassador de Denmarke a la*

a followed by blotted symbol

Haye, which my Lord signed in bed. After that, I to bed and the Doctor, and sleep well.

23.   The Doctor and I waked very merry, only my eye was very red and ill in the morning from yesterday's hurt.

In the morning came infinite of people on board from the King, to go along with him.

My Lord, Mr. Crew, and others go on shore to meet the King as he comes off from shore.

Where (Sir R. Stayner bringing His Majesty into the boat) I hear that His Majesty did with a great deal of affection kiss my Lord upon his first meeting.

The King, with the two Dukes, the Queen of Bohemia, Princesse Royalle, and Prince of Orange, came on board; where I in their coming in kissed the Kings, Queen and Princesses hands, having done the other before. Infinite shooting off of the guns, and that in a disorder on purpose, which was better then if it had been otherwise.

All day nothing but Lords and persons of Honour on board, that we were exceeding full.

Dined in a great deal of state, the Royall company by themselfs in the coach, which was a blessed sight to see.

I dined with Dr. Clerke, Dr. Quarterman, and Mr. Darcy in my Cabbin.

This morning Mr Lucy came on board, to whom and his company of the King's guard in another ship my Lord did give three dozen of bottles of wine. He made friends between Mr. Pierce and I.

After dinner, the King and Duke upon the   [1] altered the name of some of the Shipps, *viz.* the *Nazeby* into *Charles* – The *Richard, James*; the *Speaker, Mary* – The *Dunbar* (which was not in company with us) the *Henery – Winsby, Happy returne – Wakefield, Richmond – Lamport,*[2] the *Henretta – Cheriton*, the *Speedwell – Bradford*, the *Successe*.

That done, the Queen, Princess Royall, and Prince of Orange took leave of the King, and the Duke of Yorke went on board the *London*, and the Duke of Glocester the *Swiftsure* – which

1. ? supply 'quarter-deck table':   2. *Langport*. These old names de-
cf. above, p. 152.   rived from the Revolution.

done, we weighed Ancre, and with a fresh gale and most happy weather we set sail for England – all the afternoon the King walking here and there, up and down (quite contrary to what I thought him to have been), very active and stirring.

Upon the Quarter-deck he fell in discourse of his escape from Worcester.[1] Where it made me ready to weep to hear the stories that he told of his difficulties that he had passed through. As[a] his travelling four[b] days and three nights on foot, every step up to the knees in dirt, with nothing but a green coat and a pair of country breeches on and a pair of country shoes, that made him so sore all over his feet that he could scarce stir.

Yet he was forced to run away from a miller and other company that took them for rogues.[2]

His sitting at table at one place, where the master of the house,[3] that had not seen him in eight years, did know him but kept it private; when at the same table there was one that had been of his own Regiment at Worcester, could not know him but made him drink the Kings health and said that the King was at least four fingers higher then he.

Another place,[4] he was by some servants of the house made to drink, that they might know him not to be a Roundhead, which they swore he was.

a followed by blank half-line
b repl. '3'

---

1. In September 1651, after his defeat there. This was one of the first occasions on which Charles could speak openly of his six weeks' adventures without endangering those who had helped him. In October 1680 he dictated a full account to Pepys at Newmarket: it survives (in Pepys's shorthand and longhand versions, together with several other accounts which Pepys collected) in PL 2141, and was published from the longhand by Sir David Dalrymple in *An account of the preservation of King Charles II* (1766 etc.), and from the shorthand and longhand by W. Matthews in *Charles II's escape* (1966). The incidents here told by the King (and which do not include the famous hiding in the oak) are in their correct sequence, and can be recognised (despite changes of detail) in the 1680 account: see Dalrymple (1766 ed.), pp. 15–17, 35–8, 64–5, 67–9, 71. Cf. also R. Ollard, *The escape of Charles II*.

2. At Evelin Mill, near Madeley, Salop.

3. George Norton of Abbotsleigh, near Bristol.

4. Thomas Symonds's house at Hambledon, Hants.

In another place, at his Inn,[1] the master of the[a] house, as the King was standing with his hands upon the back of a chair by the fire-side, he kneeled down and kissed his hand privately, saying that he would not ask him who he was, but bid God bless him whither that he was going.   Then the difficulty of getting a boat[2] to get into France, where he was fain to plot with the master thereof to keep his design from the four men and a boy (which was all his ship's company), and so got to Feckam in France.

At Roane he looked so poorly that the people went into the rooms before he went away, to see whether he had not stole something or other.   In the evening I went up to my Lord to write letters for England – which we sent away, with word of our coming, by Mr. Edw. Pickering.   The King supped alone in the coach.   After that I got a dish, and we four supped in my cabin as at noon.

About bed-time my Lord Bartlet[3] (who I had offered my service to before) sent for me to get him a bed, who with much ado I did get to bed to my Lord Middlesex in the great Cabbin below; but I was cruelly troubled before I could dispose of him and quit myself of him.

So to my Cabbin again, where the company still was and were telling more of the King's difficultys.   As, how he was fain to eat a piece of bread and cheese out of a poor boy's pocket.[4]

How at a Catholique house,[5] he was fain to lie in the priests hole a good while in the house for his privacy.

After that our company broke up, and the Doctor and I to bed.   We have all the Lords Commissioners on board us, and many others.   Under sail all night and most glorious weather.

24.   Up, and made myself as fine as I could with the Linning stockings and wide Canons that I bought the other day at Hague. Extraordinary press of Noble company and great mirth all the

a repl. 'his'

---

1. The George at Brighton.
2. The *Surprise*, a coal-brig. The master (Nicholas Tettersell) had recognised him. They sailed from Shoreham.
3. Berkeley (of Berkeley), one of

six peers deputed by the House of Lords to present an address to the King.
4. The other accounts omit this.
5. Moseley Hall, Staffs., home of the Whitgreaves.

day. There dined with me in my Cabbin (that is, the Carpenters)
Dr. Earle and Mr. Hollis, the King's Chaplins. Dr. Scarborough,
Dr. Quarterman, and Dr. Clerke, Physicians; Mr. Darcy and
Mr. Fox (both very fine gentlemen), the King's servants. Where
we had brave discourse.

Walking upon the Decks, where persons of Honour all the
afternoon – among others, Thom. Killigrew[1] (a merry droll,
but a gentleman of great esteem with the King): among many
merry stories, he told one how he writ a letter three or foui days
ago to the Princesse Royall about a Queen ⟨Dowager⟩ of Judæa
and Palestine that was in The Hague incognita, that made love to
the King, &c.; which was Mr. Cary (a Courtiers) wife that had
been a Nun, who are all married to Jesus.

At supper the three Doctors of Physique again at my Cabbin –
where I put Dr. Scarborough in mind of what I heard him say
about the use of the eyes. Which he owned, that children do
in every day's experience look several ways with both their eyes,
till custom teaches them otherwise. And that we do now see
but with one eye – our eyes looking in Paralell lynes.

After this discourse I was called to write a pass for my Lord
Mandeville to take up horses to London. Which I wrote in
the King's name and carried it to him to sign, which was the
first and only one that ever he signed in the ship *Charles*. To
bed – coming in sight of land a little before night.

25. By the morning we were come close to the land and
everybody made ready to get on shore.

The King and the two Dukes did eat their breakfast before
they went, and there being set some Shipps diet before them,
only to show them the manner of the Shipps diet, they eat of
nothing else but pease and pork and boiled beef.

I had Mr. Darcy at my cabin and Dr. Clerke, who eat with
me and told me how the King had given 50*l* to Mr. Sheply for
my Lord's servants, and 500*l* among the officers and common
men of the ship. I spoke with the Duke of York about business, who called me Pepys by name, and upon my desire did
promise me his future favour.

1. Courtier, dramatist, and wit: manager of the first Theatre Royal:
he had been in exile with the King, see below, p. 297, n. 2. (A).
and later in this year became patentee-

Great expectation of the King's making some Knights, but there was none. About noon (though the Brigantine that Beale made was there ready to carry him), yet he would go in my Lord's barge with the two Dukes; our captain steered, and my Lord went along bare with him. I went, and Mr. Mansell and one of the King's footmen, with a dog that the King loved (which shit in the boat, which made us laugh and me think that a King and all that belong to him are but just as others are) went in a boat by ourselfs; and so got on shore when the King did, who was received by Generall Monke with all imaginable love and respect at his entrance upon the land at Dover. Infinite the Croud of people and the gallantry of the Horsmen, Citizens, and Noblemen of all sorts.[1]

The Mayor of the town came and gave him his white staffe, the badge of his place, which the King did give him again. The Mayor also presented him from the town a very rich Bible, which he took and said it was the thing that he loved above all things in the world.[2]

A Canopy was provided for him to stand under, which he did; and talked awhile with Generall Monke and others; and so into a stately coach there set for him; and so away straight through the towne toward Canterbury without making any stay at Dover.

The Shouting and joy expressed by all is past imagination. I seeing that my Lord did not stir out of his barge, I got into a boat and so into his barge, whither Mr. John Crew stepped and spoke a word or two to my Lord; and so returned. We back to the ship; and going, did see a man almost drowned, that fell out of his boat into the sea but with much ado was got out.

1. Cf. *Merc. Pub.*, 31 May, p. 342 (and other newspapers); Rugge, i, f.98+; John Price, *A letter written from Dover ... May 26* (1660); T. Gumble, *Life of Gen. Monck* (1671), pp. 383–4.

2. When presented with another Bible by a group of London ministers on 29 May, the King 'thanked them for it, and said that he would make that book the rule of his life and government . . .': HMC, *Rep.*, 12/7/25.

Neither the Dover nor the London Bible – the latter costing £150 – seems to have survived in the royal libraries. The former was fastened with gold clasps: Rugge, i, f.98r. It was presented in fact not by the Mayor (Thomas Broome) but by the chaplain to the corporation, John Reading (minister of St Mary's), an aged loyalist, once chaplain to Charles I.

My Lord almost transported with joy that he hath done all this without any the least blur and obstruccion in the world that would give an offence to any, and with the great Honour that he thought it would be to him.

Being overtook by the Brigantine, my Lord and we went out of our barge into it; and so went on board with Sir W. Battin[1] and the Vice- and Rear-Admiralls.

At night my Lord supped, and Mr. Tho. Crew, with Captain Stoakes. I supped with the Captain, who told me what the King had given us. My Lord returned late and at his coming did give me order to cause the marke to be gilded, and a Crowne and *C. R.* to be made at the head of the Coach table, where the King today with his owne hand did mark his Highth – which accordingly I caused the painter to do; and is now done, as is to be seen.[2]

26. Thanks to God,*a* I got to bed in my own poor Cabbin and slept well till 9 a-clock this morning.

All the great company and Mr. North and Dr. Clerke being gone, I find myself very uncouth* all this day for want thereof. My Lord dined with the Vice-Admirall today (who is as officious, poor man, as any spaniel can be; but I believe all to no purpose, for I believe he will not hold his place).[3]

So I dined*b* commander at the Coach table today, and all the officers of the ship with me, and Mr. White of Dover.[4] After

a MS. 'got'   *b* repl. 'supped'

1. Sir William Batten (d. 1667); soon to be, as Surveyor of the Navy (from June onwards), a colleague and neighbour of Pepys at the Navy Office.

2. The King had apparently caught his head against a beam. Cf. W. Blundell, *Crosby Records* (ed. Gibson), p. 90: 'I was present in the ship (about five miles from Dover) two or three hours before King Charles II landed in England ... when the King (by reason of an accident) took his own measure, standing under a beam in the cabin, upon his place he made a mark with a knife. Sundry tall persons went under it, but there were none that could reach it.' Charles's height was given as 'above two yards' in the official description issued to aid in his capture after Worcester fight in 1651: *CSPD 1651*, p. 476. His funeral effigy now at Westminster Abbey measures 6 ft 2 ins.

3. Lawson (republican and Anabaptist in the past) now won the King's favour. He was knighted in September 1660 and was given several commands before his death in 1665.

4. Thomas White, navy agent.

a game or two at nine-pins, to work all the afternoon, making of above 20 orders.

In the evening, my Lord having been ashore (the first time that he hath been ashore since he came out of the Hope, having resolved not to go till he had brought his Majesty into England), returned on board with a great deal of pleasure.

I supped with the Captain in his Cabbin with young Captain Cuttance; and afterwards a messenger from the King came with a letter; and to go into France. And by that means we supped again with him at 12 a-clock at night.

This night the Captain told me that my Lord had appointed me 30*l*. out of the 1000 Duckets which the King had given to the ship, at which my heart was very much joyed.

To bed.

27. *Lords day.* |
Called up by John Goods to see the Garter and Heralds coate which lay in the coach, brought by Sir Edwd. Walker, King at armes, this morning for my Lord.

My Lord hath summoned all the commanders on board him to see the ceremony.[1] Which was thus:

Sir Edw., putting on his Coate and having laid the George and Garter and the King's letter to my Lord upon a Crimson Cushion (in the coach, all the commanders standing by), makes three congees to him, holding the Cushion in his arms. Then laying it down with the things upon it upon a chair – he takes the letter and delivers it to my Lord, which my Lord breaks open and gives him to read. It was directed to "Our trusty and well beloved Sir Edw. Montagu, Knight, one of our Generalls at sea, and our Companion elect of our Noble Order of the Garter." The contents of the letter is to show that the Kings of England have for many years made use of this Honour as a special mark of favour to persons of good extraction and virtue (and that many Emperors, Kings and Princes of other countries

---

1. The ceremony, held in Mountagu's cabin, began at 6 a.m. Walker's description of the occasion is in BM, Add. 37998, ff.90v–91r; for an account of the ceremony in general, see E. Ashmole, *Institution ... of the ...* order of the Garter (1672), ch. x, esp. pp. 308–9. For the King's letters granting the honour to Monck and Mountagu (Canterbury, 26 May), see *CSPD 1659–60*, p. 447.

have borne this honour^a) and that whereas my Lord is of a noble family and hath now done the King such service by sea at this time as he hath done, he doth send him this George and Garter to wear as Knight of that Order, with a dispensation for the other ceremony of the Habitt of the Order and other things till hereafter when it can be done.

So the Herald, putting the ribbon about his neck and the garter about his left leg – he salutes him with joy as Knight of the Garter, and that was all.

After that was done and the Captain and I had breakfasted with Sir Edwd while my Lord was writing of a letter¹ – he took his leave of my Lord and so to shore again to the King at Canterbury, where he yesterday gave the like Honour to Generall Monke, who are the only two for many years that have had the Garter given them before they had other Honours, of Earldome or the like, excepting only the Duke of Buckingham, who was only Sir George Villiers when he was made Knight of the Garter.²

A while after, Mr. Tho. Crew and Mr. John Pickering (who had stayed long enough to make all the world see him to be a fool) took ship for London.

So there now remains no stranger with my Lord but Mr. Hetly,³ who had been with us a day before the King went from us.

My Lord and the ship's company down to Sermon. I stayed above to write and look over my new song-book,⁴ which came last night to me from London in lieu of that that my Lord had of me. The officers being all on board, there was not room for me at table, so I dined in my Cabbin; where among other things,

a MS. 'honours'

---

1. After the ceremony, according to Walker's account, Mountagu 'desired Garter to stay some small time untill that hee had by a letter under his hand unto his Majestie as well as Garter's report made due acknowledgment for this transcendent favour'. After which Garter left at about 7 a.m.

2. This was in April 1616, four months before he was raised to the peerage. It was in early July 1660

that Mountagu received an earldom and Monck a dukedom. The honours were, however, already promised by letters from the King: Harris, i. 187.

3. William Hetley, of Brampton, Hunts.; a friend of Mountagu and a relative by marriage of the royalist branch of the Cromwell family.

4. ? a new copy of Playford's *Select ayres and dialogues* (1659); not in the PL. (E).

Mr. Dunn brought me a Lobster and a bottle of oyle instead of a bottle of Vinegar, whereby I spoiled my dinner.

Many orders in the ordering of ships this afternoon. Late to a sermon. After that up to the Lieutenant's Cabbin, where Mr. Sheply, I, and the Minister supped. And after that I went down to W. Howe's Cabbin and there with a great deal of pleasure sang till it was late. After that to bed.

28. Called up at 2 in the morning for letters for my Lord from the Duke of Yorke – but I went to bed again till 5. Trimmed early this morning.

This morning the Captain did call over all the men in the ship (not the boys) and gave every one of them a Duckett of the King's money that he gave the ship – and the officers according to their Quality.

For my share, I received in the Captain's Cabbin 60. Ducketts.[1] The rest of the morning busy writing letters. So was my Lord, that he would not come to dinner.

After dinner, to write again in order to sending to London. But my Lord did not finish his, so we did not send to London today.

A great part of the afternoon at nine-pins with my Lord and Mr. Hetly. I lost about 4s.

Supped with my Lord, and after that to bed.

This night I had a strange dream of bepissing myself, which I really did; and having kicked the clothes off, I got cold and found myself all muck-wet in the morning and had a great deal of pain in making water, which made me very melancholy.

29. *The Kings birth day.*

Busy all the morning writing letters to London; among the rest, one to Mr. Chetwind to give me an account of the fees due to the Herald for the Order of the Garter,[2] which my Lord desires to know.

After dinner, got all ready and sent away Mr. Cooke to London with a letter and token to my wife.

---

1. About £27.
2. See the lists of fees in E. Ash-   mole, *Institution ... of the ... order of the Garter* (1672), p. 311.

After that, abroad to Shoare[1] with my Lord (which he offered
me of himself, saying that I had a great deal of work to do this
month – which was very true).

On shore we took Horses. My Lord and Mr. Edwd:, Mr.
Hetly and I, and three or four servants – and had a great deal of
pleasure in riding. Among other things, my Lord showed me
a house that cost a great deal of money and is built in so barren
and inconvenient a place that my Lord calls it the Fooles house.

At last we came upon[a] a very high Cliffe[2] by the sea-side; and
riding under it, we having laid great wagers – I and D. Mathews,
that it was not so high as Pauls – my Lord and Mr. Hetly that
it was. But we riding under it, my Lord made a pretty good
measure of it with two sticks, and found it not to be above
35 yards high and Pauls now is reckoned to be about 90.[3] From
thence toward the Barge again. And in our way found the
people at Deale going to make a bone-Fire for joy of the day, it
being the King's birthday; and had some guns which they did
give fire to at my Lord's coming by – for which I did give them
20s. among them to drink.

While we were on the top of the cliff, we saw and heard our
guns in the fleet go off for the same joy. And it being a pretty
fair day, we could see above 20 miles into France.

Being returned on board, my Lord called for Mr. Sheplys
book of Pauls,[4] by which we were confirmed in our wager.
After that to supper and then to Musique, and so to bed.

The pain that I had got last night by cold is not yet gone, but
troubles me in the time of pissing.

This day it is thought that the King doth enter the city of
London.[5]

a repl. 'to'

---

1. Sc. to Deal, the fleet being now
anchored in the Downs.
2. Kingsdown.
3. Dugdale gives the height of the
tower as 260 ft: *Hist. St Paul's Cath.*
(1658), p. 11. Evelyn used it as a
measure of the height of a precipice
in the Alps: *Diary*, c. May 1646. The
spire, taken down in 1561, had been an

additional 274 ft: Dugdale, loc. cit.
Making calculations of this sort was a
favourite diversion of Mountagu's:
see his notebook (1655–68) in Bodl.,
MS. Lyell empt. 29.
4. Probably Dugdale's *History*.
5. Descriptions in Evelyn, 29 May,
and newspapers.

30. About 8 a-clock in the morning, the Lieutenant came to me to know whether I would eat a dish of Mackrell, newly-ketched this morning, for my breakfast – which the Captain and we did in the coach.

All yesterday and today I have a great deal of pain in making water and in my back, which made me afeared.   But it proved nothing but cold which I took yesterday night.

All this morning making up my accounts, in which I counted that I have made myself now worth about 80*l*, at which my heart was glad and blessed God.

Many Dover-men come and dine with my Lord.   My Lord at nine-pins in the afternoon.   In the afternoon, Mr. Sheply told me how my Lord had put me down for 70 Gilders[1] among the money which was given to my Lord's servants, which my heart did much rejoice at.

My Lord supped alone in his chamber.   Sir R. Stayner supped with us; and among other things, told us how some of his men did grumble that no more of the Dukes money came to their share and so would not receive any.   Whereupon he called up those that had taken it, and gave them three shares apiece more – which was very good, and made good sport among the seamen. To bed.

31.   This day my Lord took Phisique – and came not out of his chamber.

All the morning making orders.   After dinner, a great while below in the great Cabbin, trying with W. Howe some of Mr. Lawes's songs, perticularly that of *What is a kisse*,[2] with which we had a great deal of pleasure.

After that to making of orders again.

The captain of the *Assistance*, Captain Sparling, brought me this afternoon a pair of silk stockings, of a light blue, which I was much pleased with.

The Captain and I to supper.   And after that, a most pleasant walk till 10 at night with him upon the Deck, it being a fine evening.

---

1. About £7.
2. A setting of Herrick's lyric 'Among thy fancies, tell me this', entitled 'The Kisse. *A Dialogue*': Henry Lawes, *Ayres, and dialogues . . . the third book* (1658), pp. 29–31.   (E).

My pain was gone again that I had yesterday, blessed be God.

This day, the Month end, I in very good health. And all the world in a merry mood because of the King's coming. I expect every minute to hear by Mr. Cooke how my poor wife doth.

This day I begun to teach Mr. Edwd., who I find to have a very good Foundation laid for his Latin by Mr. Fuller.

I find myself in all things well as to body and mind, but only for the absence of my wife.*a*

a oblique line, below, follows entry

JUNE

1. This morning Mr. Sheply disposed of the money that the Duke of Yorke did give my Lord's servants and 22 Duccatons[1] came to my share, whereof he spoke to me to give Jasper something, because my Lord had left him out. ⟨I did give Mr. Sheply the fine payre of buckskin gloves that I bought myself about five year ago.⟩

My Lord took Phisique today – and so came not out all day. The Captain on shore all day.

After dinner, Captain Jefferys and W. Howe and the Lieutenant and I to nine-pins – where I lost about two shillings. So fooled away all the afternoon.

At night Mr. Cooke comes from London with letters – leaving all things there very gallant and joyful. And brought us word that the Parliament had ordered the 29 of May, the King's birthday, to be for ever kept as a day of thanksgiving for our redemption from tyranny and the King's return to his Government, he entering London that day.[2]

My wife was in London when he came thither, and hath been there a week with Mr. Bowyer and his wife.

My poor wife hath not been well a week before; but thanks be to God, is well again. She would fain see me and be at her house again, but we must be content. She writes me word how the Joyces go very rich and grow very Proud; but it is no matter. And that there was a talk that I should be knighted by the King; which they laugh at, but I think myself happier in my wife and estate then they are in theirs.

To bed. ⟨The Captain came on board when I was going to bed, quite fuddled; and himself the next morning told me so

a addition crowded in between paragraphs at end of line

---

1. About £6 7s.

2. A committee was appointed by the Commons to bring in a bill for this purpose on 30 May (*CJ*, viii. 49); the consequent act was 12 Car. II c. 14. In 1661 a form of prayer for the occasion was ordained in Convocation. It was printed, along with those for the other 'state holy-days' (e.g. Charles I's execution, 30 January), in all Anglican prayer-books until 1859.

too; that the Vice-Admirall, Rear-Admirall, and he had been drinking all day.$\rangle^a$

2. Being with my Lord in the morning about business in his Cabbin, I took occasion to give him thanks for his love to me in the share that he had given me of his Majestys money and the Dukes. He told me that he hoped to do me a more lasting kindness, if all things stand as they are now between him and the King – but says "We must have a little patience and we will rise together. In the meantime I will do you all the good Jobbs I can." Which was great content for me to hear from my Lord.

All the morning with the Captain, computing how much the 30 ships that came with the King from Scheveling their pay comes to for a month (because the King promised to give them all a month's pay) and it comes to 6538*l*: and the *Charles* perticularly, 777*l*. I wish we had the money. All the afternoon with two or three captains in the Captain's cabin, drinking of white wine and sugar and eating pickled oysters – where Captain Sparling told us the best Story that ever I heard; about a gentleman that persuaded a country fellow to let him gut his oysters or else they would stink.

At night writing letters to London and Weymouth; for my Lord being now to sit in the House of Peeres,[1] he endeavours to get Mr. Edwd. Mountagu for Weymouth and Mr. George for Dover.

Mr. Cooke late with me in my cabin while I wrote to my wife; and drank a bottle of wine and so took leave of me upon his Journy, and I to bed.

3. Waked in the morning by one who when I asked who it was, he told me one from Bridewell, which proved Captaine Holland.[2] I rose presently to him. He is come to get an order for the setting out of his ship, and to renew his commission.

a addition crowded into bottom of page

---

1. He had been promised an earldom on 26 May; the patent was sealed on 12 July.

2. Philip Holland; a friend of Pepys prominent in the naval service of the Commonwealth. His house,

in Bridewell precinct (near to the house of correction), was not far from that of Pepys's father. He had commanded Mountagu's ship, the *Assurance*, in the Baltic, 1659.

He tells me how every man goes to the Lord Mayor to set down their names as such that do accept of his Majestys pardon; and showed me a certificate under the Lord Mayor's hand that he had done so.[1] At sermon in the morning. After dinner into my cabin to cast my accounts up; and find myself to be worth near 100*l*, for which I bless Almighty God – it being more then I hoped for so soon; being, I believe, not clearly worth 25*l* when I came to sea, besides my house and goods.[2]

Then to set my papers in order, they being increased much upon my hand through want of time to put them in order. The ship's company all this while at sermon. After sermon my Lord did give me instructions to write to London about business; which done, after supper to bed.

4. Waked in the morning at 4 a-clock to give some money to Mr. Hetly, who was to go to London with the letters that I writ yesterday night. After he was gone, I went and lay down in my gowne upon my bed again an hour or two. At last, waked by a messenger come for a post-warrant for Mr. Hetly and Mr. Creed, who stood to give so little for their horses that the man would not let them have any without a warrant – which I sent them.

All the morning getting Captain Hollands commission done, which I did, and he at noon went away; I took my leave of him upon the Quarter-deck with a bottle of sack, my Lord being just set down to dinner.

Then he being gone, I went to dinner; and after dinner to my cabin to write.

This afternoon I showed my Lord my accounts, which he passed; and so I think myself to be worth near 100*l* now. In the evening I made an order for Captain Sparling of the *Assistance* to go to Middleburgh to fetch over some of the King's goods and took the opportunity to send all my Duch money, there being 70 Duckatoones and 29 gold Ducketts to be changed if he

---

1. Soldiers and sailors were among the first to claim the pardon offered· in the King's Declaration of Breda. The Lord Mayor issued and signed printed certificates for this purpose: *CSPD 1660–1*, p. 37.

2. Pepys had received fees as admiral's secretary as well as gifts from the King and the Duke of York. He owned a lease of his house, not the freehold.

can for English money; which is the first venture that ever I made, and so I have been since a little afeared of it.[1] After supper some Musique and so to bed.

This morning, the King's proclamacion against drinking, swearing and debauchery was read to our ships' companies in the fleet; and indeed, it gave great satisfaction to all.[2]

5. A-bed late. In the morning my Lord went on shore with the Vice-Admirall a-fishing; and at dinner returned.

In the afternoon I played at nine-pins with my Lord; and when he went*a* in again, I got him to sign my accountts for 115*l*: and so upon my private balance, I find myself confirmed in my estimate that I am worth 100*l*.

In the evening in my cabin a great while, getting the song without book, *Help, helpe Divinity* &c.[3]

After supper my Lord called for the Lieutenant's Gitterne, and with two Candlesticks with money in them for Symballs we made some barber's Musique,[4] with which my Lord was much pleased.

So to bed.

6. In the morning I had letters come that told me, among other things, that my Lord's place of Clerke of the Signett[5] was

a repl. 'gone'

---

1. The venture failed, and Pepys had to change the coins at Backwell's in London: below, p. 183.

2. *A proclamation against debauched and profane persons, who, on pretence of regard to the King, revile and threaten others, or spend their time in taverns and tippling houses, drinking his health* ... (30 May): *CSPD 1660–1*, p. 2; a copy was sent to Pepys on 2 June: ib., p. 35. Printed in *Somers Tracts* (ed. Scott), vii. 423–5. It had been occasioned by loyal excesses committed on the King's birthday (29 May).

3. 'Help, help, O help, divinity of love'; Henry Lawes's setting of Henry Hughes's poem (referring to

Henrietta-Maria's landing in a storm at Bridlington, 1643), printed in Lawes's *Second book of ayres and dialogues* (1655), pp. 1–3: Willa McC. Evans, *H. Lawes*, p. 211; W. Maynard in *Music and Letters*, 33/335+. (E).

4. Gitterns or similar simple instruments were normally kept in barbers' shops for waiting customers to play on. Hence 'barber's music' was a sort of unskilled popular music. Cf. W. Chappell, *Popular music of olden time*, pp. 101–4, 148; Sir F. Bridge in *Occ. papers Pepys Club*, i. 105; W. L. Woodfill, *Musicians in Engl. soc.*, p. 203. (E).

5. But see above, p. 128, n. 1.

fallen to him.   Which he most lovingly did tell me that I should execute, in case he could not get a better imployment for me at the end of the year – because he thought that the Duke of Yorke would command all, but he hoped that the Duke would not remove me but to my advantage.

I had a great deal of talk about my uncle Robt:,[1] and he told me that he could not tell how his mind stood as to his estate.[a] But he would do all that lay in his power for me.

After dinner came Mr. Cooke from London, who told me that my wife he left well at Huntsmore, though her health not altogether so constant as it used to be, which my heart is troubled for.   Mr. Moores letters tell me that he thinks my Lord will be suddenly sent for up to London.   And so I get myself in readiness to go.

My letters tell me:

That Mr. Calamy had preached before the King in a Surplice. This I heard afterward to be false.[2]

That my Lord Generall Monke and three more Lords are made Commissioners for the Treasury.[3]

That my Lord hath some great place conferred on him, and they say Master of the Wardrobe.[4]

a   MS. 'state'

───────────

1. Robert Pepys of Brampton, Hunts.   For Pepys's inheritance from him, see below, ii. 135 & n. 1.

2. Edmund Calamy, sen., was one of the first of the twelve or so Presbyterians made royal chaplains at this time as a reward for their party's services at the Restoration.   They were not required to use the Prayer Book or to wear surplices, to which they objected.   Henry Townshend's *Diary* (ed. Willis Bund, i. 48, 6 June) has the story that Calamy asked to be excused wearing the surplice, only to be told that the King would not in that case bother him to preach at all. Cf. W. Kennett, *Register* (1728), p. 162; M. Sylvester, *Reliq. Baxt.* (1696), bk i, pt ii. 229; R. Wodrow, *Hist. sufferings Church of Scotland* (1828–30), i. 42.

3. The other lords were the Earl of Southampton, Lord Robartes and Lord Colepeper; the Lord Chancellor (Sir Edward Hyde), Sir Edward Nicholas and Sir William Morice (Secretaries of State) were also included.   The patent was sealed on 19 June.

4. See below, p. 175 & n. 5.

That the two Dukes[1] do haunt the Parke much, and that they were at a play, *Madam Epicene*,[2] the other day.

That Sir Ant. Cooper, Mr. Hollis and Mr. Annesly, late president of the Council of State, are made privy-counsellors to the King.[3]

At night very busy sending Mr. Donne away to London. I wrote to my father for a coat to be made me against I come to London, which I think will not be long.

At night Mr. Edwd: Mountagu came on board and stayed long up with my Lord.

7. I to bed, and about one in the morning W. Howe called me up to give him a letter to carry to my Lord that came to me today, which I did. And so to sleep again. About 3 in the morning the people begun to wash the deck and the water came pouring into my mouth, which wakened me; and I was fain to rise and get on my gown, and sleep leaning upon my table.

This morning Mr. Mountagu went away again.

After dinner came Mr. John Wright and Mr. Moore, with the sight of whom my heart was very glad. They brought an order for my Lord's coming up to London – which my Lord resolved to do tomorrow.

All the afternoon getting my things in order to set forth tomorrow. At night walked up and down with Mr. Moore, who did give me an account of all things at London. Among others, how the Presbyters would be angry if they darst, but they will not be able to do anything.

Most of the commanders on board and supped with my Lord.

Late at night came Mr. Edw. Pickering from London, but I could not see him this night.

---

1. York and Gloucester, brothers of the King.

2. *Epicœne, or The silent woman*, a comedy by Ben Jonson: first acted in 1609, published in 1616, and now performed by Michael Mohun and other players at the Red Bull Theatre in St John's St, Clerkenwell: *Dram. records of Sir Henry Herbert* (ed.

Adams), p. 82. This is the first record of a post-Restoration performance. (A).

3. All had been prominent rebels, but were Presbyterians and recent converts to a restoration. They were admitted to the Privy Council at the end of May, and later raised to the peerage.

I went with Mr. Moore to the Maister's Cabbin, and saw him there in order to going to bed.

After that to my own Cabbin to put things in order and so to bed.

8.[1]   Out early.   Took horse at Deale.   I troubled much with the King's Gittar[2] and Fairebrother, the rogue that I entrusted with the carrying of it on foot, whom I thought I had lost.

Came to Canterbury; dined there.   I saw the Minster and the remains of Beckett's tombe.[3]

Collonell Dixwell's horse taken by a soldier and delivered to my Lord, and by him to me to carry to London.   To Sittingburne and then to Rochester.

Mr. Hetly's mistake about dinner.

At Chatham and Rochester, the ships[4] and bridge.[5]

Came to Gravesend.   A good handsome wench I kissed, the first that I have seen a great while.

Supped with my Lord.   Drank late below with Penrose, the Captain: to bed late, having first laid out all my things against tomorrow to [put] myself in a walking garbe.   Weary and hot, to bed to Mr. Moore.

---

1. From 8 to 17 June the diary is written in rough-note form: see above, p. c, n. 14. (WM).

2. The guitar, easier to play than the lute, was coming into favour, especially among the English upper classes. (E).

3. A roughly contemporary view of the cathedral (by Hollar) is in N. Battely's *Cantuaria Sacra*, published with W. Somner's *Antiq. of Canterbury* (1703 ed.).   Early 18th-century prints of the interior are in J. Dart, *Hist. and antiq. ... of Canterbury* (1726).   Both the shrine (1220) and the old tomb (1170–1220) of Archbishop Becket had been destroyed at the Reformation.   All that Pepys can have seen is there still – the worn hollows around the site of the tomb made by the feet of pilgrims, in the Trinity Chapel.

4. On the evening of 28 May the greatest ships of the navy had been reviewed at Chatham by the King: *Merc. Pub.*, 31 May, p. 349.

5. The stone bridge over the Medway at Rochester (built c. 1392; rebuilt end 15th century; pulled down 1856) was generally held to be the most remarkable of English bridges. It had 11 arches and was 560 ft long. Descriptions c. this period, in S. de Sorbière, *Relation* (Cologne, 1667), pp. 20–1; *Arch. Cant.*, 6/62, 64, 72; C. Fiennes, *Journeys* (ed. Morris), p. 122; views in *Drawings of Engl. in 17th cent.* (ed. P. H. Hulton), ii, pls 14–16, 19; Magalotti, p. 360. A painting (c. 1734) is reproduced in Frederick F. Smith, *Hist. Rochester*, opp. p. 336.

9. Up betimes. 25s the reckoning for very beer. Paid the house and by boats to London, six boats. Mr. Moore, W. Howe and I, and then the child in the room of W. Howe.

Landed at the Temple. To Mr. Crews. To my father's and put myself into a handsome posture to wait upon my Lord. Dined*a* there.

To Mr. Crews again. In the way met Dr Clerke and Mr. Pierce.

To White-hall with my Lord and Mr. Edw. Mountagu. Found the King in the parke. There walked. Gallantry great.

To Will How till 10 at night. Back and to my fathers.

10. *Whitsunday.* Up and to my Lord's. To Mr. Merstons,[1] where Monsieur Impertinent. At my father's found my wife. After dinner, my wife and I to walk in Lincolnes-Inne walks. After prayers she home and I to my Lord. Stayed there: and so to my father's, where I met Mr. Fairebrother. To bed with my wife.

11. Betimes to my Lord. Extreme much people and business. So with him to White-hall to the Duke.

Back with him by coach and left him in Covent-guarden. I back to Wills and the hall to see my friends. Then to the Leg in Kingstreete with Mr. Moore and sent for Limpertinent to dinner with me. After that, with Mr. Moore about privy Seale business to Mr.*b* Watkins.[2] So to Mr. Crews. Then towards my father's; met my Lord and with him to Dorset-house to the Chancellor. So to Mr. Crews and saw my Lord at Supper, and then home. Went to see Mrs. Turner, and so to bed.

12. Visited by the two Pierces. Mr. Blackburne. Dr. Clerke and Mr. Creede, and did give them a ham of Bacon.

So to my Lord and with him to the Duke of Glocester. So to Mr. Crews and look over my papers and business to set them

---

a repl. 'Died'   *b* repl. 'to'

---

1. The longhand is clear, but this must be Robert Mossom, whose Anglican services in the Savoy Pepys so often attended at this time with 'Monsieur Impertinent' (Butler).

2. Underclerk in the Privy Seal office. Mountagu had a clerkship there; Pepys and Moore were to act as his deputies.

in order a little; very hot weather. The two Dukes dined at the Speakers this day[1] and I saw there a fine entertainment and dined with the pages.

To Mr. Crews, whither came Mr. Greatorex, and with him to Faithornes,[2] and so to the Devil taverne. To my Lord's and stayed till 12 at night about business: so to my father's. My father and mother in bed – who had been with my uncle Fenner &c. and my wife all the day and expected me. But I found Mr. Cooke there, and so to bed.

13. To my Lord's. And thence to the Treasurer's of the Navy.[3] With Mr. Creede and Pierce the Purser to Rawlinsons, whither my uncle Wight came, and I spent 12s. upon them. So to Mr. Crews, where I blotted a new carpet that was hired, but got it out again with fair water.

By water with my Lord in a boat to Westminster and to the Admiralty, now in a new place.[4]

After business done there, to the Renish wine-house with Mr. Blackeburne, Creed, and Wivell.

So to my Lord's lodgings and to my father's, and to bed.

14. Up to my Lord and from him to the Treasurer of the Navy for 500l. After that to a tavern with Washington the purser – very gallant and eat and drank. To Mr. Crews and laid the money.

To my Lady Pickering with the plate that she did give my Lord the other day.

Then to Wills and met Will Symons and Doling and Luellin,

---

1. The Dukes of Gloucester and of York had recently addressed letters of thanks to the Commons for the grants of supply made to them: *CJ*, viii. 56, 59. Their entertainment was one of a series to which members of the royal family were treated at this time.

2. William Faithorne, sen., draughtsman, engraver and print-seller, from whom Pepys later made many purchases. (OM).

3. His office was then in Leadenhall St. (R).

4. It had moved from Derby House in Cannon Row, Westminster (where it had been since January 1655), to Whitehall Palace, on the Duke of York's taking office as Lord High Admiral. Pepys refers below, at p. 229, to 'the Admiralty chamber'. (R).

and with them to the bull=head, and then to a new ale-house in Brewers-yard, where Winter that had the fray with Stoakes,[1] and from them to my father's.

15. All the morning at the Comissioners of the Navy about getting out my bill for 50*l* for the last Quarter[2] – which I got done with a great deal of ease, which is not common.

After that with Mr. Turner[3] to the Dolphin and drank. And so by water to W. Symons's – where D. Scobell with his wife, a pretty and rich woman. Mrs. Symons a very fine woman. Very merry after dinner with marrying of Luellin and D. Scobells kinswoman that was there.[4] Then to my Lord, who told me how the King hath given him the place of the Great Wardrobe.[5]

My Lord resolves to have Sarah[6] again. I to my father's, and then to see my uncle and aunt Fenner. So home and to bed.

16. Rose betimes and abroad in one shirt,[7] which brought me a great cold and pain. Murford took me to Harvys by ⟨my⟩ father's to drink and told me of a business that I hope to get 5*l* by.[8]

1. William Winter, merchant, had been in dispute with Capt. John Stoakes over a prize taken c. 1657 in the Mediterranean: *CSPD 1659–60*, pp. 289–90.

2. For Pepys's entertainment (and that of his clerk) as secretary to the Generals of the Fleet for the past 91 days. Bill registered at the Navy Treasury on the 18th: PRO, Adm. 20/1, p. 84. The Commissioners' office was the Navy Office in Seething Lane.

3. Thomas Turner, Clerk-General to the Navy Office.

4. Llewellyn never married in earnest. For mock-weddings, see *Comp.*: 'Games etc.'

5. Mountagu's patent was dated 30 June. The Mastership of the Great Wardrobe was one of the principal household offices, carrying with it fees and allowances, a house at Puddle Dock and an establishment, staffed (in 1670) by 40 assistants, which acted as the central depot for all clothes, robes, furnishings etc., for the use of the King and his household.

6. A former housekeeper; in trouble in 1657 for misbehaviour: *Letters*, p. 9. For a later misdemeanour, see below, iii. 288.

7. Until the widespread use of knitted underwear in the 19th century men commonly wore two shirts in cold weather.

8. The grant of a naval commission for a friend: see below, pp. 178, 180. William Murford was a timber merchant and entrepreneur.

To my Lord, and so to White-hall with him about the Clerk of the Privy Seales place which he is to have.

Then to the Admiralty, where I wrote some letters. Here Collonell Thomson told me as a great secret, that the *Nazeby* was on fire when the King was there – but that it is not known; when God knows, it is quite false.

Dined at Mr. Crews, and after dinner with my Lord to White-hall. Court attendance infinite tedious. Got a piece of gold of Major Holmes for the horse of Dixwells that I brought to town. Back with my Lord to my Lady Wrights and stayed while it had done raining, which it hath not done a great while.

After that, at night home to my father's and to bed.

17. *Lords day.* Lay long abed.

To Mr. Messums; a good sermon. This day the Organs did begin to play at White-hall before the King.[1]

Dined at my father's. After dinner to Mr. Messums again, and so in the garden and heard Chappells father preach, that was page to the protector.

And just by the window that I stood at, there sat Mrs. Butler the great beauty.

After sermon to my Lord and then into grays Inne walks, where Mr. Edwd. and I saw many beauties.

So to my father's, where Mr. Cooke, W. Bowyer, and my Cozen Joyce Norton supped. To bed.

18. To my Lord, where much business and some hopes of getting some money thereby. With him to the parliament-house, where he did entend to have gone to have made his appearance today, but he met Mr. Crew upon the stairs and would not go in.

---

1. Cf. Rugge, i, f.103r. The organ in Whitehall Chapel, like many church organs, had been taken down during the revolution. It was recovered through John Playford's efforts and erected in its old place soon after the Restoration. 'Father' Bernard Smith's new organ there, built under John Hingston's supervision, was apparently completed by October 1662. Cf. below, pp. 195, 283; A. Freeman, *Father Smith*, p. 2; W. L. Sumner, *The Organ* (1962), pp. 140, 145. (E).

He went to Mrs. Browns and stayed till word was brought him what was done in the House.[1] This day they made an end of the twenty men to be excepted from[a] pardon to their estates.[2]

By barge to Stepny with my Lord, where at Trinity-house we had great entertainment.[3]

With my Lord there went Sir W. Pen, Sir H. Wright, Hetly, Pierce, Creed, Hill, I and other servants.

Back again to the Admiralty and so to my Lord's lodgings, where he told me that he did look after the place of the Clerk of the Acts[4] for me. So to Mr. Crews and my father's and to bed. My wife went this day to Huntsmoore for her things, and I was very lonely all night.

This evening my wife's brother Balty came to me to let me know his bad condition and to get a place for him, but I perceive he stands upon a place for a gentleman that may not stain his family; when God help him, he wants bread.

19. Call[ed] on betimes by Murford, who showed me five pieces to get a business done for him, which I am resolved to do.

Much business at my Lord's. This morning my Lord went into the House of Commons and there had the thanks of the House, in the name of the parliament and the Commons of Eng-

a repl. 'for'

---

1. Mountagu was due to receive the thanks of the House (below, p. 178, n. 1), but his visit was presumably postponed by the arrival of a message from the King asking the Commons to speed the passage of the bill of indemnity and oblivion: *CJ*, viii. 66–7. Mrs Browne was Elizabeth, second wife of John Browne, Clerk of the Parliaments: his first wife (d. 1634) was Temperance Crew, aunt of Mountagu's wife. The Brownes lived in Old Palace Yard in the Clerk's official residence.

2. *CJ*, viii. 67.

3. This being Trinity Monday, when the corporation met to elect its officers for the year.

4. The office which Pepys held until he became Secretary to the Admiralty in 1673, and in which he made his reputation as an administrator. The Clerk of the Acts was secretary to the Navy Board, which conducted the civil administration of the navy. The Admiralty consisted at this period of the Admiral (the Duke of York), his secretary (Coventry) and a small staff of clerks. The royal patent for Pepys's appointment was issued on 13 July.

land, for his late service to his King and Country.[1]   A motion was made for a reward for him, but it was quashed by Mr. Annesly, who above most men is engaged to my Lord's and Mr. Crews families.[2]

Meeting with Captain Stoakes at White-hall, I dined with him and Mr. Gallop, a parson (with whom afterwards I was much offended at his importunity and impertinence, such another as Elborough),[3] and Mr. Butler, who complimented much after the same manner as the parson did.   After that toward my Lord's at Mr. Crews, but was met with by a servant of my Lady Pickering – who took me to her and she told me the story of her husband's case and desired my assistance with my Lord, and did give me, wrapped up in paper, 5*l* in silver.[4]   After that to my Lord, and with him to White-hall and my Lady Pickering.   He went at night with the King to Baynards Castle[5] to supper, and I home to my father's to bed.   My wife and the girl and dog came home today.   We were [told] of W. Howe being sick today; but he was well at night.

When I came home I found a Quantity of Chocolatte left for me, but I know not from whom.

20.   Up by 4 in the morning to write letters to sea and a Comission for him that Murford solicits for.[6]

Called on by Captain Sparling, who did give me my Duch

---

1. 'My Lord', said the Speaker, 'You have landed our Sovereign upon the safest Shore, that ever *English* King set his Foot upon; the Hearts of his People': *CJ*, viii. 68.   Sandwich kept a copy of the resolution: Sandwich MSS, Letters from Ministers, i, ff. 27-8.

2. There appears to be no other notice of this motion.   For Annesley's relations with Mountagu at this time, see *Comp.*: 'Annesley, Arthur, 1st Earl of Anglesey.'

3. Robert Elborough (also a parson) had been a schoolfellow of Pepys.

4. Cf. her gift of plate to her brother Sandwich: above, p. 174. Her husband, Sir Gilbert Pickering,

had been a prominent Commonwealthsman, and Lord Chamberlain to both Oliver and Richard Cromwell.   The Commons had excepted him from the Act of Indemnity on 9 June, when it promised him a special punishment to fit his case: *CJ*, viii. 60.   Hence his wife's anxiety.   In the end, by a vote of 6 August, he escaped with exclusion from public office, on the motion of Sandwich: *LJ*, xi. 118; HMC, *Sutherland*, p. 155.

5. The Earl of Pembroke (lessee of Baynard's Castle) was the host; the Dukes of York and Gloucester were among the other guests: *Merc. Pub.*, 21 June, p. 400.

6. See above, p. 175 & n. 8.

money again, and so much as he had changed into English
money, by which my mind was eased of a great deal of trouble –
and some other sea-Captains. I did give them a good morning
draught. And so to my Lord, who lay long in bed this day,
because he came home late from supper with the King. With
my Lord to the Parliament-house; and after that, with him to
Generall Monkes, where he dined at the Cockepitt. I home
and dined with my wife, now making all things ready there
again.

Thence to my Lady Pickering, who did give me the best
intelligence about the Wardrobe. Afterward to the Cockepitt
to my Lord with Mr. Townsend, one formerly and now again to
be imployed as Deputy of the Wardrobe.

Thence to the Admiralty, and despatched away Mr. Cooke to
sea – whose business was a letter from*ᵃ* my Lord about Mr. G.
Mountagu to be chosen as a parliament-man in my Lord's room
at Dover.[1]   And another to the Vice-admirall to give my Lord
a constant account of all things in the fleet, merely that he may
thereby keep up his power there. Another letter to Captain
Cuttance, to send the Barge that brought the King on Shoare to
Hinchingbrooke by Lynne.[2]

To my own house, meeting G. Vines and drank with him at
Charing-cross, now the King's-head taverne.

With my wife to my father's, where met with Swan, an old
Hypocrite, and with him, his friend and my father, and my Cozen
Scott to the beare tavern. To my father's and to bed.

21. To my Lord; much business. With him to the Council-
chamber, where he was sworne; and the charge of his being
admitted privy-Councellor is 26*l*.[3]

a repl. 'to'

---

1. Sandwich resigned his seat at
Dover after his elevation to the peerage, and George Mountagu was
elected on 16 August. Letters on
this election are in PRO, Adm.
2/1745, f.2*v*; *CSPDAdd. 1660–85*, pp.
4–5.

2. From King's Lynn it would go
direct to Hinchingbrooke by the
Ouse.

3. This remained the standard fee
into at least Anne's reign: E. C.
Hawtrey (ed.), *Private diary of William
1st Earl Cowper* (1833), p. 3.

To the Dogg tavern at Westminster, where Murford with Captain Curle, Captain of the *Maria*, and two friends of theirs, went to drink. The Captain did give me five pieces in gold and a silver can for my wife for the Comission I did give him this day for his ship, dated the 20th of April 1660 last.

Thence to the parliament-door and came to Mr. Crews to dinner with my Lord. Forth with my Lord to the great Wardrobe to see it – where Mr. Townsend brought us to the Governors of some poor children in tawny clothes, who have been maintained there these eleven years. Which put my Lord to a stand how to dispose of them – that he may have the house for his use.[1] The children did sing finely, and my Lord did bid me give them five pieces in gold at his going away.

Thence back to White-hall; where, the King being gone abroad, my Lord and I walked a great while in the   discoursing of the simplicity of the Protector[2] in his losing all that his father had left him. My Lord told me that the last words that he parted with the protector with when he[3] went to the Sound, were that he should rejoice more to see him in his grave at his returne home then that he should give way to such things as were then in haching and afterwards did ruine him. And the Protector said that whatever G. Mountagu, my Lord Broghill, Jones, and the Secretary[4] would have him to do, he would do it, be it what it would[a] be. Thence to my wife, meeting Mr. Blagrave, who went home with me and did give me a lesson* upon the flagelette and hanselled my silver can with my wife and I.

a repl. 'will'

---

1. The Great Wardrobe occupied a site on the n. side of the modern Queen Victoria St. In June 1649 the government had granted it to the city Corporation for the Poor (established in 1647): *CJ*, vi. 226. Sandwich had ousted them by early 1661 (below, ii. 97), despite a piteous petition on behalf of the poor children: Carte 74, f.501r.

2. Richard Cromwell.
3. Mountagu.
4. Perhaps the name of Sandwich's cousin was included out of politeness, but it is certain that the rest were Richard Cromwell's closest advisers. They were Lord Broghill (cr. Earl of Orrery, 1660), Col. Philip Jones and Secretary Thurloe.

To my father's, where Sir Tho. Honywood[1] and his family were come of a sudden, and so we forced to lie all together in the little chamber, three storeys high.

22. To my Lord, where much business. With[a] him to White-hall; where the Duke of Yorke not being up, we walked a good while in the Shield gallery. Mr. Hill (who for these two or three days hath constantly attended my Lord) told me of an offer of 500*l* for a Barronets dignity,[2] which I told my Lord of in the Balcone in this gallery, and he said he would think of it.

I to my Lord's and gave order for horses to be got to draw my Lord's great coach to Mr. Crews.

Mr. Morrice the upholster came himself today to take notice what Furniture we lack for our lodgings at White-hall.

My dear friend Mr. Fuller of Twickenham and I dined alone at the Sun taverne, where he told me how he hath the grant of being Deane of St. Patrickes in Ireland,[3] and I him my condition; and both rejoiced one for another.

Thence to my Lord and had the great coach to Brighams, who went with me to the Half-Moone and gave me a can of good Julipp and told me how my Lady Monke deals with him and others for their places, asking him 500*l*, though he was formerly the King's coachmaker and sworn to it.[4]

My Lord abroad, and I to my house and set things in a little order there. So with Mr. Moore to my father's, I staying with Mrs. Turner, who stood at her door as I passed. Among other things, she told me for certain how my old Lady Middlesex beshit herself the other day in the presence of the King, and

a repl. 'to'

---

1. Of Markes Hall, Essex; late M.P. for the county. With his brothers he used rooms in John Pepys's house as his London lodgings.

2. This would be payment for the grant of the title: cf. below, p. 221 & n. 2. £300–400 was said to be a common price: HMC, *Rep.*, 5/1/205. Hill, who solicited it on someone else's behalf, may have been Pepys's neighbour, John Hill of Axe Yard.

Baronetcies had been commonly sold ever since their introduction in 1611, but little of the revenue from their sale (even from the official fee) at this time reached the Crown.

3. The patent was issued on 3 July and he was installed on 22 October.

4. Thomas Brigham was appointed coachmaker to the Duke of York in November.

people took notice of it. Thence called at my father's; and so to Mr. Crews, where Mr. Hetly had sent a letter for me and two pair of silk stockings, one for W. Howe and the other for me.

To Sir H. Wrights to my Lord, where he was, and took direction about business; and so by link home about 11 a-clock.

To bed, the first time since my coming from sea, in my own house, for which God be praised.

23. By water with Mr. Hill towards my Lord's lodgings and so to my Lord. With him to White-hall, where I left him and went to Mr. Holmes to deliver him the horse of Dixwells that had stood these fourteen days at the bell.

So to my Lord's lodgings, where Tom Guy came to me; and there stayed to see the King touch people of the King's evil.[1] But he did not come at all, it rayned so. And the poor people were forced to stand all the morning in the rain in the garden. Afterwards, he touched them in the banquetting-house.

With my Lord to my Lord Frezendorfes, where he dined today – where he told me that he had obtained a promise of the Clerk of the Acts place for me, at which I was glad.

Met with Mr. Chetwind and dined with him at Hargraves, the cornechandler in St. Martins-lane, where a good dinner.

1. Scrofula, a tubercular infection of the soft tissues, generally the glands; allegedly healed by the touch of a consecrated king. See Sir R. Crawfurd, *King's Evil*; Marc Bloch, *Les rois thaumaturges*; J. Hastings (ed.), *Encyl. religion and ethics*, vii. 736+. In England ceremonies had been held frequently since the reign of Edward III. Under Henry VII an office was added to the service book; it appears (modified and in English) in some prayer books printed during the reign of Charles I and up to 1719. See Pepys's eye-witness account, below, ii. 74 & n. 1. There was a great revival of the practice at the Restoration: see John Browne, *Charisma Basi-* *licon* (1684); Lower, *Relation* (1660), pp. 74–8. At this period the sufferers attended a service at which prayers were offered, and were given a gold coin ('touchpiece'), touched by the ruler, which they hung around their necks. On this occasion over 600 are said to have attended at Whitehall Palace. The King thereafter appointed Fridays for the ceremony and limited the number to 200: *Merc. Pub.*, 28 June, p. 407; *Parl. Intell.*, 9 July, p. 437. The ceremony went out of use under the Hanoverians; Dr Johnson, as a little boy in Anne's reign, is said to have been among the last to have been 'touched'.

Where he showed me some good pictures and an instrument he called an Angelique. With him to London. Changed all my Dutch money at Backwells for English. And then to Cardinalls Cap with him and the City Remembrancer,[1] who paid for all.

Back to Westminster, where my Lord was – and discoursed with him a while about his family matters. So he went away; I home and wrote letters into the country, and to bed.

24. *Sonday*. Drank my morning draught at Harpers[2] and bought a pair of gloves there. So to Mr. G. Mountagu and told him what I had received from Dover about his business; likely to be chosen there.

So home, and thence with my wife toward my father's. She went thither; I to Mr. Crews, where I dined and my Lord at my Lord Montagus of Boughton in Little Queenstreete.

In the afternoon to Mr. Messums with Mr. Moore, and we sat in Mr. Butlers pew. Then to White-hall looking for my Lord, but in vain; and back again to Mr. Crews, where I found him and did give him letters. Among others, some simple ones from our Lieutenant, Lieutenant Lambert, to him and myself, which made Mr. Crew and us all laugh. I went to my father's to tell them*a* that I could not come to supper; and so after my business done at Mr. Crews, I went home, and my wife within a little while after me.

My mind all this while full of thoughts for my place of Clerk of the Acts.

25. With my Lord to White-hall all the morning. I spoke with Mr. Coventry about my business, who promised me all the assistance I could expect. Dined with young Mr. Powell, lately come from the Sound, being amuzed* at our great changes here. Mr. Southerne now Clerke to Mr. Coventry. At the Leg in King-street. Thence to the Admiralty, where I met with Mr. Turner of the Navy Office, who did look after the

a repl. 'that'

---

place of Clerk of the Acts. He was very civil to me and I to him, and shall be so.

There came a letter from my Lady Monke to my Lord about it this evening. But he refused to come to her; but meeting in White-hall with Sir Tho. Clerges, her brother, my Lord returned answer that he would not desist in my business. And that he believed that Generall Monke would take it ill if my Lord should name the officers in his army. And therefore he desired to have the naming of one officer in the fleet.

With my Lord by coach to Mr. Crews and very merry by the way, discoursing of the late changes and his good fortune.

Thence home; and then with my wife to Dorsett-house to deliver a list of the names of the Justices of peace for Huntington-shire[1] – by coach, taking Mr. Fox part of the way with me that was with us with the King on board the *Nazeby*, who I find to have married Mrs. Whittle that lived at Mr. Geeres's so long.[2] A very civil gentleman.

At Dorsett-house I met with Mr. Kipps my old friend, with whom the world is well changed, he being now seal-bearer to the Lord Chancellor,[3] at which my wife and I are very well pleased, he being a very good-natured man.

Home, and late writing letters. Then to my Lord's lodgings, this being the first night of his coming to White-hall to lie since his coming from sea.

26. Up, and was called on by Mr. Pinckny, to whom I paid 16*l* for orders that he hath made for my Lord's Cloakes and coats. Then to my Lord's lodgings. My Lord dined at his lodgings all alone today. I went to Secretary Nicholas to carry him my Lord's resolutions about his title which he hath chosen, and that

1. Mountagu, a deputy-lieutenant for the county, was submitting to the Chancellor names of suitable persons for appointment.
2. Elizabeth Whittle had lived in Salisbury Court when Pepys was a boy, at Mr Geere's (or Gery's), a relative of Mountagu. Pepys had 'a

great opinion' of her in those days and made anagrams on her name: below, p. 290. In c. 1654 she had married Stephen Fox, later Pay-master-General of the Army.
3. He had been a servant of George Mountagu.

is Portsmouth.[1] I met with Mr. Throgmorton, a merchant, who went with me to the old Three Tons at Charing-cross – who did give me five pieces of gold for to do him a small piece of service about a Convoy to Bilbo, which I did.

In the afternoon, one Mr. Watts came to me, a merchant, to offer me 500*l* if I would desist from the Clerk of the Acts place. I pray God direct me in what I do herein.

Went to my house, where I found my father and carried him and my wife by water to White-fryers, and myself to puddle wharfe to the Wardrobe to Mr. Townsend, who went with me to Backewell the goldsmith's; and there we chose a 100*l* worth*a* of plate for my Lord to give Secretary Nicholas.*b*2 Back and supped at my father's; and so home. To bed.

27. With my Lord to the Duke, where he spoke to Mr. Coventry to despatch my business of the Acts, in which place everybody gives me joy, as if I were in it; which God send.

Dined with my Lord and all his officers of his Regiment, who invited my Lord and his friends, as many as he would bring, to dinner at the Swan at Dowgate, a poor house and ill dressed but very good fish and plenty. Here Mr. Symons the Chyrurgeon told me how he was likely to lose his estate that he had bought, at which I was not a little pleased.[3]

To Westminster and with W. Howe by coach to the Speaker's, where my Lord supped with the King; but we could not get in.

a repl. 'of'   *b* repl. 'Morr' -

---

1. He changed his mind and chose Sandwich: below, p. 196 & n. 5. In the secretary's warrant issued this day the titles of the earldom (Portsmouth) and barony (Hinchingbrooke) are altered to 'Sandwich' and 'St Neot's' respectively: BM, Egerton 2551, f.33*r*. Mountagu had no close connection with either Portsmouth or Sandwich, but both had maritime interests, and (what was also important) a political value as parliamentary constituencies returning two members each. Huntingdon (which would have been the most obvious territorial title for him to take) was already an earldom in the Hastings family.

2. The usual gift made by a newly-minted earl to the Secretary of State issuing a warrant for his title. Cf. below, p. 192, n. 3.

3. The estate had been confiscated from the church: cf. below, p. 230.

So back again; and after a song or two in my chamber[1] in the dark – which doth (now that the bed is out) sound very well, I went home and to bed.

28.   My brother Tom came to me with Patternes to choose for a suit.   I paid him all to this day, and did give him 10*l* upon account.

To Mr. Coventry, who told me that he would do me all right in my business.

To Sir G. Downing, the first visit I have made him since he came.   He is so stingy a fellow, I care not to see him.[2]   I quite cleared myself of his office, and did give him liberty to take anybody in.   Hawly and he are parted too, he going to serve Sir Tho. Ingram.[3]

I went also this morning to see Mrs. Pierce the Chyrurgeon.[4] I found her in bed in her house in Margaret churchyard – her husband returned to sea.   I did invite her to go to dinner with me and my wife today.   After all this to my Lord, who lay a-bed till 11 a-clock, it being almost 5 before he went to bed, they supped so late last night with the King.

This morning I saw poor Bishop Wren going to Chappell, it being a thanksgiving-day for the King's Returne.[5]

After my Lord was awake, I went up to him to the Nursery, where he doth lie; and having talked with him a little, I took leave and carried my wife and Mrs. Pierce to Cloathworkers-hall

---

1. In Mountagu's lodgings: above, p. 59. Pepys gave up this room to Will Howe: below, p. 222.

2. He had arrived from Holland in May. His meanness is well attested by other evidence, and may have been another facet of his commercial acumen.

3. Merchant; later member of the Council for Trade.   Several months later Hawley appears to be still in Downing's service, and announces that he is looking for a job with the Bishop of London: below, ii. 9.

4. The surgeon's wife.

5. Matthew Wren, Bishop of Ely since 1638, and enemy of the Puritans, had been imprisoned in the Tower for 18 years during the revolution.   He was the uncle of Sir Christopher Wren.   This thanksgiving service was appointed by the King (on the address of both houses) to be held in all churches: Steele, no. 3222.   Similar services were held in later years on 29 May: see below, ii. 109 & n. 2. The preacher on this occasion in Whitehall Chapel was Sheldon.

to dinner, where Mr. Pierce the purser met us.[1]   We were invited
by Mr. Chaplin the victualler, where Nich. Osborne was.   Our
entertainment very good.   A brave hall.   Good company and
very good Musique.   Where among other things, I was pleased
that I could find out a man by his voice, whom I had never seen
before, to be one that sung behind the Curtaine formerly at
Sir W. Davenants opera.[2]   Here Dr. Gauden and Mr. Gauden
the victualler dined with us.[3]   After dinner to Mr. Rawlinson's
to see him and his wife.   And would have gone to my aunt
Wight, but that her only child, a daughter, died last night.

Home and to my Lord, who supped within; and Mr. Edwd.
Mountagu, Mr. Tho. Crew and others with him sat up late.   I
home and to bed.

29.   This day or two my maid Jane hath been lame, that we
cannot tell what to do for want of her.   Up and to White-hall,
where I got my warrant from the Duke to be Clerk of the Acts.[4]
Also, I got my Lord's warrant from the Secretary for his Honour
of Earle of Portsmouth and Vicount Mountagu of Hinchingbrooke.

So to my Lord to give him an account of what I had done.
Then to Sir Geffery Palmer[5] to give them to him to have bills
drawn upon them – who told me that my Lord must have some
good Latinist to make the preamble to his patent, which must
express his late service in the best terms that he can; and he told
me in what high flaunting terms Sir J. Greenville hath caused

1. The Court Minutes of the Company record a meeting on this day
but make no mention of a dinner.
The hall in Mincing Lane was a 16th-
century building reconstructed in
1633–4.   Both Pepys (in 1677–8)
and his host, Francis Chaplin (in
1668–9), later served as Masters of
the Company.

2. Either *The siege of Rhodes*, first
presented at Rutland House in 1656, or
The cruelty of the Spaniards in Peru,
first presented at the Cockpit Theatre,
Drury Lane, in 1658.   (A).

3. John Gauden, Dean of Bocking,
Essex, in November appointed Bishop
of Exeter; and his brother Denis
Gauden, victualler to the navy in
several ports and in October appointed Surveyor-General of Victualling.
The latter was to become a close
associate of Pepys.

4. PRO, Adm. 2/1725, f.8r (copy);
directed to the Attorney-General;
copy wrongly dated 20 June.

5. Attorney-General.

his to be done in, which he doth not like; but that Sir Rd. Fanshaw hath done Generall*ᵃ* Monkes very well.[1]

Back to Westminster; and meeting Mr. Townsend in the
palace – he and I and another or two went and dined at the Leg
there.   Then to White-hall, where I was told by*ᵇ* Mr. Huchinson
at the Admiralty that Mr. Barlow my Predecessor, Clerk of the
Acts, is yet alive and coming up to town to look after his place[2] –
which made my heart sad a little.   At night told my Lord
thereof and he bade me to get possession of my patent; and he
would do all that could be done to keep him out.*ᶜ* This night
my Lord and I looked over the list of the Captains, and marked
some that my Lord hath a mind to have put out.   Home and
to bed.   Our wench very lame, abed these two days.

30.   Betimes to Sir Rd. Fanshaw to draw up the preamble to
my Lord's patent.

So to my Lord and with him to White-hall, where I saw a great
many fine Antique heads of marble that my Lord Northumberland hath given the King.[3]   Here meeting with Mr. De Cretz,

a repl. 'his'   *b* l.h. repl. s.h. 'at'   *c* repl. 'our'

---

1. Mountagu's patent (12 July:
PRO, C 66/2923 no. 9) is printed in
Pepysiana, pp. 282+; the preamble
to Monck's in F. Peck, *Desiderata
Curiosa* (1779), pp. 514–15. 'The
common Custom, about Preambles
to Patents of Honour, (which Patents
are prepared by Mr. Attorney-General
in all Points except the Preamble,
which is left to the Order of the Person to be prepared), is to employ
some Chaplain, or rhetorical Scholar,
who is set on Work to pump hard
for Elogiums, and, by Dint of Elo-
quence, to varnish out his Majesty's
gracious Act': R. North, *Life of . . .
Guilford* (1742), p. 276.   Sir Richard
Fanshawe, the diplomatist, was now
persuaded to draw up the preamble
for Mountagu. He was a classical
scholar, linguist and author; for his
services to the royalists he had recently

been appointed a Master of Requests
and Latin Secretary.   Monck's patent
(creating him Duke of Albemarle)
was passed on 7 July; Grenville's (as
Earl of Bath) not until 20 April 1661.
Pepys's own patent of appointment
(from the Lord High Admiral) was
in English.

2. Thomas   Barlow,   appointed
jointly with Dennis Fleming in 1639,
had held the sole reversion since
Fleming's death.

3. Algernon Percy, 10th Earl of
Northumberland, had been a prominent member of the 'Whitehall
group' of collectors and patrons before
the Civil War: O. Millar in *Burlington Mag.*, 97/255–6. Many of the
antique busts that survive in the royal
collection appear to have been bought
by Charles I from Mantua: A. H.
Scott-Elliot, ib., 101/218–27. (OM).

he looked over many of the pieces in the gallery with me and told me whose hands they were, with great pleasure.[1]

Dined at home and Mr. Hawly with me upon six of my pigeons which my wife is resolved to kill here.

This day came Will[2] my boy to me, the wench continuing lame so that my wife could not be longer without somebody to help her. In the afternoon with Sir Edwd. Walker at his lodgings by St. Gyles's church for my Lord's pedigree, and carried it to Sir Rd. Fanshaw.

To Mr. Crews, and there took money and paid Mrs. Anne, Mrs. Jemimahs maid, off quite. And so she went away and another came to her. To White-hall with Mr. Moore, where I met with a letter from Mr. Turner of the Navy office, offering me 150*l* to be joined with me in my patent, and to advise me how to improve the advantage of my place and to keep off Barlow.

To my Lord's till late at night, and so home.[a]

a followed by blank page

---

1. Emanuel de Critz (Serjeant-Painter to the King) had known the collection of Charles I very well and during the revolution had purchased a number of royal works of art which he returned to the Crown at the Restoration. On the eve of the Restoration a committee of the House of Lords had been formed to rehabilitate as far as possible the great collections formed by Charles I, and on 23 May 1660 John Webb had asked the committee to be allowed to hang in the King's residences in London the pictures that had been reassembled and to have them recorded in an inventory by de Critz: HMC, *Rep.*, 7/1/88–93. (OM).

2. Surname unknown.

1. This morning came home my fine Camlott cloak with gold buttons – and a silk suit; which cost me much money and I pray God to make ⟨me⟩ be able to pay for it. I went to the cook's and got a good joint of meat, and my wife and I dined at home alone.

In the afternoon to the Abbey, where a good sermon by a stranger, but no Common Prayer yet.[1]

After sermon called in at Mrs. Crisps, where I saw mine-Heer Roder that is to marry Sam Hartlibs sister, a great fortune for her to light on, she being worth nothing in the world.[2] Here I also saw Mrs. Greenlife, who is come again to live in Axeyard with her new husband, Mr. Adams. Then to my Lord's, where I stayed a while. So to see for Mr. Creed, to speak about getting a copy of Barlow's patent. To my Lord's, where late at night comes Mr. Morland, whom I left prating with my Lord, and so home.

2. Infinite of business, that my heart and head and all was full.

Met with Purser Washington, with whom and a lady, a friend of his, I dined at the Bell Taverne in King's-street; but the rogue had no more manners then to invite me thither and to let me pay my club. All the afternoon with my Lord, going up and down the town. At 7 at night he went home, and there the

---

1. For the services at the Abbey at this time, see below, p. 201 & n. 1. The Prayer Book came back into use gradually after the Restoration – royal chapels and cathedrals leading the way – but it was not read in all churches until use of the revised version became compulsory in August 1662. For the diary's information, see below, pp. 201, 215, 261, 282 & 289. Cf. Evelyn, 8 July 1660; M. H. Nicolson (ed.), *Conway Letters*, p. 163; R. P. Bosher, *Making of Restoration settlement*, pp. 163–4.

2. Nan, daughter of Samuel Hartlib, sen. (writer on religious and economic affairs and a neighbour of the Pepyses in Axe Yard), was married on 10 July to Jan Roder (Roth), a merchant of Utrecht, who with his father (a merchant of Amsterdam) had befriended Charles II in exile. In a letter of 3 August 1660, Nan's father denied these stories that she had married a fortune. See G. H. Turnbull, *Hartlib, Dury, and Comenius*, pp. 2, 112–13.

Principall officers of the Navy;[1] among the rest, myself was reckoned one. We had order to meet tomorrow to draw up such an order of the Council as would put us into action before our patents were passed[2] – at which my heart was glad.

At night supped with my Lord, he and I together in the great dining-room alone by ourselfs, the first time that ever I did it in London. Home to bed. My maid pretty well again.

3. All the morning, the officers and commissioners of the Navy, we met at Sir G. Carteret's[3] chamber and agreed upon orders for the Council to supersede the old and impower us to act.

Dined with Mr. Stephens, the Treasurer's man of the Navy,[4] and Mr. Turner, to whom I offered 50*l* out of my own purse for one year and the benefit of a clerk's allowance beside – which he thanked me for; but I find he hath some design yet in his head, which I could not think of.[5]

In the afternoon my heart was quite pulled down by being told that Mr. Barlow was to enquire today for Mr. Coventry. But at night I met with my Lord, who told me that I need not fear, for he would get me the place against the world.

And when I came to W. Howe, he told me that Dr. Petty[6] hath been with my Lord and did tell him that Barlow was a

---

1. The Principal Officers of the Navy Board; see *Comp.*: 'Navy; Navy Board'.

2. These orders were issued by the Privy Council on 4 July, and had the effect of bringing the existing (temporary) Admiralty commissions to an end, of empowering the new Navy Board to act, and of having all papers delivered to Pepys as Clerk: PRO, PC 2/54, p. 63; copies in PL 2867, p. 350; Rawl. A 466, ff. 10+; Rawl. C 256, pp. 1+; BM, Stowe 327, f.227r. The patents were issued later – those of Carteret (Treasurer), Slingsby (Comptroller), Batten (Surveyor) and Pett (Commissioner) on 4 July, of Pepys on 13 July, and of

Berkeley and Penn (Commissioners) on 18 August. The date of a patent did not always at this period bear an exact relation to the date at which the officer began to perform his duties. In this case all the Principal Officers were paid their salaries from 24 or 25 June.

3. Sir George Carteret, Bt; Treasurer of the Navy and *ex officio* senior Principal Officer.

4. Anthony Stevens was cashier in the office of the Navy Treasurer.

5. See below, p. 228 & n. 2.

6. William Petty (the pioneer social statistician) was Barlow's agent, receiving power of attorney on 23 July: below, p. 305 & nn. 2 & 4.

sickly man and did not entend to execute the place himself; which put me in great comfort again.

Till 2 in the morning writing letters and things for my Lord to send to sea. So home to my wife to bed.

4. Up very early in the morning; and landing my wife at White-Friars stairs, I went to the bridge[1] and so to the Treasurer's of the Navy, with whom I spoke about the business of my office; who put me into very good hopes of my business. At his house comes Comissioner Pett; and I and he went to view the houses in Seething-lane belonging to the Navy, where I find the worst very good; and had great fears in my mind that they will shuffle me out of them, which troubles me.[2]

From thence to the Excise Office in Broad-street, where I received 500*l* for my Lord by appointment of the Treasurer; and went afterward down with Mr. Ruddyard and drank my morning draught with him and other officers. Thence to Mr. Backewells the goldsmith, where I took my Lord's 100*l* in plate for Mr. Secretary Nicholas, and my own piece of plate, being a state-dish and cup in chased-work, for Mr. Coventry; cost me above 19*l*.[3] Carried these and the money by coach to my Lord's at White-hall; and from thence carried Nicholas's plate to his house and left it there, intending to speak with him anon. So to Westminster-hall; where meeting with Monsieur L'impertinent and W. Bowyer, I took them to the Sun tavern and gave them a lobster and some wine, and sat talking like a fool with them till 4 a-clock. So to my Lord's and walking all the afternoon in White-hall Court, in expectation of what shall be done in the Council as to our business. It was strange to see how all the people flocked together bare to see the King looking out of the Council window.

1. London Bridge: the only bridge across the Thames in the London area until Westminster Bridge was opened in 1750. (R).

2. These houses were built on to the Navy Office, between Crutched Friars and Seething Lane: Pepys was to live in one from 1660 until the fire which destroyed them and the Office in 1673. The practice of having the Principal Officers live in official accommodation at the Navy Office was one of the most useful innovations of the revolutionary and Restoration periods.

3. Gifts of plate were customarily made on receiving appointments or titles, their value being fixed by the value and standing of the grant. Cf. above, p. 185 & n. 2.

At night my Lord told me how my orders that I drow last night, about giving us power to act, are granted by the Council – at which he and I were very glad. Home and to bed, my boy lying in my house this night the first time.

5. This morning my brother Tom brought me my Jackanapes coat with silver buttons. It rained this morning, which makes us fear that the glory of this great day will be lost, the King and Parliament being to be intertained by the City today with great pomp.[1]

Mr. Hater was with me today, and I agreed with him to be my clerk.[2]

Being at White-hall, I saw the King – the Dukes and all their attendants go forth in the rain to the City and bedaggled many a fine suit of clothes. I was forced to walk all the morning in White-hall, not knowing how to get out because of the rain.

Met with Mr. Cooling, my Lord Chamberlins secretary, who took me to dinner among the gentlemen wayters – and after dinner into the wine-cellar. He told me how he hath a project for all us Secretaries to join together and get money by bringing all business into our hands.

Thence to the Admirallty, where Mr. Blackburne and I (it beginning to hold up) went and walked an hour or two in the park, he giving of me light in many things in my way in this office that I go about.[3] In the evening I got my present of plate carried to Mr. Coventry's.

At my Lord's at night comes Dr. Petty to me to tell me that Barlow was come to town and other things, which put me into a despair and I went to bed very sad.

6. In the morning with my Lord at White-hall, got the order of the Council for us to act.

1. The King, the two Dukes, the Privy Council and both Houses of Parliament were entertained at Guildhall. Descriptions in [John Tatham], *Londons glory represented by time, truth and fame* . . . (1660); *Parl. Intell.*, 9 July, pp. 445–6; Rugge, i, ff.106*v*–107*r*; Mundy, v. 118–19.

2. Thomas Hater (Hayter), of

whose ability and industry Pepys came to think highly. He rose to become a successor to Pepys (Joint-Clerk of the Acts in 1673, Secretary to the Admiralty in 1679) and Comptroller in 1680. All this despite his being (at any rate in the diary period) a Quaker or Anabaptist.

3. Cf. above, p. 27, n. 3.

From thence to Westminster-hall; and there met with the Doctor that showed us so much kindness at The Hague[1] and took him to the Sun tavern and drank with him.

So to my Lord's and dined with W. Howe and Sarah, thinking it*a* might be the last time that I might dine with them together.

In the afternoon, my Lord and I and Mr. Coventry and Sir G. Carteret went and took possession of the Navy Office, whereby my mind was a little cleared but my hopes not great.

From thence, Sir G. Carteret and I to the Treasurer's Office, where he set some things in order there. And so home, calling upon Sir Geffery Palmer, who did give me advice about my patent which put me to some doubt to know what to do – Barlow being alife.

Homeward called at Mr. Pims about getting me a coat of velvett,[2] and he took me to the Half-Moone, and there the house so full that we stayed above half an hour before we could get anything. So to my Lord's, where in the dark W. Howe and I did sing Extemporys, and I find by use that we are able to sing a bass and a treble pretty well.[3] So home and to bed.

7. To my Lord. One with me to buy a clerk's place with me, and I did demand 100*l*. To the Council-chamber, where I took out an order for the advance of the salaries of the officers of the Navy, and I find mine to be raised to 350*l*. per annum.[4] Thence to the Change, where I bought two fine prints of Ragotts from Rubens;[5] and afterward dined with my uncle and Aunt Wight,

a repl. 'thinking'

---

1. See above, pp. 143–4.

2. William Pym, of the Strand, was Sandwich's tailor (and Clarendon's), and this was Pepys's first velvet coat: below, p. 232.

3. Pepys would be the bass. Music MSS in the PL have songs transposed for Pepys to bass pitch. (E).

4. From £182 p.a.; Privy Council order, 4 July: PRO, PC 2/54, pp. 59–60; cf. below, iii. 279 & n. 2. There had been no Clerk of the Acts since the Civil War: the work had been done by one of the Navy Commissioners at a salary of £250:

Oppenheim, pp. 347, 350. By the order of 4 July the Treasurer was to receive £2000 p.a.; the Comptroller's salary was raised from £275 to £500, and the Surveyor's from £245 to £490. In all cases the income was greatly increased by fees: cf. below, p. 223, n. 1.

5. The earliest reference in the diary to the purchase of prints for what was to become a very fine collection. The engraver was the Frenchman, François Ragot (d. 1670), who executed a number of engravings after Rubens. (OM).

where her sister Con and her husband was. After that to Mr. Rawlinsons with my uncle; and thence to the Navy Office, where I begin to take an inventory of the papers and goods and books of the office. To my Lord's. Late writing letters. So home to bed.

8. *Lords day.* To White-hall to chapel, where I got in with ease by going before the Lord Chancellor with Mr. Kipps. Here I heard very good Musique, the first time that I remember ever to have heard the Organs and singing-men in Surplices in my life.[1] The Bishop of Chichester[2] preached before the King and made a great flattering sermon, which I did not like that clergy should meddle with matters of state. Dined with Mr. Luellin and Salsbury at a cook's shop.[3] Home, and stayed all the afternoon with my wife till after sermon; there till Mr. Fairebrother[4] came to call us out to my father's to supper. He told me how he had perfectly procured me to be made Maister in arts by proxy – which did somewhat please me, though I remember my Cosen Rogr. Pepys was the other day dissuading me from it.[5]

While we were at supper came*a* W. Howe to supper to us. And after supper went home to bed.

a repl. 'Mr.'

---

1. After the Restoration, these usages (together with the Book of Common Prayer) returned first in the chapels royal, cathedrals and college chapels. Cf. above, p. 176 & n. 1.

2. Henry King, one of the nine bishops of the old *régime* alive at the Restoration. Several of his sermons were printed, but not apparently this one.

3. For London cookshops, see W. C. Hazlitt, *Old cookery books*, pp. 245+; F. T. Phillips, *Hist. Company of Cooks, London.* They were eating-houses which also sent cooked dishes out, but they were not usually allowed to sell drink.

4. Fellow of King's College, Cambridge.

5. The grace, 26 June, is printed in W. Kennett, *Register* (1728), p. 188. It referred to Pepys as '*apud mare ... occupatissimus*'. Residence was no longer required at Cambridge for masters who did not intend to become fellows. For the cost, see below, p. 222. Roger Pepys himself had taken no degree from Christ's College. But this was usual for anyone not needing a degree for professional purposes.

9.   All the morning at Sir G. Palmers, advising about getting my Bill[1] drawn.   From thence to the Navy Office, where in the afternoon we met and sat; and there I begun to sign bills[2] in the office the first time.   From thence Captain Holland and Mr. Browne of Harwich[3] took me to a tavern and did give me a collacion.   From thence to the Temple to further my bills being done; and so home to my Lord and thence to bed.

10.   This day I put on first my new silk suit, the first that ever I wore in my life.   This morning came Nan Pepys's husband Mr. Hall to see me, being lately come to town – I had never saw him before.   I took him to the Swan tavern with Mr. Eglin and there drank our morning draught.   Home, and called my wife and took her to Dr. Clodius's to a great wedding of Nan Hartlib to mynheer Roder, which was kept at Goring-house with very great state, cost, and noble company.   But among all the beauties there, my wife was thought the greatest.   After dinner I left the company and carried my wife to Mrs. Turner's. I went to the Atturny-generalls and had my bill, which cost me seven pieces.   Called my wife and set her home.   And finding my Lord in White-hall garden, I got him to go to the Secretarys; who did, and desired the despatch of his and my bills to be signed by the King.[4]

His bill is to be Earle of Sandwich, Viscount Hinchingbrooke, and Baron of St. Neots.[5]

Home, with my mind pretty quiet, and to bed – not returning, as I said I would, to see the bride put to bed.

11.   With Sir Wm. Pen by water to the Navy Office, where

---

1. The Attorney-General's warrant for his appointment as Clerk of the Acts.   Pepys got it on the 10th; had it made into a 'King's Bill' on the 11th; on the 12th obtained a privy seal writ and on the 13th the letters patent.   The enrolment of the patent is in PRO, C 66/2742, no. 2.

2. Warrants to the Navy Treasurer, which had to be signed by two of the Principal Officers.

3. John Browne, Storekeeper.

4. The secretary's warrants are in BM, Egerton 2551, ff.33r,56r.   That for Pepys is subscribed: 'despatch this with what expedicion you can'.

5. The patent was issued on 12 July.   Mountagu's first intention had been to take his title from Portsmouth: above, pp. 184–5.

we met and despatched business.   And that being done, we went
all to dinner to the Dolphin upon Major Bournes[1] invitation.

After that to the Office again, where I was vexed, and so was
Commissioner Pett, to see a busy fellow come to look out the
best lodgings for my Lord Barkely, and the combining between
him and Sir W. Pen; and endeed, was troubled much at it.[2]

Home to White-hall and took out my bill, signed by the
King – and carried it to Mr. Watkins of the Privy Seale to be
despatched there; and going home to take a crap, I borrowed a
pair of sheets of Mr. Howe and by coach went to the Navy
Office and lay (Mr. Hater my clerk with me) at Comissioner
Willoughby's[3] house, where I was received by him very civilly
and slept well.

12.   Up early, and by coach to White-hall with Comissioner
Pett; where after we had talked with my Lord, I went to the
Privy Seal and got my bill perfected there and at the Signett:
and then to the House of Lords and met with Mr. Kipps, who
directed me to Mr. Beale to get my patent ingrossed.

But he not having time to get it done in Chancery-hand, I
was forced to run all up and down Chancery-lane and the Six
Clerks' Office,[4] but could find none that could write that hand
that were at leisure: and so in a despair went to the Admiralty,
where we met the first time there – my Lord Mountagu,[5] my
Lord Barkely, Mr. Coventry, and all the rest of the Principall
Officers and Comissioners, only the Controller[6] who is not yet
chosen.   At night to Mr. Kipps's lodgings; but not finding him,
I went to Mr. Spong's[7] and there I found him and got him to
come to me to my Lord's lodgings at 11 a-clock of night, where

1. Nehemiah Bourne, Navy Commissioner from 1651 until the Restoration.

2. Lord Berkeley of Stratton had
just been appointed a Commissioner
of the Navy on 4 July, along with
Penn and Peter Pett. Both he and
Penn had been associates of the Duke
of York during his exile; Berkeley
had served as his governor.   Pepys
never liked him.

3. Francis Willoughby, lately Navy
Commissioner; Pepys succeeded him
in the tenancy of this house: below,
p. 208.

4. The Six Clerks, with their staff,
conducted the office business of
Chancery.

5. Lord Sandwich.

6. See below, p. 240 & n. 1.

7. Chancery clerk.

I got him to take my bill to write it himself (which was a great providence that he could do it) against tomorrow morning.

I late writing letters to sea by the post. And so went home to bed, in great trouble because I heard at Mr. Beales today that Barlow hath been there and said that he would make a stop in that business.

13. Up early, the first day that I put on my black Camlott coat with silver buttons.*a*   To Mr. Spong, whom I found in his night-gown* writing of my patent; and he had done as far as he could after*b* the &c.*1* by 8 a-clock.

It being done, we carried it to Worcester-house to the Chancellors, where Mr. Kipps (a strange providence that he should now be in condition to do me this kindness, which I never thought him capable of doing for me)*2* got me the Chancellors *Recepi* to my Bill. And so carried it to Mr. Beale for a Dockett; but he was very angry, and unwilling to do it, because he said it was ill-writ (because I had got it writ by another hand and not by him); but by much importunity I got Mr. Spong to go to his office and make an end of my patent, and in the mean-time Mr. Beale to be preparing my Dockett; which being done, I did give him two pieces, after which it was strange how civil and tractable he was to me.

From thence I went to the Navy Office, where we despatched much business and resolved of the houses for the Officers and Comissioners, which I was glad of, and I got leave to have a door made me into the leads. From thence, much troubled in mind about my patent – I went to Mr. Beale again, who had now finished my patent and made it ready for the Seal. And about an hour after I was to meet him at the Chancellors; so I went away toward Westminster and in my way met with Mr. Spong and went with him to Mr. Lilly and eat some bread and cheese and drank with him, who still would be giving me

a   repl. 'bottoms'   *b*   MS. ? 'for'

---

1. I.e. after the opening words: 2. See above, p. 184 & n. 3.
'Charles by the Grace of God, etc.'.

counsel of getting my patent out, for fear of another change and my Lord Montagu's fall.[1]

After that to Worcester-house, where by Mr. Kipps means and my pressing in Generall Mountagu's name to the Chancellor, I did beyond all expectation get my seal passed; and while it was doing in one room, I was forced to keep Sir G. Carteret (who by chance met there, ignorant of my business) in talk while it was a-doing. Went home and brought my wife with me into London and some money, with which I paid Mr. Beale 9*l* – in all; and took my patent of him and went to my wife again, whom I had left in a coach at the door of Hinde Court, and there presented her with my patent, at which she was overjoyed.[2]

So to the Navy Office and showed her my house, and were both mightily pleased at all things there, and so to my business.

So home with her, leaving her at her mother's door. I to my Lord's, where I despatched an order for a ship to fetch Sir R. Honywood[3] home, for which I got two pieces of my Lady Honywood by young Mr. Powell. Late writing letters. And great doings of Musique at the next house, which was Whallys; the King and Dukes there with Madam Palmer, a pretty woman that they have a fancy to to make her husband a cuckold.[4] Here, at the old door that did go into those lodgings, my Lord and I and W. Howe did stand listening a great while to the Musique. After that, home to bed.

This day I should have been at Guild hall to have borne wit-

1. William Lilly, the astrologer, who lived in the Strand, seems to have been well known to Spong: below, pp. 273–4. Perhaps it was Lilly's prognostications which made Spong fearful.

2. It seems probable from this entry that Elizabeth Pepys's parents lived in Hind Court at this period – perhaps until 1662: see below, iii. 232. The diary never gives any explicit information, and Pepys was not allowed by his wife to visit them.

3. Sir Robert Honywood, one of the commissioners appointed in 1659 to mediate between Sweden and Denmark. The *Happy Return* brought him home in August: *CSPD 1659–60*, p. 1; ib., *1660–1*, p. 201.

4. Barbara Villiers (daughter of the 2nd Viscount Grandison; cr. Duchess of Cleveland, 1670) had, as a young beauty of 19, married Roger Palmer in 1659. They lived in King St, Westminster, in a house recently occupied by Maj.-Gen. Edward Whalley, the regicide, who had taken sudden flight to New England. Barbara had already become the King's mistress.

ness for my brother Hawly against Blacke* Coller;[1] but I could
not, at which I was troubled.

To bed with the greatest quiet of mind that I have had a great
while, having eat nothing but a bit of bread and cheese at Lilly's
today, and a bit of bread and butter after I was a-bed.

14. Up early and advised with my wife for the putting of
all our things in a readiness to be sent to our new house. To
my Lord's, where he was in bed very late. So with Major Toll-
hurst and others to Harpers, and I sent for my barrel of pickled
oysters and there eat them. While we were doing so, comes in
Mr. Pagan Fisher the poett and promises me what he had long
ago done, a book in praise of the King of France with my armes
and a dedication to me, very handsome.[2] After him comes in Mr.
Sheply this morning, come from sea yesterday – whom I was
glad to see that he may ease me of the trouble of my Lord's
business.

So to my Lord's, where I stayed doing his business and taking
his commands. After that to Westminster-hall, where I paid
all my debts in order to my going away from thence. Here I
met with Mr. Eglin, who would needs take me to the Leg in
King's-street and give me a dish of meat to dinner; and so I
sent for Monsieur Limpertinent, where we sat long and were
merry.

After that, parted; and I took Mr. Butler with me into
London by coach and showed him my house at the Navy Office.
And did give order for the laying in coals. So into Fanchurch-street and there did give him a glass of wine at Rawlinson's, and was trimmed in the street. So to my Lord's late

---

1. Possibly the case (of ejectment
from lands) in which John Collier
was defendant: PRO, KB 125/92,
n.p.

2. *Epinicion vel elogium Lodovici
XIIII*[ti] by Payne Fisher (*'Paganus Pisca-
tor'*) had been published in (?) 1658 on
the capture of Dunkirk. The diary
does not record its receipt nor has it
survived in the PL. On 28 July the
poet tried to borrow money from

Pepys. The dedication would be
printed or written (for a consideration) on a page inserted into a specially
bound presentation copy. A MS.
dedication by Fisher to Pepys, in
Latin, survives in a copy of Fisher's
Tombs . . . in St Paul's . . . [1684], now
in the Harvard College Library.
For Pepys's arms, see below, iii. 50 &
n. 3.

writing letters; and so home, where I find my wife hath packed up all her goods in the house, fit for a removal. So to bed.

15. *Lords day.* Lay long in bed to recover my rest. Going forth, met with Mr. Sheply and went and drank my morning draught with him at Wilkinsons, and my Brother Spicer. After that to Westminster Abbey, and in Henry the 7ths chapel heard part of a sermon, the first that ever I heard there.[1] To my Lord's and dined all alone at the table with him.

After dinner, he and I alone fell to discourse, and I find him plainly to be a Scepticke in all things of religion and to make no great matter of anything therein, but to be a perfect Stoicke. In the afternoon to Henry the 7ths chapel, where I heard service and a sermon there. After that, meeting W. Bowyer, he and I to the park and walked a good while till night.

So to Harpers and drank together; and Captain Stokes came to us and so I fell into discourse of buying paper at the best hand in my office, and the Captain promised me to buy it for me in France.[2] After that to my Lord's lodgings, where I wrote some business and so home. My wife at home all this day, she having no clothes out, all being packed up yesterday. For this month I have wholly neglected anything of news, and so have beyond belief been ignorant how things go. And now, by my patent, my mind is in some quiet; which God keep. I was not at my father's tonight, I being afeared to go for fear he should still solicit me to speak to my Lord for a place in the Wardrobe, which I dare not do because of my own business yet. My wife and I mightily pleased with our new house that we hope to have.

My patent hath cost me a great deal of money, about 40*l* – which is the only thing at present which doth trouble me much. In the afternoon[3] to Henry the 7ths chapel – where I heard a sermon and spent (God forgive me) most of my time in looking

<hr />

1. Pepys's own orthodoxy and his reference later in this entry to the 'service' make it clear that the Anglicans were now using the chapel, while the Independents (in possession of the abbey during the revolution) still worshipped elsewhere in the building.

2. France was England's main source of paper both for printing and writing. For a similar deal in office paper (by Peter Pett), see PRO, Adm. 20/6, p. 59.

3. Pepys here repeats his account of the afternoon's doings. He wrote these passages on 19 July.

upon Mrs. Butler.   After that with W. Bowyer to walk in the
parke.   Afterward to my Lord's lodgings; and so home to bed,
having not been at my father's today.

16.   This morning it proved very rainy weather, so that I
could not remove my goods to my house.   I to my office and
did business there; and so home, it being then sunshine, but by
the time that I got to my house it begun to rain again, so that I
could not carry my goods by cart as I would have done.   After
that to my Lord's; and so home and so to bed.

17.   This morning (as endeed all the mornings nowadays)
much business at my Lord's.

There came to my house before I went out, Mr. Barlow, an
old consumptive* man and fair-conditioned – with whom I did
discourse a great while; and after much talk, I did grant him
what he asked – *viz.*, 50*l* per annum if my salary be not encreased
and 100*l* per annum in case it be to 350*l*.; at which he was very
well pleased to be paid as I received my money, and not otherwise.[1]

Going to my Lord's I find that my Lord had got a great cold
and kept his bed.   And so I brought him to my Lord's bedside,
and my Lord and he and I did agree together to this purpose what
I should allow him.

That done and the day proving fair, I went home and got all
my goods packed up and sent away.   And my wife and I and
Mrs. Hunt went by coach, overtaking the carts a-drinking in
the Strand – being come to my house and set in the goods; and
at night sent my wife and Mrs. Hunt to buy something for supper;
they bought a Quarter of lamb; and so we eat it but it was not
half roasted.

Will, Mr. Blackburnes nephew, is so obedient that I am greatly

---

1. Pepys's patent revoked the life
appointment of Thomas Barlow, but
the above arrangement, lasting until
Barlow's death in 1665, made assurance doubly sure. Their correspondence about it is in Rawl. A 174,
ff. 307+.   Pepys was still uncertain
about the new rates of salary awarded
to the Principal Officers because their
patents of appointment, issued after
the council order of 4 July fixing the
new rates, had specified the old, lower
rates.   But on 16 July the Admiral's
warrant put the council order into
effect: Duke of York, *Mem. (naval)*,
pp. 65–6.

glad of him.[1] At night, he and I and Mrs. Hunt home by water to Westminster.

I to my Lord; and after having done some business with him in his chamber in the Nursery,[2] which hath been now his chamber since he came from sea, I went on foot with a link-boy to my house – where I find my wife in bed and Jane washing the house, and Will. The boy sleeping and a great deal of sport I had before I could wake him. I to bed, the first night that I ever lay here with my wife.

18. This morning the carpenter made an end of my door out of my chamber upon the leads. This morning we met at the office. I dined at my house in Seething-lane. And after that, going about 4 a-clock to Westminster, I met with Mr. Carter and Mr. Cooke coming to see me in a coach, and so I returned home.

I did also meet with Mr. Pierce the surgeon, with a porter with him with a barrel of Lemons which my man Burr sends me from sea.

I took all these people home to my house and did give them some drink; and after them comes Mr. Sheply, and after a little stay we all went by water to Westminster as far as the New Exchange.

Thence to my Lord about business; and being in talk, in comes one with half a Bucke from Hinchingbrooke, and it smelling a little strong, my Lord did give it me, though it was as good as any could be.

I did carry it to my mother (where I had not been a great while, and endeed had no great mind to go, because my father did lie upon me continually to do him a kindness at the Wardrobe, which I could not do because of my own business being so fresh with my Lord); but my father was not at home, and so I did leave the venison with her to dispose of as she pleased.

---

1. William Hewer, a boy of just under 18, now introduced by his uncle, Robert Blackborne, into Pepys's service. He lived to become Pepys's closest friend and companion, making a career in the Navy Office and rising to become a Commissioner of the Navy under James II.

2. In Whitehall Palace.

After that home; where Wll. Ewre now was and did lie*a* this night with us, the first night.

My mind very quiet; only, a little trouble*b* I have for the great debts which I have still upon me to the Secretary, Mr. Kipps, and Mr. Spong for my patent.

19. I did lie late a-bed. I and my wife by water. Landed her at White-friars with her boy, with an Iron of our new range which is already broke and my wife will have changed, and many other things she hath to buy with the help of my father today.

I to my Lord and find him in bed. This day I received my commission to swear people the oath of allegeance and supremacy delivered me by my Lord.[1]

After talk with my Lord I went to Westminster-hall, where I took Mr. Michell and his wife (and Mrs. Murford we sent for afterward) to the Dogg tavern, where I did give them a dish of anchoves and olives and paid for all. And did talk of our old discourse when we did use to talk of the King, in the time of the Rump, privately. After that to the Admiralty Office in White-hall, where I stayed and writ my last observations for these four days last past.

Great talk of the difference between the Episcopall and Presbyterian clergy, but I believe it will come to nothing.[2]   So home and to bed.

20. We sat at the office this morning (Sir W. Batten and Mr. Pett being upon a Survey to Chatham):[3] this morning I sent my

a repl. 'now'   *b* repl. 'troubled'

1. By a parliamentary resolution of 11 June (*CJ*, viii. 61), these commissions were to be issued to all persons nominated by the Lord General and the Lord High Admiral, the government being anxious to have the oaths taken by all members of the armed forces.

2. Throughout the country, disputes were occurring over the possession of livings between the puritan incumbents put in during the revolu-tion and the extruded Anglicans, and a pamphlet war between the two sides on more general issues was now reaching a climax. On 16 July the Commons had had a long debate on ecclesiastical policy, lasting until 10 p.m.: *Diary of Henry Townshend* (ed. Willis Bund), i. 55.

3. Batten (Surveyor) was making an inspection of ships and stores; Peter Pett (Commissioner at Chatham) accompanied him.

wife to my father's and with him to go buy 5*l*-worth of pewter. After we rose at the office, I went to my father's, where my uncle Fenner and all his crew and Captain Holland and his wife and my wife were at dinner at a venison pasty, of the venison that I did give my mother the other night.

I did this time show so much coldness to W. Joyce that I believe all the table took notice of it.

After that to Westminster about my Lord's business, and so home – my Lord having not been well these [two]*ᵃ* or three days. And I hear that Mr. Barnwell¹ at Hinchingbrooke is fallen sick again. Home and to bed.

21. This morning Mr. Barlow hath appointed for*ᵇ* me to bring him what form I would have the agreement between [him and]*ᵃ* I to pass, which I did to his lodgings at the Golden eagle in the new street between Fetter-lane and Shoe-lane.²

Where he liked it very well; and I from him went to get Mr. Spong to engross it in Duplicates.

To my Lord and spoke to him about the business of the Privy Seale for me to*ᶜ* be sworn, though I got nothing by it but to do Mr. Moore a kindness – which he did give me a good answer to.³ Went to the Six Clerks' Office to Mr. Spong for the writings, and dined with him at a club* at the next door, where we had three voices to sing catches. So to my house to write letters and so to Whitehall about business of my Lord's concerning his creation, and so home and to bed.

22. *Lords day.* All the last night it had rained hard. My Brother Tom came this morning the first time to see me, and I paid him all that I owe my father to this day. Afterward I went out and looked into several churches; and so to my uncle Fenners, whither my wife was got before me; and we, my father and mother and all the Joyces and my aunt Bell, whom I had not seen many a year before. After dinner, I to White-

a MS. blotted   *b* repl. 'me'   *c* repl. 'for'

1. Sandwich's steward.
2. Now Little and Great New Sts. (R).
3. Pepys was to act for Sandwich, and Moore was to deputise for Pepys. In fact, Pepys found the work lucrative: below, p. 213.

hall (my wife to church with K. Joyce), where I found my
Lord at home and walked in the garden with him, he showing
me all the respect that can be. I left him – and went to walk
in the park, where great endeavouring to get into the Inward
park, but could not. And one man was basted by the keeper
for carrying some people over on his back through the water.

Afterward to my Lord's, where I stayed and drank with Mr.
Sheply; and having first sent to get a pair of oares, it was the
first time that ever I went by water on the Lord's day.[1] Home,
and at night had a chapter[2] read; and I read prayers out of the
Common Prayer book, the first time that ever I read prayers in
this house.[3] So to bed.

23. This morning, Mr. Barlow comes to me and he and I
went forth to a Scrivener in FanChurch-street, whom we find
sick of the gout in bed, and signed and sealed our agreement
before him.

He urged to have these[a] words (*in Consideracion whereof*) to be
interlined, which I granted, though against my will.

Met this morning at the office; and afterward Mr. Barlow
by appointment comes and dined with me. And both of us
very pleasant and pleased. After dinner to my Lord, who
took me to Secretary Nicholas; and there, before him and
Secretary Morris, my Lord and I, upon our knees, together
took our oaths of Allegiance and Supremacy and the oath of the
Privy Seale – of which I was much glad, though I am not likely
to get anything by it at present; but I do desire, for fear of a
turn-out of our office. That done and my Lord gone from
me, I went with Mr. Cooling and his Brother and Sam Hartlibb,
little Jenings and some others to the King's-head tavern at
Charing-cross; where after drinking, I took boat and so home.
Where we supped merrily among ourselfs (our little boy proving
a droll); and so after prayers, to bed.

a   repl. ? 'this'

---

1. Because of his official position
Pepys was not subject to the general
rules against Sunday hire.

2. Of the Bible; a common ellipsis:
cf. below, p. 270; iv. 189; *Tangier
Papers*, p. 13; Samuel Johnson,

Diaries, Prayers etc. (1958 ed.), p. 313.
One of the few occasions on which
Pepys records reading the Bible.

3. For family prayers, see J. H.
Overton, *Life in Engl. church*, pp.
334+.

This day my Lord had heard that Mr. Barnwell was dead, but it is not so yet, though he be very ill.

I was troubled all this day with Mr. Cooke; being willing to do him good, but my mind is so taken up with my own business that I cannot.

24. To White-hall, where I did acquaint Mr. Watkins[1] with my being sworn into the Privy Seale, at which he was much troubled, but put it up and did offer me a kinsman of his to be my clerk, which I did give him some hope of, though I never entend it. In the afternoon I spent much time walking in White-hall court with Mr. Bickerstaffe, who was very glad of my Lord's being sworn, because of his business with his Brother Baron, which is referred to my Lord Chancellor and to be ended tomorrow. Baron hath got a grant beyond sea to come in before the Reversioners of the Privy Seal.[2] This afternoon Mr. Mathews[3] came to me to get a certificate of my Lord's and my being sworn, which I put in some forwardness; and so home and to bed.

25. In the morning at the office, and after that 《my dining with Mr. Creede and seeing the Butlers ought to be placed in yesterdays account, it being put here by mistake》 down to White-hall, where I met with Mr. Creed, and with him and a Welch Schoolmaster, a good scholar but a very pedagogue, to the ordinary at the Leg in King's-street. I got my certificate of my Lord's and my being sworn. This morning[4] my Lord took leave of the House of Commons – and had the thanks of the House for his great services to his country.

In the afternoon (but this is a mistake, for it was yesterday in the afternoon) Monsieur Limpertinent and I met, and I took him to the Sun and drank with him; and in the evening going away, we met his mother and sisters and father coming down-

1. Of the Privy Seal Office.
2. The dispute was about a Privy Seal clerkship. Usually reversionary interests were respected at the Restoration. This was an exception made because of Baron's services to the King in exile. (He had brought him news of his restoration.) See J. C.

Sainty in *Bull. Inst. Hist. Res.*, 41/155 n. For the Chancellor's ruling in Baron's favour, see below, p. 236.
3. John Matthews of the Privy Seal Office.
4. A mistake; Sandwich resigned from the Commons on the 24th, not the 25th: *CJ*, viii. 101.

stairs from the Gate-house, where they lodge. Where I did
the first time salute them all; and very pretty Madam Frances
is endeed. After that, very late home and called in Tower
streete and there at a barber's was trimmed the first time. Home
and to bed.

26. Early to White-hall, thinking to have a meeting of my
Lord and the Principal Officers; but my Lord could not, it
being the day that he was to go and be admitted in the House
of Lords, his patent being done, which he presented upon his
knee to the Speaker; and so it was read in the House and he
took his place.[1]

I at the Privy Seal Office with Mr. Hooker, who brought me
acquainted with Mr. Crofts of the Signet, and I invited them to
a dish of meat at the Leg in King-street; and so we dined there
and I paid for all and had very good light given me as to my
imployment there. Afterward to Mr. Pierces, where I should
have dined but I could not; but found Mr. Sheply and W. Howe
there. After we had drunk hard, we parted, and I went away
and met with Dr. Castle, who is one of the clerks of the Privy
Seale, and told him how things was with my Lord and I – which
he received very gladly. I this day was told how Baron, against
all expectation and law, hath got the place of Bickerstaffe; and
so I question whether he will not lay claim to wait the next
month;[2] but my Lord tells me that he will stand for it.

In the evening met with T. Doling, who carried me to St.
James's fair;[3] and there meeting with W. Symons and his wife
and Luellin and D. Scobells wife and cousin, we went to Woods
at the Pell-mell (our old house for clubbing)[4] and there we spent
till 10 at night. At which time I sent to my Lord's for my clerk
Will to come to me, and so by link home to bed. Where I
find Comissioner Willoughby had sent for all his things away
out of my bedchamber; which is a little disappointment, but it
is better then pay too dear for them.

1. *LJ*, xi. 107.
2. The clerks of the Privy Seal
took duty for a month at a time.
3. Held for the 14 days following
St James's day (25 July) in the road
from St James's Palace to Tyburn.

4. A weekly meeting of young
government clerks which Pepys and
his friends held 'in Cromwell's time':
below, 5 July 1665. Taverns and
inns were much used for club meetings of this sort.

27. The last night Sir W. Batten and Sir W. Penn came to their houses at the office. Met this morning and did business till noon. Dined at home and from thence to my Lord's, where Will, my clerk, and I were all the afternoon making up my accounts; which we had done by night, and I find myself worth about 100*l* after all my expenses.

At night, I sent to W. Bowyer to bring me a 100*l* bag that he hath in his hands of my Lord's in keeping, out*a* of which I paid Mr. Sheply all that remains due to my Lord upon my balance, and took the rest home with me late at night. We got a coach, but the horses were tired and would not carry us further then St. Dunstans, so we light and took a link; and so home, weary, to bed.

28. Early in the morning I rose, and a boy brought me a letter from Poet Fisher, who tells me that he is upon a panegyrique of the King,[1] and desired to borrow a piece of me; and I sent him half a piece.

To Westminster about business; and there dined with Mr. Sheply and W. Howe; afterward meeting with Mr. Henson, he had formerly had the brave clock that went with bullets (which is now taken away from him by the King, it being his goods),[2] I went with him to the Sun tavern and sent for Mr. Butler, who was now all full of his high discourse in praise of Ireland, whither he and his whole family is going by Collonell Dillons persuasion – but so many lies I never heard in praise of anything as he told of Ireland.[3] So home late at night and to bed.

a repl. 'in which'

---

1. Untraced; it may have appeared anonymously or pseudonymously or in collaboration. Payne Fisher was most unlikely to have missed this opportunity: that he had composed both a panegyric and a threnody on Oliver Cromwell would not have deterred him.

2. For this bullet (or rolling-ball) clock, see *Comp.*: 'Hanson, Edward.'

3. Col. Cary Dillon (later 5th Earl of Roscommon), an Irish soldier who rose to become a member of the Irish Privy Council, was at this time paying court to Frances Butler. He did not in fact marry her, but he succeeded in persuading her brother to go to Ireland: cf. below, iii. 299.

29. *Lords day*. I and my boy Will to White-hall; and I with my Lord to White-hall chapel, where I heard a cold sermon of the Bishop of Salsbury, Duppa, and the ceremonies did not please me, they do so overdo them.[1]

My Lord went to dinner to Kensington – with my Lord Camden,[2] so I dined and took Mr. Borfett, my Lord's chaplain, and his friend along with me with Mr. Sheply at my Lord's.

In the afternoon, with Dick Vines and his Brother Payton,[3] we walked to Lisson greene and Marybone – and back again. And finding my Lord at home, I got him to look over my accounts, which he did approve of and signed them; and so we are even to this day. Of this I was glad; and do think myself worth in good clear money about 120*l*. Home late, calling in at my father's without stay. To bed.

30. Sat at our office today; and my father came this day, the first time to see us at my new house, and Mrs. Crisp by chance came in and sat with us. Looked over our house and advised about the furnishing of it.[4] This afternoon I got my 50*l*, due to me for my first Quarter salary as Secretary to my Lord,[5] paid to Tho. Hater for me, which he received and brought home to me, of which I am full glad.

To Westminster and, among other things, met with Mr. Moore and took him and his friend, a bookseller in Paul's church-yard, to the Rhenish wine-house; and drinking there, the sword-bearer of London (Mr. Man) came to ask for us; with whom we sat late, discoursing about the worth of my office of Clerk of the Acts, which he hath a mind to buy and I asked four years' purchase: we are to speak more of it tomorrow. Home on foot; and seeing him at home in Butlersbury, he lent me a torch, which Will carried; and so home.

1. Brian Duppa as Lord Almoner and Gilbert Sheldon as Dean of the Chapel Royal made Whitehall Chapel the headquarters of the Laudian revival at this time.

2. At Campden House on what is now Campden Hill; the largest house in the parish after Holland House. (R).

3. *Recte* Blayton, Vines's brother-in-law.

4. At 17 March (above, p. 90) Pepys remarks on the fine furnishings of Mrs Crisp's house in Axe Yard.

5. For 91 days' service, ending 10 June: PRO, Adm. 20/1, no. 596.

31. To White-hall, where my Lord and the Principal Officers met and had great discourse about raising of money for the Navy; which is in very sad condition, and money must be raised for it.   Mr. Blackeburne, Dr. Clerke, and I to the Quakers[1] and dined there.   I back to the Admiralty and there was doing things in order to the calculating of the debts of the Navy[2] and other business all the afternoon.   At night I went to the Privy Seale, where I found Mr. Crofts and Mathews making up all their things to leave the office tomorrow to those that came to wait the next month.   I took them to the Sun tavern and there made them drink, and discoursed concerning the office and what I was to expect tomorrow about Baron, who pretends to the next month.

Late home, by Coach so far as Ludgate with Mr. Mathews, and thence home on foot with W. Hewre with me, and so to bed.

1. Unidentified: possibly Edward Billing, of Millway, Westminster.

2. See below, p. 226 & n. 4.

AUGUST.

1. Up very early, and by water to White-hall to my Lord's; and there up to my Lord's lodging (W. Howe being now ill of the goute at Mr. Pierces) and there talked with him*a* about the affairs of the Navy and how I was now to wait today at the Privy Seale. Comissioner Pett was with me, whom I desired to make my excuse at the office for my absence this day.

Thence to the Privy Seale Office, where I got (by Mr. Mathews means) possession of the books and table, but with some expectation of Barons bringing of a warrant from the King to have this month.[1]

Nothing done this morning, Baron having spoke to Mr. Woodson and Groome (clerks to Mr. Trumball of the Signet) to keep all work in their hands till the afternoon, at which time he expected to have his warrant from the King for this month.

I took at noon Mr. Hooper[2] to the Leg in King's-street and did give him his dinner, who did still advise me much to act wholly*b* myself in the Privy Seale; but I told him that I could not, because I have other business to take up my time.

In the afternoon at the office again, where we had many things to sign; and I went to the Council-chamber and there got my Lord to sign the first bill, and the rest all myself – but received no money today. After I had signed all, I went with Dicke Scobell and Luellin to drink at a bottle-beer house in the Strand; and after staying there a while (having sent W. Ewre home before), I took boat and homewards went, and in Fish-street bought a lobster; and as I had bought it I met with Winter and Mr. Delabarr and there, with a piece of Sturgeon of theirs, we went to the Sun tavern in that street and eat them. Late home and to bed.

2. To Westminster by water with Sir W. Batten and Sir W. Penn (our servants in another boat) to the Admiralty; and

a 'him' repeated   *b* MS. 'highly'

---

1. See above, p. 208, n. 2.   2. An official of the Privy Seal.

from thence I went to my Lord's to fetch him thither. Where we stayed all the morning about ordering of money for the victuallers and advising how to get a sum of money to carry on the business of the Navy. From thence, dined with Mr. Blackburne at his house with his friends (his wife being in the country and just upon her return to London), where we were very well treated and merry.

From thence, W. Ewre and I to the office of Privy Seale, where I stayed all the afternoon and received about 40*l* for yesterday and today, at which my heart rejoiced for God's blessing to me, to give me this advantage by chance – there being of this 40*l* about 10*l* due to me for this day's work. So great is the present profit of this office above what it was in the King's time; there being the last month about 300 bills, whereas in the last King's time it was much to have 40.[1] With my money, home by coach.

It being the first time that I could get home before our gates were shut since I came to the Navy Office.

When I came home, I find my wife not very well of her old pain in the lip of her *chose*, which she had when we were first married.[2]

I went and cast up the expense that I laid out upon my former house (because there are so many that are desirous of it and I am in my mind loath to let it go out of my hands, for fear of a turn). I find my layings-out to come to about 20*l*, which with my fine* will come to about 22*l* to him that shall hire my house of me.

To bed.

1. Fees for writing privy seal warrants ('bills') were the main source of income for the clerks. In the early months of the Restoration, when many new appointments to office were being made, this income might be considerable, and much larger than the official salaries, particularly because until November 1661 no rates for fees were established: below, ii. 209, 214. Cf. Sandwich's remarks to Pepys on 16 August (below, p. 223) and Pepys's accounts summarised below at p. 238 and ii. 2. Pepys received less, however, for pardons, of which there were many in this post-revolutionary period: below, pp. 310, 312. Some were issued free, others at a reduced rate: Rawl. A 174, f.261r.

2. Diagnosed as spasmodic dysmenorrhoea: Sir D'Arcy Power in *Occ. papers Pepys Club*, i. 78+, esp. p. 90. It is clear from later entries that the trouble abated.

3. Up betimes this morning; and after the Barber had done with me, then to the office, where I and Sir W. Penn only did meet and despatch business.[1]   At noon my wife and I by coach to Dr Clerkes to dinner.   I was very much taken with his lady, a comely, proper woman (though not handsome); but a woman of the best language that ever I heard any in my life.   Here dined Mrs. Pierce and her husband.

After dinner I took leave to go to Westminster, where I was at the Privy Seale Office all day, signing things and taking money – so that I could not do as I had intended; that is, to return to them and go to the Red Bull play-house.[2]   But I took coach and went to see whether it was done or no; and I find it done, so I returned to Dr Clerkes, where I find them and my wife; and by and by took leave and went away home.

4. To White-hall, where I found my Lord gone with the King by water to dine at the Tower with Sir J. Robinson, Lieutenant;[3]   I found my Lady Jemimah at my Lord's, with whom I stayed and dined all alone.   After dinner to the Privy Seal Office, where I did business.   So to a Committee of Parliament (Sir Hen. Finch, Chaireman) to give them an answer to an order of theirs, that we could not give them any account of the accounts of the Navy in the year 36, 37, 38, 39, 40 – as they desire.[4]   After that I went and bespoke some linen of Betty Lane in the Hall; and after that to the Trumpett, where I set and talked with her, &c.

At night, it being very rainy and it thundering and lightening exceedingly, I took coach at the Trumpet-door, taking Monsieur Limpertinent along with me as far as the Savoy, where he said he went to lie with Cary Dillon, and is still upon the mind of going (he and his whole family) to Ireland.   Having set him

---

1. Two were a quorum for most business.

2. In St John's St, Clerkenwell; an open-air playhouse, at this time used by a troupe headed by Michael Mohun. (A).

3. The King went there in order to act as godfather at the christening of Sir John Robinson's child: Mundy, v. 120.

4. The Committee for Public Debts had been empowered to examine persons, papers and witnesses on 1 June: *CJ*, viii. 52.   An enquiry into the debts of the navy had been ordered by the House of Commons on 17 July and the Navy Board produced its estimate on 13 August: ib., viii. 91; BM, Add. 9311, f.69r.

down, I made haste home;*a* and in the Court-yard, it being very dark, I heard a man enquire for my house; and having asked his business, he told me that my man William (who went this morning out of town to meet his aunt Blackburne) was come home not very well to his mother, and so could not come home tonight; at which I was very sorry. I find my wife still in pain. To bed, having not time to write letters; and endeed, having so many to write to all places that I have no heart to go about them.

Mrs. Shaw did die yesterday; and her husband so sick that he is not like to live.[1]

5. *Lords day.* My wife being much in pain, I went this morning to Dr. Williams (who had cured her once before of this business) in Holborne, and he did give me an oyntment which I sent home by my boy and a plaster, which I took with me to Westminster (having called and seen my mother in the morning as I went to the Doctors), where I dined with Mr. Sheply (my Lord dining at Kensington).

After dinner to St. Margaretts, where the first time I ever heard Common Prayer in that church. I sat with Mr. Hill in his pew – Mr. Hill that married in Axe-yard and that was aboard us in the Hope;*b* church done, I went and Mr. Sheply to see W. How at Mr. Pierces, where I stayed singing of songs and psalms an hour or two, and were very pleasant with Mrs. Pierce and him. Thence to my Lord's, where I stayed and talked and eat and drank with Mr. Sheply. After that to Westminster-stairs, where I saw a fray between Myn-heer Clinke (a Duchman that was at Hartlibs wedding) and a waterman, which made good sport. After that I got a Gravesend boat that was come up to fetch some reed[2] on this side the bridge, and got them to carry me to the Bridge, and so home – where I found my wife.

After prayers, I to bed to her, she having had a very bad night

a repl. ? 'with'   *b* repl. 'Downes'

1. Sarah, wife of Robert Shaw of Axe Yard (an Exchequer colleague), was buried in St Margaret's, Westminster on 5 August. Her husband survived.

2. Used for breaming ships (cleaning their bottoms by burning off tar) and (in war-time) for loading fireships.

of it. This morning before I was up, Will came home pretty well again, he having been only weary with riding, which he is not used to.

6. This morning at the office; and that being done, home to dinner all alone, my wife being ill in pain a-bed – which I was troubled at, and not a little impatient. After dinner to White-hall at the Privy Seale all the afternoon; and at night with Mr. Man to Mr. Rawlinson's in Fanchurch-street, where we stayed till 11 a-clock at night; so home and to bed – my wife being all this day in great pain.

This night Mr. Man offered me 1000*l* for my office of Clerk of the Acts, which made my mouth water; but yet I dare not take it till I speak with my Lord to have his consent.

7th. This morning to White-hall to the Privy Seale and took Mr. Moore and myself and dined at my Lord's with Mr. Sheply. While I was at dinner, in comes Sam Hartlibb and his Brother-in-law,[1] now knighted by the King, to request my promise of a ship for them to Holland, which I had promised to get for them. After dinner to the Privy Seale all the afternoon.

At night, meeting Sam Hartlibb, he took me by coach to Kensington to my Lord of Hollands.[2] I stayed in the coach while he went in about his business. He staying long, I left the coach and walked back again before on foot (a very pleasant walk) to Kensington, where I drank and stayed very long waiting for him; at last he came; and after drinking at the Inn, we went toward Westminster.

Here I endeavoured to have looked out Jane that formerly lived at Dr Williams at Cambrige, whom I had long thought to live at present here; but I found myself in an errour, meeting one in the place where I expected to have found her, but she proves not she, though very like her.

We went to the Bullhead, where he and I sat and eat and drank till 11 at night; and so home on foot. Found my wife pretty well again, and so I to bed.

---

1. Sir John Roder, knighted on 5 August.

2. Holland House, built in 1607. Sam Hartlib, jun., was a council clerk.

Claims were now being made on the Crown by the administrators of the late Earl's estate: *CSPD 1660–1*, p. 66.

8. We met at the office; and after that, to dinner at home; and from thence with my wife by water to Catau Sterpin,[1] with whom and her mistress Pye we sat discoursing of Kates marriage to Monsieur Petit, her mistress and I giving the best advice we could for her to suspend her marriage till Monsieur Petit had got some place that may be able to maintain his life,*a* and not for him to live upon the portion that she shall bring him.[2] From thence to Mr. Butlers to see his daughters, the first time that ever we made a visit to them. We find them very pretty; and Collonell Dillon there, a very merry and witty companion; but methinks they live in a gaudy but very poor condition. From thence, my wife and I entending to see Mrs. Blackburne, who had been a day or two ago to see my wife, but my wife was not in condition to be seen. But she not being at home, my wife went to her mother's and I to the Privy Seale. At night from the Privy Seale, Mr. Woodson and Mr. Jenings and I, to the Sun taverne till it was late; and from thence to my Lord's, where my wife was come from Mrs. Blackburnes to me; and after I had done some business with my Lord, she and I went to Mrs. Hunts, who would needs have us to lie at her house tonight, she being with my wife so late at my Lord's with us, and would not let us go home tonight.

We lay there all night very pleasantly and at ease, I taking my pleasure with my wife in the morning, being the first time after her being eased of her pain.

9. Left my wife at Mrs. Hunts and I to my Lord's. And from thence with Judge-Advocate Fowler, Mr. Creed and Mr. Sheply to the Rhenish wine-house, and Captain Hayward of the *Plymouth*, who is now ordered to carry my Lord Winchelsea Embassador to Constantinople.[3] We were very merry, and Judge-Advocate did give Captain Hayward his oath of Allegiance and Supremacy. Thence to my office of Privy Seale; and having signed some things there, with Mr. Moore and Deane Fuller to

a symbol blotted

---

1. See above, p. 16, n. 6.
2. They were married on 16 October: *Harl. Soc. Reg.*, 40/313.
3. John Hayward was soon afterwards displaced from his command (below, p. 224) and the *Plymouth* prevented from setting off until early October: *CSPD 1660–1*, pp. 273, 309; cf. HMC, *Finch*, i. 80.

the Leg in King-street; and sending for my wife, we dined there – very merry, and after dinner parted. After dinner, with my wife to Mrs. Blackburne to visit her. She being within, I left my wife there; and I to the Privy Seal, where I despatch some business; and from thence to Mrs. Blackburne again, who did treat my wife and I with a great deal of civility and did give us a fine collation of collar of beef, &c.

Thence, I having my head full of drink through having drunk so much Rhenish wine in the morning and more in the afternoon at Mrs. Blackburne. Came home and so to bed, not well; and very ill all night.

10. I had a great deal of pain all night and a great looseness upon me, so that I could not sleep. In the morning I rose with much pain and to the office I went and dined at home; and after dinner, with great pain in my back, I went by water to White-hall to the Privy Seale; and that done, with Mr. Moore and Creed to Hideparke by coach and saw a fine foot-race, three times round the park, between an Irishman and Crow that was once my Lord Claypooles footman[1] (by the way, I cannot forget that my Lord Claypoole did the other day make enquiry of Mrs. Hunt concerning my house in Axeyard and did set her on work to get it of me for him, which methinks is a very great change): Crow beat the other above two miles.

Returned from Hide-parke; I went to my Lord's and took Will (who waited for me there) by coach and went home taking my lute home with me [which] hath been all this while since I came from sea at my Lord's for him to play on. To bed, in some pain still.

For this month or two, it is not imaginable how busy my head hath been, so that I have neglected to write letters to my Uncle Robt. in answer to many of his, and to other friends; nor endeed have I done anything as to my own family; and especially this

1. John Claypole was a son-in-law of Oliver Cromwell; 'Lord' by virtue of office (Lord of the Bed-chamber to the Protector) and of membership of Cromwell's Upper House. He had a taste for sport (somewhat to the dismay of the godly): hence perhaps the racing footman. Footmen were often athletic (cf. the 'running footman' who trotted alongside coaches, saving them from spills) and Irishmen had a reputation for fleetness of foot.

month, my waiting at the Privy Seale makes me much more unable to think of anything, because of my constant attendance there after I have done at the Navy Office. But blessed be God for my good chance of the Privy Seale; where I get every day, I believe, about 3*l* per diem. This place I got by chance and my Lord did give it me by chance, neither he nor I thinking it to be of the worth that he and I find it to be.

Never since I was a man in the world was I ever so great a stranger to public affairs as now I am, having not read a news-book or anything like it, or enquired after any news, or what the Parliament doth or in any wise how things go. Many people look after my house in axe-yard to hire it of me, so that I am troubled with them; and I have a mind to get the money to buy goods for my house at the Navy Office, and yet I am loath to put it off, because that Mr. Man bids me 1000*l* for my office, which is so great a sum that I am loath to settle myself at my new house, lest I should take Mr. Man's offer in case I find my Lord willing to it.

11. I rose today without any pain, which makes me think that my pain yesterday was nothing but from my drinking too much the day before.

To my Lord this morning, who did give me order to get some things ready against the afternoon for the Admiralty where he would meet. To the Privy Seale and from thence, going to my own house in Axe yard, I went into Mrs. Crisps, where I met with Mr. Hartlibb, for whom I writ a letter for my Lord to*ᵃ* sign for a ship for his Brother and sister, who went away hence this day to Gravesend, and from thence to Holland.[1] I find by discourse with Mrs. Crisp[2] that he is very jealous of her, for that she is yet very kind to her old servant Meade. Thence to my Lord's to dinner with Mr. Sheply; so to the Privy Seale. And at night home; and then sent for the barber and was trimmed in the kitchen, the first time that ever I was so. I was vexed this night that Wll Ewere was out of doors till 10 at night; but was pretty well satisfied again when my wife told me that he wept because I was angry; though

a repl. 'for'

---

1. See above, p. 190 & n. 2.   2. (? Diana) Crisp, the daughter.

endeed, he did give me a good reason for his being out, but I thought a good occasion to let him know that I do expect his being at home. So to bed.

12. *Lordsday.* To my Lord; and with him to White-hall chapel, where Mr. Calamy preached and made a good sermon up[on] these words: "To whom much is given, of*a* him much is required."[1]   He was very officious with his three reverences to the King, as others do.[2] After sermon a brave Anthem of Captain Cookes, which he himself sung,[3] and the King was well pleased with it.   My Lord dined at my Lord Chamberlins[4] and I at his house with Mr. Sheply.   After dinner I did give Mr. Donne, who is going to sea, the key of my Cabbin and direction for the putting up of my things.   After that I went to walk; and meeting Mrs. Lane of Westminster-hall, I took her to my Lord's and did give her a bottle of wine in the garden, where Mr. Fairebrother of Cambrige did come and find us and drank with us.

After that I took her to my house,[5] where I was exceeding free in dallying with her, and she not unfree to take it.

At night home and called at my father's, where I found Mr. Fairebrother; but I did not stay but went homewards and called in at Mr. Rawlinsons, whither my uncle Wight was coming; and did come, but was exceeding angry (he being a little fuddled, and I think it was that I should see him in that case) as I never saw him in all my life – which I was somewhat troubled at. Home and to bed.

13. A sitting-day at our office.   After dinner to White-hall to the Privy Seal, whither my father came to me and stayed talking with me a great while, telling me that he had propounded Mr. John Pickering for Sir Tho Honiwoods daughter – which

a repl. 'to'

---

1. A loose recollection of Luke, xii. 48.

2. Calamy meant to demonstrate that Presbyterians were as loyal as Anglicans.

3. Presumably this was a verse-anthem, of which Henry Cooke

(Master of the Children of the Chapel Royal) sang the solo verses himself. (E).

4. The Earl of Manchester, Sandwich's first cousin.

5. The empty house in Axe Yard.

I think he doth not deserve for his own merit: I know not what he may do for his estate.

My father and Creed and I to the old Renish wine-house and talked and drank till night. Then my father home, and I to my Lord's, where he told me that he would suddenly go into the country; and so did commend the business of his sea-commission to me in his absence.[1] After that home by coach; and took my 100*l* that I had formerly left at Mr. Rawlinson's home with me, which is the first that ever I was maister*a* of at once. To prayers and to bed.

14. To the Privy Seale and thence to my Lord's, where Mr. Pim the Taylor and I agreed upon making me a velvet coat. From thence to the Privy Seale again, where Sir Samll Morland came in with a Barronets grant to pass, which the King hath given him to make money of.[2] Here he stayed with me a great while and told me the whole manner of his serving the King in the time of the Protector and how Thurlows bad usage made him to do it. How he discovered Sir R. Willis; and how he hath sunk his fortune for the King; and that now the King hath given him a pension of 500*l* per annum out of the Post Office for life and the benefit of two Barronets; all which doth make me begin to think that he is not so much fool as I took him to be.[3]

Home by water to the Tower, where my father, Mr. Fairebrother and Cooke dined with me. After dinner in comes young Captain Cuttance of the *Speedwell*, who is sent up for the gratuity given the seamen that brought the King over.[4] He

a repl. 'worth

---

1. The Admiral's warrant for the issue of a commission to Sandwich as Vice-Admiral had been made out on 28 July: PRO, Adm. 2/1725, f.21*v*.

2. For the sale of baronetcies, see above, p. 181, n. 2. Morland (here acting as broker in the grant of the title to someone else) paid in the fee of £1095 to the Exchequer on 22 October: *CTB*, i. 78. His own baronetcy dated from 18 July.

3. The pension ran from Michael-

mas 1660: *CTB*, i. 72. For the Morland-Willys affair, see above, p. 141 & n. 1.

4. One month's wages were paid to officers and men of Sandwich's fleet which had brought over the King: PRO, Adm. 20/1, pp. 120-7; Adm. 106/3117, n.p. Pepys later claimed a gratuity for his own 'labour-extraordinary at sea': below, ii. 51.

brought me a ferkin of butter for my wife, which is very welcome. My father after dinner takes leave, after I had given him 40s for the last half-year for my Brother John at Cambrige.

I did also make even with Mr. Fairebrother for my degree of Maister of Arts, which cost me about 9*l*. 16*s*-00*d*. To Whitehall, and my wife with me by water, where at the Privy Seale and elsewhere all the afternoon. At night home with her by water, where I made good sport with having the girl and the boy comb my head before I went to bed, in the kitchen.

15. To the office; and after dinner by water to White-hall, where I find the King gone this morning by 5 of the clock to see a Duch pleasure-boat[1] below bridge, where he dines, and my Lord with him. The King doth tire all his people that are about him with early rising since he came.[2]

To the office. All the afternoon I stayed there. And in the evening went to Westminster-hall, where I stayed at Mrs. Michells; and with her and her husband sent for some drink and drunk with them: by the same token,*a* she and Mrs. Murford and another old woman of the Hall were going a-gossiping* tonight. From thence to my Lord's, where I found him within and he did give me direction about his business in his absence, he entending to go into the country tomorrow morning. Here I lay all night in the old chamber, which I have now given up to W. How, with whom I did entend to lie; but he and I fell to play with one another, so that I made him to go lie with Mr. Sheply. So I lay alone all night.

16. This morning my Lord (all things being ready) carried me by coach to Mr. Crews, in the way talking how good he

---

a 'by the same token' repeated but bracketed

---

1. The yacht *Mary*, presented to the King by the city of Amsterdam. It was at this period that yachts were introduced into England – together with the word itself – from Holland. Previously, state barges had served as royal pleasure-boats. Charles II, a skilful seaman, himself led the fashion for yacht-sailing.

2. Charles was often up very early – sometimes at dawn – for hunting, sailing, or tennis. Cf., e.g., HMC, *Hastings*, ii. 140-1.

did hope my place would be to me and, in general, speaking that it was not the salary of any place that did make a man rich, but the opportunities of getting money while he is in the place:[1] where he took leave and went into the coach, and so for Hinching-brooke: my Lady Jem and Mr. Thomas Crew in the coach with him.

Thence to Whitehall about noon, where I met with Mr. Madge, who took me along with him and Captain Cooke (the famous singer) and other Maisters of Musique to dinner at an ordinary above Charing*a*-cross, where we dined, all paying their club. Thence to the Privy Seal, where there hath been but little work these two days. In the evening, home.

17. To the office and that done, home to dinner, where Mr. Unthanke my wife's tailor dined with us, we having nothing but a dish of sheep's trotters. After dinner, by water to White-hall, where a great deal of business at the Privy Seale. At night I and Creede and the Judge-Advocate went to Mr. Pim the Taylors, who took us to the Half Moon, and there did give us great store of wine and Anchoves, and would pay for them all.

This night I saw Mr. Creed show many the strangest eva-sions to shift off his drink[2] that ever I saw in my life.

By coach home and to bed.

a s.h. repl. s.h. 'Charg'-

---

1. For almost all government servants, from ministers of state to doorkeepers, the incidental profits of office – fees, gratuities and *douceurs* – amounted to much more than the official salary. Hence the high price of offices: a secretaryship of state sold for £10,000 (below, iii. 226, n. 2); a com-missionership of the navy for £2000 (*CSPD 1667-8*, p. 227). Pepys's own office had recently been valued by a prospective purchaser at £1000: above, p. 216. (After Pepys's tenure it was worth much more.) The system, though open to abuse, served a useful purpose by bringing salaries (fixed before the 16th-century infla-tion) to a reasonable level at a minimal cost to the government, and it was common to all European states. Nor did it necessarily lead to corruption. For details about Pepys, see above, Introduction, pp. cxxiii-iv, and *Comp.*: 'Wealth'; for the subject in general, see K. W. Swart, *Sale of offices in 17th cent.*; G. E. Aylmer, *King's Servants*; L. Stone in *Essays . . . in honour of Tawney* (ed. F. J. Fisher), pp. 89+.

2. It was often customary for each member of a drinking party in turn to propose and pay for a toast: to 'shift it off' was to miss one's turn: cf. [W. King], *Journey to Engl.* (1700), p. 19. John Creed, as a Puritan, may have objected to toasts on principle.

18. This morning I took my wife toward Westminster by water and landed her at White-friars, with 50s.*ᵃ* to buy her a petticoat. And I to the Privy Seale. By and by comes my wife to tell me that my father hath persuaded her to buy a most fine cloth of 26s per yard and a rich lace, that the petticoat will come to 5l,¹ at which I was somewhat troubled; but she doing it very innocently, I could not be angry.

I did give her more money and sent her away; and I and Creede and Captain Hayward (who is now unkindly put out of theᵇ *Plymouth* to make way for Captain Allen to go to Constantinople, and put into his ship the *Dover*, which I know will trouble my Lord)² went and dined at the Leg in King's-street, where Captain Ferrers, my Lord's Cornett, comes to us – who after dinner took me and Creed to the Cockepitt play, the first that I have had time to see since my coming from sea, *The Loyall Subject*, where one Kinaston, a boy, acted the Dukes sister but made the loveliest lady that ever I saw in my life – only, her voice not very good.³ After the play done, we three went to drink, and by Captain Ferre[r]s means, Mr. Kinaston and another that acted Archas the Generall⁴ came to us and drank with us. Thence home by coach; and after being trimmed, leavingᶜ my wife to look after her little bich, which was just now a-whelping, I to bed.

19. *Lords day.* In the morning my wife tells me that the bich hath whelp[ed] four young ones and is very well after it, my wife having had a great fear that she would die thereof, the dog that got them being very big.

a MS. '50l'   *b* repl. 'his'
c 'after being trimmed' repeated but crossed out

---

1. Gowns were often worn so as to show the upper petticoat which was, therefore, very ornamental: Cunnington, pp. 175–6.

2. John Hayward had served the Protectorate and had been with Sandwich on both the Baltic and the Dutch voyages of 1659 and 1660. Thomas Allin had been a consistent royalist.

3. The play was a tragicomedy by John Fletcher, first acted in 1618, and published in 1647. Edward Kynaston, playing Olympia, and now nearly 20, was one of the last actors to play feminine roles in the Elizabethan tradition. The theatre was the Cockpit, Drury Lane. (A).

4. Probably Thomas Betterton. (A).

This morning Sir W. Batten, Pen and myself went to church[1] to the church-wardens to demand a pew, which at present could not be given us, but we are resolved to have one built. So we stayed and heard Mr. Mills,[2] a very good Minister.

Home to dinner, where my wife had on her new petticoat that she bought yesterday, which endeed is a very fine cloth and a fine lace; but that being of a light colour and the lace all silver, it makes no great show.

Mr. Creed and my Brother Tom dined with me. After dinner my wife went and fetched the little puppys to us, which are very pretty ones. After they were gone, I went up to put my papers in order; and finding my wife's clothes lie carelessly laid up, I was angry with her, which I was troubled for. After that, my wife and I went and walked in the garden; and so home to bed.

20. Office day. As Sir W. Pen and I were walking in the garden, a messenger came to me from the Duke of Yorke to fetch me to the Lord Chancellor. So (Mrs. Turner with her daughter The being come to my house to speak with me about a friend of hers to send to sea) I went with her in her coach as far as Worcester-house; but my Lord Chancellor being gone to the House of Lords, I went thither and (there being a law case tried before them this day) got in;[3] and there stayed all the morning, seeing their manner of sitting on Woolpacks, &c., which I never did before.

After the House was up, I spoke to my Lord and had order from him to come to him at night. This morning Mr. Creed did give me the papers that concern my Lord's sea-commission, which he left in my hand and went to sea this day to look after the gratuity-money.[4] The afternoon at the Privy Seale; where reckoning with Mr. Moore, he had got 100*l* for me together, which I was glad of, guessing that the profits of this month to me would come to 100*l*.

In the evening I went all alone to drink at Mrs. Harpers, where

1. St Olave's, Hart St, the Navy Office's parish church: for the pew, see below, p. 230 & n. 2.

2. Daniel Milles, Rector since April 1657.

3. *LJ*, xi. 134; HMC, *Rep.*, 7/127. The public were admitted to trials but not to debates.

4. See above, p. 221.

I found Mrs. Crisps daughter, with whom and her friends I stayed and drank. And so with W. Ewre by coach to Worcester-house, where I light, sending him home with the 100*l* that I received today. Here I stayed and saw my Lord Chancellor come into his Great Hall, where wonderful how much company there was to expect him at a Seale.[1]

Before he would begin any business, he took my papers of the state of the debts of the fleet and there viewed them before*ª* all the people and did give me his advice privately how to order things to get as much money as we can of the parliament.[2]

That being done, I went home, where I find all my things come home from sea (sent by my desire by Mr. Dun), of which I was glad, though many of my things are quite spoiled with mould, by reason of lying so long a-shipboard and my cabin being not tight.*ᵇ* I spent much time to dispose of them tonight, and so to bed.

21. This morning I went to White-hall with Sir W. Penn by water, who in our passage told me how he was bred up under Sir W. Batten.[3] We went to Mr. Coventry's chamber, and consulted of drawing my papers of debts of the Navy against the afternoon for the Committee.[4] So to the Admiralty, where

a repl. 'and'   *b* repl. 'night'

---

1. Some sealing-days, like this, were public; others private: Sir H. C. Maxwell-Lyte, *Hist. notes on Great Seal*, p. 298. Cf. Pepys's later account of sealing-day at the Privy Seal: below, ii. 156.

2. Hyde was chairman of the Treasury Commission.

3. Penn may have been referring to the very earliest years of his service, before the civil wars, or to the period (1642–4) in which he was under Batten's command in the parliamentary navy. See Penn, i. 3–4.

4. The Commons' committee to examine the navy's debts appointed on 2 August (*CJ*, viii. 109), of which Col. John Birch, whom Pepys saw in the afternoon, was in charge.

Birch had written to the Navy Board on 9 August asking for a statement. Pepys's secretarial copy of the statement (13 August) and of Birch's letter is in PL 2265, no. 8. The accounts are dated 27 June. The committee reported to the Commons on 12 November: for its conclusions, see *CJ*, viii. 182. £678,000 was owing for wages, victuals and stores, and £273,255 for the ships about to be paid off. For the difficulties involved in arriving at correct figures, see Ehrman, pp. 165+. Thomas Turner, Clerk-General of the office, later charged for six books of Dutch paper 'to write the debts of the Navy into'; PRO, Adm. 20/1, p. 135, no. 853.

W. Ewre and I did them; and after that he went to his aunts
Blackburne (who hath a kinswoman died at her house today, and
was to be buried tonight, by which means he stayed very late
out); and I to Westminster-hall, where I met Mr. Crew and dined
with him; where there dined one Mr. Hickeman, an Oxford
man, who spoke very much against the heighth of the new
old-clergy, for putting out many of the religious fellows of
colleges and enveighing against them for their being drunk –
which if true, I am sorry to hear.¹

After that toward Westminster, where I called on Mr. Pim
and there found my velvet coat (the first that ever I made)²
done, and a velvet mounteer, which I took to the Privy Seal
Office and there locked them up, and went to the Queenes
Court and there, after much waiting, spoke with Collonell
Birch, who read my papers and desired some addition; which
done, I returned to the Privy Seale, where little to do, and with
Mr. Moore toward London, and in our way meeting Monsieur
Etchar (Mr. Mountagu's man) about the Savoy, he took us to
the Brazen-nose taverne and there drank; and so parted and I
home by coach; and there, it being post-night, I wrote to my
Lord to give him notice that all things are well. That Generall
Monke is made Lieutenant of Ireland, which my Lord Roberts

---

1. A royal visitation of Oxford,
designed to evict all college and university officers unlawfully intruded
during the revolution, had begun on
31 July with the dismissal of several
Heads of Houses. Henry Hickman
(a friend of the Crews, once lecturer
at Brackley church and tutor to
Nathaniel Crew) had himself been
ejected from his fellowship at Magdalen on 6 August: *Rest. visit. Oxf.*
(ed. F. J. Varley, Camden Misc.
xviii), p. 10. He was one of the
most prominent of Oxford Puritans,
and was here objecting on behalf of
the 'religious' dons to the high-
handedness of the old fellows newly
restored. Anthony Wood's comment, on the other hand, was:
'Whereas great cruelty was acted in
the Presbyterian Visitation 12 years
before, now nothing but moderation,
and a requital in a manner of good for
evil...': *Hist. univ. Oxford* (1786–
96), vol. ii, pt ii. 701.

2. Not worn until 22 April 1661,
on the occasion of the King's coronation entry.

(made Deputy) doth not like of, to be Deputy to any man but the King himself.[1]   After that to bed.

22. Office. Which done, Sir W. Penn took me into the garden and there told me how Mr. Turner doth entend to petition the Duke for an Allowance Extra as one of the Clerks of the Navy,[2] which he desired me to join with him in the furthering of.   Which I promised to do, so that it did not reflect upon me or to my damage to have any other added, as if I*a* was not able to perform my place; which he did wholly disown to be any of his intention, but far from it.

I took Mr. Hater home with me to dinner, with whom I did advise, who did give me the same counsel.

After dinner he and I to the office about doing something more as to the debts of the Navy then I had done yesterday. And so I to White-hall to the Privy Seale; and having done there, with my father (who came to see me) to Westminster-hall and the parliament-house to look for Collonell Birch; but found him not.   In the House, after the Committee was up, I met with Mr. G. Mountague and joyed him in his entrance (this being his third day) for Dover.   Here he made me sit all alone in the House, none but he and I, half an hour, discoursing how things stand; and in short he told me how there was like to be many factions at Court between Marquis Ormond,[3] Generall Monke,

a repl. ? 'as'

---

1. Monck (since 7 July Duke of Albemarle) had been appointed to the lord-lieutenancy in June but intended to stay in England and rule through a resident deputy. Robartes had been made Lord Deputy on 25 July, but wished to be responsible to the King (who had appointed him) and to have the full powers of his predecessors in the post. He resigned and was made Lord Privy Seal in May 1661, while Albemarle in turn was replaced as Lieutenant by Ormond in February 1662. Robartes later served as Lord Lieutenant (with no success),

in 1669–70. Cf. Clarendon, *Life*, i. 463–6 (he speaks of Robartes's 'intolerable pride'); HMC, *Sutherland*, p. 195 (14 August).

2. Thomas Turner, Clerk-General to the office, had held the same post under the Commonwealth, and had been a claimant to the Clerkship of the Acts at the Restoration. He now became clerk to the Comptroller, receiving an extra £30 p.a. by order of the Duke of York (22 September).

3. Lord High Steward; the greatest figure in Irish affairs at this time.

and the Lord Roberts, about the business of Ireland. As there is
already between the two Houses about the Act of Indemnity[1]
and in the House of Commons between the Episcopalian and
Presbyterian men.[2]

Thence to my father (walking with Mr. Hering, Minister of
St. Brides) and took them to the Sun tavern, where I found
George (my old Drawer) come again. From thence by water;
landed them at Black-friars, and so home and to bed.

23. By water to Doctors Commons to Dr. Walker to give
him my Lord's papers to view over concerning his being im-
powered to be Vice-Admirall under the Duke of Yorke.[3]
Thence, meeting with Mr. Pinkeny, he and I to a morning
draught and thence by water to White-hall to the Parliament
house, where I spoke with Collonell Birch; and so to the Admiralty chamber, where we and Mr. Coventry have a meeting
about several businesses. Among others, it was moved that
Phin Pett (kinsman to the Commissioner) of Chatham should
be suspended his imployment till he had answered to some
articles put in against him; as, that he should formerly say that
the King was a bastard and his mother a whore.[4]

Thence to Westminster-hall, where I met with my father
Bowyer and Mr. Spicer, and them I took to the Leg in King's-
street and did give them a dish or two of meat; and so away to
the Privy Seale, where the King being out of Towne, we have
had nothing to do these two days.[5]   To Westminster-hall, where

1. The act dealing with the regicides was to occupy much parliamentary time. Four conferences between the Houses were held before
they could agree on its terms, the
last beginning on the 24th.

2. The bill concerning church
livings had been debated this day:
CJ, viii. 130. Cf. above, p. 204
& n. 2.

3. For the papers and the appointment, see above, p. 221 & n. 1.
Doctors' Commons (near St Paul's)
housed the society of lawyers practis-
ing civil (Roman) law in the Court of

Admiralty (where Dr Walter Walker
was an advocate) and in the ecclesiastical courts.

4. Phineas Pett had been confirmed
as Assistant Master-Shipwright,
Chatham, on 11 June, but was dismissed on 15 October. The Pett
family (so numerous and powerful in
naval affairs and so fond of office)
attracted many enemies.

5. Privy Seal warrants were made
out only on the authority of 'King's
bills' issued, under the sign manual,
from the Signet Office. Cf. below,
p. 303.

I met with W. Symons, T. Doling and Mr. Booth, and with them to the Dogg, where we eat a Muske millon (the first that I have eat this year) and were very merry with W. Symons, calling him Mr. Deane, because of the Deanes lands that his uncle had left him, which are like to be lost all.[1]

Thence home by water; and very late at night writing letters to my Lord to Hinchingbrooke and also to the Vice-Admirall in the Downes; and so to bed.

24. Office; and then with Sir W. Batten and Sir W. Penn to the parish church to find out a place where to build a seat or a gallery to sit in; and did find one, which is to be done speedily.[2] Thence with them to dinner at a tavern in Thames-street, where they were invited to a roasted haunch of venison and other very good victuals and company.

Thence to White-hall to the Privy Seale, but nothing to do. At night by land to my father's, where I found my mother not very well. I did give her a pint of sack.[3] My father came in and Dr T. Pepys, who talked with me in French a great while about looking out of a place for him. But I find him a weak man and speaks the worst French that ever I heard of one that hath been so long beyond sea.[4]

---

1. From his uncle, Henry Scobell, late Clerk of Parliament and registrar of the commission for the sale of the lands of deans and chapters, Symons had inherited two manors confis-cated from the Dean and chapter of St Paul's. All such lands were now restored.

2. It contained at least three pews (below, iii. 177) and was used for the first time on the following 11 Novem-ber. It was built on the s. side of the nave and was approached from the churchyard by a covered staircase of which a view (c. 1736) is given in A. Povah, *St Olave, Hart St*, opp. p. 102. It was removed in 1853, a tablet now marking the position of the outside staircase, and the memorial to Pepys (1884) that of the gallery itself. Pay-ments for the work, October–Decem-ber 1660 (entered under 'Extra Service on the Seas'), are in PRO, Adm. 20/1, pp. 135, 193, 298: ib., 20/3, p. 15. Both material and workmen came from Deptford yard.

3. For the medicinal use of wine, see R. Burton, *Anat. Melancholy* (ed. Shilleto), i. 255; A. L. Simon, *Hist. wine trade in Engl.*, vol. iii, ch. xvi.

4. Dr Thomas Pepys (first cousin of the diarist's father), aged 39, had been abroad studying medicine at Leyden and Padua. Pepys always regarded him as unemployable.

Thence into Paul's churchyard and bought Barkley's *Argenis*[1] in Latin; and so home and to bed.

I find at home that Captain Bun hath sent me four dozen bottles of wine to me today.[2]

The King came back to White-hall tonight.[3]

25. This morning Mr. Turner and I by coach from our office to Whitehall (in our way I calling on Dr Walker for the papers I did give him the other day, which he had perused and find that the Dukes counsel hath abated something of the former draught which Dr. Walker drew for my Lord) to Sir G. Carteret, where we three made up an estimate of the debts of the Navy for the Council.[4]

At noon I took Mr. Turner and Mr. Moore to the Leg in King-street and did give them a dinner; and afterward to the Sun tavern and did give Mr. Turner a glass of wine, there coming to us Mr. Fowler the Apothecary (the Judge's son) with a book of lute lessons which his father had left there for me, such as he formerly did use to play when a young man and had the use of his hand.

To the Privy Seale and found some business now again to do there.

To Westminster-hall for a new half-shirt of Mrs. Lane; and so home by water. Wrote letters by the post to my Lord and

1. A political romance by the Scottish satirist, John Barclay (d. 1621). It eulogised Henry IV of France and Elizabeth of England, criticised Philip II, and roundly denounced all faction and conspiracy. First published in 1621 in Latin, it was translated into many languages and had passed through 40 editions by 1693. A copy of the Leyden–Rotterdam edition of 1659–69 (in Latin; PL 1368–9) was added to the PL after 1700: PL, 'Supellex Literaria, Additamenta', f. 9r. Close by St Paul's churchyard were many booksellers' shops; Pepys usually made his purchases at this time at Joseph Kirton's.

2. Thomas Bunn of the *Essex* had just returned from a voyage to Spain: *CSPD 1660–1*, pp. 110, 315.

3. He had been deer-hunting in the country: *CSPVen. 1659–61*, p. 191.

4. The same estimate (of the debts at 27 June) which Pepys mentions above at 21 August. A copy, deriving from this meeting of 25 August, is in BM, Add. 9312, f.1r. A Council committee had been appointed on 1 August to investigate the debts with Sandwich's help (PRO, PC 2/54, p. 102); they appear to have left most of the work to the committee of the Commons appointed on the following day.

to sea. This night W. Eure brought me home from Pims my velvet coat and cap, the first that ever I made. So to bed.

26. *Lords day*. With Sir W. Penn to the parish church, where we are placed in the highest pew of all, where a stranger preached a dry and tedious long sermon. Dined at home, and with my wife to church again in the afternoon.

Home again and walked in the garden and on the leads till night; and so to supper and to bed.

27. This morning comes one with a vessel of Northdowne ale[1] from Mr. Pierce the purser to me. And after him, another with a brave Turkey-carpet and a Jarre of Olives from Captain Cuttance and a pair of fine Turtle-doves from John Burr to my wife. These things came up today in our smack; and my boy Ely came along with them and came after office was done to see me. I did give him half a crowne because I saw that he was ready to cry to see that he could not be entertained* by me here.[2]

In the afternoon to the Privy Seale, where good stir[a] of work now toward the end of the month. From thence with Mr. Mount, Luellin and others to the Bullhead till late, and so home. Where about 10 a-clock Major Hart came to me – whom I did receive with wine and a dish of Anchoves, which made me so dry that I was ill with them all night and was fain to have the girl rise to fetch me some drink.

28. At home looking over my papers and books and house as to the fitting of it to my mind till 2 in the afternoon. Some time I spent this morning beginning to teach my wife some skill in Musique, and find her apt beyond imagination.

To the Privy Seale where great stir of work today. Collonell Scroope is this day excepted out of the Act of Indemnity, which

a ? 'store'

---

1. Margate ale: Northdown was in the parish of St John the Baptist.

2. Eliezer Jenkins had served Pepys on the Dutch voyage.

hath been now long in coming out, but it is expected tomorrow.[1] I carried home 80*l* from Privy Seale by coach; and at night spent a little more time with my wife about her Musique with great content.

This day I heard my poor mother hath these two days been very ill, and I fear she will not last long.

To bed – a little troubled that I fear my boy Will is a thief and hath stole some money of mine – perticularly a letter that Mr. Jenkins did leave the last week with me with half a crown in to send to his son.

29. Office day. Before I went to the office, my wife and I examined my boy Will about his stealing*a* of things, as we doubted yesterday; but he denied all with the greatest subtility and confidence in the world. To the office; and after office, then to the church, where we took another view of the place where we had resolved to build a gallery; and have set men about doing it. Home to dinner; and there I find that my wife hath discovered my boy's theft and a great deal more then we imagined. At which I was vexed and entend to put him away.

To my office at Privy Seale in the afternoon; and from thence at night to the Bull-head with Mount, Luellin and others; and thence to my father's; and he being at my uncle Fenner's, I went thither to him, and there sent for my boy's father and talked with him about his son and had his promise that if I will send home his boy, he will take him notwithstanding his indentures.

Home at night; and find that my wife hath found out more, of the boy's stealing 6s. out of W. Ewres closet and hid it in the house of office – at which my heart was troubled. To bed and caused the boy's clothes to be brought up to my chamber. But after we were all a-bed, the wench (which lies in our chamber) called us to listen of a sudden; which put my wife into such a

a repl. 'still'

---

1. Adrian Scroope was one of the regicides. The Commons, on 9 June and 13 August, had allowed him the benefit of the Act, since he had surrendered; but the Lords had voted otherwise, and on this day the Lower House concurred: *CJ*, viii. 60-1, 118, 139-40. It was the large number of debates about the application of the bill to particular cases which had delayed its passage.

fright that she shook, every joynt of her, and a long time that I could not get her out of it. That noise was the boy, we did believe, was got in a desperate mood out of his bed to do himself or Wm. some mischief. But the wench went down and got a candle lighted; and finding the boy in bed and locking the doors fast, with a candle burning all night, we slept well, but with a great deal of fear.

30. We found all well in the morning below-stairs, but the boy in a sad plight over seeming sorrow; but he is the most cunning rogue that ever I met with of*a* his age.

To White-hall, where I met with the Act of Indemnity (so long talked of and hoped for), with the Act of Rate for Polemony and for Judiciall proceedings.[1]

At Westminster-hall I met with Mr. Pagett the lawyer and dined with him at Heaven.[2] This afternoon my wife went to Mr. Pierces wife's child's christening. And was urged to be godmother, but I advised her beforehand not to do it; so she did not, but as proxy for my Lady Jemimah. This the first day that ever I saw my wife wear black patches since we were married.[3] My Lord came to town today; but coming not home till very late, I stayed till 10 at night; and so home on foot. Mr. Sheply and Mr. Childe this night at the tavern.

31. Early to wait upon my Lord at White-hall; and with him to the Duke's chamber. So to my office in Seething-lane. Dined at home; and after dinner to my Lord again; who told me that he is ordered to go suddenly to sea and did give me some orders to be drawing upon against his going.[4] This after-

a repl. 'in'

---

1. *An act for free and general pardon, indemnity and oblivion; An act for the speedy provision of money for disbanding and paying off the forces; An act for confirmation of judicial proceedings.* All had received royal assent on the 29th, and had been published on the same day: 12 Car. II c.'s 11, 9 and 12. The act concerning judicial proceedings confirmed all judicial decisions made since 1642.

2. For Heaven, see above, p. 31 & n. 2.

3. Pepys had met with patches in Holland on 14 May 1660.

4. Sandwich sailed from the Downs on 7 September to bring from Holland the King's sister, Mary (Princess Royal and Princess Dowager of Orange): Sandwich, p. 80.

noon I agreed to let my house quite out of my hands to Mr. Dalton (of the wine-cellar to the King, with whom I have drunk in the old wine-cellar two or three times) for 41*l*. At night, made up even at Privy Seale for this month against tomorrow to give up possession; but we know not to whom – though we most favour Mr. Bickerstaffe, with whom and Mr. Mathewes we drank late after office was done at the Sun, discoursing what to do about it tomorrow against Baron; and so home and to bed. Blessed be God all things continue well with and for me; I pray God fit me for a change of my fortune.[a]

> *a* followed by long oblique line and sixteen blank pages

SEPTEMBER.

1. *Saturday.*

This morning I tooke*ᵃ* care to get a vessel to carry my Lord's things to the Downes on Monday next. And so to White-hall to my Lord, where he and I did look over the Commission drawn for him by the Dukes counsel, which I do not find my Lord to be displeased with, though short of what Dr. Walker did formerly draw for him.[1]

Thence to the Privy Seale to see how things went there; and I find that Mr. Baron had by a severe warrant from the King got possession of the office from his Brother Bickerstaffe, which is very strange and much to our admiration, it being against all open Justice.[2]

Mr. Moore and I and several others being invited today by Mr. Goodman, a friend of his, we dined at the Bull-head upon the best venison pasty that ever I eat of in my life; and with one dish more, it was the best dinner I ever was at. Here rise in discourse at table a dispute between Mr. Moore and Dr. Clerke, the former affirming that it was essentiall to a Tragedy to have the argument of it true, which the Doctor denyed and left to me to be judge – and the cause to be determind next Tuesday morning at the same place upon the eating of the remains of the pasty, and the loser to spend 10s.[3]

All this afternoon sending express to the fleet to order things against my Lord's coming – and taking direction of my Lord about some rich furniture to take along with him for the Princesse.[4]

a repl. symbol rendered illegible

1. See above, p. 221 & n. 1; p. 231.
2. For this dispute, see above, p. 207 & n. 2. The King's warrant was dated 29 August: *CSPD Add. 1660-85*, p. 9. Bickerstaffe was appointed to a clerkship in June 1662.
3. At this time there was an increasing desire in some quarters for verisimilitude in drama. Ben Jonson had professed 'truth of Argument'

and 'integrity in the *Story*' as principles of tragic composition in his address *To the reader* in *Sejanus* (1605). Most Restoration critics, however, were in general agreement with Thomas Rymer's assertion in *The tragedies of the last age* (1678) that history cannot illustrate truths 'universal and eternal' as well as fiction can. (A).
4. See above, p. 234, n. 4.

And talking of this, I hear by Mr. Townsend that there is the greatest preparacion against the Prince de Ligne's coming over from the King of Spaine that ever was in England for any Imbassador.[1]

Late home; and what with business and my boy's roguery, my mind being unquiet, I went to bed.

2. Sunday.
To Westminster. My Lord being gone before my coming to Chappell, I and Mr. Sheply told out my money and made even for my privy Seale fees and gratuity mony[2] &c. to this day between my Lord and I.

After that to Chappell, where Dr Ferne, a good honest sermon upon: "the Lord is my Shield."[3] After sermon, a dull Anthem; and so to my Lord's (he dining abroad) and dined with Mr. Sheply. So to St. Margaretts and heard a good sermon upon the text: "Teach us the old way," or something like it[4] – wherein he run over all the new tenets in Policy and Religion which have brought us into all our late divisions.

From church to Mrs. Crisp's (having sent Will Ewre home to tell my wife that I would not come home tonight because of my Lord's going out erly tomorrow morning); where I sat late and did give them a great deal of wine, it being a farewell-cup to Laud Crisp.[5] I drank till the daughter began to be very loving to me and kind, and I fear is not so good as she should be.

To my Lord's and to bed with Mr. Sheply.

3. Up and to Mr.   the Goldsmith near the new

1. He came as Spanish ambassador-extraordinary to congratulate Charles II on his restoration. For the full magnificence of his embassy, see F. Leuridant, *Une ambassade du Prince de Ligne*. For the money spent by the English government on his entertainment, see *CSPD 1660–1*, p. 181; cf. *CSPVen. 1659–61*, pp. 191, 201. Thomas Townshend's department (the Great Wardrobe) furnished Camden House (in the city) and two neighbouring houses for him: PRO, PRO 30/24, bdle 4, no. 118.

2. The gratuity for his service on the voyage to Holland: see above, p. 221, n. 4.

3. A loose recollection of 2 Sam. xxii. 3; or Ps. iii. 3; or Ps. xxviii. 7. The chapel was that of Whitehall Palace, and the preacher Henry Ferne, Master of Trinity College, Cambridge, and Dean of Ely.

4. Possibly 1 Kings, viii. 36: 'that thou teach them the good way wherein they should walk'.

5. The Crisps' son, now entering Sandwich's service.

Exchange (where I bought my wedding ring); and there with much ado got him to put a gold ring to the Jewell which the King of Sweden did give my Lord – out of which my Lord hath now taken the King's picture and entends to make a George of it.[1]

This morning at my Lord's I had an opportunity to speak with Sir G. Downing, who hath promised me to[a] give me up my bond[2] and to pay me for my last Quarter while I was at Sea, that so I may pay Mr. Moore and Hawly.

About noone, my Lord having taken leave of the King in the Shield Gallery (where I saw with what kindnesse the King did hugg my Lord at his parting), I went over with him and saw him in his Coach at Lambeth and there took leave of him, going to the Downes. Which put me in mind of his first voyage that ever he made;[3] which he did begin like this, from Lambeth. In the afternoon with Mr. Moore to my house to cast up our Privy Seale accounts, where I find that my Lord's comes to 400 and odd pounds, and mine to 132*l* – out of which I do give him as good as 25*l*. for his pains, with which I doubt he is not Satisfyed – but my heart is full glad.[4] Thence with him to Mr. Crews and did fetch as much money as did make even our accounts between him and I.

Home; and there found Mr. Cooke come back from my Lord for me to get him some things bought for him to be brought

a repl. 'long'

---

1. The medal given by Charles X to Sandwich in August 1659 on his departure from the Sound: Harris, i. 154; cf. Whinney and Millar, p. 89. It was bequeathed in his will to his wife, and was there described as a 'jewell set with dyamonds on the one side And a Picture case on the other side': PCC, Eure, 113.

2. The recognizances Pepys entered into when admitted as Downing's clerk in the Exchequer.

3. To the Mediterranean in February 1656.

4. Detailed accounts (by Pepys and Moore) for March–July 1661 (Rawl. A 174, ff. 259–62) make clear some of the principles on which fees were divided. Each of the four clerks of the office took charge for a month at a time, and the fees for the four months were then divided equally among them and the Lord Privy Seal. A deputy was paid an agreed proportion of his principal's share. Sandwich's share in the second quarter of 1661 had dropped to £176 1*s*. 8*d*., Moore's to £3 7*s*. 9*d*.

after him – a toilette Capp and Combe case of Silke to make use of in Holland (for he is to go himself to The Hague) which I am to do tomorrow morning.

This day my father and my uncle Fenner and both his sons have been at my house to see it; and my wife did treat them nobly with wine and Anchoves.

By reason of my Lord's going today I could not get to the office to meet today.

4. I did many things this morning at home before I went out – as looking over the Joyners, who are flooring my dining-roome – and doing business with Sir Wms. both[1] at the office. And so to White-hall and so to the bull head where we had the remaynes of our pasty, where I did give my verdict against Mr. Moore upon last Saturdays wager. Where Dr. Fuller[2] coming in doth confirme me in my verdict.

From thence to my Lord's and dispatcht Mr. Cooke away with the things to my Lord. From thence to Axeyard to my house; where standing at the door, Mrs. Diana[3] comes by, whom I took into my house upstairs and there did dally with her a great while, and find that in Latin *"nulla puella negat."*

So home by water; and there sat up late, putting my papers in order and my money also, and teaching my wife her Musique lesson, in which I take great pleasure.

So to bed.

5. To the Office.
From thence by Coach, upon the desire of the Principal Officers, to a Maister of Chancery to give Mr. Stowell[4] his oath, whereby he doth swear that he did hear Phineas Pett say very high words[a] against the King a great while ago.[5]

Coming back, our Coach broke; and so Stowell and I to Mr. Rawlinsons and after a glass of wine parted. And I to the

a repl. 'orders'

---

1. Sir William Batten and Sir William Penn.

2. Thomas Fuller the author; he and Pepys decided that tragedies need not be historically true.

3. Probably Diana Crisp.

4. ? Robert Sewell, Storekeeper, Chatham.

5. See above, p. 229.

office; home to dinner, where (having put away my boy in the morning) his father brought him again, but I did so clear up the boy's roguery to his father that he could not speak against my putting him away; and so I did give him 10s for the boy's clothes that I made him and so parted and I tore his Indenture.

All the afternoon with the*a* Principal Officers at Sir W. Battens about Petts business (where I first saw Collonell Slingsby, who hath now his patent for Comp[t]roller)[1] but did bring it to no issue. This day I saw our *Dedimus* to be Sworne in the Peace by, which will be shortly.

In the evening, my wife being a little impatient, I went along with her to buy her a necklace of pearle which will cost 4*l* 10s – which I am willing to comply with her in, for her incouragement and because I have lately got money, having now above 200*l* in Cash beforehand in the world.[2]

Home; and having in our way bought a rabbett and two*b* little lobsters, my wife and I did supp late; and so to bed.

Great newes nowaday of the Duc D'Anjou's desire to marry the Princesse Henriette.[3]

Hugh Peters is said to be taken.[4]   And the Duke of Glocester is fallen ill and is said will prove the small-pox.

6.   To White-hall by water with Sir W. Battin; and in our passage told me how Comissioner*c* Pett did pay himself for the entertainment that he did give the King at Chattam at his coming in,[5] and 20s a day all the time that he was in Holland – which I wonder at.   And so I see there is a great deal of envy between them two.

At White-hall I met with Comissioner Pett, who told me how Mr. Coventree and Fairebanke his Sollicitor are falling out.   One

a l.h. repl. l.h. 'Sr.'.   *b* l.h. repl. '2'   *c* l.h. repl. s.h. 'com'-

---

1. Issued on 31 August.
2. On 30 April 1666 Pepys gave her a pearl necklace costing £80.
3. Philippe, Duc d'Anjou, afterwards Duc d'Orleans, brother of Louis XIV, married Henrietta, youngest sister of Charles II, in March 1661.

4. The leading preacher of the New Model army, in hiding since 18 June when he was excluded from the Act of Indemnity; arrested on 2 September in Southwark (*DNB*).
5. A banquet at Chatham on 28 May when the King reviewed the fleet: *Merc. Pub.*, 31 May, p. 349.

complaining of the other for taking too great fees[1] – which is too true.

I find that Comissioner Pett is under great discontent and is loath to give too much money for his place, and so doth greatly desire me to go along with him in what we shall agree to give Mr. Coventree. Which I have promised him, but am unwilling to mix my fortune with him that is going down the wind.

We all met this morning afterward at the Admiralty, where our business is to get provision of victualls ready for the ships in the Downes; which we did, Mr. Gauden promising to go himself thither and see it done.[2] Dined, Will and I, at my Lord's upon a joynt of meat that I send Mrs. Sarah for.

Afterwards to my house and sent all my books to my Lord's, in order to send them to my house that I now dwell in. Home and to bed.

7. An office day; and in the afternoon at home all the day, it being the first that I have been at home all day since I came hither.

Putting my papers, books and other things in order, and writing of letters. ⟨This day my Lord set sail from the Downes for Holland.⟩[a][3]

8. All day also at home. At night sent for by Sir W. Penn, with whom I sat late, drinking a glass of wine – and discoursing; and I find him to be a very Sociable man, and an able man and very Cunning.

9. *Sunday.* In the morning with Sir W. Pen to church; and a very good sermon of Mr. Mills.

a addition crowded into end of line

---

1. There was no establishment of fees fixed by the Admiral until April 1661; now and later the matter caused much dispute. The solicitor was an intermediary between Coventry and those who sought favours of him.

2. Denis Gauden was victualler of the Navy. The ships were the *Dartmouth* and *Happy Return*, about to go to the Canaries, and the *Plymouth*, bound for Constantinople with the new English ambassador. The Duke of York had on the 3rd ordered them to be victualled: PRO, Adm. 2/1745, f.6r.

3. See above, p. 234, n. 4.

Home to dinner, and Sir W. Pen with me to such as I had; and it was very handsome, it being the first time that he ever saw my wife or house since we came hither.

Afternoon, to church with my wife. And after that home and there walked with Major Hart (who came to see me) in the garden, who tells me that we are all like to be speedily disbanded, and then I lose the benefit of a Muster.[1] After supper to bed.

10. *office day*. news brought us of the Dukes intention to go tomorrow to the fleet for a day or two to meet his sister. Collonell Slingsby and I to White-hall, thinking to proffer our service to the Duke to wait upon him; but meeting with Sir G. Carteret, he sent us in all haste back again to hire two Catches for the present use of the Duke. So we returned and landed at the Beare at the bridge-foot, where we saw Suthwark faire (I having not at all seen Bartlmew fayre);[2] and so to the towre-wharfe, where we did hire two Catches. So to the office and found Sir W. Batten at dinner with some friends upon a good Chine of beef, on which I eat heartily, I being very hungry.

Home, where Mr. Snow (whom afterwards we called one another Cosen)[3] came to me to see me; and with him and one Shelston, a simple fellow that looks after an imployment (that was with me just upon my going to sea last), to a taverne, where till late with them. So home, having drunk too much; and so to bed.

11. At Sir W. Battens with Sir W. Pen we drank our morn-

---

1. Sandwich's regiment (q.v. above, p. 7) was disbanded in November: below, p. 295 & n. 3. The order in which the regiments were disbanded was determined by lots drawn in full Privy Council in the presence of the King; in this case on 28 September: *Merc. Pub.*, 11 October, p. 644. Sandwich's was among the last regiments to be paid off. Pepys as colonel's Secretary and Muster-Master (at any rate in name) was paid for each muster.

2. Southwark Fair, originally authorised to run from 7 to 9 September (W. de G. Birch, *Hist. charters London*, p. 82), had like most fairs extended its duration, and now lasted for 14 days. Bartholomew Fair ran at this time from 23 August to 6 September.

3. ? John Snow of Blackwall (see below, ii. 30); related to Pepys through a marriage connection with the Glascocks.

ing draught, and from thence for an houre in the office and despatch a little business.

Dined at Sir W. Battens; and by this time I see that we are like to have a very good correspondency and neighbourhood, but chargeable. All the afternoon at home looking over my Carpenters. At night I called Tho. Hater out of the office to my house to sit and talk with me. After he was gone, I caused the Girle to wash the wainscote of our parler, which she did very well; which caused my wife and I good sport. Up to my chamber to read a little, and write my Diary for three or four days past.

The Duke of Yorke did go today by break-of-day to the Downes. The Duke of Glocester ill. The House of Parliament was to adjourne today: I know not yet whether it be done or no.[1]

To bed.

12. *office day.* This noon I expected to have had my Cosen Snow and my father come to dine with me, but it being very rainy they did not come.

My Brother Tom came to my house with a letter from my Brother John, wherein he desires some books – Barthol. *Anatomy*;[2] Rosinus *Roman antiquities*,[3] and Gassendus *astronomy*.[4] The last of which I did give him, and an angell toward my father's buying of the others.

At home all the afternoon looking after my workmen in my house, whose lazinesse doth much trouble me.

This day the Parliament adjourned.[5]

1. It did not adjourn until the 13th: *CJ*, viii. 175.

2. Probably Thomas Bartholinus, *Anatomia* (5th ed., Leyden, 1651, or 6th ed., The Hague, 1660). Pepys retained a copy of the latter: PL 1479.

3. Johannes Rosinus, *Antiquitatum romanorum corpus absolutissimum ex variis scriptoribus collect.* (1st ed., Basle, 1583; many times reissued). Pepys kept a copy of the Amsterdam edition of 1685: PL 1869. The work was said to be most useful to both students and teachers – too useful, since it saved them the trouble of going to the original authors.

4. Pierre Gassendi, *Institutio Astronomica* (1st ed., Paris, 1647). Pepys retained the 1683 edition (London): PL 1224.

5. A mistake; see above, n. 1.

13. old East comes to me in the morning with letters and I did give him a bottle of Northdown ale, which made the poor man almost drunk.

In the afternoon my wife went to the buriall of a child of my Cozen Scotts. And it is observable that within this month my aunt Wight was brought to bed of two girles – my Cozen Stradwick of a girl and a boy, and my Cozen Scott of a boy, and all died.

I in the afternoon to Westminster, where Mr. Dalton was ready with his money to pay me for my house; but our writings not being drawn, it could not be done today. I met with Mr. Hawly, who was removing his things from Mr. Bowyers, where he hath lodged a great while, and I took him and W. Bowyer to the Swan and drank; and Mr. Hawly did give me a little black Rattoon, painted and gilt.

Home by water.

This day the Duke of Glocester dyed of the small-pox – by the great negligence of the Doctors.[1]

14. *office day.* I got 42*l.* 15*s.* 00*d* appointed me by bill for my imployment of Secretary to the 4th of this month,[2] it being the last money I shall receive upon that scoare.

My wife went this noon to see my mother, who I hear is very ill, at which my heart is very sad.

In the afternoon Luellin comes to my house and takes me out to the Miter in Woodstreete, where Mr. Samford, W. Symons and his wife, and Mrs. Scobell. Mr. Mount and Chetwin. Where we were very merry – Luellin being drunk and I being to defend the ladies from his kissing them, I kissed them myself very often with a great deal of mirth. parted very late, they by Coach to Westminster and I on foot.

1. They had forecast recovery and had prescribed nothing: HMC, *Sutherland,* p. 156; *CSPVen. 1659-61,* p. 198.

2. For 78 days' service (at £200 p.a.) as secretary to Mountagu, Admiral of the summer fleet. This was to cover also the wage of Pepys's clerk. PRO, Adm. 20/1, no. 1350.

15. Met very early at our office this morning to pick out the 25 ships which are to be first payd off.[1]

After that, to Westminster and dined with Mr. Dalton in his office, where we had one great Court dish. But our*a* papers not being done, we could [not] make an end of our business till Monday next.

Mr. Dalton and I over the water to our Landlord Vanly, with whom we agreed as to Daltons becoming his tenant. Back to Westminster, where I met with Dr. Castle, who chidd me for some errors in our Privy Seale business; among the rest, for letting the Fees of the six judges pass unpaid.[2] Which I know not what to say to till I speak with Mr. Moore. I was much troubled for fear of being forced to pay*b* the money myself. Called at my father's going home and bespoke mourning for myself for the death of the Duke of Glocester. I found my mother pretty well. So home to bed.

16. *Sunday*. To Dr. Hardys church[3] and sat with Mr. Rawlinson and heard a good sermon upon the occasion of the Dukes death. His text was – "And is there any evil in the city and the Lord hath not done it?"[4]

Home to dinner – having some sport with Wm: who never hath been at Common-prayer before.

After dinner, I alone to Westminster, where I spent my time walking up and down in Westminster Abbey all sermon time

a repl. 'my'   *b* MS. 'paid'

---

1. A bill providing £140,000 for the complete disbandment of the army and paying off part of the navy had been passed on 13 September: *LJ*, xi. 171; 12 Car. II c. 20. The ships were paid as they came into harbour – 17 being still unpaid on 5 December: *CJ*, viii. 243. For Pepys's figures for the 25 ships (£161,132 10s. altogether), see ib., p. 176.

2. The mistake may have been due

to the fact that several judges now appointed had also received appointments to the bench under Charles I or the Interregnum. See E. Foss, *Judges of Engl.*, vii. 3+.

3. St Dionis Backchurch, of which Nathaniel Hardy had recently been made Rector.

4. A loose recollection of Amos, iii. 6.

with Ben. Palmer and Fetters the Wachmaker – who tell me that my Lord of Oxford is also dead of the small-pox. In whom his Family dyes, after 600 years having the honour in their family and name.[1] From thence to the parke, where I saw how far they have proceeded in the pellmell and in making of a river through the parke, which I have never seen before since it was begun.[2] Thence to White-hall garden, where I saw the King in purple mourning for his brother.

So home; and in my way met with Dinah, who spoke to me and told me she hath a desire to speak to [me] about some business when I come to Westminster again – which she spoke in such a manner that I was afeared she might tell me something that I would not hear of our last meeting at my house at Westminster.

Home, it being very dark. There was a gentleman in the poultry had a great and dirty fall over a water-pipe that lay along the Channell.

17. office very earely about casting up the debts of those 25 shipps which are to be paid off – which we are to present to the Comittee of parliament tomorrow.[3]

I did give my wife 15*l* this morning to go to buy mourning things for her and I, which she did. Dined at home and Mr. Moore with me. Afterwards to White-hall to Mr. Dalton and drank in the Seller, where Mr. Vanly according to appointment was.

---

1. The report was mistaken: the Earl (20th in succession since 1142) had smallpox (HMC, *Sutherland*, p. 156), but did not die until 1703, when the main line of the family did indeed become extinct for lack of legitimate male heirs. They had held the title for 500 (not 600) years. In 1625 the succession had been saved only by a second cousin (the 20th Earl's father) who after some difficulty established his right to the title.

2. Work on the new Mall (replacing the old Pall Mall) was probably completed by January 1661, when a keeper was appointed: *CTB*, i. 394. The canal and lake were also made at this time, the water being brought from the Thames. Soldiers were employed in the digging. HMC, *Hastings*, ii. 141; Rugge, i, ff.129*v*, 130*r*.

3. See above, p. 245, n. 1. This committee continued to sit during the parliamentary adjournment (13 September–6 November).

Then forth to see the Prince de Ligne, Spanish Embassador, come in to his audience, which was done in very great State.[1]

That being done, Dalton, Vanly, Scrivener and some friends of theirs and I to the Axe and signed and sealed our writings; and then to the Wine Seller again, where I received 41*l* for my interest in my house, out of which I paid my landlord to Michaelmas next; and so all is even between him and I, and I freed of my poor little house. Home by linke with my money under my arme. So to bed, after I had looked over the things my wife hath bought today; with which being not very well pleased, they costing too much, I went to bed in a discontent.

Nothing yet from Sea, where my Lord and the Princesse is.[2]

18. At home all the morning, looking over my workmen in my house. After dinner, Sir W. Batten, Pen, and myself by Coach to Westminster-hall, where we met Mr. Wayte that belongs to the Treasurer; and so we went up to the Committee of Parliament which are to consider of the debts of the army and navy, and did give in our account of the 25 shipps. Collonell Birch was very impertinent and troublesome.[3] But at last we did agree to fit the accounts of one ship more perfectly for their view within a few days, that they might see what a trouble it is to do what they desire. From thence, Sir Williams both going by water home, I took Mr. Wayte to the Rhenish wine-house and drank with him and so parted.

Thence to Mr. Crews and spoke with Mr. Moore about the business of paying of Baron our share of the dividend.[4] So on foot home, by the way buying a hatt-band and other things for my mourning tomorrow. So home and to bed. ⟨This day I

1. The audience was in the Banqueting House, Whitehall, and the procession consisted of 50 coaches. Accounts in F. Leuridant, *Une ambassade du Prince de Ligne . . .*, pp. 23+; Evelyn; Mundy, v. 120-1; *Merc. Pub.*, 20 September, p. 608. The cavalcade consisted of '16 ritch coaches, one especially comparable to His Majesties, drawne with sixteen faire blacke horses' (Mundy). This was the only audience de Ligne was

given, and it was said that he went away sad to think he was not to be allowed to repeat the splendid occasion: HMC, *Le Fleming*, p. 26.

2. They did not set sail from Holland until the 20/30th.

3. John Birch long remained a vigorous critic of Pepys and of the government's naval administration (e.g. in the debates of 1677-8).

4. Privy seal fees, divided between the clerks and the Lord Privy Seal.

heard that the Duke of Yorke, upon the news of the death of his brother yesterday, came hither by post last night.⟩

19. *office day*. I put on my mourning and went to the office. At noon, thinking to have found my wife in hers, I found that the taylor had failed her, at which I was vexed because of an invitacion that we have to a dinner this day; but after having waited till past one a-clock, I went and left her to put on some other clothes and come after me to the Miter tavern in Woodstreete (a house of the greatest note in London), where I met W. Symons and D. Scobell and their wifes. Mr. Samford, Luelling, Chetwind, one Mr. Vivion, and Mr. White, formerly chaplin to the Lady Protectresse (and still so, and one they say that is likely to get my Lady Francesse for his wife).[1]

Here we were very merry and had a very good dinner – my wife coming after me hither to us. Among*a* other pleasures, some of us fell to Handycapp, a sport that I never knew before, which was very good. We stayed till it was very late and it rained sadly; but we made shift to get coaches and so home and to bed.

20. At home and at the office and in the garden, walking with both Sir Wms. all the morning. After dinner to Whitehall to Mr. Dalton and with him to my house and took away all my papers that were left in my closet; and so I have now nothing more in the house or to do with it. We called to speak

a MS. 'away'

---

1. 'The Lady Protectresse' was Elizabeth, widow of Oliver Cromwell; at her death in 1665 she left her property in the hands of Jeremiah White, who had been chaplain both to her and to her husband: *CSPD 1665–6*, p. 299. Frances was her fourth daughter, who from 1658 until her marriage in 1663 to Sir John Russell, was the widow of Robert Rich. Pepys's story is at variance with that given by Oldmixon, who knew White well. According to him (*Hist. Engl.*, 1730, p. 426), White had paid court to Lady Frances some years before. Discovered on his knees before her by the Protector (who planned to break off the affair), he quickly explained that he was asking permission to marry her gentlewoman, whereupon Oliver had him married to the gentlewoman immediately. The marriage, says Oldmixon, was not very happy and lasted for fifty years.

with my landlord Beale, but he was not within; but spoke with the old woman, who takes it very ill that I did not let her have it,[1] but I did give her an answer. From thence to Sir G. Downing and stayed late there (he having sent for me to come to him), which was to tell me how my Lord Sandwich hath disappointed him of a ship to bring over his child and goods, and made great complaint thereof; but I got him to write a letter to Lawson, which it may be may do the businesse for him, I writing another also about it. While he was writing, his Lady and I had a great deal of discourse in praise of Holland.

By water to the Bridge, and so to Major Harts lodgings in Cannon-streete, who used me very kindly with wine and good discourse, perticularly upon the ill method which Collonell Birch and the Comittee use in disbanding of the army – and the navy; promising the Parliament to save them a great deal of money, when we judge that it will cost the King more then if they had nothing to do with it, by reason of their delayes and scrupulous enquirys into the accounts of both.

Home and to bed.

21. *office day.* There all the morning and afternoon till 4 a-clock. Then to White-hall, thinking to have put up my books at my Lord's, but am disappointed for want of a chest which I have at Mr. Bowyers. Back by water about 8 a-clock; and upon the water saw [the] corps of the Duke of Gloucester*a* brought down Somersett-house stairs to go by water to Westminster to be buried tonight.[2] I landed at the old Swan[3] and went to the Hoope taverne and (by a former agreement) sent for Mr. Chaplin, who with Nich Osborne and one Daniel came to us and there we drank off two or three quarts of wine, which was very good (the drawing of our wine causing a great quarrell in the

a MS. 'Yorke'

---

1. I.e. the lease which Pepys had just sold to Dalton. The 'old woman' was Alice, wife of Francis Beale.

2. He was buried at about midnight in Henry VII's chapel, Westminster Abbey: HMC, *Le Fleming,* p. 26. Funerals, especially of grand

and wealthy personages, were commonly held at night, to the light of torches which were extinguished at the grave.

3. Presumably the stairs of that name, not the Old Swan tavern. (R).

house between the two drawers which should draw us the best, which caused a great deal of noise and falling out till the maister parted them and came up to us and did give us a large account of the liberty that he gives his servants all alike, to draw what wine they will to please his customers); and eat above 200 wallnutts. About 10 a-clock we broake upp. And so home; in my way I called in with them at Mr. Chaplins, where Nich. Osborne did give me a barrell of Samphire[1] and showed me the Keyes of Mardyke fort, which he that was commander of the fort sent him as a token when the fort was demolished;[2] which I was mightily pleased to see and will get them of him if I can.

Home, where I find my boy (my mayd's brother)[3] come out of the country today; but was gone to bed and so I could not see him tonight.

I to bed.

22. This morning I called up the boy to me and find him a pretty well-looked boy, and one that I think will please me.

I went this morning to Westminster by land along with Luellin, who came to my house this morning to get me to go with him to Captain Allen to speak with him for his brother to go with him to Constantinople; but could not find him. We walked on to Fleetstreete, where at[a] Mr. Standings in Salsbury-court we drank our morning draught and had a pickled herring. Among other discourse here, he told me how the pretty woman that I always loved at the beginning of Cheapeside that sells children's coates was served by the Lady Bennett (a famous Strumpet), who by counterfeiting to fall into a swoune upon the sight of her in her shop, became acquainted with her and at last got her ends of her to lie with a gallant that had hired her to Procure this poor soul for him. To Westminster to my Lord's; and there in the house of office vomited up all my breakfast, my stomach

a l.h. repl. s.h. 'we'

---

1. A commonly used pickle.
2. Mardyke, in Flanders (four miles east of Dunkirk), having been taken from the Spaniards in September 1657, the Council of State ordered its fort to be slighted in August 1659:

CSPD 1659-60, p. 142. Sandwich had commanded the naval force at the time of its capture.
3. Jane's brother, Wayneman Birch, who succeeded Will.

being ill all this day by reason of the last night's debauch. Here I sent to Mr. Bowyers for my chest and put up my books and sent them home.[1] And stayed here all day in my Lord's chamber and upon the leads gazing upon Diana, who looked out at a window upon me. At last I went out to Mr. Harpers, and she standing over the way at the gate, I went over to her and appointed to meet tomorrow[a] in the afternoon at my Lord's. Here I bought a hanging jack. From thence by coach home (by the way at the New Exchange I bought a pair of Short black stockings to wear over a pair of silk ones for mourning; and here I met with The. Turner and Joyce[2] buying of things to go into mourning too for the Duke, which is now the mode of all the ladies in towne), where I writ some letters by the post to Hinchingbrooke to let them know that this day Mr. Edwd Pickering is come from my Lord and says that he left him well in Holland and that he will be here within three or four days.

To bed, not well of my last night's drinking yet. I had the boy up tonight for his sister to teach him to put me to bed, and I heard him read, which he doth pretty well.

23. *Lords day.* My wife got up to put on her mourning today and to go to church this morning. I up and set down my Journall for these five days past. This morning came one from my father's with a black cloth coate, made of my short cloak, to walk up and down in. To church, my wife and I with Sir W. Battin, where we heard of Mr. Mills a very good sermon upon these words: "So run that you may obtaine."[3]

After dinner I all alone to Westminster: at White-hall I met with Mr. Pierce and his wife (she newly come forth after childbirth) both in mourning for the Duke of Glocester. She went with Mr. Childe to White-hall Chappell and Mr. Pierce with me to the abby, where I expected to hear Mr. Baxter or Mr. Rowe their farwell sermon in the abby. And there in Mr.

a repl. 'this after'-

---

1. Cf. above, p. 241.
2. Joyce Norton, a cousin of the Turners as well as of Pepys.
3. 1 Cor., ix. 24.

Symons's pewe I sat and heard Mr. Rowe.[1] Before sermon I laughed at the reader, who in his prayer desire[d] of God that He would imprint his word on the thums of our right hands and on the right great toes of our right feet.[2] In the middst of sermon some plaster fell from the topp of the Abbey, that made me and all the rest in our pew afeared, and I wished myself out.

After sermon, with Mr. Pierce to White-hall and from thence to my Lord, but Diana did not come according to our agreement. So calling at my father's (where my wife had been this afternoon but was gone home), I went home.

This afternoon, the King having news of the Princesses being come to Margetts, he and the Duke of Yorke went down thither in Barges to her.

24. *office day.* From thence to dinner by Coach with my wife to my Cozen Scotts – and the company not being come, I went over the way to the Barbers. So thither again to dinner, where was my uncle Fenner and my aunt, my father and mother and others. Among the rest, my Cozen Rich. Pepys, their elder brother, whom I have not seen these fourteen years, ever since he came from New England.[3] It was strange for us to go a-gossiping to her, she having newly buried her child that she was brought to bed of.[4]

I rose from table and went to the Temple church, where I had appointed Sir W. Batten to meet him; and there at Sir Henige Finch, Sollicitor-Generall's Chamber, before him and Sir W. Wilde, Recorder of London (whom we sent for from his chamber), we were sworn Justices of Peace for Middlesex, Essex, Kent, and Southampton; with which Honour I did find my mind mightily pleased, though I am wholly ignorant in the

---

1. Since 1650 an Independent congregation had met in the Abbey, John Rowe being its second minister after 1654. It now moved first to Smithfield, and then to Holborn: I. Boseley, *Ministers of the Abbey Independent Church*, pp. 141+. Richard Baxter, leader of the moderate Puritans, had never been a pastor of this church, but had used its pulpit: M. Sylvester, *Reliq. Baxt.* (1696), bk i,

pt ii. 301–2; R. Baxter, *The vain religion of the formal hypocrite* (1660).

2. See Exod., xxix. 20; also Lev., viii. 23 and xiv. 14.

3. Richard Pepys of Ashen, Essex, eldest son of Richard Pepys, Lord Chief Justice of Ireland (d. 1659), was in Boston, Mass., c. 1634–46. He was the elder brother of Judith Scott.

4. Her infant son had been buried on the 13th.

duty of a Justice of Peace.[1] From thence with Sir Wm to White-hall by water (old Mr. Smith[2] with us) intending to speak with Secretary Nicholas about the augmentacion of our Salarys.[3] But he being forth, we went to the Three Tuns tavern – where we drank awhile, and then came in Collonell Slingsby and another gentleman and sat with us. From thence to my Lord's to enquire whether they have had anything from my Lord or no.

Knocking at the door, there passed by Monsieur L'impertinent, for whom I took a Coach and went with him to a dancing-meeting in Broadstreete, at the house that was formerly the Glasse house (Luke Channell Maister of the Schoole) where I saw good dancing. But it growing late and the room very full of people, and so very hott, I went home.

25. To the office, where Sir W. Batten, Collonell Slingsby, and I sat a while; and Sir R. Ford coming to us about some business, we talked together of the interest of this kingdom to have a peace with Spain and a war with France and Holland[4] – where Sir R. Ford talked like a man of great reason and experience. And afterwards did send for a Cupp of Tee (a China drink) of which I never had drank before) and went away.[5]

Then came Collonell Birch and Sir R. Browne (by a former appointment) and with them from Towre-wharf in the barge belonging to our office we went to Deptford to pay off the ship *Successe*.[6] Which (Sir G. Carteret and Sir W. Penn after-

---

1. It was customary to make the Principal Officers of the Navy justices for the counties in which the royal dockyards were situated. For Pepys's work as a J.P., see below, p. 316; iii. 137. The officers lacked similar powers in the city itself until an act of 1664: below, iv. 82 & n. 1.

2. ? Robert Smith, Navy Office messenger.

3. The new and increased rates of pay fixed at the appointment of the new officers in July were not enrolled in the Exchequer until February 1663. A Council order of 22 September now gave authority for the payment of the higher rates although the process of enrolment was not yet complete: BM, Add. 9314, f.iv.

4. This new policy satisfied the major mercantile interests. Ford was one of the greatest of the merchants trading with Spain.

5. It was imported *via* Holland from c. 1658, but cost c. £2 per lb. The brackets are Pepys's own.

6. The *Old Success*, in harbour since November 1658 and now paid off at a cost of £3228: PRO, Adm. 20/1, p. 107. Cf. *Merc. Pub.*, 11 October, p. 645. Col. John Birch and Sir Richard Browne were two of the parliamentary commissioners appointed to disband the forces.

wards coming to us) we did, Collonell Rich[1] being a mighty busy man and one that is the most indefatigable and forward to make himself work of any man that ever I knew in my life. At the globe we had a very good dinner, and after that to the pay again; which being finished, we returned by water again. And I from our office with Collonell Slingsby by Coach to Westminster (I setting him down at his lodgings by the way) to enquire for my Lord's coming thither (the King and the Princesse coming up the River this afternoon as we were at our pay); and I find him gone to Mr. Crews, where I find him well; only, had got some brush upon his foot which was not well yet. My Lord told me how the ship that brought the Princesse and him (the *Tredagh*) did knock six times upon the Kentish Knock, which put them in great fear for the ship; but got off well. He told me also how the King hath knighted Vice-admirall Lawson and Sir Rich. Stayner.[2] From him late, and by Coach home – where the playsterers being at work in all the rooms in my house, my wife was fain to make a bed upon the ground for her and I; and so there we lay all night.

26. *office day.* That done, to the church, where we did consult about our gallery.[3] So home to dinner, where I found Mrs. Hunt, who brought me a letter[4] for me to get my Lord to sign for her Husband, which I shall do for her.

At home with the workmen all the afternoon, our house being in a most sad pickle.

In the evening to the office, where I fell a-reading of Speeds geography[5] for a while.

So home, thinking to have found Will at home; but he not being come home but gone somewhere else, I was very angry;

1. *Recte* Birch.
2. On the 24th. Stayner had previously been knighted by Cromwell in 1657.
3. See above, p. 230, n. 2.
4. Possibly a certificate of loyalty which John Hunt required in order to keep his job in the Excise: see below, p. 257 & n. 2.

5. John Speed, *A prospect of the most famous parts of the world* (1631), PL 2901 (1); or one of the two excerpts from it (*Theatre of the empire of Great Britain*, PL 2901 (2), and *England, Wales, Scotland and Ireland described and abridged from a farr larger volume*), both of which had been published in several editions by 1660.

and when he came, did give him a very great check for it, and so I went to bed.

27. To my Lord at Mr. Crews and there took order about some business of his; and from thence home to my workmen all the afternoon. In the evening to my Lord's and there did read over with him and Dr Walker my Lord's new commission for Sea and advised thereupon how to have it drawn. So home and to bed.

28. *office day*. This morning Sir W. Batten, Collonell Slingsby, went with Collonell Birch and Sir Wm Doyly to Chattam to pay off a ship there.[1] So only Sir W. Pen and I left here in town.

All the afternoon at home among my workmen; work till 10 or 11 at night; and did give them drink and were very merry with them – it being my luck to meet with a sort of Drolling workmen upon all occasions. To bed.

29. All day at home to make an end of our dirty work of the playsterers; and indeed, my Kitchin is now so handsome that I did not*a* repent of all the trouble that I have been put to to have it done.

This day or yesterday I hear Prince Robt. is come to Court; but welcome to nobody.[2]

30. *Lords day*. To our parish church both forenoon and afternoon, all alone.

At night went to bed without prayers, my house being everywhere foule above-stairs.

a l.h. repl. s.h. 're'-

---

1. The *Hound*: PRO, Adm. 20/1, p. 107.

2. Prince Rupert, first cousin of Charles II, had in the Civil War and afterwards quarrelled with Charles I and most of the royalists, including Hyde. Since 1654 he had absented himself from Court. The King now gave him an annuity (which ran from this day) but nothing else: *CSPD 1660-1*, p. 355. He was not admitted to the Privy Council until April 1662.

1. Early to my Lord to White-hall; and there he did give me some work to do for him and so with all haste to the office.

Dined at home, and my father by chance with me. After dinner he and I advised about hangings for my rooms, which are now almost fit to be hung,[1] the painters beginning to do their work today.[2]

After dinner he and I to the Miter, where with my uncle Wight (whom my father fetched thither), while I drank a glass of wine privately with Mr. Mansell (a poor Reformado of the *Charles*) who came to see me.

Here we stayed and drank three or four pints of wine and so parted.

I home to look after my workmen; and at night to bed.

The Comissioners are very busy disbanding of the army, which they say doth cause great robbing.[3] My layings out upon my house in Furniture are so great that I fear I shall not be able to go through them without breaking one of my bags of 100*l*, I having but 200*l* yet in the world.

2. With Sir W. Pen by water to White-hall – being this morning visited before I went out by my brother Tom, who told me that for his lying out-of-doors a day and a night my father hath forbid him to come any more into his house – at which I was troubled and did soundly chide him for doing so; and upon confessing his fault, I told him I would speak to my father.

1. Wallpapers were not widely used until well on into the 18th century. Cf. below, pp. 261, 269.

2. William Brewer's bills (10 November 1660–24 June 1661) for 'divers painted workes' at the Navy Office and at several lodgings there, including Pepys's, are in PRO, Adm. 20/1, pp. 191, 197; ib., 20/2, p. 106.

They amount to over £50. Pepys's house was clear of the painters by Christmas Day.

3. Cf. Rugge (i, f.134*v*): 'Nov. 1660. Great robings of houses and highways in and about London.' Albemarle on 28 August had issued an order forbidding soldiers to create disturbances at theatres: BM, Egerton 2542, f.405*r*.

At White-hall I met with Captain Clerke and took him to the Legg in King-streete and did give him a dish or two of meat, and his purser that was with him, for his old kindness to me on board.[1] After dinner I to Westminster-hall, where I met with Mrs. Hunt and was forced to wait upon Mr. Scawen at a committee to speak for her Husband, which I did.[2] After that met with Luellin and Mr. Fage and took them both to the Dogg and did give them a glass of wine. After that at Wills I met with Mr. Spicer; and with him to the abby to see them at vespers there, where I find but a thin congregacion allready. So that I see religion, be it what it will, is but a humour, and so the esteem of it passeth as other things do. From thence with him to see Robin Shaw, who hath been a long time ill and I have not seen him since I came from Sea. He is much changed, but in hopes to be well again. From thence by Coach to my father's and discoursed with him about Tom and did give my advice to take him home again, which I think he will do in prudence rather then put him upon learning the way of being worse.

So home; and from home to Major Hart, who is just going out of towne tomorrow and made much of me and did give me the oaths of Supremacy and allegiance – that I may be capable of my arreares.[3]

So home again, where my wife tells me what she hath bought today; *viz*, a bed and furniture for her chamber, with which, very well pleased, I went to bed.

3. With Sir W. Batten and Pen by water to White-hall, where a meeting of the Dukes of Yorke and Albermarle, my Lord Sandwich and all the Principal Officers, about the Winter gard; but we determined of nothing.

From thence to my Lord's, who sent a great iron chest to White-hall; and I saw it carried into the King's closet, where I saw most incomparable pictures. Among the rest, a book open

---

1. During the voyage to Holland: see, e.g., above, p. 104.
2. Robert Scawen, whom Pepys knew well as a commissioner for disbanding the forces, had been recently appointed one of the commissioners for regulating the Excise. John Hunt either now or shortly afterwards held a sub-commissionership under him.
3. The pay due to him as secretary to Sandwich's regiment.

upon a deske which I durst have sworn was a reall book, &c.[1]

Back again to my Lord and dined all alone with him, who doth treat me with a great deal of respect. And after dinner did discourse an houre with me and advise about getting of some way to get himself some money to make up for all his great expenses – saying that he believed he might have anything that he would ask of the King.

This day Mr. Sheply and all my Lord's good[s] came from sea – some of them laid at the Wardrobe and some brought to my Lord's house.

From thence to our office, where we met and did business: and so home and spent the evening looking upon the painters that are at work in my house.

This day I heard the Duke speak of a great design that he and my Lord of Pembrooke have, and a great many others, of sending a venture to some parts of affrica to dig for gold=ore there. They entend to admit as many as will venture their money, and so make themselfs a company. 250*l* is the lowest share for every man. But I do not find that my Lord doth much like it.[2]

At night Dr Fairebrother (for so he is lately made of the Civil law) brought home my wife by Coach, it being rainy weather, she having been abroad today to buy more furniture for her house.

4. *Thursday.* This morning I was busy looking over papers at the office all alone. And being visited by Lieutenant Lambert of the *Charles* (to whom I was formerly much beholden to),[3]

1. The King's Closet contained some of the most important and highly prized small pictures in the reconstituted royal collection. The inventory of Charles II's pictures (MS., c. 1667; in the office of the Surveyor of the Queen's Pictures) lists some 160 pictures, drawings and miniatures in this room (nos 305-465 in the section ff. 18-26 dealing with Whitehall). The illusionist picture is presumably *A picture of a book upon the closet door*, recorded in James II's collection: *Cat. of the collection . . . belonging to King James the Second*

(1758), p. 12, no. 136. It was later at Kensington Palace, but is not recorded in the inventories of the royal collection after 1714. (OM).

2. The Royal African Company, incorporated 18 December 1660, consisted of the Duke of York and 31 others; Pembroke was the chairman of the governing body. Sandwich (with William Coventry and Carteret) became a member. C. T. Carr (ed.), *Select charters of trading companies, 1530-1707*, pp. 172-7.

3. On the Baltic voyage, 1659.

I took him along with me to a little alehouse hard by our office, whither my Cozen Tho. Pepys the Turner had sent for me to show me two Gentlemen that had a great desire to be known to me, the one his name is Pepys, of our family, but one that I never heard of before, and the other a younger son of Sir Tho. Bendishes,[1] and so we all called Cosins.

After sitting awhile and drink[ing], my two new Cosins, myself and Lieutenant Lambert went by water to White-hall; and from thence I and Lieutenant Lambert to Westminster Abbey, where we saw Dr Fruen[2] translated to the Archbishopric of Yorke.

Here I saw the Bishops of Winchester, Bangor, Rochester, Bath and Wells, and Salisbury,[3] all in their habitts, in King Henry the 7ths chappell. But Lord, at their going out, how people did most of them look upon them as strange Creatures, and few with any kind of love or Respect.

From thence we two to my Lord's, where we took Mr. Sheply and W. Howe to the Rayne Deare and had some oysters, which were very good, the first I have eat this year. So back to my Lord's to dinner; and after dinner Lieutenant Lambert and I did look upon my Lord's Modell,[4] and he told me many things in a ship that I desired to understand.

From thence by water, I (landing Lieutenant Lambert at Black-friars) went home and there by promise met with Rob. Shaw and Jack Spicer, who came to see me; and by the way I met upon Tower hill with Mr. Pierce the surgeon and his wife and took them home and did give them good wine, ale, and anchoves. And stayed them till night, and so adieu.

Then to look upon my paynters that are now at work in my house. At night to bed.

---

1. Sir Thomas Bendish, until 1660 ambassador at Constantinople; his aunt had married Pepys's great-uncle, John Pepys of Cottenham. He had five sons.

2. Accepted Frewen, formerly Bishop of Coventry and Lichfield.

3. I.e. Brian Duppa (recently translated from Salisbury), William Roberts, John Warner, William Pierce and Humphrey Henchman. The last-named was a bishop-designate, not being consecrated until 28 October.

4. A ship model. For Pepys's collection of them, see below, iii. 163 & n. 1.

5. *Office day.* Dined at home; and all the afternoon at home to see my paynters make an end of their work, which they did today to my content; and I am in great joy to see my house likely once again to be cleane.   At night to bed.

6.   All this morning Collonell Slingsby and I at the office getting a Catch ready for the Prince de Ligne to carry his things away today, who is now going home again.[1]

About noon comes my Cosen H. Alcock, for whom I wrote a letter for my Lord to sign to my Lord Broghill for some preferment in Ireland, whither he is is now a-going.

After him comes Mr. Creed, who brought me some books from Holland with him, well bound[2] and good books, which I thought he did entend to give me, but I find that I must pay him.

He dined with me at my house; and from thence to Whitehall together, where I was to give my Lord an account of the Stacions and Victualls of the fleet in order to the choosing of a fleet fit for him to take to sea to bring over the Queene.[3]

But my Lord not coming in before 9 at night, I stayed no longer for him, but went back again home and so to bed.

7.   *Lordsday.*   To White-hall on foot, calling at my father's to change my long black Cloake for a short one (long cloaks being now quite out); but he being gone to church, I could not get one, and therefore I proceeded on and came to my Lord before he went to Chappell; and so went with him, where I heard Dr. Spurstow[4] preach before the King a poor dry sermon; but a very good Anthemne of Captain Cookes afterwards.

Going out of the Chappell, I met with Jack Cole my old friend (whom I had not seen a great while before), and have promised to renew acquaintance in London together.   To my Lord's and dined with him; he all dinner time talking French to me and telling me the story how the Duke of Yorke hath got my Lord Chancellors daughter with child, and that she doth lay it to him,

---

1. For de Ligne's embassy, see above, p. 237 & n. 1. For his departure, see *CSPVen. 1659–61*, p. 207.

2. Cf. above, p. 140 & n. 2.

3. The Queen Mother, Henrietta-Maria.

4. William Spurstowe, a leading Presbyterian minister; recently made chaplain to the King. This was the only occasion on which he preached in the Chapel Royal: M. Sylvester, *Reliq. Baxt.* (1696), bk i, pt ii. 229.

and that for certain he did promise her marriage and had signed it with his blood, but that he by stealth had got the paper out of her Cabinett. And that the King would have him to marry her, but that he will not.[1] So that the thing is very bad for the Duke and them all; but my Lord doth make light of it, as a thing that he believes is not a new thing to the Duke to do abroad.[a] Discoursing concerning what if the Duke should marry her, my Lord told me that among his father's many old sayings that he had writ in a book of his,[2] this is one: that he that doth get a wench with child and marries her afterward it is as if a man should shit in his hat and then clap it upon his head.

I perceive my Lord is grown a man very indifferent in all matters of Religion, and so makes nothing of these things.

After dinner to the Abby, where I heard them read the church-service, but very Ridiculously, that endeed I do not in my mind like it at all. A poor cold sermon of Dr. Lambs, one of the Prebends, in his habitt, came afterwards; and so all ended. And by my troth a pitiful sorry devocion it is that these men pay.

So walked home by land. And before supper I read part of the Maryan persecution in Mr. Fuller.[3] So to supper, prayer, and to bed.

8. *office day*. And my wife being gone out to buy some household stuff, I dined all alone. And after dinner to Westminster, in my way meeting Mr. Moore coming to me, who went back again with me, calling in several places about business: at my father's about gilded leather for my dining room, at Mr. Crews about money, at my Lord's about the same; but meeting not Mr. Sheply there, I went home by water and Mr. Moore with me, who stayed and supped with me till almost 9 at night. We love one another's discourse, so that we cannot part when we do meet.

a l.h. repl. s.h. 'br'-

---

1. Much of this is fabrication. Anne Hyde had secretly married the Duke at her father's house on 3 September; a son was born on 22 October. The Duke had entered a contract of marriage in November 1659. Sandwich was using French in front of the servants. For the public acknowledgement of the marriage, see below, p. 320 & n. 4.

2. Untraced.

3. Thomas Fuller, *The church-history of Britain*, bk viii; PL 2437 (1656 ed.).

He tells me that the profit of the Privy Seale is much fallen – for which I am very sorry.   He gone, and I to bed.

9.   This morning, Sir W. Batten with Collonell Birch to Deptford to pay off two ships.   Sir W. Pen and I stayed to do business, and afterward together to White-hall, where I went to my Lord and found him in bed not well.   And saw in his chamber his picture,[2] very well done; and am with child[a] till I get it copyed out, which I hope to do when he is gone to sea.

To White-hall again, where at Mr. Coventrys chamber I met with Sir W. Pen again, and so with him to Redriffe by water and from thence walked over the fields to Deptford (the first pleasant walk I have had a great while); and in our way had a great deal of merry discourse, and find him to be a merry fellow and pretty good-natured and sings very bawdy songs.

So we came and find our Gentlemen and Mr. Prin at the pay.

About noon we dined together and were very merry at table, telling of tales.

After dinner to the pay of another ship[3] till 10 at night.   And so home in our barge, a clear Moone-shine night and it was 12 a-clock before we got home – where I find my wife in bed and part of our chambers hung today by the Upholster; but not being well done, I was fretted, and so in a discontent to bed.

I find Mr. Prin a good honest, playne man, but in his discourse not very free or pleasant.

Among all the tales that passed among us today, he told us of one Damford, that being a black* man did scald[b] his beard with mince-pye, and it came up again all white in that place and so continued to his dying day.   Sir W. Pen told us a good jest about some Gentlemen blinding of the drawer, and who he cached was to pay the recko[n]ing.   And so they got away, and the master of the house coming up to see what his man did, his man got hold of him, thinking it to be one of the Gentlemen, and told him that he was to pay the reckoning.

a lower corner of page blotted　　　　　*b* repl. 'slald'

---

1. The *Griffin* and the *Hector*: PRO, Adm. 20/1, pp. 108, 109.
2. The portrait by Lely; for the portrait and Pepys's copy, see below,

p. 271 & n. 1.   (OM).
3. Probably the *Great President*: PRO, Adm. 20/1, pp. 108-9.

10. *office day* all the morning. In the afternoon with the Upholster seeing him do things to my mind; and to my content he did fit my chamber and my wife's. At night comes*ª* Mr. Moore and stayed late with me to tell me how Sir Hards: Waller (who only pleads guilty), Scott, Cooke, Peters, Harrison, &c. were this day arraigned at the bar at the Sessions-house, there being upon the bench the Lord Mayor, Generall Monke, my Lord of Sandwich, &c.; such a bench of noblemen as hath not been ever seen in England.¹

They all seem to be dismayed and will all be condemned without Question. In Sir Orland. Brigeman's charge, he did wholly rip up the unjustnesse of the war against the King from the beginning, and so it much reflects upon all the Long Parliament; though the King hath pardoned them, yet they must hereby confess that the King doth look upon them as traytors.²

Tomorrow they are to plead what they have to say. At night to bed.

11. In the morning to my Lord's, where I met with Mr. Creed, and with him and Mr. Blackburne to the Rhenish wine-house – where we sat drinking of healths*ᵇ* a great while, a thing which Mr. Blackburne formerly would not upon any terms have done.³ After we had done there, Mr. Creed and I to the Leg in King-street to dinner, where he and I and my Will had a good udder to dinner; and from thence to walk in St. James's Park – where we observed the several engines at work to draw up water, with which sight I was very much pleased.

Above all the rest, I liked best that which Mr. Greatorex

a l.h. repl. s.h. 'Mr.'   *b* l.h. preceded by blot and s.h. 'healths'

---

1. Sir Hardress Waller and 31 other regicides had been indicted before a grand jury of Middlesex on the previous day at Hicks's Hall; on this day began their trial at the Session House (Old Bailey) before a commission of oyer and terminer. Two (not one, as Pepys states) pleaded guilty – Waller and George Fleetwood: *State Trials* (ed. Howell), v. 998, 1005. The Lord Mayor was Sir Thomas Aleyn.

2. The charge given to the grand jury on the day before by Sir Orlando Bridgeman, Lord Chief Baron of the Exchequer, is printed in *State Trials*, v. 988–94. He was concerned to prove that levying war against the King's authority (as well as against the King himself) was treason. He did not mention the Long Parliament directly.

3. Puritans objected to the drinking of healths as a pagan custom.

brought, which is one round thing going within all with a pair
of stairs round;*a* which being laid at an angle of 45 doth carry
up the water with a great deal of ease.[1] Here in the park we met
with Mr. Salsbury, who took Mr. Creed and me to the Cockpitt[2]
to see *The Moore of Venice*, which was well done.[3] Burt acted the
Moore; by the same token, a very pretty lady that sot by me
cried to see Desdimona smothered.

From thence with Mr. Creed to Hercles pillers, where he and
I drank; and so parted and I went home.

12. *office day* all the morning. And from thence with Sir
Wm Batten and the rest of the officers to a venison pasty of his
at the Dolphin, where dined withal Collonell Washington, Sir
Edw. Brett and Major Norwood, very noble company.[4] After
dinner I went home, where I found Mr. Cooke, who told me
that my Lady Sandwich is come to town today, whereupon I
went to Westminster to see her; and found her at supper, so she
made me sit down all alone with her; and after supper stayed and
talked with her – she showing most extraordinary love and
kindness and did give me good assurance of my Uncles resolution
to make me his heire.[5] From thence home and to bed.

a 'round' repeated

1. Probably a version of the Archi-
medean screw – a wooden spiral tube
consisting of a worm inside a cylinder.
Cf. the fire-engine worked by 'a
sucking-worm': J. Houghton, *Coll.
for improvement of husbandry and
trade*, 9 August 1695 (engravings in PL
2972, pp. 76–7, 78). For the improvements being made at this time in the
gardens and the lake, see above, p.
246; and cf. *CTB*, i. 693. Ralph
Greatorex was an inventor and mathematical instrument maker.
2. In Drury Lane. From 8 October until 4 November 1660 this
theatre was used by a new troupe

known as His Majesty's Comedians,
including Mohun, Hart, Clun and
Cartwright from the Red Bull
Theatre and Burt, Betterton and
Kynaston from the former Cockpit
company. (A).
3. Cast in Downes, pp. 6–7. The
play was Shakespeare's *Othello*, which
had been acted in 1604 and published
in 1622. (A).
4. All three were officers high in
the King's favour.
5. Robert Pepys lived at Brampton
near Hinchingbrooke, whence Lady
Sandwich had just returned.

13. To my Lord's in the morning, where I met with Captain Cuttance. But my Lord not being up, I went out to Charing-cross to see Major-Generall Harrison hanged, drawn, and quartered – which was done there – he looking as cheerfully as any man could do in that condition.[1] He was presently cut down and his head and his heart shown to the people, at which there was great shouts of joy. It is said that he said that he was sure to come shortly at the right hand of Christ to judge them that now have judged him. And that his wife doth expect his coming again.[2]

Thus it was my chance to see the King beheaded at White-hall[3] and to see the first blood shed in revenge for the blood of the King at Charing-cross. From thence to my Lord's and took Captain Cuttance and Mr. Sheply to the Sun taverne and did give them some oysters. After that I went by water home, where I was angry with my wife for her things lying about, and in my passion kicked the little fine Baskett which I bought her in Holland and broke it, which troubled me after I had done it.

Within all the afternoon, setting up shelfes in my study. At night to bed.

14. *Lords day.* early to my Lord's, in my way meeting with Dr. Fairebrother, who walked with me to my father's back again; and there we drank our morning draught, my father being gone to church and my mother asleep in bed. Here he caused me to put my hand, among a great many Honourable hands, to a paper or Certificate on his behalfe.[4]

To White-hall Chappell, where one Dr Crofts made an in-different sermon and after it an anthemne, ill sung, which made the King laugh. Here I first did see the Princesse Royall since she came into England. Here I also observed how the Duke of Yorke and Mrs. Palmer did talke to one another very wantonly

1. Thomas Harrison, the regicide, had been condemned on the 11th. Cf. his hagiographer: he was 'mighty cheerful to the astonishment of many': *The speeches and prayers of Maj. Gen. Harrison . . .* (1660), p. 6. Secretary Nicholas reported that he died 'under a hardness of heart that created horror in all who saw him': *CSPD 1660–1*, p. 312.
2. The views attributed to Harrison and his wife were commonly attributed to all Fifth-Monarchists.
3. See below, p. 280.
4. An ex-royalist, he was job hunting. Cf. also above, p. 69 & n. 1.

through the hangings that parts the King's closet and the closet where the ladies sit.

To my Lord's, where I found my wife; and she and I did dine with my Lady (my Lord dining with my Lord Chamberlain), who did treat my wife with a very great deal of respect.

In the evening we went home through the rain by water in a sculler, having borrowed some coates of Mr. Sheply.   So home wet and dirty, and to bed.

15. office all the morning. My wife and I by water; I landed her at White-friers, who went to my father's to dinner, it being my father's wedding day, there being a very great dinner and only the Fenners and Joyces there. ⟨This morning Mr. Carew was hanged and quartered at Charing-Crosse – but his Quarters by a great favour are not to be hanged up.⟩[a1]

I was forced to go to my Lord's to get him to meet the officers of the Navy this afternoon, and so could not go along with her. But I missed my Lord, who was this day upon the bench at the Sessions-house. So I dined there and went to White-hall, where I met with Sir W. Batten and Pen, who with the Comptroller, Treasurer, and Mr. Coventry (at his Chamber) made up a list of such ships as are fit to be kept out for the Winter guard[2] – and the rest to be paid off by the Parliament when they can get money, which I doubt will not be a great while.

That done, I took Coach and called my wife at my father's; and so homewards, calling at Tho. Pepys the Turner's for some things that we wanted.   And so home, where I fell to read *The fruitlesse precaution* (a book formerly recommended by[b] Dr Clerke at sea to me),[3] which I read in bed till I had made an end of it and do find it the best-writ tale that ever I read in my life.   After that done, to sleep, which I did not very well do because that

a   addition crowded into bottom of page   *b*   l.h. repl. s.h. 'to'

---

1. John Carew was a regicide, but also (being a republican and a Fifth-Monarchist) an opponent of Cromwell. The Commons had only by a small majority excepted him from the Act of Indemnity, and now, after his condemnation and execution, his

quarters were granted to his brother and given decent burial that night.

2. Thirty-five are listed in PRO, Adm. 2/1745, f.11r.   Large ships were unable to ride out the winter seas.

3. See above, p. 135 & n. 2.

my wife, having a stopping in her nose, she snored much, which I never did hear her do before.

16. This morning my Brother Tom came to me, with whom I made even for my last Cloathes to this day. And having eaten a dish of anchoves with him in the morning, my wife and I did entend to go forth to see a play at the Cockpitt[1] this afternoon; but Mr. Moore coming to me, my wife stayed at home and he and I went out together, with whom I called at the upholsters and several other places that I have business with; and so home with him and from thence to the Cockpitt, where understanding that *Wit without money*[2] was acted, I would not stay, but went home again by water, by the way reading of the other two stories that are in the book that I read last night, which I do not like so well as that.

Being come home, Will told me that my Lord hath a mind to speak with me tonight; so I returned by water, and coming there, it was only to enquire how the ships were provided with Victualls that are to go with him to fetch over the Queen,[a][3] which I gave him a good account of.

He seemed to be in a melancholly humour, which I was told by W. Howe was for that he hath lately lost a great deal of money at cards, which he fears he doth too much addict himself to nowadays. So home by water and to bed.

17. *office day.* At noon comes Mr. Creede to me, whom I took along with me to the feathers in Fishstreete, where I was invited by Captain Cuttance to dinner – a dinner made by Mr. Dawes and his brother. We have two or three dishes of meat well done. Their great designe[b] was to get me concerned in a business of theirs about a vessel of theirs that is in the service, hired by the King,[4] in which I promise to do them all the service

a followed by blot   *b* l.h. repl. s.h. 'dis'-

---

1. In Drury Lane. (A).
2. A comedy by John Fletcher, first acted c. 1614 and published in 1639. (A).
3. See above, p. 260.
4. Probably the *Seaflow* ketch of

50 tons, hired on 24 June 1660 at £18 per month, of which Henry Dawes was part-owner. But she was not released until February 1662. PRO, Adm. 20/3, p. 76.

I can. From thence home again with Mr. Creed; where I finding Mrs. The Turner and her aunt Dike, I would not be seen but walked in the garden till they were gone. Where Mr. Spong came to me. They being gone and Mr. Creed, Mr. Spong and I went to our Musique to sing; and he being gone, my wife and I went to put all my books in order in [my] closet, and I to give her her books. After that to bed.

18. This morning, it being expected that Collonell Hacker and Axtell should die, I went to Newgate but found that they were reprieved till tomorrow.[1] So I to my aunt Fenners, where with her and my uncle I drank my morning draught. So to my father's and did give order for a pair of black bayes linings to be made me for my breeches against tomorrow morning, which was done.

So to my Lord's, where I spoke with him and he would have had me dine with him; but I went thence to Mr. Blackburnes, where I met my wife and my Will's father and mother (the first time that ever I saw them),[2] where we have a very fine dinner. Mr. Creed was also there. This day, by her high discourse, I find Mrs. Blackburne to be a very high Dame and a Costly one.

Home with my wife by Coach. This evening comes Mr. Chaplin and N. Osborne[3] to my house, of whom I made very much and kept them with me till late, and so to bed.

At my coming home, I find that The Turner hath sent for a pair of Doves that my wife hath promised her. And because she did not send them in the best Cage, she sent them back again with a Scornefull letter with which I was angry, and yet pretty well pleased that she was crossed.

---

1. Col. Francis Hacker and Col. Daniel Axtel had been condemned as regicides on the 15th. Hacker had commanded the guard at the King's execution; Axtel at his trial: *State Trials* (ed. Howell), v. 1146–85. The reprieve was possibly ordered out of consideration for Hacker's relatives, some of whom were royalists and were allowed the disposal of his body: *CSPD 1660–1*, pp. 316, 339,

494. Peter Mundy (v. 126) says that it was because the 18th was St Luke's day.

2. Thomas Hewer, of St Sepulchre's parish, was a stationer who supplied the Navy Office.

3. Both were concerned with navy victualling. Francis Chaplin was a provision merchant and Osborne was (now or later) clerk to Denis Gauden, the navy victualler.

19. office in the morning. This morning my Dining room was finished with greene Serge hanging and gilt leather, which is very handsome.[1]

This morning Hacker and Axtell were hanged and Quarterd, as the rest are.[2]

This night I sat up late to make up my accounts ready against tomorrow for my Lord; and I find him to be above 80*l* in my debt, which is a good sight and I bless God for it.

20. This morning one came to me to advise with me where to make me a window into my cellar in lieu of one that Sir W. Batten had stopped up; and going down into my cellar to look, I put my foot into a great heap of turds, by which I find that Mr. Turners house of office is full and comes into my cellar, which doth trouble me; but I will have it helped.[3]

To my Lord's by land, calling at several places about business. Where I dined with my Lord and Lady; where he was very merry and did talk very high how he would have a French Cooke and a Master of his Horse,[4] and his lady and child to wear black paches; which methought was strange, but he is become a perfect Courtier; and among other things, my Lady saying that she would have a good Merchant for her daughter Jem, he answered that he would rather see her with a pedlar's pack at her back, so she married a Gentleman rather then that she should marry a Citizen.

This afternoon, going through London and calling at Crowes the upholster in Saint Bartholmew.- I saw the limbs of some of our new Traytors set upon Aldersgate, which was a sad sight to see; and a bloody week this and the last have been, there being

1. The serge would be for curtains and the gilt leather for the walls.

2. Of these two only Axtel's body was quartered: *Merc. Pub.*, 25 October, p. 674.

3. Water-closets had not yet been adopted even by the well-to-do. They are said to have been invented by Sir John Harington (a godson of Queen Elizabeth who published books on the subject), but required a good water-supply and elaborate plumbing. Lawrence Wright, *Clean and decent*, passim, esp. pp. 71-3.

4. On 15 November Lady Sandwich was to hire a French maid, and not long afterwards Sandwich had a suit costing £200 made in France for the coronation (below, ii. 83) and appointed Ferrer as his Master of the Horse. For the spread of French influences, see C. Bastide, *Anglo-French entente in 17th cent.*, ch. iv.

ten hanged, drawn, and Quarterd.[1] Home; and after writing a letter to my Uncle by the post, I went to bed.

21. *Lords day.* To the Parish church in the morning, where a good sermon by Mr. Mills.

After dinner to my Lord's, and from thence to the Abby, where I met with Spicer and D. Vines and others of the old Crew:[2] so leaving my boy at the abby against I came back, we went to Prices by the Hall back-doore; but there being no drink to be had,[3] we went away; and so to the Crowne in the Palace-yard[a] – I and George Vines by the way calling at their house, where he carried me up to the top of his turret, where there is Cookes head set up for a traytor, and Harrison's on the other side of Westminster hall. Here I could see them plainly, as also a very fair prospect about London. From the Crowne to the Abbey to look for my boy, but he is gone thence; and so he being a novice, I was at a loss what was become of him. I called at my Lord's (where I found Mr. Adams, Mr. Sheply's friend) and at my father's, but found him not. So home, where I found him; but he had found the way home well enough, of which I was glad. So after supper and reading of some chapters,[4] I went to bed. This day or two my wife hath been troubled with her boyles in the old place, which doth much trouble her.

Today at noon (God forgive me), I strung my Lute, which I have not touched a great while before.

22. *office day.* After that to dinner at home upon some ribbs of roast beef from the Cookes (which of late we have been forced to do because of our house being alway under the painters' and other people's hands, that we could not dress it ourselfs): after dinner to my Lord's, where I find all preparing[b] for my Lord's going to sea to fetch the Queene tomorrow.

At night my Lord came home, with whom I stayed long and talked of many things. Among others, I got leave of him to

a followed by blot   *b* l.h. repl. s.h. 'pre'-

---

1. Cf. *Merc. Pub.*, 25 October, p. 677; Mundy, v. 126–7.

2. Exchequer colleagues.

3. Perhaps because it was service-time: cf. above, p. 54 & n. 1.

4. Of the Bible: see above, p. 206, n. 2.

have his picture, that was done by Lilly, coppyed.[1] And talking of religion, I find him to be a perfect Sceptique, and said that all things would not be well while there was so much preaching, and that it would be better if nothing but Homilys were to be read in churches.[2]

This afternoon (he told me), there hath been a meeting before the King and my Lord Chancellor of some Episcopalian and Presbyterian Divines; but what hath passed he could not tell me.[3]

After I had done talk with him, I went to bed with Mr. Sheply in his Chamber, but could hardly get any sleep all night, the bed being ill-made and he a bad bedfellow.

23. We rise early in the morning to get things ready for my Lord. And Mr. Sheply going to put up his pistolls (which were charged with bullets) into the Holsters, one of them flew off. And it pleased God, that the mouth of the gun being downward, it did us no hurt; but I think I never was in more danger in my life. Which put me into a great fright.

About 8 a-clock my Lord went; and going through the garden, my Lord met with Mr. Wm. Mountagu, who told him of an estate of land lately come into the King's hand, that he hath a mind my Lord should beg.[4] To which end, my Lord writ a

1. Lely had already painted at least two portraits of Sandwich; this was probably the portrait (head and shoulders in black, wearing the insignia of the Garter) later at Hinching-brooke. The copyist was Emanuel de Critz: see below, pp. 290, 292, 301. The copy was bought at the Pepys Cockerell sale of 1848 by Lord Braybrooke and is now at Audley End: R. J. B. Walker, *Audley End . . . Cat. of the pictures* (1954), p. 7. De Critz made a repetition from Pepys's copy (below, p. 292), and copies of the design are not uncommon, e.g. in the National Portrait Gallery (609). (OM).

2. A common view among the upper classes. The homilies issued by royal authority (2 vols, 1547, 1571; PL 2376 [1673 ed.]) enjoined political obedience, and were used as substitutes for sermons by parsons not licensed to preach.

3. The conference at Worcester House, resulting in the issue of the King's Declaration of 25 October: see below, p. 278. The meeting had been broken up by the news that the Duchess of York was in labour, and none of the participants seems to have been sure what had been agreed on.

4. On 2 November a warrant was issued for the grant to Sandwich of the manors of Liveden and Church-field, Northants.: *CSPD 1660–1*, p. 351.

letter presently to my Lord Chancellor[1] to do it for him; which (after leave taken of my Lord at White-hall bridge)[2] I did carry to Warwick-house to him and have a fair promise of him that he would do it this day for my Lord. In my way thither I met the Lord Chancellor and all the Judges riding on Horse back and going to Westminster Hall, it being the first day of the Terme – which was the first time I ever saw any such Solemnity.[3]

Having done there, I returned to White-hall; where meeting with my Brother Ashwell and his Cosen Sam. Ashwell and Mr. Mallard, I took them to the Leg in King-street and gave them a dish of meat for dinner and paid for it. From thence going to White-hall, I met with Catau. Stirpin in mourning, who told me that her Mistress was lately dead of the small-pox and that herself was now married to Monsieur Petit, as also what her mistress hath left her, which was very well.[4] She also took me to her Lodging at a Ironmongers in King-streete – which was but very poor; and I find by a letter that she showed me of her Husbands to the King that he is a right Frenchman and full of their own projects (he having a design to reforme the Universitys and to institute Schooles for the learning of all languages, to speak them naturally and not by rule), which I know will come to nothing.[5]

From thence to my Lord's, where I went forth by Coach to Mrs. Packer's with my Lady and so to her house again. From thence I took my Lord's picture and carried it to Mr. De Cretz to be copied.

So to White-hall, where I met Mr. Spong[6] and went home with him and played and sang, and eat with him and his mother.

---

1. Presumably a mistake for 'my Lord Chamberlain', the Earl of Manchester (Sandwich's cousin) who lived at Warwick House.
2. The public pier and landing stairs for the palace. (R).
3. The procession, later discontinued because of Clarendon's gout, was revived by Shaftesbury, but only once, in 1673, allegedly because of the judges' indifferent horsemanship: Louise F. Brown, *Shaftesbury*, p. 217.

4. Elizabeth Pye, her mistress, had left her the sum of £200, her wearing apparel and her linen.
5. Nothing appears to be known of this proposal. For methods of teaching languages, see K. Lambley, *Teaching of French language*. Pepys's scepticism about Frenchmen derived perhaps from experience of his father-in-law's projects.
6. John Spong, mathematical instrument maker.

After supper we looked over many books and instruments of his, especially his Wooden Jack in his Chimny that go with the Smoak; which indeed is very pretty.

I find him to be as ingenious and good-natured a man as ever I met with in my life and cannot admire him enough, he being so plain and illiterate a man as he is.

From thence by Coach home and to bed – which was welcome to me after a night's absence.

24. I lay and slept long today. *Office day.* I took occasion to be angry with my wife before I rise about her putting up of half a crowne of mine in a pepper box, which she hath forgot where she hath lain it. But we were friends again, as we are always. Then I rise to Jack Cole, who came to see me. Then to the office. So home to dinner – where I find Captain Murford, who did put 3*l* in my hands for a friendship I have done him; but I would not take it, but bid him keep it till he hath enough to buy my wife a necklace.[1]

This afternoon, people at work in my house to make a light in my yard into my sellar.

To White-hall; in my way met with Mr. Moore who went back with me.

He tells me among other things that the Duke of Yorke is now sorry for his lying with my Lord Chancellor's daughter, who is now brought to bed of a boy.[2]

From White-hall to Mr. De Cretz, who I find about my Lord's picture. From thence to Mr. Lilly's;[3] where not finding Mr. Spong, I went to Mr. Greatorex, where I met him; and so to an alehouse, where I bought of him a drawing pen and he did show me the manner of the Lamp glasses, which carry the light a great way. Good to read in bed by and I intend to have one of them.

So to Mr. Lillys with Mr. Spong; where well received, there

1. William Murford was a timber merchant and entrepreneur. He was soon to offer Pepys a share in a light-house project (below, ii. 41) and from the beginning of his acquaintance with Pepys had pressed gifts on him (e.g. above, p. 177). The diary records no gift of a necklace by him to Mrs Pepys.

2. Charles, Duke of Cambridge, b. 22 October; d. 5 May 1661.

3. William Lilly, astrologer, of the Strand.

being a Clubb there tonight among his friends – among the rest, Esquire Ashmole,[1] who I find a very ingenious Gentleman; with him we two sang afterward in Mr. Lillys study. That done, we all parted and I home by Coach, taking Mr. Booker[2] with me – who did tell me a great many fooleries what may be done by Nativitys; and blaming Mr. Lilly for writing to please his friends and to keep in with the times (as he did formerly to his owne dishonour) and not according to the rules of Art, by which he could not well erre, as he hath done.[3]

I set him downe at Limestreete end; and so home, where I found a box of Carpenters tooles sent by my Cozen Tho. Pepys, which I have bespoake of him for to imploy myself with some-times.

To bed.

25. All the day at home, doing something in order to the fitting of my house.

In the evening to Westminster about business: so home and to bed. This night the vault at the end of my Sellar was emptyed.[4]

26. *office*.

My father and Doctor[a] Tho. Pepys dined at my house, the last of whom I did almost fox with Marget ale. My father is mightily pleased with my ordering of my house. I did give him money to pay several bills.

a l.h. repl. s.h. 'my'

---

1. Elias Ashmole, antiquary and herald; a friend of Lilly and much concerned with astrology, who had this day taken up his duties as a Comptroller of the Excise for London: C. H. Josten (ed.), *Ashmole*, ii. 800.

2. John Booker, astrologer.

3. Lilly was mercenary by his own confession (see his *Hist. of his life and times*, 1822, esp. p. 88), and was sus-pected of having been in the pay of every successive government of the past twenty years. Certainly his popular annual almanacks successfully adjusted themselves to each change

of *régime*. He claimed, however, that the government pension he had been given in 1648 was for only two years, and for foreign intelligence, not astrological prophecy: op. cit., pp. 145–6. In 1660 his almanacks lay under some disrepute because of his failure to foresee any of the changes in English government in 1659–60, or the defeat and death of his foreign patron, Charles Gustavus of Sweden.

4. Turner, Pepys's neighbour, charged the Navy Treasury on 26 October with 31s. 7d. for this opera-tion: PRO, Adm. 20/1, p. 133.

After that, I to Westminster to White-hall, where I saw the Duc de Soissons[1] go from his audience with a very great deal of state. His own coach all red velvet, covered with gold lace, and drawn by six barbes, and attended with 20 pages very rich in clothes.

To Westminster-hall and bought, among other books, one of the Life of our Queene. Which I read at home to my wife; but it was so sillily writ that we did nothing but laugh at it: among other things, it is dedicated to that Paragon of virtue and beauty, the Duchesse of Albemarle.[2]

Great talk, as if the Duke of Yorke doth now own the marriage between him and the Chancellor's daughter.

27. In London and Westminster all this day, paying of money and buying of things for my house.

In my going, I went by chance by my new Lord Mayors house (Sir Rd. Browne) by goldsmiths hall, which is now in fitting; and endeed, it is a very pretty house.[3]

In coming back, I called at Pauls churchyard and there I bought Alsted, *Encyclopædia*,[4] which cost me 38*s*.

1. *Recte* the Comte de Soissons, French ambassador-extraordinary sent to congratulate Charles II on his restoration. The audience had been held in the Banqueting House of Whitehall; he was now returning to Somerset House. Other descriptions in *Parl. Intell.*, 29 October, p. 702; Rugge, i, f.131r.

2. John Dauncey, *The history of the thrice illustrious Princess Henrietta Maria de Bourbon, Queen of England*, just published, was inscribed to 'the Paragon of Vertue and Beauty, her Grace, the Dutchesse of Aubemarle'. The epistle dedicatory ended with the prayer 'that the Rising Sun of your Graces Vertues and Honours may still soar higher, but never know a declension'. The rest of the book was in similar style. Not in the PL. To most people (including Pepys) the Duchess was a slut.

3. Before the building in the 18th century of the Mansion House as an official residence for the Lord Mayor, each kept his mayoralty in his own house or in one acquired for it. Browne kept his in Camden House, Maiden Lane (now Gresham St), north of Goldsmiths' Hall, then or later the house of Ald. Sir Thomas Bludworth: Rugge, i, f.125r; Stow, *Survey* (ed. Strype, 1720), bk v. 147. (R).

4. A Latin work compiled by Johann Heinrich Alsted (d. 1638), German Protestant divine and pedagogue; arranged (as was usual until the early 18th century) by subjects, not alphabetically; a very influential encyclopaedia in its day: in Cotton Mather's words, 'a *North-West Passage* to *all the Sciences*': qu. S. E. Morison, *Harvard Coll. in 17th cent.*, i. 158. PL 2523-4 (1st ed., 2 vols, folio, Herborn 1630) may be the copy here referred to.

Home and to bed – my wife being much troubled with her old pain.[1]

28. *Lords day*.

There came some pills and plaisters this morning from Dr. Williams for my wife.

I to Westminster Abbey, where with much difficulty going round by the Cloysters, I got in, this day being a great day for the Consacrating of five Bishopps, which was done after sermon;[2] but I could not get into Hen. 7. chappell, so I went to my Lord's where I dined with my Lady and my young Lord and Mr. Sidny[3] (who was sent for from Twicknham yesterday to see my Lord Mayors show tomorrow); Mr. Childe did also dine with us.

After dinner to White-hall Chappell; my Lady and my Lady Jemimah and I up to the King's Closet (who is now gone to meet the Queene); so meeting with one Mr. Hill,[4] that did know my Lady, he did take us into the King's closet and there we did stay all the service time – which I thought a great honour.[5]

We went home to my Lord's lodgings afterward; and there I parted with my Lady and went home – where I did find my wife pretty well after her Phisique.   So to bed.

29.[a]   I up earely, it being my Lord Mayors day[6] (Sir Rich.

a   blot in MS.

---

1. See above, p. 213, n. 2.
2. The first consecration of bishops since 1644. The service was conducted by Brian Duppa, Bishop of Winchester; the preacher John Sudbury, Prebendary of Westminster. The new bishops were those of London (Sheldon), Salisbury (Henchman), Worcester (Morley), Lincoln (Sanderson) and St Asaph (Griffith). After further consecrations in the following December and January only two sees remained to be filled. J. Sudbury, *Sermon preached at the consecration of . . . Gilbert, Lord Bishop of London . . .* (1660); *Parl. Intell.*, 29 October, p. 702; Rugge, i, f.131r.
3. Sandwich's sons here referred to

were Viscount Hinchingbrooke (whom Pepys has previously called 'Mr Edward' or 'the child') and Sidney, his younger brother.
4. Probably Roger Hill, musician of the Chapel Royal.
5. Admission to the King's Closet (where the royal entourage assembled before proceeding into chapel) was in theory limited to peers, privy councillors, and gentlemen of the bedchamber: BM, Stowe 562, f.7r-v.
6. The date of Lord Mayor's Day was altered from 29 October to 9 November after the calendar reform of 1752, when eleven days were cancelled from the English calendar.

Browne); and neglecting my office, I went to the Wardrobe,
where I met my Lady Sandwich and all the Children. Where
after drinking of some strang*a* and incomparable good Clarett of
Mr. Rumballs,[1] he and Mr. Townsend did take us and set the
young Lords at one Mr. Nevills, a draper in Pauls churchyard;
and my Lady and my Lady Pickering and I to one Mr. Isackson's,
a linendraper at the Key in Cheapside – where there was a company of fine ladies and we were very civilly treated and had a
very good place to see the pageants; which were many and I
believe good for such kind of things but in themselfs but poor
and absurd.[2] After the ladies were placed, I took Mr. Townsend
and Isackson to the next door, a tavern, and did spend 5*s* upon
them. The show being done, with much ado we got as far as
Pauls, where I left my Lady in the coach and went on foot with
my Lady Pickering to her lodging, which was a poor one in
Black-fryers, where she never invited me to go in at all with
her – which methought was very strange for her to do.

So home, where I was told how my lady Davis[3] was now
come to our next lodgings and hath locked up the leads doore
from me, which put me into so great a disquiet that I went to
bed and could not sleep till morning at it.

30. Within all the morning and dined at home, my mind
being so troubled that I could not mind nor do anything till I

a possibly 'strange'

---

1. William Rumbold; he and
Thomas Townshend were officials
of the King's Wardrobe.
2. Described by John Tatham
(author of the verses declaimed on
this occasion) in *The royale oake,
with other various and delightfull scenes
presented on the water and the land,
celebrated in honour of the deservedly
honoured Sir Richard Brown* ... (1660);
reprinted in R. T. D. Sayle, *Lord
Mayors' pageants of the Merchant
Taylers' Co.*, pp. 130+. The tab-
leaux consisted of scenes peopled with
allegorical figures who gave tongue in
verse written for the occasion. They
greeted the Lord Mayor on his progress by water in the morning to the
law courts at Westminster, and on his
progress after the Guildhall dinner
to his house. See F. W. Fairholt,
Lord Mayors' pageants (1843–4); R.
Withington, *Engl. Pageantry*; and cf.
*A calendar of dramatic records in the
books of the Livery Companies of
London, 1485–1640* (Malone Soc.,
Collections, vols iii and v).
3. Wife of John Davis, just appointed clerk to Lord Berkeley of
Stratton, Navy Commissioner.

speak with the Comptroller to whom the lodgings belong. In the afternoon, to ease my mind, I went to the Cockpitt all alone and there saw a very fine play called *The Tamer tamed*,[1] very well acted.

That being done, I went to Mr. Crews, where I had left my boy; and so with him and Mr. Moore (who would go a little way with me home, as he will always do) to the Hercules pillers to drink, where we did read over the King's Declaracion in matters of Religion, which is come out today. Which is very well penned I think; to the Satisfaccion of most people.[2]

So home, where I am told that Mr. Davis's people have broke open the bolt of my chamber door that go upon the leads; which I went up to see and did find it so, which did still trouble me more and more. And so I sent for Griffith[3] and got him to search their house to see what the meaning of it might be; but can learn nothing tonight. But I am a little pleased that I have found this out.

I hear nothing yet of my Lord whether he be gone for the Queene from the Downes or no; but I believe he is, and that he is now upon coming back again.

31. *office day.* Much troubled all this morning in my mind about the business of my walk in the leades. I speak of it to the Comptroller and the rest of the principall officers, who are all un-willing to meddle in anything that may anger my Lady Davis; and so I am fain to give over for the time that she doth continue therein.

1. Designed as a sequel to Shake-speare's *The taming of the shrew*, John Fletcher's comedy, *The woman's prize, or The tamer tamed*, was first acted about 1606 and published in 1647. The theatre was the Cockpit in Drury Lane. (A).

2. *His Majestie's declaration to all his loving subjects . . . concerning ecclesiastical affairs*; issued on 25 October: copy in BM, E 1075 (20), dated 30 October; reprinted in E. Cardwell (ed.), *Doc. annals Church of Engl.* (1844), ii. 285–301; probably written by Hyde, but based, to a remarkable extent, on draft proposals made by the Presbyterians; generally known as the Worcester House Declaration. It promised a limited episcopacy and referred dis-puted points of liturgy and ceremonial to a synod. There is no doubt that it pleased all moderate Presbyterians; see, e.g., below, pp. 282–3. But it came to nothing when the Commons rejected a bill confirming it in the following November.

3. William Griffith (Griffin), door-keeper to the Navy Office.

Dined at home; and after dinner to Westminster-hall, where I met with Billing the Quaker at Mrs. Michells shop, who is still of the former opinion he was of against the Clergymen of all sorts, and a cunning fellow I find him to be.[1] Home, and there I have news that Sir W. Pen is resolved to ride to Sir W. Batten's country house[2] tomorrow and would have me to go with him. So I sat up late, getting together my things to ride in, and was fain to cut a pair of old bootes to make leathers for those that I was to wear. To bed.

This month I conclude with my mind very heavy for the loss of the leades – as also for the greatnesse of my late expenses. Insomuch that I do not think that I have above 150*l* clear money in the world. But I have, I bless God, a great deal of good Houshold stuffe.

I hear today that the Queen is landed at Dover and will be here on Friday next the 2 of November.[3]

My wife hath been so ill of late of her old pain[4] that I have not known her this fortnight almost, which is a pain to me.

1. A government agent wrote of Edward Billing in 1662: 'noe man more busie sturring up and downe, inquyreing after newes then he': *Extracts from State Papers . . . 1654–72* (ed. N. Penney), p. 156.

2. The Rectory Manor House, Church Hill, Walthamstow, Essex. Penn later had a house not far away at Wanstead.

3. The Queen [Mother] had landed at Dover on the 30th. Cf. *CSPD 1660–1*, p. 326.

4. See above, p. 213, n. 2.

1. This morning Sir W. Pen and I were mounted carely. And have very merry discourse all the way, he being very good company.

We came to Sir Wm. Battens, where he lives like a prince, and we were made very welcome. Among other things, he showed us my Lady's closet, where there was great store of rarities. As also a chaire which he calls King Harrys chair, where he that sits down is catched with two irons that come round about him, which makes good sport.[1] Here dined with us two or three more country gentlemen; among the rest, Mr. Christmas my old Schoolfellow, with whom I had much talk. He did remember that I was a great roundhead when I was a boy, and I was much afeared that he would have remembered the words that I said the day that the King was beheaded (that were I to preach upon him, my text should be: "The memory of the wicked shall rot"); but I found afterward that he did go away from schoole before that time.[2]

He did make us good sport in imitating Mr. Case, Ash, and Nye, the ministers[3] – which he did very well. But a deadly drinker he is, and grown exceeding fat. From his house to an alehouse near the church, where*a* we sat and drank and were merry; and so we mounted for London again – Sir W. Batten with us. We called at Bowe and drank there, and took leave of Mr. Johnson of Blackwall,[4] who dined with us and rode with us thus far.

a MS. 'were'

---

1. A variety of joke-chair said to have been invented by Pope Paul V, and associated by Evelyn with Italian 'treachery' rather than, as here, with Henry VIII: Evelyn, ii. 254 & n. 3. Cf. the chair 'with an engine' in John Ford's *The broken heart*, IV, 4.

2. Pepys had been present at the King's execution: above, p. 265.

The text is a loose recollection of Prov., x. 7.

3. Thomas Case and Simeon Ashe were leading Presbyterians, Philip Nye one of the most prominent Independents; all were well-known London preachers. Mimicry of preachers was a favourite game.

4. Henry Johnson, shipbuilder.

So home by moone-light, it being about 9 a-clock before we got home.

2. office. Then dined at home, and by chance Mr. Holliard[1] called at dinner-time and dined with me – with whom I have great discourse concerning the cure of the King's evil, which he doth deny altogether any effect at all.

In the afternoon I went forth and saw some silver bosses put upon my new Bible,[2] which cost me 6s-6d the making and 7s. 6d the silver; which with 9s-6d the book, comes in all to 1-3-6 my Bible in all. From thence with Mr. Cooke, that made them, and Mr. Stephens the silversmith to the tavern and did give them a pint of wine. So to White-hall, where when I came I saw the boats going very thick to Lambeth and all the stairs to be full of people: I was told the Queene was a-coming, so I got a sculler for sixpence to carry me thither and back again; but I could not get to see the Queen.[3] So came back and to my Lord's, where he was come and I Supt with him, he being very merry, telling merry stories of the country Mayors how they entertained the King all the way as he came along and how the country gentlewomen did hold up their heads to be kissed by the King, not taking[a] his hand to kiss as they should do. I took leave of my Lord and Lady, and so took coach at White-hall and carried Mr. Childe as far as the Strand, and myself got as far [as] ludgate by all the bonefires, but with a great deal of trouble – and there the Coachman desired that I would release him, for he darst not go further for the fires. So he would have had a shilling or 6d for bringing of me so far; but I had but 3d about me and did give him that. In Pauls churchyard I called at Kirton's; and there they had got a Masse book for me,

a repl. 'giving'

1. Thomas Hollier (Holliard) of St Thomas's Hospital, the surgeon who had operated on Pepys for the stone in 1658.

2. Not in the PL; probably the new edition published this year at Cambridge by John Field, with engravings by John Ogilby.

3. Cf. Rugge, i, f.132v: 'Hir comming was very privett, Lambeth-way wher the Kinge the Queene Duke of York Prince Edward and the rest tooke water att Lambeth and crossed the Thames and all safely arrived at Whitehall.'

which I bought and cost me 12s.   And when I came home, sat
up late and read in it – with great pleasure to my wife to hear
that that she long ago was so well acquainted with.[1]   So to bed.

I observed this night very few bonfires in the City, not above
three in all London for the Queenes coming;   whereby I guess
that (as I believed before) her coming doth please but very few.[2]

3. *Saturday.* At home all the morning.   In the afternoon
to White-hall – where my Lord and Lady were gone to kiss
the Queens hand.

To Westminster-hall where I met with Tom Doling and we
two took Mrs. Lane to the ale-house, where I made her angry
with commending of Tom Newton and her new sweetheart to
be both too good for her – so that we parted with much anger,
which made Tom and I good sport.   So home to write letters
by the post, and so to bed.

4. *Lords day.*   In the morn to our own church, where Mr.
Mills did begin to nibble at the Common Prayer[3] by saying
"Glory*ª* be to the Father," &c after he had read the two psalms.
But the people have beene so little used to it that they could not
tell what to answer.   This Declaracion of the King's[4] doth give

a l.h. repl. l.h. 'Gloria'

---

1. Her parents were Protestant,
but Catholic friends had tried to
convert her in her youth in Paris:
Family Letters, p. 28. She seems to
have given her husband cause to fear
that she was a Catholic in 1668: see
below, 6 December 1668. The missal
which Pepys retained in his library
was a magnificent vellum folio
(*Missale ad usum Sarum*), printed by
Pynson in 1520 (PL 2795). When
accused of being a Papist, in the
Commons' debate of 16 February
1674, Pepys denied ever having had a
Popish book in his house: Grey, ii.
427.

2. According to Rugge (i, f.132*v*),
there were few bonfires because she
had not travelled through the city,
and few knew of her arrival. Richard
Baxter, the Puritan, detected disturbances in the river-tides caused by the
passage across the water of the popish
Queen Mother; 'there were that day
on the *Thames* three Tides in about
Twelve hours, to the common
admiration of the People': M. Sylvester, *Reliq. Baxt.* (1696), bk i, pt ii.
283.

3. Its use was not compulsory until
after the Act of Uniformity (May
1662): cf. above, p. 190, n. 1.

4. See above, p. 278, n. 2.

the Presbyters some satisfaction and a pretence*a* to read the Common Prayer which they could not do before because of their former preaching against it.

After dinner to Westminster, where I went to my Lord; and having spoke with him, I went to the abby, where the first time that ever I heard the organs in a Cathedrall.[1] Thence to my Lord's, where I found Mr. Pierce the Chyrurgeon and with him and Mr. Sheply (in our way calling at the Bell to see the seven Flanders mares that my Lord hath bought lately) to*b* his house, where we drank several bottles of Hull ale. Much company I find to come to her;[2] and cannot wonder at it, for she is very pretty and wanton.

Thence to my father's, where I find my mother in greater and greater pain of the Stone. I stayed long and drank with them, and so home – and to bed. My wife seemed very pretty today, it being the first time that I have given her leave to weare a black patch.[3]

5. *Office day.* Being disappointed of money, we failed of going to Deptford to pay off the *Henriette* today.

Dined at home; and at home all the day and at the office at night, to make up an account of what the debts of 19 of the 25 ships that should have been paid off is encreased since the adjournment of the Parliament – they being to sit again tomorrow.[4] This 5 of November is observed exceeding well in the City; and at night great bonefires and fireworks. At night Mr. Moore came and sat with me, and there I took a book and he did instruct me in many law=notions, in which I took great pleasure. To bed.

6. In the morning with Sir W. Batten and Pen by water to Westminster; where at my Lord's I met with Mr. Creed and

a l.h. repl. s.h. 'pretence'   *b* MS. 'he'

---

1. The Abbey organ was despoiled during the Interregnum; an instrument (? the same) was 'sett up' this month (Rugge, i, f.134*r*); 'Father' Smith repaired and added to an organ there in 1666: A. Freeman, *Father Smith*, p. 3; P. A. Scholes, *Puritans and music*, ch. xv; W. L. Sumner, *The Organ* (1962), pp. 128, 145. (E).

2. Sc. Mrs Pearse.

3. But cf. above, p. 234.

4. Cf. *CJ*, viii. 182.

with him to see my Lord's picture (now almost done); and thence to Westminster-hall, where we found the Parliament met today. And thence, meeting with Mr. Chetwind, I took them to the Sun and did give them a barrel of oysters and have good discourse; among other things, Mr. Chetwind told me how he did fear that this late business of the Duke of Yorke's[1] will prove fatal to my Lord Chancellor.

From thence Mr. Creed and I to Wilkinsons and dined together; and in great haste thence to our office, where we met all commonly,*a* for the sale of two ships by an inch of candle (the first time that ever I saw any of this kind), where I observed how they do invite one another and at last how they all do cry; and we have much to do to tell who did cry last.[2] The ships were the *Indian* sold for 1300*l*, and the *Halfe moone* sold for 830*l*.[3]

Home and fell a-reading of the tryalls of the late men that were hanged for the King's death; and found good satisfaccion in reading thereof.[4]

At night to bed; and my wife and I did fall out about the dog's being put down into the Sellar, which I have a mind to have done because of his fouling the house; and I would have my will. And so we went to bed and lay all night in a Quarrell.

a word uncertain

---

1. His secret marriage (3 September) with the Chancellor's daughter.

2. This was the usual method of auction-sale. A section of wax candle an inch in length was lit for each lot, and the successful bidder was the one who shouted immediately before the candle went out. At 3 September 1662 Pepys has more details. See also John Hollond, *Discourses* (ed. Tanner), pp. 284–5; *N. & Q.*, 17 January 1863, p. 49. Sales of government property were usually advertised in the newspapers and on the Royal Exchange.

3. Both were prizes; the *Indian*

a 4th-rate, and the *Half-Moon* a 5th-rate. For their sale, see PRO, Adm. 106/3520, f.3r (which gives the second price as £850); Adm. 2/1732, f.52r (order of 20 October); below, p. 301. Cf. the Navy Board's report on these and other decayed ships, 4 September: Duke of York, *Mem.* (*naval*), pp. 1–2.

4. Many accounts were published, but this is probably *An exact and most impartial accompt of the . . . trial . . . of nine and twenty regicides* (1660); PL 1430, pp. 1+. Thomason dated his copy 31 October: BM, E 1047 (3).

This night I was troubled all night with a dream that my wife was dead, which made me that I slept ill all night.

7. *office day.* This day my father came to dine at my house; but being sent for in the morning, I could not stay but went by water to my Lord; where I dined with him, and he in a very merry humour (present Mr. Borfett and Childe).[1]

At dinner he, in discourse of the great opinion of the virtue, gratitude (which he did account the greatest thing in the world to him and hath therefore in his mind been often troubled in the late times how to answer his gratitude to the King, who raised his father)[2] did say that that was it that did bring [him] to his obedience to the King. And did also bless himself with his good fortune, in comparison to what it was when I was with him in the Sound – when he darst not owne his correspondence with the King.[3] Which is a thing that I never did hear of to this day before; and I do from this raise an opinion of him to be one of the most secret men in the world – which I was not so convinced of before.

After dinner he bade all go out of the room, and did tell me how the King hath promised him 4000*l* per annum for ever and hath already given him a bill under his hand (which he showed me) for 4000*l* that Mr. Fox is to pay him.[4] My Lord did advise with me how to get this received and to put out 3000*l* into safe hands at use, and the other he will make use of for his present occasion. This he did advise with me about with much Secresy.

After all this he called for the Fiddles and books, and we two and W. Howe and Mr. Childe did sing and play some psalmes of Will. Lawes[5] and some songs. And so I went away.

1. Dr William Child was a musician who taught music to Sandwich; Samuel Borfett later became one of Sandwich's chaplains.

2. Sir Sidney Mountagu, Sandwich's father, had been a royalist in the Civil War. It was James I who had 'raised' him, making him a Master of Requests and a Knight of the Bath in 1616.

3. Cf. above, p. 125 & n. 1.

4. This grant was made to support Sandwich's title. A secretary's warrant for its payment from royal lands was made out on 27 March 1661 (BM, Egerton 2551, f.139*r*), but not until 1663 was it decided from what funds it should be paid: *CSPD 1663–4*, pp. 9, 35, 94, 640; *CTB*, i. 609. Stephen Fox was Comptroller of the King's Household.

5. Henry and William Lawes, *Choice psalmes put into musick for three voices* (1648). (E).

So I went to see my Lord's picture, which is almost done and doth please me very well.

Then to White-hall to find out Mr. Fox; which I did, and did use me very civilly; but I did not see his lady, whom I have so long known when she was a maid, Mrs. Whittle. From thence, meeting my father Bowyer (whom I have not seen a great while), I took him to Harpers and there drank with him. Among other things in discourse, he told me how my wife's Brother hath a horse at grasse with him, which I was troubled to hear, it being his boldnesse upon my scoare.

Home by Coach and read late in the last night's book of Tryalls, and told my wife about her Brothers horse at Mr. Bowyers, who is also much troubled for it – and doth entend to go tomorrow to enquire the truth.

To bed.

notwithstanding this was the first day that the King's proclamacion against Hackny Coaches coming into the streets to stand to be hired, yet I got one tonight to carry me home.[1]

8. This morning Sir Wm. and the Treasurer and I went by barge with Sir Wm. Doyly and Mr. Prin to Deptford to pay off the *Henrietta*,[2] and have a good dinner. I went to Mr. Davys's[3] and saw his house (where I was once before, a great while ago) and I find him a very pretty man. In the afternoon Comissioner Pett and I went on board the Yaght;[4] which endeed is one of the finest things that ever I saw for neatness and room in

1. See *A proclamation to restrain the abuses of hackney coaches in the cities of London, and Westminster, and the suburbs thereof*: Steele, no. 3267; reprinted *N. & Q.*, 6 August 1853, pp. 122–3. It had been issued on 18 October and was to come into effect on 6 November, not on the 7th as Pepys states. London streets, designed for horsemen and pedestrians, were now being blocked by coaches and carts.

2. Her wages amounted to £8190 16s. 1d. and the pay went on from 8 a.m. until 1 a.m. the next day: PRO, Adm. 20/1, p. 109; *Parl. Intell.*, 12 November, p. 735. D'Oyly and Prynne were parliamentary commissioners appointed to supervise the paying-off of the armed forces. Cf. *CSPD 1660–1*, p. 353.

3. John Davis, Storekeeper at Deptford dockyard.

4. The Dutch yacht, *Mary*: see above, p. 222 & n. 1.

so small a vessel. Mr. Pett is to make one to out-do this for the Honour of his country, which I fear he will scarce better.[1]

From thence with him as far as Ratcliffe, where I left him going by water to London; and I (unwilling to leave the rest of the officers) went back again to Deptford; and being very much troubled with a sudden loosenesse, I went into a little alehouse at the end of Ratcliffe and did give a groat for a pot of ale and there I did shit. So went forward in my walk with some men that were going that way a great pace, and in our way we met with many merry seamen that have got their money paid them today.

We sat very late, doing this work and waiting for the tide: it being mooneshine, we got to London before two in the morning. So home, where I found my wife up, who showed me her head, which was very well dressed today, she having been to see her father and mother.

So to bed.

9.   Lay long in bed this morning, though an office day, because of our going to bed late last night. Before I went to my office, Mr. Creed came to me about business; and also Mr. Carter, my old Cambridge friend, came to give me a visit; and I did give them a morning draught in my study. So to the office; and from thence to dinner with Mr. Wivell at the Hoope taverne, where we have Mr. Sheply, Talbott and Adams, Mr. Chaplin and Osborne; and our dinner given us by Mr. Adis and another, Mr. Wine, the King's fishmonger. Good sport with Mr. Talbot, who eats no sort of Fish and there was nothing else till we sent for a neat's tongue.

From thence to White-hall, where I find my Lord hath an organ set up today in his dining-room; but it seems an ugly one, in the form of Bridewell.[2]

---

1. Pepys later concluded that Pett's yacht (the *Catherine*) was 'much beyond the Dutch man's': below, ii. 12.

2. Possibly the organ-case resembled Bridewell Hospital (originally a Tudor royal palace: illust. in E. G. O'Donoghue, *Bridewell Hosp.*, opp. pp. 56, 58).

Thence I went to Sir Harry Wrights, where my Lord was busy at Cards; and so I stayed below with Mrs. Carter and Evans (who did give me a lesson* upon the Lute) till he came downe; and having talked with him at the door about his late business of money, I went to my father's and stayed late, talking with my father about my Sister Pall's coming to live with me if she would come and be as a servant (which my wife did seem to be pretty willing to do today); and he seems to take it very well and entends to consider of it.   Home and to bed.

10.   Up early: Sir W. Batten and I to make up an account of the Wages of the officers and mariners at sea, ready to present to the Committee of Parliament this afternoon.   Afterwards came the Treasurer and Comptroller and sat all the morning with us – till the business was done.

So we broke up, leaving the thing to be writ over fair and carried to Trinity-house for Sir W. Battens hand; which staying very long, I found (as appointed) the Treasurer and Comptroller at White-hall and so we went with a foule copy to the Parliament-house, where we met with Sir Tho. Clerges and Mr. Spry;[1] and after we have given them good satisfaccion, we parted.

The Com[p]troller and I to the Coffee-house, where he showed me the state of his Case; how the King doth owe him above 6000*l*.[2]   But I do not see great likelihood for them to be paid, since they begin already in Parliament to dispute the paying of the just Sea=debts, which were always promised to be paid and will be the undoing of thousands if they be not paid.

So to White-hall to look but could not find Mr. Fox; and then to Mr. Moore at Mr. Crews, but missed of him also.   So to Pauls churchyard and there bought *Montelion*, which this

1. The two M.P.'s appointed by the Commons on the 8th to present the report on the navy's debts. They presented it on the 12th: *CJ*, viii. 179, 182; *Parl. Hist.*, iv. 143–4. See also Duke of York to Navy Board, 9 November: PRO, Adm. 2/1745, f.13r.

2. In May 1660 Slingsby had addressed a petition to the King referring, among other things, to £5,800 owed him by the late King 'for arms delivered': *CSPD 1660–1*, p. 16.

year doth not prove so good as the last was; and so after reading it, I burned it.[1]

After reading of that and the Comedy of *The Rump*,[2] which is also very silly, I went to bed. ⟨This night going home, Will and I bought a goose.⟩[a]

11. *Lords day.* This morning I went to Sir W. Batten's about going to Deptford tomorrow. And so eating some hog's pudding of my Lady's making, of the hog that I saw a-fattening the other day at her house,[3] he and I went to church into our new Gallery (the first time that ever it was used and it not being yet quite finished);[4] there came after us Sir W. Pen, Mr. Davis, and his eldest son. There being no women this day, we sat in the foremost pew and behind us our servants; but I hope it will not be always so, it not being handsome for our servants to sit so equal with us.

This day also did Mr. Mills begin to read all the Common prayer, which I was glad of.

Home to dinner. And then walked to White-hall, it being very cold and foule and rainy weather. I found my Lord at home; and after giving him an account of some business, I returned and went to my father's, where I found my wife. And there we supped and Dr. Tho Pepys (who my wife told me after I was come home that he hath told my Brother Tho that he loved my wife so well that if she have a childe he would never marry, but leave all that he hath to my childe); and after supper

a addition crowded into end of line

---

1. *Montelion, the prophetical almanac for the year 1661* was a skit on astrological prophecies, and on those of William Lilly in particular. Shortlived and anonymous, it has been attributed to John Phillips, Milton's nephew; according to Wood (*L. & T.*, i. 13), this number (the second to appear) was by Thomas Flatman. See Wing, M 2491–2b. Astrologers' almanacks regularly appeared in large numbers in the late autumn, giving their readers (for a few pence) foreknowledge of the

events of the following year. Pepys often read them, and preserved in his library a collection of those issued for 1688: PL 425, 426. For almanacks, see *The Library* (ser. 4), 10/361+; *EHR*, 80/322+.

2. *The Rump, or The mirror of the late times*, a satirical comedy of the Cromwellian *régime* by John Tatham, published in 1660; not in the PL. (A).

3. At Walthamstow: on 1 November.

4. See above, p. 230 & n. 2.

we walked home, my little boy carrying a link and Will leading my wife.

So home and to prayers and to bed.

I should have said that before I got to my Lord's this day I went to Mr. Foxes at White-hall, where I first saw his lady, formerly Mrs. Eliz. Whittle (whom I had formerly a great opinion of and did make an Anagram or two upon her*a* name) when I was a boy. She proves a very fine lady and mother to fine children.

Today I agreed with Mr. Fox about my taking of the 4000*l* of him that the King hath given my Lord.

12. Lay long in bed today. Sir Wm. Batten went this morning to Deptford to pay off the *Wolfe*. Mr. Comptroller and I sat a while at the office to do business; and then I went with him to his house in Limestreete (a fine house and where I never was before); and from thence by Coach (setting down his sister at the new Exchange) to Westminster-hall – where first I met with Jack Spicer and agreed with him to help me to tell money this afternoon. Then to De Cretz, where I saw my Lord's picture finished[1] – which doth please me very well. So back to the hall, where by appointment I met the Comptroller; and with him and three or four Parliament men I dined at Heaven.[2] And after dinner called at Will's on Jack Spicer and took him to Mr. Foxes, who saved me the labour of telling me the money by giving me 3000*l* by content (the other 1000*l* I am to have on thursday next), which I carried by Coach to the Exchequer and put it up in a chest in Spicers office. From thence walked to my father's, where I found my wife (who hath been with my father today buying of a tablecloth and a dozen of napkins of Diaper, the first that ever I bought in my life).

My father and I took occasion to go forth; and went and drank at Mr. Standings, and there discoursed seriously concerning my sister's coming to live with me – which I have much mind for her good to have, and yet I am much afeared of her ill-nature.

a repl. 'his'

---

1. See above, p. 271 & n. 1.   2. For Heaven, see above, p. 31, n. 2.

Coming home again, he and I and my wife, my mother and Pall, went all together into the little Roome, and there I told her plainly what my mind was: to have her come not as a sister in any respect but as a servant – which she promised me that she would, and with many thanks did weep for joy. Which did give me and my wife some content and satisfaccion.

So by coach home and to bed.

The last night, I should have mentioned how my wife and I was troubled all night with the sound of drums in our ears – which in the morning we found to be Mr. Davys's jack. But not knowing the cause of its going all night, I understand today that they have had a great feast today.

13. earely going to my Lord's, I met with Mr. Moore (who was going to my house; and endeed I find to be a most careful, painful, and able man in business) and took him by water to the Wardrobe and showed him all the house; and endeed there is a great deal of roome in it – but very ugly till my Lord hath bestowed great cost upon it.

Thence parting with him – I went to White-hall and there did give my Lord an account of my receiving of some of his money yesterday and how I do advise for his disposing of it, which he likes well.

So to the Exchequer and there took Spicer and his fellow Clarke to the Dogg taverne and did give them a peck of oysters; and so home to dinner. Where I find my wife making of pyes and tarts to try her oven with (which she hath never yet done); but not knowing the nature of it, did heat it too hot and so did a little overbake her things, but knows how to do better another time.

At home all the afternoon. At night made up my accounts*a* of my Sea expences in order to my clearing of my imprest bill of 30*l* which I had in my hands at the beginning of my voyage – which I entend to show to my Lord tomorrow.[1] To bed.

a repl. 'sea'

---

1. Pepys obtained the imprest from Sandwich who had been given £500 by the Navy Treasury: above, pp. 82, 104. Sandwich's accounts (29 July–14 November) were signed on the 14th: Carte 74, f.276r.

14. *Office day*. But this day was the first that we do begin to sit in the afternoons and not in the forenoons.[1]   And therefore I went into Cheapeside to Mr. Beachamp's the goldsmith to look out a piece of plate to give Mr. Fox from my Lord for his favour about the 4000*l* – and did choose a guilt Tankard.   So to Pauls churchyard and bought *Cornelianum Dolium*.[2]   So home to dinner; and after that to the office till late at night; and so Sir W. Pen, the Comptroller and I to the Dolphin, where we found Sir W. Batten (who is seldom a night from hence); and there we did drink a great Quantity of Sack.   And did tell many merry stories, and in good humours we were all.   So home and to bed.

15.   To Westminster; and it being very cold upon the Water, I went all alone to the Sun and drank a draught of mulled White wine.   And so to Mr. de Cretz, whither I sent for J. Spicer (to appoint him to expect me this afternoon at the office with the other 1000*l* from White-hall); and here we stayed and did see him give some finishing touches to my Lord's picture; so that at last it is complete to my mind, and I leave mine with him to copy out another for himself, and took the originall by a porter with me to my Lord's – where I found my Lord within and stayed hearing him and Mr. Childe[3] playing upon my Lord's new Organ – the first time I ever heard it.

My Lord did this day show me the Kings picture which was done in Flanders, that the King did promise my Lord before he ever saw him and that we did expect to have had at sea before the King*ᵃ* came to us.   But it came but today.   And endeed it

a l.h. repl. s.h. 'came'

---

1. This was for the convenience of those members of the Board who were also members of Parliament, which had reassembled on 6 November.

2. A Latin comedy, published in 1638, and variously attributed to Thomas Randolph and Richard Braithwait; described in *European Mag.*, 37 (1800)/343. This copy is probably PL 218 (1). (A).

3. William Child, later organist of St George's Chapel, Windsor, and one of the organists at Whitehall Chapel. (E).

is the most pleasant and the most like him that ever I saw picture in my life.[1]

As dinner was coming to table, my wife came hither and I got her carried into my Lady (who took phisique today and was just now hiring of a French maid that was with her, and could not understand one another till my wife came to interpret): here I did leave my wife to dine with my Lord (the first time that ever he did take notice of her as my wife, and did seem to have[a] a great esteem for her); and did myself walk homewards (hearing that Sir W. Pen was gone before in a coach) to overtake him and with much ado at last did in Fleetestreete; and there I went into him and there was Sir Arnold Brames; and we all three to Sir W. Batten's to dinner, he having a couple of servants married today; and so there was a great number of Merchants and others of good Quality, on purpose after dinner to make an offering, which when dinner was done, we did;[2] and I did give 10*s* and no more, though I believe most of the rest did give more and did believe that I did so too.

From thence to White-hall again by water to Mr. Fox's; and there by two porters I carried away the other 1000*l*. He was not within himself, but of his Kinsman I have it and did give him 4*l* and other servants something.

But whereas I did entend to have given Mr. Fox himself a piece of plate of 50*l*, I was demanded a 100*l* for the fee of the office, at 6*d* a pound – at which I was surprized; but however, I did leave it there till I speak with my Lord.

a repl. 'take'

---

1. A full length, still (1965) in the possession of the Sandwich family (on loan to the Ministry of Works); painted at the end of the Interregnum by an hitherto unidentified artist (Mr David Piper has suggested Simon Luttichuys) and one of the most impressive portraits painted of the King before the Restoration. Roy. Acad., *The age of Charles II* (1960–1, no. 34). Reproduced below, ii. opp. p. 109. (OM).

2. The registers of St Olave's record as the only marriage this day that of Thomas Peake and Martha Webb: *Harl. Soc. Reg.*, 46/275. It was usual for a prosperous householder's friends and neighbours to give 'offerings' of this sort at the marriage of his servants: cf. HMC, *Rep.*, 10/2/80, 81 [1602].

So I carried it to the Exchequer; where at Wills I found Mr. Spicer, and so lodged it in his office with the rest.

From thence, after a pot of ale at Wills, I took boat in the darke and went for all that to the old Swan, and so to Sir W. Battens; and leaving some of the gallants at Cards, I went home.

Where I find my wife much satisfyed with my Lord's courtesy and respect to her.   And so after prayers to bed.

16.   Up earely to my father's, where by appointment Mr. Moore came to me; and he and I to the Temple, and thence to Westminster-hall to speak with Mr. Wm. Mountagu about his looking upon the title of those lands which I do take as Security for 3000*l* of my Lord's money.[1]

That being done, Mr. Moore and I parted; and in the Hall I met with Mr. Fontleroy (my old acquaintance, whom I have not seen in a long time) and he and I to the Swan; and in discourse he seems to be wise and say little, though I know things are changed against his mind.

Thence home by water, where my father, Mr. Snow and Mr. Moore did dine with me.   After dinner Mr. Snow and I went up together to discourse about the putting out of 80*l* to a man which lacks the money and would give me 15*l* per annum for eight years for it – which I did not think profit enough; and so he seemed to be disappointed by my refusal of it.   But I would not now part with my money easily.

He seems to do it as a great favour to me, to offer me to come in upon a way of getting of money which they call Bottummary. Which I do not yet understand, but do believe there may be something in that of great profit.[2]

After we were parted, I went to the office and there we sat all the afternoon.   And at night we went to a barrel of oysters at Sir W. Battens.   And so home, and I to the setting of my papers in order, which did keep me up late.   So to bed.

---

1. See below, p. 310 & n. 2. William Mountagu was Sandwich's principal legal adviser.

2. 'Bottomry' was a form of mortgage (often advertised in the newspapers) in which a shipowner mort-gaged his ship as security for repayment of a loan.   Rates were high because if the ship foundered, the lenders got nothing.   The diary has no trace of any such venture by Pepys.

17. In the morning to White-hall, where I inquired at the Privy Seale Office for a form for a nobleman to make one his Chaplin. But I understanding that there is not any, I did draw up one; and so to my Lord's and there did give him to sign it for Mr. Turner[1] to be his first Chaplin: I did likewise get my Lord to sign my last Sea accounts, so that I am even to this day when I have received the ballance of Mr. Creed.

I dined with my Lady and my Lady Pickering, where her son John dined with us, who doth continue a foole, as he ever was since I knew him. His mother would fain marry him to get a portion for his sister Betty,[2] but he will not hear of it.

Hither came Major Hart this noon, who tells me that the Regiment is now disbanded[3] and that there is some money coming to me for it. I took him to my Lord to Mr. Crews; and from thence with Mr. Sheply and Mr. Moore to the devill tavern, and there we drank. So home and wrote letters by the post: then to my Lyra viall[4] and to bed.

18. *Lords day.* In the morning to our own church, where Mr. Powell (a crooke legged man that went formerly with me to Pauls schoole) preached a good sermon.

In the afternoon too to our own church and my wife with me (the first time that she and my Lady Battin came to sit in our new pew); and after sermon my Lady took us home and there we supped with her and Sir W. Batten and Pen and were much made of – the first time that ever my wife was there. So home and to bed.

19. *office day.* After we have done a little at the office this morning, I went along with the Treasurer in his Coach to White-

---

1. John Turner, Rector of Eynesbury, Hunts. (a living in Sandwich's gift), 1649–89. Formal appointment as chaplain to a nobleman would permit a certain amount of non-residence, by virtue of an act of 1529.

2. 'Well-bred and comely . . . but very fat': below, iv. 308.

3. In Shropshire on 12 November,

its arrears amounting to over £16,000: *Merc. Pub.*, 15 November, p. 727. For Pepys's pay, see below, p. 304.

4. Either his bass viol 'tuned lyraway', or a smaller, specially made instrument. The lyra-viol was distinguished by its tuning. (E)

hall. And in our*ᵃ* way, in discourse do find him a very good-natured man. And talking of those men who now stand condemned for murdering the King, he says that he believes that if the law would give leave, the King is a man of so great compassion that he would wholly acquit them.

Going to my Lord's, I met with Mr. Sheply; and so he and I to the Sun and I did give him a morning draught of Muscadine. And so to see my Lord's picture at De Cretz and he says it is very like him; and I say so too. After that to Westminster-hall, and there hearing that Sir W. Batten was at the Leg in the Palace,¹ I went thither and there dined with him and some of the Trinity-house men who have obtained something today at the House of Lords concerning the Ballast*ᵇ* Office.²

After dinner I went by water to London to the Globe in Cornehill and there did choose two pictures³ to hang up in my house, which my wife did not like when*ᶜ* I came home and so I sent the picture of Paris back again. To the office, where we sat all the afternoon till night. So home; and there came Mr. Beachamp to me with the gilt tankard,⁴ and I did pay him for it 20*l.* So to my Musique and sat up late at it. And so to bed, leaving my wife to sit up till 2 a-clock that she might call the wench up to wash.

20. About 2 a-clock my wife wakes me and comes to bed; and so both to sleep and the wench to wash.

I rise and with Will to my Lord's by land, it being a very hard frost and the first we have had this year. There I stayed

a repl. 'his'   *b* l.h. repl. s.h. ? 'quarry'   *c* repl. 'when'

---

1. I.e. in New Palace Yard. (R).
2. On this day the Lords confirmed to Trinity House their right to provide 'lastage and ballastage' to ships in the Thames, without prejudice to the lawsuit then pending: *LJ*, xi. 188. The monopoly of digging gravel from the river eastwards of London Bridge and of selling it as ships' ballast was a valuable one, and since the Restoration Trinity House's possession of it had been challenged by the executors

and assigns of William Mountjoy, a patentee: BM, Egerton 2542, f.478r. In 1663 the dispute was settled in favour of the corporation. HMC, *Rep.*, 8/1/sect. 1. 249*b*–254*b*; *CSPD 1661–2*, p. 415: ib., *1662–3*, p. 134; *LJ*, xi. 60.
3. Probably engravings; bought from John Cade, stationer in Cornhill. (OM).
4. See above, p. 292.

with my Lord and Mr. Sheply, looking over my Lord's accounts and to set matters straight between him and Sheply. And he did commit the viewing of those accounts to me – which was a great joy to me to see that my Lord doth look upon me as one to put trust in.[1]

Then to the Organ, where Mr. Childe and one Mr. Mackworth (who plays finely upon the viallin) were playing, and so we played till dinner. And then dined – where my Lord in a very good humour and kind to me.

After dinner to the Temple, where I met Mr. Moore and discoursed with him about the business of putting out my Lord's 3000*l*; and that done, Mr. Sheply and I to the new Play-house near Lincolnes Inn fields (which was formerly Gibbons's tennis-court), where the play of *Beggers' bush*[2] was newly begun. And so we went in and saw it. It was well acted (and here I saw the first time one Moone,[3] who is said to be the best actor in the world, lately come over with the King); and endeed it is the finest play-house, I believe, that ever was in England.

From thence, after a pot of ale with Mr. Sheply at a house hard by, I went by link home, calling a little by the way at my father's and my uncle Fenner's, where all pretty well. And so home, where I found the house in a washing pickle; and my wife in a very joyful condition when I told her that she is to see the Queene next Thursday.

Which puts me in mind to say that this morning I found my Lord in bed late, he having been with the King, Queene, and Princesse at the Cockpitt[4] all night, where Generall Monke treated them; and after supper, a play – where the King did put a great affront upon Singleton's Musique, he bidding them

---

1. Although no longer Sandwich's principal man of business in London, Pepys continued to audit his accounts until Sandwich's death. Shipley was steward at Hinchingbrooke.

2. *The beggar's bush*, a comedy by Fletcher and Massinger; acted in 1622 and published in 1647. The theatre was the Theatre Royal, Vere St, at which Thomas Killigrew's King's

Company played from 8 November 1660 to the beginning of May 1663. During this period Pepys generally refers to it as 'the Theatre'. (A).

3. Michael Mohun; he probably played Goswin: Genest, i. 337. (A).

4. The private royal theatre in Whitehall Palace; one of the earliest references to its use for plays after the Restoration. (A).

stop and bade the French Musique play[1] – which my Lord says doth much out-do all ours.

But while my Lord was rising, I went to Mr. Foxes and there did leave the Gilt Tankard for Mrs. Fox; and then to the Counting-house to him, who hath invited me and my wife to dine with him on Thursday next, and so to see the Queene and Princesses.

21. Lay long in bed. This morning my Cosen Tho. Pepys the Turner sent me a Cupp of Lignum vitæ for a token. This morning my wife and I went to Paternoster-Rowe and there we bought some greene watered Moyre for a morning wastcoate. And after that we went to Mr. Cades to choose some pictures for our house. After that my wife went home and I to Popes head[2] and bought me an aggat heafted knife which cost me 5s. So home to dinner; and so to the office all the afternoon. And at night to my viallin (the first time that I have played on it since I came to this house) in my dining roome; and afterwards to my Lute there – and I took much pleasure to have the neighbours come forth into the yard to hear me.

So downe to supper and sent for the barber, who stayed so long with me that he was locked into the house and we were fain to call up Griffith to let him out. So up to bed, leaving my wife to wash herself[3] and to do other things against tomorrow to go to Court.

22. This morning came the Carpenters to make me a door at the other side of my house, going into the Entry – which I was much pleased with.

---

1. For French influences in English music, see R. North (ed. Rimbault), p. 99 n.; id. (ed. Wilson), pp. 300, 349; J. A. Westrup, *Purcell*, p. 27. Some time in 1660–1 Charles instituted a string band (which included John Singleton) in imitation of the French court's '*vingt-quatre violons du Roi*'. The first known reference to them is below, ii. 86. At the above entry Pepys may be referring to a visiting band. (E).

2. Pope's Head Alley, well-known for its cutlers' shops. (R).

3. This may have involved a bath; one of the few occasions on which the subject is mentioned in the diary. A rub-down with a cloth, followed by a sprinkling of scented water, was the usual method employed by women at this period. See Neville Williams, *Powder and paint*, pp. 13, 46; Lawrence Wright, *Clean and decent*, passim.

At noon my wife and I walked to the old Exchange; and there she bought her a white whiske and put it on, and I a pair of gloves; and so we took coach for White-hall to Mr. Foxes – where we found her within, and an alderman of London paying a 1000*l* or 1400*l* in gold upon the table for the King,[1] which was the most gold that ever I saw together in my life.

Mr. Fox came in presently and did receive us with a great deal of respect. And then did take my wife and I to the Queenes presence-Chamber. Where he got my wife placed behind the Queenes chaire and I got into the Crowd;[2] and by and by the Queen and the two princesses came to dinner. The Queen, a very little plain old woman and nothing more in her presence in any respect nor garbe then any ordinary woman. The Princesse of Orange I have often seen before. The Princess Henriettee is very pretty, but much below my expectation[3] – and her dressing of herself with her haire frized short up to her eares[4] did make her seem so much the less to me.

But my wife, standing near her with two or three black paches on and well dressed, did seem to me much handsomer then she.

Dinner being done, we went to Mr. Foxes again, where many gentlemen dined with us, and most princely dinner – all provided for me and my friends; but I bringing none but myself and wife, he did call the company to help to ⟨eate⟩ up so much good

---

1. Probably part of a loan of £100,000 from the city which had just been negotiated: Sharpe, ii. 385–6. Cf. *CTB*, i. 73, 237; *CSPD Add. 1660–85*, pp. 41–2.

2. Members of the royal family dined in semi-public on certain days of the week. The Household Ordinances (c. 1660–70) empowered the gentleman-usher to admit 'Persons of good Fashion and good Appearance that have a desire to see Us at Dinner', and to exclude 'any Inferior, Mean or Unknown People': BM, Stowe 562, ff. 3v, 5v. The King dined at a raised table enclosed by a rail.

3. She was generally held to be charming rather than good-looking. Her slimness was unkindly remarked on by Louis XIV, who (having tastes that were baroque in these matters as in others) asked his brother why he was so anxious to wed the bones of the Holy Innocents. C. H. Hartmann, *The King my brother*, pp. 21–2.

4. A style fashionable in the 1660's: 'corkscrew curls massed on each side above the ears and wired out away from the face. The front hair . . . strained back . . . , and the back hair brushed up . . . and twisted into a small flat "bun" ': Cunnington, p. 181.

victualls.   At the end of the dinner, my Lord Sandwich's health
in the gilt tankard that he did give Mrs. Fox the other day.

After dinner I have notice given me by Will,*a* my man,
that my Lord did enquire for me; so I went to find him, and
met him and the Duke of Yorke in a Coach going towards
Charing-Crosse.   I endeavoured to fallow them, but I could
not; so I returned to Mr. Fox and after much kindness and
good discourse, we parted from thence.

I took Coach for my wife and I homewards; and I light at
the Maypoole in the Strand and sent my wife home.

I to the new playhouse and saw part of *The Traytor* (a very
good Tragedy); where Moone did act the Traytor very well.[1]

So to my Lord's and sat there with my Lady a great while
talking.   Among other things, she took occasion to enquire (by
Madam Dury's late discourse with her) how I did treate my
wife's father and mother.   In which I did give her a good
account.   And she seemed to be very well opinioned of my wife.

From thence to White hall at about 9 at night. And there,
with*b* Loud the page that went with me, we could not get out
of Henry the 8ths gallery into the further part of the boarded*c*
gallery where my Lord was walking with my Lord Ormond.
And we had a key of Sir S. Morland, but all would not do;
till at last, by knocking, Mr. Harrison the Dore=keeper did open
us the door.

And after some talk with my Lord about getting a Katch to
carry my Lord St. Albans goods to France[2] – I parted and went
home on foot, it being very late and dirty.   And so weary to bed.

23.   This morning, standing looking upon the workmen
doing of my new doore to my house – there comes Captain
Straughan the Scott (to whom the King hath given half of the

a repl. 'Will'   *b* repl. 'we'   *c* l.h. repl. s.h. 'Lord'

---

1. *The Traitor*, a tragedy by James
Shirley, acted in 1631 and published
in 1635; now at the TR, Vere St.
Michael Mohun played Lorenzo.
(A).

2. Henry Jermyn, Earl of St Albans,
had been in France as ambassador-
extraordinary since July.

money that the two ships lately sold do bring);[1] and he would needs take me to the Dolphin and give me a glass of wine and a peck of oysters, he and I. He did talk much what he is able to advise the King for good husbandry in his ships – as by ballasting them with lead oare and many other tricks. But I do believe that he is a knowing man in sea business. Home and dined. And in the afternoon to the office, where till late. And that being done, Mr. Creed did come to speak with me and I took him to the Dolphin, where there was Mr. Pierce the Purser and his wife and some friends of theirs. So I did spend a Crowne upon them – behind the barr, they being akinned to the people of the house and this being the house where Mr. Pierce was apprentice.

After they were gone, Mr. Creed and I spent an houre in looking over the account which he doth intend to pass in our office for his Contingencys,[2] which I did advise about and approve or disapprove of as I saw cause.

After an hour being serious at this, we parted about 11 a-clock at [night]; and so I home and to bed – leaving my wife and the maid at their Linnen to get up.

24. To my Lord's. Where after I had done talking with him – Mr. Townsend, Rumball, Blackburne, Creed and Sheply and I to the Renish wine-house; and there I did give them two quarts of Wormwood wine. And so we broke up.

So we parted, and I and Mr. Creed to Westminster-hall and looked over a book or two, and so to my Lord's – where I dined with my Lady – there being Mr. Childe and Mrs. Bochett,[3] who are never absent at dinner there – under pretence of a wooing. From thence I to Mr. De Cretz and did take away my Lord's

---

1. Cf. above, p. 284. The Duke of York's orders to this effect are in PRO, Adm. 2/1745, ff. 16*v*, 20*r*; the other half was to go towards the building of the two royal yachts. Capt. John Strachan ('Honest Strachan') had been navy agent at Leith since before the Civil War.

2. John Creed had been Deputy-Treasurer to Sandwich's fleet in the spring of 1660. Contingency money was a fund for casual expenditure.

3. Probably related to Samuel Borfett, later Sandwich's chaplain. (Pepys spells the name variously.) William Child was a widower.

picture¹ which is now finished for me, and I paid 3*l*-10*s* for it and the frame – and am very well pleased with it and the price.

So carried it home by water, Will being with me. At home I have a fire made in my Closett and put my papers and books and things in order. And that being done, I fell to entering those two good songs of Mr. Lawes, *Helpe, helpe, O helpe* &c. and *O King*ᵃ *of heaven and Hell* in my song book – to which I have got Mr. Childe to set the base to the Theorbo.² And that done, to bed.

25. *Lords day.* In the forenoon I alone to our church. And after dinner I went and ranged about to many churches. Among the rest, to the Temple, where I heard Dr. Wilkins a little (late maister of Trinity in Cambrige); and that being done, to my father's to see my mother, who is troubled much with the Stone. And that being done, I went home, where I have a letter brought me from my Lord to get a ship ready to carry the Queenes things over to France – she being to go within five or six days.³ So to supper and to bed.

26. *Office day.* To it all the morning. And dined at home, where my father came and dined with me – who seems to take much pleasure to have a son that is neat in his house, I being now making my new door into the entry, which he doth please himself much with.

After dinner to the office again and there till night. And that being done, the Comptroller and I to the Miter to a glass of wine – where we fell in discourse of poetry, and he did repeat some verses of his own making, which were very good.

a MS. 'God'

1. See above, p. 271, n. 1. (OM).
2. For these songs, see above, p. 76, n. 2, p. 169, n. 3. Pepys probably had Henry Lawes's *Second book of ayres and dialogues* (1655) containing them, but for accompaniment it provided only unfigured bass-lines. This entry suggests that he was copying them into a MS. book, with accompaniments in tablature for theorbo provided by Child. (E).

3. The Queen Mother was to take Princess Henrietta to France for her marriage to the Duc d'Anjou (later Orleans). They did not in fact leave Whitehall for Portsmouth until 2 January, and because of bad weather and the Princess's illness did not sail until the 25th: *CSPD 1660-1*, pp. 476, 487, 488.

Home; there hear that my Lady Batten hath given my wife a visitt (the first that ever she made her), which pleased me exceedingly. So after supper to bed.

27. To White-hall – where I find my Lord gone abroad to the Wardrobe, whither he doth now go every other morning, and doth seem to resolve to understand and look after that business himself.

From thence to Westminster-hall; and in King-streete, there being a great stop of coaches,[1] there was a falling-out between a drayman and my Lord Chesterfield's coachman, and one of his footmen killed. At the Hall I met with Mr. Creed; and he and I to Hell[2] to drink our morning draught. And so I to my Lord's again, where I find my wife. And she and I dined with him and my Lady and great company of my Lord's friends, and my Lord did show us great respect.

As soon as dinner was done, my wife took her leave and went with Mr. Blackburne and his wife to London to a christening of a Brother's child of his on Tower-hill.

And I to a play – *The Scornfull Lady*.[3]

And that being done, I went homewards and met Mr. Moore, who hath been at my house, and I took him to my father's and we three to Standing's to drink. Here Mr. Moore told me how the House hath this day voted the King to have all the Excize for ever.[4]

This day I do also hear that the Queenes going to France is stopped, which doth like me well, because then the King will be in town the next month, which is my month again at the Privy Seale.[5]

---

1. Traffic-blocks became much commoner in the narrow streets of London with the growth of population, trade and wheeled traffic in the 17th century. See N. G. Brett-James, *Growth of Stuart London*, ch. xvii. Pepys was once held up for 1½ hours: below, ii. 231.

2. An eating-place in New Palace Yard. (R).

3. A comedy by Beaumont and Fletcher, first published in 1616, and now acted by Thomas Killigrew's company at the TR, Vere St. (A).

4. The King was to have half the duties for life, and the other half was settled on the Crown in perpetuity: *CJ*, viii. 193.

5. The office would then be busier (and more profitable): see above, p. 229 & n. 5.

From thence home – where when I came, I do remember that I did leave my boy Waineman at White-hall with order to stay there for me in the Court – at which I was much troubled; but about 11 a-clock at night the boy came home well. And so we all to bed.

28. This morning I went to White-hall to my Lord's, where Major Hart did pay me 23. 14. 09, due to me upon my pay in my Lord's troop at the time of our disbanding – which is a great blessing to have without taking any care*a* in the world for.[1] But now I must put an end to any hopes of getting any more so; but I bless God for this.

From thence with Mr. Sheply and Pinkny to the Sun and did give them a glass of wine and a peck of Oysters for joy of my getting of this money.

So home, where I find that Mr. Creed hath sent me the 11*l*. 05*s*. 00 that is due to me upon the remaynes of account for my sea business[2] – which is also so much clear money to me; and my bill of impresse for 30*l*[3] is also cleared.   So that I am wholly clear as to the Sea in all respects.   To the office and was there till late at night – and among the officers do hear that we may have our Salaryes allowed by the Treasurer,[4] which doth make me very glad and praise God for it.

Home to supper; and Mr. Hater supped with me, whom I did give order to take up my money of the Treasurer[5] tomorrow if it can be had.

So to bed.

29. In the morning, seeing a great deal of foule water come into my parler from under the particion between me and Mr. Davis, I did step thither to him and tell him of it, and did seem

a possibly 'law'

---

1. See above, p. 242 & n. 1.
2. See above, p. 295.
3. Paid on account by Creed on 5 April: above, p. 104.
4. The Lord Treasurer: see above, p. 253 & n. 3. Pepys was to have £350 p.a. instead of £300; see above,

p. 202 & n. 1. The Navy Treasurer's ledger shows the revised figure as early as the first payment, authorised on 29 September: PRO, Adm. 20/1, p. 210, no. 1320.
5. The Navy Treasurer.

very ready to have it stopped. And did also tell me how thiefs did attempt to rob his house last night, which doth make us all afeared.

This noon, I being troubled that the workmen that I have to do my door were called to Mr. Davis away, I sent for them, which Mr. Davis sent to enquire a reason of and I did give him a good one, that they were come on purpose to do some work with me that they had already begun, with which he was well pleased; and I glad, being unwilling to anger him.[a]

In the afternoon Sir W. Batten and I met and did sell the ship *Church* for 440*l*, and we asked 391*l*;[1] and that being done, I went home; and Dr. Petty came to me about Mr. Barlow's money,[2] and I being a little troubled to be so importuned before I have received it and that they would have it stopped in Mr. Fenn's[3] hands, I did force the Doctor to go fetch the letter of Atturny that he hath to receive it,[4] only to make him some labour, which he did bring; and Mr. Hater came along with him from the Treasury with my money for the first Quarter (Michaelmas last) that ever I received for this imployment; so I paid the Doctor 25*l* and had 62*l*. 10*s* for myself and 7*l* 10*s*. to myself also for Will's salary, which I do entend yet to keep for myself.[5]

With this my heart is much rejoiced and do bless Almighty God that he is pleased to send me so sudden and unexpected a payment of my salary so soon after my great disbursements – so that now I hope I am worth 200*l* again.

In a great ease of mind and spirit, I fell about the auditing of Mr. Sheplys last accounts with my Lord, by my Lord's desire. And about that I sat till 12 a-clock at night, till I begun to doate; and so to bed – with my heart praising God for his mercy to us.

a MS. 'them'

---

1. The *Church* was a 5th-rate; recently a hulk at Harwich. According to a letter from the Duke of York to the Board (3 December) she fetched £510: PRO, Adm. 2/1745, f.17*v*.

2. See above, p. 202 & n. 1. William Petty was the social statistician; a fellow mathematician of Barlow's.

3. Paymaster to the Navy Treasurer.

4. 23 July; Pepys kept it among his papers: Rawl. A 174, f.319*r*.

5. £30 p.a. was the normal salary for a Navy Board clerk; Pepys kept the money since Will Hewer was boarding with him. See below, iv. 353. For the payments to Pepys, by warrants of 29 September (£87 10*s*. for himself and £25 for his two clerks Hayter and Hewer), see PRO, Adm. 20/1, nos 1322, 1320.

30. *Office day.* To the office in the morning, where Sir G. Carter[e]t did give us an*a* account how Mr. Holland doth entend to prevail with the parliament that his project of discharging*b* the seamen all at present by tickett and so to promise interest to all men that will lend money upon them at 8 per cent for so long as they are unpaid – whereby he doth think to take away the growing debt, which doth now lie upon the kingdom for*c* lack of present money to discharge the seamen.[1] But this we are troubled at, as some diminucion to us.

I having two barrells of Oysters at home, I caused one of them and some wine to be brought to the inner room in the office, and there the Principal Officers did go and eat them.

So we sat till noon; and then to dinner. And to it again in the afternoon till night.

At home I sent for Mr. Hater and broke the other barrell with him.*d* And did afterward sit down, discoursing of sea tearmes to learn of him. And he being gone, I went up and sat till 12 at night again to make an end of my Lord's accounts – as I did the last night. Which at last I made a good end of; and so to bed.

a l.h. repl. s.h. 'the' *b* repl. symbol rendered illegible
 c repl. 'by' *d* l.h. repl. s.h. 'them'

---

1. John Hollond was an experienced naval official: between 1635 and 1653 he had been in turn Paymaster, Commissioner, and Surveyor. Pepys kept some of his earlier memoranda (1636) on pay-tickets: PL 2875, pp. 273–5. His present scheme came to nothing; additional funds were provided by a tax: see below, p. 308; ii. 18, n. 3.

DECEMBER.

1. *Saturday.* This morning, observing some things to be laid up not as they should be by the girl, I took a broom and basted her till she cried extremely, which made me vexed, but before I went out I left her appeased: and so to White-hall, where I found Mr. Moore attending for me at the Privy Seale. But nothing to do today.

I went to my Lord St. Alban's lodgings and found him in bed talking to a priest (he looked like one) that leaned along over the side of the bed. And there I desired to know his mind about making the Katch stay longer which I got ready for him the other day.[1] He seems to be a fine civil gentleman.

To my Lord's and did give up my audit of those accounts which I have been these two days about, and were well received by my Lord. I dined with my Lord and Lady and we have a venison pasty. Mr. Sheply and I went into London; and calling upon Mr. Pinkny the goldsmith, he took us to the tavern and gave us a pint a wine; and there fell into our company old Mr. Flower and another gentleman, who did tell us how a Scotch Knight was killed basely the other day at the Fleece in Covent-garden – where there hath been a great many formerly killed.[2] So to Paul's churchyard and there I took the little man at Mr. Kirton's[3] and Mr. Sheply to Ringstead's at the Star; and after a pint of wine – I went home, my brains somewhat troubled with so much wine; and after a letter or two by the post, I went to bed.

2. *Lords day.* My head not very well and my body out of order by last night's drinking – which is my great folly. To

---

1. See above, p. 300. St Albans was one of the leading Catholics at court.

2. According to Rugge (i, f.136r) the murderer was a Scotsman named 'Balindin' [Ballantyne] and his victim Sir John 'Gooscall' [? Godshall].

Aubrey remarked in his *Miscellanies* published in 1696, that this tavern 'was very unfortunate for *Homicides*' (p. 31), and that it had become a private house.

3. The hunchback apprentice at Kirton's bookshop: above, p. 53.

church, and Mr. Mills made a good sermon; so home to dinner.
My wife and I all alone to a leg of mutton, the sawce of which
being made sweet, I was angry at it and eat none, but*a* only dined
upon the Marrowbone that we [had] beside.

To church in the afternoon. And after sermon took Tom.
Fuller's *Church History* and read over Henry the 8ths life – in
it.[1] And so to supper and to bed.

3. This morning I took a resolucion to Rise*b* early in the morning; and so I rose by candle, which I have not done all this
winter. And spent my morning in fidling till time to go to the
office. Where Sir G. Carteret did begin again discourse concerning Mr. Hollands proposition, which the King doth take
very ill. And so Sir George, in lieu of that, doth propose that
the seamen shall have half in present money and tickets for the
other half, to be paid in three months after. Which we judge to
be very practicable. After office, home to dinner – where came
in my Cosen Snow by chance, and I have a very good Capon to
dinner. So to the office again till night and so home. And
then came Mr. Davis of Deptford (the first time that ever he
was at my house) and after him Monsieur L'impertinent, who is
to go to Ireland tomorrow and so came to take his leave of me.
They both find me under the barbers hand. But I have a bottle
of good sack in the house and so made them very wellcome.

Mr. Davis sat with me a good while after the other was gone,
talking of his hard usage and of the endeavours to put him out
of his place in the time of the late Comissioners, and he doth
speak very highly of their Corrupcion.

After he was gone, I fell a-reading *Cornelianum Dolium*[2] till
11 a-clock at night, with great pleasure; and after that to bed.

4. To White-hall to Sir G. Carteret's Chamber, where all the
officers met; and so we went up to the Duke of Yorke and he
took us into his Closet and we did open to him our project of

a MS. 'by'　　　*b* word blotted

---

1. Bk v; pp. 163–255 in the folio
edition of 1656.
2. See above, p. 292, n. 2; 'a witty

but indelicate ... comedy': *DNB*,
'Randolph, Thomas'. (A).

stopping the growing charge of the fleet, by paying them in hand one moyety and the other four months hence. This he doth like; and we returned by his order to Sir G. Carteret's chamber, and there we did draw up this design in order to be presented to the parliament. From thence I to my Lord's and dined with him and told him what we have done today.

Sir Tho. Crew dined with my Lord today and we were very merry with Mrs. Bockett, who dined there still, as she hath always done lately.[1] After dinner Sir Tho. and my Lady went to the playhouse to see *The Silent Woman*.[2] I home by water; and with Mr. Hater in my chamber all alone, he and I did put this morning's design into words. Which being done, I did carry it to Sir W. Batten's where I found some gentlemen with him (Sir W. Pen among the rest, pretty merry with drink) playing at Cards; and there I stayed looking upon them till one a-clock in the morning; and so Sir W. Pen and I went away, and I to bed.

This day the parliament voted that the bodies of Oliver, Ireton, Bradshaw, and   [3], should be taken up out of their graves in the abby and drawn to the gallows and there hanged and buried under it.[4] Which (methinks) doth trouble me, that a man of so great courage as he was should have that dishonour, though otherwise he might deserve it enough.

5. This morning the Proposall which I writ the last night I showed to the Officers this morning, and was well liked of. And I wrote it fair for Sir G. Carteret to show to the King; and so it is to go to the Parliament.[5]

I dined at home; and after dinner went to the new Theatre[6] and

1. Cf. above, p. 301, n. 3.

2. See above, p. 171. This performance was evidently given by Thomas Killigrew's company at the TR, Vere St, since Killigrew had the sole right to produce Jonson's plays. See Nicoll, p. 296. (A).

3. Supply 'Pride'.

4. *CJ*, viii. 197; the word used was 'carcases' not 'bodies'. Sentence on these leading regicides was to be executed on 30 January next, the anni-

versary of their crime. All had died before the Restoration, and had recently been attainted by parliament. See below, ii. 24, n. 3; 27, n. 1. The three mentioned had been buried among the kings and queens in Westminster Abbey; Pride, at Nonsuch.

5. A statement of the navy debts was recorded in the *Commons' Journals* for 5 December (viii. 243-4), but this proposal is not mentioned.

6. See above, p. 297, n. 2. (A).

there I saw *The Merry Wifes of Windsor* acted.   The humours
of the Country gentleman and the French Doctor very well done;
but the rest but very poorly, and Sir J. Falstaffe as bad as any.[1]

From thence to Mr. Will Mountagu's chamber to have sealed
some writings tonight between Sir R. Parkhurst and myself,
about my Lord's 2000*l*;[2] but he not coming, I went to my
father's.   And there found my mother still ill of the stone and
hath just newly voided one, which she hath let drop into the
Chimny; and could not*a* find it to show it me.   From thence
home and to bed.

6.   This morning some of the Comissioners of Parliament
and Sir W. Batten went to Sir G. Carteret's office here in town
and paid off the *Chesnutt*.[3]   I carried my wife to White-friers
and landed her there; and myself to White-hall to the Privy
Seale, where abundance of Pardons to seal; but I was much
troubled for it, because that there is no fees now coming for them
to me.[4]   Thence Mr. Moore and I alone to the Legg in King Street
and dined together on a Neats tongue and udder.

From thence by coach to Mr. Crews to my Lord, who told
me of his going out of town tomorrow to settle the Militia in
Huntingtonshire.[5]   And did desire me to lay up a box of some
rich jewells and things that were*b* in it, which I promised to

a MS. 'and'   b MS. 'there'

---

1. Falstaff was probably played by
William Cartwright, one of Thomas
Killigrew's players, who took that
role in I Henry IV: below, 2 November 1667. Shakespeare's comedy was
written c. 1600 and published in 1602
(in a garbled form) and in the 1623
Folio. Unlike so many others of his
plays, this one was not altered for
presentation on the Restoration stage.
(A).

2. A mortgage secured on Sir
Robert Parkhurst's land: above, pp.
285, 294; below, iv. 94. Evelyn
speaks of Parkhurst as a spendthrift:
24 August 1681.

3. PRO, Adm. 20/1, no. 734.
The commissioners were those appointed to pay off the forces. Carteret's office was the Navy Treasury
in Leadenhall St; he also had an
apartment in Whitehall Palace.

4. No fees were charged for many
of the pardons issued by the King at his
restoration.

5. Sandwich had been a Deputy-
Lieutenant for the county since 1643;
his cousin the Earl of Manchester was
Lord-Lieutenant.

do. After much free discourse with my Lord, who tells me his mind as to his enlargeing his family, &c, and desiring me to look him out a Mayster of the horse and other servants,[1] we parted. From thence I walked to Greatorexe's (he was not within); but there I met with Mr. Jonas Moore,[2] and took him to the Five bells and drank a glass of wine and left him. So to the Temple, where Sir R. Parkhurst (as was intended the last night) did seal the writings and is to have the 2000*l* told tomorrow.

From thence by water to Parliament-stayres and there at an alehouse to Doling (who is suddenly to go into Ireland to venture his fortune), Simonds (who is at a great loss for 200*l* present money, which I was loath to let him have; though I could now do it and do love him and think him honest and sufficient, yet loathness to part with money did dissuade me from it), Luellin (who was very drowzy from a doase that he hath got the last night), Mr. Mount and several others; among the rest, one Mr. Pierce, formerly an army=man, who did make us the best sport for songs and stories in a Scoch tone (which he doth very well) that ever I heard in my life. I never knew so good a companion in all my observation.

From thence to the bridge by water, it being a most pleasant mooneshine night, with a waterman that did tell such a company of bawdy stories how once he carried a lady from Putny in such a night as this and she bid him lie down by her, which he did and did give her content; and a great deal more roguery.

Home and found my girle knocking at the door (it being 11 a-clock at night), her mistress having sent her out for some triviall business, which did vex me when I came in; and so I took occasion to go up and to bed in a pett.

Before I went forth this morning, one came to me to give me notice that the Justices of Middlesex do meet tomorrow at Hickes hall[3] and that I, as one, am desired to be there; but I fear I cannot be there, though I much desire it.

7. This morning the Judge-Advocate Fowler came to see me, and he and I sat talking till it was time to go to the office.

---

1. Pepys's friend Robert Ferrer became Master of the Horse.
2. The mathematician.

3. Their sessions-house in Clerkenwell.

To the office – and there stayed till past 12 a-clock; and so I left the Comptroller and Surveyor and went to White-hall to my Lord's.   Where I find my Lord gone this morning to Huntington – as he told me yesterday he would.   I stayed and dined with my Lady, there being Loud the Page's mother there and dined also with us, and seemed to have been a very pretty woman and of good discourse.

Before dinner I examined Loud in his Latin and find him a very pretty boy and gone a great way in Latin.

After dinner I took a box of some things of value that my Lord hath left for me to carry to the Exchequer.   Which I did, and left them with my Brother Spicer – who also hath this morning paid 1000*l* for me by appointment to Sir R. Parkhurst. So to the Privy Seale, where I signed a deadly number of Pardons, which doth trouble me to get nothing by.   Home by water; and there was much pleased to see that my little room is likely to come to be finished soon.

I fell a-reading in Fuller's *history of Abbys*[1] and my wife in *Grand Cyrus*[2] till 12 at night; and so to bed.

8.   To White-hall to the privy Seale.   And thence to Mr. Pierce's Chyrurgeon to tell them that I would call them by and by to go to dinner.   But I going into Westminster-hall, met with Sir G. Carteret and Sir W. Pen (who were in a great fear that we have committed an errour of 100000*l* in our late account given in to the Parliament, in making it too little); and so I was fain to send word to Mr. Pierces to come to my house and also to leave the key of the Chest with Mr. Spicer of the Chest wherein my Lord's money is; and went along with Sir W. Pen by water to the office.   And there with Mr. Huchinson we did find that we were in no mistake.   And so I went to dinner with my wife and Mr. and Mrs. Pierce the Chyrurgeon to Mr. Pierce the Purser (the first time that ever I was at his house), who doth live very

---

1. Thomas Fuller, *Church-hist. Brit.*, bk vi.

2. *Artamène, ou Le grand Cyrus*, the fashionable and interminable novel by Madeleine de Scudéri (d. 1701), leader of the *précieuses*; first published in 1649–53 in ten volumes.   An English translation had been issued in 1653–5 and re-issued in June 1660 (*Trans. Stat. Reg.*, ii. 269) which Pepys later records that he possessed: below, 21 May 1667.   He did not retain any version in the PL.

plentifully and finely. We have a lovely Chine of beef and other good things, very complete – and*ᵃ* drank a great deal of wine. And her daughter played after dinner upon the virginalls, and at night by lanthorne home again; and Mr. Pierce and his wife being gone home – I went to bed, having drank so much wine that my head was troubled – and was not very well all night. And the Winde, I observed, was ris exceedingly this night before I went to bed.[1]

9. *Lords day.* Being called up earely by Sir W. Batten, I rose and went to his house and he told me the ill news that he hath this morning from Woolwich: that the *Assurance* (formerly Captain Hollands ship, and now Captain Stoakes, designed for Guiny and manned and victualled), was by a gust of wind sunk down to the bottom. Twenty men drowned.[2] Sir Wms both went by barge thither to see how things are – and I am sent to the Duke of Yorke to tell him. And by boat, with some other company going to White-hall from the old Swan, I went to the Duke. And first calling upon Mr. Coventry at his Chamber, I went to the Duke's bed-side (who hath sat up late last night and lay long this morning), who was much surprized therewith.

This being done, I went to Chappell and sat in Mr. Blagraves pew and there did sing my part along with another before the King – and with much ease.[3]

From thence going to my Lady, I met with a letter from my Lord (which Andrew hath been at my house to bring me, but missed me) commanding me to go to Mr. Denham to get a man to go to him tomorrow to Hinchingbrooke to Contrive with

---

a preceded by blot

1. Dr D. J. Schove writes: 'This gale (probably from the south-west) was severe all over England. York and Beverley minsters were damaged by it. See *Mirabilis Annus* (1661), pp. 47–8; J. Goad, *Astro-Meteorologica* (1686), p. 293; *Yorks. Arch. Journ.*, 37/142.'

2. The night's storm had taken the ship by surprise; both master and mate were ashore, the guns were not lashed, and many portholes were open. See the report of an enquiry in PRO, Adm. 2/1745, ff. 21*r*, 23*v*; Duke of York, *Mem.* (naval), pp. 10–11. Cf. also *Merc. Pub.*, 13 December, p. 807.

3. Thomas Blagrave was one of the gentlemen of the Chapel Royal; Pepys was singing (? at sight) with the choir. Cf. the similar occasion on 29 December 1661. (E).

him about some alteracions in his house; which I did, and got Mr. Kennard.[1]

Dined with my Lady and stayed all the afternoon with her; and had infinite of talk of all kind of things, especially of beauty of men and women, with which she seems to be much pleased to talk of.

From thence at night to Mr. Kennard and took him to Mr. Denham the Surveyors – where while we could not speak with him, his chief man (Mr. Cooper) did give us a cup of good sack. From thence with Mr. Kennard to my Lady, who is much pleased with him; and after a glass of sack there we parted – having taken order for a horse or two for him and his servant, to be gone tomorrow.

So to my father's, where I sat while they were at supper; and I find my mother below stairs and pretty well.

Thence home, where I hear that the Comptroller hath some business with me, and (with G[r]iffin's lanthorne) I went to him and there stayed in discourse an houre, till late. Among other things, he showed me a design of his, by the King's making an order of Knights of the Sea, to give encouragement for persons of honour to undertake the service of the sea; and he hath done it with great pains and very ingeniously.[2]

So home and to prayers and to bed.

10. Up exceeding early to go to the Comptroller, thinking to have gone with him to White-hall. But he not being up and it being a very fine bright Moonshine morning, I went and walked all alone twenty turns in Cornhill, from gracious-streete corner to the Stockes and back again – from 6 a-clock till past 7 – so long that I was weary: and going to the Controller's, thinking to find him ready, I find him gone. At which I was troubled, and being weary, went home. And from thence with my wife by water to Westminster. And put her to my father Bowyer's

1. John Denham (the poet) was Surveyor-General of the King's Works; Thomas Kennard (Kinward) was Master-Joiner under him. For the alterations, see below, ii. 49 & n. 1. Sandwich had just arranged for five marble mantelpieces to be

brought over from Italy: Carte 73, f.502r.

2. Nothing came of this proposal. Pepys mentions it again, in the 1680's, in his *Naval Minutes* (pp. 52–3, 90, 117–18).

(they being newly come out of the country); but I could not stay there, but left her there. I to the hall and there met with Collonell Slingsby: so hearing that the Duke of Yorke is gone down this morning to see the ship sunk yesterday at Woolwich, he and I returned by his Coach to the office. And after that to dinner. After dinner he came to me again and sat with me at my house. And among other discourse, he told me that it is expected that the Duke will marry the Lord Chancellor's daughter at last. Which is likely to be the ruine of Mr.*ᵃ* Davis and my Lord Barkely,[1] who have carried themselfs so high against the Chancellor – Sir Ch. Barkely swearing that he and others have lain with her often, which all believe to be a lie.[2]

He and I in the evening to the Coffee-house in Cornhill, the first time that ever I was there. And I find much pleasure in it through the diversity of company – and discourse.

Home and find my wife at my Lady Battens, and have made a bargain to go see the ship sunk at Woolwich, where both the Sir Wms. are still, since yesterday. And I do resolve to go along with them. From thence home and up to bed – having first been in my study; and to ease my mind did go to cast up how my cash stands, and I do find, as near as I can, that I am worth in money clear 240*l* – for which God be praised.

This afternoon there was a Couple of men with me, with a book in each of their hands, demanding money for polemony; and I overlooked the book and saw myself set down *Samuel Pepys, gent.*, 10*s* for himself and for his servants 2*s*. Which I did presently pay without any dispute;[3] but I fear I shall not escape

a repl. 'my'

---

1. Lord Berkeley of Stratton, Commissioner of the Navy; John Davis was his clerk.

2. Sir Charles Berkeley (Berkeley of Stratton's nephew; cr. Earl of Falmouth, 1664) was spreading these stories in order to prevent the marriage. But it had been celebrated in secret on 3 September. He later withdrew the charges and obtained the Duke's pardon: Clarendon, *Life*, i. 397. See Gramont, pp. 159+; Lister, ii. 73–9; C. H. Hartmann, *The King's friend*, pp. 37+; Marvell, i. 142, 201 ('The pious Mother Queen heareinge her Son/Was thus enamour'd with a butterd bun . . .').

3. He had reason to expect to be charged £10 as an esquire under the act (12 Car. II c. 9), as in fact he was charged in 1667 under the next poll-tax: below, 20 March 1667. But his office was not specifically named in the statute, as many others were. For his being an esquire, see above, pp. 96–7.

so, and therefore I have long ago laid by 10*l*: for them; but I think I am not bound to discover myself.

11.[a]   My wife and I up very early this day.   And though the weather was bad and the wind high, yet my Lady Batten and her mayde and we two did go by our barge to Woolwich (my Lady being very fearful), where we found both Sir Wms: and much other company, expecting the weather to be better that they might go about weighing up[1] the *Assurance*, which lies there (poor ship, that I have been twice merry in in Captain Hollands time)[2] under water; only the upper deck may be seen, and the masts.   Captain Stoakes is very melancholly; and being in search for some clothes and money of his, which he says he hath lost out of his Cabbin, I did the first office of a Justice of Peace to examine a seaman thereupon.   But could find no reason to commit him.

This last tide, the *Kingsale* was also run aboard, and lost her mainmast, by another ship; which makes us think it ominous to the Guiny voyage – to have two of her ships spoilt[b] before they go out.[3]

After dinner, my Lady being very fearefull, she stayed and kept my wife there; and I and another gentleman, a friend of Sir W. Pen's, went back in the barge; very merry by the way, and I went as far as White-hall in her.   To the Privy Seale, where I signed many pardons and some few things else.   From thence, Mr. Moore and I into London to a taverne near my house and there we drank and discoursed of ways how to put out a little money to the best advantage.   And at present he hath persuaded me to put out 250*l* for 50*l* per annum for eight years – and I think I shall do it.

Thence home – where I find the wench washing: and I up to my study, and there did make up an even 100*l* and sealed it to lie by.   After that to bed.

a repl. '12'   *b* MS. 'spilt'

---

1. A weighted line would be passed under the wreck at low tide; the ends would be secured to two lighters, and the ship would rise at high water.

2. Philip Holland commanded the *Assurance*, 1653–60. She went on the Baltic expedition of 1659.

3. Five other ships sailed early the next year: Mundy, v. 131, n.

12.^a Troubled for the absence of my wife. This morning I went (after the Comptroller and I have sat an hour at the office) to White-hall to dine with my Lady. And after dinner to the Privy Seale and sealed abundance of pardons, and little else. From thence to the Exchequer and did give my mother Bowyer[1] a visit, and her^b daughters – the first time that I have seen them since I went last to sea. From thence, up with J. Spicer to his office and took 100*l*; and by Coach with it as far as my father's, where I called to see them and my father did offer me six pieces of gold in lieu of six pounds that he borrowed of me the other day;[2] but it went against me to take of him, and therefore did not, though I was afterward a little troubled that I did not.

Thence home and told out this 100*l* and sealed it up with the other last night, it being the first 200*l* that ever I saw together of my own in my life – for which God be praised.

So to my Lady Battens and sat an hour or two and talked^c with her daughter and people, in the absence of her father and mother and my wife, to pass away the time. After that home and to bed – reading myself asleep while the wench sat mending my breeches by my bedside.

13.^d All the day long looking upon my workmen, who this day begin to paint my Parlour. Only at noon my Lady Batten and my wife came home, and so I step to my Lady's, where was Sir John Lawson and Captain Holmes; and there we dined and had very good red wine of my Lady's own making in England.[3]

14.^e Also, all this day looking upon my workmen; only met

---

a   repl. '13'   *b*   l.h. repl. s.h. 'his'
c   'talked' repeated twice and twice crossed out
d   repl. '14'   *e*   repl. '15'

---

1. Elizabeth, wife of Robert Bowyer: she and her husband ('my father Bowyer') were two of Pepys's most generous friends.

2. His father had presumably borrowed silver coins, which were now declining in value in comparison with gold.

3. Sc. at Walthamstow, Essex, her country house.

with the Comptroller at the office a little both forenoon and afternoon; and at night step a little with him to the Coffee-house, where we light upon very good company and have very good discourse concerning insects and their having a genera-tive faculty as well as other Creatures.[1]

This night in discourse the Comptroller told me, among other persons that were heretofore the principall officers of the Navy, there was one Sir Peter Bucke a Clerk of the acts, of which to myself I was not a little proud.[2]

15.[a] All day at home looking upon my workmen. Only, at noon Mr. Moore came and brought me some things to sign for the Privy Seale and dined with me; we have three eales, that my wife and I bought this morning of a man that cried them about, for our dinner. And that was all I[b] did today.

16. In the morning to church; and then dined at home. In the afternoon I to White-hall, where I was surprized with the news of a plott against the King's person and my Lord Monkes –

a repl. '16'   b repl. 'we'

---

1. The long-held theory (dating back to Pliny and Aristotle) that insects were generated from putre-faction (or sweat or even dust) was still current. On the work of the 17th-century physiologists (in sev-eral countries) establishing that ova must be present if dead flesh is to generate worms, see K. J. Franklin, *Short hist. physiology*, p. 69; F. J. Cole, *Early theories sexual generation;* C. E. Raven, *Engl. naturalists, John Ray*, pp. 375+. For discussions in the Royal Society in 1661, see Birch, i. 22, 23, 24. Cf. below, ii. 105, n. 4. Aubrey (i. 292) relates that Harrington the republican, im-prisoned in 1660 and 'being a gentle-man of a high spirit and a hot head . . . grew to have a phancy that his perspiration turned to flies, and some-times to bees . . .'.

2. Peter Buck (d. 1625) had been made Clerk in 1600, and knighted in 1604. Pepys envied him his title: cf., e.g., below, iii. 40. But Buck (a very corrupt officer, in fact) was the exception: no other 17th-century Clerk of the Acts was knighted, though it was usual for the other Principal Officers to receive the honour. Pepys was at this moment the only one of the five resident officers below the rank of knight.

and that since last night there is about 40 taken upon suspicion;[1] and among others, it was my lot to meet with Simon Beale the Trumpet, who took me and Tom. Doling into the guard in Scotland-yard and showed us Major-Generall Overton.[2] Where I heard him deny that he is guilty of any such things, but that whereas it is said that he is found to have brought many armes to towne, he says it was only to sell them, as he will prove by oath.

From thence with Tom. Doling and Boston and D. Vines (who we met by the way) to Prices and there we drank; and in discourse I learned a pretty trick to try whether a woman be a maid or no, by a string going round her head to meet at the end of her nose; which if she be not, will come a great way beyond.

Thence to my Lady and stayed with her an hour or two talking of the Duke of York and his Lady, the Chancellor's daughter, between whom she tells me that all is agreed and he will marry her.[3] But I know not how true yet.

It rained hard, and my Lady would have had me have the coach, but I would not; but to my father's, where I met my wife and there supped; and after supper by linke home and to bed.

17. All day looking after my workmen; only, in the afternoon to the office, where both Sir Wms. were come from Woolwich and tell us that contrary to their expectations, the *Assurance* is got up without much damage to her body; only to the goods that she hath within her, which argues her to be a strong, good ship.[4]

This day my parlour is gilded, which doth please me well.

18. All day at home without stirring out at all, looking after my workmen.

1. Overton's Plot; hatched by discontented sectaries and disbanded soldiers, allegedly under the lead of Maj.-Gen. Lambert, at the time a prisoner in the Tower. Its aims were said to include the burning of Whitehall Palace, and the killing of the King and Albemarle: *CSPVen. 1659–61*, pp. 228, 230–1; M. P. Ashley, *John Wildman*, pp. 161+. Some examinations of those arrested are summarised in *CSPD 1660–1,* pp. 413, 416+.

2. Reputedly military leader of the Fifth-Monarchists.

3. See above, p. 315, n. 2.

4. She was eventually sold in 1698. Anthony Deane, Assistant-Shipwright, Woolwich, who was to become a lifelong associate of Pepys, was principally responsible for the success of the operation: NWB, p. 49.

19. At noon I went and dined with my Lady at White-hall; and so back again to the office; and after that home to my workmen. ⟨This night Mr. Gawden sent me a great Chine of beef and half a dozen of Toungs.⟩*a*

20. All day at home with my workmen, that I may get all done before Christmas. This day I hear that the Princess Royall hath the small-pox.

21. By water to Whitehall (leaving my wife at White-friers going to my father's, with him to buy her a muffe and Mantle); there I signed many things at the Privy Seale. And carried 200*l* from thence to the Exchequer and laid it up with Mr. Hales; and afterward took him and W. Bowyer to the Swan and drank with them. They told me that this is St. Thomas day and that by an old Custome this day the Exchequer men have formerly, and do entend this night, to have a supper – which, if I could, I promised to come to; but did not.[1]

To my Lady and dined with her. She told me how dangerously ill the Princess Royall is: and that this morning she was said to be dead.[2] That she hears that she hath married herself to young Jermin,[3] which is worse then the Duke of Yorkes marrying the Chancellor's daughter – which is now publicly owned.[4]

After dinner to the office all the afternoon. At seven at night I walked through the dirt to White-hall to see whether my Lord be come to town; and I find him come – and at supper; and I supped with him. He tells me that my aunt at Brampton hath voided a great Stone (the first time that ever

a addition crowded in between entries

---

1. The feast of St Thomas the Apostle was a *dies non* observed by all courts of law; any other reason for this Exchequer supper has not been traced. See also 21 December 1661, when it is celebrated by a dinner. The feast had not been revived at the restoration of the Exchequer in 1654. In 1670 the clerks of the Receipt were upbraided for observing several holi-

days in excess of the legal number: *CTB*, iii (pt i), p. 568.
2. She died on the 24th.
3. Henry Jermyn, favourite nephew and adopted heir of the Earl of St Albans. There was no truth in this report.
4. Evelyn kissed the Duchess's hand on the 22nd. For the secrecy of the marriage, see above, p. 261, n. 1.

I heard she was troubled therewith) and cannot possibly live long.[1] That my uncle is pretty well, but full of pain still.

After supper home and to bed.

22.   All the morning with my paynters – who will make an end of all this day, I hope.   At noon I went to the Sun tavern on Fish-streete hill to a dinner of Captain Teddimans, where was my Lord Inchiquin (who seems to be a very fine person), Sir W. Pen, Captain Cuttance, and one Mr. Lawrence (a fine gentleman now going to Algier) and other good company; where we have a very fine dinner, good Musique and a great deal of Wine.[2] We stayed here very late: at last, Sir W. Pen and I home together, he so overgone with wine that he could hardly go; I was forced to lead him through the street and he was in a very merry and kind moode.   I home (found my house clear of the workmen and their work ended), my head troubled with wine; and I, very merry, went to bed – my head akeing all night.

23.   *Lordsday.*
In the morning to church, where our pew all covered with Rosemary and baize.[3]   A stranger made a dull sermon.

Home and found my wife and maid with much ado have made shift to spit a great Turkey sent me this week from Charles Carter my old Collegue, now Minister in Huntingtonshire.[4] But not at all roasted; and so I was fain to stay till 2 a-clock; and after that to church with my wife and a good sermon there was, and so home.

All the evening at my book;[5] and so to supper and to bed.

1. Ann, wife of Robert Pepys, died in October 1661.

2. This dinner party seems to have been associated with Algiers. Thomas Teddiman, who gave it, had in early August commanded the ship which brought home Lord Inchiquin and Henry Lawrence, both prisoners of the Algiers pirates: *CSPD 1660–1*, p. 183. Inchiquin's son was still in their hands, but a ransom was on its way to free him: ib., pp. 355, 402; Rugge, i, ff. 84*r*, 114*r*.

3. Bays were, with holly, ivy and rosemary, the commonest evergreens used in Christmas decoration.

4. Carter had been at Magdalene with Pepys.   He became Rector of Irthlingborough, Northants., in 1664.

5. Probably Fuller's *Church-history of Britain*, which Pepys was reading at this time.

24. In the morning to the office; and there Comissioner Pett (who seldom comes there) told me that he hath lately presented a piece of plate (being a Cople of flagons) to Mr. Coventree, but he did not receive them – which did also put me upon doing the same too.[1] And so after dinner I went and chose a payre of Candlsticks, to be made ready for me at Alderman Backwell's. So to the office again in the afternoon, till night; and so home and with the paynters till 10 at night, making an end of my house and the arch before my door; and so this night I was rid of their and all other work, and my house was made ready against tomorrow, being Christmas day. This day the Princesse Royall[2] dyed at Whitehall.

25. *Christmas day.*

In the morning very much pleased to see my house once more clear of workmen and to be clean; and endeed it is so far better then it was, that I do not repent of my trouble that I have been at.

In the morning to church; where Mr. Mills made a very good sermon. After that home to dinner, where my wife and I and my brother Tom (who this morning came to see my wife's new mantle put on, which doth please me very well) – to a good shoulder of Mutton and a Chicken. After dinner to church again, my wife and I, where we have a dull sermon of a stranger which made me sleep; and so home; and I, before and after supper, to my Lute and Fullers *History*, at which I stayed all alone in my Chamber till 12 at night; and so to bed.

26. In the morning to Alderman Backwells for the Candle-sticks for Mr. Coventry; but they being not done, I went away; and so by Coach to Mr. Crews and there took some money of Mr. Moores for my Lord, and so to my Lord's, where I found Sir Thom. Bond[3] (whom I never saw before) with a message from the Queene about vessells for the carrying over of her goods; and so I with him to Mr. Coventree, and thence to the office

1. Perhaps in similar expectation of their being returned? See below, ii. 10.

2. Aged 29; see below, p. 323, n. 1.

3. Comptroller of the Household to the Queen [Mother].

(being soundly washed going through the Bridge) to Sir Wm. Batten and Pen (the last of whom took physique today and so I went up to his Chamber); and there having made an end of that business, I returned to White-hall by water and dined with my Lady Sandwich - who at table did tell me how*a* much fault was laid upon Dr. Frazer and the rest of the Doctors for the death of the Princesse.[1]

My Lord did dine this day with Sir Henry Wright in order to his going to sea with the Queene.

Thence to my father Bowyers, where*b* I met my wife and with her home by water.

27. In the morning to Alderman Backewelles again, where I found the Candlsticks done and went along with him in his Coach to my Lord's and left the candlesticks*c* with Mr. Sheply. I stayed in the garden talking much with my Lord, who doth show me much of his love and doth communicate his mind in most things to me, which is my great content.

Home; and with my wife to Sir W. Batten's to dinner, where much and good company. Good and much entertainment. My wife, not very well, went home. I stayed late there, seeing them play at cards; and so home and to bed.

This afternoon there came in a strange lord to Sir W. Batten's by a mistake and enters discourse with him, so that we could not be rid of him till Sir Arn. Brames and Mr. Bens and Sir Wm. fell a-drinking to him till he was drunk, and so sent him away. About the middle of the night I was very ill, I think with eating and drinking too much; and so I was forced to call the mayde (who pleased my wife and I in her running up and down so inocently in her smock) and vomited in the bason; and so to sleep, and in the morning was pretty well - only got cold and so have pain in pissing, as I used to have.

a MS. 'whose' or 'hows'   *b* repl. 'and'   *c* repl. 'c'-

---

1. The illness had lasted only five days, and the doctors had disagreed whether it was measles, spotted fever or smallpox (Marvell, ii. 13) - diseases often confused at this time. Alexander Fraizer (Frazier) had been the King's physician-in-ordinary since June, and because of his intrigues with the revolutionary government during the Interregnum had many enemies at court.

28. *office day*. There all the morning. Dined at home alone with my wife; and so stayed within all the afternoon and evening at my lute, with great pleasure; and so to bed with great content.

29. Within all the morning. Several people to speak with me. Mr. Sheply for 100*l*. Mr. Kenard and Warren the Merchant – about deales[1] for my Lord. Captain Robt. Blake, lately come from the Streights, about some Florence wine for my Lord. And with him I went to Sir W. Pen; who offering me a barrel of oysters, I took them both home to my house (having by chance a good piece of roastebeefe at the fire for dinner); and there they dined with me and sat talking all the afternoon – good company. Thence I to Alderman Backewells and took a brave State=plate and Cupp in lieu of the Candlsticks that I had the other day, and carried them by Coach to my Lord's and left them there: and so back to my father's and saw my mother; and so to my uncle Fenners, whither my father came to me and there we talked and drank, and so away. I home with my father, he telling me how bad wifes both my Cozen Joyces make to their Husbands, which I much wondered at. After talking of my sister's coming to me next week, I went home and to*a* bed.

30. *Lords day*. Lay long in bed; and being up, I went with Will to my Lord's, calling in at many churches in my way. There I found Mr. Sheply in his Venetian cap taking physic in his chamber. And with him I sat till dinner.

My Lord dined abroad and my Lady in her chamber. So Mr. Hetly, Childe and I dined together. And after dinner Mr. Childe and I spent some time at the lute; and so promising me to prick me some lessons* to my Theorbo, he went away to see Henery Laws, who lies very sick.

I to the abby and walked there, seeing the great confusion of people that came there to hear the organs.[2] So home, calling in at my father's; but stayed not, my father and mother being both forth.

a l.h. repl. s.h. 'to'

---

1. Wood for the alterations at Hinchingbrooke: see above, p. 313–14. William Warren, timber merchant, was soon to become an important associate of Pepys.

2. See above, p. 283 & n. 1.   (E).

At home I fell a-reading of Fuller's *Church History* till it was late, and so to bed.

31. At the office all the morning. And after that home; and not staying to dine, I went out and in Paul's churchyard I bought the play of *Henery the fourth*.[1] And so went to the new Theatre[2] (only calling at Mr. Crews and eat a bit with the people there at dinner) and there saw it acted; but my expectation being too great, it did not please me as otherwise I believe it would; and my having a book I believe did spoil it a little.

That being done, I went to my Lord's, where I found him private at cards with my Lord Lauderdale and some persons of Honour; so Mr. Sheply and I over to Harpers and there drank a pot or two, and so parted – my boy taking a catt home with him from my Lord's, which Sarah hath given him for my wife, we being much troubled with mice.

At Whitehall enquiring for a coach, there was a Frenchman with one eye that was going my way; so he and I hired the coach between us and he set me down in Fanchurch-street. Strange how this[a] fellow, without asking, did tell me all what he was, and how he hath run away from his father and come into England to serve the King, and now going back again &c.

Home and to bed.

a symbol blotted

---

1. Probably Part I of Shakespeare's history play, written about 1597; nine editions were published between 1598 and 1639. Downes (p. 7) mentions Shakespeare's *Henry IV* as one of the plays acted by Killigrew's company and the cast which he lists is for Part I. PL 2635 (1685 Folio). (A).

2. See above, p. 297, n. 2. (A).

London
in the sixteen-sixties

Western half (omitting most minor streets & alleys)

0   220   440   660 yds

☐ Area of Great Fire

Tyburn Gibbet

TO OXFORD

1 St Martin-in-the-Fields
2 The Cockpit
3 Axe Yard
4 Holbein Gate
5 King St Gate
6 Westminster Hall
7 St Margaret's Church
8 The Gatehouse
9 The King's Playhouse, Drury Lane
10 The New Exchange
11 The Maypole
12 St Clement Danes Church
13 Clare Market
14 The Duke's Playhouse, Lincoln's Inn Fields
15 Temple Bar
16 St Dunstan-in-the-West
17 The Rolls Chapel
18 St Andrew's Church, Holborn

Burlington House

Clarendon House

Berkeley House

Piccadilly

St James's Fields (being developed

Berkshire House

St James's Palace

TO KNIGHTSBRIDGE AND KENSINGTON

The Mall

St James's Park

Goring House

Canal

TO CHELSEA

Petty France

Based on a map prepared by the late Professor T. F. Reddaway

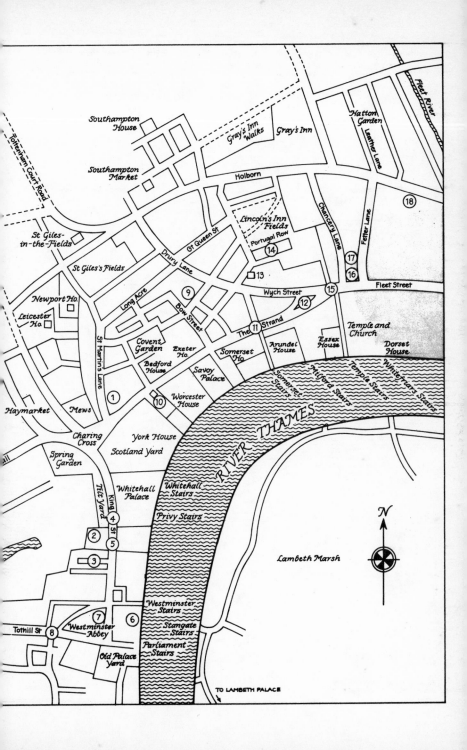

St James's Church
Clerkenwell
The Charterhouse
Bunhill Fields
Upper Moorfields
Artillery Ground
Bun Hill
Moorfields
Bedlam
London Wall
Smithfield
St Bartholomews
Holborn
Fleet River
Shoe Lane
Old Bailey
Warwick Lane
Paternoster Row
St Paul's
Bridewell
Blackfriars Stairs
Paul's Wharf
Baynard's Castle
Puddle Wharf and Stairs
Falcon Stairs
Upper Ground
Bear Garden
SOUTHWARK
St Margaret's Hill
St George's Fields
TO CLAPHAM
Bermondsey

St John Street
Goswell St
Old St
Aldersgate Street
Long Lane
Barbican
Jewen Street
Duck St
Redcross Street
Whitecross Street
Coleman Street
Lothbury Throgmorton St
London Wall
Bishopsgate
St Mary Axe
Wormwood Street
St Martin's La.
Foster Lane
Wood Street
Milk St
King St
Old Jewry
Cheapside
Old Change
Friday St
Lambeth Hill
Ludgate Hill
Watling St
Thames Street
Queenhithe
Three Cranes
Dowgate
Steelyard
Old Swan
Cannon Street
Fish Street Hill
Pudding La.
Botolph La.
Gracechurch St
Lime Street
Fenchurch St
Tower Street
Mincing La.
Water La.
Mark Lane
Threadneedle Street
Cornhill
Leadenhall St
Poultry
Lion Quay
Botolph's Wharf
Custom House
LONDON BRIDGE
St Thomas's Hospital

N

Based on a map prepared by the late Professor T. F. Reddaway

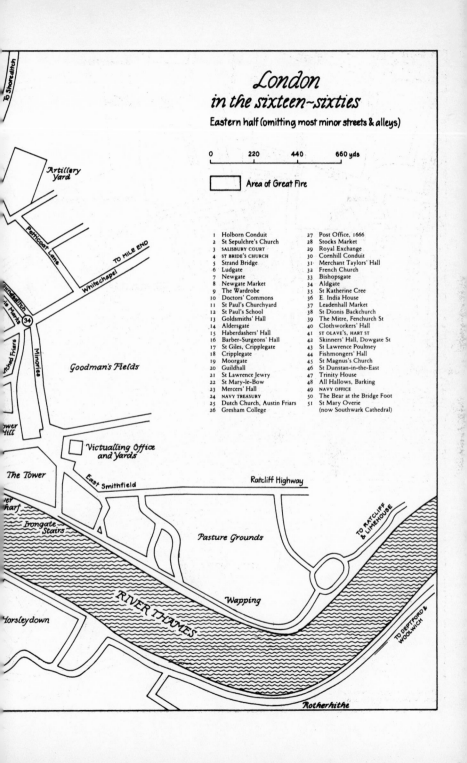

London
in the sixteen-sixties

Eastern half (omitting most minor streets & alleys)

0   220   440   660 yds

Area of Great Fire

1   Holborn Conduit
2   St Sepulchre's Church
3   SALISBURY COURT
4   ST BRIDE'S CHURCH
5   Strand Bridge
6   Ludgate
7   Newgate
8   Newgate Market
9   The Wardrobe
10 Doctors' Commons
11 St Paul's Churchyard
12 St Paul's School
13 Goldsmiths' Hall
14 Aldersgate
15 Haberdashers' Hall
16 Barber-Surgeons' Hall
17 St Giles, Cripplegate
18 Cripplegate
19 Moorgate
20 Guildhall
21 St Lawrence Jewry
22 St Mary-le-Bow
23 Mercers' Hall
24 NAVY TREASURY
25 Dutch Church, Austin Friars
26 Gresham College

27 Post Office, 1666
28 Stocks Market
29 Royal Exchange
30 Cornhill Conduit
31 Merchant Taylors' Hall
32 French Church
33 Bishopsgate
34 Aldgate
35 St Katherine Cree
36 E. India House
37 Leadenhall Market
38 St Dionis Backchurch
39 The Mitre, Fenchurch St
40 Clothworkers' Hall
41 ST OLAVE'S, HART ST
42 Skinners' Hall, Dowgate St
43 St Lawrence Poultney
44 Fishmongers' Hall
45 St Magnus's Church
46 St Dunstan-in-the-East
47 Trinity House
48 All Hallows, Barking
49 NAVY OFFICE
50 The Bear at the Bridge Foot
51 St Mary Overie
    (now Southwark Cathedral)

TO Shoreditch

Artillery Yard

Petticoat Lane

Whitechapel

TO MILE END

34

...gate Marks

...ford Friars

Minories

Goodman's Fields

...wer ...ill

Victualling Office and Yards

The Tower

East Smithfield

Ratcliff Highway

...wharf

Irongate Stairs

Pasture Grounds

TO RATCLIFF & LIMEHOUSE

Horsleydown

RIVER THAMES

Wapping

TO DEPTFORD & WOOLWICH

Rotherhithe

SELECT LIST OF PERSONS

ADMIRAL, the: James, Duke of York, Lord High Admiral of England

ALBEMARLE, 1st Duke of (Lord Monke): Captain-General of the Kingdom

ARLINGTON, 1st Earl of (Sir Henry Bennet): Secretary of State

ASHLEY, 1st Baron (Sir Anthony Ashley Cooper, later 1st Earl of Shaftesbury): Chancellor of the Exchequer

ATTORNEY-GENERAL: Sir Geoffrey Palmer

BACKWELL, Edward: goldsmith–banker

BAGWELL, Mrs: Pepys's mistress; wife of ship's carpenter

BALTY: Balthasar St Michel; brother-in-law; minor naval official

BATTEN, Sir William: Surveyor of the Navy

BETTERTON (Baterton), Thomas: actor in the Duke's Company

BIRCH, Jane: maidservant

BOOKSELLER, my: Joshua Kirton (until the Fire)

BOWYER, my father: Robert Bowyer, senior Exchequer colleague

BRISTOL, 2nd Earl of: politician

BROUNCKER (Bruncker, Brunkard, Brunkerd), 2nd Viscount: Commissioner of the Navy

BUCKINGHAM, 2nd Duke of: politician

CARKESSE (Carcasse), James: clerk in the Ticket Office

CARTERET, Sir George: Treasurer of the Navy and Vice-Chamberlain of the King's Household

CASTLEMAINE, Barbara, Countess of: the King's mistress

CHANCELLOR, the: see 'Lord Chancellor'

CHILD, the: usually Edward, eldest son and heir of Sandwich

CHOLMLEY, Sir Hugh: courtier, engineer

COCKE, Capt. George: hemp merchant

COFFERER, the: William Ashburnham

COMPTROLLER (Controller), the: the Comptroller of the Navy (Sir Robert Slingsby, 1660–1; Sir John Mennes, 1661–71)

COVENTRY, Sir William: Secretary to the Lord High Admiral, 1660–7; Commissioner of the Navy

CREED, John: household and naval servant of Sandwich

CREW, 1st Baron: Sandwich's father-in-law; Presbyterian politician

CUTTANCE, Sir Roger: naval captain

DEANE, Anthony:　shipwright

DEB:　*see* 'Willet, Deborah'

DOWNING, Sir George:　Exchequer official, ambassador to Holland and secretary to the Treasury Commission

DUKE, the:　usually James, Duke of York, the King's brother; occasionally George (Monck), Duke of Albemarle

DUKE OF YORK:　*see* 'James, Duke of York'

EDWARD, Mr:　Edward, eldest son and heir of Sandwich

EDWARDS, Tom:　servant

EVELYN, John:　friend, *savant*; Commissioner of Sick and Wounded

FENNER, Thomas (m. Katherine Kite, sister of Pepys's mother):　ironmonger

FERRER(s), Capt. Robert:　army captain; Sandwich's Master of Horse

FORD, Sir Richard:　Spanish merchant

FOX, Sir Stephen:　Paymaster of the Army

GAUDEN, Sir Denis:　Navy victualler

GENERAL(s), the:　Albemarle, Captain-General of the Kingdom, 1660–70; Prince Rupert and Albemarle, Generals-at-Sea in command of the Fleet, 1666

GIBSON, Richard:　clerk to Pepys in the Navy Office

GWYN, Nell:　actress (in the King's Company) and King's mistress

HARRIS, Henry:　actor in the Duke's Company

HAYTER, Tom:　clerk to Pepys in the Navy Office

HEWER, Will:　clerk to Pepys in the Navy Office

HILL, Thomas:　friend, musician, Portuguese merchant

HINCHINGBROOKE, Viscount (also 'Mr Edward', 'the child'):　eldest son of Sandwich

HOLLIER (Holliard), Thomas:　surgeon

HOLMES, Sir Robert:　naval commander

HOWE, Will:　household and naval servant of Sandwich

JAMES, DUKE OF YORK:　the King's brother and heir presumptive (later James II); Lord High Admiral

JANE:　usually Jane Birch, maidservant

JOYCE, Anthony (m. Kate Fenner, 1st cousin):　innkeeper

JOYCE, William (m. Mary Fenner, 1st cousin):　tallow-chandler

JUDGE-ADVOCATE, the:　John Fowler, Judge-Advocate of the Fleet

KNIPP (Knepp), Elizabeth:　actress in the King's Company

LADIES, the young, the two, the:　often Sandwich's daughters

LAWSON, Sir John:　naval commander

LIEUTENANT OF THE TOWER:　Sir John Robinson

L'IMPERTINENT, Mons.:　[?Daniel] Butler, friend, ? clergyman

LORD CHAMBERLAIN: Edward Mountagu, 2nd Earl of Manchester; Sandwich's cousin

LORD CHANCELLOR: Edward Hyde, 1st Earl of Clarendon (often referred to as Chancellor after his dismissal, 1667)

LORD KEEPER: Sir Orlando Bridgeman

LORD PRIVY SEAL: John Robartes, 2nd Baron Robartes (later 1st Earl of Radnor)

LORD TREASURER: Thomas Wriothesley, 4th Earl of Southampton

MARTIN, Betty (b. Lane): Pepys's mistress; shopgirl

MENNES (Minnes), Sir John: Comptroller of the Navy

MERCER, Mary: maid to Mrs Pepys

MILL(E)S, John: Rector of St Olave's, Hart St; Pepys's parish priest

MONCK (Monke), George (Lord): soldier. *See* 'Albemarle, 1st Duke of

MONMOUTH, Duke of: illegitimate son of Charles II

MOORE, Henry: lawyer; officer of Sandwich's household

MY LADY: usually Jemima, wife of Sandwich

MY LORD: usually Sandwich

NELL, NELLY: usually Nell Gwyn

PALL: Paulina Pepys; sister

PEARSE, (Pierce), James: surgeon to Duke of York, and naval surgeon

PENN, Sir William: Commissioner of the Navy and naval commander (father of the Quaker leader)

PEPYS, Elizabeth (b. St Michel): wife

PEPYS, John and Margaret: parents

PEPYS, John (unm.): brother; unbeneficed clergyman

PEPYS, Tom (unm.): brother; tailor

PEPYS, Paulina (m. John Jackson): sister

PEPYS, Capt. Robert: uncle, of Brampton, Hunts.

PEPYS, Roger: 1st cousin once removed; barrister and M.P.

PEPYS, Thomas: uncle, of St Alphege's, London

PETT, Peter: Commissioner of the Navy and shipwright

PICKERING, Mr (Ned): courtier, 1662–3; Sandwich's brother-in-law and servant

POVEY, Thomas: Treasurer of the Tangier Committee

PRINCE, the: usually Prince Rupert

QUEEN, the: (until May 1662) the Queen Mother, Henrietta-Maria, widow of Charles I; Catherine of Braganza, wife of Charles II (m. 21 May 1662)

RIDER, Sir William: merchant

ROBERT, Prince: Prince Rupert

RUPERT, Prince: 1st cousin of Charles II;   naval commander

St MICHEL, Alexander and Dorothea: parents-in-law

St MICHEL, Balthasar ('Balty';   m. Esther Watts):   brother-in-law; minor naval official

SANDWICH, 1st Earl of: 1st cousin once removed, and patron; politician and naval commander

SHIPLEY, Edward: steward of Sandwich's household

SIDNY, Mr: Sidney Mountagu, second son of Sandwich

SOLICITOR, the: the Solicitor-General, Sir Heneage Finch

SOUTHAMPTON, 4th Earl of: Lord Treasurer

SURVEYOR, the: the Surveyor of the Navy (Sir William Batten, 1660–7;   Col. Thomas Middleton, 1667–72)

TEDDEMAN, Sir Thomas: naval commander

THE: Theophila Turner

TREASURER, the: usually the Treasurer of the Navy (Sir George Carteret, 1660–7;   1st Earl of Anglesey, 1667–8);   sometimes the Lord Treasurer of the Kingdom, the Earl of Southampton, 1660–7

TRICE, Tom: step-brother; civil lawyer

TURNER, John (m. Jane Pepys, distant cousin):   barrister

TURNER, Betty and Theophila: daughters of John and Jane Turner

TURNER, Thomas: senior clerk in the Navy Office

VICE-CHAMBERLAIN, the: Sir George Carteret, Vice-Chamberlain of the King's Household and Treasurer of the Navy

VYNER, Sir Robert: goldsmith–banker

WARREN, Sir William: timber merchant

WARWICK, Sir Philip: Secretary to the Lord Treasurer

WIGHT, William: uncle (half-brother of Pepys's father); fishmonger

WILL: usually Will Hewer

WILLET, Deborah: maid to Mrs Pepys

WILLIAMS ('Sir Wms. both'):   Sir William Batten and Sir William Penn, colleagues on the Navy Board

WREN, Matthew: Secretary to the Lord High Admiral, 1667–72

SELECT GLOSSARY

A Large Glossary will be found in the *Companion*. This Select Glossary is restricted to usages, many of them recurrent, which might puzzle the reader. It includes words and constructions which are now obsolete, archaic, slang or dialect; words which are used with meanings now obsolete or otherwise unfamiliar; and place names frequently recurrent or used in colloquial styles or in non-standard forms. Words explained in footnotes are not normally included. The definitions given here are minimal: meanings now familiar and contemporary meanings not implied in the text are not noted, and many items are explained more fully in *Companion* articles and in the Large Glossary. A few foreign words are included. The spellings are taken from those used in the text: they do not, for brevity's sake, include all variants.

ABLE: wealthy
ABROAD: away, out of doors
ACCENT (of speech): the accentuation and the rising and falling of speech in pronunciation
ACCOUNTANT: official accountable for expenditure etc.
ACHIEVEMENT: hatchment, representation of heraldic arms
ACTION: acting, performance
ACTOR: male or female theatrical performer
ADDES: adze
ADMIRAL SHIP: flagship carrying admiral
ADMIRATION; ADMIRE: wonder, alarm; to wonder at
ADVENTURER: investor, speculator
ADVICE: consideration
AFFECT: to be fond of, to be concerned
AFFECTION: attention
AGROUND: helpless
AIR: generic term for all gases
ALL MY CAKE WILL BE DOE: all my plans will miscarry
ALPHABET: index, alphabetical list
AMBAGE: deceit, deviousness

AMUSED, AMUZED: bemused, astonished
ANCIENT: elderly, senior
ANGEL: gold coin worth *c.* 10*s.*
ANGELIQUE: small archlute
ANNOY: molest, hurt
ANOTHER GATE'S BUSINESS: different altogether
ANSWERABLE: similar, conformably
ANTIC, ANTIQUE: fantastic
APERN: apron
APPRENSION: apprehension
APPROVE OF: criticise
AQUA FORTIS (FARTIS): nitric acid
ARTICLE: to indict
ARTIST: workman, craftsman, technician, practitioner
ASTED: Ashtead, Surrey
AYERY: airy, sprightly, stylish

BAGNARD: bagnio, prison, lock-up
BAILEY, BAYLY: bailiff
BAIT, BAŸTE: refreshment on journey (for horses or travellers). *Also* v.
BALDWICK: Baldock, Herts.
BALLET: ballad, broadside

BAND: neckband

BANDORE: musical instrument resembling guitar

BANQUET: course of fruits, sweets and wine; slight repast

BANQUET-, BANQUETING-HOUSE: summer-house

BARBE (s.): Arab (Barbary) horse

BARBE (v.): to shave

BARN ELMS: riverside area near Barnes, Surrey

BARRECADOS (naval): fenders

BASE, BASS: bass viol; thorough-bass

BASTE HIS COAT: to beat, chastise

BAVINS: kindling wood, brushwood

BAYLY: *see* 'Bailey'

BAYT(E): *see* 'Bait'

BEARD: facial hair, moustache

BEFOREHAND, to get: to have money in hand

BEHALF: to behave

BEHINDHAND: insolvent

BELL: to throb

BELOW: downstream from London Bridge

BELOW STAIRS: part of the Royal Household governed by Lord Steward

BEST HAND, at the: the best bargain

BEVER: beaver, fur hat

BEWPERS: bunting, fabric used for flags

BEZAN, BIZAN (Du. *bezaan*): small yacht

BIGGLESWORTH: Biggleswade, Beds.

BILL: (legal) warrant, writ; bill of exchange: Bill of Mortality (weekly list of burials; *see* iii. 225, n. 2)

BILLANDER (Du. *bijlander*): bilander, small two-masted merchantman

BIRD'S EYE: spotted fabric

BIZAN: *see* 'Bezan'

BLACK (adj.): brunette, dark in hair or complexion

BLACK(E)WALL: dock on n. shore of Thames below Greenwich used by E. Indiamen

BLANCH (of coins): to silver

BLIND: out of the way, private, obscure

BLOAT HERRING: bloater

BLUR: innuendo; charge

BOATE: boot or luggage compartment on side of coach

BODYS: foundations, basic rules; structure; (of ship) sectional drawings

BOLTHEAD: globular glass vessel with long straight neck

BOMBAIM: Bombay

BORDER: *toupée*

BOTARGO: dried fish-roe

BOTTOMARYNE, BOTTUMARY, BUMMARY: mortgage on ship

BOWPOTT: flower pot

BRAINFORD: Brentford, Mdx.

BRAMPTON: village near Huntingdon in which Pepys inherited property

BRANSLE: branle, brawl, group dance in duple measure

BRAVE (adj.): fine, enjoyable

BRAVE (v.): to threaten, challenge

BREAK BULK: to remove part of cargo

BREDHEMSON, BRIGHTHEMSON: Brighton, Sussex

BRIDEWELL-BIRD: jailbird

BRIDGE: usually London Bridge; also jetty, landing stairs

BRIEF: collection authorised by Lord Chancellor for charity

BRIG, BRIGANTINE: small vessel equipped both for sailing and rowing

BRIGHTHEMSON: *see* 'Bredhemson'

BRISTOL MILK: sweet sherry

BROTHER: brother-in-law; colleague

BRUMLY: Bromley, Kent

BRUSH (s.): graze

BUBO: tumour

BULLEN: Boulogne

BULLET: cannon-ball

BUMMARY: *see* 'Bottomaryne'

BURNTWOOD: Brentwood, Essex

BURY (of money): pour in, salt away, invest

BUSSE: two- or three-masted fishing boat

CABALL: inner group of ministers; knot

CABARETT (Fr. *cabaret*): tavern

CALES: Cadiz

CALICE, CALLIS: Calais

CALL: to call on/for; to drive

CAMELOTT, CAMLET, CAMLOTT: robust, ribbed cloth made of wool or goat hair

CANAILLE, CHANNEL, KENNEL: drainage gutter (in street); canal (in St James's Park)

CANCRE: canker, ulcer, sore

CANNING ST: Cannon St

CANONS: boot-hose tops

CANTON (heraldic): small division of shield

CAPER (ship): privateer

CARBONADO: to grill, broil

CARESSE: to make much of

CARRY (a person): to conduct, escort

CAST OF OFFICE: taste of quality

CATAPLASM: poultice

CATCH: round song; (ship) ketch

CATT-CALL: whistle

CAUDLE: thin gruel made with wine

CELLAR: box for bottles

CERE CLOTH: cloth impregnated with wax and medicaments

CESTORNE: cistern

CHAFE: heat, anger

CHALDRON: 1½ tons (London measure)

CHAMBER: small piece of ordnance for firing salutes

CHANGE, the: the Royal (Old) Exchange

CHANGELING: idiot

CHANNELL: *see* 'Canaille'

CHANNELL ROW: Cannon Row, Westminster

CHAPEL, the: usually the Chapel Whitehall Palace

CHAPTER: usually of Bible

CHARACTER: code, cipher; verbal portrait

CHEAP (s.): bargain

CHEAPEN: to ask the price of, bargain

CHEQUER, the: usually the Exchequer

CHEST, the: the Chatham Chest, the pension fund for seamen

CHILD, with: eager, anxious

CHIMNEY/CHIMNEY-PIECE: structure over and around fireplace

CHIMNEY-PIECE: picture over fireplace

CHINA-ALE: ale flavoured with china root

CHOQUE: a choke, an obstruction

CHOUSE: to swindle, trick

CHURCH: after July 1660, usually St Olave's, Hart St

CLAP: gonorrhoea

CLERK OF THE CHEQUE: principal clerical officer of a dockyard

CLOATH (of meat): skin

CLOSE: shutter; (of music) cadence

CLOUTERLY: clumsily

CLOWNE: countryman, clodhopper

CLUB (s.): share of expenses, meeting at which expenses are shared *Also* v.

CLYSTER, GLISTER, GLYSTER: enema

COACH: captain's state-room in large ship

COCK ALE: ale mixed with minced chicken

COCKPIT(T), the: usually the theatre in the Cockpit buildings, Whitehall Palace; the buildings themselves

COD: small bag; testicle

CODLIN TART: apple (codling) tart

COFFEE: coffee-house

COG: to cheat, banter, wheedle

COLEWORTS: cabbage

COLLAR DAY: day on which knights of chivalric orders wore insignia at court

COLLECT: to deduce

COLLIER: coal merchant; coal ship

COLLOPS: fried bacon

COLLY-FEAST: feast of collies (cullies, good companions) at which each pays his share

COMEDIAN: actor

COMEDY: play

COMFITURE (Fr. *confiture*): jam, marmalade

COMMEN, COMMON GUARDEN: Covent Garden

COMMONLY: together

COMPASS TIMBER: curved timber

COMPLEXION: aspect

COMPOSE: to put music to words. *Also* Composition

CONCEIT (s.): idea, notion

CONCLUDE: to include

CONDITION (s.): disposition; social position, state of wealth

CONDITION (v.): to make conditions

CONDITIONED: having a (specified) disposition or social position

CONGEE: bow at parting

CONJURE: to plead with

CONJUROR: wizard who operates by conjuration of spirits

CONSIDERABLE: worthy of consideration

CONSTER: to construe, translate

CONSUMPTION: (any) wasting disease. *Also* 'Consumptive'

CONTENT, by/in: by agreement, without examination, at a rough guess

CONVENIENCE: advantage

CONVENIENT: morally proper

CONVERSATION: demeanour, behaviour; acquaintance, society

COOLE: cowl

CORANT(O): dance involving a running or gliding step

COSEN, COUSIN: almost any collateral relative

COUNT: reckon, estimate, value

COUNTENANCE: recognition, acknowledgement

COUNTRY: county, district

COURSE, in: in sequence

COURSE, of: as usual

COURT BARON: manorial court (civil)

COURT-DISH: dish with a cut from every meat

COURT LEET: local criminal court

COUSIN: *see* 'Cosen'

COY: disdainful; quiet

COYING: stroking, caressing

CRADLE: fire-basket

CRAMBO: rhyming game

CRAZY: infirm

CREATURE (of persons): puppet, instrument

CRUSADO: Portuguese coin worth 3s.

CUDDY: room in a large ship in which the officers took their meals

CULLY: dupe; friend

CUNNING: knowledgeable; knowledge

CURIOUS: careful, painstaking, discriminating; fine, delicate

CURRANT: out and about

CUSTOMER: customs officer

CUT (v.): to carve meat

CUTT (s.): an engraving

DAUGHTER-IN-LAW: stepdaughter

DEAD COLOUR: preparatory layer of colour in a painting

DEAD PAYS: sailors or soldiers kept on pay roll after death

DEALS: sawn timber used for decks, etc.

DEDIMUS: writ empowering J.P.

DEFALK: to subtract

DEFEND: to prevent

DEFY (Fr.): to mistrust. *Also* Defyance

DELICATE: pleasant

DELINQUENT: active royalist in Civil War and Interregnum

DEMORAGE: demurrage, compensation from the freighter due to a shipowner for delaying vessel beyond time specified in charter-party

DEPEND: to wait, hang

DEVISE: to decide; discern

DIALECT: jargon

DIALL, double horizontal: instrument telling hour of day

DIRECTION: supervision of making; arrangement

DISCOVER: to disclose, reveal

DISCREET: discerning, judicious
DISGUST: to dislike
DISPENSE: outgoings
DISTASTE (s.): difference, quarrel, offence. *Also* v.
DISTINCT: discerning, discriminating
DISTRINGAS: writ of distraint
DOATE: to nod off to sleep
DOCTOR: clergyman, don
DOE: dough. *See* 'All my cake . . .'
DOGGED: determined
DOLLER: *see* 'Rix Doller'
DORTOIRE: dorter, monastic dormitory
DOTY: darling
DOWNS, the: roadstead off Deal, Kent
DOXY: whore, mistress
DRAM: timber from Drammen, Norway
DRAWER: tapster, barman
DRESS: to cook, prepare food
DROLL: comic song
DROLLING, DROLLY: comical, comically
DRUDGER: dredger, container for sweetmeats
DRUGGERMAN: dragoman, interpreter
DRY BEATEN: beaten without drawing blood
DRY MONEY: hard cash
DUANA: divan, council
DUCCATON: ducatoon, large silver coin of the Netherlands worth 5s. 9d.
DUCKET(T): ducat, foreign gold coin worth 9s.
DUKE'S [PLAY] HOUSE, the: playhouse in Lincoln's Inn Fields used by the Duke of York's Company from June 1660 until 9 November 1671; often called 'the Opera'. Also known as the Lincoln's Inn Fields Theatre (LIF)
DULL: limp, spiritless

EARTH: earthenware
EASILY AND EASILY: more and more slowly

EAST INDIES: the territory covered by the E. India Company, including the modern sub-continent of India
EAST COUNTRY, EASTLAND: the territory (Scandinavia and Baltic area) covered by the Eastland Company
EFFEMINACY: love of women
ELECTUARY: medicinal salve with a honey base
EMERODS: haemorrhoids
ENTENDIMIENTO (Sp.): understanding
ENTER (of horse): to break in
ENTERTAIN: to retain, employ
EPICURE: glutton
ERIFFE: Erith, Kent
ESPINETTE(S): spinet, small harpsichord
ESSAY: to assay
EVEN (adv.): surely
EVEN (of accounts): to balance
EVEN (of the diary): to bring up to date
EXCEPT: to accept
EXPECT: to see, await

FACTION: the government's parliamentary critics
FACTIOUS: able to command a following
FACTOR: mercantile agent
FACTORY: trading station
FAIN: to be forced; to like
FAIRING: small present (as from a fair)
FALCHON: falchion, curved sword
FAMILY: household (including servants)
FANCY (music): fantasia
FANFARROON: fanfaron, braggart
FARANDINE, FARRINDIN: *see* 'Ferrandin'
FASHION (of metal, furniture): design, fashioning
FAT: vat
FATHER: father-in-law (similarly with 'mother' etc.)
FELLET (of trees): a cutting, felling
FELLOW COMMONER: undergraduate

paying high fees and enjoying privileges

FENCE: defence

FERRANDIN, FARRINDIN, FARANDINE: cloth of silk mixed with wool or hair

FIDDLE: viol; violin

FINE (s.): payment for lease

FINE FOR OFFICE (v.): to avoid office by payment of fine

FIRESHIP: ship filled with combustibles used to ram and set fire to enemy

FITS OF THE MOTHER: hysterics

FLAG, FLAGGMAN: flag officer

FLAGEOLET: end-blown, six-holed instrument

FLESHED: relentless, proud

FLOOD: rising tide

FLUXED (of the pox): salivated

FLYING ARMY/FLEET: small mobile force

FOND, FONDNESS: foolish; folly

FOND: fund

FORCE OUT: to escape

FORSOOTH: to speak ceremoniously

FORTY: many, scores of

FOXED: intoxicated

FOX HALL: Vauxhall (pleasure gardens)

FOY: departure feast or gift

FREQUENT: to busy oneself

FRIENDS: parents, relatives

FROST-BITE: to invigorate by exposure to cold

FULL: anxious

FULL MOUTH, with: eagerly; openly, loudly

GALL: harass

GALLIOTT: small swift galley

GALLOPER, the: shoal off Essex coast

GAMBO: Gambia, W. Africa

GAMMER: old woman

GENERAL-AT-SEA: naval commander (a post, not a rank)

GENIUS: inborn character, natural ability; mood

GENT: graceful, polite

GENTILELY: obligingly

GEORGE: jewel forming part of insignia of Order of Garter

GERMANY: territory of the Holy Roman Empire

GET UP ONE'S CRUMB: to improve one's status

GET WITHOUT BOOK: to memorise

GHOSTLY: holy, spiritual

GIBB-CAT: tom-cat

GILDER, GUILDER: Dutch money of account worth 2s.

GIMP: twisted thread of material with wire or cord running through it

GITTERNE: musical instrument of the guitar family

GLASS: telescope

GLEEKE: three-handed card game

GLISTER, GLYSTER: see 'Clyster'

GLOSSE, by a fine: by a plausible pretext

GO TO ONE'S NAKED BED: to go to bed without night-clothes

GO(O)D BWYE: God be with ye, good-bye

GODLYMAN: Godalming, Surrey

GOODFELLOW: convivial person, good timer

GOODMAN, GOODWIFE (Goody): used of men and women of humble station

GOOD-SPEAKER: one who speaks well of others

GORGET: neckerchief for women

GOSSIP (v.): to act as godparent, to attend a new mother; to chatter. *Also* s.

GOVERNMENT: office or function of governor

GRACIOUS-STREET(E): Gracechurch St

GRAIN (? of gold): sum of money

GRAVE: to engrave

GREEN (of meat): uncured

GRESHAM COLLEGE: meeting-place of Royal Society; the Society itself

GRIEF: bodily pain

GRUDGEING, GRUTCHING: trifling complaint, grumble

GUEST: nominee; friend; stranger

GUIDE: postboy

GUILDER: *see* 'Gilder'

GUN: cannon, salute

GUNDALO, GUNDILOW: gondola

GUNFLEET, the: shoal off Essex coast

HACKNEY: hack, workhorse, drudge

HAIR, against the: against the grain

HALF-A-PIECE: gold coin worth *c.* 10s.

HALF-SHIRT: sham shirt front

HALFE-WAY-HOUSE: Rotherhithe tavern halfway between London Bridge and Deptford

HALL, the: usually Westminster Hall

HAND: cuff

HANDSEL: to try out, use for first time

HAND-TO-FIST: hastily

HANDYCAPP: handicap, a card game

HANG IN THE HEDGE: to be delayed

HANGER: loop holding a sword; small sword

HANGING JACK: turnspit for roasting meat

HANK: hold, grip

HAPPILY: haply, perchance

HARE: to harry, rebuke

HARPSICHON, HARPSICHORD: keyboard instrument of one or two manuals, with strings plucked by quills or leather jacks, and with stops which vary the tone

HARSLET: haslet, pigmeat (esp. offal)

HAT-PIECE: protective metal skull cap

HAVE A GOOD COAT OF [HIS] FLEECE: to have a good share

HAVE A HAND: to have leisure, freedom

HAVE A MONTH'S MIND: to have a great desire

HAWSE, thwart their: across their bows

HEAD-PIECE: helmet

HEART: courage

HEAVE AT: to oppose

HECTOR: street-bully, swashbuckler

HERBALL: botanical encyclopaedia; *hortus siccus* (book of dried and pressed plants)

HERE (Du. *heer*): Lord

HIGH: arrogant, proud, high-handed

HINCHINGBROOKE: Sandwich's house near Huntingdon

HOMAGE: jury of presentment at a manorial court

HONEST (of a woman): virtuous

HOOKS, off the: out of humour

HOPE, the: reach of Thames downstream from Tilbury

HOPEFUL: promising

HOUSE: playhouse; parliament; (royal) household or palace building

HOUSE OF OFFICE: latrine

HOY: small passenger and cargo vessel, fore-and-aft rigged

HOYSE: to hoist

HUMOUR (s.): mood; character, characteristic; good or ill temper

HUMOUR (v.): to set words suitably to music

HUSBAND: one who gets good/bad value for money; supervisor, steward

HYPOCRAS: hippocras, red or white wine (flavoured)

ILL-TEMPERED: out of sorts, ill-adjusted (to weather etc.; cf. 'Temper')

IMPERTINENCE: irrelevance, garrulity, folly. *Also* 'Impertinent'

IMPOSTUME: abscess

IMPREST: money paid in advance by government to public servant

INDIAN GOWN: loose gown of glazed cotton

INGENIOUS, INGENUOUS: clever, intelligent

INGENUITY: wit, intelligence; freedom

INGENUOUS: *see* 'Ingenious'

INSIPID: stupid, dull

INSTITUCIONS: instructions

INSTRUMENT: agent, clerk

INSULT: to exult over

INTELLIGENCE: information

INTRATUR: warrant authorising payment by Exchequer

IRISIPULUS: erysipelas

IRONMONGER: often a large-scale merchant, not necessarily a retailer

JACK(E): flag used as signal or mark of distinction; rogue, knave. *See also* 'Hanging Jack'

JACKANAPES COAT: monkey jacket, sailor's short close-fitting jacket

JACOB(US): gold sovereign coined under James I

JAPAN: lacquer, lacquered

JARR, JARRING: quarrel

JEALOUS: fearful, suspicious, mistrustful. *Also* Jealousy

JERK(E): captious remark

JES(S)IMY: jasmine

JEW'S TRUMP: Jew's harp

JOCKY: horse-dealer

JOLE (of fish): jowl, a cut consisting of the head and shoulders. *See also* 'Pole'

JOYNT-STOOL: stout stool held together by joints

JULIPP: julep, a sweet drink made from syrup

JUMBLE: to take for an airing

JUMP WITH: to agree, harmonise

JUNK (naval): old rope

JURATE (of Cinque Ports): jurat, alderman

JUSTE-AU-CORPS: close-fitting long coat

KATCH: (ship) ketch

KEEP A QUARTER: to make a disturbance

KENNEL: *see* 'Canaille'

KERCHER: kerchief, head-covering

KETCH (s.): catch, song in canon

KETCH (v.): to catch

KING'S [PLAY] HOUSE, the: playhouse in Vere St, Clare Market, Lincoln's Inn Fields, used by the King's Company from 8 November 1660 until 7 May 1663; the playhouse in Bridges St, Drury Lane, used by the same company from 7 May 1663 until the fire of 25 January 1672. Also known as the Theatre Royal (TR)

KITLIN: kitling, kitten, cub

KNEES: timbers of naturally angular shape used in ship-building

KNOT (s.): flower bed; difficulty; clique, band

KNOT (v.): to join, band together

KNOWN: famous

LACE: usually braid made with gold- or silver-thread

LAMB'S-WOOL: hot ale with apples and spice

LAMP-GLASS: magnifying lens used to concentrate lamp-light

LAST: load, measure of tar

LASTOFFE: Lowestoft, Suff.

LATITUDINARIAN: liberal Anglican

LAVER: basin of a fountain

LEADS: flat space on roof top, sometimes boarded over

LEAN: to lie down

LEARN: to teach

LEAVE: to end

LECTURE: weekday religious service consisting mostly of a sermon

LESSON: piece of music

LETTERS OF MART: letters of marque

LEVETT: reveille, reveille music

LIBEL(L): leaflet, broadside; (in legal proceedings) written charge

LIE UPON: to press, insist

LIFE: life interest

LIFE, for my: on my life

LIGHT: window

LIGNUM VITAE: hard W. Indian wood with medicinal qualities, often used for drinking vessels

LIMB: to limn, paint

LIME (of dogs): to mate

LINK(E): torch

LINNING: linen

LIPPOCK: Liphook, Hants.

LIST: pleasure, desire

LOCK: waterway between arches of bridge

LOMBRE: *see* 'Ombre'

LONDON: the city of London (to be distinguished from Westminster)

LOOK: to look at/for

LOOK AFTER: to have eyes on

LUMBERSTREETE: Lombard St

LUTE: pear-shaped instrument with six courses of gut strings and a turned-back peg-box; made in various sizes, the larger instruments having additional bass strings

LUTESTRING: lustring, a glossy silk

LYRA-VIALL: small bass viol tuned for playing chords

MAD: whimsical, wild, extravagant

MADAM(E): prefix used mainly of widows, elderly/foreign ladies

MAIN (adj.): strong, bulky

MAIN (s.): chief purpose or object

MAISTER: expert; professional; sailing master

MAKE (s.): (of fighting cocks) match, pair of opponents

MAKE (v.): to do; to copulate

MAKE LEGS: to bow, curtsey

MAKE SURE TO: to plight troth

MALLOWS: St Malo

MAN OF BUSINESS: executive agent, administrator

MANAGED-HORSE (cf. Fr. *manège*): horse trained in riding school

MANDAMUS: royal mandate under seal

MARGARET, MARGETTS: Margate, Kent

MARGENTING: putting margin-lines on paper

MARK: 13s. 4d.

MARMOTTE (Fr., term of affection): young girl

MARROWBONE: Marylebone, Mdx

MASTY: burly

MATCH: tinderbox and wick

MATHEMATICIAN: mathematical instrument-maker

MEAT: food

MEDIUM: mean, average

METHEGLIN: strong mead flavoured with herbs

MINCHIN-LANE: Mincing Lane

MINE: mien

MINIKIN: treble string of a viol

MISTRESS (MRS.): prefix used of unmarried girls and women as well as of young married women

MISTRESS: sweetheart

MITHRYDATE: drug used as an antidote

MODEST (of woman): virtuous

MOHER (Sp. *mujer*): woman, wife

MOIS, MOYS: menstrual periods

MOLD, MOLDE, MOLLE (archit.): mole

MOLEST: to annoy

MOND: orb (royal jewel in form of globe)

MONTEERE, MOUNTEERE: riding cap; close-fitting hood

MOPED: bemused

MORECLACK(E): Mortlake, Surrey

MORENA (Sp.): brunette

MORNING DRAUGHT: drink (sometimes with snack) usually taken mid-morning

MOTHER-IN-LAW: stepmother (similarly with 'father-in-law' etc.)

MOTT: sighting line in an optical tube

MOUNTEERE: *see* 'Monteere'

MOYRE: moire, watered silk

MUM: strong spiced ale

MURLACE: Morlaix, Brittany

MUSCADINE, MUSCATT: muscatel wine

MUSIC: band, choir, performers

MUSTY: peevish

NAKED BED: *see* 'Go to one's n.b.'

NARROWLY: anxiously, carefully

NAUGHT, NOUGHT: worthless, bad in condition or quality, sexually wicked

NAVY: Navy Office

NAVY OFFICERS: Principal Officers of the Navy – i.e. the Comptroller, Treasurer, Surveyor, Clerk of the Acts, together with a variable number of Commissioners; members of the Navy Board. Cf. 'Sea-Officers'

NEARLY: deeply

NEAT (adj.): handsome

NEAT(s.): ox, cattle

NEITHER MEDDLE NOR MAKE: to have nothing to do with

NEWSBOOK: newspaper (weekly, octavo)

NIBBLE AT: to bite at

NICOTIQUES: narcotics, medicines

NIGHTGOWN(E): dressing gown

NOISE: group of musical instruments playing together

NORE, the: anchorage in mouth of Thames

NORTHDOWNE ALE: Margate ale

NOSE: to insult, affront

NOTE: thing deserving of note, note of credit

NOTORIOUS: famous, well-known

NOUGHT: see 'Naught'

OBNOXIOUS: liable to

OBSERVABLE (adj.): noteworthy, notorious

OBSERVABLE (s.): thing or matter worthy of observation

OF: to have

OFFICE DAY: day on which a meeting of the Navy Board was held

OFFICERS OF THE NAVY: see 'Navy Officers'

OLEO (Sp. *olla*): stew

OMBRE (Sp. *hombre*): card game

ONLY: main, principal, best

OPEN: unsettled

OPERA: spectacular entertainment (involving use of painted scenery and stage machinery), often with music

OPERA, the: the theatre in Lincoln's Inn Fields. *See* 'Duke's House, the'

OPINIASTRE, OPINIASTREMENT (Fr.): stubborn, stubbornly

OPPONE: to oppose, hinder

ORDER: to put in order; to punish

ORDINARY (adj.): established

ORDINARY (s.): eating place serving fixed-price meals; peace-time establishment (of navy, dockyard, etc.)

OUTPORTS: ports other than London

OVERSEEN: omitted, neglected; guilty of oversight

OWE: to own

PADRON (?Sp., ?It. *patrone*): master

PAGEANT: decorated symbolic float in procession

PAINFUL: painstaking

PAIR OF OARS: large river-boat rowed by two watermen, each using a pair of oars. Cf. 'Scull'

PAIR (OF ORGANS/VIRGINALS): a single instrument

PALACE: New Palace Yard

PALER: parlour

PANNYARD: pannier, basket

PARAGON: heavy rich cloth, partly of mohair

PARALLELOGRAM: pantograph

PARCEL: share, part; isolated group

PARK, the: normally St James's Park (Hyde Park is usually named)

PARTY: charter-party

PASQUIL: a lampoon

PASSION: feeling, mood

PASSIONATE: touching, affecting

PATTEN: overshoe

PAY: to berate, beat

PAY A COAT: to beat, chastise

PAYSAN (Fr.): country style

PAY SAUCE: to pay dearly

PENDANCES, PENDENTS: lockets; earrings

PERPLEX: to vex

PESLEMESLE: pell-mell, early form of croquet

PETTY BAG: petty cash

PHILOSOPHY: natural science

PHYSIC: laxative, purge

PHYSICALLY: without sheets, uncovered

PICK: pique

PICK A HOLE IN A COAT: to pick a quarrel, complain

PICKAROON (Sp. *picarón*): pirate, privateer

PIECE: gold coin worth *c.* 20*s.*

PIECE (PEECE) OF EIGHT: Spanish silver coin worth 4*s.* 6*d.*

PIGEON: coward

PINK(E): small broad-beamed ship; poniard, pointed weapon

PINNER: coif with two long flaps; fill-in above low *décolletage*

PIPE: measure of wine (c. 120 galls.)

PIPE (musical): flageolet, after 16 Apr. 1668 usually a recorder, specified as such

PISTOLE: French gold coin worth 16*s.*

PLACKET: petticoat

PLAT(T): plate, plan, chart, map; arrangement; level; [flower] plot

PLATERER: one who works silver plate

PLAY (v.): to play for stakes

PLEASANT: comical

POINT, POYNT: piece of lace

POINT DE GESNE: Genoa lace

POLE: head; head-and-shoulder (of fish); poll tax

POLICY: government; cunning; self-interest

POLLARD: cut-back, stunted tree

POMPOUS: ceremonious, dignified

POOR JACK: dried salt fish

POOR WRETCH: poor dear

POSSET: drink made of hot milk, spices, and wine (or beer)

POST (v.): to expose, pillory

POST WARRANT: authority to employ posthorses

POSY: verse or phrase engraved on inside of ring

POWDERED (of meat): salted

PRACTICE: trick

PRAGMATIC, PRAGMATICAL: interfering, conceited, dogmatic

PRATIQUE: ship's licence for port facilities given on presentation of clean bill of health

PRESBYTER JOHN: puritan parson

PRESENT (s.): shot, volley

PRESENT, PRESENTLY: immediate, immediately

PRESS BED: bed folding into or built inside a cupboard

PREST MONEY (milit., naval): earnest money paid in advance

PRETTY (of men): fine, elegant, foppish

PREVENT: to anticipate

PRICK: to write out music; to list

PRICK OUT: to strike out, delete

PRINCE: ruler

PRINCIPLES (of music): natural ability, rudimentary knowledge

PRISE, PRIZE: worth, value, price

PRIVATE: small, secret, quiet

PRIZE FIGHT: fencing match fought for money

PROPRIETY: property, ownership

PROTEST (a bill): to record non-payment; represent bill after non-payment

PROUD (of animals): on heat

PROVOKE: to urge

PULL A CROW: to quarrel

PURCHASE: advantage; profit; booty

PURELY: excellently

PURL(E): hot spiced beer

PUSS: ill-favoured woman

PUT OFF: to sell, dispose of, marry off

PYONEER: pioneer (ditch digger, labourer)

QU: cue

QUARREFOUR: crossroads

QUARTERAGE: any salary or sum paid quarterly

QUARTRE: position in dancing or fencing

QUEST HOUSE: house used for inquests, parish meetings

QUINBROUGH: Queenborough, Kent

QUINSBOROUGH: Königsberg, E. Prussia

RACE: to rase, destroy

RAKE-SHAMED: disreputable, disgraceful

RARE: fine, splendid

RATE: to berate, scold

RATTLE: to scold

RATTOON: rattan cane

READY: quick, accomplished

REAKE: trick

RECEPI: writ of receipt issued by Chancery

RECITATIVO (*stilo r.*): the earliest type of recitative singing

RECONCILE: to settle a dispute, to determine the truth

RECORDER: family of end-blown, eight-holed instruments (descant, treble, tenor, bass)

RECOVER: to reconcile

RECOVERY (legal): process for re-establishment of ownership

REDRIFFE: Rotherhithe, Surrey

REFERRING: indebted, beholden to

REFORM: to disband

REFORMADO: naval/military officer serving without commission

REFRESH (of a sword): to sharpen

RELIGIOUS: monk, nun

REPLICACION (legal): replication, plaintiff's answer to defendant's plea

RESEMBLE: to represent, figure

RESENT: to receive

RESPECT: to mean, refer to

RESPECTFUL: respectable

REST: wrest, tuning key

RETAIN (a writ): to maintain a court action from term to term

REVOLUTION: sudden change (not necessarily violent)

RHODOMONTADO: boast, brag

RIDE POST: to travel by posthorse, to ride fast

RIGHT-HAND MAN: soldier on whom drill manoeuvres turn

RIGHTS, to: immediately, directly

RIS (v.): rose

RISE: origin

RIX DOLLER: Dutch or N. German silver coin (*Rijksdaalder, Reichsthaler*) worth c. 4s. 9d.

ROCKE: distaff

ROMANTIQUE: having the characteristics of a tale (romance)

ROUNDHOUSE: uppermost cabin in stern of ship

ROYALL THEATRE, the: *see* 'Theatre, the'

RUB(B): check, stop, obstacle

RUFFIAN: pimp, rogue

RUMP: remnant of the Long Parliament

RUMPER: member or supporter of the Rump

RUNLETT: cask

RUNNING: temporary

SACK: white wine from Spain or Canaries

SALT: salt-cellar

SALT-EELE: rope's end used for punishment

SALVE UP: to smooth over

SALVO: excuse, explanation

SARCENET: thin taffeta, fine silk cloth

SASSE (Du. *sas*): sluice, lock

SAVE: to be in time for

SAY: fine woollen cloth

SCALE (of music): key; gamut

SCALLOP: scalloped lace collar

SCALLOP-WHISK: *see* 'Whiske'

SCAPE (s.): adventure

SCAPE (v.): to escape

SCARE-FIRE: sudden conflagration

SCHOOL: to scold, rebuke

SCHUIT (Du.): canal boat, barge

SCONCE: bracket, candlestick

SCOTOSCOPE: spy-glass for use in dark

SCOWRE: to beat, punish

SCREW: key, screw-bolt

SCRUPLE: to dispute

SCULL, SCULLER: small river-boat rowed by a single waterman using one pair of oars. Cf. 'Pair of oars'

SEA-CARD: chart

SEA-COAL: coal carried by sea

SEA-OFFICERS: commissioned officers of the navy. Cf. 'Navy Officers'

SECOND MOURNING: half-mourning

SEEL (of a ship): to lurch

SEEM: to pretend

SENNIT: sevennight, a week

SENSIBLY: perceptibly, painfully

SERPENT: variety of firework

SERVANT: suitor, lover

SET: sit

SET UP/OFF ONE'S REST: to be certain, to be content, to make an end, to make one's whole aim

SEWER: stream, ditch

SHAG(G): worsted or silk cloth with a velvet nap on one side

SHEATH (of a ship): to encase the hull as a protection against worm

SHIFT (s.): trial; dressing room

SHIFT (v.): to change clothes; to dodge a round in paying for drinks (or to get rid of the effects of drink)

SHOEMAKER'S STOCKS: new shoes

SHOVE AT: to apply one's energies to

SHROUD: shrewd, astute

SHUFFLEBOARD: shovelboard, shove-ha'penny

SHUTS: shutters

SILLABUB, SULLYBUB, SYLLABUB: sweetened milk mixed with wine

SIMPLE: foolish

SIT: to hold a meeting

SIT CLOSE: to hold a meeting from which clerks are excluded

SITHE: sigh

SKELLUM: rascal, thief

SLENDERLY: slightingly

SLICE: flat plate

SLIGHT, SLIGHTLY: contemptuous; slightingly, without ceremony

SLIP A CALF/FILLY: to abort

SLOP(P)S: seamen's ready-made clothes

SLUG(G): slow heavy boat; rough metal projectile

SLUT (not always opprobrious): drudge, wench

SMALL (of drink): light

SNAP(P) (s.): bite, snack, small meal; attack

SNAP (v.): to ambush, cut down/out/off

SNUFF: to speak scornfully

SNUFFE, take/go in: to take offence

SOKER: old hand; pal; toper

SOLD(E)BAY: Solebay, off Southwold, Suff.

SOL(L)ICITOR: agent; one who solicits business

SON: son-in-law (similarly with daughter etc.)

SON-IN-LAW: stepson

SOUND: fish-bladder

SOUND, the: strictly the navigable passage between Denmark and Sweden where tolls were levied, but more generally (and usually in Pepys) the Baltic

SPARROWGRASS: asparagus

SPEAK BROAD: to speak fully, frankly

SPECIALITY: bond under seal

SPECIES (optical): image

SPEED: to succeed

SPIKET: spigot, tap, faucet

SPILT, SPOILT: ruined

SPINET: single-manual wing-shaped keyboard instrument with harpsichord action

SPOIL: to deflower; injure

SPOTS: patches (cosmetic)

SPRANKLE: sparkling remark, *bon mot*

SPUDD: trenching tool

STAIRS: landing stage

STAND IN: to cost

STANDING WATER: between tides

STANDISH: stand for ink, pens, etc.

STATE-DISH: richly decorated dish; dish with a round lid or canopy

STATESMAN: Commonwealth's-man

STATIONER: bookseller (often also publisher)

STEEPLE: tower

STEMPEECE: timber of ship's bow

STICK: blockhead

STILLYARD, the: the Steelyard

STIR(R): commotion

STOMACH: courage, pride; appetite

STOMACHFULLY: proudly

STONE-HORSE: stallion

STOUND: astonishment

STOUT: brave, courageous

STOWAGE: storage, payment for storage

STRAIGHTS, STREIGHTS, the: strictly the Straits of Gibraltar; more usually the Mediterranean

STRANG: strong

STRANGERS: foreigners

STRIKE (nautical): to lower the top-sail in salute; (of Exchequer tallies) to make, cut

STRONG WATER: distilled spirits

SUBSIDY MAN: man of substance (liable to pay subsidy-tax)

SUCCESS(E): outcome (good or bad)

SUDDENLY: in a short while

SULLYBUB: *see* 'Sillabub'

SUPERNUMERARY: seaman extra to ship's complement

SURLY: imperious, lordly

SWINE-POX: chicken-pox

SWOUND: to swoon, faint

SYLLABUB: *see* 'Sillabub'

SYMPHONY: instrumental introduction, interlude etc., in a vocal composition

TAB(B)Y: watered silk

TABLE: legend attached to a picture

TABLE BOOK: memorandum book

TABLES: board games

TAILLE, TALLE (Fr. *taille*): figure, shape (of person)

TAKE EGGS FOR MONEY: to cut one's losses, to accept something worthless

TAKE A CRAP: to defecate

TAKE OUT: to learn; perform

TAKE POST: to ride hired posthorses

TAKING (s.): condition

TALE: reckoning, number

TALL: fine, elegant

TALLE: *see* 'Taille'

TALLY: notched wooden stick used by the Exchequer in accounting

TAMKIN: tampion, wooden gun plug

TANSY, TANZY: egg pudding flavoured with tansy

TARGETT: shield

TARPAULIN: 'tar', a sea-bred captain as opposed to a gentleman-captain

TAXOR: financial official of university

TEAR: to rant

TELL: to count

TEMPER (s.): moderation; temperament, mood; physical condition

TEMPER (v.): to moderate, control

TENDER: chary of

TENT: roll of absorbent material used for wounds; (Sp. *tinto*) red wine

TERCE, TIERCE: measure of wine (42 galls.; one-third of a pipe)

TERELLA: terrella, spherical magnet, terrestrial globe containing magnet

TERM(E)S: menstrual periods

THEATRE, the: before May 1663 usually Theatre Royal, Vere St; afterwards usually Theatre Royal, Drury Lane (TR)

THEM: *see* 'Those'

THEORBO: large double-necked tenor lute

THOSE: menstrual periods

THRUSH: inflammation of throat and mouth

TICKELED: annoyed, irritated

TICKET(T): seaman's pay-ticket

TIERCE: *see* 'Terce'

TILT: awning over river-boat

TIMBER: wood for the skeleton of a ship (as distinct from plank or deals used for the decks, cabins, gun-platforms etc.)

TIRE: tier

TOKEN, by the same: so, then, and

TONGUE: reputation, fame

TOPS: turnovers of stockings

TOUCHED: annoyed

TOUR, the: coach parade of *beau monde* in Hyde Park

TOUSE: to tousle/tumble a woman

TOWN(E): manor

TOY: small gift

TOYLE: foil, net into which game is driven

TRADE: manufacture, industry

TRANSIRE: warrant allowing goods through customs

TRAPAN, TREPAN: (surg.) to perforate skull; cheat, trick, trap, inveigle

TREASURY, the: the Navy Treasury or the national Treasury

TREAT: to handle (literally)

TREAT, TREATY: negotiate, negotiation

TREBLE: treble viol

TREPAN: *see* 'Trapan'

TRIANGLE, TRYANGLE: triangular virginals

TRILL(O): vocal ornament consisting of the accelerated repetition of the same note

TRIM: to shave

TRUCKLE/TRUNDLE-BED: low bed on castors which could be put under main bed

TRYANGLE: *see* 'Triangle'

TRY A PULL: to have a go

TUITION: guardianship

TUNE: pitch

TURK, the: used of all denizens of the Turkish Empire, but usually here of the Berbers of the N. African coast, especially Algiers

TURKEY WORK: red tapestry in Turkish style

TURKY-STONE: turquoise

TUTTLE FIELDS: Tothill Fields

TWIST: strong thread

UGLY: unpleasant, offensive

UMBLES (of deer): edible entrails, giblets

UNBESPEAK: cancel, countermand

UNCOUTH: out of sorts or order, uneasy, at a loss

UNDERSTAND: to conduct oneself properly; (s.) understanding

UNDERTAKER: contractor; parliamentary manager

UNHAPPY, UNHAPPILY: unlucky; unluckily

UNREADY: undressed

UNTRUSS: to undo one's breeches, defecate

UPPER BENCH: name given in Interregnum to King's Bench

USE: usury, interest

USE UPON USE: compound interest

VAPOURISH: pretentious, foolish

VAUNT: to vend, sell

VENETIAN CAP: peaked cap as worn by Venetian Doge

VESTS: robes, vestments

VIALL, VIOL: family of fretted, bowed instruments with six gut strings; the bowing hand is held beneath the bow and the instrument held on or between the knees; now mostly superseded by violin family

VIRGINALS: rectangular English keyboard instrument resembling spinet; usually in case without legs

VIRTUOSO: man of wide learning

WAISTCOAT, WASTECOATE: warm undergarment

WAIT, WAYT (at court etc.): to serve a turn of duty (usually a month) as an official

WARDROBE, the: the office of the

King's Great Wardrobe, of which Lord Sandwich was Keeper; the building at Puddle Wharf containing the office; a cloak room, dressing room

WARM: comfortable, well-off

WASSAIL, WASSELL: entertainment (e.g. a play)

WASTCOATE: *see* 'Waistcoat'

WASTECLOATH: cloth hung on ship as decoration between quarter-deck and forecastle

WATCH: clock

WATER: strong water, spirits

WAY, in/out of the: accessible/inaccessible; in a suitable/unsuitable condition

WAYTES: waits; municipal musicians

WEATHER-GLASS(E): thermometer (or, less likely, barometer)

WEIGH (of ships): to raise

WELLING: Welwyn, Herts.

WESTERN BARGEMAN (BARGEE): bargee serving western reaches of Thames

WESTMINSTER: the area around Whitehall and the Abbey; not the modern city of Westminster

WHISKE: woman's neckerchief

WHITE-HALL: royal palace, largely burnt down in 1698

WHITSTER: bleacher, launderer

WIGG: wig, cake, bun

WILDE: wile

WIND (s.): wine

WIND LIKE A CHICKEN: to wind round one's little finger

WINDFUCKER: talkative braggart

WIPE: sarcasm, insult

WISTELY: with close attention

WITTY: clever, intelligent

WONDER: to marvel at

WOODMONGER: fuel merchant

WORD: utterance, phrase

WOREMOODE: wormwood

WORK: needlework. *Also* v.

WRETCH: *see* 'Poor wretch'

YARD: penis

YARE: ready, skilful

YILDHALL: Guildhall

YOWELL: Ewell, Surrey